Handbook of
Forensic Genetics

Biodiversity and Heredity in Civil and Criminal Investigation

Security Science and Technology

ISSN: 2059-1063

Series Editor: Chris Hankin *(Imperial College London, UK)*

Published

Security Science and Technology – Vol. 2

Handbook of Forensic Genetics

Biodiversity and Heredity in Civil and Criminal Investigation

Editors

Antonio Amorim
University of Porto, Portugal

Bruce Budowle
University of North Texas Health Science Center, USA

World Scientific

NEW JERSEY · LONDON · SINGAPORE · BEIJING · SHANGHAI · HONG KONG · TAIPEI · CHENNAI · TOKYO

Published by

World Scientific Publishing Europe Ltd.

57 Shelton Street, Covent Garden, London WC2H 9HE

Head office: 5 Toh Tuck Link, Singapore 596224

USA office: 27 Warren Street, Suite 401-402, Hackensack, NJ 07601

Library of Congress Cataloging-in-Publication Data
Names: Amorim, Antonio, 1952– , author. | Budowle, Bruce, 1953– , author.
Title: Handbook of forensic genetics : biodiversity and heredity in civil and criminal investigation /
    Antonio Amorim & Bruce Budowle.
Other titles: Security science and technology ; v. 2.
Description: New Jersey : World Scientific, [2016] | Series: Security science
    and technology ; volume 2 | Includes bibliographical references.
Identifiers: LCCN 2015049553 | ISBN 9781786340771 (hc : alk. paper)
Subjects: | MESH: Forensic Genetics
Classification: LCC RA1057.55 | NLM W 750 | DDC 614/.1--dc23
LC record available at http://lccn.loc.gov/2015049553

British Library Cataloguing-in-Publication Data
A catalogue record for this book is available from the British Library.

Desk Editors: Dipasri Sardar/Mary Simpson

Typeset by Stallion Press
Email: enquiries@stallionpress.com

Printed in Singapore

Contents

Foreword

For more than a century, forensic science has contributed to criminal and civil investigations. Science has a special role in providing hopefully a more objective view for reconstructing a crime or event and is embraced by lay and technical people alike. However, science, with its seemingly objective veneer, has limitations that must be understood so that the interpretation of forensic results is valid and reliable. The drive towards better technology and practices under the umbrella of quality must be sought and continue to progress. Latent print identification was the first application to be fully exploited by the forensic sciences, and for many years it was heralded as the gold standard of forensic science. Many other applications, such as handwriting, trace evidence, microscopic hair comparisons, ballistics to name a few, have ensued. Yet, many have lacked the documentation to support validity and today some of the tenets of various disciplines are being called into question. Then along comes forensic genetics, a recent new comer to the physical evidence realm. It has only been 30 years since its inception. To be fair, forensic genetics has been around for a substantially longer timeframe, owing to the use of polymorphic protein markers such as ABO blood group, phosphoglucomutase-1, esterase D, transferrin, group specific component and haptoglobin. Regardless, the advent of molecular biology tools made it possible to analyze directly DNA found in biological samples and has provided a discriminating ability that rivals, if not exceeds, the class and individualizing methodologies that analyze other forms of forensic evidence.

The field of forensic genetics, fully immersed in molecular biology, population genetics, statistics, bioinformatics and quality assurance, has become the prominent field among the forensic science disciplines. Yet, it was the way of greater scrutiny and greater demands that drove forensic DNA analyses development, validation and implementation that has had the largest impact on the forensic science field. Solid-based principles of molecular biology and population genetics were relied upon. These principles were used to develop methods that were tested and validated to ensure and demonstrate a more robust capability than other forensic science applications. Moreover, the much sought peer-review process was vibrant and constructive with thought and philosophy added to better develop the procedures employed and to motivate the science community's constituents to continue to improve. Indeed, the field has embraced debate and open discussion to advance capabilities. All the efforts to date have led to forensic genetics being the most validated and understood of the forensic disciplines, and those efforts contribute substantially to provide a safer and more secure society.

Even with the gold standard moniker of forensic genetics, there is still a need to improve current capabilities. As an example, clearly, mixture interpretation is still vexing. Not all practitioners are correctly interpreting results, and consensus has yet to be attained. No doubt with advancements such as probabilistic modeling and hypothesis building more mixture evidence will be interpreted and the outcomes substantiated. The largest obstacle that confronts forensic genetics practitioners from implementing current approaches properly and embracing newer ways to analyze biological evidence is the ever challenging translational aspects of the science. Caseworkers are busy, and the demands on them for throughput are huge. These already burdened individuals do not have the time and resources to benefit from the continued advances in forensic genetics, nor to keep abreast of current practices. While no one should advocate that every cutting edge research endeavor must be implemented, it should be requisite that the methods that are employed be performed properly and that the user be able to explain the general bases for the analytical method and the manner(s) that the results are interpreted. In addition, improvements need to be translated more effectively. An infrastructure of education and training is essential. We all have a responsibility to facilitate transfer of science from the developers to the users, and the community must find the way to maintain proficiency and embrace the developments that will continue to be presented.

In this regard, we have brought together scientists, who have dedicated their careers to developing and validating various aspects of forensic genetics, to produce this book. The topics have a wide range, from basics to novel applications, so that one can appreciate the breadth that the field of forensic genetics has. Moreover, this book intends to contribute to the translation of forensic genetics to the community, and users can have another source to facilitate understanding. This book was written to be a resource that describes the fundamentals of the field. Representative topics are provided to initiate and educate the reader. Forensic genetics continues to evolve as a scientific discipline, and the advances in the field have been exciting and significant. We hope that the book will serve as a foundational text to stimulate the current and next generation of scientists.

We all are aware that there continue to develop novel ways of disseminating and retrieving information that in some ways have turned obsolete the classical ways of communicating science.[1] The power and dynamics of the internet — still not fully exploited — are tempered by the volatility, instability and lack of quality control

---

[1]For instance, because of the speed of information dissemination, the recent informative special issue — Butler JM (2015) Introduction and issue summary: New trends in forensic genetics. *Forensic Sci Int Genet.* 18:1–3 — could not be incorporated in this book.

which impact confidence in the huge amount of available information. Both the editors and the contributors, however, seek publication in a much more responsible, controlled and peer-reviewed fashion than those who fill the contents of a webpage without the benefit of peer-review. We hope that this book in its traditional format, especially when coupled with available electronic media, will still have and will go on having a role in communicating science.

We also recognize that the final product now achieved is different from what we perceived when starting the project. As in any human enterprise, many contrivances (some unpredictable) occurred stemming from particular personal approaches or philosophies and others related to local or global political, professional and health problems. However, we believe that the different views of the contributors only makes this book more relevant to supporting and advancing the field of forensic genetics. We especially want to take the opportunity to thank the contributors for their efforts and patience dealing with our prodding and edit requests.

Fort Worth and Porto,
October 12, 2015
Bruce Budowle
Antonio Amorim

Guide to Readers

All chapters of this book can be read independently, provided some basic knowledge of genetics. For beginners, it is advisable to begin with Chapters 1–4 in order to grasp the basic genetic concepts and essential biological foundations and Chapter 9 for an overview of the standard methodological analysis of DNA as forensic evidence.

Chapters 5–8 are of a more advanced nature and deal with the most common types of issues faced when dealing with genetic evidence, namely: kinship, sampling error, ancestry estimation and last but not least, mixtures.

DNA databases in general (with special emphasis on autosomal) are discussed in Chapter 11; when involving Y chromosome in Chapter 12, and mitochondrial databasing is referred in Chapter 14.

Advanced level reading on X chromosome, its special features and its recent and growing interest in forensics is provided in Chapter 10.

A state-of-the-art and future perspectives of forensic genetics technology is given in Chapter 13, with a specific development in mitochondrial genomics in Chapter 14.

Specific chapters are devoted to types of applications of particular importance, such as: missing persons identification (15), pharmacogenetics (16), phenotype inference from DNA (17), and ancestry estimation (7) for humans, while those using non-human DNA evidence are dealt with in Chapters 18–23.

Last, but not least, an approach to the paramount problems of standardization, regulation and quality assurance can be found in Chapter 24.

List of Contributors

Marc W. Allard (marc.allard@fda.hhs.gov)
Food and Drug Administration, Office of Regulatory Science
Division of Microbiology, HFS-712
5100 Paint Branch Parkway, College Park, MD 20740, USA

Antonio Amorim (aamorim@ipatimup.pt)
Instituto de Investigação e Inovação em Saúde
Universidade do Porto, Portugal

Instituto de Patologia e Imunologia Molecular da
Universidade do Porto (IPATIMUP)
Rua Júlio Amaral de Carvalho 45
4200-135 Porto, Portugal
Faculdade de Ciências
Universidade do Porto, Portugal

Ricardo Araújo (raraujo@ipatimup.pt)
Instituto de Investigação e Inovação em Saúde
Universidade do Porto, Portugal

Instituto de Patologia e Imunologia Molecular da
Universidade do Porto (IPATIMUP)
Rua Júlio Amaral de Carvalho 45
4200-135 Porto, Portugal

Barbara van Asch (bva@sun.ac.za)
Department of Genetics
Faculty of Agrisciences, Stellenbosch University
Private Bag X1, Matieland 7602, South Africa

Qasim Ayub (qa1@sanger.ac.uk)
The Wellcome Trust Sanger Institute
Wellcome Trust Genome Campus, Hinxton, UK

Ingo Bastisch (ingo.bastisch@gmail.com)
BKA (Federal Criminal Police Office)
Wiesbaden, Germany

Kayla Baylor (kbayl1@unh.newhaven.edu)
Forensic Science Department
Henry C. Lee College of Criminal Justice & Forensic Sciences
University of New Haven, 300 Boston Post Road
West Haven, CT 06516, USA

C.P. (Kees) van der Beek (k.v.d.beek@nfi.minvenj.nl)
Netherlands Forensic Institute, DNA-database department
PO Box 24044, 2490 AA The Hague, The Netherlands

Eric W. Brown (Eric.Brown@fda.hhs.gov)
Forensic Science Program, 325 Natural Science Bldg
Western Carolina University, Cullowhee, NC 28723, USA

Bruce Budowle (bruce.budowle@unthsc.edu)
Department of Molecular and Medical Genetics
Institute of Applied Genetics, University of North Texas Health
Science Center, Fort Worth, TX, USA

Center of Excellence in Genomic Medicine Research (CEGMR)
King Abdulaziz University, Jeddah, Saudi Arabia

Amke Caliebe (caliebe@medinfo.uni-kiel.de)
Institute of Medical Informatics and Statistics
Christian-Albrechts University of Kiel, Kiel, Germany

Sherryn A. Ciavaglia (sherryn.ciavaglia@flinders.edu.au)
School of Biological Sciences
Flinders University, South Australia, Australia

Science and Advice for Scottish Agriculture, Edinburgh, UK

Heather Miller Coyle (HCoyle@newhaven.edu)
Forensic Science Department
Henry C. Lee College of Criminal Justice & Forensic Sciences
University of New Haven, 300 Boston Post Road
West Haven, CT 06516, USA

James M. Curran (j.curran@auckland.ac.nz)
University of Auckland Department of Statistics
Private Bag 92019, Auckland 1142, New Zealand

Thore Egeland (thore.egeland@gmail.com)
IKBM, Norwegian University of Life Sciences
Ås, Norway

Manuel García-Magariños (manugm1981@hotmail.com)
IKBM, Norwegian University of Life Sciences, Ås, Norway
Department of Mathematics, University of A Coruña, Spain

Fernando González-Candelas (fernando.gonzalez@uv.es)
Unidad Mixta Infección y Salud Pública
FISABIO-Universidad de Valencia
CIBER en Epidemiología y Salud Pública
Instituto Cavanilles de Biodiversidad y Biología Evolutiva
Edificio Institutos de Investigación. Parque Científico
C/Catedrático José Beltrán, 2, 46980-Paterna, Valencia, Spain

Leonor Gusmão (lgusmao@ipatimup.pt)
DNA Diagnostic Laboratory (LDD)
State University of Rio de Janeiro (UERJ), Rio de Janeiro, Brazil

IPATIMUP — Institute of Molecular Pathology and Immunology
University of Porto, Porto, Portugal

Instituto de Investigação e Inovação em Saúde
Universidade do Porto, Porto, Portugal

Marc Haber (mh25@sanger.ac.uk)
The Wellcome Trust Sanger Institute
Wellcome Trust Genome Campus
Hinxton, UK

René L.M. Huel (rene.huel@icmp.int)
International Commission on Missing Persons
The Hague, Netherlands

Jodi A. Irwin (Jodi.Irwin@ic.fbi.gov)
FBI Laboratory, Quantico, VA, USA

Rebecca S. Just (rebecca.s.just.ctr@mail.mil)
FBI Laboratory, Quantico, VA, USA

Sree Kanthaswamy (sree.kanthaswamy@asu.edu)
School of Mathematical and Natural Sciences
New College of Interdisciplinary Arts and Sciences
Arizona State University (ASU)
Glendale, AZ, USA

Manfred Kayser (m.kayser@erasmusmc.nl)
Department of Genetic Identification
Erasmus MC University Medical Center Rotterdam
Rotterdam, The Netherlands

Kenneth K. Kidd (kenneth.kidd@yale.edu)
Department of Genetics, Yale University School of Medicine
New Haven, CT 06520, USA

Michael Krawczak (krawczak@medinfo.uni-kiel.de)
Institute of Medical Informatics and Statistics
Christian-Albrechts University of Kiel, Kiel, Germany

Adrian Linacre (adrian.linacre@flinders.edu.au)
School of Biological Sciences, Flinders University
Adelaide, Australia

Jillian Ng (jllng@ucdavis.edu)
Molecular Anthropology Laboratory
University of California, Davis, CA, USA

Robert Oldt (rfoldt@ucdavis.edu)
Molecular Anthropology Laboratory
University of California, Davis, CA, USA

Walther Parson (Walther.parson@gmail.com)
Institute of Legal Medicine
Medical University of Innsbruck, Innsbruck, Austria

Forensic Science Program, The Pennsylvania State University
University Park, PA, USA

Thomas J. Parsons (thomas.parsons@icmp.int)
International Commission on Missing Persons
The Hague, Netherlands

Filipe Pereira (fpereirapt@gmail.com)
Interdisciplinary Centre of Marine and Environmental Research
(CIIMAR/CIMAR), University of Porto
Rua dos Bragas 289, Porto 4050-123, Portugal

Vânia Pereira (vania.pereira@sund.ku.dk)
Section of Forensic Genetics, Department of Forensic Medicine
Faculty of Health and Medical Sciences,
University of Copenhagen Frederik V's Vej, 11 DK-2100
Copenhagen Ø, Denmark

Nádia Pinto (npinto@ipatimup.pt)
IPATIMUP — Institute of Molecular Pathology and Immunology
University of Porto, Porto, Portugal

Instituto de Investigação e Inovação em Saúde
Universidade do Porto, Porto, Portugal

Lutz Roewer (lutz.roewer@charite.de)
Department of Forensic Genetics
Institute of Legal Medicine and Forensic Sciences
Charité, Universitätsmedizin Berlin, Germany

Antti Sajantila (antti.sajantila@helsinki.fi)
Department of Forensic Medicine
University of Helsinki, Helsinki, Finland

Department of Molecular and Medical Genetics
Institute of Applied Genetics
University of North Texas Health Science Center
Fort Worth, TX, USA

Torben Tvedebrink (tvede@math.aau.dk)
Department of Mathematical Sciences
Aalborg University, Denmark

Chris Tyler-Smith (cts@sanger.ac.uk)
The Wellcome Trust Sanger Institute
Wellcome Genome Campus, Hinxton
Cambs. CB10 1SA, UK

Susan Walsh (walshsus@iupui.edu)
Department of Biology
Indiana University–Purdue University Indianapolis (IUPUI)
Indianapolis, IN, USA

Mark R. Wilson (wilsonm.3@battelle.org)
Applied Genomics Battelle, Inc.
2001 Jefferson Davis Hwy, Suite 1203
Arlington, VA 22202-3619, USA

CHAPTER 1

Definition and Purpose

Antonio Amorim

Faculty of Sciences, University of Porto, Portugal
IPATIMUP/I3S, Porto, Portugal
Department of Molecular and Medical Genetics,
Institute of Applied Genetics,
University of North Texas Health Science Center, Fort Worth, TX, USA

Bruce Budowle

University of North Texas Health Science Center,
Fort Worth, TX, USA
Center of Excellence in Genomic Medicine Research (CEGMR),
King Abdulaziz University,
Jeddah, Saudi Arabia

The development and application of molecular tools to characterize biological evidence ushered in the field of forensic genetics (FG). Its growth has been phenomenal and the success stories are many and continue to arise every day. Indeed, FG has become the gold standard for the forensic science disciplines (Lynch, 2003). However, such accolades can give us a false sense of security and sometimes make us complacent regarding our achievements and more so our limitations. Therefore, it is important at times to step back and reflect on the practices and issues that confront FG, or for that matter, any applied science.

1

All applied sciences necessarily define themselves by the problems they address and the manner that they intend to solve such problems. FG is no exception, and has been defined with relative ease; either rather succinctly by Jobling and Gill (2004) as:

The application of genetics for the resolution of legal cases

or more descriptively as:

The application of genetics to human and non-human material (in the sense of a science with the purpose of studying inherited characteristics for the analysis of inter- and intra-specific variations in populations) for the resolution of legal conflicts

which was used when launching one of the leading journals in the FG field (Forensic Science International: Genetics; Anonymous, 2007).

These definitions are rather telling of the view of the participants of FG as they both reflect more so a traditional, one-sided view of how FG serves the legal arena. That is, genetics and the expert(s) provide support in the 'resolution' of already established 'legal cases' or 'conflicts'. In classical terms, before any contribution of FG, there typically is a legal confrontation (either civil or criminal) by representing parties, with two (or more) conflicting positions on a specific issue. These conflicting views are defined and held by public or private entities, and carried out within the legal framework of a court system. An exemplary situation is the criminal case in which the government prosecution claims that a certain suspect has committed a crime and the defence maintains that it was committed by someone else. In this scenario, both parties may agree on the material existence of the crime and they just may differ on its authorship. In this context, when biological evidence is associated with the commission of the crime, the contribution of experts to examine or produce evidence may help the court to decide the ultimate issue of guilt or innocence. For instance, if a sexual offence has been committed and a suspect identified (by non-genetic evidence, such as eye-witnesses, image recordings, etc.), a biological sample collected from the victim's body can be examined in order to obtain the genetic profile of the source of this biological evidence. The FG expert, asked to perform the analyses, should act simply as an expert witness, independent of both parties and provide the results of the analysis regarding the potential source of the evidence (as well as those who cannot be the source of the evidence).

However, FG's role has expanded substantially and is far more diverse in how it serves the society. There has been an increasing importance of FG in the investigation phase to develop a suspect long before the conflict between "sides" may enter into the process. In addition, the evidence may contribute to the preparation of the case itself, contribute more so to pleadings and dismissal of cases, and just as importantly even serve in prevention of crime. In contrast to the comparison of genetic evidence with a designated suspect (or victim), the use of DNA databases and DNA profile searches occur routinely where no suspect has been identified. Here, if the same biological material is available, it is possible to perform the same genetic analysis as in a classically-defined setting, but instead there are no conflicting sides at this point. The genetic profile is used to generate investigative leads with the goal to ultimately lead to the identification of the true source of the crime scene evidence. Then, one would expect the classical role to begin.

The strength of an association between a suspect (or victim) and biological evidence with FG is more and more frequently serving as a way to reduce to the judicial workload. FG is used to resolve identity, prior to the courtroom setting and supporting pleadings instead of further legal action. For example, in the classical approach, FG is increasingly used to evaluate preliminarily the feasibility of the legal action, as in a paternity case in which both the alleged father and the mother (or the legal representative of the child) agree to perform a genetic test. In some countries, this is in fact a routine procedure and is regulated by law. Indeed, in many modern societies, either by suspicion by the government or simply to reduce slowness and unnecessary expenses inherent to litigation, as well as many civil cases are increasingly being solved extra-judicially (Almog, 2014).

FG does contribute to the 'resolution of legal conflicts' but — paradoxically — is indeed in many instances preventing 'legal conflicts' that take place in the courtroom setting. Various sections of this book will delve further into these facets of FG and how it contributes to source attribution.

1 What Makes FG Different from Other Forensic Disciplines?

It is also important to consider what makes FG distinct among other forensic disciplines. As mentioned above, FG enjoys a prestigious place among forensic sciences, often presented as the golden standard. Although a lot of this prestige is owed to DNA technology itself and its high resolution and sensitivity of detection, the high status is grounded on a solid theoretical and genetic basis, substantial validation and quality assurance practices, and a wealth of peer-reviewed literature. Moreover, it is well known that genetic information as stored in DNA is itself of a digital nature, and the theoretical framework initiated by Mendel has been chemically and biologically validated. Indeed the significance of evidence is presented within the framework of population genetics theory, so that evidential value is not purely empirical. Many calculations performed on FG data involve consideration of expected values and are not dependent solely on previous observations.

In contrast with many traditional forensic science disciplines, FG does not rely upon the assumption of discernible uniqueness (every object, being unique, leaves discernibly unique marks or traces, so that if two marks are indistinguishable, they must have been made by the same agent, while conversely if two marks are observed as different, they should have distinct producers (Saks and Koehler, 2005)). FG does not employ observations in such a direct, naïve fashion — but instead embraces similarities of the components of a "DNA profile" and measurement error in its classifications. Out of a range of possible values for a certain measurement, the data are extracted and only the fact of belonging to a specific unambiguously defined group (e.g. an allele) is used to define a DNA profile. This approach is shown in Table 1, where the distribution of DNA fragments' sizes for a specific Y-chromosome marker observed in a human population sample is displayed.

Although the measurement results could occupy a range of possible values in the scale, they present a clustered distribution

Table 1:   Observed size range, mean size and standard deviation values computed from a precision study on 58 individuals for a Y-chromosome marker (DYS438). Modified from (Shewale *et al.*, 2004).

Allele	Observed range	Mean	Standard deviation
8	296.37–296.77	296.57	0.09
9	301.69–302.24	301.96	0.12
10	307.02–307.89	307.45	0.17
11	312.41–313.43	312.92	0.19
12	317.67–318.86	318.26	0.22
13	322.98–324.19	323.58	0.23

allowing a less ambiguous classification (than marks from other types of forensic evidence) into well-defined types, numerically labeled in this case. All typings classified as '8' are considered operationally indistinguishable, and belonging to a different type than '9', '10' and so forth. So, in one manner instead of looking for individualization, FG seeks classification based on known shared marks (Evett, 1995; Cole, 2009). Of course, if a sufficient number of characteristics are tested, the number of individuals sharing the same composite profile becomes infinitesimal, so that, with a modest financial and technical effort, individualization can be achieved in practical terms.

The theoretical foundations of FG have additional consequences, some immediately achievable while others constitute near and long term goals. The field, compared with fingerprints, handwriting, tool marks and other pattern recognition applications, continues to move to minimize 'expert opinion' or reduce the subjective component of data interpretation. What constitutes an allele is rarely questioned, as might be done for a point from a latent print (Jackson *et al.*, 2006). More explicit assumptions and the existence of formal protocols, often promulgated by commonly used commercial kits, are key factors to consensus of profile determination. This more objective analysis platform promulgated in FG supports the analysis, and in some situations interpretation, of DNA evidence with less incorporation of human intervention (Gill *et al.*, 1996; Power *et al.*, 2008). But even the gold standard has limitations that should be openly discussed and addressed. The most evident is mixture interpretation where there still is a good degree of subjectivity, on which there is substantial discussion in the peer-reviewed literature to improve, some of it reflected in this book. What is noteworthy is the degree of discussion of such limitations and perhaps the gold standard is not about the problems, but the status is deserved because of the field's capability to debate the issues.

The early debates on population genetics and calculating the rarity of a DNA profile have pretty much subsided. Estimating the frequency of a genetic profile is well established and only very subtle issues are discussed. In the FG context, population genetics theory allows: (i) the calculation of expected values (and thus to control the sampling quality and robustness) and also (ii) the estimation of the frequency of profiles not previously observed (Amorim, 2013). In contrast, other forensic science disciplines must rely on frequency estimations that are purely empirical and that may not be representative of the population of that item or material.

2 Current Situation and Problems — A Dynamic Discipline

Having extolled the virtues of FG, it would seem that we support, that it should have the highest prestige of the forensic disciplines. We caution such a view based on an unrivalled technological advance (which indeed exists, but it is not causal) and that DNA is almost phenomenal in its abilities (Amorim, 2012). These perceptions by themselves are not justified, since many other forensic disciplines use methods and technologies that are at least as sophisticated as those employed in FG. The DNA, as remarkable as it may be, is just a molecule and does not possess any magical properties.

With the exception of very extreme applications, such as those involving so-called low copy number (LCN), or low-template DNA (LTDNA) analyses (Dror and Hampikian, 2011; Gill *et al.*, 2012; Budowle *et al.*, 2009b; Schneider *et al.*, 2011; Pascali and Prinz, 2012 and references therein), one does not witness situations, more common in other disciplines, where the same evidence is interpreted in diametrically opposed manners by the experts. Indeed, in this context of difference of opinions by experts in FG, the contention is almost exclusively on the strength of the association rather on the development of results. That being said, Balding (2013) appropriately opined when commenting on the UK Forensic Science Regulator report on LTDNA (Caddy, 2008) which, while classifying the underlying science as "sound" and profiling results "fit for purpose", although admitting that there was a lack of agreement "on how LTDNA profiles are to be interpreted": "Without valid methods of assessing evidential strength, a technique cannot be fit for purpose in the criminal justice system". FG, unlike many of its sister forensic disciplines, is well positioned to debate the issues and effectively move forward to improve upon interpretation.

The most pressing FG issues and debates, except for extreme applications, are in hypothesis formulation (Buckleton *et al.*, 2014; McKenna, 2013), interpretation of results, documentation and communication and less about technology and profile generation (for a recent review, see Ludwig and Fraser (2014)). A wide gap persists between leaders in the field of FG and its practitioners on how to address the formal framework for interpretation of some results, e.g. mixture evidence. Also communication between experts and between experts and laypersons needs to improve. These persistent limitations require a concerted effort from all involved in FG (Biedermann, 2013; Kruse, 2013; Mullen *et al.*, 2014). Some of the detected weaknesses have been analyzed in detail with appalling results, depicting situations in which practitioners may incorrectly apply well-defined interpretation principles (de Keijser and Elffers, 2012). This gap is heterogeneous across the various types of expertize and legal systems (Gill, 2009; Lynch *et al.*, 2009), but is sufficiently general and prevalent to cause individual and collective concerns (Kaye, 2010). Some of these and the proposed improvements deserve discussion. There is also a need to communicate well to the police, jurists, and other stakeholders the meaning of genetic evidence so its strengths and just importantly its limitations can be appreciated. Otherwise, the value of DNA evidence may not be applied properly. It is distressing how heterogeneous (or even the lack) of education and training of practitioners is within the forensic disciplines (Houck, 2013), including FG. Not surprisingly, the education and training disparity are felt much more on the statistical side rather than in technology updating, and a possible cause was attributed to the poor relations between academic researchers and practitioners (Robertson, 2012), but also may be attributed to a lack of realization of the importance of statistics (Budowle *et al.*, 2009a; Krane *et al.*, 2010; Budowle, 2010; Fenton, 2011). Education and training are essential and are a key to success in any discipline, notwithstanding FG. We all have a responsibility to improve the education and training of practitioners in FG, which is well reflected in the US President's DNA Initiative–DNA Analysts training website (http://projects.nfstc.org/pdi/). In this context, the extinction of the Forensic Science Service was a prime example of a dismal policy trend towards dealing with forensic science as an enterprise, in the sense of a business organization (Anonymous, 2013). The consequences are yet to be completely comprehended (Jackson, 2013), but are recognized as a travesty (Budowle *et al.*, 2011).

FG does deserve some praise for its early embracement of quality assurance. There still is a need for adopting standards, principles or guidelines to remedy detected problems, or at least the most egregious problems. Indeed the implementation of standards and guidelines is well entrenched for laboratory practices (Willis, 2014), but is now acknowledged as being required also for the formalization of the logical and statistical framework. The urgency of developing such measures has been institutionally recognized (e.g. Aitken *et al.*, 2010; Association of Forensic Science Providers, 2009) but unfortunately the community's consensus on the recommendations is still out of reach (Biedermann *et al.*, 2014).

Finally, despite the profound differences between adversarial and inquisitorial judicial systems (Coyle, 2012), bias is an issue that must be appreciated. Some have intimated that the lack of independence of practitioners and police services is viewed as a source of biases (Dror and Hampikian, 2011). Such positions may misdirect the cause of bias and give a false sense of ridding if a laboratory is independent from the police. All human beings are biased. Bias does not mean that people are intentionally trying to slant their interpretations. It is a natural human tendency to fit "things" by confirmation or by context. We need to continue to build systems that address bias no matter where the analyst is employed or whether one side of the "conflict" seeks the assistance of the analyst. We in FG must be ever vigil and even more so open to constructive criticism to improve. We all want FG to continue to rightly enjoy the prestige of being the gold standard.

References

C. Aitken, P. Roberts and G. Jackson. Fundamentals of probability and statistical evidence in criminal proceedings. Guidance for Judges, Lawyers, Forensic Scientists and Expert Witnesses. Royal Statistical Society's Working Group on Statistics and the Law. The Royal Statistical Society, London, 2010.

J. Almog. Forensics as a proactive science. *Science and Justice*, 54(5): 325–326, 2014.

A. Amorim. Opening the DNA black box: Demythologizing forensic genetics. *New Genetics and Society*, 31(3):259–270, 2012.

A. Amorim, Basic principles. In *Encyclopedia of Forensic Sciences*, J. A. Siegel, P. J. Saukko (eds.), 2nd edn., vol. 1, pp. 211–213. Academic Press, Waltham, 2013.

Anonymous. Launching forensic science international daughter journal in 2007. *Forensic Science International: Genetics*, 1:1–2, 2007.

Anonymous. Forensics fiasco. *Nature*, 500(7460):5, 2013.

Association of Forensic Science Providers. Standards for the formulation of evaluative forensic science expert opinion. *Science & Justice*, 49(3): 161–164, 2009.

D. J. Balding. Evaluation of mixed-source, low-template DNA profiles in forensic science. *Proceedings of the National Academy of Sciences USA*, 110(30):12241–12246, 2013.

A. Biedermann. Your uncertainty, your probability, your decision. *Frontiers in Genetics*, 4:148, 2013.

A. Biedermann, J. Vuille and F. Taroni. DNA, statistics and the law: a cross-disciplinary approach to forensic inference. *Frontiers in Genetics*, 5:136, 2014.

B. Budowle. Author reply to Commentary on: A perspective on errors, bias, and interpretation in the forensic sciences and direction for continuing advancement. *Journal of Forensic Sciences*, 55(1):275–276, 2010.

B. Budowle, M. C. Bottrell, S. G. Bunch, R. Fram, D. Harrison, S. Meagher, C. T. Oien, P. E. Peterson, D. P. Seiger, M. B. Smith, M. A. Smrz, G. L. Soltis and R. B. Stacey. A perspective on errors, bias, and interpretation in the forensic sciences and direction for continuing advancement. *Journal of Forensic Sciences*, 54(4):798–809, 2009a.

B. Budowle, A. J. Eisenberg, A. van Daal. Validity of low copy number typing and applications to forensic science, *Croatian Medical Journal*, 50(3):207–217, 2009b.

B. Budowle, M. K. Kayser and A. Sajantila. The demise of UK's Forensic Science Service (FSS): Loss of world-leading engine of innovation and development in the forensic sciences. *BMC Investigative Genetics* 2:4, 2011.

J. Buckleton, J. A. Bright, D. Taylor, I. Evett, T. Hicks, G. Jackson and J. M. Curran. Helping formulate propositions in forensic DNA analysis. *Science & Justice*, 54(4):258–261, 2014.

B. Caddy, G. Taylor and A. Linacre. *A Review of Low Template DNA Analysis*. UK Home Office, London, 2008.

S. A. Cole. Forensics without uniqueness, conclusions without individualization: The new epistemology of forensic identification. *Law, Probability and Risk*, 8:233–255, 2009.

H. M. Coyle. The importance of scientific evaluation of biological evidence — data from eight years of case review. *Science & Justice*, 52(4):268–270, 2012.

I. Dror and G. Hampikian. Subjectivity and bias in forensic DNA mixture interpretation. *Science & Justice*, 51(4):204–208, 2011.

I. W. Evett. Avoiding the transposed conditional. *Science & Justice*, 35(2):127–131, 1995.

N. Fenton. Science and law: Improve statistics in court. *Nature*, 479(7371): 36–37, 2011.

P. Gill. When DNA goes on trial. *Nature*, 460:34–35, 2009.

P. Gill, A. Urquhart, E. Millican, N. Oldroyd, S. Watson, R. Sparkes and C. P. Kimpton. A new method of STR interpretation using inferential logic — development of a criminal intelligence database. *International Journal of Legal Medicine*, 109(1):14–22, 1996.

P. Gill, L. Gusmão, H. Haned, W. R. Mayr, N. Morling, W. Parson, L. Prieto, M. Prinz, H. Schneider, P. M. Schneider and B. S. Weir. DNA commission of the International Society of Forensic Genetics: Recommendations on the evaluation of STR typing results that may include drop-out and/or drop-in using probabilistic methods. *Forensic Science International: Genetics*, 6(6):679–688, 2012.

M. M. Houck. Intellectual infrastructure: a modest critique of forensic science. *Science & Justice*, 53(1):1, 2013.

G. Jackson. The impact of commercialization on the evaluation of DNA evidence. *Frontiers in Genetics*, 4:227, 2013.

G. Jackson, S. Jones, G. Booth, C. Champod and I. W. Evett. The nature of forensic science opinion — a possible framework to guide thinking and practice in investigations and in court proceedings. *Science & Justice*, 46(1):33–44, 2006.

M. A. Jobling and P. Gill, Encoded evidence: DNA in forensic analysis. *Nature Reviews Genetics*, 5(10):739–751, 2004.

D. H. Kaye. The good, the bad, the ugly: The NAS report on strengthening forensic science in America. *Science & Justice*, 50(1):8–11, 2010.

J. de Keijser and H. Elffers. Understanding of forensic expert reports by judges, defense lawyers and forensic professionals. *Psychology, Crime & Law*, 18(2):191–207, 2012.

D. E. Krane, S. Ford, J. R. Gilder, K. Inman, A. Jamieson, R. Koppl, I. L. Kornfield, D. Michael Risinger, N. Rudin, M. S. Taylor and W. C. Thompson. Commentary on: A perspective on errors, bias, and interpretation in the forensic sciences and direction for continuing advancement. *Journal of Forensic Sciences*, 55(1):273–274, 2010.

C. Kruse. The Bayesian approach to forensic evidence: Evaluating, communicating, and distributing responsibility. *Social Studies of Science*, 43(5):657–680, 2013.

A. Ludwig and J. Fraser. Effective use of forensic science in volume crime investigations: Identifying recurring themes in the literature. *Science & Justice*, 54(1):81–88, 2014.

M. Lynch. God's signature: DNA profiling, the new gold standard in forensic science. *Endeavour*, 27(2):93–97, 2003.

M. Lynch, S. A. Cole, R. McNally and K. Jordan. *Truth Machine: The Contentious History of DNA Fingerprinting*. University of Chicago Press, Chicago, 2009.

L. McKenna. Understanding DNA results within the case context: Importance of the alternative proposition. *Frontiers in Genetics*, 4:242, 2013.

C. Mullen, D. Spence, L. Moxey and A. Jamieson. Perception problems of the verbal scale. *Science & Justice*, 54(2):154–158, 2014.

V. Pascali and M. Prinz. Highlights of the conference The hidden side of DNA profiles: Artifacts, errors and uncertain evidence. *Forensic Science International: Genetics*, 6(6):775–777, 2012.

T. Power, B. McCabe and S. A. Harbison. FaSTR DNA: A new expert system for forensic DNA analysis. *Forensic Science International: Genetics*, 2(3): 159–165, 2008.

President's DNA Initiative–DNA Analysts training website. http://projects.nfstc.org/pdi/, accessed March 7, 2016.

J. Robertson. Truth has many aspects. *Science & Justice*, 52(1):62–66, 2012.

M. J. Saks and J. J. Koehler. The coming paradigm shift in forensic identification science. *Science*, 309(5736):892–895, 2005.

P. M. Schneider, J. M. Butler and A. Carracedo. Publications and letters related to the forensic genetic analysis of low amounts of DNA. *Forensic Science International: Genetics*, 5(1):1–2, 2011.

J. G. Shewale, H. Nasir, E. Schneida, A. M. Gross, B. Budowle and S. K. Sinha. Y-chromosome STR system, Y-PLEX 12, for forensic casework: development and validation. *Journal of Forensic Sciences*, 49(6):1278–1290, 2004.

S. Willis. Accreditation — Straight belt or life jacket? Presentation to Forensic Science Society Conference November 2013. *Science & Justice*, 54(6):505–507, 2014.

CHAPTER 2

Mendelian Genetics, Modes of Transmission and Genomics

Antonio Amorim

Faculty of Sciences,
University of Porto and IPATIMUP / I3S, Porto, Portugal

> *There is grandeur in this view of life, with its several powers, having been originally breathed into a few forms or into one; and that, whilst this planet has gone cycling on according to the fixed law of gravity, from so simple a beginning endless forms most beautiful and most wonderful have been, and are being, evolved.*
>
> Charles Darwin (1859) *"On the Origin of Species by Means of Natural Selection,"* p. 490.

Perhaps Charles Darwin was exaggerating poetically on the seemingly infinite forms of life but undoubtedly the current and past biodiversity — some, if not most of which was unknown to him and still unknown to us — is prodigious. At the same time, he was publishing his most famous work, another researcher outside the scientific arena, Gregor Mendel, was determining how the distinctive characteristics of living beings are transmitted from parents to offspring. In his words (Mendel, 1866) "[..] so far, no generally applicable law governing the formation and development of hybrids has been successfully formulated", since "among all the numerous experiments made, not one has been carried out to such an extent and in such a way as to make it possible to determine the number of different forms under which the offspring of the hybrids appear, or to arrange these forms with certainty according to their separate generations, or definitely to ascertain their statistical relations". He concluded that "to undertake a labor of such far-reaching extent […] appears, however, to be the only right way by which we can finally reach the solution of a question the importance of which cannot be overestimated in connection with the *history of the evolution of organic forms*" (italics are ours).

His work and the importance of his results remained unrecognized for far too many years. Yet, still today his role as founder of a new discipline and creator of a formal theory with no parallel in Biology is not properly acknowledged (Rehmeyer, 2010).

This chapter presents a post-DNA version of his theories as well as the biological bases underlying the different primary modes of transmission observed in the biosphere, highlighting the evolutionary constraints responsible for the sometimes strange forms of transmitting (genetic) information from parents to offspring. For some cases of special forensic interest, specific chapters in this book already are devoted to kinship; therefore a general framework will be provided.

1 Reproduction

Embedded in the very definition of life is reproduction, that is, to contribute to the creation of new living beings of the same kind. This creation is achieved generally through two different mechanisms: either a single progenitor divides itself producing two (or more) genetically "identical" offspring or two (or more) progenitors combine their genetic material to give rise to one (or more) genetically similar offspring. The former mechanism is termed **clonal** or **asexual** reproduction while the latter is known as **sexual** reproduction. Somewhat intermediate cases, in which pieces of genetic information from one donor can be incorporated in the basic genetic makeup of an offspring provided by progenitor(s) can be found across the entire range of life and will be specifically addressed later in this chapter. In the remainder of this section, if not explained otherwise, sexual reproduction will refer to the standard cases in which each offspring requires two progenitors and clonal to the purely budding-like mechanism. For readers interested in the remarkable diversity of widely different forms of sex, we refer them to the recent update presented by the Tree of Sex Consortium (2014).

Asexual reproduction from the genetics point of view seems trivial and uninteresting: an offspring will carry (barring copy errors, i.e. **mutations**) the same exact genetic information as its progenitor. Conversely, sexual reproduction presents far more complexity, since many approaches are possible: does an offspring receive all the information from both progenitors, doubling its genetic endowment?; Does each progenitor contribute (exactly) half of their genetic complement, so that an offspring will receive the same amount of overall genetic information present in the previous generation?; or Does each sex specialize to some degree, so that one provides the offspring with a sex-specific part of information (or only a variable part, in a way that determines the sex of the offspring)?

All these possible modes of sexual reproduction (except the first one) are observed in a stable, regular form in many biological groups. But to make things more complex, in a plethora of organisms some of these disparate modes of transmission coexist, so that in the same species part of the genetic information can be democratically transmitted by both sexes, while other parts are exclusively transmitted either by males or females or by both, but in different quantities.

In order to try to make this conundrum a bit clearer to the reader, before addressing Mendel's theory, we will interrupt this conceptual and formal approach and will provide next an overview of the biological bases of inheritance.

2 Biological Bases of Inheritance

Despite the enormous variety of contemporary forms of life, as far as we know, all replication of genetic information is based upon a single chemical, deoxyribonucleic acid (DNA). That is true even for ribonucleic acid (RNA) viruses, which may not be considered, strictly speaking, living entities as they depend ultimately for reproduction on DNA-based living beings. We shall ignore if in the past alternative chemical species for storage of genetic information were used or even some extant forms of life that may still be discovered to do so.

Fortunately, while diversity of reproduction is considerable, the common chemical basis ensures sufficient uniformity to allow for a common technological toolkit for all required forensic analyses. This unity, however, does not convey that because there is a common technical theme(s) for forensic genetics, there is not a vast array of different biological systems built up over geological time; indeed, there are many.

This diversity is not, contrary to early speculations on evolution and still present in descriptive metaphors, easily accommodated into a kind of genealogical tree relating all forms of life to founding ancestors (a single one, according to some) which arose billions of years ago in a prebiotic Earth. A network represents better fact that the phenomenon called **horizontal** (or **lateral or vertical**) **transfer** of DNA (Soucy *et al.*, 2015), refers to the exchange of pieces of DNA between organisms in a manner other than "traditional" reproduction. The genetic makeup of virtually all species is thus a jigsaw puzzle in which the presence of dissonant relationships are recognized. Fortunately, for practical cases, this transfer is so far in our distant past or of so limited an amount that in terms of forensic applications (with the exception of microbial and viral forensics; see the chapter on this topic and Ragan *et al.*, 2009; Koonin 2015; Maddison *et al.*, 2007) it can be neglected.

Another uniformity of the living world is that basic living components are made up of a single unit or multiples of these units. The name of this unit is the **cell**, and can be defined as the smallest unit which is able to replicate independently. The cell consists of a more or less structured fluid enclosed within a membrane, containing a vast array of molecules, including necessarily DNA.

This apparent simplicity of the basic unit of life masks a profound gap between two quite different types of cells: prokaryotic and eukaryotic. **Prokaryotic cells** are characterized by the absence of an internal structure, a **nucleus**, enveloping the DNA; in contrast, **eukaryotic cells** possess a nucleus in which DNA is contained — except during cell division. The differences between these two types of cells are not only morphological, limiting ourselves to those that have direct genetic consequences. The differences can be summarized as follows: (1) each prokaryotic cell has a single DNA molecule (although non-essentially some ancillary, transitory, smaller molecules, such as plasmids, can occur), and it is not organized into complex macromolecular architectures; (2) although some forms of so-called parasexuality can occur, prokaryote reproduction is typically clonal; (3) prokaryotes are unicellular (or if colonial they do not show differentiation), while (4) eukaryotic cells, believed to result from the fusion of prokaryotic cells (the symbiotic theory), contain various organelles (that seem to be the remnants of ancestral free-living prokaryotes) some of them with their own DNA (in the most complex case, plastids and mitochondria) and (5) eukaryote reproduction is (at least potentially) sexual and the nuclear DNA exists at some point of the life cycle in a duplicate state.

A main concept to retain from this diversity summary is that each eukaryotic cell is a genetically heterogeneous collection of portions of genomes formed into bodies known as **chromosomes**, each one predictably with its own but similar mode of transmission. We are now ready to address Mendel's work with a new focus and an extended framework. It is somewhat surprising that Mendel solved the more complex mode of transmission, i.e. sexual reproduction. We begin by presenting this work and then generalize it to the primary modes of transmission observed in eukaryotes, using the human example, which is a good model for mammalians, and for obvious forensic genetics applications. Other examples will be dealt in other chapters of this book.

Mendelian Theory of Inheritance and Modes of Transmission

First of all, Mendel limited his research to cases where observed differences in a specific characteristic(s) between members of a population were clear-cut, i.e. all members could be classified into discrete groups without ambiguity. It is believed that, when studying seed color in his experimental model (*Pisum sativum*), Mendel was not ignorant of the differences existing among 'yellow' or 'green' peas, but he took advantage of the gap between these characteristics, just classifying them into two phenotypic groups. **Phenotype** will refer to each of the classes into which members of a population can be grouped according to their appearance for a specific characteristic. Mendel hypothesized that, if the observed differences are of a hereditary nature, there should be some place in the cell where the information for the characteristic should be stored. We now know that location — it is a specific region of DNA called a **locus** (plural: loci) and specifically for the characteristic a **gene**. He further thought that some difference in content of that information should be responsible for the observable alternative, that is, in modern parlance, that a locus could contain alternative forms (differences in DNA sequence), called **alleles**. Mendel reasoned further that, in order to avoid the Russian doll paradox, the number of copies of this information should be reduced in each generation of sexual reproduction, so that both parents should generate gametes (female ovules and male spermatozoa) containing only half of the information which, when fusing to form an egg, would reconstruct the amount present in each progenitor. Therefore, each locus can be present in double copy (**diploidy**), as in the cells of the body of progenitors and in single copy (**haploidy**), as in gametes. Another term is **genotype**, which is the specific genetic state of occupancy of a locus in a cell or individual. If the diploid cell possesses two different alleles at a specific locus, it is said to be **heterozygous**, and if the alleles are identical the genotype is referred to as **homozygous**. Lastly, Mendel observed that the discrete trait could disappear in one generation and reappear in the next one. Thus, he deduced that these heritable entities were unchanged as they passed form parent to offspring. We now know this observation to be the result of **dominant** and **recessive** alleles (or traits).

Using these definitions, the Mendelian theory of inheritance can be summarized as follows:

1. For each observable characteristic (phenotype), two copies of genetic information (genes, alleles) at a locus exist in each individual, defining the corresponding genotype.
2. An individual transmits to each offspring only one of these copies, each one with a probability = 1/2.

An example of application of the theory can be given by the classical ABO blood group (Owen, 2000; Landsteiner, 1900). Suppose a father has phenotype *A* and mother is phenotypically *B*. Surprisingly, one of their children does not resemble any of them and is phenotype *O*. Is this observation genetically possible without invoking non-paternity? Yes, if we recognize that the relationship between phenotype and genotype is not absolute and not always the result of a homozygote genotype; in fact, alleles *A* and *B* are **co-dominant**, but **dominant** over O (which is **recessive**), so that phenotype to genotype relationship can be explained as follows:

Phenotype	Genotype
A	*AA* or *AO*
B	*BB* or *BO*
AB	*AB*
O	*O*

Thus, the situation that one child does not seem to fit to the parents' blood groups is perfectly explainable, and qualitatively and quantitatively predictable:

	Father *B* (*BO*) gametes	
	B 1/2	*O* 1/2
Mother *A* (*AO*) gametes		
A 1/2	*AB* (*AB*) 1/4	*A* (*AO*) 1/4
O 1/2	*B* (*BO*) 1/4	*O* (*OO*) 1/4

We have concluded the description of the Mendelian theory as applied to a single characteristic in a specific **mode of transmission**, the **homogametic** (meaning the gametes carry equal amount of information for this locus) **diploid** model. For reasons that will become clear below it also is designated as **autosomal** mode of inheritance.

There are mechanisms, other than that of autosomal inheritance in mammalians. We will briefly describe these remaining ones (as they are addressed in more detail in other chapters). One of the organelles in, for example, animals' cells is the mitochondrion (plural: mitochondria), which possesses its own DNA (of prokaryotic type, **mtDNA**) and is exclusively transmitted by females to the offspring of both sexes. It is therefore a sexual mode of transmission, haploid and **heterogametic.** Spermatozoa also contain mitochondria, but they do not survive in the zygote after fertilization. Thus, the mtDNA genome has an exclusive maternal transmission. Note that a person's mtDNA is identical to the one his/her mother carries and to brothers and sisters (i.e. to anybody in the maternal line, barring mutation). From this maternal inheritance point of view, an individual is not genetically related to his/her father! Furthermore, a male will not transmit his mother's mtDNA to his offspring. These features of mtDNA transmission mode, combined with a lack of recombination, limit the diversity and hence discrimination power of mtDNA for many forensic applications. However, in kinship analyses, where the maternal reference sample is multiple generations distant from the individual or item of interest, mtDNA can be more informative than the more widely used autosomal markers.

An almost symmetrical situation occurs with a substantial part of one of the nuclear DNA molecules, the Y chromosome, which is exclusively transmitted from fathers to sons. Again it is a haploid molecule with a heterogametic mode of transmission, but in this case male-driven (also called **holandric**). In this regard, a son's sister and mother are completely unrelated to him while he is identical to all paternally related members of his lineage (again barring mutation).

Nuclear DNA molecules are complexed with an array of proteins, variable according to the cell cycle, constituting morphological entities visible under a common microscope and thus dubbed colored bodies, or **chromosomes**. In humans, for instance, there are two sets of 23 different chromosomes (or

23 homologous chromosome pairs) in each female somatic cell. In males, however there are also 46 chromosomes, but only 22 homologous pairs, the remaining two chromosomes being conspicuously different and not identical to any member of the 22 pairs. Mammals have evolved a chromosomal sex-determining mechanism, in which the male sex determining gene is located in a small chromosome, called the **Y chromosome**. So normal males have 22 pairs of **autosomes** and two heterologous **heterosomes**: X and Y, while females possess, besides the 22 pairs of autosomes, a homologous pair of heterosomes: XX. However, since the mechanism of cell division for gamete production requires, for correct apportionment of chromosomes in the daughter cells some pairing (and material exchange) between chromosomes, some regions of both sex chromosomes must be maintained homologous. These regions are called **pseudoautosomal**, since despite being located on the sex chromosomes, they behave, in terms of genetic transmission and recombination as if they were autosomal. It becomes clear that the holandric mode equates to the **Y-chromosome specific** DNA, better named (will see why when dealing with the analysis of the transmission of various characteristics at the same time) **non-recombining region of Y chromosome** (**NRY**).

DNA occurring in the **X-chromosome specific region** will behave as if it were an autosome in females and as haploid in males. It is therefore dubbed **heterogametic haplodiploid** (males being the heterogametic sex). This mode of inheritance can be visualized in the following scheme, where the indexed numbers represent alleles at an X-specific locus:

			Father X_1Y gametes	
			X_1	Y
Mother X_2X_3 gametes	X_2 1/2		X_1X_2 1/2	X_2Y 1/2
	X_3 1/2		X_1X_3 1/2	X_3Y 1/2
			female	male

3 Simultaneous Analysis of the Transmission of Multiple Markers

When Mendel addressed the problem of studying the transmission of two loci at the same time, he speculated that it would be done in an **independent transmission** fashion, and provided some fitting experimental results to support his hypothesis. Independent transmission means that to calculate the probability of a certain type of gamete with many loci, one can just multiply the probabilities for each of them. So in the simple case of two heterozygous loci, the probability of one allele at one locus being transmitted with another allele at a different locus would be $1/2 \times 1/2 = 1/4$.

This hypothesis proved not to be absolute. Although for many pairs of loci the observed proportions proved to fit the expectations under the assumption of independence, in a large number of cases, there is clear violation of this simple model. We will begin by analyzing what can happen with a pair of autosomal markers for which the Mendel experimental strategy is followed: obtaining a double heterozygote resulting from parents which are doubly opposite homozygotes ($A1 \times B2$; A and B represent alleles at the first locus; 1 and 2 alleles at the second locus). In the following table, the double heterozygote ($AB/12$) possible gametogenesis for a pair of autosomal loci is presented:

Gametes	Proportions under			
	Independence	Absolute linkage	Linkage with recombination	
A1	1/4	1/2	$1/2(1-r)$	Old combination
A2	1/4	0	$1/2(r)$	*New combination*
B1	1/4	0	$1/2(r)$	*New combination*
B2	1/4	1/2	$1/2(1-r)$	Old combination

In this table, under the heading 'independence' the expected proportions are listed under the original Mendelian hypothesis while in the second (**absolute linkage**), there are only two possible gametes and the two loci are transmitted without **recombination**, reproducing intact the original arrangements of the parental generation. In the third column, there is some degree of disruption of the original combinations, a degree which is measured by the **recombination fraction**, *r*.

The biological basis for this association or independence of alleles at different loci is due to the special type of cell division that occurs in the formation of gametes in which the amount of genetic material is reduced in half, so that from the diploid mother cell, four haploid gametes are formed. The following scheme depicts what happens in this complex cell division (each horizontal line represents a chromosome and both loci under study are assumed **linked**):

Mother cell	DNA duplication	Recombination	Gametes
A 1	*A* 1	*A* 1	
			———— *A* 1
			———— *A*2
		)(	
			———— *B*1
			———— *B*2
B 2	*B* 2	*B* 2	

If the loci are sufficiently apart in the chromosome, recombination always occurs between them, and thus they behave independently ($r = 1/2$), i.e. as if they were on different chromosomes. The shorter the physical distance between two loci, the smaller the probability of recombination is and r tends to 0, or absolute linkage. Note, however that the relationship between distance and *r* is not necessarily linear and that recombination, at a finer scale, tends to occur in specific sequence contexts, which are **recombination hotspots** (Pääbo, 2003).

Obviously in normal circumstances, recombination can occur only between homologous chromosomes and is therefore limited to the diploid and haplodiploid genomic regions. Then, for humans and most mammals, recombination is restricted to autosomes and pseudoautosomal regions (in both sexes) and to X-chromosome specific regions (but only in females). Conversely, the mitochondrial genome as well as the Y-specific region (NRY) does not recombine and all loci within these regions behave in the same manner as a single locus. The forensic and evolutionary consequences of these differences in the capacity of reshuffling the genomic contents are enormous and will be explored in specific chapters of this book.

4 Generalization of Mendelian Theory to Population Analysis

All the above theories were applied to a context where either genetic composition of offspring can be predicted given parents' genotypes, or inversely, parents' composition is inferred from offspring genotypes. If Mendelian theory were limited to this field of application (called familial genetics), its application to forensics would be limited. Fortunately, soon after the rediscovery of Mendel's work, a generalization, now called **Hardy–Weinberg principle,** was undertaken (Hardy, 1908).

The Hardy–Weinberg principle is very easily formalized for a single autosomal locus, if a set of simplifying assumptions are accepted. Namely, there is a relationship between allele frequencies and genotype frequencies such that the genotype distribution is expected to be obtained by squaring the sum of allele frequencies. This relationship holds if mating occurs at random between individuals, irrespective of their genotypes; population size is considered infinite; and there is no mutation, migration or selection (all genotypes are equally successful in reproduction). Note that these conditions are rarely met, especially in humans, and yet the Hardy–Weinberg principle generally can be met for the majority of loci studied in a population sample. In the simplest case of an autosomal locus with just two alleles, A and a, with frequencies p and q, we will have the relationship

$$(p + q)^2 = p^2 + 2pq + q^2.$$

or:

female male	A p	a q
A P	AA P^2	Aa pq
a q	aA qp	Aa q^2

This formulation (a binomial expansion) is easily generalized to multiple allele situations (a multinomial expansion) and only applies to autosomal (and pseudoautosomal loci). In haploid loci, it does not apply as genotype = allele for all NRY chromosome or mtDNA loci. For X-linked loci, a slightly different form is depicted, again for a biallelic locus in the following chessboard format (with a further assumption: equal allele frequencies in male and female gene pools):

female male	X_A p	X_a q
X_A P	$X_A X_A$ P^2	$X_A X_a$ pq
X_a q	$X_a X_A$ qp	$X_a X_a$ q^2
Y	$X_A Y$ p	$X_a Y$ q

The population analysis of two loci is not always straightforward and still today is plagued with conceptual confusions and mistakes. However, a simple explanation is possible and was advanced as early as 1922 by Felix Bernstein (Crow, 1993). Let us use the two locus example given above: autosomal with alleles A and B for the first locus and alleles 1 and 2 for the second locus. Recall that four types of gametes are defined: $A1$, $A2$, $B1$ and $B2$. Each of these different types of gametes, obtained by combining one allele from each of the loci under consideration and which are physically linked is called a **haplotype**. The Hardy–Weinberg equilibrium can be generalized to more than one locus, using this concept by stating that the genotype distribution is expected to be obtained by squaring the sum of haplotype frequencies. So, denoting by x_1, x_2, x_3 and x_4, the frequencies of haplotypes A1, A2, B1 and B2, respectively, we will have:

$$(x_1 + x_2 + x_3 + x_4)^2 = x_1^2 + x_2^2 + x_3^2 + x_4^2 + 2x_1x_2 + 2x_1x_3$$
$$+ 2x_1x_4 + 2x_2x_3 + 2x_2x_3 + 2x_2x_4 + 2x_3x_4.$$

Male \ Female	A1 x_1	A2 x_2	B1 x_3	B2 x_4
A1 x_1	A1/A1 x_1^2	A1/A2 x_1x_2	A1/B1 x_1x_3	A1/B2 x_1x_4
A2 x_2	A1/A2 x_1x_2	A2/A2 x_2^2	A2/B1 x_2x_3	A2/B2 x_2x_4
B1 x_3	A1/B1 x_1x_3	A2/B1 x_2x_3	B1/B1 x_3^2	B1/B2 x_3x_4
B2 x_4	A1/A2 x_1x_4	A2/B2 x_2x_4	B1/B2 x_3x_4	B2/B2 x_4^2

So things would seem to fit well. But this formulation does not address the question: How to relate allele and haplotype frequencies?

If we assume that there is no gametic or haplotypic association, they are simply obtained by multiplying the frequencies of the alleles involved, i.e.

	1	2
	u	v
A	$A1$	$A2$
P	pu	pv
B	$B1$	$B2$
q	qu	qv

If so, then the algebra above can be reformulated directly in terms of allele frequencies:

$$(p + q)^2 (u + v)^2 = (pu + pv + qu + qv)^2 = (x_1 + x_2 + x_3 + x_4)^2.$$

This assumption, however, is frequently violated and haplotype frequencies are not equal to the product of allele frequencies, a situation in which there is **gametic association**, (rather unfortunately) commonly named **linkage disequilibrium (LD)**.

When LD is present, we will observe

$$x1 = pu + D,$$
$$x2 = pv - D,$$
$$x3 = qu - D,$$
$$x4 = qv + D.$$

The quantity D, which measures how strong is the departure from Hardy–Weinberg proportions due to gametic association, is called **gametic determinant**. It varies between $-1/4$ and $+1/4$; being 0 when there is no LD. This statistic, appropriate for the analysis of a pair of biallelic loci, has some undesirable properties, since it depends upon the gene frequencies at both loci. Indeed the theoretical maximum absolute value is only attainable in the very special case of equally frequent (0.5) alleles at both loci. For instance, an apparently modest value of 0.14 is indeed the maximum D value for the situation depicted in the table below, since $D_{max} = 0.7 - (0.8 \times 0.7)$:

	1	2
	0.7	0.3
A	A1	A2
0.8	0.7	0.1
B	B1	B2
0.2	0	0.2

Therefore, in order to make any comparisons between populations in terms of the degree of LD, some kind of standardization is required, as is commonly achieved by converting D into

$$D' = D/D_{max}.$$

It is very important to remember that LD or genetic association is an essentially different concept from linkage (hence the misfit of using the word 'linkage' when referring to LD) and often are confused. Two important misconceptions are associated with this confusion and must be clarified. The first is to the erroneous assumption that unlinked loci must have no LD. In fact, gametic association can occur between loci on different chromosomes. The most common reason for such a situation is that the population under analysis results from recent admixture between parental populations with different allele/gene frequencies. In this case, even under random mating and maximum recombination, D is halved in each generation (i.e. $D_1 = D_0 - rD_0$). It is of course more probable to observe LD between physically close loci, since the smaller the recombination fraction, the slower is the approach to equilibrium. Thus, LD can be explored to estimate time frames for admixture events. However, it is also possible that two closely linked loci can be in gametic equilibrium in a population, provided sufficient time as recombination or recurrent mutation can breakdown initial LD.

The second misunderstanding is rooted in the fact that linkage is a property relating to the physical location of a pair of loci. If two loci are linked, they have this property in all normal individual members of a species and in all of its populations. In contrast, LD is an historical and demographic property in which non-alleles of a pair of loci do not appear, in a specific population, at the expected frequency under random association. Thus, not only in a given population some pairs of non-alleles may show significant LDs while others do not, but also that some populations may show significant LDs for some haplotypes' distributions while other populations do not.

These strange properties of LD require consideration when structuring databases, particularly for recently admixed populations (as there are many modern, cosmopolitan urban conglomerates). There are obvious forensic implications that must be addressed to make the best use of such population data sets.

A final cautionary word is warranted for the special case of sex chromosomes. Although pseudoautosomal markers at a single locus analysis level behave exactly as autosomal markers, when analyzed multifactorially among them or with X or Y linked loci, they can show bizarre properties. Since recombination in pseudoautosomal regions (PARs) occurs mainly in males, LDs in PARs occur much more often than would be expected. Also odd is that LD is expected to occur between PAR markers and both Y and X specific markers, which again drives very interesting properties to explore in forensic and evolutionary terms.

5 Genomics and Non-Mendelian Genetics

A common assumption to the theoretical framework is the constancy of the number of copies of a locus in each cell. For instance, at an autosomal locus, each somatic cell is assumed to possess two copies, while gametes carry just one. This assumption is now known to be violated for a non-negligible proportion of the DNA of complex genomes and reaching considerable frequencies in the populations of a given species. Indeed, not only copy number variants (CNVs) abound, but also reach polymorphic proportions copy number polymorphisms (CNPs), over 15% of the assembled human genome sequence (Estivill and Armengol, 2007). This type of variation, technically still hard to detect, is not uniform over the genome (Makino *et al.*, 2013), being particularly common at the Y chromosome (Jobling, 2008), and introduces a further complexity in the relationship between phenotype and genotype (Gautam *et al.*, 2012) bringing a new dimension in the forensic field (Repnikova *et al.*, 2013).

All in all, in this 'omics' era, a truly global genomic approach is still theoretically and technologically daunting and ethically debatable. If some conclusion is to be drawn now for the general implications for forensics, it must be formulated in the cautionary form that we need more than ever to appreciate and understand the various modes and mechanisms of transmission and associations in order to properly interpret the significance of DNA evidence.

References

J. F. Crow. Felix Bernstein and the first human marker locus. *Genetics*, 133(1):4–7, 1993.

C. Darwin. *On the Origin of Species by Means of Natural Selection, or the Preservation of Favoured Races in the Struggle for Life*, 1st edn. John Murray, London, 1859.

X. Estivill and L. Armengol. Copy number variants and common disorders: Filling the gaps and exploring complexity in genome-wide association studies. *PLoS Genetics*, 3(10):1787–1799, 2007.

P. Gautam, P. Jha, D. Kumar *et al.* Spectrum of large copy number variations in 26 diverse Indian populations: Potential involvement in phenotypic diversity. *Human Genetics*, 131(1):131–143, 2012.

G. H. Hardy. Mendelian proportions in a mixed population. *Science*, 28(706):49–50, 1908.

M. A. Jobling. Copy number variation on the human Y chromosome. *Cytogenetic and genome Research*, 123(1–4):253–262, 2008.

E. V. Koonin. The turbulent network dynamics of microbial evolution and the statistical tree of life. *Journal of Molecular Evolution*, 80(5–6): 244–250, 2015.

K. Landsteiner. *Zur Kenntnis der antifermentativen, lytischen und agglutinierenden Wirkungen des Blutserums und der Lymphe. Zentralblatt Bakteriologie*, 27:357–362, 1900.

D. R. Maddison, K.-S. Schulz and W. P. Maddison. The tree of life web project. *Zootaxa*, 1668:19–40, 2007.

T. Makino, A. McLysaght and M. Kawata. Genome-wide deserts for copy number variation in vertebrates. *Nature Communications*, 4:2283, 2013.

G. Mendel. Versuche über Pflanzen-Hybriden, Verhandlungen des natur-forschenden Vereines, Abhandlungen. Brünn, 4:3–47, 1866. English translation at http://www.mendelweb.org/Mendel.html, accessed March 8, 2016.

R. Owen. Karl Landsteiner and the first human marker locus. *Genetics*, 155:995, 2000.

S. Pääbo. The mosaic that is our genome. *Nature*, 421(6921):409–412, 2003.

M. A. Ragan, J. O. McInerney and J. A. Lake. The network of life: genome beginnings and evolution. Introduction. *Philosophical Transactions of the Royal Society B: Biological Sciences*, 364(1527):2169–2175, 2009.

J. Rehmeyer. Darwin, the Reluctant Mathematician. In *The Best Writing on Mathematics 2010*, M. Pitici (ed.), pp. 377–379. Princeton University Press, New Jersey, 2010.

E. A. Repnikova, J. A. Rosenfeld, A. Bailes, C. Weber, L. Erdman, A. McKinney, S. Ramsey, S. Hashimoto, D. Lamb Thrush, C. Astbury, S. C. Reshmi, L. G. Shaffer, J. M. Gastier-Foster and R. E. Pyatt. Characterization of copy number variation in genomic regions containing STR loci using array comparative genomic hybridization. *Forensic Science International: Genetics*, 7(5):475–481, 2013.

S. M. Soucy, J. Huang and J. P. Gogarten. Horizontal gene transfer: Building the web of life. *Nature Reviews Genetics*, 16(8):472–482, 2015.

Tree of Sex Consortium. Tree of sex: A database of sexual systems. *Scientific Data*, 1:140015, 2014.

Further Reading

A. Amorim. Basic principles. In *Encyclopedia of Forensic Sciences*, J. A. Siegel, P. J. Saukko (eds.), 2nd edn., vol. 1, pp. 211–213. Academic Press, Waltham, 2013a.

A. Amorim. Population Genetics. In S. Maloy, K. Hughes (eds.) *Brenner's Encyclopedia of Genetics*, 2nd edn., pp. 407–411. Elsevier, New York, 2013b.

M. Hamilton. *Population Genetics*. Wiley-Blackwell, Chichester (and the companion website, 2009, http://www.blackwellpublishing.com/hamiltongenetics/).

CHAPTER 3

Evolutionary and Population Genetics in Forensic Science

Qasim Ayub, Marc Haber and Chris Tyler-Smith

The Wellcome Trust Sanger Institute,
Wellcome Genome Campus, Hinxton, United Kingdom

1 Introduction

One aim that is central to much of forensic genetics is to assign a
DNA sample of interest to a relevant source, which may be a species,
population, family or individual depending on the circumstances.
The main elements necessary for an assignment are choosing a suitable set of variants to type in the DNA sample and matching them
to some reference database or other sample, such as one provided
by a suspect; but other elements such as predicting the phenotype
of the donor of the sample also may be involved sometimes. For an
assignment to be achieved, it is necessary to understand the properties of different categories of DNA variants, how they are distributed
among species, populations and other groups, and how they may be
linked to phenotypes. Several relevant aspects are covered in other
chapters in this book: (Mendelian genetics, Types of genomes and
markers, databases, etc.) Here, we provide an introduction to

evolutionary and population genetics, so that the reader can under-stand why it is easy to assign a DNA sample to a species as long as that species is represented in databases, or to determine whether or not two samples come from the same individual, but often much more difficult to assign to a population or breed, or to make reliable inferences about phenotype. We will focus mainly on humans because of their central importance to forensic genetics, but also refer sometimes to other species.

The organization of this chapter is as follows: first, we introduce the basic biological and demographic processes that shape the pat-terns of genetic variation in a population. Next, we provide an overview of the measures of genetic diversity. We conclude with our current understanding of origins and divergence of modern humans.

2 Processes Shaping Genetic Diversity

2.1 *Biological Processes*

2.1.1 Mutation and mutation rates

Any change in DNA nucleotide sequence is referred to as a muta-tion and this change is the fundamental means of generating new alleles and hence genetic variation. Evolutionary and forensic stud-ies mostly focus on changes that are transmitted from one individual to another and are present in the cells that form the egg or sperm in diploid organisms like humans. These changes result in genetic patterns that define individuals and populations. Mutations also occur somatically in normal tissues and in diseases (such as cancer); however, these are not inherited and the resulting genetic profile is usually unpredictable, making these types of changes less interesting for forensic scientists, except in some very specific situations like distinguishing identical twins. The starting state of a variant is referred to as "ancestral", and the state after a mutation as "derived".

Mutations occur in different sizes ranging from single nucleotide polymorphisms/variants (SNPs/SNVs), which arise by insertion, deletion or base substitutions involving only one nucleotide, to insertions, deletions or duplications involving a few to millions of nucleotides and chromosomal aneuploidies, rearrangements, translocations and chromothripsis, a recently described phenomenon by which massive multiple chromosomal rearrangements occur as a single mutational event, usually in somatic cells in cancer or certain congenital disorders (Maher and Wilson, 2012).

The rate of occurrence of mutations differs between species and even between different regions of the genome of a single species. The mutation rate of a wild-type *E. coli* bacterial strain is $\sim 1 \times 10^{-3}$ per genome per generation (Lee *et al.*, 2012). In humans, mutation rates have been estimated by sequence comparisons with chimpanzees, within pedigrees, or more recently from sequences from ancient humans who died number of years ago (ya) (Nachman and Crowell, 2000; Fu *et al.*, 2014; Soares *et al.*, 2009, Kuroki *et al.*, 2006; Xue *et al.*, 2009; Mendez *et al.*, 2013; Poznik *et al.*, 2013; Butler, 2006; Zhivotovsky *et al.*, 2004; Shi *et al.*, 2010; Burgarella and Navascués, 2011; Helgason *et al.*, 2015) (Figure 1). Pedigree-based analysis of parent–child trios estimates that the autosomal mutation rate is $2.97{-}4.00 \times 10^{-10}$ mutations per nucleotide per year, introducing around 70 ± 24 (mean $\pm$ standard deviation) new mutations in each individual (Kong *et al.*, 2012), while that reported from ancient DNA is 4.30×10^{-10} mutations per nucleotide per year (Fu *et al.*, 2014). In animals including humans, the paternal mutation rate is substantially higher than the maternal (ratio = 3.9 in humans) because of the larger number of cell divisions necessary to produce sperm than eggs (Kong *et al.*, 2012). The age of the father at conception of the child, therefore, has a major influence, contributing about two mutations per year (Kong *et al.*, 2012).

Since the mutation rate is low, copies of the same variant in different individuals are usually identical by descent from a common ancestor in which the mutation first arose. This low mutation rate forms the basis for one well-established, population-genetic model, the infinite alleles model, where the possibility of back mutations and recurrent mutations is ignored (Kimura and Crow, 1964). For slow-mutating SNPs, the infinite allele model appears to be a reasonable approximation to biological reality.

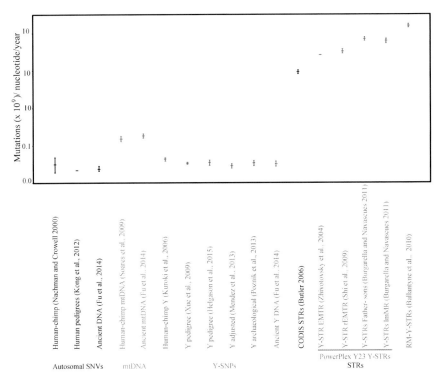

Figure 1: Mutation rates ($\times 10^9$/nucleotide/year).

Note: Published mutation rates for autosomal, mitochondrial (mtDNA) and Y-chromosomal SNPs and STRs are shown along with their 95% confidence intervals (where available; vertical lines).

However, in forensic DNA analysis, Short or Simple Tandem Repeats (STRs) also known as microsatellites, are more commonly used. These short segments of DNA, which are tandemly repeated several times, have a higher mutation rate than SNPs and are consequently multi-allelic, and much more polymorphic (Figure 1). There may be sequence variation within copies of the repeated units, and the number of repeat units changes rapidly. The high mutation rate of the STRs, which introduces variation into a population over short evolutionary times, makes them a useful tool for the elucidation of human population history and for forensic identity testing purposes. For example, most tests in paternity and disaster cases today use around 15 STRs. These have a match probability for unrelated individuals in the order of 10^{-20}, making STR profiling a powerful and standard tool for individual identification.

2.1.2 Recombination and linkage disequilibrium

Genetic recombination is the mechanism by which DNA sequences are reassorted between generations. The crossing over and exchange of DNA segments between homologous chromosomes during cell division (prophase I of meiosis) results in variation by producing new combinations of alleles. Combinations of alleles on the same chromosome are known as haplotypes. Recombination's shuffling process continually generates novel combinations of alleles, allowing an almost infinite number of possible haplotypes in a complete genome. The non-random inheritance of loci closed together in a haplotype is often expressed in terms of linkage disequilibrium (LD). One popular measure of LD between pairs of SNPs is the disequilibrium coefficient denoted r^2, which is estimated from the allelic frequencies (Pritchard and Przeworski, 2001). Genetic markers that are close to each other on a chromosome have a higher r^2 and share similar genealogies as opposed to those that are further apart ($r^2 \leq 0.1$). In the absence of evolutionary forces other than random mating and Mendelian segregation, recombination will act over multiple generations to reduce the amount of LD between two physically linked markers. LD decays approximately exponentially over time at a rate that depends on the linkage distance, or recombination fraction. The recent flow of genetic data have allowed fine-scale estimation of recombination rates which revealed hotspots of recombination containing binding sites for PR domain containing 9 (PRDM9), a zinc finger protein essential for proper meiotic progression, interspersed with stretches of relatively little recombination. The consequence is a block-like structure, with blocks showing high internal LD separated from other blocks by low LD between them (The International HapMap Consortium, 2005). In forensics, statistical tests may assume that variants assort independently, and so such variants must not be in LD, most simply achieved by choosing variants on different chromosomes. Mitochondrial DNA and the male-specific part of the

Y chromosome do not recombine, so the variants in these genomic regions are in complete LD, and thus require different statistical treatments than for autosomal markers.

2.1.3 Genetic drift

Genetic drift refers to the random change in allele frequencies from one generation to the next (Wright, 1931). This change occurs by chance since individuals in a population contribute different numbers of offspring to the next generation. The amount of genetic drift depends on several factors such as population size and growth. It eventually leads to the fixation or loss of variants. This effect occurs faster in a small population, where the variation tends to be low. Genetic drift has its greatest effect in population isolates, such as island populations or groups who do not mix with others for social reasons (Wright, 1943).

2.1.4 Natural selection

As Wright observed "selection, whether in mortality, mating or fecundity, applies to the organism as a whole and thus to the effects of the entire gene system…" (Wright, 1931). In its modern interpretation, natural selection is the differential reproduction of genetically distinct individuals within a population. It is governed by differences among individuals in traits such as mortality, fertility, mating success and the viability of the offspring, which are collectively referred to as components of fitness. The fitness of a genotype is a measure of the individual's ability to survive and reproduce. The evolutionary success of an individual is determined by their fitness relative to other genotypes in the population.

Some variants reduce the fitness of the carrier and will be selected against (purifying selection), while others increase fitness giving a selective advantage to its carriers and undergo positive selection. Population geneticists assume that most variants do neither of these things, and are therefore neutral.

The fitness of diploid organisms is determined by the interaction between the two homologous variants at a locus. If both chromosomes carry the same version of a variant, they are homozygous; if they carry different versions, then they are heterozygous for that variant. Several models can be considered for a non-neutral variant, including overdominance and underdominance, where the heterozygote has the highest or the lowest fitness, respectively. Overdominance creates a balanced polymorphism maintaining variability in a population. One classic example of a balanced polymorphism in humans is a mutation in the beta-globin gene which confers protection against malaria when heterozygous, but causes sickle-cell disease when homozygous (Rosenthal, 2011). A classic example of positive selection is the SNP rs4988235 $(c.-13910 C > T)$, which influences lactase (LCT) gene expression in adulthood and confers lactose tolerance in north-western Europeans, Central and south Asians (Gallego Romero *et al.*, 2012; Enattah *et al.*, 2002, 2007). The cis-regulatory variant is located in a region on chromosome 2, that is, in high LD in Europeans and has been identified as being under selection in several genomic scans of selection (Figure 2). Individuals with the derived T allele, present at a frequency of 51% in Europeans, are able to digest the milk sugar, lactose, as adults. The selection was an adaptation to the increased utilization of milk obtained from domesticated animals in human diets during and after the Neolithic period. Such variants can be useful in forensic analysis to help identify likely population of origin.

2.2 Demographic Processes

2.2.1 Census and effective population sizes

Effective population size, designated N_e, is a concept that was introduced by Wright (1931) and is widely used in population genetics. It refers to the size of an idealized population fitting simple population-genetic models that experiences the same amount of long-term genetic drift, and thus carries the same amount of variation, as the observed population. In contrast, the census population size includes individuals of all ages and is an official snapshot in time of a population inhabiting a particular part of the world.

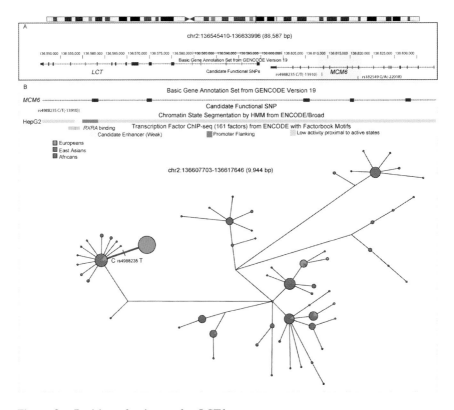

Figure 2:   Positive selection at the *LCT* locus.

Note: (A) An ~89 kb region on chromosome 2 (vertical red line on the ideogram) that spans the *LCT* and *MCM6* genes showing GENCODE (Version 19) transcript annotation. Exons are represented by boxes, the lines connecting them are introns and the arrowheads indicate the direction of transcription. The *MCM6* region highlighted in blue contains the intronic variant rs4988235. The *T* (A on the forward strand) allele of rs4988235 is associated with the ability to digest the milk sugar, lactose, as an adult, and lies in a deoxyribonuclease (DNase I) hypersensitivity region indicating open chromatin. The Encyclopedia of DNA Elements (ENCODE) annotation shows that the variant lies in a candidate enhancer region in a liver cell line (HepG2) that binds the RXRA transcription factor. (B) The lower panel shows a median-joining haplotype network of a region (highlighted in blue in panel A), that is, in high LD ($r^2 \geq 0.95$) in Europeans. Phased haplotypes in three continental populations that were generated by the Phase I of the 1000 Genomes Project were used to construct this network. The derived T allele for the regulatory variant rs4988235 lies on the branch (red) leading towards the most frequent haplotype found in Europeans (large green circle).

Generally population censuses are held once in a decade. Genetic N_e values for humans are typically 10,000–20,000, while the world census size is over 7,000,000,000. This large difference reflects the fact that the human population does not match simple population-genetic models: it was perhaps around 10,000–20,000 some 200,000 ya, but has subsequently increased enormously.

2.2.2 Migration and admixture

The movement of genetic variants from one population to another is known as gene flow. It is the consequence of individual or group migration from one inhabited area to another and the reproductive success of the migrant in his/her new location. Very simple models of migration are often used: the *n*-island model (Wright, 1931) assumes a meta-population is split into equal sized islands with equal migration rates. The stepping-stone model (Kimura and Weiss, 1964) introduces the idea of geographical substructure by only allowing gene flow between adjacent sub-populations. The isolation-by-distance model (Wright, 1943) considers a continuous population where mating choices are limited by distance, leading to genetic similarity in neighborhoods. Clearly, migration processes are far more complex than these models allow. Migrants are rarely a random sample of their source population; they are often age-structured, sex biased, and related to one another (kin-structured migration) (Jobling *et al.*, 2013).

Genetic admixture results from interbreeding between previously separated populations and results in the introduction of new variants and haplotypes. It is ubiquitous in humans. There is evidence, for example, that all non-African human populations are admixed with Neanderthals, an extinct type of human. Prominent examples of recent admixture in human populations include African–Americans and Latinos. African–Americans descend primarily from admixture between African slaves and Europeans, whereas Latinos represent admixture between Native Americans and Europeans, with or without an African component.

2.2.3 Non-random mating

Selection of mates in humans is influenced by phenotypic traits such as skin color or stature or by abstract traits such as cultural affiliation. The genetic consequence is that the allelic frequencies drift almost independently within subgroups of the population, and new mutations tend to stay within the limits of the subgroups.

The most common non-random mating pattern among humans is positive assortative mating, in which individuals mate with others who are "similar". The net evolutionary effect of this mating pattern is a progressive decrease in genetic diversity and increase in the number of homozygous genotypes in the population. A less common non-random mating pattern is the negative assortative mating, in which individuals select mates "different from themselves". This leads to increased diversity and a progressive increase in the frequency of heterozygous genotypes.

Humans have intentionally or unintentionally influenced the mating of other animals and plants in a process called artificial selection, in which breeding is regulated to preserve particular traits. There is evidence that this type of practice started early in the prehistory with key species such as dogs, cattle, wheat and rice. The consequence is a decrease in diversity across the genome of these species with runs of homozygosity (ROH) often spanning millions of base pairs at selected loci.

3 Measuring Genetic Diversity and Selection

3.1 *Measures of Molecular Diversity*

A simple measure of diversity is generated by counting the number of alleles at a locus or by calculating the mean number of alleles over a range of loci. Such summary statistics allow comparisons between populations and can inform about some demographic processes such population bottlenecks or admixture events when the mean number of alleles is low or high. Other measures of diversity take into account haplotypes or average comparisons between pairs of individuals/DNA sequences.

A simple and widely used measure of the degree of DNA variation within a population is nucleotide diversity, a concept developed by Nei (1987). It is defined as the average number of nucleotide differences per site between any two randomly chosen DNA sequences from a given population, and is denoted by π.

Early comparisons of human populations using simple measurements of genetic diversity were able to present plausible models on human origins and migrations. For example, Vigilant *et al.* (1991) used the average number of nucleotide differences per 100 bp for comparing pairs of individuals from a population. Using just 610 nucleotides and 189 individuals, they showed that Africans had the greatest genetic diversity and suggested an African origin of human mitochondrial DNA.

3.2 *Measures of Genetic Distance between Populations*

There are a number of measures for genetic distance. These usually make assumptions about the mechanisms driving population divergence. A common measure for genetic distance between two populations is the fixation index or F_{ST}. It is a measure of population differentiation and genetic structure and is estimated from the mean and variance of variant frequencies between the two populations (Weir and Cockerham, 1984). Another widely used measure of genetic distance is Nei's standard genetic distance (Nei, 1972). It assumes that differences arise due to mutation and genetic drift. Cavalli-Sforza and Edwards defined a measure that assumes genetic drift only and populations are considered as points in a multi-dimensional space (Cavalli-Sforza and Edwards, 1967). The measure is suitable for constructing phylogenetic trees and has been used with microsatellite data (Bowcock *et al.*, 1994).

3.3 *Clustering Methods for Inference on Individual Ancestry*

Individuals in a population can be grouped based on their genetic resemblance. The consequence for forensic science is that an individual's ancestry can be predicted based on their genetic information, together with previous knowledge of worldwide genetic diversity. Population sub-structure and its components need to be taken into consideration when estimating a match probability. Two main methods that are generally used for clustering individuals and populations include distance- and model-based methods.

Distance-based methods are based on calculating pairwise genetic distances between a set of individuals or populations. The information from the resulting distance matrix is then reduced to two or three dimensions by a method such as multi-dimensional scaling (MDS) and represented graphically for identification of clusters. Principal component analysis (PCA) is an alternative and very widely-used method that uses the raw data from allele frequencies rather than genetic distances (Price *et al.*, 2006). Each extracted component/axis represents a percentage of the total variation between individuals or populations (Figure 3).

Model-based methods assume that observations from each cluster are random draws from some parametric model. The widely-used ones assign individuals to *K* ancestral populations on the basis of their genotypes, while simultaneously estimating population allele frequencies using maximum-likelihood or Bayesian statistical methods (Pritchard *et al.*, 2000). These methods are implemented in software such as STRUCTURE (Pritchard *et al.*, 2000) and ADMIXTURE (Figure 3) (Alexander *et al.*, 2009).

In forensic DNA analysis, samples obtained from a crime scene may be of unknown ancestry. We can apply these methods and assign them to a continental origin or geographical area with high confidence. There are also a number of commercial personal genetic testing ventures that provide ancestry-related information. Some use ancestry informative markers (AIMs), variants with large allele frequency differences among populations from different geographical regions (Halder *et al.*, 2008; Bauchet *et al.*, 2007). Although many of these are anonymous and have no apparent phenotypic consequences, they also include several variants like the *LCT/MCM6* variant associated with lactose tolerance mentioned above and others that are linked to phenotypic traits like eye, hair and skin color (Table 1). Specialized forensic kits use the HIrisPlex system for prediction of hair and eye color from DNA profiling (Walsh *et al.*, 2013). Genotyping AIMs in samples of unknown ancestry can identify with high confidence the continental origins of an individual and determine what proportion of ancestry is likely to be derived from each geographical region.

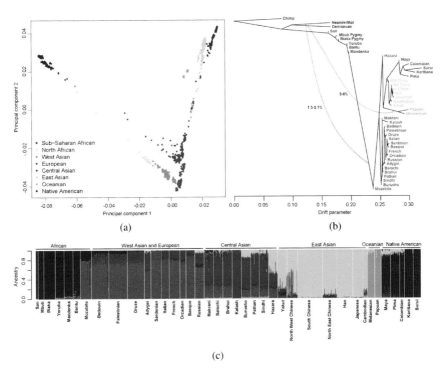

Figure 3:   Individual ancestry and population relationships based on genome-wide DNA variants using the Human Genome Diversity Project (HGDP) dataset.

Note: (A) Principal component analysis using hundreds of thousands of SNPs from each of the 1,041 individuals in the HGDP dataset. Each individual is represented by a point on the plot and is colored according to his or her geographic location. The clustering of points of the same color illustrates how human genetic diversity is correlated with geography. (B) A maximum likelihood tree of population relationships using genome-wide allele frequency data. The tree was rooted using the chimpanzee genome sequence. In addition, the genomes of two archaic humans, Neanderthal and Denisova, were also used in the comparison. The population split of Neanderthals and Denisovans from modern humans was estimated to have occurred at least 550,000 ya. However, genetic studies have shown that several gene flow events occurred among Neanderthals, Denisovans and early non-African modern humans after their initial divergence. (C) World population structure inferred by ADMIXTURE. Each thin vertical line (which merge into apparently solid blocks of color in the figure) is partitioned into colored segments representing ancestry probabilities of an individual from six inferred ancestral populations.

Table 1: Selected ancestry informative markers and variants associated with skin, eye and hair color adapted from Walsh *et al.* (2012).

Variation	Chr	Position$	Variant*	Gene	Consequence	Change**	Phenotype
rs3827760	2	108897145	A/G	*EDAR*	Missense	Val370Ala	Hair thickness, teeth, glands
rs4988235	2	135851076	G/A	*MCM6/LCT*	Intronic		Lactase persistence
rs16891982	5	33951588	C/G	*SLC45A2*	Missense	Leu374Phe	Eye & hair pigmentation
rs28777	5	33958854	C/A	*SLC45A2*	Intronic		Hair pigmentation
rs12203592	6	396321	C/T	*IRF4*	Intronic		Eye & hair pigmentation
rs4959270	6	457748	C/A	*EXOC2*	Intergenic		Hair pigmentation
rs683	9	12709305	A/C	*TYRP1*	3_prime_UTR_variant		Hair pigmentation
rs1042602	11	89178528	C/A	*TYR*	Missense	Ser192Tyr	Hair & skin
rs1393350	11	89277878	G/A	*TYR*	Intronic		Eye pigmentation
rs12821256	12	88934558	T/C	*KITLG*	Intergenic		Hair pigmentation
rs12896399	14	92307319	G/T	*SLC24A4*	Intergenic		Eye pigmentation
rs2402130	14	92334859	G/A	*SLC24A4*	Intronic		Hair pigmentation
rs1800407	15	27985172	C/T	*OCA2*	Missense	Arg419Gln	Eye & hair pigmentation
rs12913832	15	28120472	A/G	*HERC2*	Intronic		Eye & hair pigmentation
rs1426654	15	48134287	G/A	*SLC24A5*	Missense	Thr111Ala	Skin pigmentation
rs17822931	16	48224287	C/T	*ABCC11*	Missense	Gly180Arg	Ear wax
rs312262906	16	89919342	InsA	*MC1R*	Frameshift	Asn29LysfsTer14	Red hair

rs1805005	16	89919436	G/T	*MC1R*	Missense	Val60Leu	Hair pigmentation
rs1805006	16	89919510	C/A	*MC1R*	Missense	Asp84Glu	Hair pigmentation
rs2228479	16	89919532	G/A	*MC1R*	Missense	Val92Met	Hair pigmentation
rs11547464	16	89919683	G/A	*MC1R*	Missense	Arg142His	Hair pigmentation
rs1805007	16	89919709	C/T	*MC1R*	Missense	Arg151Cys	Hair pigmentation
rs201326893	16	89919714	C/A	*MC1R*	Stop gained	Tyr152Stop	Red hair
rs1110400	16	89919722	T/C	*MC1R*	Missense	Ile155Thr	Hair pigmentation
rs1805008	16	89919736	C/T	*MC1R*	Missense	Arg160Trp	Hair pigmentation
rs885479	16	89919746	G/A	*MC1R*	Missense	Arg163Gln	Hair pigmentation
rs1805009	16	89920138	G/C	*MC1R*	Missense	Asp294His	Hair pigmentation
rs2378249	20	34630286	A/G	*PIGU*	Intronic		Hair pigmentation

Chr = chromosome.

$ Variant position in Human Reference version GRCh38.

* Ancestral/Derived variant alleles.

** amino acid change, if any.

3.4 *TMRCA*

The time to most recent common ancestor (TMRCA) is another term used to describe the relatedness between individuals or haplotypes. In human genealogy, TMRCA refers to the number of generations that separate a set of individuals from their most recent genealogical common ancestor. The term is also used to describe a common ancestor of individual DNA sequences at a locus. TMRCAs of different loci within a particular pair of individuals vary substantially and can be several orders of magnitude older than the genealogical TMRCA.

If we go back in time, then all humans presently alive would be related to everyone else; surprisingly, perhaps, the genealogical MRCA of all living humans lived just a few centuries ago (Rohde *et al.*, 2004). In forensics, the aim is often to estimate how long ago samples of interest share an ancestor at a particular locus such as mtDNA or the Y chromosome. This estimate employs a mutation rate, which in itself is uncertain. Increasing the length of sequence or number of markers that are genotyped can increase confidence in estimates for the TMRCA.

4 Genetic Diversity in Humans

4.1 *Comparison of Humans with other Species*

Each human is genetically distinct because of both the assortment of variation from the population they inherit and the new mutations they carry; a few genetic differences which arise during development can be detected even between 'identical' (monozygotic) twins, who develop from a single zygote. Differences between individuals form the basis of DNA-based forensic analysis, and there are large variation databases for humans and other species commonly assayed in DNA forensics (Table 2).

Allele frequencies differ slightly in different human populations and more so in geographically isolated populations mainly due to genetic drift and in some instances natural selection. These differences are of significance not only from the evolutionary or forensic

Table 2: Useful links for large scale variation datasets.

Databases url
1000 Genomes Project http://browser.1000genomes.org/index.html
The ALlele FREquency Database (ALRED) http://alfred.med.yale.edu/
dbSNP http://www.ncbi.nlm.nih.gov/SNP/
Dog Genome SNP Database (DoGSD) http://dogsd.big.ac.cn/
CANINE CODIS database https://www.vgl.ucdavis.edu/forensics/CANINECODIS.php
HGDP-CEPH browser http://spsmart.cesga.es/search.php?dataSet=ceph_stanford
MITOMAP: A human mitochondrial genome database http://www.mitomap.org/ MITOMAP
SNPedia http://www.snpedia.com/index.php/SNPedia
Simons Genome Diversity Project Dataset https://www.simonsfoundation.org/life-sciences/simons-genome-diversity-project-dataset/
Y-STR Haplotype Reference Database (YHRD) https://yhrd.org/

point of view, but also from the medical point of view such as the prevalence of the sickle cell variant in malaria-endemic regions of Africa.

In general, any two unrelated human individuals picked at random from a world sample are 99.9% identical. Human populations from different parts of the world are so similar because we share a common origin within the last few hundred thousand years, a recent time from an evolutionary perspective. There is more genetic diversity in Africans than in people from other continents, for reasons explained below. The low genetic variation in humans overall is remarkable in comparison to other apes: for example, the recent sequencing of 79 great ape genomes identified more than double the number of SNPs found in over a thousand diverse humans (Prado-Martinez *et al.*, 2013; The 1000 Genomes Project Consortium, 2010).

4.2 Modern Human Origins and Spread

Modern humans are the sole surviving "rational man" species from the many forms of human ancestors who have lived over the past millions of years since our separation from the chimpanzee lineage some 6–7 million ya. Over the last four decades, archeological, fossil and genetic data have provided evidence in favor of a predominantly recent African origin of modern humans. Specifically, by 200,000 ya the fossil record from Africa shows the earliest appearance of anatomically modern skeletal features, with the Omo and Herto skulls from Ethiopia, representing likely ancestors of modern humans 195,000–160,000 ya (Weaver, 2012; McDougall *et al.*, 2005; White *et al.*, 2003). The fossil record also indicates that the first out-of-Africa migration of anatomically modern humans occurred before 100,000 ya (Schwarcz and Grun, 1992), into the Levant, where modern humans lived around 90,000 ya. However, it is believed that the geographical range of anatomically modern humans later retracted back to Africa, due to their inability to thrive in the harsher, colder, and more arid non-tropical environment of the Levant soon after 90,000 ya. This event is indicated by the lack of archaeological records of modern humans from the Levant between 90,000 and 60,000 ya (Bar-Yosef, 1992). Furthermore, archaeology indicates that these humans appear to have been behaviorally pre-modern and to have been replaced by Neanderthals during the colder period.

During the same period of ~100,000–60,000 ya, evidence for modern human behavior begins to appear in the archaeological record in Africa. There is much controversy about what constitutes modern human behavior, but there is some consensus about it being associated with increasingly diverse materials used in toolmaking, long-distance transport of some of these materials and the appearance of decorative arts such as ochre use and bead construction. Subsequently, archaeological and genetic data suggest a date of around 70,000–60,000 ya for a second expansion out of Africa of fully modern (i.e. both anatomically and behaviorally modern) humans and the origin of all current non-African populations (Stringer, 2012; Henn *et al.*, 2012; Quintana-Murci *et al.*, 1999). The timing, number of exits and routes used by these fully modern humans in their spread out of Africa all remain controversial (Balter, 2011; Macaulay *et al.*, 2005). Dates between 100,000 and 50,000 ya, one or two exits, and the use of either a Northern route *via* Egypt and Sinai, or a Southern route across the Bab el Mandeb strait into Arabia have been proposed, with some support for the Northern route (Pagani *et al.*, 2015). Despite these uncertainties, there is clear evidence that the wayfarers reached Australia by ~50,000 ya. The expansion was accompanied by a continuous decrease of genetic diversity with increasing distance from Africa, a pattern that is consistent with a serial founder model where new populations are formed from a subset of the expanding wave outward from Africa. (Mele *et al.*, 2012; Henn *et al.*, 2012; DeGiorgio *et al.*, 2009; Li *et al.*, 2008). This origin explains why there are no discrete human 'races', and why any attempt to categorize humans into distinct categories will inevitably fail.

The simple out-of-Africa model of human expansion has been revised in the last few years in the light of results from ancient DNA research. Analyses of DNA obtained from bones of two archaic human groups, the Neanderthals and Denisovans, suggest that there was a limited amount of gene flow from archaic to modern humans. This admixture with archaic hominins most likely occurred in separate brief episodes (Green *et al.*, 2010; Reich *et al.*, 2010), giving rise to a "leaky replacement" model. One episode occurred at an early stage of the out-of-Africa expansion introducing ~2% Neanderthal gene flow into all non-Africans, and the second occurred only in the ancestors of populations in Oceania introducing ~5% Denisovan gene flow. It is estimated that New Guineans, Australian aboriginals and Bougainville Islanders received 4–6% of their genetic material from archaic Denisovans and that it occurred most likely in South East Asia (Reich *et al.*, 2011). This result suggests that the archaic Denisovans were spread throughout Asia and not restricted

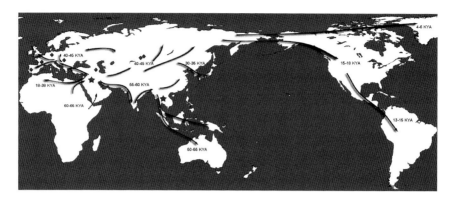

Figure 4:   Out of Africa expansion of modern humans.

Note: The map shows a 2015 view of the routes and dates of the initial expansion waves that led to anatomically and behaviorally modern humans populating the world after the out-of-Africa migration event. There are two possible routes that modern humans could have used to exit Africa: via Egypt towards the Levant or across the Bab-el-Mandeb strait into Arabia. Pagani *et al.* (2015) suggest that the northern route was more probable but genetic and archaeological investigations are still on-going. Modern humans migrated out of Africa around 60,000 ya and inter-bred with at least two archaic distinct human groups that inhabited Eurasia at that time. Blue and purple diamonds show sites where Neanderthal and Denisovans remains have been found respectively. Stars show putative locations of archaic and modern human admixture.

to the Altai Mountain region in Siberia, where the sequenced bone sample was discovered. These admixture events with archaic humans indicate the complexity of modern human origins (Figure 4), and additional admixture events are likely.

Genetic studies have proposed that admixture with archaic humans could have introduced a few beneficial alleles which helped modern humans to adapt to non-African environments. For example, Neanderthal alleles are enriched for genes affecting keratin filaments which make up most of the outer layer of human skin (Sankararaman *et al.*, 2014). On the other hand, Denisovans appear to have provided genetic variation that enabled high-altitude adaptation in Tibetans (Huerta-Sanchez *et al.*, 2014). These studies show that archaic alleles from extinct species continue to shape human biology and that modern human origin has been more complex than we imagined a decade ago.

Ancient DNA sequences have also changed our perceptions about origins of modern Europeans and shown multiple population expansions and contractions. Present-day Europeans are now considered to be a mixture of eastern and western hunter-gatherer populations and Near Eastern farmers with some genetic input from an ancestral north Eurasian population best represented by fossil material from Siberia, the Málta boy skeleton, with later contributions from Bronze Age Yamnaya people as well as migrations within the historical period (Haak *et al.*, 2015; Lazaridis *et al.*, 2014; Raghavan *et al.*, 2014).

5 Conclusions

Population and evolutionary genetics explain the origin of modern human population structure and relationships. Extant human populations are related by descent from a common African ancestral population, and population sub-structure has arisen subsequently, including by small amounts of admixture with archaic humans. Geographical structure is limited in amount and is gradual rather than showing abrupt changes. It provides a basis for genetic ancestry inference, but also needs to be accounted for in DNA-based forensic analyses. Most genetic variants have no impact on phenotype (i.e. they are neutral), but a few do affect phenotype and allow some limited information about appearance to be obtained from a DNA sample.

References

D. H. Alexander, J. Novembre, K. Lange. Fast model-based estimation of ancestry in unrelated individuals. *Genome Research*, 19:1655–1664, 2009.

M. Balter. Was North Africa the launch pad for modern human migrations? *Science*, 331:20–23, 2011.

O. Bar-Yosef. The role of western Asia in modern human origins. *Philosophical Transactions of the Royal Society B: Biological Sciences*, 337:193–200, 1992.

M. Bauchet, B. Mcevoy, L. N. Pearson, E. E. Quillen, T. Sarkisian, K. Hovhannesyan, R. Deka, D. G. Bradley and M. D. Shriver. Measuring European population stratification with microarray genotype data. *The American Journal of Human Genetics,* 80:948–956, 2007.

A. Bowcock, A. Ruiz-linares, J. Tomfohrde, E. Minch, J. Kidd and L. Cavalli-Sforza. High resolution of human evolutionary trees with polymorphic microsatellites. *Nature,* 368:455–457, 1994.

C. Burgarella and M. Navascués, Mutation rate estimates for 110 Y-chromosome STRs combining population and father–son pair data. *European Journal of Human Genetics,* 19:70–75, 2011.

J. M. Butler. Genetics and genomics of core short tandem repeat loci used in human identity testing. *Journal of Forensic Sciences,* 51:253–265, 2006.

L. L. Cavalli-Sforza and W. Edwards. Phylogenetic analysis models and estimation procedures. *The American Journal of Human Genetics,* 19:233–257, 1967.

M. DeGiorgio, M. Jakobsson and N. A. Rosenberg. Out of Africa: Modern human origins special feature: explaining worldwide patterns of human genetic variation using a coalescent-based serial founder model of migration outward from Africa. *Proceedings of the National Academy of Sciences USA,* 106:16057–16062, 2009.

N. S. Enattah, T. Sahi, E. Savilahti, J. D. Terwilliger, L. Peltonen and I. Jarvela. Identification of a variant associated with adult-type hypolactasia. *Nature Genetics,* 30:233–237, 2002.

N. S. Enattah, A. Trudeau, V. Pimenoff, L. Maiuri, S. Auricchio, L. Greco, M. Rossi, M. Lentze, J. K. Seo, S. Rahgozar, I. Khalil, M. Alifrangis, S. Natah, L. Groop, N. Shaat, A. Kozlov, G. Verschubskaya, D. Comas, K. Bulayeva, S. Q. Mehdi, J. D. Terwilliger, T. Sahi, E. Savilahti, M. Perola, A. Sajantila, I. Jarvela and L. Peltonen. Evidence of still-ongoing convergence evolution of the lactase persistence T-13910 alleles in humans. *American Journal Human Genetics,* 81:615–625, 2007.

Q. Fu, H. Li, P. Moorjani, F. Jay, S. M. Slepchenko, A. A. Bondarev, P. L. Johnson, A. Aximu-Petri, K. Prufer, C. De Filippo, M. Meyer, N. Zwyns, D. C. Salazar-Garcia, Y. V. Kuzmin, S. G. Keates, P. A. Kosintsev, D. I. Razhev, M. P. Richards, N. V. Peristov, M. Lachmann, K. Douka, T. F. Higham, M. Slatkin, J. J. Hublin, D. Reich, J. Kelso, T. B. Viola and S. Paabo. Genome sequence of a 45,000-year-old modern human from western Siberia. *Nature,* 514:445–449, 2014.

I. Gallego Romero, C. Basu Mallick, A. Liebert, F. Crivellaro, G. Chaubey, Y. Itan, M. Metspalu, M. Eaaswarkhanth, R. Pitchappan, R. Villems,

D. Reich, L. Singh, K. Thangaraj, M. G. Thomas, D. M. Swallow, M. Mirazon Lahr and T. Kivisild. Herders of Indian and European cattle share their predominant allele for lactase persistence. *Mol Biol Evol,* 29:249–260, 2012.

R. E. Green, J. Krause, A. W. Briggs, T. Maricic, U. Stenzel, M. Kircher, N. Patterson, H. Li, W. Zhai, M. H. Fritz, N. F. Hansen, E. Y. Durand, A. S. Malaspinas, J. D. Jensen, T. Marques-Bonet, C. Alkan, K. Prufer, M. Meyer, H. A. Burbano, J. M. Good, R. Schultz, A. Aximu-Petri, A. Butthof, B. Hober, B. Hoffner, M. Siegemund, A. Weihmann, C. Nusbaum, E. S. Lander, C. Russ, N. Novod, J. Affourtit, M. Egholm, C. Verna, P. Rudan, D. Brajkovic, Z. Kucan, I. Gusic, V. B. Doronichev, L. V. Golovanova, C. Lalueza-Fox, M. De La Rasilla, J. Fortea, A. Rosas, R. W. Schmitz, P. L. Johnson, E. E. Eichler, D. Falush, E. Birney, J. C. Mullikin, M. Slatkin, R. Nielsen, J. Kelso, M. Lachmann, D. Reich and S. Paabo, A draft sequence of the Neandertal genome. *Science,* 328:710–722, 2010.

W. Haak, I. Lazaridis, N. Patterson, N. Rohland, S. Mallick, B. Llamas, G. Brandt, S. Nordenfelt, E. Harney, K. Stewardson, Q. Fu, A. Mittnik, E. Banffy, C. Economou, M. Francken, S. Friederich, R. G. Pena, F. Hallgren, V. Khartanovich, A. Khokhlov, M. Kunst, P. Kuznetsov, H. Meller, O. Mochalov, V. Moiseyev, N. Nicklisch, S. L. Pichler, R. Risch, M. A. Rojo Guerra, C. Roth, A. Szecsenyi-Nagy, J. Wahl, M. Meyer, J. Krause, D. Brown, D. Anthony, A. Cooper, K. W. Alt and D. Reich. Massive migration from the steppe was a source for Indo-European languages in Europe. *Nature,* 522:207–211, 2015.

I. Halder, M. Shriver, M. Thomas, J. R. Fernandez and T. Frudakis. A panel of ancestry informative markers for estimating individual biogeographical ancestry and admixture from four continents: utility and applications. *Human Mutation,* 29:648–658, 2008.

A. Helgason, A. W. Einarsson, V. B. Guethmundsdottir, A. Sigurethsson, E. D. Gunnarsdottir, A. Jagadeesan, S. S. Ebenesersdottir, A. Kong and K. Stefansson. The Y-chromosome point mutation rate in humans. *Nature Genetics,* 47:453–457, 2015.

B. M. Henn, L. L. Cavalli-Sforza and M. W. Feldman. The great human expansion. *Proceedings of the National Academy of Sciences U S A,* 109:17758–17764, 2012.

E. Huerta-Sanchez, X. Jin, Asan, Z. Bianba, B. M. Peter, N. Vinckenbosch, Y. Liang, X. Yi, M. He, M. Somel, P. Ni, B. Wang, X. Ou, Huasang, J. Luosang, Z. X. Cuo, K. Li, G. Gao, Y. Yin, W. Wang, X. Zhang, X. Xu,

H. Yang, Y. Li, J. Wang, J. Wang and R. Nielsen. Altitude adaptation in Tibetans caused by introgression of Denisovan-like DNA. *Nature*, 512:194–197, 2014.

M. Jobling, E. Hollox, M. Hurles, T. Kivisild and C. Tyler-Smith. *Human Evolutionary Genetics*. New York, Garland Science, 2013.

M. Kimura and J. F. Crow. The number of alleles that can be maintained in a finite population. *Genetics*, 49:725–738, 1964.

M. Kimura and G. H. Weiss, The stepping stone model of population structure and the decrease of genetic correlation with distance. *genetics*, 49:561–576, 1964.

A. Kong, M. L. Frigge, G. Masson, S. Besenbacher, P. Sulem, G. Magnusson, S. A. Gudjonsson, A. Sigurdsson, A. Jonasdottir, W. S. Wong, G. Sigurdsson, G. B. Walters, S. Steinberg, H. Helgason, G. Thorleifsson, D. F. Gudbjartsson, A. Helgason, O. T. Magnusson, U. Thorsteinsdottir and K. Stefansson. Rate of de novo mutations and the importance of father's age to disease risk. *Nature*, 488:471–475, 2012.

Y. Kuroki, A. Toyoda, H. Noguchi, T. D. Taylor, T. Itoh, D. S. Kim, D. W. Kim, S. H. Choi, I. C. Kim, H. H. Choi, Y. S. Kim, Y. Satta, N. Saitou, T. Yamada, S. Morishita, M. Hattori, Y. Sakaki, H. S. Park and A. Fujiyama. Comparative analysis of chimpanzee and human Y chromosomes unveils complex evolutionary pathway. *Nature Genetics*, 38:158–167, 2006.

I. Lazaridis, N. Patterson, A. Mittnik, G. Renaud, S. Mallick, K. Kirsanow, P. H. Sudmant, J. G. Schraiber, S. Castellano, M. Lipson, B. Berger, C. Economou, R. Bollongino, Q. Fu, K. I. Bos, S. Nordenfelt, H. Li, C. De Filippo, K. Prufer, S. Sawyer, C. Posth, W. Haak, F. Hallgren, E. Fornander, N. Rohland, D. Delsate, M. Francken, J. M. Guinet, J. Wahl, G. Ayodo, H. A. Babiker, G. Bailliet, E. Balanovska, O. Balanovsky, R. Barrantes, G. Bedoya, H. Ben-Ami, J. Bene, F. Berrada, C. M. Bravi, F. Brisighelli, G. B. Busby, Cali, F. M. Churnosov, D. E. Cole, D. Corach, L. Damba, G. Van Driem, S. Dryomov, J. M. Dugoujon, S. A. Fedorova, I. Gallego Romero, M. Gubina, M. Hammer, B. M. Henn, T. Hervig, U. Hodoglugil, A. R. Jha, S. Karachanak-Yankova, R. Khusainova, E. Khusnutdinova, R. Kittles, T. Kivisild, W. Klitz, V. Kucinskas, A. Kushniarevich, L. Laredj, S. Litvinov, T. Loukidis, R. W. Mahley, B. Melegh, E. Metspalu, J. Molina, J. Mountain, K. Nakkalajarvi, D. Nesheva, T. Nyambo, L. Osipova, J. Parik, F. Platonov, O. Posukh, V. Romano, F. Rothhammer, I. Rudan, R. Ruizbakiev, H. Sahakyan, A. Sajantila, A. Salas, E. B. Starikovskaya,

A. Tarekegn, D. Toncheva, S. Turdikulova, I. Uktveryte, O. Utevska, R. Vasquez, M. Villena, M. Voevoda, C. A. Winkler, L. Yepiskoposyan, P. Zalloua, *et al.* Ancient human genomes suggest three ancestral populations for present-day Europeans. *Nature,* 513:409–413, 2014.

H. Lee, E. Popodi, H. Tanga and P. L. Foster. Rate and molecular spectrum of spontaneous mutations in the bacterium *Escherichia coli* as determined by whole-genome sequencing. *PNAS USA,* 109:E2774–E2783, 2012.

J. Z. Li, D. M. Absher, H. Tang, A. M. Southwick, A. M. Casto, S. Ramachandran, H. M. Cann, G. S. Barsh, M. Feldman, L. L. Cavalli-Sforza and R. M. Myers, Worldwide human relationships inferred from genome-wide patterns of variation. *Science,* 319:1100–1104, 2008.

V. Macaulay, C. Hill, A. Achilli, C. Rengo, D. Clarke, W. Meehan, J. Blackburn, O. Semino, R. Scozzari, F. Cruciani, A. Taha, N. K. Shaari, J. M. Raja, P. Ismail, Z. Zainuddin, W. Goodwin, D. Bulbeck, H. J. Bandelt, S. Oppenheimer, A. Torroni and M. Richards, Single, rapid coastal settlement of Asia revealed by analysis of complete mitochondrial genomes. *Science,* 308:1034–1036, 2005.

C. A. Maher and R. K. Wilson, Chromothripsis and human disease: piecing together the shattering process. *Cell,* 148:29–32, 2012.

I. Mcdougall, F. H. Brown and J. G. Fleagle, Stratigraphic placement and age of modern humans from Kibish, Ethiopia. *Nature,* 433:733–736, 2005.

M. Mele, A. Javed, M. Pybus, P. Zalloua, M. Haber, D. Comas, M. G. Netea, O. Balanovsky, E. Balanovska, L. Jin, Y. Yang, R. M. Pitchappan, G. Arunkumar, L. Parida, F. Calafell, J. Bertranpetit and C. Genographic, Recombination gives a new insight in the effective population size and the history of the old world human populations. *Molecular Biology and Evolution,* 29:25–30, 2012.

F. L. Mendez, T. Krahn, B. Schrack, A. M. Krahn, K. R. Veeramah, A. E. Woerner, F. L. Fomine, N. Bradman, M. G. Thomas, T. M. Karafet and M. F. Hammer, An African American paternal lineage adds an extremely ancient root to the human Y chromosome phylogenetic tree. *The American Journal of Human Genetics,* 92:454–459, 2013.

M. W. Nachman and S. L. Crowell, Estimate of the mutation rate per nucleotide in humans. *Genetics,* 156:297–304, 2000.

M. Nei. Genetic distance between populations. *The American Naturalist,* 106:283–292, 1972.

M. Nei. *Molecular Evolutionary Genetics.* New York, Colombia University Press, 1987.

L. Pagani, S. Schiffels, D. Gurdasani, P. Danecek, A. Scally, Y. Chen, Y. Xue, M. Haber, R. Ekong, T. Oljira, E. Mekonnen, D. Luiselli, N. Bradman, E. Bekele, P. Zalloua, R. Durbin, T. Kivisild and C. Tyler-Smith. Tracing the route of modern humans out of Africa by using 225 human genome sequences from Ethiopians and Egyptians. *The American Journal of Human Genetics*, 96:986–991, 2015.

G. D. Poznik, B. M. Henn, M. C. Yee, E. Sliwerska, G. M. Euskirchen, A. A. Lin, M. Snyder, L. Quintana-Murci, J. M. Kidd, P. A. Underhill and C. D. Bustamante, Sequencing Y chromosomes resolves discrepancy in time to common ancestor of males versus females. *Science*, 341:562–565, 2013.

J. Prado-Martinez, P. H. Sudmant, J. M. Kidd, H. Li, J. L. Kelley, B. Lorente-Galdos, K. R. Veeramah, A. E. Woerner, T. D. O'connor, G. Santpere, A. Cagan, C. Theunert, F. Casals, H. Laayouni, K. Munch, A. Hobolth, A. E. Halager, M. Malig, J. Hernandez-Rodriguez, I. Hernando-Herraez, K. Prufer, M. Pybus, L. Johnstone, M. Lachmann, C. Alkan, D. Twigg, N. Petit, C. Baker, F. Hormozdiari, M. Fernandez-Callejo, M. Dabad, M. L. Wilson, L. Stevison, C. Camprubi, T. Carvalho, A. Ruiz-Herrera, L. Vives, M. Mele, T. Abello, I. Kondova, R. E. Bontrop, A. Pusey, F. Lankester, J. A. Kiyang, R. A. Bergl, E. Lonsdorf, S. Myers, M. Ventura, P. Gagneux, D. Comas, H. Siegismund, J. Blanc, L. Agueda-Calpena, M. Gut, L. Fulton, S. A. Tishkoff, J. C. Mullikin, R. K. Wilson, I. G. Gut, M. K. Gonder, O. A. Ryder, B. H. Hahn, A. Navarro, J. M. Akey, J. Bertranpetit, D. Reich, T. Mailund, M. H. Schierup, C. Hvilsom, A. M. Andres, J. D. Wall, C. D. Bustamante, M. F. Hammer, E. E. Eichler and T. Marques-Bonet. Great ape genetic diversity and population history. *Nature*, 499:471–475, 2013.

A. L. Price, N. J. Patterson, R. M. Plenge, M. E. Weinblatt, N. A. Shadick and D. Reich. Principal components analysis corrects for stratification in genome-wide association studies. *Nature Genetics*, 38:904–909, 2006.

J. K. Pritchard and M. Przeworski. Linkage disequilibrium in humans: models and data. *The American Journal of Human Genetics*, 69:1–14, 2001.

J. K. Pritchard, M. Stephens and P. Donnelly. Inference of population structure using multilocus genotype data. *Genetics*, 155:945–959, 2000.

L. Quintana-Murci, O. Semino, H. J. Bandelt, G. Passarino, K. Mcelreavey and A. S. Santachiara-Benerecetti. Genetic evidence of an early exit of Homo sapiens sapiens from Africa through eastern Africa. *Nature Genetics*, 23:437–441, 1999.

M. Raghavan, P. Skoglund, K. E. Graf, M. Metspalu, A. Albrechtsen, I. Moltke, S. Rasmussen, T. W. Stafford, Jr. L. Orlando, E. Metspalu, M. Karmin, K. Tambets, S. Rootsi, R. Magi, P. F. Campos, E. Balanovska, O. Balanovsky, E. Khusnutdinova, S. Litvinov, L. P. Osipova, S. A. Fedorova, M. I. Voevoda, M. Degiorgio, T. Sicheritz-Ponten, S. Brunak, S. Demeshchenko, T. Kivisild, R. Villems, R. Nielsen, M. Jakobsson and E. Willerslev. Upper Palaeolithic Siberian genome reveals dual ancestry of Native Americans. *Nature*, 505:87–91, 2014.

D. Reich, R. E. Green, M. Kircher, J. Krause, N. Patterson, E. Y. Durand, B. Viola, A. W. Briggs, U. Stenzel, P. L. Johnson, T. Maricic, J. M. Good, T. Marques-Bonet, C. Alkan, Q. Fu, S. Mallick, H. Li, M. Meyer, E. E. Eichler, M. Stoneking, M. Richards, S. Talamo, M. V. Shunkov, A. P. Derevianko, J. J. Hublin, J. Kelso, M. Slatkin and S. Paabo. Genetic history of an archaic hominin group from Denisova Cave in Siberia. *Nature*, 468:1053–1060, 2010.

D. Reich, N. Patterson, M. Kircher, F. Delfin, M. R. Nandineni, I. Pugach, A. M. Ko, Y. C. Ko, T. A. Jinam, M. E. Phipps, N. Saitou, A. Wollstein, M. Kayser, S. Paabo and M. Stoneking. Denisova admixture and the first modern human dispersals into Southeast Asia and Oceania. *The American Journal of Human Genetics*, 89:516–528, 2011.

D. L. Rohde, S. Olson and J. T. Chang, Modelling the recent common ancestry of all living humans. *Nature*, 431:562–566, 2004.

P. J. Rosenthal. Lessons from sickle cell disease in the treatment and control of malaria. *The New England Journal of Medicine*, 364:2549–2551, 2011.

S. Sankararaman, S. Mallick, M. Dannemann, K. Prufer, J. Kelso, S. Paabo, N. Patterson and D. Reich, The genomic landscape of Neanderthal ancestry in present-day humans. *Nature*, 507:354–357, 2014.

H. P. Schwarcz and R. Grun, Electron spin resonance (ESR) dating of the origin of modern man. *Philosophical Transactions of the Royal Society B: Biological Sciences*, 337:145–148, 1992.

W. Shi, Q. Ayub, M. Vermeulen, R.-G. Shao, S. Zuniga, K. Van Der Gaag, P. De Knijff, M. Kayser, Y. Xue and C. Tyler-Smith. A worldwide survey of human male demographic history based on Y-SNP and Y-STR data from the HGDP–CEPH populations. *Molecular Biology and Evolution*, 27:385–393, 2010.

P. Soares, L. Ermini, N. Thomson, M. Mormina, T. Rito, A. Rohl, A. Salas, S. Oppenheimer, V. Macaulay and M. B. Richards, Correcting for purifying selection: an improved human mitochondrial molecular clock. *The American Journal of Human Genetics*, 84:740–759, 2009.

C. Stringer. Evolution: What makes a modern human. *Nature*, 485:33–35, 2012.

The 1000 Genomes Project Consortium. A map of human genome variation from population-scale sequencing. *Nature*, 467:1061–1073, 2010.

The International Hapmap Consortium. A haplotype map of the human genome. *Nature*, 437:1299–1320, 2005.

L. Vigilant, M. Stoneking, H. Harpending, K. Hawkes and A. C. Wilson, 1991. African populations and the evolution of human mitochondrial DNA. *Science*, 253:1503–1507, 1991.

S. Walsh, F. Liu, A. Wollstein, L. Kovatsi, A. Ralf, A. Kosiniak-Kamysz, W. Branicki and M. Kayser. The HIrisPlex system for simultaneous prediction of hair and eye colour from DNA. *Forensic Science International: Genetics*, 7:98–115, 2013.

T. D. Weaver. Did a discrete event 200,000–100,000 years ago produce modern humans? *Journal of Human Evolution* , 63:121–126, 2012.

B. S. Weir and C. C. Cockerham, Estimating F-statistics for the analysis of population structure. *Evolution*, 38:1358–1370, 1984.

T. D. White, B. Asfaw, D. Degusta, H. Gilbert, G. D. Richards, G. Suwa and F. C. Howell, Pleistocene *Homo sapiens* from Middle Awash, Ethiopia. *Nature*, 423:742–747, 2003.

S. Wright. Evolution in Mendelian populations. *Genetics*, 16:97–159, 1931.

S. Wright. Isolation by Distance. *Genetics*, 28:114–138, 1943.

Y. Xue, Q. Wang, Q. Long, B. L. Ng, H. Swerdlow, J. Burton, S. Carl, R. Taylor, Z. Abdellah, Y. Zhao, D. Asan, G. Macarthur, M. A. Quail, N. P. Carter, H. Yang and C. Tyler-Smith. Human Y chromosome base substitution mutation rate measured by direct sequencing in a deep-rooting pedigree. *Current Biology*, 19:1453–1457, 2009.

L. A. Zhivotovsky, P. A. Underhill, C. Cinnioglu, M. Kayser, B. Morar, T. Kivisild, R. Scozzari, F. Cruciani, G. Destro-Bisol, G. Spedini, G. K. Chambers, R. J. Herrera, K. K. Yong, D. Gresham, I. Tournev, M. W. Feldman and L. Kalaydjieva, The effective mutation rate at Y chromosome short tandem repeats, with application to human population-divergence time. *The American Journal of Human Genetics*, 74:50–61, 2004.

CHAPTER 4

Probability and Likelihood

Amke Caliebe and Michael Krawczak

Institute of Medical Informatics and Statistics, Christian-Albrechts, University of Kiel, Kiel, Germany

"Probability theory is nothing but common sense reduced to calculation."

Pierre Simon de Laplace, *Théorie Analytique des Probabilités*, 1812

1 Probability as a Mathematical Concept

Probability theory is a comparatively young mathematical discipline despite the fact that humans have been occupied with the (apparent) randomness of natural events throughout their cultural history. In fact, with the indisputable exception of biological death, most events that matter to us as human beings are 'random' in the sense that they have at least two realistic outcome options. Which option was, is, may or will eventually come true is uncertain to us either because we lack critical knowledge to make such judgment or because the required knowledge does not exist in the first place. The major goal of probability theory is to formalize and quantify this uncertainty. To this end, mathematicians have decided to define 'probability' as a mathematical function P that assigns a real number $P(A)$ to an abstract entity A called an 'event'.

1.1 Different Interpretations of Probability

The first scientific (so-called 'classical') interpretation of probability was given by French scholar Pierre Simon Laplace (1749–1827) as the ratio of the number of favourable events to the total number of possible events (Stigler, 1990). In this sense, the probability of rolling doubles with a pair of fair dice equals 1/6 because there are 36 possible results (treating the two dice as distinguishable), six of which are doubles. Around the mid-19th century, the problems and paradoxes of the classical interpretation of probability motivated the development of a more advanced concept. In his 1866 book 'Logic of Chance', English philosopher John Venn (1834–1923) was among those who laid the foundations of the 'frequentist theory' of probability, which holds that probabilities only make sense in the context of well-defined random experiments (Salmon, 1981). In the view of a frequentist, the relative frequency of occurrence of a particular experimental outcome in a large series of replications of that experiment is a measure of its probability. Thus, for a frequentist, the probability of rolling doubles with a certain pair of dice equals 1/6 if and only if a long run of throws with these dice yields doubles in every sixth throw on average. Arguably, frequentism is still by far the most commonly held view of 'probability' among natural scientists.

In the 1930s, Russian mathematician Andrei Nikolaevich Kolmogorov (1903–1987; Figure 1) finally built up probability theory rigorously from three fundamental axioms in a way comparable to Euclid's treatment of geometry (Vovk, 2001):

1. $P(A) \geq 0$,
2. $P(\Omega) = 1$,
3. $P(A + B) = P(A) + P(B)$.

The first axiom mandates that probabilities should not be negative, which is a sensible but nevertheless arbitrary convention. The second axiom introduces the all-encompassing event Ω that corresponds to the union of all possible events. For example, Ω is the event that throwing a single die results in an integer number between one and six. Since, by definition, there is certainty about the occurrence of Ω, this event is (again sensibly but arbitrarily)

Figure 1:   Andrei Nikolaevich Kolmogorov (1903–1987), Soviet mathematician.

Note: Kolmogorov is widely considered one of the most prominent mathematicians of the 20th century. He made major advances in different scientific fields, including probability theory, topology, turbulence and classical mechanics. (Copyright 2015, The Science Photo Library.)

assigned unity as the maximum possible probability. The third axiom deals with the union $A+B$ of mutually exclusive events, such as the outcome of a coin toss (which is either heads or tails). A natural requirement for a probability to match our intuitive understanding of it would be that the probability of the occurrence of A or B equals the sum of the two individual probabilities. This is the assertion of the third axiom (which, in its mathematically correct form, refers not only to two but to a countable, potentially infinite number of events). Kolmogorov's axiomatization has achieved the status of orthodoxy in mathematics, and it is what mathematicians typically have in mind when they think of 'probability'.

1.2 *Probabilistic Models*

Every treatment of uncertainty that is grounded in the mathematical principles of probability theory requires the presence of an underlying model which, in turn, is characterized by its parameters. Even a comparatively simple task like quantifying the uncertainty of a coin toss involves a parametric model, namely $P(\text{heads}) = \alpha$ and $P(\text{tails}) = 1 - \alpha$, where parameter α equals the probability of heads. However, the choice of an appropriate model for a given type of uncertainty is not within the domain of probability theory itself but constitutes an inductive process, drawing upon prior experience (empirical models) or knowledge (mechanistic models) or both. Only after a model has been selected, any subsequent formal treatment of uncertainty is deductive and follows the mathematical rules of probability theory.

A text book example of a probabilistic model is provided by Mendel's first law ('Law of Segregation') which, although originally conceived by its namesake on the basis of empirical observations, invokes a mechanistic abstraction of the process of genetic inheritance (Figure 2). Mendel's first law implies that the genotype probabilities

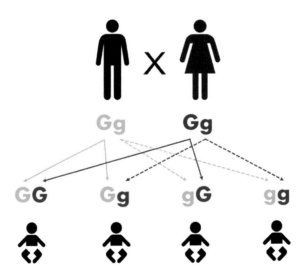

Figure 2: Mendel's first law, the 'Law of Segregation'.

Note: Without mutation, the offspring of a pair of Gg heterozygotes are of either three genotypes, namely GG, Gg or gg. The probability of each offspring genotype depends upon the segregation probability θ, i.e. the probability that a parent passes allele G rather than allele g to an offspring. If $\theta = 1/2$, the genotype probabilities are $1/4$, $1/2$ and $1/4$, respectively; if $\theta < 1/2$, then $P(\text{GG}) < 1/4$, $P(\text{Gg}) < 1/2$ and $P(\text{gg}) > 1/4$.

among the offspring of a Gg × Gg mating of two heterozygotes equal $P(\text{GG}) = 1/4$, $P(\text{Gg}) = 1/2$ and $P(\text{gg}) = 1/4$. The parameter of this model, namely the meiotic transmission probability of $1/2$, derives from an understanding of the underlying biological mechanism and, in principle, does not need to be ascertained or verified empirically. However, given our present-day understanding of genetics, such orthodoxy is not justified because the true parameter of the model may differ from its theoretical value due to segregation distortion (e.g. genotype-dependent prenatal selection) or mutation. To take this possibility properly into account, the model needs to be revised in the light of empirical data and the parameter changed accordingly, if necessary. In any case, once established, an improved model would be interpreted and used in the same deductive fashion as its predecessor.

2 Statistics: The Art of Building Models

The adaptation of probabilistic models to real data is the domain of statistics, which indeed can be described as the art of giving sensible answers to meaningful questions about model parameters. For example, once it has been accepted that the body height of females and males follows a normal distribution with expected values (or 'population means') μ_F and μ_M, respectively, the Student t-test evidentially is a good tool to clarify whether μ_F equals μ_M in the light of some empirical height measurements. Another important task of statistics is parameter estimation. Estimation of population parameters is necessary if the population of interest cannot be comprehensively assessed for the characteristic(s) in question, as is usually the case in practice. A complete census, by contrast, would reveal, say the exact average family income per year, or the exact sex ratio, or the exact proportion of retired people in a given country. Estimation also is necessary if the population of interest (at least in principle) is infinitely large. For example, the number of times a given dice can be thrown is potentially unlimited so that its probability of showing 6 in a single throw in the future can only be estimated, but never determined exactly.

2.1 *The Bayesian-frequentist Controversy*

Ideally, making scientific inference about a model parameter θ on the basis of some empirical data D should yield $P(\theta = \theta_0|D)$, the posterior probability that θ equals some θ_0 in the light of D. In fact, one of the main objectives of forensic genetics can be couched in terms of inferring a model parameter, namely the kinship coefficient θ of an observed pair of trace donor and suspect. The genetic data D (usually a match between the genetic profiles of the two individuals) form the basis of balancing the prosecution hypothesis $\{\theta = 1\}$ against the defence hypothesis $\{\theta = 0\}$ (or $\{\theta = x > 0\}$ in rare instances where a blood relative of the suspect is reasonably considered to be the trace donor). Adoption of a certain probabilistic model immediately yields $P(D|\theta = \theta_0)$, the probability of the data D assuming that a certain θ_0 is the true value of θ. In the forensic genetics context, $P(D|\theta = 0)$ is referred to as the 'random match probability', a key quantity that will be addressed in more detail in the second half of this chapter.

Whilst $P(\theta = \theta_0|D)$ may be the most coveted quantity, however, only $P(D|\theta = \theta_0)$ is usually available. Fortunately, a formal connection between $P(\theta = \theta_0|D)$ and $P(D|\theta = \theta_0)$ can be made by Bayes' Theorem, a progression of insights expounded by English 18th century philosopher and Presbyterian minister Thomas Bayes (1701–1761) in his famous 'Essay towards solving a Problem in the Doctrine of Chances'. In modern mathematical notation, Bayes' Theorem reads

$$P(\theta = \theta_0 \mid D) = \frac{P(D \mid \theta = \theta_0) \cdot P(\theta = \theta_0)}{\sum_{x} P(D \mid \theta = x) \cdot P(\theta = x)}, \tag{1}$$

where $P(\theta = x)$ denotes some prior distribution of θ on its possible values x. As simple as the theorem may look, the question whether the invoked prior distribution truly exists, or can reasonably be assumed to exist, was at the heart of the so-called 'Bayesian-frequentist controversy' — a debate among statisticians that lasted for decades and more than once verged on personal vendetta (McGrayne, 2011). Is it sensible to ascribe some kind of randomness to the parameters of a probabilistic model? In the one camp were the frequentists who were willing to answer in the affirmative only if θ resulted from an experiment, or if such an experiment was at least theoretically possible. The Bayesians, on the other hand, maintained that a prior distribution of θ could always be found through experimental work, theoretical knowledge or subjective judgement. At least an 'uninformed' prior distribution could be defined, for example, by giving each value x of θ equal weight.

2.2 Fisher and the Likelihood: A 'Third Way'

It is not surprising that a pragmatic way out of the gridlock between Bayesians and frequentists was devised by Sir Ronald Aylmer Fisher (1890–1962; Figure 3), an English statistician of such empirical impetus that many geneticists still regard him as one of their own

Figure 3:   Sir Ronald Aylmer Fisher (1890–1962), English statistician and geneticist.

Note: Fisher's contributions to statistics include methods of experimental design and data analysis. In genetics, he showed that Mendel's laws and Darwin's theory of natural selection are in full accord. In recognition of his many achievements, Fisher was knighted in 1952. (Copyright 2015, The Science Photo Library.)

breed (in fact, Fisher was Balfour Professor of Genetics at the University of Cambridge for 14 years).

Fisher clearly disapproved of the Bayesians' axiomatic insistence on the availability of a prior distribution for θ, but at the same time acknowledged that the long-run frequency was not the only sensible way of looking at probability (Pawitan, 2013). As a 'third way', Fisher proposed to interpret $P(D|\theta = x)$ as a function of x called the 'likelihood' of x. Of course, the likelihood function $L(x)$ depends upon the observed data, but the data are treated as fixed in Fisher's concept whereas the model parameter is regarded as variable. In mathematical terms, the likelihood function is only well-defined given the observed data, which means that L is exclusive to the universe in which D is observed, and may look different in other universes where other data are observed.

It must be emphasized that the likelihood $L(\theta_0)$ is not the probability of θ_0 being the true value of θ, but rather a measure of rationale belief in θ_0. In fact, the likelihood function cannot be a probability for formal reasons because it fails the third of Kolmogorov's axioms. Usually,

$$
\begin{aligned}
L(\theta_0 \vee \theta_1) &= P(D|\theta = \theta_0 \vee \theta = \theta_1) \neq P(D|\theta = \theta_0) + P(D|\theta = \theta_1) \\
&= L(\theta_0) + L(\theta_1)
\end{aligned}
\tag{2}
$$

which means that likelihoods do not add up (in Equation (2), symbol $\vee$ denotes the logical connection 'or').

The likelihood concept has major applications in statistics. Right from the start, Fisher himself seems to have been motivated by the problem of parameter estimation, and the likelihood function provides a 'good' solution to this problem. Thus, Fisher proposed to estimate θ by $\hat{\theta}$, defined via

$$
L(\hat{\theta}) = \max_{\theta} L(\theta)
\tag{3}
$$

and called it the 'maximum likelihood' estimator of θ. The underlying (maximum likelihood) principle can be phrased as "accept that value of θ as the best guess that would have rendered your observation D most probable". In addition to being intuitively appealing, the maximum likelihood estimator also usually has some highly desirable mathematical properties for large sample sizes: it gives the correct answer on average, it is rather stable and it allows researchers to benefit in terms of accuracy from increasing their sample sizes.

The second common use of likelihood is in statistical testing where the so-called 'likelihood ratio (LR) test' allows easy comparison of two probabilistic models (the null model and the alternative model). Decision making about the rejection or non-rejection of the null model is based upon the LR

$$\mathrm{LR} = \frac{\max_{\theta \in \Theta_0} L(\theta)}{\max_{\theta \in \Theta_A} L(\theta)}, \tag{4}$$

where Θ_0 and Θ_A denote the parameter spaces of the null and the alternative model, respectively.

The LR test is particularly useful in situations where the null model is a special case of the alternative model, i.e. where Θ_0 is a subspace of Θ_A. Under the null model, $-2 \cdot \ln(\mathrm{LR})$ follows a chi-squared distribution with degrees of freedom equal to the difference in dimensions between Θ_0 and Θ_A, provided that the sample size is large enough. Notably, this convenient property is also accepted, without objection, by frequentists because the test only exploits a certain functional quality of the LR without touching upon its interpretation.

3 Likelihood Ratios in Forensics: The Match Probability

In forensics, the LR is generally used to quantify the evidential value of some genetic data D related to a case of interest. Given an appropriate model, the conditional probability of D can be calculated assuming either the prosecution hypothesis H_P or the defence hypothesis H_D, which yields

$$\mathrm{LR} = \frac{L(H_P)}{L(H_D)} = \frac{P(D \mid H_P)}{P(D \mid H_D)}. \tag{5}$$

The LR thus expresses both (i) how much more probable the genetic data are under the prosecution rather than the defence hypothesis and (ii) how much more likely (not probable, see Section 2.2) the prosecution hypothesis is than the defence hypothesis in the light of the genetic data.

A common setting for the forensic use of the LR is that of a biological trace, left at a crime scene by an unknown donor, and the concomitant presence of a suspect. In the simplest situation, DNA of sufficient quantity and quality is available from both subjects to allow unambiguous genotyping for a selection of genetic markers, and the two profiles 'match', i.e. they comprise identical genotypes for all markers. There are two possible explanations for a genetic match, namely the prosecution hypothesis that trace donor T and suspect S are one and the same person $\{T = S\}$, and the defence hypothesis that the two are different persons $\{T \neq S\}$. Leaving technical issues aside, $P(D|T = S) = L(H_P)$ is unity so that the evidential value of D rests entirely on the so-called 'match probability' $P(D|T \neq S)$. Since the match probability equals the likelihood of the defence hypothesis in the light of the match, $L(H_D)$, the LR in this situation is just the inverse of the match probability, i.e.

$$\text{LR} = \frac{1}{P(D \,|\, T \neq S)}. \tag{6}$$

3.1 *Which Match Probability?*

Explicit calculation of a match probability requires specification, under the defence hypothesis, of how the suspect got involved into the case. The simplest but nevertheless most popular assumption is that the (male) suspect is a 'random man' which means that he was drawn at random from a particular population. In this case, the match probability is equated to the probability of randomly drawing the suspect genetic profile from the population pool of profiles which, in turn, is estimated using an appropriate database. Often, the match probability then is referred to as the 'random match probability'.

There has been considerable concern about the 'random man' assumption in the past (Balding, 2004, 2005; Balding and Nichols, 1994) because a suspect rarely if ever becomes a suspect by chance alone. This holds true even for a so-called 'cold match' where the suspect was identified via the successful search of a forensic genetic database because the latter is rarely representative of the overall population. Instead, it seems reasonable to imply that there is always a special 'suspect population' that differs to some unknown extent from the 'database population' used for generating match probabilities. In a structured population, for example, it may be reasonable to assume that the suspect and the trace donor came from the same but unknown sub-population, particularly because there is a match. Ignoring this fact leads to match probabilities that are no longer conservative (i.e. favorable to the defendant). One possible solution to this problem is the inclusion, into the match probability calculation, of some kind of measure F (often also abbreviated as θ) of the allele frequency variation among sub-populations (Balding and Nichols, 1994; National Research Council, 1996; Steele and Balding, 2014; Weir and Cockerham, 1984). With this procedure, for example, the match probability between two homozygotes AA at a single autosomal locus equals

$$P(\text{AA} \mid H_D) = \frac{[2F + (1-F)p] \cdot [3F + (1-F)p]}{(1+F) \cdot (1+2F)}, \qquad (7)$$

where p is the population frequency of allele A. The proposed adjustments could be shown to be conservative even in cases where suspect and trace donor belong to different sub-populations.

Another type of problem arises if the defence claims that the trace donor is a relative of the suspect. In this case, the match probability depends upon the presumed kinship coefficient θ_0 between suspect and trace donor (see Section 2.1) and, usually, would be much larger than under the 'random man' assumption. The likelihood of the prosecution hypothesis is $L(1) = P(D|\theta = 1)$, which equals unity again, whereas the likelihood of the defence hypothesis is $L(\theta_0) = P(D|\theta = \theta_0)$. Note that $\{\theta_0 = 0\}$ represents the special case of the 'random man' hypothesis.

If the trace is a mixture of contributions from multiple donors, or if the trace DNA is of such low quality or quantity that dropouts and dropins have to be taken into consideration, the calculation of match probabilities gets even more difficult. In this case, the choice of an appropriate model under the defence hypothesis could be problematic because, for example, neither the number of trace contributors nor the relevant dropin and dropout rates are usually known with certainty. It may well be fair and sensible in this situation to calculate the match probability under different plausible models and to adopt the maximum of the obtained results for decision making, although other methods have been proposed as well (Brenner *et al.*, 1996; Buckleton *et al.*, 1998, 2007; Perez *et al.*, 2011).

3.2 *Posterior Odds vs. Likelihood Ratio*

The LR by itself is difficult to interpret and therefore provides little guidance to the evaluation of forensic evidence. The LR is a ratio of genetic data probabilities but what is needed for making a judgment in a criminal case are the posterior odds (PO) in favor of, or against, the prosecution hypothesis being correct. These two quantities are linked by Bayes' Theorem (see Equation (1)):

$$\text{PO} = \frac{P(H_P \mid D)}{P(H_D \mid D)} = \text{LR} \cdot \frac{P(H_P)}{P(H_D)}. \tag{8}$$

Calculating the PO from the LR thus requires knowledge of the prior odds $P(H_P)/P(H_D)$, i.e. of the relative prior probabilities of the prosecution and defence hypothesis before the genetic data became known. Note that Equation (8) is often verbalized as "posterior odds equal LR times prior odds". Determination of the prior odds is the responsibility of the court or jurors and has to take all external evidence for the identity of suspect and trace donor into account (i.e. all evidence except the genetic data). Therefore, quantification of the prior odds is a highly subjective process and the result usually varies from juror to juror. Moreover, the prior odds are not necessarily fixed but may change during the course of a trial as more and more external evidence becomes available. In cases where no external evidence is available (e.g. because the suspect was identified by a database search), the prior odds may even be close to zero and therefore difficult to quantify sensibly in the first place (see Section 3.3). The subjectivity and shakiness of the prior odds are the main reason why the LR rather than the PO is usually communicated in court.

Uncertainty about the prior odds also implies that the decision between defence and prosecution hypothesis cannot be construed as a statistical test, based upon the LR. Statistical tests give full priority to the long-term proportion of wrong decisions under the null hypothesis and, by declaring them irrelevant, deliberately neglect all additional information included in prior probabilities. On the other hand, reporting the LR helps demarcating two different concerns, namely (i) the objective evaluation of genetic evidence and (ii) the subjective evaluation of external evidence. Focusing on the LR thus expresses the view that the contribution in court of genetics experts should be confined to their primary technical expertize.

One way to solve the dilemma of uncertain prior odds, and to eventually align LRs and PO, would be to increase the information content of the genetic data beyond good and evil. In other words, the genetics experts should ensure that the LR is so large in a given case that the PO exceed the threshold for making a decision on $\{T = S\}$ under all reasonable prior odds (a situation commonly paraphrased in criminal cases as being "beyond a reasonable doubt"). It is important to remember, however, that the hypotheses at stake so far were concerned with whether the suspect donated the trace or not. Occasionally, this question may be only distantly related to the question of guilt or innocence. For example, most spouses of a murder victim are likely to have left a biological trace on the victim without actually being involved in the crime. The effect of large LRs in such instances can be illustrated by defining two novel hypotheses comprising whether the suspect was the (or a) perpetrator of the crime (H_P^*) or not (H_D^*). The PO^* in favor of H_P^* are calculated as

$$\text{PO}^* = \frac{P(H_P^* \mid D)}{P(H_D^* \mid D)} = \frac{P(H_P^* \mid D, H_P) \cdot \text{PO} + P(H_P^* \mid D, H_D)}{P(H_D^* \mid D, H_P) \cdot \text{PO} + P(H_D^* \mid D, H_D)}. \tag{9}$$

If the LR and, hence, the PO are large enough for the left-hand term in both the numerator and the denominator to dominate the right-hand term, formula (9) reduces to

$$\mathrm{PO}^* \approx \frac{P(H_P^* \mid D, H_P)}{P(H_D^* \mid D, H_P)} = \frac{P(H_P^* \mid H_P)}{P(H_D^* \mid H_P)} = \frac{P(H_P \mid H_P^*) \cdot P(H_P^*)}{P(H_P \mid H_D^*) \cdot P(H_D^*)}$$

$$= \mathrm{LR}^* \cdot \frac{P(H_P^*)}{P(H_D^*)}. \tag{10}$$

Simultaneous conditioning on D and H_P is equivalent to conditioning on H_P alone because H_P logically implies D. Not surprisingly, the last term in formula 10 closely resembles the last term in formula 8 because the 'proof' of $\{S = T\}$ indeed constitutes a new observation that replaces the genetic match D, and that yields a new LR^* weighing H_P^* against H_D^*. LR^* is not necessarily of the same magnitude as LR, and for the spouse murder alluded to above, LR^* may even be close to unity irrespective of LR. Notably, formula 10 is valid only if the external evidence included in prior odds $P(H_P^*)/P(H_D^*)$ does not overlap with the evidence used for calculating PO because one and the same information cannot be used twice in the same chain of reasoning.

Irrespective of whether concretization of a threshold is necessary or not in practice, minimum posterior probabilities of H_P^* of 95% or 99% have been propagated for criminal cases, corresponding to PO^* of 19:1 and 99:1, respectively (Franklin, 2006; Tillers and Gottfried, 2006; Weinstein and Dewsbury, 2006; Weiss, 2003). Of course, in order to be meaningful in the first place, any PO^* threshold must take the relative costs of wrong decisions into account, thereby acknowledging the fact that, in criminal cases, incriminating (and eventually convicting) an innocent person is generally deemed a much graver mistake than letting a guilty person go free. In civil cases such as paternity disputes, the thresholds may have to be chosen differently (Clermont, 2009; Krawczak and Schmidtke, 1992; Weiss, 2003).

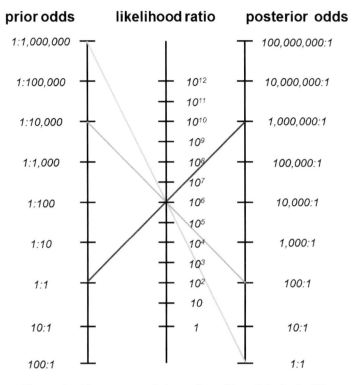

Figure 4:   Nomogram relating prior odds to PO via the LR.

So-called 'nomograms' (Figure 4) are a helpful means to graphically illustrate in court how LRs are converted into PO under different prior odds (Fagan, 1975; Meester and Sjerps, 2004; National Research Council, 1996; Riancho and Zarrabeitia, 2002). As an example, suppose that the LR or LR* in a given case equals 1,000,000. If the prior odds were 1:1 (corresponding to a 50% prior probability of the prosecution hypothesis H_P or H_P^*) due to some convincing external evidence, the posterior odds (PO or PO*) would equal 1,000,000:1 (red line in Figure 4) and therefore exceed any sensible threshold by several orders of magnitude. Prior odds of 1:10,000, in turn, would yield posterior odds equal to 100:1 (blue line) and therefore end up in a value near possible decision-relevant thresholds. However, if the prior odds are much smaller, say 1:1,000,000, as may be plausible for a cold match, the resulting posterior odds are 1:1 (green line) which clearly would be insufficient for decision making in criminal cases.

3.3 The Database Controversy

The so-called 'database controversy' nicely illustrates both, the utility of the LR in forensics and the difficulty to comprehend the underlying theory. The controversy invokes two scenarios labeled 1 and 2 before (Balding, 2002; Berger *et al.*, 2015). In scenario 1, a suspect was identified through external evidence and a genetic match was subsequently obtained between the suspect and a trace. In scenario 2, the suspect was identified through a successful database search where they yielded the only match. In which scenario would the genetic data yield a smaller match probability and therefore be ascribed larger evidential value?

Opposing answers were given to this question, each with seemingly convincing arguments supporting it. Those favoring scenario 1 (National Research Council, 1996; Schneider *et al.*, 2010; Stockmarr, 1999) argued that the database search resembles the multiple testing problem in statistics, and the NRC consequently proposed as the match probability in scenario 2 the product of the match probability in scenario 1 and the size *N* of the database. Stockmarr (1999) came to the same conclusion by calculating the LR under a modified prosecution hypothesis that he deemed more appropriate, namely "the trace donor was included in the database" rather than "the trace donor and the suspect are the same person". What sounded like a bit of a quibble was in fact used by Stockmarr (1999) to argue that scenario 2 involved N two-person comparisons rather than one, as in scenario 1.

Eventually, the advocates of scenario 1 yielding the smaller match probability were proven wrong (Balding, 2002; Balding and Donnelly, 1996; Donnelly and Friedman, 1999). In fact, the match probability in scenario 1 is even a little larger than in scenario 2 because, in the latter, there is additional evidence in favor of the prosecution hypothesis, namely that none of the other individuals in the database matched the trace. The argument used by the NRC was invalid because, contrary to the multiple testing problem, there is only exactly one trace donor involved in the type of criminal case considered. The modification of the prosecution hypothesis by Stockmarr (1999) was invalidated by the notion that his new hypothesis was simply irrelevant to the prosecution (Dawid, 2001; Donnelly and Friedman, 1999).

Why did the database controversy arise in the first place? Indeed, it may seem plausible at first glance that the LR of a match should be larger in scenario 1 than in scenario 2, but this is due to the fact that LRs, prior odds and PO are easily confused. For moderately sized databases, the LRs are about the same but the prior odds differ greatly between the two scenarios. In scenario 1, the suspect is identified beforehand and the prior odds for the prosecution hypothesis are therefore large. In scenario 2, the prior odds are very small since no external evidence was available. This results in much smaller PO in scenario 2 than in scenario 1, and the controversy seems to have arisen from an attempt to blame this difference on the genetic data rather than the prior odds.

4 Conclusions

- Probability and likelihood are two sides of the same coin. The probability of observing a particular set of data under a certain hypothesis equals the likelihood of that hypothesis in the light of the data, once the data have been observed.
- The likelihood of a hypothesis must not be confused with its probability. Quantification of the latter requires knowledge of the prior probabilities of all hypotheses of interest, which in turn requires evaluation of all evidence other than the data.
- When a genetic match between a trace and a suspect is evaluated in forensic practice, two hypotheses are usually at stake, namely the prosecution hypothesis (identity of the two) and the defence hypothesis (non-identity).
- Although the posterior odds in favor or against the prosecution hypothesis are the sought-after quantity for decision making in

court, expert communication of the results of a forensic genetic analysis is usually confined to the LR because this self-restriction obviates the need for (subjective) quantification of the prior odds.

References

D. J. Balding. The DNA database search controversy. *Biometrics*, 58:241–244, 2002.

D. J. Balding. Comment on: Why the effect of prior odds should accompany the likelihood ratio when reporting DNA evidence. *Law, Probability and Risk*, 3:63–64, 2004.

D. J. Balding. *Weight-of-Evidence for Forensic DNA Profiles.* John Wiley & Sons, New Jersey, 2005.

D. J. Balding and P. Donnelly. Evaluating DNA profile evidence when the suspect is identified through a database search. *Journal of Forensic Sciences*, 41:603–607, 1996.

D. J. Balding and R. A. Nichols. DNA profile match probability calculation: How to allow for population stratification, relatedness, database selection and single bands. *Forensic Science International*, 64:125–140, 1994.

C. E. Berger, P. Vergeer and J. S. Buckleton. A more straightforward derivation of the LR for a database search. *Forensic science international: Genetics*, 14:156–160, 2015.

C. H. Brenner, R. Fimmers and M. P. Baur. Likelihood ratios for mixed stains when the number of donors cannot be agreed. *International Journal of Legal Medicine*, 109:218–219, 1996.

J. S. Buckleton, J. M. Curran and P. Gill. Towards understanding the effect of uncertainty in the number of contributors to DNA stains. *Forensic Science International: Genetics*, 1:20–28, 2007.

J. S. Buckleton, I. W. Evett and B. S. Weir. Setting bounds for the likelihood ratio when multiple hypotheses are postulated. *Science & Justice*, 38:23–26, 1998.

K. M. Clermont. Standards of Proof Revisited. Cornell Law Faculty Publications Paper 13, 2009.

A. P. Dawid. Comment on Stockmarr's "Likelihood ratios for evaluating DNA evidence when the suspect is found through a database search". Biometrics, 57:976–980, 2001.

P. Donnelly and R. D. Friedman. DNA database searches and the legal consumption of scientific evidence. *Michigan Law Review*, 97:931–984, 1999.

T. J. Fagan. Nomogram for Bayes's Theorem. *New England Journal of Medicine*, 293:257, 1975.

J. Franklin. Case comment—United States v. Copeland, 369 F. Supp. 2d 275 (E.D.N.Y. 2005): Quantification of the 'proof beyond reasonable doubt' standard. *Law, Probability and Risk*, 5:159–165, 2006.

M. Krawczak and J. Schmidtke. The decision theory of paternity disputes: Optimization considerations applied to multilocus DNA fingerprinting. *Journal of Forensic Sciences*, 37:1525–1533, 1992.

S. B. McGrayne. *The Theory that Would Not Die: How Bayes' Rule Cracked the Enigma Code, Hunted Down Russian Submarines & Emerged Triumphant from Two Centuries of Controversy*. Yale University Press, New Haven CT, 2011.

R. Meester and M. Sjerps. Why the effect of prior odds should accompany the likelihood ratio when reporting DNA evidence. *Law, Probability and Risk*, 3:51–62, 2004.

National Research Council. *The Evaluation of Forensic DNA Evidence*. National Academy Press, Washington DC, 1996.

Y. Pawitan. *In All Likelihood: Statistical Modelling and Inference Using Likelihood*. OUP, Oxford, 2013.

J. Perez, A. A. Mitchell, N. Ducasse, J. Tamariz and T. Caragine. Estimating the number of contributors to two-, three-, and four-person mixtures containing DNA in high template and low template amounts. *Croatian Medical Journal*, 52:314–326, 2011.

J. A. Riancho and M. T. Zarrabeitia. The prosecutor's and defendant's Bayesian nomograms. *International Journal of Legal Medicine*, 116: 312–313, 2002.

W. Salmon. John Venn's Logic of Chance. In J. Hintikka, D. Gruender, E. Agazzi(eds.) *Probabilistic Thinking, Thermodynamics and the Interaction of the History and Philosophy of Science. Proceedings of the 1978 Pisa Conference on the History and Philosophy of Science*, Volume 2. Springer Netherlands, Dordrecht, pp. 125–138, 1981.

P. M. Schneider, H. Schneider, R. Fimmers, W. Keil, G. Molsberger, W. Pflug, T. Rothämel, M. Eckert, H. Pfeiffer and B. Brinkmann. *Allgemeine Empfehlungen der Spurenkommission zur statistischen Bewertung von DNA-Datenbank-Treffern. Rechtsmedizin*, 20:111–115, 2010.

C. D. Steele and D. J. Balding. Choice of population database for forensic DNA profile analysis. *Science & Justice*, 54:487–493, 2014.

S. Stigler. *The History of Statistics: The Measurement of Uncertainty Before 1900.* Harvard University Press, Cambridge MA, 1990.

A. Stockmarr. Likelihood ratios for evaluating DNA evidence when the suspect is found through a database search. *Biometrics*, 55:671–677, 1999.

P. Tillers and J. Gottfried. Case comment—United States v. Copeland, 369 F. Supp. 2d 275 (E.D.N.Y. 2005): A Collateral Attack on the Legal Maxim That Proof Beyond A Reasonable Doubt Is Unquantifiable? *Law, Probability and Risk*, 5:135–157, 2006.

V. Vovk. Kolmogorov's complexity conception of probability. In *Probability Theory: Philosophy, Recent History and Relations to Science*, V. F. Hendricks, K. F. Jørgensen (eds.), pp. 51–69. Kluwer, Dordrecht, 2001.

J. B. Weinstein and I. Dewsbury. Comment on the meaning of 'proof beyond a reasonable doubt'. *Law, Probability and Risk*, 5:167–173, 2006.

B. S. Weir and C. C. Cockerham. Estimating F-Statistics for the Analysis of Population-Structure. *Evolution*, 38:1358–1370, 1984.

C. Weiss. Expressing scientific uncertainty. *Law, Probability and Risk*, 2:25–46, 2003.

CHAPTER 5

Kinship

Manuel García-Magariños[*,†] *and Thore Egeland*[*]

[*]IKBM, Norwegian University of Life Sciences, Ås, Norway
[†]Department of Mathematics, University of A Coruña, Spain

1 Introduction

Analysis of relationship cases have been carried out in forensic studies for several decades. Standard forensic problems, including paternity issues, inmigration cases and inheritance claims, can be expressed in terms of identifying a particular pedigree between the individuals of interest. Victim identification in mass disasters (DVI) usually requires detection of relationships with living relatives. This has been the case, for instance, for the identification of victims in the 9/11 attacks (Brenner and Weir, 2003) or the Swissair flight disaster (Leclair *et al.*, 2004). Kinship studies have also shed light in order to establish the truth regarding some historical figures, like assassination of the Tsar Nicholas II and his family (Gill *et al.*, 1995) or the discovery that the former president of the United States Thomas Jefferson had had a child with a slave (Foster *et al.*, 1998). Use of probabilistic and statistical procedures is essential in order to provide with numerical estimations allowing to test and solve these problems.

This chapter is divided in sections reviewing the two most common approaches to relationship analysis in the forensic science.

The presentation of the classical methods is followed by explanations of methods needed when complicating factors like mutation, silent alleles, dropout and sampling uncertainty cannot be ignored. Finally a new approach, the parametric approach, is introduced.

2 Classical Methods

2.1 Motivational Example

Throughout this chapter we will return several times to the data in Table 1 and Figure 1 to illustrate methods. Genotype data for an alleged father (AF) and a child (CH) is shown for three markers. AF and CH share respectively 1, 0 and 2 alleles for these markers. If AF is the father of CH, a mutation must have occurred for *PENTA_E*, assuming artefacts like genotyping error can be disregarded. Alternative fathers may be an unrelated man or a brother. The statistical evaluation of the indicated hypotheses will be discussed later and exemplified.

2.2 Likelihood Ratio

Biostatistical evaluations for the study of family relationships between two or more individuals follow likelihood ratio (LR) principles. These calculations are based on the ideas of Essen-Möller (1938), and were extended by Gurtler in the 1950's. For a pairwise relationship between two individuals A_1, A_2 with data for marker i, $g_i = (g_{i1}, g_{i2})$, and given mutually exclusive hypotheses

$$\begin{cases} H_0: \text{Individuals } A_1, A_2 \text{ have a relationship } x, \\ H_1: \text{Individuals } A_1, A_2 \text{ are unrelated.} \end{cases}$$

Table 1: Genotype data for a child and alleged father (AF) along with LR-s.

Marker	CH	AF	Allele Freq.	LR	LR (mut)
TH01	6/9	6/7	$p_6 = 0.209$, $p_7 = 0.2126$, $p_9 = 0.141$	1.196	1.198
PENTA_E	7/9	8/10	$p_7 = 0.15$, $p_8 = 0.25$, $p_9 = 0.35$, $p_{10} = 0.25$	0.000	0.013
TPOX	8/8	8/8	$p_8 = 0.559$	1.789	1.782
Total				0	0.028

Note. For all markers, remaining alleles are lumped into a rest allele. The rightmost column is based on a mutation model described in the text ('stepwise stationary' with mutation rate 0.005 and range 0.1).

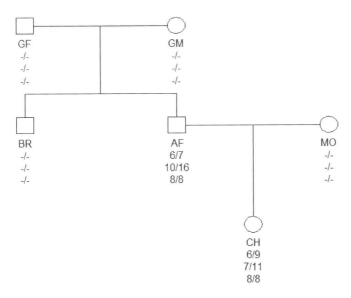

Figure 1: Various versions of this pedigree are used for examples throughout.

the LR is calculated as

$$LR_i = \frac{\Pr(g_i \mid H_0)}{\Pr(g_i \mid H_1)}. \qquad (1)$$

For the particular example in Table 1, the LR for the TH01 marker is

$$
\begin{aligned}
LR_{\text{TH01}} &= \frac{\Pr(CH = 6/9, \, AF = 6/7 \mid H_0)}{\Pr(CH = 6/9, \, AF = 6/7 \mid H_1)} \\
&= \frac{\Pr(CH = 6/9 \mid AF = 6/7, H_0)}{\Pr(CH = 6/9)} = \frac{1}{4 p_6} = 1.196.
\end{aligned}
$$

Given a set of independent markers and provided Hardy–Weinberg equilibrium (HWE) is fulfilled, the product rule can be applied and the combined LR is the product of each single value

$$LR = \prod LR_i. \qquad (2)$$

In the example $LR_{PENTA\_E} = 0$ and $LR_{TPOX} = 1.789$ so the combined LR is

$$LR = LR_{TH01} \times LR_{PENTA\_E} \times LR_{TPOX} = 0.$$

Conditions under which HWE and the product rule are fulfilled will be addressed below. The term paternity index (PI) is used for the LR in paternity cases like the example in Figure 1, where hypotheses are stated as

$$\begin{cases} H_0: \text{AF is the biological father of C}, \\ H_1: \text{An unrelated man to AF is the biological father of C}. \end{cases}$$

2.3 Probability of Paternity

A straightforward application of Bayes theorem using prior probabilities π_0, π_1 for both hypotheses allows calculation of the posterior probability of paternity as

$$\Pr(H_0 \mid g) = \frac{LR\pi_0}{LR\pi_0 + \pi_1}. \tag{3}$$

For the marker TH01 in the example and assuming equal priors $\pi_0 = \pi_1 = 0.5$, the posterior is

$$\Pr(H_0 \mid g) = \frac{1.196 \times 0.5}{1.196 \times 0.5 + 0.5} = 0.545.$$

If the priors are changed in order to take into account a low prior for paternity, $\pi_0 = 0.1$, the posterior takes the value $\Pr(H_0 \mid g) = 0.117$. Figure 2 indicates how the value of the posterior changes as a function of the prior π_0 and also as a function of the frequency of the shared allele between the alleged father and the child. Although posterior probabilities seem to be highly dependent on priors with only one marker, this effect is usually diluted when a large number of markers is used.

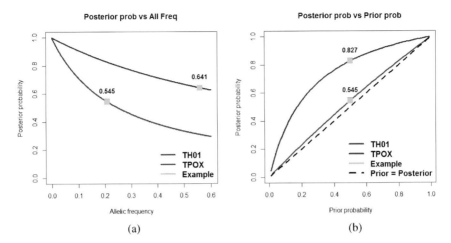

Figure 2: Effect of the allelic frequency for the common marker (a) and the prior probability of H_0 (b) on the posterior probability of the null hypothesis. Values obtained in the example are remarked.

Prior values are commonly guessed based on subjective belief. The standard $\pi_0 = \pi_1 = 0.5$ is used in many forensic laboratories as in most cases there is no evidence-based information on which the priors may be determined. However, a quantitative estimation of the priors influence on the posterior probability is desirable (Hubig *et al.*, 2013). Calculation of posterior probabilities is optional, as the LR is the value communicated in court and civil cases in many countries. The Neyman–Pearson lemma of statistics states that the LR alone provides the most powerful criterion for distinguishing between any two simple hypothesis (Balding *et al.*, 2013).

2.4 *Random Man not Excluded*

Selection of markers is based on their discriminant ability, usually measured by the power of exclusion. The power of exclusion in a paternity study may be defined as the proportion of men who do not possess the required paternal allele. If the possible paternal alleles at a locus are A_1, A_2, ..., A_n (often there is only one or two), the exclusion power of this locus is

$$PE_l = \left(1 - \sum Pr(A_i)\right)^2 \qquad (4)$$

and, for a set of L loci

$$PE = 1 - \prod_{l=1}^{L}(1 - PE_l). \tag{5}$$

The power of exclusion for the three markers of our example can be calculated as $PE_{TH01} = 0.423$, $PE_{PENTA\_E} = 0.25$, $PE_{TPOX} = 0.194$, so the joint value is $PE = 0.651$. Therefore, the power of exclusion values depend on the number of alleles and allelic frequencies, the relationship being tested, etc.

The Random Man Not Excluded (RMNE) method (Li and Chakravarty, 1988) seeks to determine the fraction of the population that would not be excluded from a certain relationship. This amounts to calculation of the PE, or equivalently to the calculation of

$$RMNE = 1 - PE.$$

The RMNE method is a simpler method when compared to LR calculation, but does not fully use the genetic evidence other than to establish a non-exclusion. Nonetheless, some debate has arisen about the ability of both (Buckleton and Curran, 2008). A recent study by Slooten and Egeland (2014) has shed light on the mathematical relation between RMNE and LR. There, it is proved that

$$RMNE = E\,[LR^{-1}(\mathcal{H}_1)], \tag{6}$$

under the reasonable assumption that LR should be a finite number. $LR(\mathcal{H}_1)$ is the random variable of the values of LR when H_1 is true. The expected LR for truly related individuals exceeds than the inverse of the RMNE; however, it is inevitably also possible to obtain a LR that is smaller.

3 Complicating Factors

3.1 *Mutation*

Mutations between alleles are relatively common, specifically with forensic markers. Based on mutation rates and ranges, mutation matrices can be obtained indicating the probability of mutation between alleles. A much cited paper in the field is Ohta and

Kimura (1973). For a duo with genotypes AF = a/b and CH = c/d, the LR may be written

$$\text{LR} = \frac{1}{4} \frac{\left(m_{ac} + m_{bc}\right)p_d + \left(m_{ad} + m_{bd}\right)p_c}{p_c p_d}, \tag{7}$$

where m_{kl} is the probability that allele k ends up as l. Note that a, b, c and d are variables and may or may not differ. Consider the marker PENTA_E in our example. Then $a = 7$, $b = 9$, $c = 8$ and $d = 10$. A stepwise stationary model was specified with mutation rate 0.005 and range 0.1; then (details omitted) $m_{8,7} = 2.4e^{-3}$, $m_{10,7} = 4.5e^{-5}$, $m_{8,9} = 2.4e^{-3}$ and $m_{10,9} = 4.5e^{-3}$ and the LR for the marker PENTA_E is LR = 0.013. (Recall that the combined LR = 0 if the value for one marker is 0. This may be unreasonable if all other markers give positive values. The problem is then resolved by allowing for mutations.)

3.2 Silent Alleles

When an individual is apparently homozygote and there may be silent alleles, represented by S, frequencies of the silent allele, p_s, need to be taken into account. Of course, solving the biological uncertainty about the homozygous nature of the marker should always be the aim, but this is not often possible, hence numeric solutions can be applied instead. Silent allele frequencies for several forensic markers are available at http://www.cstl.nist.gov/strbase/NullAlleles.htm. The remaining allele frequencies and the one of the silent allele should still add to one.

Consider now marker TPOX in our example. Both the alleged father and the child have initially been reported as homozygote, but there are serious doubts about the presence of a silent allele in both individuals. We will represent then the observed profile for both as $G^*_{AF} = 8$ and $G^*_C = 8$, indicating they could be either 8/8 or 8/S. Assume the silent allele frequency as $p_s = 0.05$. Then, marginal and conditional probabilities for the genotypes can be calculated as

$$\Pr(G^*_{AF} = 8) = \Pr(G^*_C = 8) = p_8^2 + 2p_8 p_S,$$

$$\Pr(G_{AF} = 8/8 \,|\, G_{AF}^* = 8) = \frac{p_8}{p_8 + 2p_S},$$

$$\Pr(G_{AF} = 8/S \,|\, G_{AF}^* = 8) = \frac{2p_S}{p_8 + 2p_S}.$$

Analogously, the probability of G_C^* conditional on G_{AF}^* under the null hypothesis is

$$\begin{aligned}
\Pr(G_C^* = 8 \,|\, &G_{AF}^* = 8, H_0) \\
&= \Pr(G_C^* = 8 \,|\, G_{AF} = 8/8)\Pr(G_{AF} = 8/8 \,|\, G_{AF}^* = 8) \\
&\quad + \Pr(G_C^* = 8 \,|\, G_{AF} = 8/S)\Pr(G_{AF} = 8/S \,|\, G_{AF}^* = 8) \\
&= \frac{(p_8 + p_S)p_8}{p_8 + 2p_S} + \frac{(p_8 + p_S / 2)2p_S}{p_8 + 2p_S} \\
&= \frac{(p_8 + p_S)^2 + p_8 p_S}{p_8 + 2p_S}
\end{aligned}$$

and so the LR for paternity is

$$\mathrm{LR} = \frac{\Pr(G_C^* = 8 \,|\, G_{AF}^* = 8, H_0)}{\Pr(G_C^* = 8)} = \frac{(p_8 + p_S)^2 + p_8 p_S}{p_8(p_8 + 2p_S)^2} = 1.643.$$

3.3 Dropout

Over the past few years, the field of forensic genetics has been introduced to more sensitive methods that allow for samples with very small amounts of DNA to be analyzed. Allelic dropout in relationship problems may commonly appear in cases with DNA degraded samples. Partial profiles can lead to falsely considering markers as homozygous or to exclude markers. The ISFG DNA commission recommends the use of a probabilistic approach which includes dropout for forensic case work (Gill *et al.*, 2012). Three models for dropout are studied in Drum *et al.* (2014) and exemplied for relationship problems.

Sampling uncertainty

Calculation of a LR value is based on allelic frequencies for a given set of markers. It is general practice for a laboratory to validate population databases before proceeding to report any results arising from their estimates. The process of validation may include issues about the size of the database, the method of selection of the samples, and dependence effects. Uncertainty in the estimate due to the database is often called sampling error, where error does not refer to an analytical error but rather the variation that would occur if a different sample of individuals were taken to create the database. A list of methods addressing for sampling uncertainty can be found in Buckleton *et al.* (2005).

3.4 *Various Forms of Dependence*

In order to obtain correct LR values, HWE must be fulfilled. The Hardy–Weinberg law is a statement of independence between alleles at one locus. Given a marker with alleles A_1, A_2, ..., A_n and their corresponding allelic frequencies p_1, p_2, ..., p_n, the Hardy–Weinberg law states that the single-locus frequency of a combination $A_i A_j$ is

$$\begin{cases} p_i^2 & \text{if } A_i = A_j, \\ 2 p_i p_j & \text{if } A_i \neq A_j. \end{cases} \tag{8}$$

This law will be exactly true in all generations after the first if a number of assumptions are met. These assumptions are: infinite population, random mating and absence of disturbing forces like selection, migration or mutation. It may also be true or approximately true under some circumstances if these assumptions are not entirely met. Statistical tests can be carried out looking for significant deviations of the HWE in genetic markers. These tests take into account the fact that human populations are finite and hence small non-significant deviations from the numerical values in (8) can be found.

Continuous discussion can be found in the forensics literature about which genetic markers are the more suitable in kinship studies. In most cases, analyses with widely known commercial kits of STR markers provide powerful statistical evidence favoring one of the hypotheses. The more recent advent of new genotyping technologies have given rise to SNP markers. As a consequence, some controversy has arised regarding the potential for SNP as possible replacements of STR loci. This possibility has been mainly discarded (Gill, 2001; Gill *et al.*, 2004; Amorim and Pereira, 2005; Butler *et al.*, 2007). This does not mean to say that SNP markers will not fulfill an important role in forensics. The low polymorphism of SNP markers leads to a large increase of the probability of two individuals sharing identity- by-state (IBS) alleles. Small arrays of approximately 50 loci are comparable to existing STR multiplexes with 13–17 markers. Regarding kinship studies, in those cases where the statistical evidence is insufficient, the common practice is to extend the set of markers being used. Many studies have carried out such an approach, remarking the fact that SNP markers are incomparably less prone to mutation than STRs.

Traditionally, likelihood-based approaches to relationship estimation have used unlinked genetic markers. Hence, most of the paternity cases and further family studies make use of the product rule as indicated in (2), implying the assumption of within and between locus independence is frequently carried out. The product rule's assumption of independence needs to be carefully, as it is not entirely true in many situations. In one way or another, population databases are usually an incomplete mixing of subpopulations with differing allele frequencies, producing mild within and between locus allelic associations. A clear example of this is the U.S. population, composed by population groups with very different ancestries. As a consequence, the product rule has a tendency to overstate the value of the forensic evidence by a small amount, hence favoring the prosecution (Buckleton *et al.*, 2001).

There are some relationships that cannot be distinguished using just unlinked markers. Halfsiblings, uncle–nephew and grandparent–grandchild pairwise relationships are undistinguishable on the basis of data at independently segregating loci. Nevertheless, they have distinct consequences for data at linked loci, since each one provides different probabilities that the two relatives share one IBD gene at two linked loci (Thompson, 1998). Likelihoods must be calculated numerically and the Lander–Green algorithm is the basic engine in modern computing packages. This algorithm is based on a hidden Markov model for the unobserved IBD status along the chromosome (Egeland and Sheehan, 2008).

A common occurrence in human populations is the breach of the assumption of random mating. Many population groups tend to isolate themselves, mainly for geographical reasons. This translates to cryptic relatedness (Astle and Balding, 2009), an increased probability that two unrelated individuals share IBD alleles, usually expressed as θ or F_{st} in the forensic literature. In such cases, algorithms that take substructuring into consideration should be used. The method of Balding and Nichols (1994) can be used to evaluate LRs for paternity duos and trios when population substructure exists. The sampling formula to account for the presence of substructure measured by θ indicates that if x alleles are type "a" out of a total of n alleles sampled, then the probability that the next allele "a" is given by

$$\frac{x\theta + (1-\theta)p_a}{1+(n-1)\theta}. \tag{9}$$

Probabilities in the numerator and denominator of the LR in (1) can then be corrected using this sampling formula. Take for instance the TH01 marker in the motivational example

$$\Pr(\mathrm{CH} = 6/9 \mid \mathrm{AF} = 6/7, H_0) = \frac{1}{2}\frac{1-\theta}{1+\theta}p_9,$$

$$\Pr(\mathrm{CH} = 6/9 \mid H_1) = 2\frac{\theta + (1-\theta)p_6}{1+\theta}\frac{1-\theta}{1+2\theta}p_9.$$

and so the LR is recalculated as

$$\mathrm{LR}_{\mathrm{TH01}} = \frac{\Pr(\mathrm{CH} = 6/9 \mid \mathrm{AF} = 6/7, H_0)}{\Pr(\mathrm{CH} = 6/9 \mid H_1)} = \frac{(1+2\theta)}{4[\theta + (1-\theta)p_6]}.$$

Realistic examples with $\theta = 0.01$ and $\theta = 0.03$ can then be calculated, obtaining

$$\mathrm{LR}_{\mathrm{TH01}} = 1.176 \ (\theta = 0.01),$$

$$\mathrm{LR}_{\mathrm{TH01}} = 1.139 \ (\theta = 0.03).$$

4 The Parametric Approach

The classical approach to solve kinship cases by means of LR calculation has been the prevailing procedure for many years. Nonetheless, this does not mean it is problem-free. One of the shortcomings associated to the classical approach is that the LR distribution is unknown. Although mean, variance and other parameters of LR have been calculated (Slooten and Egeland, 2014), they are dependent on the nature of the markers used, namely number of alleles and allele frequencies. Furthermore, knowledge of the parameters does not mean the distribution corresponds to any known parametric distribution. This implies that p-values cannot be calculated as there is no reference test statistic. This is also associated with lack of LR threshold values with statistical significance. Verbal interpretations are provided in Evett and Weir (1998), though they lack mathematical support. Another problem is verbal formulation of the hypotheses, which is a potential source of misinterpretations (Amorim, 2008) and produces a contrast with many other application of statistics in different sciences, where hypotheses are formulated based on parameters. Besides, a common practice in forensics is that $H_0 \cup H_1$ does not usually cover the entire space of events. This gives rise to errors in those cases where the tested relationship is closer than the tested one.

4.1 *Identity-By-Descent (IBD)*

The concept of identity-by-descent (Cotterman, 1940), usually mentioned as IBD, refers to two individuals sharing two copies of the same allele from a common ancestor within the pedigree being considered. Figure 3 shows the nine condensed identity states that can be found between two individuals, as defined by Jacquard

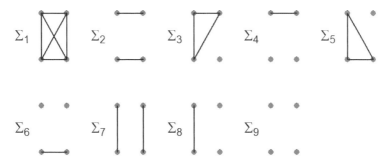

Figure 3:   IBD states between pairs of alleles.

(1972). Dots in each row represent the alleles from each individual, while connections represent IBD. States Σ_1–Σ_6 show cases where IBD alleles can be found within the same individual, hence they are a result of inbreeding. For non-inbreeding pairwise relationships, let us denote $\kappa = (\kappa_0, \kappa_1, \kappa_2)$ the probabilities of sharing 0, 1 or 2 IBD alleles, respectively,

$$\begin{cases} \kappa_0 = \Pr(\Sigma_9), \\ \kappa_1 = \Pr(\Sigma_8), \\ \kappa_2 = \Pr(\Sigma_7), \end{cases}$$

fulfilling $\kappa_0 + \kappa_1 + \kappa_2 = 1$. Hence, pairwise relationships can be represented as points in the 2D simplex

$$K^* = \{(\kappa_0, \kappa_1) \in \mathbb{R}^2 : \kappa_0 \geq 0, \kappa_1 \geq 0, \kappa_0 + \kappa_1 \leq 1\}.$$

Estimation of IBD probabilities has the advantage of providing a continuous measure of the amount of DNA shared by two people. Table 3 indicates the values of $\kappa = (\kappa_0, \kappa_1, \kappa_2)$ for the most common pairwise relationships. Their location in K^* is shown in Figure 4. The term avuncular encompasses three relationships which are indistinguishable from an IBD point of view: half-siblings, grandparent–grandchild and uncle–nephew.

Estimation of pairwise relationships from genotype data is carried out by maximizing the likelihood with respect to κ. For a

Table 3: IBD probabilities for the most common pairwise relationships.

Relationship	$\kappa = (\kappa_0, \kappa_1, \kappa_2)$
Parent–child	$(0, 1, 0)$
Siblings	$\left(\frac{1}{4}, \frac{1}{2}, \frac{1}{4}\right)$
Avuncular	$\left(\frac{1}{2}, \frac{1}{2}, 0\right)$
First cousins	$\left(\frac{3}{4}, \frac{1}{4}, 0\right)$
Double first cousins	$\left(\frac{9}{16}, \frac{6}{16}, \frac{1}{16}\right)$
Half-siblings cousins	$\left(\frac{7}{16}, \frac{8}{16}, \frac{1}{16}\right)$
First-second cousins	$\left(\frac{21}{32}, \frac{10}{32}, \frac{1}{32}\right)$
Unrelated	$(1,0,0)$

Note. Half-siblings cousins refers to the relationship of individuals who share a parent, while the other two are siblings. First-second cousins means that two parents are siblings and the other two are avuncular.

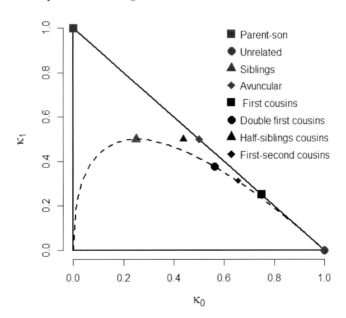

Figure 4: Space of pairwise relationships in $\mathbb{R}^2$.

marker i with genotypes g_{i1}, g_{i2} for the two individuals, the likelihood of a κ value is calculated as (Thompson, 1975)

$$
\begin{aligned}
L_i(\kappa) &= \Pr\left(g_{i1}, g_{i2} \mid \kappa\right) \\
&= \Pr\left(g_{i1}, g_{i2} \mid \Sigma_9\right)\kappa_0 + \Pr\left(g_{i1}, g_{i2} \mid \Sigma_8\right)\kappa_1 + \Pr\left(g_{i1}, g_{i2} \mid \Sigma_7\right)\kappa_2 \\
&= \Pr\left(g_{i1}\right)\Pr\left(g_{i2}\right)\kappa_0 \\
&\quad + \Pr\left(g_{i1} \mid g_{i2}, \mathrm{PC}_{gi1-gi2}\right)\Pr\left(g_{i2}\right)\kappa_1 + \Pr(g_{i1})I_{gi1=gi2}\left(1-\kappa_0-\kappa_1\right),
\end{aligned}
$$

where $\mathrm{PC}_{gi1-gi2}$ denotes a parent–child relationship and I_E is the indicator function of an event E. Assuming independence, the likelihood for a set of N markers is

$$
L(\kappa) = \prod_{i=1}^{N} L_i(\kappa).
$$

Likelihoods for separate markers can be easily calculated for the example in Table 1.

$$
L_{\mathrm{TH01}}(\kappa) = 4p_6^2 p_7 p_9 \kappa_0 + p_6 p_7 p_9 \kappa_1,
$$

$$
L_{\mathrm{PENTA\_E}}(\kappa) = 4p_7 p_8 p_9 p_{10},
$$

$$
L_{\mathrm{TPOX}}(\kappa) = p_8^4 \kappa_0 + p_8^3 \kappa_1 + p_8^2 \kappa_2.
$$

Maximum likelihood estimates for κ are obtained as

$$
\hat{\kappa} = \underset{\kappa \in K^*}{\operatorname{argmax}} \, L(\kappa).
$$

5 Discussion

The question remains: what value should be reported to a courtroom? LR is reported in some countries while the posterior probability is the method of choice in others. A similar segmentation can be found in the scientific field, in what seems to be a very controversial issue. David Balding and colleagues supported the posterior probability as a way to include further evidence by means of priors:

> We believe that such an approach is inappropriate. How could these very different sets of evidence be accounted for in a hypothesis testing framework? We believe that the only logical method of weighing the DNA evidence in conjunction with the other evidence is to use Bayes' rule. In the legal context, Bayes' rule makes clear the distinction between the domain of the expert witness, the likelihood ratio, and the domain of the court, the assessment of other evidence (Balding *et al.*, 1994).

On the other trench, many other experts stand up for the LR between exclusive hypotheses as the best choice in order to communicate results in court:

> The ratio of the probability of the observations given the prosecution proposition to the probability of the observations given the defence proposition, which is known as the likelihood ratio, provides the most appropriate foundation for assisting the court in establishing the weight that should be assigned to those observations. A verbal scale based on the notion of the likelihood ratio is the most appropriate basis for communication of an evaluative expert opinion to the court (Aitken *et al.*, 2011; Buckleton *et al.*, 2014).

Both values are calculated from allelic frequencies of independent loci. These are estimated using population databases of anonymous individuals, often victims and suspects of previous cases, classified into ethnic groups. However, relationship cases are usually constrained to specific sub-populations and the question arises of how much allelic frequencies in these sub-populations differ. It is the duty of the forensic expert to explain how these statistical issues have been overcome in order to obtain reliable results.

Differences between legal systems are also remarkable. Few similarities can be found among the courtrooms in continental Europe, the UK and the US. Although many scholars prefer the inquisitorial legal system of most of mainland Europe to the adversarial system implemented in the US and the UK, the strong incentive to probe for weaknesses inherent in the latter system provides an important safeguard (Balding, 2005).

Ethical issues are also important and familial searching is one example in this context. Searching of DNA databases is becoming a significant aspect of criminal investigations. Familial searching refers to the process whereby a DNA profile obtained from a crime scene fails to match any existing profile, but is used in order to seek a relative, by means of the increased likelihood of similarity between the DNA profiles of those who have a direct genetic relationship. In some countries like The Netherlands, familial searching is admissible and regulated by rules whereas in other countries this procedure is not allowed. Knowledge of the methods and limitations of kinship analysis is obviously important for those who work in a paternity lab. However, relationship inference is also relevant in other forensic areas and for applications in human genetics. Finally, controversies regarding the admissibility of familial searching shows that also the informed citizen could benefit from some understanding and hopefully this chapter helps.

References

C. Aitken, C. E. H. Berger, J. S. Buckleton, C. Champod, J. Curran, A. P. Dawid, I. W. Evett, P. Gill, J. González-Rodríguez and G. Jackson. Guest editorial. Expressing evaluative opinions: A position statement. *Science and Justice*, 51:1–2, 2011.

A. Amorim and L. Pereira. Pros and cons in the use of SNPs in forensic kinship investigation: a comparative analysis with STRs. *Forensic Science International*, 150:17–21, 2005.

A. Amorim. A cautionary note on the evaluation of genetic evidence from uni-parentally transmitted markers. *Forensic Science International: Genetics*, 2:376–378, 2008.

W. Astle and D. J. Balding. Population structure and cryptic relatedness in genetic association studies. *Statistical Science*, 24:451–471, 2009.

D. J. Balding and R. A. Nichols. A method for quantifying differentiation between populations at multi-allelic loci and its implications for investigating identity and paternity. *Genetica*, 96:3–12, 1994.

D. J. Balding, P. Donnelly and R. A. Nichols. DNA fingerprinting: A review of the controversy: Comment: Some causes for concern about DNA profiles. *Statistical Science*, 9:248–251, 1994.

D. Balding. A question of significance. *Significance*, 20–23, 2005.

D. J. Balding, M. Krawczak, J. S. Buckleton and J. M. Curran. Decision-making in familial database searching: KI alone or not alone? *Forensic Science International: Genetics*, 7:52–54, 2013.

C. H. Brenner and B. S. Weir. Issues and strategies in the DNA identification of World Trade Center victims. *Theoretical Population Biology*, 63:173–178, 2003.

J. S. Buckleton, S. Walsh and S. A. Harbison. The fallacy of independence testing and the use of the product rule. *Science and Justice*, 41:81–84, 2001

J. Buckleton, C. M. Triggs and S. J. Walsh. *Forensic DNA Evidence Interpretation.* CRC Press, Boca Raton, USA, 2005.

J. Buckleton and J. Curran. A discussion of the merits of random man not excluded and likelihood ratios. *Forensic Science International: Genetics*, 2:343–348, 2008.

J. Buckleton, J. A. Bright, D. Taylor, I. Evett, T. Hicks, G. Jackson and J. M. Curran. Helping formulate propositions in forensic DNA analysis. *Science and Justice*, 54:258–261, 2014.

J. M. Butler, M. D. Coble and P. M. Vallone. STRs vs. SNPs: Thoughts on the future of forensic DNA testing. *Forensic Science on Medicine and Pathology*, 3:200–205, 2007.

C. W. Cotterman. A calculus for statistico-genetics. Ph.D. Thesis: Ohio State University. Published in *Genetics and Social Structure*. Dowden: Hutchinson and Ross, 1940.

G. Dørum, D. Kling, C. Baeza-Richer, M. García-Magariños, S. Saebo, S. Desmyter and T. Egeland. Models and implementation for relationship problems with dropout. *International Journal of Legal Medicine* 129: 411–423, 2015.

T. Egeland, P. Mostad, B. Mevag and M. Stenersen. Beyond traditional paternity and identification cases. Selecting the most probable pedigree. *Forensic Science International: Genetics*, 110:4759, 2000.

T. Egeland and N. Sheehan. On identification problems requiring linked autosomal markers. *Forensic Science International: Genetics*, 2:219–225, 2008.

E. Essen-Möller. Die Beweiskraft der Ähnlichkert in Vaterschaftsnachweis. Theoretische Grundlagen. *Mitteilungen der Anthropologischen Gesellschaft in Wien*, 68:9–53, 1938.

I. W. Evett and B. S. Weir. *Interpreting DNA Evidence.* Sinauer Associates, Inc. Sunderland, USA, 1998.

E. A. Foster, M. A. Jobling, P. G. Taylor, P. Donnelly, P. de Knijff, R. Mieremet T. Zerjal, and C. Tyler-Smith. Jefferson fathered slave's last child. *Nature,* 396:27–28, 1998.

P. Gill, P. L. Ivanov, C. Kimpton, R. Piercy, N. Benson, G. Tully, I. Evett, E. Hagelberg and K. Sullivan. Identification of the remains of the Romanov family by DNA analysis. *Nature,* 6:130–135, 1995.

P. Gill. An assessment of the utility of single nucleotide polymorphisms (SNPs) for forensic purposes. *International Journal of Legal Medicine,* 114:204–210, 2001.

P. Gill, D. J. Werrett, B. Budowle and R. Guerrieri. An assessment of whether SNPs will replace STRs in national DNA databases. *Science and Justice,* 44:51–53, 2004.

P. Gill, L. Gusmao, H. Haned, W. Mayr, N. Morling, W. Parson, L. Prieto, M. Prinz, H. Schneider, P. Schneider and B. Weir. DNA commission of the International Society of Forensic Genetics: Recommendations on the evaluation of STR typing results that may include drop-out and/or drop-in using probabilistic methods. *Forensic Science International: Genetics,* 6:679–688, 2012.

M. Hubig, J. Sanft, H. Muggenthaler and G. Mall. Setting the boundaries of prior influence on kinship relation testing: The case of many hypotheses. *International Journal of Legal Medicine,* 127:1055–1063, 2013.

A. Jacquard. Genetic information given by a relative. *Biometrics,* 28:1101–1114, 1972.

D. Kling, A. O. Tillmar and T. Egeland. Familias 3 — Extensions and new functionality. *Forensic Science International: Genetics,* 13:121–127, 2014.

B. Leclair, C. J. Fregeau, K. L. Bowen and R. M. Fourney. Enhanced kinship analysis and STR-based DNA typing for human identification in mass fatality incidents: The Swissair flight 111 disaster. *Journal of Forensic Sciences,* 49:1–15, 2004.

C. C. Li and A. Chakravarty. An expository review of two methods of calculating the paternity probability. *American Journal of Human Genetics,* 43:197–205, 1988.

T. Ohta and M. Kimura. A model of mutation appropriate to estimate the number of electrophoretically detectable alleles in a finite population. *Genetical Research,* 22:201–204, 1973.

K. J. Slooten and T. Egeland. Exclusion probabilities and likelihood ratios with applications to kinship problems. *International Journal of Legal Medicine*, 128:415–425, 2014.

E. A. Thompson. The estimation of pairwise relationships. *Annals of Human Genetics*, 39:173–188, 1975.

E. A. Thompson and T. R. Meagher. Genetic linkage in the estimation of pairwise relationship. *Theoretical and Applied Genetics*, 97:857–864, 1998.

CHAPTER 6

Assessing Sampling Error in DNA Evidence

James M. Curran

University of Auckland, Department of Statistics,
Private Bag 92019,
Auckland 1142,
New Zealand

1 Introduction

A person whose DNA profile matches that found in an evidential stain can be associated with the crime for which the stain was recovered. Typical examples include those of a suspect having the same profile as a stain at the crime scene or having possessions that carry a stain with a victim's profile. Other situations include a stain profile that, when compared to profiles from several family members, does not exclude the possibility it came from a missing member of that family. In each case, it is usual to attach numerical weight to the event of the observed match in order to aid interpretation by investigators or triers of fact in court. As these weights are generally based on sample frequencies of the allelic components of the profile, they are subject to sampling error and here we take up the question of how best to convey information about the size of this error.

The quantity of primary interest is the likelihood ratio (LR). To simplify the discussion, we will initially limit ourselves to the single source case, although some of the methods discussed in this chapter can be easily extended to take into account mixed stains with multiple contributions.

We consider a case where DNA has been recovered from a stain found at a scene. There are no more than two alleles present at any locus, and the evidence is considered to have arisen from a single contributor. The authorities have apprehended a single suspect who has the same genotype as the crime scene stain. We disregard at this time issues of peak height, stutter, allelic dropout and drop-in. We propose two alternative propositions, or hypotheses, concerning the evidence, *E*. These are:

H_p	the suspect, *S* is the only donor to this stain
H_d	some other person, unrelated to *S* is the only donor to this stain

These hypotheses are mutually exclusive, but not mutually exhaustive. That is, if they were mutually exhaustive then if one of these hypotheses is true, then the other must be false. The key point is these are not the only pair of hypotheses that we might propose, and perhaps more importantly, they might *both* be false. For example, it is possible to consider a set of hypotheses such as

H_p	the suspect, *S* and two unrelated individuals are the only donors to this stain
H_d	four unrelated individuals are donors to this stain

even if these bear no relation to the facts of the case.

We restrict ourselves here to these very simple hypotheses as several of the methods described were developed for the first pair of hypotheses only.

The usual measure of the strength of the evidence Evett and Weir (1998) is the LR, and is expressed as a ratio the probability of the evidence calculated under the assumption that each of the two hypotheses in turn is true. That is

$$LR = \frac{\Pr(E \mid H_p)}{\Pr(E \mid H_d)}.$$

In this very simple situation, the LR reduces to the reciprocal of the random match probability. That is

$$LR = \frac{1}{P}.$$

The LR should be estimated for the population to which the true offender is supposed to belong. This is rarely, if ever known and usual practice is to estimate the LR in each of the major racial subgroups present in the population of interest.

This limitation to a single population is in the interests of simplicity, although methodology does exist to consider multiple populations in certain circumstances.

The quantities $\Pr(E \mid H_p)$ and $\Pr(E \mid H_d)$ are functions of genotype probabilities, although these are usually reduced to allele probabilities by assuming linkage equilibrium (LE), and occasionally Hardy–Weinberg Equilibrium (HWE). The allele probability, p_{A_i} is the true, but unknown probability of observing an allele of type A_i in the population of interest. We estimate these allele probabilities with allele frequencies. That is, we estimate the probability of observing allele A_i in the population with a frequency calculated from a finite sample of individuals, usually some sort of DNA database, of size N. This process of sampling induces what statisticians refer to as sampling error, or sometime sampling uncertainty. Sampling uncertainty arises by the very act of sampling. It is a result of not knowing the true value exactly because only a subset of the population has been sampled. Sampling error decreases as the sampling fraction, the ratio the sample size to the population size, approaches one.

There have been several methods suggested to characterize the sampling uncertainty of an estimated match probability, generally through the use of confidence intervals. The first NRC forensic DNA report (National Research Council, 1992) suggested that the frequency of each constituent allele be replaced by a binomial upper confidence limit, and these limits then multiplied across alleles. Another simple approach, although one with some empirical support was suggested by the second NRC forensic DNA report (National Research Council, 1996) and was to multiply and divide the estimated match probability by a factor of 10. That is, we estimate the match probability and then make it 10 times smaller, by dividing it by 10, and make it 10 times larger by multiplying it by 10. Using this method, the resulting interval from $\hat{P}/10$ to $10 \times \hat{P}$ could be used to convey uncertainty in $\hat{P}$. Weir (1996) suggested a bootstrapping approach by resampling individuals in some population sample. Chakraborty *et al.* (1993) appealed to the asymptotic normality of the logarithm of the product of allele frequencies to provide an analytical expression for the confidence interval, and this was extended by the second National Research Council report (1996) to allow for population structure. Balding (1995) gave both a likelihood support interval and a "conservative Bayesian estimate." Curran *et al.* (2002) developed a suggestion given by Balding (1995) which makes use of the posterior distribution of the allele probabilities updated by the database counts. We will describe each of these methods in some detail and compare their respective performances by way of simulation.

2 Method

We consider here, DNA profiles from single contributors consisting of genotypes $A_{l1}A_{l2}$ present at the lth of L loci, where L is usually greater than 10 for modern multiplexes. The two alleles at each locus may or may not be the same. We will assume that alleles are discrete categories that can be determined without ambiguity for DNA extracted from a sample. This is usually true for STR loci, but may not be the case for the less commonly used VNTR loci. If allele

A_{li} has a population probability of p_{li}, then, an appropriate estimate for the LR at locus l taking into account population substructure is given by

$$\text{LR}_l = \begin{cases} \dfrac{(1+\theta)(1+2\theta)}{[2\theta+(1-\theta)p_{l1}][3\theta+(1-\theta)p_{l1}]}, & A_{l1}=A_{l2} \\[4mm] \dfrac{(1+\theta)(1+2\theta)}{2[\theta+(1-\theta)p_{l1}][\theta+(1-\theta)p_{l2}]}, & A_{l1}\neq A_{l2}. \end{cases} \tag{1}$$

The reciprocals of these equations appear as Equations (4.10a) and (4.10b) in the second NRC report (National Research Council, 1996). The LRs are the reciprocal of the probabilities of a person in the population having genotype $A_{l1}A_{l2}$ given that one person in the same population is known to have the genotype $A_{l1}A_{l2}$. The quantity θ is the coancestry coefficient and describes the structure of the population through the low-level of relatedness which we expect to find between individuals. In particular, it allows use of population-wide allele probabilities in the absence of knowledge of the probabilities in the specific subpopulation relevant to the crime in question. When this substructure is either absent or is ignored, θ can be set to zero, and then these quantities simplify to

$$\text{LR}_l = \begin{cases} \dfrac{1}{p_{l1}^2}, & A_{l1}=A_{l2} \\[4mm] \dfrac{1}{2p_{l1}p_{l2}}, & A_{l1}\neq A_{l2}. \end{cases} \tag{2}$$

It is customary, regardless of the value of θ, to multiply over loci to get the overall LR,

$$\text{LR} = \prod_{l=1}^{L} \text{LR}_l.$$

This last expression is known as the "product rule." It should be noted that this expression does not carry an implicit assumption of linkage equilibrium, or independence between loci. The LR is a product of conditional probabilities, regardless of the value of θ. If A and C are genotypes (of two different people) at one locus and B and D are genotypes of the same people at different loci, then independence between loci would imply that

$$\Pr(A \text{ and } B \mid C \text{ and } D) = \Pr(A \mid C \text{ and } D) \Pr(B \mid C \text{ and } D),$$

whereas the expression in the product rule is

$$\Pr(A \mid C) \Pr(B \mid D).$$

These two quantities are not equivalent, and it is only a numerical "coincidence" that they are equal to each other when $\theta = 0$.

It is usual to use the allele proportions, or sample frequencies, $\hat{p}_{li}$, as estimates of the population values p_{li}. These sample frequencies are obtained from a sample of n_l individuals from the population (not from the specific relevant subpopulation) who were genotyped at locus l. We denote the corresponding estimated LRs as $\widehat{\text{LR}}_i$ and $\widehat{\text{LR}}$. We wish to assess the sampling uncertainty associated with $\widehat{\text{LR}}$.

2.1 Products of Confidence Limits and Factors of 10

The first NRC suggested replacing the allele frequency $\hat{p}_{li}$ with its binomial-based confidence limit

$$\hat{p}_{li} + z^*_{(1-\alpha)} \sqrt{\hat{p}_{li}(1 - \hat{p}_{li}) / 2n_l},$$

where as $z^*_{1-\alpha}$ is the point from the standard normal distribution such that $\Pr(Z < z^*_{(1-\alpha)}) = 1 - \alpha$. This suggestion is clearly invalid as confidence limits for products are not obtained as products of confidence limits, and hence we give it no further attention.

Similarly, the second NRC suggestion of constructing the interval

$$(\widehat{\text{LR}} / 10, 10\widehat{\text{LR}}),$$

has limited applicability as there must at least be an effect of sample size. That is, we expect any method which attempts to deal with sampling uncertainty to become more accurate as the sample size increases. This method does have the merit of simplicity and is based on empirical observation, and so has been included in this study.

2.2 Normal Approximation Approach

Methods based on asymptotic normality have the advantage of leading to relatively simple analytical expressions. Chakraborty *et al.* (1993) derived a set of expressions for the approximate distribution of

$$\log_e(\hat{P}),$$

where $\hat{P}$ is the random match probability. Beecham and Weir (2011) extended this procedure to deal with both population substructure and mixed stains where the LR is the only relevant quantity.

The procedure assumes that $\log_e(\hat{P})$ is normally distributed, so that a two-sided $100(1 - \alpha)\%$ confidence interval for $\hat{P}$ is given by

$$(\hat{P}/C, C\hat{P}),$$

where

$$C = z^{*}_{(1-\alpha/2)} \sqrt{\text{Var}\left[\log_e(\hat{P})\right]}.$$

The task is to compute the variance of $\log_e(\hat{P})$. Assuming LE, this reduces to computing the variance of $\log_e(\hat{P}_l)$, as

$$\text{Var}\left[\log_e(\hat{P})\right] = \text{Var}\left[\log_e\left(\prod_{l=1}^{L}\hat{P}_l\right)\right],$$

$$= \text{Var}\left[\sum_{l=1}^{L}\log_e\left(\hat{P}_l\right)\right],$$

$$= \sum_{l=1}^{L}\text{Var}\left[\log_e\left(\hat{P}_l\right)\right],$$

when the loci are independent. This expression is correctly given for $\theta = 0$ in (Chakraborthy *et al.*, 1993) and (National Research Council, 1996)

$$\mathrm{Var}\left[\log_e\left(\hat{P}_i\right)\right] \approx \begin{cases} \dfrac{2(1-p_{l1})}{n_l p_{l1}}, & A_{l1} = A_{l2} \\[2mm] \dfrac{p_{l1} + p_{l2} - 4 p_{l1} p_{l2}}{2 n_l p_{l1} p_{l2}}, & A_{l1} \neq A_{l2}. \end{cases} \tag{3}$$

However, Weir (1996) showed that the expressions given for $0 < \theta < 1$ are not correct as the formulae do not account for between population variation. The correct expressions are

$$\mathrm{Var}\left[\log_e\left(\hat{P}_i\right)\right] \approx \begin{cases} p_{i1}(1-p_{i1})(1-\theta)^2\left(\theta + \dfrac{1-\theta}{2n_i}\right) \\[2mm] \left(\dfrac{5\theta + 2(1-\theta)p_{i1}}{\left[3\theta + (1-\theta)p_{i1}\right]\left[2\theta + (1-\theta)p_{i1}\right]}\right)^2, & A_{i1} = A_{i2} \\[4mm] (1-\theta)^2\left(\theta + \dfrac{1-\theta}{2n_i}\right)\left(\dfrac{p_{i1}\left(1-p_{i1}\right)}{\left[\theta + (1-\theta)p_{i1}\right]^2}\right) \\[2mm] -\dfrac{2 p_{i1} p_{i2}}{\left[\theta + (1-\theta)p_{i1}\right]\left[\theta + (1-\theta)p_{i2}\right]} + \dfrac{p_{i2}(1-p_{i2})}{\left[\theta + (1-\theta)p_{i2}\right]^2}\right), & A_{i1} \neq A_{i2} \end{cases} \tag{4}$$

and these reduce to Equation (3) when $\theta = 0$. The effect of θ is shown in Table 1 for the four locus profile given in (Chakraborthy

Table 1: The effect of θ on the normal approximation confidence bounds. The values in this table are in units of 1 million, for example 2.7 is 2.7 million.

θ	Lower bound				$\widehat{\mathrm{LR}}$		Upper bound			
	99%		95%				95%		99%	
	2	7	3	2	5	2	8	6	10	0
0.001	1	9	2	3	4	8	10	1	12	7
0.01	0	3	0	6	2	6	12	1	19	7
0.03	0	06	0	11	0	8	6	6	12	5

et al., 1993). Setting θ to any value greater than zero clearly decreases the estimated LR, and taking into account between population variability increases the width of the confidence intervals. The 95% interval when $\theta = 0.03$ in this example is not very different from the NRC factor-of-10 rule.

2.3 *The Bootstrap*

Weir (1996) suggested a bootstrap approach to this problem. Bootstrapping (Efron, 1979) is a statistical procedure which is used to approximate the sampling distribution of a statistic by resampling the data. We use the term resampling to mean sampling with replacement. This resampling in some sense simulates the process of sampling from the population. It is a theoretically justified approach which can work well in practice and has become incredibly popular as computing power has increased because it can be computationally intensive.

The bootstrap procedure discussed by Weir (1996) resamples whole profiles from a sample of individuals, usually a DNA database, taken from the population. This sampling of whole profiles preserves any within-individual allelic dependencies. The procedure is as follows:

[H] b in $1...B$ take a random sample of size N with replacement from your database, where N is equal to the size of your database; Determine the allele frequencies in your new sampled database; Calculate LR_b using the new frequencies; Sort the B LRs into ascending order so that $\text{LR}_{(1)}$ denotes the smallest and $\text{LR}_{(B)}$ denotes the largest; Let $lb = \text{LR}_{(\lfloor B \times \alpha/2 \rfloor)}$; Let $ub = \text{LR}_{(\lceil B \times 1-\alpha/2 \rceil)}$ (lb, ub) where B is an arbitrarily large number of bootstrap repetitions; and α is the desired confidence level for a two-sided $100 \times (1 - \alpha)$ confidence interval. Usually $B = 1,000$ is sufficient for most problems.

2.4 *Uniform Allele Prior Distribution*

In our previous work (Curran *et al.*, 2002), we discussed a Bayesian method introduced by Balding (1995). In fairness to

Balding, this particular method was never intended to act as an adjustment for sampling uncertainty. Its purpose is to deal with issue of unobserved alleles, or very rare alleles, and in some way is the basis of what is often referred to as the "size-bias correction." The method proposes that we place equal probability of the true value of the frequencies of the observed alleles. That is, we give equal weighting, or assign a uniform prior in Bayesian terminology, to any set of allele frequencies that add up to one. For example, if we observed a single allele A at locus l, then we say that the true value of p_A is anywhere between 0 and 1 with probability 1. That is, $p_A = 0.1$ is just as likely as $p_A = 0.9$ and so on. The approach then makes an assumption about the sampling of alleles from the population. In general, we assume multinomial sampling which implies three conditions are satisfied (National Research Council, 1992):

1. there is a finite sample size N taken from an infinite population;
2. each allele is sampled independently;
3. the probability of observing allele A_i is constant.

If these assumptions are met, then Bayesian theory allows us to update the distribution of allele probabilities based on the observed allele counts x_{A_i} in a finite sample, i.e. a database. Specifically, if a single allele A is observed x_A times in a database of N individuals and therefore $2N$ alleles, and we assume a uniform prior on p_A, then the posterior distribution of the p_A is

$$p_A \sim \text{Beta}(x_A + 1, 2N - x_A + 1) = \text{Dir}_2(x_A + 1, 2N - x_A + 1).$$

If we observe two alleles A and B with respective counts of x_A and x_B in $2N$ alleles, then the joint posterior distribution of p_A and p_B is

$$p_A, p_B \sim \text{Dir}_3(x_A + 1, x_B + 1, 2N - x_A - x_B + 1).$$

Balding used these posterior distributions to derive the expected value of the random match probability. There were minor mistakes in the original derivations which are corrected by Weir (Evett and Weir, 1998). These are

$$\frac{E[p_{0l}]}{E[P_{0l}^2]} = \begin{cases} \dfrac{(x_{l1}+4)(x_{l1}+3)}{(2N_l+5)(2N_l+4)}, & A_{l1} = A_{l2} \\[4mm] \dfrac{2(x_{l1}+2)(x_{l2}+2)}{(2N_l+6)(2N_l+5)}, & A_{l1} \neq A_{l2}. \end{cases} \tag{5}$$

One might regard this as being approximately equal to the product rule estimate that would be obtained if two copies of the questioned profile was added to the database. The rationale for doing so is that the approach lends itself to an intuitive explanation: "we have seen this profile twice; once in the defendant and once in true offender." Practical interpretations aside, there are some issues relating to this estimator. Firstly, it does not actually address the problem of sampling variation. It addresses the problem of dealing with alleles that have not been observed in the database — an issue we will return to later. Secondly, as remarked upon by Balding himself, it is an inconsistent approach in that the prior distributions are different for homozygous profiles and heterozygous profiles. In order to explain this, we need to know something about the Dirichlet distribution.

2.4.1 The Dirichlet distribution

A Dirichlet distribution is used to model the behavior a set of (random) proportions which sum to one. That is, when we write

$$\mathbf{p} = (p_1, p_2, \ldots, p_k) \sim \mathrm{Dir}_k(\boldsymbol{\alpha}),$$

we mean that the vector of values $\mathbf{p} = (p_1, p_2, \ldots, p_k)$ follow a Dirichlet distribution with parameters $\boldsymbol{\alpha} = (\alpha_1, \alpha_2, \ldots, \alpha_k)$, where $\alpha_i > 0$, $i = 1, \ldots, k$ and $\Sigma_{i=1}^k p_i = 1$. When we describe the behavior of this distribution by drawing a graph or writing down the probability density function, we do this in terms of $(p_1, p_2, \ldots, p_{k-1})$ because given knowledge of $(p_1, p_2, ..., p_{k-1})$, we can determine the value of p_k by subtraction. That is

$$p_k = 1 - \sum_{i=1}^{k-1} p_i.$$

This means we can visualize the Dirichlet distribution for $k = 2,3$. Figures 1 and 2 show several examples of 2D and 3D Dirichlet distributions for different α values. As a general rule-of-thumb, parameter values less than one tend to put more probability (density) on either very small or very large values, whereas values greater than one favor intermediate values.

We use the term 'uniform Dirichlet distribution' when all of the α_i's are set to one. The left-hand panel in Figure 1 is a 2D uniform Dirichlet distribution, and the top two panels show the equivalent uniform Dirichlet in three dimensions. You might think of the latter as being like a pizza box cut along the diagonal. The expected value, or mean, of the ith component of Dirichlet distributed random variable is

$$E[p_i] = \frac{\alpha_i}{\sum_{i=1}^{k} \alpha_i}.$$

With this definition, we can now see the inconsistency in this approach. If we use a 2D uniform Dirichlet prior for homozygous

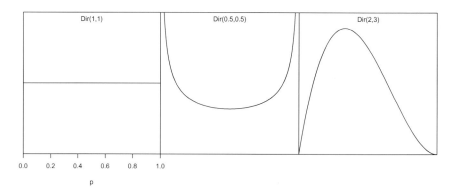

Figure 1:   2D Dirichlet distributions with different parameters.

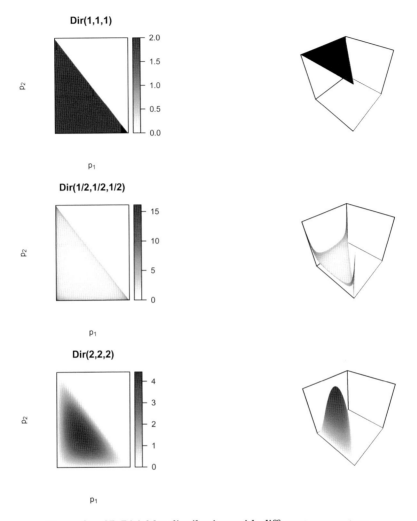

Figure 2: 3D Dirichlet distributions with different parameters.

profiles, and a 3D Dirichlet prior for heterozygous profiles, then the prior expected values for the allele probabilities are

$$E[p_{li}] = \begin{cases} \dfrac{1}{2}, & A_{l1} = A_{l2} \\[2ex] \dfrac{1}{3}, & A_{l1} \neq A_{l2}. \end{cases}$$

That is, the prior probability of an allele frequency changes depending on whether we have a homozygous or heterozygous profile. This does reflect the idea that we want to make all sets of allele probabilities equally.

2.5 The Bayesian Highest Posterior Density Method

As Balding noted in 1995, it would be more sensible to specify a prior for all possible alleles at a locus, and then update that prior based on the observed counts in a DNA database. Curran *et al.* (2002) utilized this idea. The updated distribution, the posterior distribution, can then be used to simulate 'new' sets of database frequencies, which in turn can be used to calculate the LR. This gives us a sample from the sampling distribution of the LR, and we can use this information to get an upper bound on the LR. Formally the procedure is as follows:

[H] l in $1...L$ Calculate $\mathbf{x}_l = (x_{l1}, x_{l2}, \ldots, x_{ln_l})$. That is, the set of observed allele counts in your database for each locus. Let $\alpha_{li} = x_{li} + \alpha_0$ be the updated Dirichlet parameter for the ith allele at the lth locus, with a prior parameter value of α_0. α_0 is constant across all alleles and all loci b in $1...B$ generate a new set of allele frequencies by sampling from $\mathbf{p}_l \sim \text{Dir}_{n_l}(\boldsymbol{\alpha}_l)$ at each locus. Calculate LR_b using the new frequencies. Sort the B LRs into ascending order so that $\text{LR}_{(1)}$ denotes the smallest and $\text{LR}_{(B)}$ denotes the largest. Let $lb = \text{LR}_{(\lfloor B \times \alpha/2 \rfloor)}$ and $ub = \text{LR}_{(\lceil B \times 1-\alpha/2 \rceil)}(lb, ub)$, where B is an arbitrarily large number of bootstrap repetitions, and α is the desired probability for a two-sided $100 \times (1 - \alpha)$ credible interval. A credible interval is the Bayesian equivalent of a confidence interval. Its interpretation differs in that one may make the statement that "The true value is contained within this interval with probability $(1 - \alpha)$." Usually $B = 1,000$ is sufficient for most problems.

The initial implementation used by Curran *et al.* (2002) used uniform Dirichlet priors, that is $\alpha_0 = 1$. However, work by Triggs and Curran (2006), showed that $\alpha_0 = 1/n_l$ is a less sensitive choice, where n_l is the number of allowable alleles at locus l. By *less sensitive*, we mean that the prior has less impact on the resulting intervals.

3 Simulations

We explore the performance of each of these methods through simulation. The simulations in this chapter made use of the 210 African American profiles published by Budolwe *et al.* (1999). We used the CODIS core loci from these profiles. We also made use of an unpublished New Zealand Caucasian database of 12,163 profiles which were typed using the SGM+ multiplex.

Every profile in this database was assigned an LR (assuming independence between and within loci). Using this information, a common profile (with a relatively small match LR) and a rare profile (with a very large match LR) were selected. The profiles are shown in Tables 2–6, along with the sample allele proportions. The performance of each method was tested using these "common" and "rare" profiles. More common (or rarer) profiles could have been artificially generated.

Table 2:   A common African American profile.

Locus (l)	A_{l1}	$\hat{p}_{l1}$	x_{l1}	A_{l2}	$\hat{p}_{l2}$	x_{l2}	$\widehat{LR}_l$
D3S1358	15	0.2872	112	15	0.2872	112	12.13
vWA	16	0.1389	50	17	0.1139	41	31.61
FGA	24	0.1417	51	24	0.1417	51	49.83
D8S1179	13	0.0585	21	14	0.1950	70	43.84
D21S11	29	0.0585	21	31.2	0.0557	20	153.3
D18S51	17	0.0944	34	17	0.0944	34	112.11
D5S818	12	0.4123	148	12	0.4123	148	5.88
D13S317	12	0.2699	105	12	0.2699	105	13.72
D7S820	8	0.1071	45	10	0.3524	148	13.24
CSF1PO	8	0.2625	110	11	0.1432	60	13.30
TPOX	9	0.1122	47	11	0.1957	82	22.78
THO1	7	0.1432	60	8	0.1575	66	22.17
D16S539	11	0.1692	68	11	0.1692	68	34.95
All loci							3.61×10^{18}

Table 3:   A rare African American profile.

Locus (l)	A_{l1}	$\hat{p}_{l1}$	x_{l1}	A_{l2}	$\hat{p}_{l2}$	x_{l2}	$\widehat{LR}_l$
D3S1358	14	0.0641	25	14	0.0641	25	243.31
vWA	14	0.0028	1	14	0.0028	1	127551.02
FGA	20	0.0056	2	27	0.0222	8	31887.76
D8S1179	12	0.0139	5	15	0.1783	64	201.21
D21S11	29	0.0585	21	29	0.0585	21	292.40
D18S51	14	0.0111	4	15	0.05	18	900.90
D5S818	11	0.2451	88	12	0.4123	148	4.95
D13S317	11	0.1003	39	13	0.1054	41	47.33
D7S820	10	0.3524	148	11	0.2667	112	5.32
CSF1PO	10	0.0955	40	11	0.1432	60	36.58
TPOX	8	0.1742	73	9	0.1122	47	25.58
THO1	9.3	0.0907	38	10	0.0955	40	57.74
D16S539	9	0.0274	11	10	0.0299	12	613.50
All Loci							2.17×10^{30}

The sample allele proportions from each database were used to generate 1,000 "databases" of N profiles for $N = 100$, 400, 1,000. This simulates the act of sampling from the population. As the databases were generated without any population substructure, the appropriate estimator of the match probability is given by the product rule.

An estimate of sampling error was calculated for the match probabilities estimated from each database. The normal approximation was used to give a 99% lower confidence limit. One thousand ($B = 1,000$) bootstrap samples were taken from each database for the bootstrap method and the 1st percentile recorded. One thousand ($B = 1,000$) samples from the posterior density of the allele probabilities were taken for the highest posterior density (HPD) method: the lower bound of a one-sided 99% credible/ highest posterior density interval for the LR was calculated. Balding's Bayesian method used the corrected Equation (5) from Evett and Weir (1998).

4 Results

Summaries of the performance of each of the methods are displayed in Tables 4–7. Each method generates a lower bound for the true value of the LR. The normal approximation and bootstrap are confidence bounds and as such should be interpreted in a frequentist manner. That is, on average, 99% of the intervals (from the lower bound to $+\infty$) are expected to contain the true population profile frequency. The interpretation for the Bayesian HPD is that "The true value of the LR is greater than the lower bound with probability 0.99," or "We are 99% sure that the true LR is greater than the lower bound." The factor of 10 has neither a frequentist, nor Bayesian interpretation. Similarly, Balding's estimator is really a modified estimator of location rather than an estimate taking into account sampling variability and as such does not have a probabilistic interpretation.

The ideal method should (National Research Council, 1992)

1. Give a lower bound that is lower than the true LR, a high proportion of the time.
2. Give lower bounds that are lower than the true LR, but not "too much lower."
3. Produce a distribution of lower bounds that is tightly concentrated around a central value, and become more tightly concentrated as the size of the database increases.

The proportion of times that the lower bound is lower than the true LR is called the estimated coverage. Our first requirement for an ideal method is high coverage. However, it is simple to maximize coverage, by making the lower bound absurdly small. To take this idea to the extreme, if we made the lower bound zero, then all methods would have 100% coverage, because 100% of all LRs lie between zero and infinity. However, this is of limited utility to the court because it says that the true LR offers something between no support (LR = 0) to complete support (LR = ∞) for the proposition that the suspect was the true donor of the evidence. Therefore, our second property of an ideal method is that the lower bound is not "too far"

Table 4:   Results using the African Amerian database (CODIS loci) and a common profile.

Method	N	Coverage	2.5%	97.5%	Ratio
Factor of 10	100	0.957	16.8	18.7	6.7
Log-Normal		0.974	16.9	18.6	7.4
Balding		0.902	17.2	18.8	3.7
Bootstrap		0.913	17.1	18.8	4.4
HPD		0.910	17.1	18.8	4.3
	400	1.000	17.2	18.0	9.2
		0.985	17.7	18.5	3.0
		0.764	18.0	18.8	1.4
		0.974	17.7	18.6	2.6
		0.972	17.7	18.5	2.6
	1,000	1.000	17.3	17.8	9.7
		0.984	18.0	18.5	2.0
		0.651	18.2	18.8	1.1
		0.977	18.0	18.5	1.9
		0.972	18.0	18.6	1.9
	5,000	1.000	17.4	17.7	9.9
		0.992	18.3	18.5	1.4
		0.583	18.4	18.6	1.0
		0.990	18.3	18.5	1.4
		0.991	18.3	18.5	1.4
	10,000	1.000	17.5	17.6	9.9
		0.992	18.4	18.5	1.3
		0.540	18.5	18.6	1.0
		0.991	18.4	18.5	1.2
		0.988	18.4	18.5	1.2

away from the true value. We can measure this by looking at the median ratio of the lower bound to the true value. Finally, we would like the method to be moderately consistent given different sets of data with approximately the same sample frequencies. We can meas-

Table 5:   Results using the African Amerian database (CODIS loci) and a rare profile.

Method	N	%Zero	Coverage	2.5%	97.5%	Ratio
Factor of 10	100	77	0.965	26.3	29.5	28.5
Log-Normal		77	1.000	25.1	27.5	1410.0
Balding		0	1.000	25.0	27.1	2640.0
Bootstrap		77	0.996	25.9	29.0	88.5
HPD		0	0.529	26.5	35.1	1.3
	400	13	0.878	27.4	29.9	6.2
		13	0.999	27.1	28.7	35.4
		0	0.999	27.3	29.0	18.8
		13	0.960	27.4	29.5	9.3
		0	0.850	27.4	30.6	8.4
	1,000	1	0.941	27.8	29.8	7.7
		1	0.998	27.9	29.1	8.6
		0	0.952	28.3	29.6	3.8
		1	0.939	28.1	29.7	4.9
		0	0.953	28.0	29.7	5.4
	5,000	0	1.000	28.1	28.9	9.7
		0	0.990	28.7	29.3	2.8
		0	0.762	28.9	29.7	1.4
		0	0.976	28.7	29.4	2.5
		0	0.979	28.7	29.4	2.5
	10,000	0	1.000	28.2	28.7	9.9
		0	0.992	28.9	29.4	2.1
		0	0.723	29.1	29.6	1.2
		0	0.979	28.9	29.4	1.9
		0	0.985	28.9	29.4	2.0

Table 6:   Results using the New Zealand Caucasian database (SGM+ loci) and a common profile.

Method	N	Coverage	2.5%	97.5%	Ratio
Factor of 10	100	1.000	9.3	10.2	8.5
Log-Normal		0.979	9.7	10.6	3.1
Balding		0.701	10.1	11.0	1.3
Bootstrap		0.946	9.8	10.7	2.4
HPD		0.936	9.9	10.8	2.3
	400	1.000	9.4	9.9	9.7
		0.986	10.2	10.6	1.8
		0.616	10.4	10.8	1.1
		0.973	10.2	10.6	1.7
		0.970	10.2	10.6	1.7
	1,000	1.000	9.5	9.8	9.9
		0.988	10.3	10.6	1.5
		0.581	10.5	10.8	1.0
		0.981	10.3	10.6	1.4
		0.979	10.3	10.6	1.4
	5,000	1.000	9.6	9.7	9.9
		0.987	10.5	10.6	1.2
		0.519	10.6	10.7	1.0
		0.984	10.5	10.6	1.2
		0.984	10.5	10.6	1.2
	10,000	1.000	9.6	9.7	10.0
		0.991	10.5	10.6	1.1
		0.534	10.6	10.7	1.0
		0.989	10.5	10.6	1.1
		0.991	10.5	10.6	1.1

Table 7: Results using the New Zealand Caucasian database (SGM+ loci) and a rare profile.

Method	N	%Zero	Coverage	2.5%	97.5%	Ratio
Factor of 10	100	98	1.000	18.2	19.6	105.0
Log-Normal		98	1.000	17.2	18.2	2050.0
Balding		0	1.000	17.1	18.6	1490.0
Bootstrap		98	1.000	18.0	19.2	245.0
HPD		0	0.416	18.8	25.7	0.5
	400	61	0.995	18.9	20.8	13.0
		61	1.000	18.7	20.0	45.6
		0	0.999	19.0	20.4	18.2
		61	0.995	19.0	20.7	13.5
		0	0.693	19.2	22.8	2.5
	1,000	18	0.973	19.3	21.0	8.3
		18	1.000	19.4	20.6	10.7
		0	0.958	19.8	21.0	4.1
		18	0.965	19.6	21.0	5.0
		0	0.830	19.6	21.8	4.3
	5,000	0	0.999	19.6	20.5	9.1
		0	0.991	20.2	20.9	2.7
		0	0.772	20.5	21.2	1.4
		0	0.957	20.3	21.0	2.3
		0	0.965	20.3	21.0	2.4
	10,000	0	1.000	19.7	20.3	9.5
		0	0.990	20.4	20.9	2.1
		0	0.694	20.6	21.2	1.2
		0	0.974	20.4	21.0	1.9
		0	0.977	20.4	21.0	1.9

ure this by looking at the distribution of lower bounds, and in particular an interval for the central 95%.

Tables 4–7 show our measures of performance. The coverage is in the column headed 'Coverage.' The median ratio of the true value to the lower bound is in the column 'Ratio,' and the endpoints of a 95% interval for the likely values of the lower bound are given in the columns labeled '2.5%' and '97.5%' respectively. For example, if we take from Table 4 where $N = 1,000$, we can see that the factor of 10 method has 100% coverage, that the median lower bound is 11.4 times smaller than the true value, and that the 95% of the bounds produced by the method lie between $10^{17.3}$ and $10^{17.8}$. The reader may wonder why the factor of 10 ratio is not 10. The ratio is between the true LR and lower bound, rather than the estimated LR and the lower bound which is exactly 10.

4.1 *Zeros*

There is an additional column labelled '% Zero' in the Tables 5 and 7 which gives the results for the two rare profiles. Zeros arise when one or more of the alleles in the crime scene sample has not been observed in the database, and hence has a frequency of zero. As a consequence, the factor of 10 method, the log-normal method and the bootstrap method will all yield a lower bound of zero, as the product rule estimate of the LR is zero. Balding's estimator and the HPD do not suffer from this because they make the assumption of a prior probability for each allele. It is possible to overcome the zero problem by specifying a minimum allele frequency (Budowle *et al.*, 1996), or adding a small constant to all frequencies including the zero and renormalizing. However, both approaches, and any other, are arbitrary and could not be reasonably defended to the court.

One approach that may have some justification, however, is the addition of the crime scene profile to the database. One might justify this by noting that if the alternative hypothesis is true, then we have observed the alleles in question in at least one other individual, namely the true offender.

The results from taking this approach are shown in Tables 8–11. It is apparent that the issue of zeros has been addressed, as we would

Table 8: Results using the African American database (CODIS loci) including the crime scene profile, and a common profile.

Method	N	Coverage	2.5%	97.5%	Ratio
Factor of 10	100	0.999	16.4	18.1	17.6
Log-Normal		1.000	16.5	18.1	18.0
Balding		0.993	16.8	18.4	8.5
Bootstrap		0.994	16.7	18.3	10.8
HPD		0.993	16.7	18.3	10.9
	400	1.000	17.0	17.9	12.0
		0.997	17.6	18.4	3.9
		0.866	17.9	18.7	1.8
		0.994	17.6	18.5	3.4
		0.992	17.6	18.4	3.3
	1,000	1.000	17.2	17.8	10.6
		0.996	17.9	18.5	2.2
		0.771	18.1	18.7	1.3
		0.991	17.9	18.5	2.1
		0.991	17.9	18.5	2.1
	5,000	1.000	17.4	17.7	10.2
		0.999	18.3	18.5	1.4
		0.654	18.4	18.6	1.1
		0.998	18.3	18.5	1.4
		0.998	18.3	18.5	1.4
	10,000	1.000	17.5	17.6	10.0
		0.994	18.4	18.5	1.3
		0.581	18.4	18.6	1.0
		0.995	18.4	18.5	1.3
		0.993	18.4	18.5	1.3

Table 9: Results using the African American database (CODIS loci) including the crime scene profile, and a rare profile.

Method	N	Coverage	2.5%	97.5%	Ratio
Factor of 10	100	1.000	25.0	27.6	1310.0
Log-Normal		1.000	24.1	26.3	17100.0
Balding		1.000	23.9	25.8	42400.0
Bootstrap		1.000	25.0	27.7	1370.0
HPD		1.000	24.7	27.2	3210.0
	400	0.999	26.9	28.7	48.8
		1.000	26.7	28.1	118.0
		1.000	26.9	28.3	70.6
		0.999	27.0	28.9	35.9
		1.000	26.9	28.6	55.0
	1,000	0.999	27.4	29.0	20.9
		1.000	27.6	28.8	17.9
		1.000	27.9	29.1	8.1
		0.994	27.8	29.2	10.3
		1.000	27.7	29.0	12.5
	5,000	1.000	28.0	28.8	12.0
		0.998	28.6	29.3	3.4
		0.895	28.9	29.6	1.7
		0.992	28.6	29.3	2.9
		0.996	28.6	29.3	3.1
	10,000	1.000	28.1	28.7	10.7
		0.996	28.8	29.3	2.3
		0.789	29.1	29.6	1.3
		0.991	28.8	29.4	2.1
		0.993	28.8	29.4	2.1

Table 10:   Results using the New Zealand Caucasian database (SGM+ loci) including the crime scene profile, and a common profile.

Method	N	Coverage	2.5%	97.5%	Ratio
Factor of 10	100	1.000	9.1	10.0	11.0
Log-Normal		0.996	9.6	10.5	3.9
Balding		0.850	10.0	10.8	1.7
Bootstrap		0.986	9.7	10.6	3.1
HPD		0.983	9.7	10.6	3.0
	400	1.000	9.4	9.9	10.2
		0.992	10.1	10.6	1.9
		0.694	10.3	10.8	1.1
		0.984	10.2	10.6	1.8
		0.981	10.2	10.6	1.8
	1,000	1.000	9.5	9.8	10.2
		0.990	10.3	10.6	1.5
		0.642	10.5	10.8	1.1
		0.988	10.3	10.6	1.5
		0.987	10.3	10.6	1.5
	5,000	1.000	9.6	9.7	10.0
		0.996	10.5	10.6	1.2
		0.545	10.6	10.7	1.0
		0.992	10.5	10.6	1.2
		0.992	10.5	10.6	1.2
	10,000	1.000	9.6	9.7	10.0
		0.989	10.5	10.6	1.1
		0.527	10.6	10.7	1.0
		0.986	10.5	10.6	1.1
		0.987	10.5	10.6	1.1

Table 11: Results using the New Zealand Caucasian database (SGM+ loci) including the crime scene profile, and a rare profile.

Method	N	Coverage	2.5%	97.5%	Ratio
Factor of 10	100	1.000	17.0	19.1	984.0
Log-Normal		1.000	16.3	17.8	8980.0
Balding		1.000	16.3	17.6	10300.0
Bootstrap		1.000	17.2	19.3	671.0
HPD		1.000	16.9	18.7	1700.0
	400	1.000	18.4	20.2	44.8
		1.000	18.3	19.6	106.0
		1.000	18.6	19.8	57.9
		0.998	18.7	20.6	24.8
		1.000	18.6	20.1	42.5
	1,000	1.000	19.0	20.5	18.0
		1.000	19.2	20.3	17.3
		1.000	19.6	20.6	7.8
		0.985	19.4	20.9	7.9
		1.000	19.4	20.6	10.4
	5,000	1.000	19.6	20.3	11.4
		1.000	20.2	20.8	3.3
		0.891	20.4	21.1	1.7
		0.992	20.2	20.9	2.7
		0.994	20.2	20.9	2.9
	10,000	1.000	19.7	20.2	10.5
		0.996	20.4	20.9	2.2
		0.785	20.6	21.1	1.3
		0.991	20.4	20.9	2.0
		0.993	20.4	20.9	2.1

expect, but the cost can be quite high, especially when the database is small. If we take, for example, the results in Table 9, we can see that the median ratio between the true value and the lower bound ranged from approximately 1,300–42,000 depending on the method. That is, the reported lower bound on the LR could be anywhere between 1,300 and 42,000 times smaller (three to four orders of magnitude) than the true value. One may argue that this degree of conservativeness might be warranted in the case of involving very rare alleles. However, we believe that it is an argument really against using very small databases to evaluate the LR. On the plus side, we can see that the effect of the additional profile is significantly diminished once the database reaches a moderate size (~5,000), and that it has relatively little impact when the profile in question is common.

5 Discussion

If DNA evidence is to be accompanied by estimated LR, then a prudent statistical procedure is to provide a measure of sampling uncertainty for these estimates. This is especially necessary when estimates are based on samples of just a few hundred profiles. The criticism that this provision of both an estimate and its bound(s) may confuse a jury can be met if the forensic scientist presents only the bound(s) and states that sampling effects have been considered.

The most complete discussion of sampling uncertainty is based on the sampling distribution of an estimate. This leads naturally to frequentist confidence and support intervals or Bayesian highest posterior density intervals, even if these are described only in terms of their boundaries. An unfortunate consequence of Balding's discussion of 'conservative Bayesian estimates' is that some forensic agencies have taken to presenting only point estimates based on sample allele proportions calculated by adding crime and suspect profiles to a database. These modified point estimates do not address sampling uncertainty, as is made clear in Tables 4–7, and nor were they designed to. It would be misleading to regard them as acting like confidence limits.

The relatively poor performance of normal-based limits or bootstrap limits for small sample sizes is a consequence of specific alleles not appearing in these samples. The problem disappears when θ is assigned a non-zero value. Bootstrapping will always have the disadvantage of requiring access to all the profiles in a database, as opposed to a published table of sample allele proportions and counts. Both bootstrapping and posterior distribution methods have substantial computing requirements, and this suggests use of normal-based analytical methods, especially for large sample sizes. For single-contributor stains, such as those considered here, it does appear that these normal methods are preferable. For multiple-contributor stains, however, or other complex situations involving relatives or missing persons, the match probability expressions become quite complex and it may not be simple to derive the necessary variance expressions. A general approach, with non-zero θ, would be better provided by bootstrapping or the posterior density.

Acknowledgments

The author wishes to thank Professor Bruce Weir and Dr John Buckleton who collaborated on previous research in this area. The author also would like to Professor David Balding who provided information and criticism to this work.

This work was supported in part by grant 2014-DN-BX-K028 from the US National Institute of Justice. Points of view in this document are those of the author and do not necessarily represent the official position or policies of the US Department of Justice.

References

D. J. Balding. Estimating products in forensic identification using DNA profiles. *Journal of the American Statistical Association*, 90:839–844, 1995.

G. W. Beecham and B. S. Weir. Confidence interval of the likelihood ratio associated with mixed stain DNA evidence. *Journal of Forensic Sciences*, 56:S166–S171, 2011.

B. Budowle, K. L. Monson and R. Chakraborty. Estimating minimum allele frequencies for DNA profile frequency estimates for PCR-based loci. *International Journal of Legal Medicine*, 108:173–176, 1996.

B. Budowle, T. R. Moretti, A. L. Baumstark, D. A. Defenbaugh and M. Keys. Population data on the thirteen CODIS core short tandem repeat loci in African Americans, U.S. Caucasians, Hispanics, Bahamians, Jamaicans, and Trinidadians. *Journal of Forensic Sciences*, 44:1277–1286, 1999.

R. Chakraborty, M. R. Srinivasan and S. F. Daiger. Evaluation of standard error and confidence intervals of estimated multilocus genotype probabilities and their implications in DNA. *American Journal of Human Genetic*, 52:60–70, 1993.

J. M. Curran, J. S. Buckleton C. M. Triggs and B. S. Weir. Assessing uncertainty in DNA evidence caused by sampling effects. *Science & Justice*, 42:29–37, 2002.

B. Efron. Bootstrap methods: Another look at the jackknife. *The Annals of Statistics*, 7:1–26, 1979.

I. W. Evett and B. S. Weir. *Interpreting DNA Evidence: Statistical Genetics for Forensic Scientists*. Sinauer Associates, 1998.

National Research Council (US). Committee on DNA Technology in Forensic Science. *DNA Technology in Forensic Science*. National Academy Press, 1992.

National Research Council (US). Committee on DNA Forensic Science: An Update. *The Evaluation of Forensic DNA Evidence*. National Academy Press, 1996.

C. M. Triggs and J. M. Curran. The sensitivity of the Bayesian HPD method to the choice of prior. *Science & Justice*, 46:169–178, 2006.

B. S. Weir. *Genetic Data Analysis II*. Sinauer, 1996.

CHAPTER 7

Thoughts on Estimating Ancestry

Kenneth K. Kidd

Department of Genetics, Yale University School of Medicine,
New Haven, CT 06520, USA

Use of genetic markers to determine population relationships has a long history extending back to the use of the ABO blood group system in the early 20th century. In the middle of the last century, the field of genetic anthropology got a great boost with the documentation by Harris (1969) of extensive protein polymorphism in humans. The blood group and protein polymorphism data accumulated globally were integrated and published in the book "The History and Geography of Human Genes" by Cavalli-Sforza *et al.* (1994). By then, the interest in "blood groups" for anthropology was already declining because of the demonstration of polymorphism directly in the autosomal DNA by Kan and Dozy (1978a, 1978b) and then in mitochondrial DNA (mtDNA) by Cann *et al.* (1987). The number of documented DNA polymorphisms in the nuclear DNA increased exponentially in the first decade after 1978 (Figure 1) and has now reached millions (Abecasis *et al.*, 2010; Auton *et al.*, 2015). The amount of anthropological population data for mtDNA variation also increased greatly during the 1990's and continues today. It already was abundantly clear by the late 1980's that the number of

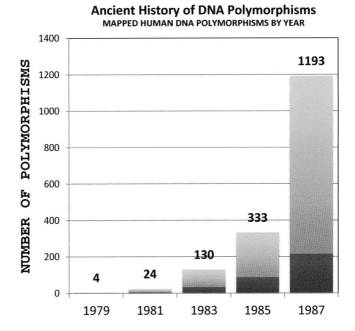

Figure 1: Histogram of the number of DNA polymorphisms cataloged and assigned D numbers by the Human Gene Mapping Workshops (Pearson *et al.*, 1987; Kidd *et al.*, 1988) during the initial period of discovery.

Note: Red shading indicates polymorphisms identified in known genes; green shading indicates polymorphisms in anonymous segments of DNA.

autosomal DNA polymorphisms (then known as restriction fragment length polymorphisms — RFLPs) exceeded all previous types of human genetic markers for anthropological research. In 1994, Cavalli-Sforza started organizing what would become the Human Genome Diversity Project.

Soon after entering the 21st century, researchers began studying autosomal single nucleotide polymorphisms (SNPs) to infer ancestry for forensic use. Variation in mtDNA and in the non-recombining part of the Y chromosome (NRY) also is informative on ancestry of an individual but each is only a single locus evolutionarily and subject to considerable chance variation. Moreover, each traces only one ancestral lineage back in time: the maternal lineage for mtDNA and the paternal lineage of men for NRY. Many genetically independent autosomal SNPs, in contrast, collectively can provide estimates of ancestry through all ancestral lineages.

A significant difference exists between the anthropology-evolution objectives of gene frequency studies to infer human history and the forensic use of genetic markers to infer ancestry of an individual. Inference of the evolutionary history of human populations since the major expansion of modern humans out of Africa needs large amounts of unbiased data to diminish the effect of random noise, i.e. random genetic drift, recent recombination, recent mutation, etc. Chip arrays with over a million SNPs and now whole genome sequencing are providing these very large amounts of data on some human populations. Such data also can provide information on an individual's ancestry when data on appropriate reference populations exist. However, efficient forensic inference of recent ancestry of an individual does not need such massive amounts of reference data. A small number of highly biased genetic markers that efficiently maximizes the differences among populations can be very effective if the appropriate reference data exist. Unfortunately, the standard short tandem repeat polymorphisms (STRPs) already being studied for standard forensic identity purposes do not provide either enough difference in allele frequencies around the world or enough independent markers to provide highly significant differences in inferred ancestry beyond certain continental extremes. SNPs, in contrast, do allow highly significant sets of markers that can provide significant assignment of ancestry to diverse biogeographic regions. This chapter focuses on the use of SNPs for ancestry inference.

1 What is Needed to use SNPs for Ancestry Inference in Forensics

Inference of ancestry requires both a panel of SNPs with allele frequencies that vary among populations and a set of reference populations with allele frequencies for those SNPs. A panel of SNPs is *a priori* good only for the set of populations used to select the SNPs and for those populations on which the SNP panel already has been tested. Also, the inference of ancestry can only be as good as the global coverage of the reference populations and the reference populations need to provide reasonable estimates of the allele frequencies of all the SNPs in the specific panel of SNPs. This requirement implies reference population sample sizes of at least a few dozen individuals. Of course, larger sample sizes are better, up to about 100–200 individuals. Beyond that, the increased accuracy of any specific allele frequency contributes minimally to the overall accuracy.

Many different statistics can and have been used to identify the SNPs to include in a panel, F_{ST} of Wright and Informativeness of Rosenberg (Rosenberg *et al.*, 2003) have both been used to identify SNPs that have large allele frequency differences among a set of populations. Large differences are not sufficient since different SNPs likely have different patterns of allele frequency variation among populations. Different sets of SNPs may have different abilities to distinguish certain populations or sets of populations. How well a set of SNPs works to constitute a panel has been evaluated using programs such as STRUCTURE and statistics such a principle components analysis (PCA) (*cf.*, Lawson and Falush, 2012). These methods can demonstrate that a panel of SNPs has information to distinguish among groups of individuals from a specific set of populations.

2 What Exists in the Forensic Literature?

Given the many published panels of SNPs for forensic inference of ancestry, the immediate focus is not the development of a new panel but the ability to determine the likely ancestry of an individual when typed for the SNPs in an existing panel. The various panels involve quite diverse sets of SNPs and reference populations. The relative merits of the various panels cannot be readily evaluated because the individual panels have often been developed based on different sets of reference populations. Before considering how well reference populations represent global diversity, let us consider first the diversity of SNPs among the published panels.

As part of our anthropology and forensic database work on ALFRED <alfred.med.yale.edu> and FROG-kb <frog.med.yale.edu>

we noticed that very few SNPs appeared in multiple publications and decided on a more systematic study. We identified 21 largely independent published panels of ancestry informative SNPs (AISNPs) and examined their union of 1,397 distinct SNPs (Soundararajan *et al.*, 2016). The 1,397 SNPs in 21 panels yield a largely empty matrix of SNPs and population allele frequencies. No SNP occurred in more than six panels; the two SNPs that occurred in six panels were the skin pigmentation SNPs, rs1426654 at SLC24A5 and rs16891982 at SLC45A2. These SNPs probably represent a general European bias. Four additional SNPs occurred in five panels; eight in four panels; 32 in three; 131 in two; and 1,220 in no more than one panel. Even among the SNPs in multiple panels, the different SNPs usually occurred in different combinations of panels. The reference population data for most of the panels involved relatively few populations in common. The "empty matrix" problem makes a comprehensive global reference database impossible for a single set of ancestry informative SNPs (AISNPs) and also makes statistical comparisons impossible among populations that have been studied for different sets of SNPs. Only 46 (3%) of the 1,397 SNPs occur in three or more panels (Figure 2). The analyses of 44 of these 46 AISNPs were able to

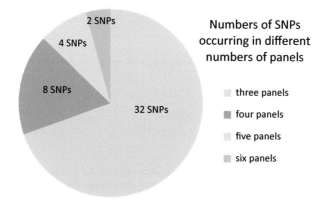

Figure 2:   The distribution of the number of ancestry informative SNPs that have been included in three or more of the 21 panels reviewed (Soundararajan *et al.*, 2016). We note that even for the SNPs that occur in the same number of panels, the specific combination of panels usually differs.

provide only five clusters of individuals when tested on 4,559 individuals from 73 populations: sub-Saharan Africa, Europe and SW Asia, South Asia, East Asia and the Americas. Thus, these 21 different panels of SNPs for ancestry inference make a strong collective statement that the forensic community does not need a completely new panel of SNPs for discrimination at the "continental" level. Ability to discriminate among five biogeographic regions is easy and of only limited value for forensics in most parts of the world given recent movements of individuals around the world. Numbers of individuals from diverse ancestries may be a small fraction of a population, but they should not be ignored in forensic investigations.

The data that have been used to search for good ancestry SNPs have not been especially good. Several problems have existed, but the primary one was the lack of a large number of SNPs typed on a global sample of populations. The most common set of publicly available reference populations is the HGDP set of small samples of 52 populations totaling a thousand individuals. Two studies have typed large numbers of SNPs on these samples (Jakobsson *et al.*, 2008; Li *et al.*, 2008). Because many of the populations have very small sample sizes, the variances of the allele frequencies are large, which is not a problem for evolutionary studies using a very large number of SNPs. However, when used as the reference populations for forensic ancestry inference the high variance does contribute to uncertainty. While the 1,000 Genomes data now provide much more robust allele frequency estimates, the sampling of populations is not globally representative. We note that of the 21 published panels of ancestry SNPs reviewed, two of the better loci (rs3811801 and rs671) with East-Asia-specific alleles have been included only in one panel and two other loci (rs1800414 and rs1229984) with East Asia specific alleles have been included in only two of the 21 panels. None of these has yet been typed in the HGDP panel.

Forensic ancestry inference is now a rapidly changing field in the sense that better SNPs are being identified because of better sets of population data to screen. Also, researchers are now collaborating to see that many more populations are being tested for those new SNPs and the best of those previously identified. Consequently, it is impossible as yet to recommend any panel of ancestry informative SNPs

(AISNPs) as the final best panel. At the moment, there are two published panels of AISNPs that have considerable reference data available: the Seldin Lab 128 (Kosoy *et al.*, 2009; Nassir *et al.*, 2009; Kidd *et al.*, 2011) and the Kidd Lab 55 (Kidd *et al.*, 2014). Currently 4,871 individuals from 119 populations provide reference data for the Seldin Lab 128 AISNPs (Kidd *et al.*, 2011) and 6,947 individuals from 125 populations provide reference data for the Kidd Lab 55 AISNPs (Rajeevan *et al.*, 2012; Pakstis *et al.*, 2015). There is some overlap between the two panels, and data on many populations exist for 169 of the union of 170 SNPs.

3 Methods for Estimating Ancestry of an Individual

All of the existing methods for ancestry inference make assumptions, and all are dependent on the specific reference populations available. This chapter does not deal with partial ancestry assignments or how to use a system like FROG-kb to infer components of admixed ancestry. Attempting allocation of ancestry to two or more different ancestral populations raises many questions of statistical accuracy as well as accuracy as a function of what populations are being considered contributors to the mixed ancestry. There are also conceptual issues. The American Society of Human Genetics Ancestry and Ancestry Testing Task Force, in its white paper (Royal *et al.*, 2010), sets forth caveats to be kept in mind in ancestry inference. Rather than repeat those caveats noting the STRUCTURE program and PCA analyses, several of the same issues arise using likelihood. Other than brief mention of those two approaches, the use of likelihood and likelihood ratios (LRs) will be explained in more detail with examples. The method is easy to apply because the computational underpinnings are available online in FROG-kb (http://frog.med.yale.edu/FrogKB/).

3.1 *STRUCTURE Analyses*

STRUCTURE requires the genotypes for all individuals, both the reference populations and the target individual. The problem with STRUCTURE is the absence of good reference genotypes for a good representation of populations. There are two datasets readily available: the HGDP panel of SNPs (Li *et al.*, 2008) <cephb.fr/hgdp> and the 1,000 genomes <1000genomes.org>. Neither is a good representation of many regions of the world. Many datasets on individuals in specific populations exist, but not all large sets of SNPs agree, and the data have not been integrated.

3.2 Likelihood Analyses

Programs such as the calculations in FROG-kb use the allele frequencies for the reference populations and calculate the probability that the target individual's multi-locus genotype could occur in each of the populations. The reference populations have to have data for all of the SNPs in a panel, but the target individual need not have data for all of them. The following elaborates on how to interpret the results of likelihood analyses, but many of the principles apply to all approaches to ancestry inference from SNP data.

4 Interpreting Results from Ancestry Inference Analyses

Several issues are important in interpreting results for an individual. First, if the actual population of origin is not included in the reference dataset, one cannot interpret the results as indicating the true origin. A *priori*, one does not know the population of origin of the target individual, and therefore, one does know whether or not the population of origin is among the reference data. Second, if very closely related populations are included in the reference dataset, the true population of origin may not be significantly different from the most likely. Third, the results for an individual whose recent ancestors are from genetically very different populations may not yield accurate ancestry inference depending on the SNPs used and the reference populations available.

The logic of using likelihood is that the population with the highest probability of the specified genotype (the target individual) is the population most likely to be the origin of the individual with that genotype. The advantage of using this statistical framework is that it becomes clear that the "most likely" may not be meaningfully different from other highly likely populations. If the LR among the more likely populations is within a factor of 10 of the most likely, there is no significant basis for distinguishing among those potential ancestral populations. Even a ratio of up to 100 includes populations that cannot be meaningfully excluded from possibly being ancestral for the specific genotype. A useful terminology is to consider all populations with a LR within an order of magnitude to be "likely" to be the population of origin. Those populations with a ratio greater than 10 and up to 100 (two orders of magnitude) should be considered to be "possible". Then those with a ratio greater than two orders of magnitude to be "unlikely". At some point, based on an investigator's level of confidence, the LR is so large as to exclude those populations.

Remembering that the AISNPs are polymorphic and while one allele may be fixed in some populations, one recognizes that different individuals from the same population will have different genotypes. Consequently, the most likely population of origin may be different for different individuals from the same population, even for close relatives. This observation can be especially true if ancestry is from one of several closely related populations. This phenomenon further emphasizes the need to consider the several higher likelihoods and LRs carefully and qualify any conclusion appropriately based on the set of reference populations used.

Let us consider an example: Figure 3 shows the FROG-kb results for two unrelated individuals from the state of Kerala in Southwest India. The input data for each individual were the genotypes for all of the SNPs in the 55 AISNP panel. The different results illustrate multiple points about ancestry inference. First, the true population of origin is not always the most likely. Second, the rank orders of all populations will differ between two individuals from the same population. Third, which populations are among those that must be considered "not significantly different" from the most likely will be different populations for different test individuals. These are all expected since most of the loci will be segregating within every population and multiple different genotypes are possible within

Population (Region, Sample Size 2N)	Probability of Genotype in each Population	Likelihood Ratio
Keralite (Asia,60)	9.1E-12	
Sri Lankan Tamil(STU) (Asia,204)	9.3E-13	9.8
Gujarati(GIH) (Asia,206)	9.0E-13	10
Sonowal Kachari (Asia,36)	5.9E-13	15
Bengali(BEB) (Asia,172)	4.2E-13	22
Indian(ITU) (Asia,204)	2.4E-13	38
Punjabi(PJL) (Asia,192)	1.6E-13	58
Mohannas (Asia,112)	9.5E-14	97
Pathan (Asia,184)	4.3E-14	2.1E+2
Hazaras (Asia,60)	1.8E-15	5.2E+3
Thoti (Asia,28)	1.7E-15	5.5E+3
Negroid Makrani (Asia,56)	1.0E-15	9.0E+3
Iranians (Asia,88)	1.0E-15	9.2E+3
Kuwaiti (Asia,32)	6.8E-16	1.3E+4
Palestinian Arabs (Asia,140)	1.6E-16	5.6E+4
Tajiks (Asia,40)	7.5E-17	1.2E+5
Smar_Tunisia (Africa,130)	2.8E-17	3.2E+5
Adygei (Europe,108)	6.4E-18	1.4E+6
Druze (Asia,212)	6.4E-18	1.4E+6
Lybia (Africa,142)	6.1E-18	1.5E+6
Kairoun_Tunisia (Africa,94)	4.7E-18	1.9E+6
Mehdia_Tunisia (Africa,92)	4.5E-18	2.0E+6
Kerkennah_Tunisia (Africa,96)	4.0E-18	2.3E+6
Nebeur_Tunisia (Africa,64)	3.0E-18	3.0E+6
Turkish_Cypriot (Asia,120)	1.9E-18	4.9E+6
Kesra_Tunisia (Africa,90)	1.6E-18	5.7E+6
Turkish (Asia,154)	1.2E-18	7.9E+6
Sardinian (Europe,68)	4.5E-19	2.0E+7
Yemenite Jews (Asia,146)	4.5E-19	2.0E+7

(a)

Figure 3: An example of the likelihoods of populations being the origin of two different individuals from the state of Kerala, Southwest India. (A) The correct population of origin is the most likely and a nearby population is the next most likely. Statistically it is not possible to make a definitive call between them; other populations from India and Pakistan are less likely, but cannot be excluded. (B) The correct population of origin is not the most likely and five others are likely populations of origin; two more are possible populations of origin that cannot be excluded.

Population (Region, Sample Size 2N)	Probability of Genotype in each Population	Likelihood Ratio
Mohannas (Asia,112)	2.5E-13	
Keralite (Asia,60)	2.2E-13	1.1
Pathan (Asia,184)	1.8E-13	1.4
Sri Lankan Tamil(STU) (Asia,204)	3.9E-14	6.4
Gujarati(GIH) (Asia,206)	3.0E-14	8.3
Indian(ITU) (Asia,204)	2.9E-14	8.5
Thoti (Asia,28)	2.5E-14	10
Bengali(BEB) (Asia,172)	2.4E-14	10
Punjabi(PJL) (Asia,192)	7.4E-15	34
Sonowal Kachari (Asia,36)	7.0E-16	3.6E+2
Iranians (Asia,88)	3.5E-16	7.3E+2
Negroid Makrani (Asia,56)	1.7E-16	1.5E+3
Kuwaiti (Asia,32)	1.6E-16	1.6E+3
Hazaras (Asia,60)	3.0E-17	8.5E+3
Palestinian Arabs (Asia,140)	1.4E-17	1.8E+4
Yemenite Jews (Asia,146)	1.4E-17	1.8E+4
Adygei (Europe,108)	6.7E-18	3.8E+4
Tajiks (Asia,40)	3.6E-18	7.0E+4
Turkish (Asia,154)	1.8E-18	1.4E+5
Sardinian (Europe,68)	1.8E-18	1.4E+5
Mehdia_Tunisia (Africa,92)	1.2E-18	2.0E+5
Smar_Tunisia (Africa,130)	1.1E-18	2.3E+5
Druze (Asia,212)	7.3E-19	3.4E+5
Kesra_Tunisia (Africa,90)	4.7E-19	5.3E+5
Turkish_Cypriot (Asia,120)	2.5E-19	1.0E+6
Uyghur (EastAsia,60)	1.2E-19	2.2E+6
Lybia (Africa,142)	1.0E-19	2.4E+6
Nebeur_Tunisia (Africa,64)	9.7E-20	2.6E+6
Roman Jews (Europe,54)	9.3E-20	2.7E+6
Kairoun_Tunisia (Africa,94)	8.5E-20	2.9E+6

(b)

Figure 3: (*Continued*)

each population. An individual who happens to be homozygous for the less frequent alleles at two loci will be less likely to originate from that population, all else being equal, than an individual homozygous for the more frequent alleles at those two loci. The impact on the likelihoods of other populations will depend on the allele frequencies at those loci in those other populations.

The two examples in Figure 3 were selected to illustrate these points, including the very large differences in ranking and LRs that can be seen. While the correct population of origin is among those in the top group in both cases, in one case, it is the second best among six populations with a likelihood within an order of magnitude of the best: these six must be considered the likely population of origin. In the other case, the correct population is the best and only one other population has a likelihood (barely) within an order of magnitude. In both cases, there are populations that must be considered "possible" as the origin of the individual.

5 Conclusion

Which ancestry panel is best? What method of estimating ancestry is best? Because the SNPs by Populations matrix is so empty, it is impossible to compare many of the different panels. Even the matrix of the 46 commonly found SNPs does not have populations typed for all 46, though there are many individuals typed for 44 of them. Still, those individuals can have their ancestry likelihoods tested against a different panel of SNPs if they are typed for the different SNPs in that panel. Until the forensic community can assemble a large set of data on multiple populations for the same set of SNPs, it will be unclear what set of SNPs is "best" for what method to distinguish among possible ancestries.

References

G. R. Abecasis, D. Altshuler, A. Auton, L. D. Brooks, R. M. Durbin, R. A. Gibbs, M. E. Hurles and G. A. McVean. A map of human genome variation from population-scale sequencing. *Nature*, 467(7319):1061–1073, 2010.

A. Auton, L. D. Brooks, R. M. Durbin, E. P. Garrison, H. M. Kang, J. O. Korbel, J. L. Marchini, S. McCarthy, G. A. McVean and G. R. Abecasis. A global reference for human genetic variation. *Nature*, 526(7571): 68–74, 2015.

R. L. Cann, M. Stoneking and A. C. Wilson. Mitochondrial DNA and human evolution. *Nature*, 325(6099):31–36, 1987.

H. Harris. Enzyme and protein polymorphism in human populations. *British Medical Bulletin*, 25(1):5–13, 1969.

M. Jakobsson, S. W. Scholz, P. Scheet, J. R. Gibbs, J. M. VanLiere, H. C. Fung, Z. A. Szpiech, J. H. Degnan, K. Wang, R. Guerreiro, J. M. Bras, J. C. Schymick, D. G. Hernandez, B. J. Traynor, J. Simon-Sanchez, M. Matarin, A. Britton, J. van de Leemput, I. Rafferty, M. Bucan, H. M. Cann, J. A. Hardy, N. A. Rosenberg and A. B. Singleton. Genotype, haplotype and copy-number variation in worldwide human populations. *Nature*, 451(7181):998–1003, 2008.

Y. W. Kan and A. M. Dozy. Antenatal diagnosis of sickle-cell anaemia by D.N.A. analysis of amniotic-fluid cells. *Lancet*, 2(8096): 910–912, 1978a.

Y. W. Kan and A. M. Dozy. Polymorphism of DNA sequence adjacent to human beta-globin structural gene: relationship to sickle mutation. *Proceedings of the National Academy of Sciences U S A*, 75(11):5631–5635, 1978b.

J. R. Kidd, F. R. Friedlaender, W. C. Speed, A. J. Pakstis, F. M. De La Vega and K. K. Kidd. Analyses of a set of 128 ancestry informative single-nucleotide polymorphisms in a global set of 119 population samples. *Investigative Genetics*, 2(1):1, 2011.

K. K. Kidd, A. M. Bowcock, P. L. Pearson, J. Schmidtke, H. F. Willard, R. K. Track and F. Ricciuti. Report of the committee on human gene mapping by recombinant DNA techniques. *Cytogenetics and Cell Genetics* , 49(1–3):132–218, 1988.

K. K. Kidd, W. C. Speed, A. J. Pakstis, M. R. Furtado, R. Fang, A. Madbouly, M. Maiers, M. Middha, F. R. Friedlaender and J. R. Kidd. Progress toward an efficient panel of SNPs for ancestry inference. *Forensic Science International: Genetics*, 10:23–32, 2014.

R. Kosoy, R. Nassir, C. Tian, P. A. White, L. M. Butler, G. Silva, R. Kittles, M. E. Alarcon-Riquelme, P. K. Gregersen, J. W. Belmont, F. M. De La Vega and M. F. Seldin. Ancestry informative marker sets for determining continental origin and admixture proportions in common populations in America. *Human Mutation*, 30(1):69–78, 2009.

L. Luca Cavalli-Sforza, P. Menozzi and Alberto Piazza. *The History and Geography of Human Genes*. Princeton University Press, 1994.

D. J. Lawson, and D. Falush. Population identification using genetic data. *Annual Review of Genomics and Human Genetics*, 13:337–361, 2012.

J. Z. Li, D. M. Absher, H. Tang, A. M. Southwick, A. M. Casto, S. Ramachandran, H. M. Cann, G. S. Barsh, M. Feldman, L. L. Cavalli-Sforza and R. M. Myers. Worldwide human relationships inferred from genome-wide patterns of variation. *Science*, 319(5866):1100–1104, 2008.

R. Nassir, R. Kosoy, C. Tian, P. A. White, L. M. Butler, G. Silva, R. Kittles, M. E. Alarcon-Riquelme, P. K. Gregersen, J. W. Belmont, F. M. De La Vega and M. F. Seldin. An ancestry informative marker set for determining continental origin: validation and extension using human genome diversity panels. *BMC Genetics*, 10:39, 2009.

A. J. Pakstis, E. Haigh, L. Cherni, A. B. ElGaaied, A. Barton, B. Evsanaa, A. Togtokh, J. Brissenden, J. Roscoe, O. Bulbul, G. Filoglu, C. Gurkan, K. A. Meiklejohn, J. M. Robertson, C. X. Li, Y. L. Wei, H. Li, U. Soundararajan, H. Rajeevan, J. R. Kidd and K. K. Kidd. 52 additional reference population samples for the 55 AISNP panel. *Forensic Science International: Genetics*, 19:269–271, 2015.

P. L. Pearson, K. K. Kidd and H. F. Willard. Report of the committee on human gene mapping by recombinant DNA techniques. *Cytogenetics and Cell Genetics*, 46(1–4):390–566, 1987.

H. Rajeevan, U. Soundararajan, A. J. Pakstis and K. K. Kidd. Introducing the Forensic Research/Reference on Genetics knowledge base, FROG-kb. *Investigative Genetics*, 3(1):18, 2012.

N. A. Rosenberg, L. M. Li, R. Ward and J. K. Pritchard. Informativeness of genetic markers for inference of ancestry. *The American Journal of Human Genetics*, 73(6):1402–1422, 2003.

C. D. Royal, J. Novembre, S. M. Fullerton, D. B. Goldstein, J. C. Long, M. J. Bamshad and A. G. Clark. Inferring genetic ancestry: opportunities, challenges, and implications. *The American Journal of Human Genetics*, 86(5):661–673, 2010.

U. Soundararajan, L. Yun, M. Shi and K. K. Kidd. Minimal SNP overlap among multiple panels of ancestry informative markers argues for more international collaboration. *Forensic Science International: Genetics*, 23:25–32, 2016.

CHAPTER 8

DNA Mixtures

Torben Tvedebrink

Department of Mathematical Sciences,
Aalborg University,
Denmark

When biological material is obtained from a scene of crime, it is often possible to produce a DNA profile from small amounts of DNA. If more than one individual has contributed DNA to the crime scene stain, the resulting DNA profile is called a DNA mixture. The analysis of DNA mixtures continues to be an area of research. In particular, the interpretation of DNA mixtures based on statistical models have received considerable attention since the first publication by Evett *et al.* (1991) on the topic more than 20 years ago. DNA mixtures is still an active research area: at the International Conference on Forensic Inference and Statistics (ICFIC) 2014 in Leiden, at least 14 presentations were devoted to the analysis of DNA mixtures.

If only a single individual has contributed DNA to an observed DNA profile, we refer to this as a single contributor stain. Single contributor stains are expected to show one or two alleles per locus for homozygous and heterozygous loci, respectively. However, if the DNA is limited in quantity or quality, there is a risk of some alleles of the contributor missing in the resulting DNA profile. This event is called allelic drop-out (or locus drop-out in case of an entire locus is missing) and implies that the DNA profile is partial. In order to assess the weight of evidence under this phenomena, the likelihood will depend on a probability of drop-out. Various methods have been proposed in order to estimate drop-out probabilities for forensic genetic samples. However, as the risk of allelic drop-out is caused by the quantity and quality of the input DNA, this should be reflected in the drop-out probability.

The main feature of DNA mixtures is the increased uncertainty attached to the evidence compared to single contributor stains. For single contributor stains, does allelic drop-out and degradation of the biological material increase the complexity of the interpretation. However, uncertainty about the number of contributors, their relative amounts of contributed DNA and their specific DNA profiles adds to this complexity.

In Section 1, more details on the detection method and artefacts caused by the data generating process are discussed. Most of these issues related equally to single contributor stains, however, for DNA mixtures their relative influence on the interpretation is enhanced. The number of contributors is discussed in Section 2 including some population genetics theory. In that section, statistical models regarding an assessment of the number of contributors based on the number of unique alleles are discussed. Statistical models for the electropherogram (*cf.* Section 1) are presented in Section 3, where we distinguish among binary, semi-continuous and continuous models. This differentiation is caused by the amount of data from the electropherogram included in the evidential calculations.

1 Capillary Electrophoresis and Electropherogram

In forensic genetics, the prevailing method of detection is capillary electrophoresis (CE), which is a method for detecting the amount of specific fragments of DNA after polymerase chain reaction (PCR) has amplified the relevant DNA fragments. By detecting the intensity of fluorescent dyes using a CCD camera, an electropherogram (EPG) is produced with peaks reflecting the amounts of fluorescent emitted (see Figure 1) by fragments of identical length. Detecting a

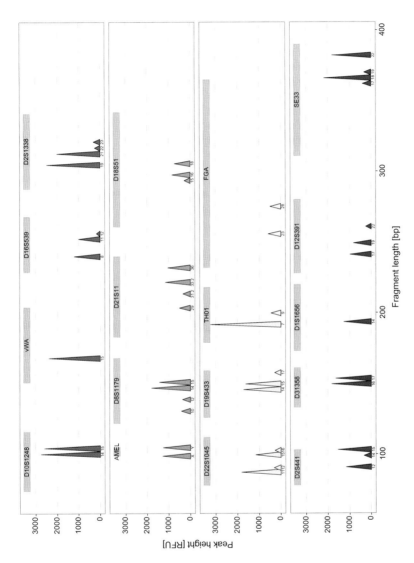

Figure 1: A stylized electropherogram (EPG) of a DNA mixture (typed using the NGM SElect™ multiplex, Applied Biosystems, 2012) showing the observed alleles as peaks measured in relative fluorescent units (RFU).

DNA profile using CE methods, only the fragment lengths are observed, implying that underlying microvariants e.g. due to SNPs are pooled together. The fluorescent intensities are additive which implies that the more fragments of identical length the higher peaks are observed in the EPG.

A side-product of the PCR process are stutters, which are DNA fragments often one repeat shorter but also can be observed one repeat larger (but typically in lower RFUs than the minus stutter peak). For each cycle in the PCR process, stutters are formed with a locus and allele specific rate. The longer the allele and simpler repeat pattern of a locus the higher the stutter rate is. This often is measured by the longest uninterrupted sequence (LUS) of the fragments, which equals the longest stretch of successive repeats of identical DNA motifs. Stutters are particularly important for DNA mixture analysis as stutter peaks of a major contributor to a DNA mixture may have heights similar to that of a minor contributor.

Since the EPG is detected using a sensitive CCD camera, the EPG is observed with background noise in between the peaks. Therefore, a detection threshold often is used for practical purposes. This threshold implies that, e.g. all peaks below 50 RFU in the EPG are discarded, which may cause some peaks of true alleles to be unobserved. DNA profiles obtained from degraded biological material tend to have smaller peaks for longer fragments of DNA. This is mainly caused by damage to the DNA strand, where the risk of broken DNA fragments increases with the length. For DNA mixtures, the total amount of purified DNA may seem sufficient for obtaining full profiles. However, due to the difference in the relative amount of contributed DNA, the risk of allelic drop-out can be severe for minor contributors even for samples with optimum input DNA amounts. This effect is even more noted for degraded DNA samples.

2 Number of Contributors

The number of contributors to a DNA mixture, m, is an essential parameter in the interpretation. Biedermann *et al.* (2012) emphasised that the number of contributors prior to analysis is unknown and therefore should have an uncertainty attached to it. Earlier Brenner *et al.* (1996) discussed the issue of computing the likelihood ratio (LR) when the number of donors cannot be agreed between the prosecutor and defence. Related to this discussion, Lauritzen and Mortera (2002) derived expressions for the number of unknown contributors relevant to consider when analyzing DNA mixtures. More recently numerous studies (e.g. Egeland *et al.*, 2003; Paoletti *et al.*, 2005; Buckleton *et al.*, 2007; Perez *et al.*, 2011) estimate and/or investigate the effect of the number of contributors to a DNA mixture.

The approach of Biedermann *et al.* (2012) used Bayesian Networks in order to demonstrate their approach of deriving a probability for the number of contributors. They argued that the approach of Haned *et al.* (2011a, 2011b) attempts to estimate the most likely number of contributors without assigning uncertainty to this estimate. Tvedebrink (2014) derived the exact distribution for the number of alleles in a *m*-person DNA mixture. Given a prior on the number of contributors, this result can be used to assess the probability of the number of contributors based on the number of observed alleles.

For most crime scene cases, it may be of value to assess the weight of the evidence for a varying number of contributors. From a logical point of view, there is no requirement for the number of contributors to be the same under the two hypotheses compared using a LR. However, for some software implementations (*cf.* Section 3.4), the number of contributors have been the same for computational purposes.

3 Statistical Models

There are generally two schools of thoughts being used in forensic genetics for evaluating the genetic evidence. One being the method computing the "probability of inclusion" (combined probability of inclusion, CPI) or alternatively "the random man not excluded" (RMNE) quantity. These approaches are inferior to the LR, framework as the LR methodology allows the probability of the evidence to be evaluated under well-formulated competing hypotheses (termed the "first principle of evidence interpretation" Evett and Weir, 1998). Thus, sound statistical literature that deals with the analysis of DNA mixtures take its point of departure using the likelihood framework.

The statistical models entering the *LR* (*cf.* Eq. (1)) have been extended to cope with more of the uncertainties and artifacts observed in the detected mixed DNA profile. Modelling these components are important in order to assess the probability of the evidence, since it is the task of the forensic geneticists to assign an evidential weight by computing the likelihood of the evidence under competing hypotheses.

For any type of statistical model, the underlying framework for assessing the weight of evidence is by computing the LR. For DNA mixtures, the evaluation can in most instances be computationally intense due to the vast number of potential genotypes. Let E evidence EPGs denote the evidence under consideration and by H_p and H_d, the hypotheses of the prosecutor and defence, respectively (there exist other naming conventions of these hypotheses). The LR is when computed as

$$\text{LR} = \frac{P(E \mid H_p)}{P(E \mid H_d)} = \frac{\sum_{g \in Gp} P(E \mid g) P(g \mid H_p)}{\sum_{g \in Gd} P(E \mid g) P(g \mid H_d)}$$
$$= \frac{\sum_{g \in Gp} L_E(g) P(g \mid H_p)}{\sum_{g \in Gd} L_E(g) P(g \mid H_d)}, \tag{1}$$

where g is a vector of DNA profiles from the set of genotypes, G_p and G_d, consistent with the two hypotheses, respectively. For a m-person DNA mixture, the sets G_p and G_d consists in general of all combinations of of m DNA profiles, where each profile may take its individual alleles from the set of alleles at each genotyped locus, $l = 1, \ldots, L$. That is, for G_d we have that

$$G_d = \{ g = (g_i)_{i=1}^{m} : g_i = (g_{il_1}, g_{il_2})_{l=1}^{L} \text{ with } (g_{il_1}, g_{il_2}) \in A_l \times A_l$$
$$\text{where } A_l = \{ A_{l1}, \ldots, A_{ln_l} \} \},$$

where A_l is the set of distinct alleles at locus l. Thus, for each locus l, we have $n_l(n_l + 1)/2$ possible states for g_i implying that $|G_d| = \Pi_{l=1}^{L}\{n_l(n_l + 1)/2\}^m$. For a three-person DNA mixture typed with the European Standard Set of loci, $L = 16$, this corresponds to 10^{95} possible profile combinations, where n_l for each locus is set to the number of reported alleles detectable with NGMSElect (Applied Biosystems, 2012). Hence, in order to make computations feasible some assumptions need to be made, e.g. conditional independence of loci etc.

In (1), $P(E \mid g) = L_E(g)$ models the EPG signal given the DNA profiles g. That is, $L_E(g)$ weighs the contribution from g to $P(E \mid H_i)$ by the goodness-of-fit to the observed data. Small values of $L_E(g)$ would correspond to E being less likely to observed given that the specific DNA profiles in g where the contributors to E. Conversely, large values would correspond to close correspondence between the observed EPG and the expectation under the model specified by L_E (Notation due to Lauritzen, 2014). A natural and important assumption is that the distribution of the EPG is independent of the assumption, i.e. $P(E \mid g)$ only depends on the proposed genotypes in g.

Most of the recent discussions regarding DNA mixture models revolve around L_E while less debate and focus is devoted to $P(g \mid H_i)$, which models the population genetic component. That is, here we measure the rarity of the DNA profiles (g) in the population. Often the population genetic models that are used compensate for sub-population structures (using the θ-correction, Balding and Nichols, 1994) and close relatedness by explicit stating this in H_p and H_d, i.e. the defence might claim it is a brother to the defendant who is the contributor to a given stain.

However, for simple crime cases, there is a single suspect or defendant to weigh the evidence against. We refer to these cases as simple query mixtures, such that the two competing hypotheses differ only as to whether the profile Q of our query person is in the mixture or not. That is, H_d is identical to H_p expect that our query profile Q is allowed to vary freely in the set of genotypes (sometimes denoted by X, e.g. Balding, 2013). As a suggestion for a common assumption (convention), Lauritzen (2014) proposed to define

$$\pi(\boldsymbol{g}) = P(\boldsymbol{g} \mid H_d) = P(\boldsymbol{g} \mid q \in \boldsymbol{g}, H_d) P(q \in \boldsymbol{g} \mid H_d) = \pi_d(\boldsymbol{g} \mid q)\pi(q), \quad (2)$$

where q is the genotype of the query person Q, and $\pi(q) = P(q \in \boldsymbol{g} \mid H_d)$ is the probability that Q's genotype is present by chance (the defence's claim stated in H_d), whereas we have $P(q \in \boldsymbol{g} \mid H_p) = 1$ (Lauritzen, 2014). Furthermore, we have that under H_p: $q \in \boldsymbol{g}$. This implies that $P(\boldsymbol{g} \mid H_p) = P(\boldsymbol{g} \mid q \in \boldsymbol{g}, H_p) = \pi_p(\boldsymbol{g} \mid q)$ in the notation of (2). Hence, we may write

$$\pi(\boldsymbol{g} \mid q) = \pi_p(\boldsymbol{g} \mid q) = \pi_d(\boldsymbol{g} \mid q),$$

which emphasize that for simple query mixtures, the distribution of the composition $\boldsymbol{g}$ given q is independent of the hypothesis.

Using the notation defined above and utilizing (2), we find that (Lauritzen, 2014):

$$\begin{aligned}
\text{LR} &= \frac{P(E \mid H_p)}{P(E \mid H_d)} = \frac{\Sigma_{\boldsymbol{g} \in G_p} L_E(\boldsymbol{g})\pi(\boldsymbol{g} \mid q)}{\Sigma_{\boldsymbol{g} \in G_d} L_E(\boldsymbol{g})\pi(\boldsymbol{g})} \\
&= \frac{1}{\pi(q)} \frac{\Sigma_{\boldsymbol{g} \in G_p} L_E(\boldsymbol{g})\pi(\boldsymbol{g})}{\Sigma_{\boldsymbol{g} \in G_d} L_E(\boldsymbol{g})\pi(\boldsymbol{g})} = \frac{P(q \in \boldsymbol{g} \mid E, H_d)}{P(q \in \boldsymbol{g} \mid H_d)},
\end{aligned} \quad (3)$$

where the last equality holds since G_p equals G_d but restricted to the cases where $q \in \boldsymbol{g}$, $G_p = G_d|_{q \in \boldsymbol{g}}$. Thus, the LR can be thought of a measure of the probability that profile q is included in the constitution of profiles, $\boldsymbol{g}$, when taking the EPG evidence, E, into account while assuming H_d is true. In the words of Lauritzen (2014): "WoE is $\log_{10}$ of ratio of probabilities that genotypes of defendant is in sample — with or without taking EPG into account", where WoE $= \log_{10}$ LR is a measure of the weight of evidence in *bans* originally introduced by Alan Turing (Good, 1979; Balding, 2013).

The various statistical models for evaluating $L_E(\boldsymbol{g})$ can be categorized into three groups: (1) the binary models (Section 3.1) where only data regarding the presence or absence of alleles are included in the LR, (2) the semi-continuous models (Section 3.2) assign probability of drop-out and drop-in to the observed and "missing" alleles, and (3) the continuous models (Section 3.3) where the specific peak heights are modelled by some statistical distribution. However, common to all methods is that $P(q \in g \mid E, H_d) \leq 1$, which implies that they satisfy the inequality that

$$\text{LR} \leq 1/P(q \in g \mid H_d) = 1/\pi(q).$$

That is, the weight of evidence from a DNA mixture (using any statistical model for L_E) can never exceed the LR one would obtain in the case of a single contributor stain with no ambiguities (e.g. drop-in or drop-out) (Lauritzen, 2014; Cowell *et al.*, 2015).

3.1 *Binary Models*

The binary models are the simplest model for evaluating $L_E(g)$. Under the binary scheme, only alleles present in the EPG are considered. This implies that the summation over G_i is greatly simplified. However, it also implies that allelic drop-out of a true contributors, S, alleles yields $\text{LR} = 0$ assuming S contributes to the evidence under H_p. In general, we may formulate

$$L_E(g) = \begin{cases} 1, & E \equiv g, \\ 0, & E \not\equiv g, \end{cases} \tag{4}$$

where $E \equiv g$ implies g is consistent with E, i.e. no alleles in E are unexplained by g and no alleles in g are missing in E. This construction implies that the LR can be evaluated using a combinatorial expression taking all possible permutations and sub-population structure into account (Curran *et al.*, 1999).

3.2 *Semi-Continuous Models*

Semi-continuous models relax the assumption of (4) by introducing the concepts of drop-out and drop-in events. That is, drop-out is the event where one or more alleles of an alleged contributor is missing in the EPG (or is below a pre-set detection threshold), whereas drop-in is the event of additional unexplained allelic components in the EPG (e.g. contamination from plasticware). Hence, the semi-continuous models are also referred to as "drop-models", where the important parameters are the drop-out probability, $P(D)$, and the probability of contamination, $P(C)$. Both of these probabilities are factors of the measuring process and depends, especially for $P(D)$, highly on the amount of input DNA, which can be poorly estimated for low amounts of DNA. Furthermore, the quantitation of input DNA is not necessarily reliable as contributors to mixtures are in different amounts and degraded DNA could be misleading. Tvedebrink *et al.* (2009) showed how the drop-out probability has a dose-response relationship with the average peak height (lower amounts of DNA increase the drop-out probability and vice versa). Furthermore, degradation of the biological material increases the risk of allelic drop-out for longer DNA fragments (Tvedebrink *et al.*, 2012).

For the semi-continuous models $L_E(g)$ can be specified through a product of drop-out and drop-in probabilities:

$$L_E(g) = P(D)^{n(D)} P(\bar{D})^{n(\bar{D})} P(C)^{n(C)} P(\bar{C})^{n(\bar{C})}, \qquad (5)$$

where $P(\bar{D}) = 1 - P(D)$ and $P(\bar{C}) = 1 - P(C)$ are the probability of complementary events to D and C, respectively, i.e. no allelic drop-out and no contamination. The n-functions count the number of (non) drop-out and (non) drop-in events needed to have g explaining E. The formulation of $L_E(g)$ in (5) is a simplification in that the drop-out probability is constant for all alleles regardless of the amount of contributed DNA, e.g. the drop-out probability for a homozygous locus is considerably less than that of an allele at a heterozygous locus (Tvedebrink *et al.*, 2012). Balding and Buckleton (2009) discuss the semi-continuous models in greater detail for some specific scenarios. Variants of the semi-continuous models are also recommended by the DNA commission of the International Society of Forensic Genetics (Gill *et al.*, 2012) in order to evaluate the genetic evidence to account for allelic drop-out and drop-in.

Common to all semi-continuous models is that $P(D)$ and $P(C)$ must be somehow estimated or assigned a distribution. This may be done by various means, however, as the drop-out probability in particular is dependent on the amount of input DNA a surrogate of this quantity should have direct influence on $P(D)$. That is, quantitative means of estimating $P(D)$ may be confounded by population genetic phenomena (Tvedebrink, 2014). One such approach was proposed by Gill *et al.* (2007) and implemented in LRmix (Haned, 2011; Haned *et al.*, 2012; Gill and Haned, 2013), where the range of drop-out probabilities was estimated using a Monte Carlo simulations: (1) each single copy of an allele drops out by a frequency $P(d)$ and (2) the total number of alleles for each simulation is compared to the observed number in the case sample. All simulations with a coinciding number of observed alleles are used to assess the plausible range for $P(d)$. However, when drop-out probabilities are used in weight of evidence calculations, they represent a total allele drop-out, i.e. all copies have dropped out, which happens with probability $P(D)$ (Haned *et al.*, 2012; Gill and Haned, 2013). However, these drop-out events are different, except in the case of a drop-out of a non-shared allele, i.e. in general we have $P(D) \neq P(d)$.

These and other drawbacks of the semi-continuous models and why fully continuous models are being considered are discussed in the next section.

3.3 Continuous Models

The continuous models for the EPG evidence E includes most of the sampled signal from the capillary electrophoresis genetic analyser. However, most methodologies retain a detection threshold, of 50 RFU say, in order to reduce the influence from the background noise. That is, the majority of models operates with allelic drop-out induces from limited amounts of DNA. The underlying assumption for the continuous models is that distribution of the peak heights from the EPG can be modelled by some statistical distribution. Examples include the normal, log-normal and gamma distributions, where the former lacks the restriction of non-negative peak heights measurements.

Furthermore, analysis of the behavior of the residuals from fitting gamma or log-normal models to the peak heights show support for the choice of these distributions. For certain parameter values, these two distributions are hard to distinguish and the specific choice of distribution are often based on some desirable mathematical properties. For the log-normal distribution, some of the attractive properties are closed form expressions for most parameter estimates when log-transforming the observed data (Taylor *et al.*, 2013a), whereas the gamma distribution have some unique additive properties which are demonstrated by Cowell *et al.* (2015). Furthermore, the gamma distribution was also utilized by Puch-Solis *et al.* (2013).

Puch-Solis and Clayton (2014), where one of the main differences between these two gamma model approaches was the estimation procedure.

For the continuous models, the underlying assumption is that by specifying the systematic components in the DNA measurement process and data generating process, the peak height measurements made by capillary electrophoresis (CE) follows a statistical distribution with probability density function *f*. Let *F* denote the associated cumulative distribution function, then

$$L_E(\boldsymbol{g}) = F(T;\psi,\boldsymbol{g})^{n(D)} \prod_{i=1}^{n(\bar{D})} f(h_i;\psi,\boldsymbol{g}), \qquad (6)$$

where, as above, $n(D)$ is the number of dropped-out alleles and T is the detection threshold, i.e. dropped-out alleles $h_i < T$ with h_i being the peak height of the *i*th allele in $\boldsymbol{g}$. Furthermore, ψ is a vector of model parameters some of which are unknown and need to be estimated.

3.4 *Software*

There are basically three ways the parameters can be eliminated (Lauritzen, 2014): (1) using known and fixed plug-in estimates, (2) integrate over the parameter space by using prior distributions (e.g. by Markov Chain Monte Carlo, MCMC) and (3) maximize the likelihood and use estimates as *known* quantities. Methods (1) and (3) are similar as they rely on plug-in estimates, however, (1) utilizes external non-case specific data or background information, whereas (3) estimates the parameter for the specific sample at hand. Cowell *et al.* (2015) is a prominent example of (3), whereas the number of solutions relying on MCMC techniques (2) is more diverse, including TrueAllele (Perlin and Sinelnikov, 2009), STRmix (Taylor *et al.*, 2013b) and LiRa (Puch-Solis and Clayton, 2014). When using MCMC to assess the unknown parameters (or their distribution), there is a risk of not sampling the entire state space of DNA profiles. Finite MCMC chains can only visit finitely many states making it probable that some high intensity region of the space is not investigated by the sampling scheme. Trying to resolve this by multiple starts with varying initial values may work, however, there is no guarantees when it comes to MCMC (which the name may indicate) converging in finite time. That is, multiple runs may yield approximately the same results, however, there is no way of knowing whether this is consistently correct — or consistently wrong. For many cases, the *WoE* is in the range of 10 to 20 bans, i.e. the LR is in the range of 10^{10}–10^{20}. However, for challenging cases, we may obtain WoE = 3 or WoE = 7. This may be challenging for MCMC methods: Recall the expression of LR in (3) where the denominator is the genotype distribution of the query profile q and the numerator the probability of q being in the sample conditioned on the EPG evidence, E. Since $P(q \in g \mid H_d)$ typically is 10^{-20} (Applied Biosystems, 2012), the numerator, $P(q \in g \mid E, H_d)$, for cases with WoE = 5 this implies that $P(q \in g \mid E, H_d) = 10^{-15}$, which is a very small probability mass to estimate reliably. On the other hand, MCMC methods allow the statistical models to be more complex as adding another parameter is reasonably inexpensive in terms of computational cost.

A common property of the continuous models are that if variance parameters in the model for the peak heights increases, such that the distribution effectively is non-informative, the continuous methods collapse into a semi-continuous model. Comparing the results from semi-continuous and continuous methods is not straight forward. However, the numerical results often tend to be similar of similar magnitude for the two types of the methods. An important distinction is the need for an *initial screening* when using semi-continuous models by a forensic caseworker to assess if e.g. any of the profile specific drop-out probabilities should be set to zero. Another pre-computation task might be assessment of whether it is appropriate to link highly unbalanced peaks to the same individual. These steps are avoided when using continuous models. Steele and Balding (2014) comment on the different software implementations.

4 Data

When comparing methods and software implementations, it is important to examine EPGs with a wide range of features: varying number of contributors sharing different number of alleles (this includes DNA mixtures involving close relatives) varying mixture proportions, low template samples with a pronounced risk for allelic drop-outs, and degraded DNA samples where longer fragments are under-amplified causing high intra-locus imbalances, etc.

One resource of DNA mixture sample is the Boston University DNA mixture data. However, it may be dangerous with a fixed "control set" as methods and software will be tuned towards this specific dataset/samples.

Currently the prevailing method for measuring DNA samples and DNA mixtures in particular is using CE. This method gives EPGs where the variability and behavior have been studied and described over the recent decades. However, with the availability and increased robustness of massively parallel sequencing (MPS, also referred to as next or second generation sequencing, NGS or SGS) new types of data emerge. Many of the same sources of variability carry over from the CE technology as PCR still is a vital part of the data generating process. However, depending on the platform, additional PCR processes take place prior to sequencing. Furthermore, for most of current sequencing platforms, there is a tendency for *preferential detection* in that the sequencer is better at sequencing shorter fragments. This is due to the fact that the base calling accuracy decreases along the sequenced fragment.

Hence, read length for repeats may be accurate (but some longer lengths maybe under represented as is with PCR/STRs and CE). Sequence accuracy (the actual base calls) will depend on level of noise and to some extent the minor contributors: in other words, similar issues are present in current methodology. Hence, similar validation, which work for CE data will be needed to define the parameters so statistical models can be developed that apply well to the generated MPS data.

References

Applied Biosystems. *AmplFiSTR®NGM SElect^{TM} PCR Amplification Kit — User Guide.* Life Technologies Corporation, 2012.

D. J. Balding. Evaluation of mixed-source, low-template DNA profiles in forensic science. *Proceedings of the National Academy of Sciences,* 110(30):12241–12246, 2013.

D. J. Balding and J. S. Buckleton. Interpreting low template DNA profiles. *Forensic Science International: Genetics,* 4(1):1–10, 2009.

D. J. Balding and R. A. Nichols. DNA profile match probability calculation: How to allow for population stratification, relatedness, database selection and single bands. *Forensic Science International,* 64:125–140, 1994.

A. Biedermann, S. Bozza, K. Konis and F. Taroni. Inference about the number of contributors to a DNA mixture: Comparative analyses of a Bayesian network approach and the maximum allele count method. *Forensic Science International: Genetics,* 6(6):689–696, 2012.

C. Brenner, R. Fimmers and M. Baur. Likelihood ratios for mixed stains when the number of donors cannot be agreed. *International Journal of Legal Medicine,* 109(4):218–219, 1996.

J. S. Buckleton, J. M. Curran and P. Gill. Towards understanding the effect of uncertainty in the number of contributors to DNA stains. *Forensic Science Internationl: Genetics,* 1(1):20–28, 2007.

R. G. Cowell, T. Graversen, S. L. Lauritzen and J. Mortera. Analysis of Forensic DNA Mixtures with Artefacts. *J R Stat Soc Ser C Appl Stat,* 64(1):1–32, 2015.

J. M. Curran, C. M. Triggs, J. S. Buckleton and B. S. Weir. Interpreting DNA mixtures in structured populations. *Journal of Forensic Science,* 44(5):987–995, 1999.

T. Egeland, I. Dalen and P. Mostad. Estimating the number of contributors to a DNA profile. *International Journal of Legal Medicine*, 117(5):271–275, 2003.

I. W. Evett, C. Buffery, G. Willott and D. Stoney. A guide to interpreting single locus profiles of DNA mixtures in forensic cases. *Journal of the Forensic Science Society*, 31(1):41–47, 1991.

I. W. Evett and B. S. Weir. *Interpreting DNA Evidence: Statistical Genetics for Forensic Scientists*, Sinauer Associates, Sunderland, MA, 1998.

P. Gill, L. Gusmão, H. Haned, W. Mayr, N. Morling, W. Parson, L. Prieto, M. Prinz, H. Schneider, P. Schneider and B. Weir. DNA commission of the International Society of Forensic Genetics: Recommendations on the evaluation of STR typing results that may include drop-out and/or drop-in using probabilistic methods. *Forensic Science International: Genetics*, 6(6):679–688, 2012.

P. Gill and H. Haned. A new methodological framework to interpret complex DNA profiles using likelihood ratios. *Forensic Science International: Genetics*, 7(2):251–263, 2013.

P. Gill, A. Kirkham and J. Curran. LoComatioN: A software tool for the analysis of low copy number DNA profiles. *Forensic Science International*, 166(2–3):128–138, 2007.

I. J. Good. Studies in the history of probability and statistics. XXXVII AM Turing's statistical work in World War II. *Biometrika*, 66(2):393–396, 1979.

H. Haned. Forensim: An open-source initiative for the evaluation of statistical methods in forensic genetics. *Forensic Science International: Genetics*, 5(4):265–268, 2011.

H. Haned *et al.* Estimating the number of contributors to forensic dna mixtures: does maximum likelihood perform better than maximum allele count? *Journal of Forensic Sciences*, 56(1):23–28, 2011a.

H. Haned *et al.* The predictive value of the maximum likelihood estimator of the number of contributors to a DNA mixture. *Forensic Science International: Genetics* 5(4):281–284, 2011b.

H. Haned, K. Slooten and P. Gill. Exploratory data analysis for the interpretation of low template DNA mixtures. *Forensic Science International: Genetics*, 6(6):762–774, 2012.

S. L. Lauritzen. *On the Statistical Analysis of DNA Mixtures*, C. Berger (Ed.), *ICFIS 2014*. Leiden University, Leiden, 2014.

S. L. Lauritzen and J. Mortera. Bounding the number of contributors to mixed DNA stains. *Forensic Science International*, 130(2–3):125–126, 2002.

D. R. Paoletti, T. E. Doom, C. M. Krane, M. L. Raymer and D. E. Krane. Empirical analysis of the STR profiles resulting from conceptual mixtures. *Journal of Forensic Sciences*, 50(6):1361–1366, 2005.

J. Perez, A. A. Mitchell, N. Ducasse, J. Tamariz and T. Caragine. Estimating the number of contributors to two-, three- and four-person mixtures containing DNA in high template and low template amounts. *Croatian Medical Journal*, 52(3):314–326, 2011.

M. W. Perlin and A. Sinelnikov. An information gap in DNA evidence interpretation. *PLoS ONE*, 4(12):e8327, 2009.

R. Puch-Solis and T. Clayton. Evidential evaluation of DNA profiles using a discrete statistical model implemented in the DNA lira software. *Forensic Science International: Genetics*, 11(0):220–228, 2014.

R. Puch-Solis, L. Rodgers, A. Mazumder, S. Pope, I. Evett, J. Curran and D. Balding. Evaluating forensic DNA profiles using peak heights, allowing for multiple donors, allelic dropout and stutters. *Forensic Science International: Genetics*, 7(5):555–563, 2013.

C. D. Steele and D. J. Balding. Statistical Evaluation of Forensic DNA Profile Evidence. In S. E. Fienberg, (Ed.), *Annual Review of Statistics and its Application*, pp. 361–384, 2014.

D. Taylor, J.-A. Bright and J. Buckleton. The interpretation of single source and mixed DNA profiles. *Forensic Science International: Genetics*, 7(5):516–528, 2013a.

D. Taylor, J.-A. Bright and J. S. Buckleton. The interpretation of single source and mixed DNA profiles. *Forensic Science International: Genetics*, 7(5):516–528, 2013b.

T. Tvedebrink. On the exact distribution of the numbers of alleles in DNA mixtures. *International Journal of Legal Medicine*, 128(3):427–437, 2014.

T. Tvedebrink, P. Eriksen, M. Asplund, H. Mogensen and N. Morling. Allelic dropout probabilities estimated by logistic regression — further considerations and practical implementation. *Forensic Science International: Genetics*, 6(2):263–267, 2012.

T. Tvedebrink, P. Eriksen, H. Mogensen and N. Morling. Statistical model for degraded DNA samples and adjusted probabilities for allelic dropout. *Forensic Science International Genetics*, 6(1):97–101, 2012.

T. Tvedebrink, P. S. Eriksen, H. S. Mogensen and N. Morling. Estimating the probability of allelic drop-out of STR alleles in forensic genetics. *Forensic Science International: Genetics*, 3(4):222–226, 2009.

CHAPTER 9

Types of Genomes, Sequences and Genetic Markers (Repeats, SNPs, Indels, Haplotypes)

Vânia Pereira

Section of Forensic Genetics, Department of Forensic Medicine,
Faculty of Health and Medical Sciences,
University of Copenhagen, Copenhagen, Denmark

Leonor Gusmão

DNA Diagnostic Laboratory (LDD),
State University of Rio de Janeiro (UERJ), Rio de Janeiro, Brazil
IPATIMUP — Institute of Molecular Pathology and Immunology,
University of Porto, Porto, Portugal
Instituto de Investigação e Inovação em Saúde,
Universidade do Porto, Porto, Portugal

Population genetics focuse on the allele/haplotype frequency varia-tion in populations, and the processes responsible for modelling that variation, namely genetic drift, selection, migration and mutation.

By studying current diversity patterns in populations, it is possi-ble to infer their past history and evolution, at different time frames (Cavalli-Sforza, 1998; Jobling *et al.*, 2003).

Forensic genetics is largely grounded in population genetic studies. In forensic genetics, the quantification of the evidentiary value of the analysis results is most often performed through likelihood ratios (LRs) that statistically compare the probabilities of a certain observation under two alternative scenarios, using the random population as reference (Collins and Morton, 1994; Gjertson *et al.*, 2007; Gill *et al.*, 2012).

Variation among individuals is the basis of both pure and applied fields. Any region of the genome whether it is coding or non-coding can be screened for genetic variants but in practice, for population and forensic genetic studies, non-coding markers are preferable since they are not directly subjected to the effects of selection and are thus expected to reflect mainly population level neutral effects, such as drift, expansions, admixture and migration (Steiper, 2010). The choice for neutral markers in the forensic field also has been recommended in order to avoid ethical concerns, since they are less prone to disclose information associated with disease or genetic susceptibility (Schneider, 1997). However, this choice is being reconsidered with the advent of higher throughput systems that allow gathering information on large portions of the genome, and ancestry, and phenotype markers are increasingly being used in forensic investigation, to obtain information on potential perpetrators of crimes with no identified suspects (Kayser and de Knijff, 2011; Walsh *et al.*, 2011; Phillips *et al.*, 2014; Warshauer *et al.*, 2015).

In a forensic context, a very wide range of scenarios can emerge that will require different genetic identification tools. In each case, the selection of the appropriate genetic markers to be investigated is ultimately associated with their variation within and/or between populations, mode of transmission and also with technical aspects, mostly related to the biological sample(s) available.

This chapter aims to give an overview on the types of genetic markers that can be used for identification purposes, highlighting the advantages and limitation of markers with different characteristics, in terms of inheritance pattern and/or sequence variation.

1 Different Types of Genomes

In eukaryotes, the great majority of the genetic material is found in the cell nucleus, and the remaining fraction is contained in the DNA of mitochondria or chloroplasts. In the nucleus of the human cells, genetic information can be located at the autosomes, the X and the Y chromosomes.

Recombination is a very important feature to take into account in genetic identification. In each generation, recombination allows the reshuffling of genetic information creating new genetic constellations that are unique. With the exception of identical twins, the probability of two persons sharing the same genetic profile is virtually nil, for recombining markers.

Depending on the presence or absence of recombination, the different types of available genomes can be separated in two main groups: recombining genomes, that allow the identification of a single individual (autosomal and X-chromosomal markers) and non-recombining genomes, that allow to discriminate parental lineages and provide information that is shared by a group of related individuals (Y chromosome — for most of its length — and mitochondrial DNA genome). Table 1 summarizes some of the characteristics

Table 1: Comparison of different genomes according to their transmission properties (adapted from Schaffner, 2004).

	Autosomes	X chromosome	mtDNA	Y chromosome
Age (years)	1,000,000	750,000	100,000	100,000
Size (Mb)	3,000	150	0.017	60
Mutation rate	Moderate	Low	Very high	High
(mutations per Mb per generation)	(0.020)	(0.015)	(1–300)	(0.033)
Recombination rate	1.1	0.8	0	0
Number of usable loci	Thousands	Hundreds	1	1
Relative effective population size (Ne)	1	$\frac{3}{4}$	$\frac{1}{4}$	$\frac{1}{4}$

Notes: Recombination rate is expressed in cM/Mb. One cM (centiMorgan) refers to the genetic distance between loci for which the recombination frequency is 1%.

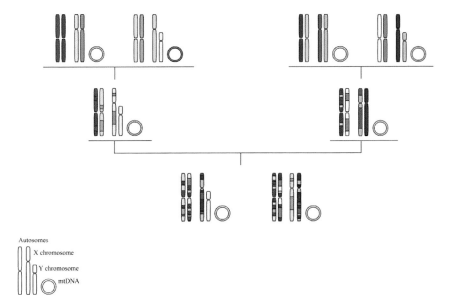

Figure 1:   Genetic transmission and recombination patterns of the different types of genomes.

of the different genomes. Figure 1 shows in more detail the different kinds of genetic information and transmission properties.

1.1 *Recombining Genomes: Autosomes and X Chromosome*

Due to recombination and the large number of chromosomes available to study, autosomes are the obvious choice when looking for variation among individuals; and autosomal DNA markers are still the main source of information for population genetic and forensic studies.

The mode of transmission of the autosomal markers is important for their choice in kinship analysis (Figure 1). Both parents contribute half of the information to their offspring and therefore, any male or female individuals maternally or paternally related will share alleles by descent with a probability that depends of the coefficient of co-ancestry between them (Pinto *et al.*, 2010, 2011).

The commercially available autosomal kits have high power of discrimination, the methods and protocols are well established, and there are guidelines developed on how to properly report data (Bar *et al.*, 1997; Morling *et al.*, 2002; Gjertson *et al.*, 2007; Prinz *et al.*, 2007; Gill *et al.*, 2012). Therefore, whether in the analysis of trace samples, individual identification or in kinship analysis, autosomal markers can provide a reliable answer in most cases.

However, situations arise where the genetic profiles obtained are not complete or the interpretation of the results is not straightforward. In these cases, it is necessary to recruit other kinds of genetic information. Combining data from markers with different characteristics or transmission properties (autosomes, mtDNA, Y chromosome and X chromosome) has been successful when addressing such complex cases (Coble *et al.*, 2009).

Although used in a more specific context, X-chromosomal markers have also some applicability in forensics, namely in situations, such as incest cases, where autosomal data fail to resolve kinship (Szibor *et al.*, 2003; Szibor, 2007; Pinto *et al.*, 2011; Gomes *et al.*, 2012).

The interest in X-chromosomal information mainly derives from its specific traits. The different number of X chromosomes present in males and females has consequences in the levels of recombination. Men have only one X chromosome that is transmitted directly to daughters without recombination, while the X chromosome inherited from the mother contains the recombined information from the two maternal X chromosomes (Figure 1).

Due to this particular mode of inheritance, the utility of X-chromosomal markers in the analysis of trace samples varies, depending on the gender of the individuals considered as well as the nature of the trace/mixture.

X-chromosomal and autosomal markers have the same power to discriminate female profiles in a population. However, because men have only one X chromosome, the power of discrimination obtained for X-chromosomal specific loci is lower than that obtained for equally diverse loci at the autosomes.

In mixtures where all contributors are female, X-chromosomal analysis has no gain in the power of discrimination when compared to autosomal markers. Moreover, there are more unlinked autosomal markers available, so the use of the X chromosome information does not present any special advantage.

Similarly, if all contributors are male, there is only one X chromosome available and therefore, only one allele per locus, which will decrease the power of discrimination compared with autosomal loci with the same diversity.

In mixtures where the contributors have different genders, the X chromosome is particularly useful when female traces need to be identified in a male background (Szibor *et al.*, 2003; Szibor, 2007). For the female and male profiles to be the same, the female will have to be homozygous for all the markers analyzed. Although possible, this is very improbable for markers with high diversity such as the short tandem repeats (STRs) selected for forensic casework (more information below in section: DNA markers).

The main area where X-chromosomal markers can contribute the most is in kinship investigation, namely in paternity cases where the putative father is not immediately available and his closest relatives must be analyzed instead. In this situation, the power of exclusion of autosomal markers decreases, and if the putative paternal grandmother is available for genotyping, X-chromosomal markers will be more informative because the putative paternal X-chromosomal haplotype can be inferred from the alleles of the paternal grandmother (Gomes *et al.*, 2012).

X-chromosomal markers also can be of interest in paternity testing, when two putative fathers are father and son and the investigated child is a female. In this situation, the analysis of the X chromosome can help to exclude paternity, since both men will not share any X chromosomal alleles by descent and will transmit their intact X-haplotype to the daughter. X-chromosomal markers also can be useful in resolving kinship testing involving two sisters or half-sisters, helping to consider or exclude paternity more efficiently than autosomal markers (Szibor *et al.*, 2003; Szibor, 2007).

Another situation where the study of X chromosomal markers can assume a special relevance is in the analysis of alternative pedigrees that are indistinguishable by the use of unlinked autosomal markers but not of X-chromosomal markers (Pinto *et al.*, 2011).

Genealogical and pedigree reconstruction over several generations also is one of the potential applications of the X-chromosome markers, as long as the lineages are not interrupted by father–son relationships (Szibor *et al.*, 2003; Szibor, 2007).

1.2 Uniparental Markers — Mitochondrial DNA and Y Chromosome

Uniparental or lineage markers — mitochondrial genome and the Y chromosome — inform about the history of female or male lineages, respectively, and can be used to study population genetic differences between male and female mediated events (Schaffner, 2004). These markers have a low effective population size (one fourth of the autosomes and one third of the X chromosomes, see Table 1) and, therefore, present accentuated genetic differences between human continental groups.

2 Mitochondria and Mitochondrial DNA

Mitochondria are organelles located in eukaryotic animal cells, responsible for energy production. Each mitochondrion contains between 100 and 10,000 copies of their own genetic information, independent from the nuclear genome — the mitochondrial DNA (mtDNA). mtDNA is a circular, double-stranded molecule of about 16,569 base pairs (bps) (Anderson *et al.*, 1981).

Although in general the mtDNA is considered monoclonal (meaning that all copies within the cell are the same), it is common for an individual to present heteroplasmy and have more than one kind of mtDNA (Gill *et al.*, 1994; Comas *et al.*, 1995; Bendall *et al.*, 1996, 1997). The accuracy to detect heteroplasmy depends on the sequencing technique used and studies refer that in order to be detected, heteroplasmy must occur in about 20% of the mtDNA molecules (Tully *et al.*, 2001).

mtDNA inheritance is uniparental and maternally mediated as only the maternal mitochondria integrate the oocytes. The process is complex and out of the scope of the current chapter, but in summary, after fertilization of the egg, the mitochondria present in the sperm are marked with ubiquitin, targeting them for destruction (Sutovsky *et al.*, 1999).

mtDNA does not recombine in each generation as does nuclear DNA and therefore, variability in the genome is only introduced by mutations (SNPs being the most frequent). Within mtDNA, the highest level of variation is located in the control region (CR) that contains about 1,122 bps (Anderson *et al.*, 1981). The CR can be further divided into three hypervariable segments — HV-I, HV-II and HV-III.

The most common type of mutation occurring in the CR are SNPs, but small insertions and deletions are also common, especially in homopolymeric regions (PolyC) located between 302–310 and 16,183–16,194.

The first forensic and population genetic investigations focused only on HV-I (position 16024–16400) and HV-II (position 44–340) and more recent studies include the full CR sequence, which is the shortest mtDNA fragment recommended by the International Society for Forensic Genetics (ISFG) for reference population data-basing purposes (Parson *et al.*, 2014). With the advent of next generation sequencing methodologies, it is now possible to sequence the complete molecule of mtDNA in a faster and cost effective manner (Parson *et al.*, 2013; King *et al.*, 2014; Mikkelsen *et al.*, 2014).

The use of mtDNA in forensics is still quite limited. The fact that it is transmitted as a single haplotype can be an advantage in the identification of victims of mass disasters or missing persons, for example, when maternal relatives are available. The downside, however, is that it does not allow discrimination at the individual level and unrelated individuals can have similar haplotypes. Whenever possible, it is advisable that mtDNA analysis in forensic genetics will be anchored with additional genetic information and/or metadata.

The biggest advantage of mtDNA analysis in forensics derives from the high number of copies present in each cell. The rate of successful DNA isolation and subsequent PCR amplification is much higher for the mtDNA than nuclear DNA, which makes the analysis of the mitochondrial genome particularly useful in ancient or degraded samples (Paabo, 1989; Parson *et al.*, 2004). In addition, although some successful strategies have been described using autosomal miniSTRs (Muller *et al.*, 2007), mtDNA has the highest success of being retrieved from hair shafts without root, which can be of great assistance in forensic casework (Wilson *et al.*, 1995; Linch *et al.*, 2001).

3 Y Chromosome

The human Y chromosome is the smallest chromosome of the nuclear genome and it contains around 58 million bps (Morton, 1991). It has two types of chromatin: hetero- and euchromatin located in different regions of the chromosome. The distal part of the long arm has heterochromatin, characterized by repetitive sequences. The size of this region is highly variable among individuals, representing in some, more than half of the length of the chromosome. Euchromatin comprises the rest of the Y chromosome and contains sequences homologous to the X chromosome, repetitive sequences and genes (Skaletsky *et al.*, 2003).

Y chromosome is male specific and is transmitted from fathers to sons (Figure 1). The Y chromosome does not recombine in the majority of its extension. The exceptions are the pseudoautosomal regions (PAR 1 and PAR 2) located at both ends of the arms that pair and can recombine with the homologous X chromosome regions during male meiosis.

Some of the characteristics discussed for the mtDNA are also common to the Y chromosome.

Like mtDNA, the male specific region of the Y chromosome is a haploid entity due to the absence of recombination. Therefore, it is paternally transmitted without recombination between generations, and as a result, DNA variation between relatives is only introduced by mutations (Jobling *et al.*, 2003). In contrast with mtDNA, however, the Y chromosome is present in just one copy per (normal) cell.

Due to the absence of recombination, Y-chromosomal analysis in paternity testing or missing person cases can only identify paternally related males and it can be helpful to disclose kinship when autosomal analyses are ambiguous. However, the applicability of Y chromosome polymorphisms in paternity testing is limited to about half of paternity cases (only in cases of male offspring), and it should be borne in mind that an outcome based solely on Y-chromosomal markers cannot exclude the paternity of any male belonging to the same paternal lineage of the true biological father. Wherever possible, to avoid or reduce this possibility, autosomal markers should be used as well. The Y-chromosomal markers can be especially useful in paternity cases in the absence of biological material belonging to the alleged father. In these situations (for example, when the alleged father is deceased), it is possible to access the complete genetic profile of his Y chromosome using any male relative in the same paternal lineage.

The Y chromosome is widely used in forensic genetics. The majority of assailants in violent crimes and sexual assault cases are male, and Y-chromosomal testing can give additional information about the perpetrator.

In the forensic context, it often is difficult to separate the extracted DNA from victim and assailant in a trace sample. Although in biological samples containing sperm cells from the assailant mixed with cells from the victim, it is possible to perform a differential analysis; however, this approach not always allows a complete separation of the two cell fractions. The differential extraction tends to fail when the fraction of sperm is very low, leading to a loss of sperm contained in the mixture (Gyllensten *et al.*, 1992; Kreike and Lehner, 1995). In other types of mixtures of body fluids from different individuals, such as blood/blood or saliva/blood, as well as in mixtures from rape cases committed by azoospermic individuals, differential extraction cannot be applied to separate male and female DNA portions. In these cases, when autosomal markers are used, the preferential amplification of the major component present in the mixture (usually the DNA of the victim) may mask or overwhelm the genetic profile of the rapist. In a mixture of male and female DNA, even in the presence of a low proportion of male material, additional genotyping of Y-chromosomal markers can provide a male-specific profile and help to distinguish between different male contributors in a mixture.

Compared to mtDNA, the Y chromosome has greater diversity, and in addition to biallelic SNPs and indels, there are many STRs that are available for forensic genetic and population studies.

Since paternal relatives will share the same Y-chromosomal haplotype, the forensic community has focused some attention on rapidly mutating markers located on the Y chromosome. It is expected that, due to higher-than-average mutation rates, these markers will provide a higher probability of distinguishing between closely related individuals and can complement current Y-STR analysis (Ballantyne *et al.*, 2014). The most recently released Y-STR commercial kits — PowerPlex®Y23 System (Promega) and Yfiler®Plus (ThermoFisher, Scientific) — already include some of these rapidly mutating markers.

Despite the wide use in forensics, Y chromosomal markers can present some statistical challenges in forensic casework. Due to lack of recombination, genetic data have to be treated as haplotypes, which present low population frequencies when a large number of loci are included. As a consequence, most population databases are mainly represented by very rare or unique haplotypes, making the statistical evaluation of genetic evidences highly dependent on the approach used to calculate match probabilities or to estimate rare or unseen haplotype frequencies in a population (Roewer *et al.*, 2000; Krawczak, 2001; Brenner, 2010, 2014; Andersen *et al.*, 2013; Caliebe *et al.*, 2015). The inclusion of some rapid mutating and highly polymorphic STRs in the new forensic kits, although increasing the probability of excluding false suspects, will accentuate the importance of sample size and coverage for an accurate statistical evaluation of the evidence in non-exclusion cases. Moreover, the use of STRs with very high mutation rates will dramatically increase the probability of observing somatic mutations in different tissues from the same individual, as well as to observe differences between paternally related individuals in kinship testing, and accurate estimates of locus/allele specific mutation rates become even more important for calculating LRs (Amorim, 2011; Pinto *et al.*, 2014).

4 DNA Markers

Before the development of PCR amplification, the first studies based on human variation relied on the information from blood group, protein and isoenzyme polymorphisms. This kind of markers had several drawbacks: they had the tendency to rapidly degrade, relatively low variability and informativeness and they required a (comparatively) large sample quantity (Jobling and Gill, 2004).

After the development of PCR, new DNA markers became available and the field of individual identification and heredity grew exponentially (Edwards *et al.*, 1991; Kimpton *et al.*, 1993; Steiper, 2010).

Genetic markers, or polymorphisms, are commonly defined as naturally occurring changes in the DNA sequence where at least two alleles have a frequency of more than 1% in the population.

Restriction Fragment Length Polymorphisms (RFLPs) were the first type of DNA variation to be applied to human identification (Gill *et al.*, 1985; Jeffreys *et al.*, 1985). Throughout the years, the advances and miniaturization of methodologies made it possible to use other types of genetic data.

Myriad DNA markers have been described for population genetic and forensic studies.

Markers with high mutation rates are very polymorphic and useful in population genetics, to study recent processes, and in forensic genetics, to distinguish between individuals. For the study of past events, slowly mutating markers are a more adequate choice, since mutation can overwrite many genetic signals (Schlotterer, 2000; Steiper, 2010). Taking advantage of their abundance in the genome as well as the ease of typing, slowly-mutating markers may also be used in forensic analysis, to infer the ethnical background of an individual, for instance, since a lower recurrence tends to produce allele frequency variations that are more geographically structured.

In order to use any kind of DNA markers in forensic and population genetic studies, there has to be a thorough assessment of several statistical parameters, not only to understand how the genome is organized, but also to correctly interpret and use the data. Parameters such as allele frequency distributions, mutation rates and power of discrimination, among others, have to be studied in order to guarantee the adequacy of using these markers in these fields.

4.1 Short Tandem Repeats, STRs

STRs are stretches of DNA sequences characterized by small repetitive motifs of usually 2–6 bps in length (Figure 2). The number of iterations is highly variable among individuals and average mutation rates are of around 2.1×10^{-3} (Brinkmann *et al.*, 1998), making them highly polymorphic. STRs occur in every region of the genome but the majority is located in non-coding regions (Ellegren, 2004).

It is widely assumed that STRs are generated by random mutations (Levinson and Gutman, 1987; Schlotterer, 2000) and that they gain and lose repeat units due to a process of DNA-replication slippage, a mutation mechanism specific to tandemly repeated sequences (Ellegren, 2000; Schlotterer, 2000).

According to the structure of the repetitive sequence, STRs can be classified into simple, compound or complex (Bar *et al.*, 1997). The structural complexity has consequences on the mutation rates and allele diversity.

The mutation model currently accepted provides an explanation on why microsatellites do not expand infinitely, assuming that two opposing mutational forces are operating. In one hand, length mutation contributes to further repeat expansion. On the other hand, longer STR alleles have an increased chance of point mutations breaking the original simple motif into smaller units with more complex substructures. Studies demonstrated that this mechanism serves as an evolutionary control that prevents the continuous growth/expansion of the STR (Ellegren, 2004).

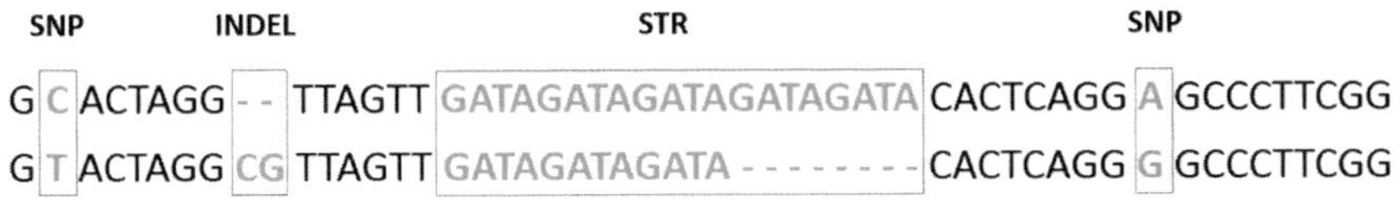

SNP	INDEL	STR	SNP
G C ACTAGG - - TTAGTT	GATAGATAGATAGATAGATA	CACTCAGG A	GCCCTTCGG
G T ACTAGG CG TTAGTT	GATAGATAGATA - - - - - - - -	CACTCAGG G	GCCCTTCGG

Figure 2:   Examples of different kinds of genomic markers: single base polymorphism (SNP), insertion/deletion (indel) and short tandem repeat (STR).

Replication slippage also can occur *in vitro* during PCR amplification and is responsible for creating 'stutter bands' — PCR products that are present in smaller quantities than the true allele and that differ in size from the main product by multiples of the length of the repeat unit. These PCR artefacts can sometimes complicate the analysis of STRs, especially in low-template or low quality samples, as well as in unbalanced mixtures from two or more contributors, but in the majority of situations they can be easily identified. Usually, STRs with four nucleotide motif units are sufficiently abundant and more stable and therefore, they have been preferred when designing the commercially available forensic kits. Although larger repeats could also be utilized due to lower stutter rates, they are not as abundant as tetrameric STRs and are also more difficult to fit in a multiplex, because of a large size range.

The analysis of STRs has become the method of choice when assessing genetic diversity in populations or to perform individual identification due to the high levels of intra-population diversity expected for these fast mutating loci and the ease of analysis and high throughput genotyping techniques where a large number of loci are simultaneously amplified (Table 2). PCR primers are fluorescently

Table 2: Comparison of the different types of DNA markers. Information is merely indicative (based on Goodwin *et al.*, 2011).

	STRs	SNPs	Indels
Frequency of occurrence	1 at every 15,000 bps	1 at every 80 bps	1 at every 7,200 bps
Average mutation rate	10^{-3}	10^{-8}	10^{-8}
Typical number of alleles	From ~5 up to 20	From 2 (up to 4)	2
Amplicon size for PCR	100bps-400 bps	~50 bps	~50 bps
Applications			
Individual identification	Yes	Limited	Limited
Ancestry inference	Limited	Yes	Yes
Phenotypic inference	No	Yes	Yes
Degraded samples	No	Yes	Yes

labelled and STR fragments are separated according to their size during capillary electrophoresis.

A vast number of STR loci has been described for human identification and commercial kits are currently available for STR typing in autosomes and the sex chromosomes. These kits have enabled the creation of standardized reference databases and allowed data comparison among labs, which ultimately will lead to better cooperation between national and international law enforcement agencies.

4.2 *SNPs*

SNPs are single nucleotide substitutions present in the genome (Figure 2). They are the most abundant polymorphisms, and make up around 85% of the human genetic variation. The latest count of human SNPs is circa 38 million (Genomes Project *et al.*, 2012), which corresponds to one SNP in every 80 base pairs, on average (Table 2).

Although in theory at each position of the DNA sequence, any of the four possible nucleotides can occur, the majority of SNPs is biallelic, which can be explained due to the low mutation rate of SNPs that renders the probability of two or more independent mutations occurring at the same exact position very low. Still, tri-allelic and tetra-allelic SNPs have been reported (Vignal *et al.*, 2002) and can be used in forensic casework to help to detect mixtures (Westen *et al.*, 2009).

Compared to STRs, SNPs are much more stable, with lower mutation rates (with a magnitude of approximately 10^{-8}, Nachman and Crowell, 2000). Therefore, they can be a valuable tool in kinship analyses or when lineage reconstruction is needed. SNPs also can be used when dealing with degraded samples or samples that have low amounts of DNA because they can be amplified and analyzed in shorter fragments than traditional STR methods.

Although SNPs are abundant throughout the genome, which is one of the advantages of this type of DNA marker, the analysis of SNPs has still not replaced STR genotyping, in part due to their lower power of discrimination per locus. The fact that most SNPs are biallelic decreases their informativity per locus and in fact, around 50 SNPs are necessary to get the same discrimination power as 12–15 STRs (Chakraborty *et al.*, 1999; Gill, 2001; Amorim and Pereira, 2005). Depending on the location in the genome and the differences in allelic frequencies between human populations, SNPs can be used in individual identification, phenotypic inference and ancestry or lineage studies (Budowle and van Daal, 2008).

Indeed, several SNP panels have been developed with different purposes. One of the most common panels, the SNPforID assay, focuses on individual identification and contains 52 autosomal SNPs (Sanchez *et al.*, 2006). This set of SNPs has been described as good complementary approach to standard STR genotyping in paternity testing (Borsting *et al.*, 2009) and several initiatives have been carried out in order to generate data from several populations (Borsting *et al.*, 2009; Phillips *et al.*, 2012; Schwark *et al.*, 2012).

4.3 *Insertion–deletion Polymorphisms, Indels*

Indels are length polymorphisms caused by insertions or deletions of nucleotides in the genome (Figure 2). Most of the indels are biallelic and around 3–15 bps, although indels of up to hundreds of base pairs have also been described (Mills *et al.*, 2006).

Studies have stated that indels may comprise between 16% and 25% of the total human variation, making them the second most abundant type of DNA polymorphisms after SNPs. It is estimated that the human genome might contain up to 2.5 million indels, with an average density of one in every 7,200 bps (Mills *et al.*, 2006) (Table 2).

In 2006, a study conducted by Mills aimed to report an initial map of human indels. Whenever possible, the study aimed to identify the ancestral allele in the chimpanzee genome. The results showed that insertions and deletions were equally common in the genome (47% insertions and 53% deletions in the human genome relative to the chimpanzee genome), leading to the conclusion that the mechanisms of insertion and deletion in the human genome have been occurring at similar rates since the last common ancestor of humans and chimpanzees, around six million years ago (Mills *et al.*, 2006).

Indels combine many of the advantages of SNPs and STRs, hence the increase in usage of indels markers in forensic and population genetic studies in recent years (Pereira *et al.*, 2009, 2012a, 2012b). Like SNPs, indels are abundant and stable markers with lower mutation rates when compared to STRs. The amplification of indels can be done in smaller fragments, increasing the success rate of DNA amplification in old and degraded samples, where traditional STR genotyping methodologies are not likely to succeed.

Compared to SNP genotyping techniques, however, the analysis of indels is less time consuming and can be carried out using the existing methods available for STR typing that combine fluorescence and capillary electrophoresis.

Despite their high occurrence in the genome, the interest in this kind of markers is very recent. The only commercially available kit for indel typing (Investigator DIPplex Kit; Qiagen), only launched in 2011, enables genotyping of 30 indels with small amplicon sizes.

Different working groups have developed panels for indel typing on autosomes and the X chromosome, and collaborative studies aiming to report allele frequencies in different populations worldwide have been carried out.

Autosomal data are starting to become available for European, African, Asian and Native American populations (Weber *et al.*, 2002; Yang *et al.*, 2005; Bastos-Rodrigues *et al.*, 2006; Pereira *et al.*, 2009; Santos *et al.*, 2010). Regarding the X chromosome, several panels have been published in the last few years: Ribeiro-Rodrigues *et al.* (2009) were the first to report a set of 13 indels, that afterwards was increased to 24 markers (Resque *et al.*, 2010) and finally, to 33 indels (Freitas *et al.*, 2010).

However, none of these panels are commercially available and most of the work to generate population data relies on the effort of the labs that developed these panels.

Somewhat related to insertion variations are NUMTs — DNA sequences homologous to mtDNA that are inserted throughout the nuclear genome (Zischler *et al.*, 1995). Some of these sequences are located in polymorphic loci and some authors have tried to address their utility in population genetic studies for reconstructing the history of modern humans (Lang *et al.*, 2012; Dayama *et al.*, 2014). In forensic genetics, these sequences gain even more importance: due to the homology with the mtDNA sequence, the amplification of NUMTs using specific mtDNA primers can sometimes produce confounding results, due to mistakenly analyzing these sequences when typing genuine mtDNA (Goios *et al.*, 2006, 2008; Dayama *et al.*, 2014).

5 Future of DNA Genotyping in Forensics

The development of next generation sequencing (NGS) methodologies over the last 10 years has made it possible to sequence whole genomes and many individuals in a single sequencing run, at a relatively low cost per base. After revolutionizing the field of clinical genetics, NGS is now taking its first steps into forensics.

Forensic genetic laboratories are starting to explore STR and SNP sequencing using NGS platforms (Seo *et al.*, 2013; Warshauer *et al.*, 2013; Dalsgaard *et al.*, 2014; Rockenbauer *et al.*, 2014; Van Neste *et al.*, 2014).

At the same time, commercial companies are working on the development of kits that combine all the DNA markers currently in use in forensics into one single multiplex.

In 2014, Thermo Fisher Scientific released two SNP typing assays for the Ion Torrent PGM™ System for human identification (HID-Ion AmpliSeq™ Identity Panel) and ancestry inference (HID-Ion AmpliSeq™ Ancestry Panel). These panels are able to sequence 124 and 165 SNPs respectively, in a single run. Data are analyzed with platform-specific software.

Illumina® is also on the race and has launched the ForenSeq™ DNA Signature Prep Kit in early 2015. The ForenSeq™ DNA Signature Prep Kit contains 29 autosomal STRs, nine X-STRs, 24 Y-STRs, 86 autosomal human identification SNPs, 56 autosomal ancestry informative SNPs and 22 autosomal SNPs associated with phenotypic traits. The ForenSeq™ DNA Signature Prep Kit will be released together with a new platform targeted for forensic genetics.

In principle, the application of NGS in forensics sounds promising and perhaps in the near future, NGS platforms will be part of forensic casework pipeline. Currently, however, there are still some challenges that have not yet been overcome.

Although the sequencing chemistry of the different platforms is more or less established and the simultaneous investigation of a great number of markers is now possible, one of the major challenges in the forensic field is to develop a sound analysis tool to report and interpret sequence data. The massive number of sequencing reads generated with NGS platforms makes the manual inspection and analysis of data virtually impossible.

The analysis software have to be thoroughly validated and accepted by the scientific community before they can be used in a real forensic context. Up to now, the solutions provided by NGS platforms have not met the forensic standards.

Moreover, sequencing of STRs will add a new level of discrimination between individuals, since besides the repeat number currently used in traditional electrophoretic methods, scientists will now have access to the actual structure of the repetitive region. This detailed information will be useful in mixture interpretation and individual identification, but the current reference STR databases used to assess the statistical weight of the evidence will not be informative for this level of molecular resolution and will need to be revised. New guidelines for allele nomenclature also will be needed and it might take a few years more until NGS methodology becomes a standard in the forensic field.

6 Conclusions

Genetic information can be retrieved from different kinds of genomic regions, allowing either the identification of paternal/ maternal lineages, or to discriminate between individuals at a more detailed level.

From the genetic information available, the choice of which markers to use will ultimately rely on the specific situation at hand. Beyond the simplest cases of kinship testing, combining markers with specific characteristics are located in regions with different transmission patterns (autosomes, mtDNA, Y chromosome and X chromosome) can help to address the more complex cases.

The forensic field is now heading towards the development of high-throughput sequencing methods where a great number of markers are simultaneously analyzed.

References

A. Amorim. A comment on "The hare and the tortoise: One small step for four SNPs, one giant leap for SNP-kind". *Forensic Science International: Genetics*, 5(4):358–360, 2011.

A. Amorim and L. Pereira. Pros and cons in the use of SNPs in forensic kinship investigation: A comparative analysis with STRs. *Forensic Science International*, 150(1):17–21, 2005.

M. M. Andersen, P. S. Eriksen and N. Morling. The discrete Laplace exponential family and estimation of Y-STR haplotype frequencies. *Journal of Theoretical Biology*, 329:39–51, 2013.

S. Anderson, A. T. Bankier, B. G. Barrell, M. H. de Bruijn, A. R. Coulson, J. Drouin, I. C. Eperon, D. P. Nierlich, B. A. Roe, F. Sanger, P. H. Schreier, A. J. Smith, R. Staden and I. G. Young. Sequence and organization of the human mitochondrial genome. *Nature*, 290(5806):457–465, 1981.

K. N. Ballantyne, A. Ralf, R. Aboukhalid, N. M. Achakzai, M. J. Anjos, Q. Ayub, J. Balazic, J. Ballantyne, D. J. Ballard, B. Berger, C. Bobillo, M. Bouabdellah, H. Burri, T. Capal, S. Caratti, J. Cardenas, F. Cartault, E. F. Carvalho, M. Carvalho, B. Cheng, M. D. Coble, D. Comas, D. Corach, M. E. D'Amato, S. Davison, P. de Knijff, M. C. De Ungria, R. Decorte, T. Dobosz, B. M. Dupuy, S. Elmrghni, M. Gliwinski, S. C. Gomes, L. Grol, C. Haas, E. Hanson, J. Henke, L. Henke, F. Herrera-Rodriguez, C. R. Hill, G. Holmlund, K. Honda, U. D. Immel, S. Inokuchi, M. A. Jobling, M. Kaddura, J. S. Kim, S. H. Kim, W. Kim, T. E. King, E. Klausriegler, D. Kling, L. Kovacevic, L. Kovatsi, P. Krajewski, S. Kravchenko, M. H. Larmuseau, E. Y. Lee, R. Lessig, L. A. Livshits, D. Marjanovic, M. Minarik, N. Mizuno, H. Moreira, N. Morling, M. Mukherjee, P. Munier, J. Nagaraju, F. Neuhuber, S. Nie,

P. Nilasitsataporn, T. Nishi, H. H. Oh, J. Olofsson, V. Onofri, J. U. Palo, H. Pamjav, W. Parson, M. Petlach, C. Phillips, R. Ploski, S. P. Prasad, D. Primorac, G. A. Purnomo, J. Purps, H. Rangel-Villalobos, K. Rebala, B. Rerkamnuaychoke, D. R. Gonzalez, C. Robino, L. Roewer, A. Rosa, A. Sajantila, A. Sala, J. M. Salvador, P. Sanz, C. Schmitt, A. K. Sharma, D. A. Silva, K. J. Shin, T. Sijen, M. Sirker, D. Sivakova, V. Skaro, C. Solano-Matamoros, L. Souto, V. Stenzl, H. Sudoyo, D. Syndercombe-Court, A. Tagliabracci, D. Taylor, A. Tillmar, I. S. Tsybovsky, C. Tyler-Smith, K. J. van der Gaag, D. Vanek, A. Volgyi, D. Ward, P. Willemse, E. P. Yap, R. Y. Yong, I. Z. Pajnic and M. Kayser. Toward male individualization with rapidly mutating y-chromosomal short tandem repeats. *Human Mutation*, 35(8):1021–1032, 2014.

W. Bar, B. Brinkmann, B. Budowle, A. Carracedo, P. Gill, P. Lincoln, W. Mayr and B. Olaisen. DNA recommendations. Further report of the DNA Commission of the ISFH regarding the use of short tandem repeat systems. International Society for Forensic Haemogenetics. *International Journal of Legal Medicine*, 110(4):175–176, 1997.

L. Bastos-Rodrigues, J. R. Pimenta and S. D. Pena. The genetic structure of human populations studied through short insertion-deletion polymorphisms. *Annals of Human Genetics*, 70(Pt 5):658–665, 2006.

K. E. Bendall, V. A. Macaulay, J. R. Baker and B. C. Sykes. Heteroplasmic point mutations in the human mtDNA control region. *The American Journal of Human Genetics*, 59(6):1276–1287, 1996.

K. E. Bendall, V. A. Macaulay and B. C. Sykes. Variable levels of a heteroplasmic point mutation in individual hair roots. *The American Journal of Human Genetics*, 61(6):1303–1308, 1997.

C. Borsting, E. Rockenbauer and N. Morling. Validation of a single nucleotide polymorphism (SNP) typing assay with 49 SNPs for forensic genetic testing in a laboratory accredited according to the ISO 17025 standard. *Forensic Science International: Genetics*, 4(1):34–42, 2009.

C. H. Brenner. Fundamental problem of forensic mathematics–the evidential value of a rare haplotype. *Forensic Science International: Genetics*, 4(5):281–291, 2010.

C. H. Brenner. Understanding Y haplotype matching probability. *Forensic Science International: Genetics*, 8(1):233–243, 2014.

B. Brinkmann, M. Klintschar, F. Neuhuber, J. Huhne and B. Rolf. Mutation rate in human microsatellites: Influence of the structure and length of the tandem repeat. *The American Journal of Human Genetics*, 62(6):1408–1415, 1998.

B. Budowle and A. van Daal. Forensically relevant SNP classes. *Biotechniques*, 44(5):603–608, 610, 2008.

A. Caliebe, A. Jochens, S. Willuweit, L. Roewer and M. Krawczak. No short-cut solution to the problem of Y-STR match probability calculation. *Forensic Science International: Genetics*, 15:69–75, 2015.

L. L. Cavalli-Sforza. The DNA revolution in population genetics. *Trends in Genetics*, 14(2):60–65, 1998.

R. Chakraborty, D. N. Stivers, B. Su, Y. Zhong and B. Budowle. The utility of short tandem repeat loci beyond human identification: Implications for development of new DNA typing systems. *Electrophoresis*, 20(8):1682–1696, 1999.

M. D. Coble, O. M. Loreille, M. J. Wadhams, S. M. Edson, K. Maynard, C. E. Meyer, H. Niederstatter, C. Berger, B. Berger, A. B. Falsetti, P. Gill, W. Parson and L. N. Finelli. Mystery solved: The identification of the two missing Romanov children using DNA analysis. *Public Library of Science One*, 4(3):e4838, 2009.

A. Collins and N. E. Morton. Likelihood ratios for DNA identification. *Proceedings of the National Academy of Sciences U S A*, 91(13):6007–6011, 1994.

D. Comas, S. Paabo and J. Bertranpetit. Heteroplasmy in the control region of human mitochondrial DNA. *Genome Research*, 5(1):89–90, 1995.

S. Dalsgaard, E. Rockenbauer, A. Buchard, H. S. Mogensen, R. Frank-Hansen, C. Borsting and N. Morling. Non-uniform phenotyping of D12S391 resolved by second generation sequencing. *Forensic Science International: Genetics*, 8(1):195–199, 2014.

G. Dayama, S. B. Emery, J. M. Kidd and R. E. Mills. The genomic landscape of polymorphic human nuclear mitochondrial insertions. *Nucleic Acids Research*, 42(20):12640–12649, 2014.

A. Edwards, A. Civitello, H. A. Hammond and C. T. Caskey. DNA typing and genetic mapping with trimeric and tetrameric tandem repeats. *The American Journal of Human Genetics*, 49(4):746–756, 1991.

H. Ellegren. Microsatellite mutations in the germline: implications for evolutionary inference. *Trends in Genetics*, 16(12):551–558, 2000.

H. Ellegren. Microsatellites: Simple sequences with complex evolution. *Nature Reviews Genetics*, 5(6):435–445, 2004.

N. S. Freitas, R. L. Resque, E. M. Ribeiro-Rodrigues, J. F. Guerreiro, N. P. Santos, A. Ribeiro-dos-Santos and S. Santos. X-linked insertion/deletion polymorphisms: Forensic applications of a 33-markers panel. *International Journal of Legal Medicine*, 124(6):589–593, 2010.

C. Genomes Project, G. R. Abecasis, A. Auton, L. D. Brooks, M. A. DePristo, R. M. Durbin, R. E. Handsaker, H. M. Kang, G. T. Marth and G. A. McVean. An integrated map of genetic variation from 1,092 human genomes. *Nature*, 491(7422):56–65, 2012.

P. Gill. An assessment of the utility of single nucleotide polymorphisms (SNPs) for forensic purposes. *International Journal of Legal Medicine*, 114(4–5):204–210, 2001.

P. Gill, L. Gusmao, H. Haned, W. R. Mayr, N. Morling, W. Parson, L. Prieto, M. Prinz, H. Schneider, P. M. Schneider and B. S. Weir. DNA commission of the International Society of Forensic Genetics: Recommendations on the evaluation of STR typing results that may include drop-out and/or drop-in using probabilistic methods. *Forensic Science International: Genetics*, 6(6):679–688, 2012.

P. Gill, P. L. Ivanov, C. Kimpton, R. Piercy, N. Benson, G. Tully, I. Evett, E. Hagelberg and K. Sullivan. Identification of the remains of the Romanov family by DNA analysis. *Nature Genetics*, 6(2):130–135, 1994.

P. Gill, A. J. Jeffreys and D. J. Werrett. Forensic application of DNA 'fingerprints'. *Nature*, 318(6046):577–579, 1985.

D. W. Gjertson, C. H. Brenner, M. P. Baur, A. Carracedo, F. Guidet, J. A. Luque, R. Lessig, W. R. Mayr, V. L. Pascali, M. Prinz, P. M. Schneider and N. Morling. ISFG: Recommendations on biostatistics in paternity testing. *Forensic Science International: Genetics*, 1(3–4):223–231, 2007.

A. Goios, A. Amorim and L. Pereira. Mitochondrial DNA pseudogenes in the nuclear genome as possible sources of contamination. *International Congress Series*, 1288:697–699, 2006.

A. Goios, L. Prieto, A. Amorim and L. Pereira. Specificity of mtDNA-directed PCR-influence of NUclear MTDNA insertion (NUMT) contamination in routine samples and techniques. *International Journal of Legal Medicine*, 122(4):341–345, 2008.

C. Gomes, M. Magalhaes, C. Alves, A. Amorim, N. Pinto and L. Gusmao. Comparative evaluation of alternative batteries of genetic markers to complement autosomal STRs in kinship investigations: Autosomal indels vs. X-chromosome STRs. *International Journal of Legal Medicine*, 126(6):917–921, 2012.

W. Goodwin, A. Linacre and S. Hadi. *An Introduction to Forensic Genetics*. John Wiley & Sons, New Jersey, 2011.

U. B. Gyllensten, A. Josefsson, K. Schemschat, T. Saldeen and U. Petterson. DNA typing of forensic material with mixed genotypes using allele-specific enzymatic amplification (polymerase chain reaction). *Forensic Science International*, 52(2):149–160, 1992.

A. J. Jeffreys, V. Wilson and S. L. Thein. Hypervariable 'minisatellite' regions in human DNA. *Nature*, 314(6006):67–73, 1985.

M. A. Jobling and P. Gill. Encoded evidence: DNA in forensic analysis. *Nature Reviews Genetics*, 5(10):739–751, 2004.

M. A. Jobling, M. Hurles and C. Tyler-Smith. *Human Evolutionary Genetics: Origins, Peoples & Disease*. Garland Science, New York, 2003.

M. Kayser and P. de Knijff. Improving human forensics through advances in genetics, genomics and molecular biology. *Nature Reviews Genetics*, 12(3):179–192, 2011.

C. P. Kimpton, P. Gill, A. Walton, A. Urquhart, E. S. Millican and M. Adams. Automated DNA profiling employing multiplex amplification of short tandem repeat loci. *PCR Methods And Applications*, 3(1):13–22, 1993.

J. L. King, B. L. LaRue, N. M. Novroski, M. Stoljarova, S. B. Seo, X. Zeng, D. H. Warshauer, C. P. Davis, W. Parson, A. Sajantila and B. Budowle. High-quality and high-throughput massively parallel sequencing of the human mitochondrial genome using the Illumina MiSeq. *Forensic Science International: Genetics*, 12:128–135, 2014.

M. Krawczak (2001). Forensic evaluation of Y-STR haplotype matches: A comment. *Forensic Science International*, 118(2–3):114–115, 2001.

J. Kreike and A. Lehner. Sex determination and DNA competition in the analysis of forensic mixed stains by PCR. *International Journal of Legal Medicine*, 107(5):235–238, 1995.

M. Lang, M. Sazzini, F. M. Calabrese, D. Simone, A. Boattini, G. Romeo, D. Luiselli, M. Attimonelli and G. Gasparre. Polymorphic NumtS trace human population relationships. *Human Genetics*, 131(5):757–771, 2012.

G. Levinson and G. A. Gutman. Slipped-strand mispairing: A major mechanism for DNA sequence evolution. *Molecular Biology and Evolution*, 4(3):203–221, 1987.

C. A. Linch, D. A. Whiting and M. M. Holland. Human hair histogenesis for the mitochondrial DNA forensic scientist. *Journal of Forensic Sciences*, 46(4):844–853, 2001.

M. Mikkelsen, R. Frank-Hansen, A. J. Hansen and N. Morling. Massively parallel pyrosequencing of the mitochondrial genome with the 454 methodology in forensic genetics. *Forensic Science International: Genetics*, 12:30–37, 2014.

R. E. Mills, C. T. Luttig, C. E. Larkins, A. Beauchamp, C. Tsui, W. S. Pittard and S. E. Devine. An initial map of insertion and deletion (INDEL) variation in the human genome. *Genome Research*, 16(9):1182–1190, 2006.

N. Morling, R. W. Allen, A. Carracedo, H. Geada, F. Guidet, C. Hallenberg, W. Martin, W. R. Mayr, B. Olaisen, V. L. Pascali, and P. M. Schneider. "Paternity Testing Commission of the International Society of Forensic Genetics: recommendations on genetic investigations in paternity cases." Paternity Testing Commission of the International Society of Forensic, *Forensic Science International*, 129(3):148–157, 2002.

N. E. Morton. Parameters of the human genome. *Proceedings of the National Academy of Sciences U S A*, 88(17):7474–7476, 1991.

K. Muller, R. Klein, E. Miltner and P. Wiegand. Improved STR typing of telogen hair root and hair shaft DNA. *Electrophoresis*, 28(16): 2835–2842, 2007.

M. W. Nachman and S. L. Crowell. Estimate of the mutation rate per nucleotide in humans. *Genetics*, 156(1):297–304, 2000.

S. Paabo. Ancient DNA: Extraction, characterization, molecular cloning, and enzymatic amplification. *Proceedings of the National Academy of Sciences U S A*, 86(6):1939–1943, 1989.

W. Parson, A. Brandstatter, A. Alonso, N. Brandt, B. Brinkmann, A. Carracedo, D. Corach, O. Froment, I. Furac, T. Grzybowski, K. Hedberg, C. Keyser-Tracqui, T. Kupiec, S. Lutz-Bonengel, B. Mevag, R. Ploski, H. Schmitter, P. Schneider, D. Syndercombe-Court, E. Sorensen, H. Thew, G. Tully and R. Scheithauer. The EDNAP mitochondrial DNA population database (EMPOP) collaborative exercises: organisation, results and perspectives. *Forensic Science International*, 139(2–3):215–226, 2004.

W. Parson, L. Gusmao, D. R. Hares, J. A. Irwin, W. R. Mayr, N. Morling, E. Pokorak, M. Prinz, A. Salas, P. M. Schneider and T. J. Parsons. DNA Commission of the International Society for Forensic Genetics: Revised and extended guidelines for mitochondrial DNA typing. *Forensic Science International: Genetics*, 13:134–142, 2014.

W. Parson, C. Strobl, G. Huber, B. Zimmermann, S. M. Gomes, L. Souto, L. Fendt, R. Delport, R. Langit, S. Wootton, R. Lagace and J. Irwin. Evaluation of next generation mtGenome sequencing using the Ion Torrent Personal Genome Machine (PGM). *Forensic Science International: Genetics*, 7(5):543–549, 2013.

R. Pereira, V. Pereira, I. Gomes, C. Tomas, N. Morling, A. Amorim, M. J. Prata, A. Carracedo and L. Gusmao. A method for the analysis of 32 X chromosome insertion deletion polymorphisms in a single PCR. *International Journal of Legal Medicine*, 126(1):97–105, 2012a.

R. Pereira, C. Phillips, C. Alves, A. Amorim, A. Carracedo and L. Gusmao. A new multiplex for human identification using insertion/deletion polymorphisms. *Electrophoresis*, 30(21):3682–3690, 2009.

R. Pereira, C. Phillips, N. Pinto, C. Santos, S. E. dos Santos, A. Amorim, A. Carracedo and L. Gusmao. Straightforward inference of ancestry and admixture proportions through ancestry-informative insertion deletion multiplexing. *Public Library of Science One*, 7(1):e29684, 2012b.

C. Phillips, M. Garcia-Magarinos, A. Salas, A. Carracedo and M. V. Lareu. SNPs as Supplements in Simple Kinship Analysis or as Core Markers in Distant Pairwise Relationship Tests: When Do SNPs Add Value or Replace Well-Established and Powerful STR Tests? *Transfusion Medicine and Hemotherapy*, 39(3):202–210, 2012.

C. Phillips, W. Parson, B. Lundsberg, C. Santos, A. Freire-Aradas, M. Torres, M. Eduardoff, C. Borsting, P. Johansen, M. Fondevila, N. Morling, P. Schneider, E. U.-N. Consortium, A. Carracedo and M. V. Lareu. Building a forensic ancestry panel from the ground up: The EUROFORGEN Global AIM-SNP set. *Forensic Science International: Genetics*, 11:13–25, 2014.

N. Pinto, L. Gusmao and A. Amorim. X-chromosome markers in kinship testing: A generalisation of the IBD approach identifying situations where their contribution is crucial. *Forensic Science International: Genetics*, 5(1):27–32, 2011.

N. Pinto, Gusmão L, Amorim A. Mutation and mutation rates at Y-chromosome specific Short Tandem Repeat Polymorphisms (STRs): A reappraisal. *Forensic Science International: Genetics*, 9 (1):20–24, 2014.

N. Pinto, P. V. Silva and A. Amorim. General derivation of the sets of pedigrees with the same kinship coefficients. *Human Heredity*, 70(3):194–204, 2010.

M. Prinz, A. Carracedo, W. R. Mayr, N. Morling, T. J. Parsons, A. Sajantila, R. Scheithauer, H. Schmitter, P. M. Schneider and G. International Society for Forensic. DNA Commission of the International Society for Forensic Genetics (ISFG): Recommendations regarding the role of forensic genetics for disaster victim identification (DVI). *Forensic Science International: Genetics*, 1(1):3–12, 2007.

R. L. Resque, S. Freitas Ndo, E. M. Rodrigues, J. F. Guerreiro, N. P. Santos, A. Ribeiro dos M. Santos, A. Zago and S. Santos. Estimates of interethnic admixture in the Brazilian population using a panel of 24 X-linked insertion/deletion markers. *American Journal of Human Biology*, 22(6):849–852, 2010.

E. M. Ribeiro-Rodrigues, N. P. dos Santos, A. K. dos Santos, R. Pereira, A. Amorim, L. Gusmao, M. A. Zago and S. E. dos Santos. Assessing interethnic admixture using an X-linked insertion-deletion multiplex. *American Journal of Human Biology*, 21(5):707–709, 2009.

E. Rockenbauer, S. Hansen, M. Mikkelsen, C. Borsting and N. Morling. Characterization of mutations and sequence variants in the D21S11 locus by next generation sequencing. *Forensic Science International: Genetics*, 8(1):68–72, 2014.

L. Roewer, M. Kayser, P. de Knijff, K. Anslinger, A. Betz, A. Caglia, D. Corach, S. Furedi, L. Henke, M. Hidding, H. J. Kargel, R. Lessig, M. Nagy, V. L. Pascali, W. Parson, B. Rolf, C. Schmitt, R. Szibor, J. Teifel-Greding and M. Krawczak. A new method for the evaluation of matches in non-recombining genomes: Application to Y-chromosomal short tandem repeat (STR) haplotypes in European males. *Forensic Science International*, 114(1):31–43, 2000.

J. J. Sanchez, C. Phillips, C. Borsting, K. Balogh, M. Bogus, M. Fondevila, C. D. Harrison, E. Musgrave-Brown, A. Salas, D. Syndercombe-Court, P. M. Schneider, A. Carracedo and N. Morling. A multiplex assay with 52 single nucleotide polymorphisms for human identification. *Electrophoresis*, 27(9):1713–1724, 2006.

N. P. Santos, E. M. Ribeiro-Rodrigues, A. K. Ribeiro-Dos-Santos, R. Pereira, L. Gusmao, A. Amorim, J. F. Guerreiro, M. A. Zago, C. Matte, M. H. Hutz and S. E. Santos. Assessing individual interethnic admixture and population substructure using a 48-insertion-deletion (INSEL) ancestry-informative marker (AIM) panel. *Human Mutation*, 31(2):184–190, 2010.

S. F. Schaffner. The X chromosome in population genetics. *Nature Reviews Genetics*, 5(1):43–51, 2004.

C. Schlotterer. Evolutionary dynamics of microsatellite DNA. *Chromosoma*, 109(6):365–371, 2000.

P. M. Schneider. Basic issues in forensic DNA typing. *Forensic Science International*, 88(1):17–22, 1997.

T. Schwark, P. Meyer, M. Harder, J. H. Modrow and N. von Wurmb-Schwark. The SNPforID Assay as a Supplementary Method in Kinship and Trace Analysis. *Transfusion Medicine and Hemotherapy*, 39(3):187–193, 2012.

S. B. Seo, J. L. King, D. H. Warshauer, C. P. Davis, J. Ge and B. Budowle. Single nucleotide polymorphism typing with massively parallel sequencing for human identification. *International Journal of Legal Medicine*, 127(6):1079–1086, 2013.

H. Skaletsky, T. Kuroda-Kawaguchi, P. J. Minx, H. S. Cordum, L. Hillier, L. G. Brown, S. Repping, T. Pyntikova, J. Ali, T. Bieri, A. Chinwalla, A. Delehaunty, K. Delehaunty, H. Du, G. Fewell, L. Fulton, R. Fulton, T. Graves, S. F. Hou, P. Latrielle, S. Leonard, E. Mardis, R. Maupin, J. McPherson, T. Miner, W. Nash, C. Nguyen, P. Ozersky, K. Pepin, S. Rock, T. Rohlfing, K. Scott, B. Schultz, C. Strong, A. Tin-Wollam, S. P. Yang, R. H. Waterston, R. K. Wilson, S. Rozen and D. C. Page. The male-specific region of the human Y chromosome is a mosaic of discrete sequence classes. *Nature*, 423(6942):825–837, 2003.

M. E. Steiper. *Human Evolutionary Biology*. Cambridge University Press, New York, 2010.

P. Sutovsky, R. D. Moreno, J. Ramalho-Santos, T. Dominko, C. Simerly and G. Schatten. Ubiquitin tag for sperm mitochondria. *Nature*, 402(6760):371–372, 1999.

R. Szibor. X-chromosomal markers: past, present and future. *Forensic Science International: Genetics*, 1(2):93–99, 2007.

R. Szibor, M. Krawczak, S. Hering, J. Edelmann, E. Kuhlisch and D. Krause. Use of X-linked markers for forensic purposes. *International Journal of Legal Medicine*, 117(2):67–74, 2003.

G. Tully, W. Bar, B. Brinkmann, A. Carracedo, P. Gill, N. Morling, W. Parson and P. Schneider. Considerations by the European DNA profiling (EDNAP) group on the working practices, nomenclature and interpretation of mitochondrial DNA profiles. *Forensic Science International*, 124(1):83–91, 2001.

C. Van Neste, M. Vandewoestyne, W. Van Criekinge, D. Deforce and F. Van Nieuwerburgh. My-Forensic-Loci-queries (MyFLq) framework for analysis of forensic STR data generated by massive parallel sequencing. *Forensic Science International: Genetics*, 9:1–8, 2014.

A. Vignal, D. Milan, M. SanCristobal and A. Eggen. A review on SNP and other types of molecular markers and their use in animal genetics. *Genetics Selection Evolution*, 34(3):275–305, 2002.

S. Walsh, F. Liu, K. N. Ballantyne, M. van Oven, O. Lao and M. Kayser. IrisPlex: A sensitive DNA tool for accurate prediction of blue and brown eye colour in the absence of ancestry information. *Forensic Science International: Genetics*, 5(3):170–180, 2011.

D. H. Warshauer, C. P. Davis, C. Holt, Y. Han, P. Walichiewicz, T. Richardson, K. Stephens, A. Jager, J. King and B. Budowle. Massively parallel sequencing of forensically relevant single nucleotide polymorphisms using TruSeq forensic amplicon. *International Journal of Legal Medicine*, 129(1):31–36, 2015.

D. H. Warshauer, D. Lin, K. Hari, R. Jain, C. Davis, B. Larue, J. L. King and B. Budowle. STRait Razor: A length-based forensic STR allele-calling tool for use with second generation sequencing data. *Forensic Science International: Genetics*, 7(4):409–417, 2013.

J. L. Weber, D. David, J. Heil, Y. Fan, C. Zhao and G. Marth. Human diallelic insertion/deletion polymorphisms. *The American Journal of Human Genetics*, 71(4):854–862, 2002.

A. A. Westen, A. S. Matai, J. F. Laros, H. C. Meiland, M. Jasper, W. J. de Leeuw, P. de Knijff and T. Sijen. Tri-allelic SNP markers enable analysis of mixed and degraded DNA samples. *Forensic Science International: Genetics*, 3(4):233–241, 2009.

M. R. Wilson, D. Polanskey, J. Butler, J. A. DiZinno, J. Replogle and B. Budowle. Extraction, PCR amplification and sequencing of mitochondrial DNA from human hair shafts. *Biotechniques*, 18(4):662–669, 1995.

N. Yang, H. Li, L. A. Criswell, P. K. Gregersen, M. E. Alarcon-Riquelme, R. Kittles, R. Shigeta, G. Silva, P. I. Patel, J. W. Belmont and M. F. Seldin. Examination of ancestry and ethnic affiliation using highly informative diallelic DNA markers: Application to diverse and admixed populations and implications for clinical epidemiology and forensic medicine. *Human Genetics*, 118(3–4):382–392, 2005.

H. Zischler, H. Geisert, A. von Haeseler and S. Paabo. A nuclear 'fossil' of the mitochondrial D-loop and the origin of modern humans. *Nature*, 378(6556):489–492, 1995.

CHAPTER 10

X Chromosome

Nádia Pinto

IPATIMUP, Institute of Molecular Pathology
and Immunology of the University of Porto/I3S, Portugal
CMUP, Center of Mathematics of the University of Porto, Portugal

Broadly speaking, forensic genetics are rooted on the estimation of kinship likelihoods and on the analyses of mixtures. Indeed, from identity to very complex pedigrees, what is at stake is generally the estimation of genetic proximity among individuals and/or samples. Interestingly, the theoretical study of X-chromosomal inheritance has been receiving greater attention from scientists focused on non-human populations, likely due to some animal species having few autosomal markers (such as Drosophila) or even none (such as honeybee, whose complete genome is haplo-diploid) (see for example Grossman and Eisen, 1989; Grossman and Fernando, 1989; Fernando and Grossman, 1990). The picture, however, has been changing and the use of X-chromosomal markers has been invoked as an added value, particularly in complex kinship cases at forensics. In this chapter, we will try to provide a global perspective on this topic.

In most mammals, the genome of females only differs from the one of males at one specific pair of chromosomes (heterosomes or gonosomal chromosomes — the 23rd pair, in humans). Indeed, normal females have two X chromosomes and males have one

X chromosome and one Y chromosome, being the other genetic information stored at pairs of homologous chromosomes (auto-somes) which recombine (i.e. exchange of genomic portions within pairs of chromosomes can occur) at both males and females.

In terms of genetic transmission, X chromosomes behave in a similar manner as autosomes in females, while in males the heterosomal pair of chromosomes does not recombine, except at small homologous regions at their extremities (the so-called pseudoautosomal — PAR — zones). For simplicity's sake, in the following when referring to the X chromosome, we mean only its specific, non-recombining part in males.

In females, X-chromosomal transmission occurs with one allele (out of two) per locus being randomly transmitted to the offspring (male or female). This transmission is, however, dissimilar in males, in which a nearly complete (PARs excepted) *en bloc* transmission of either the paternal X or Y chromosome, to each daughter or son, respectively, is observed (see Figure 1).

This mode of genetic transmission simplifies the statistical analyses for some kinship scenarios, particularly when the alleged father of a female is unavailable for testing, allowing more powerful results than those achieved with autosomes. Two paternal sisters, for example, should share the paternal X chromosome (such as a pair of paternal

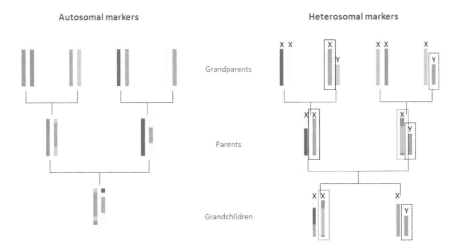

Figure 1:   Auto and heterosomal genetic transmission.

grandmother–granddaughter), so that Mendelian incompatibilities can be found in genealogies other than parenthood or identical twins, contrarily to what happens for autosomes.

On the other hand, from the point of view of clinical genetics, this lack of randomness in paternal transmission carries the drawback of genetic diseases or adverse traits linked to the X chromosome (such as haemophilia, Duchenne muscular dystrophy, Fragile X syndrome, or red–green blindness), having greater incidence than those linked to autosomes. Indeed, any daughter of a fertile male patient is carrier of the defective allele, which transmits with a half probability to any son she might have. The son will exhibit the characteristic due to the hemizygous state of the X chromosome in males.

A special feature of X-chromosome regulation of gene expression, first addressed by the Lyon hypothesis (Lyon, 1961) should be highlighted. This hypothesis posits that only one copy of X chromosome is active per cell. This chromosomal inactivation mechanism allows for X aneuploidies to be compatible with viable individuals. The most common numerically aberrant heterokaryotype is the X monosomy (corresponding to the Turner syndrome, with a prevalence of about 1 per 2000 live female births but of about 1 per 200 conceptions, most of them resulting in spontaneous and elective abortions) (Schoemaker *et al.*, 2008; Donaldson *et al.*, 2006; Iyer, 2012; Stratakis and Rennert, 1994) and the male heterokaryotypes XXY, XXXY, … (designated as Klinefelter syndrome, with a prevalence of over 1 per 500 live male births) (Bojesen *et al.*, 2003). Both are associated with higher infertility rates (parenthood being nevertheless possible through medical treatments and/or assisted reproductive procedures; see (Paduch *et al.*, 2009; Karnis, 2012) for example). On the other hand, females with X-chromosomal polysomies are likely fertile; particularly, trisomy seems to have no influence in this regard (Otter *et al.*, 2010). Regardless, individuals with abnormal X-chromosomal karyotypes are likely infertile and such unexpected genetic configuration in offspring will mislead kinship testing and should *a priori* be clearly identified in order to be appropriately considered in statistical computations.

Note, however, that all the theoretical framework presented in this chapter assumes the normal karyotypes of XX for females and XY for males.

1 X-chromosomal Relatedness: Theoretical Framework

Formally, two individuals are said to be kin-related if they can have copies of the same ancestral allele(s). Two alleles descending from the same ancestral allele are said to be identical-by-descent (or IBD) and, thus, simplifying, two individuals are said to be related if one allele of one can be IBD relative to one of the other alleles.

Indeed, the theoretical framework of relatedness is based on the concept of IBD, assuming that mutation breaks IBD and that it is considered some point in the past beyond which individuals are assumed to be unrelated. Note that two IBD alleles are, by definition, identical-by-state; however, the reciprocal is not true. Any genealogy linking a set of individuals is formally defined by a specific set of IBD probabilities, considering the several hypotheses for IBD patterns between and within the alleles of the individuals. Traditionally, such IBD patterns are graphically displayed as a set of points (or vertices, each one representing each allele of the individuals), which are linked by an edge if and only if they are assumed as IBD (Weir *et al.*, 2006).

The joint genotypic probabilities under the hypothesis of a specific genealogy only depend on the frequency of the alleles in the population and on the respective IBD probabilities. This implies that genealogies with the same IBD probabilities are undistinguishable through unlinked markers and are then said to belong to the same kinship class (see Pinto *et al.*, 2010b, 2011a, 2012d for autosomal and X-chromosomal markers, respectively). In these cases, other types of information, such as individuals' age for example, have to be considered in order to distinguish the various compatible genealogies.

1.1 *Theoretical Framework for Pairs of Individuals*

Considering the simplest case of a pair of individuals, the complete set of IBD patterns among their alleles, for the most complex case of autosomes, or for X-chromosomal markers in case of two females, can be represented through the four vertices of a square. In such IBD patterns, (a) the two top vertices of each square represent the alleles of one individual and the two at the bottom represents the two alleles of the other, and (b) two alleles are connected if and only if they are assumed as IBD (Weir *et al.*, 2006; Pinto *et al.*, 2011a).

1.1.1 Female–female pair

Assuming that it is not possible to discern maternally and paternally inherited alleles, for a pair of females there are nine IBD patterns (which are reduced to three if inbreeding is excluded) between and within their four alleles, such as for autosomal markers (see Figure 2). The joint genotypic algebraic expressions (depending on such IBD parameters and on the frequency of the alleles) are presented at Table 1.

Barring mutation, a 'mother–daughter' duo, for example, certainly share a pair of IBD X-alleles, as well as a duo 'paternal grandmother–granddaughter' or a duo 'paternal half-sisters'. Thus,

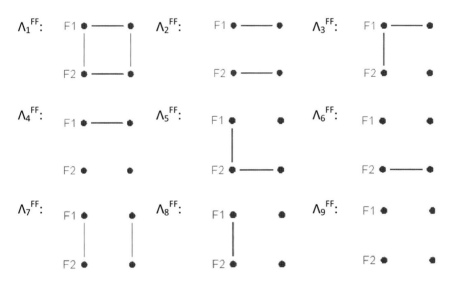

Figure 2: Complete set of identity-by-descent measures for one X-chromosome marker, considering two females: F1 and F2.

Table 1:   Joint genotypic probabilities for X-chromosome markers considering two females, the ordered genotypes of F1 and F2, the identity-by-descent probabilities Λ_t^{FF}, $t = 1,\ldots, 9$, depicted in Figure 2. The X-IBD probabilities x_t^{FF}, $t = 0, 1, 2$, represent the probability of a pair of non-inbred females sharing, respectively, none, one or two IBD X-alleles.

Genotypes	Joint X-genotypic probabilities for two females	
	General	Non-inbred females
A_iA_i, A_iA_i	$\Lambda_1^{FF}f_i + (\Lambda_2^{FF} + \Lambda_3^{FF} + \Lambda_5^{FF} + \Lambda_7^{FF})f_i^2 + (\Lambda_4^{FF} + \Lambda_6^{FF} + \Lambda_8^{FF})f_i^3 + \Lambda_9^{FF}f_i^4$	$x_2^{FF}f_i^2 + x_1^{FF}f_i^3 + x_0^{FF}f_i^4$
A_iA_i, A_jA_j	$\Lambda_2^{FF}f_if_j + \Lambda_4^{FF}f_if_j^2 + \Lambda_6^{FF}f_i^2f_j + \Lambda_9^{FF}f_i^2f_j^2$	$x_0^{FF}f_i^2f_j^2$
A_iA_i, A_iA_j	$\Lambda_3^{FF}f_if_j + (2\Lambda_4^{FF} + \Lambda_8^{FF})f_i^2f_j + 2\Lambda_9^{FF}f_i^3f_j$	$x_1^{FF}f_i^2f_j + 2x_0^{FF}f_i^3f_j$
A_iA_j, A_iA_i	$\Lambda_5^{FF}f_if_j + (2\Lambda_6^{FF} + \Lambda_8^{FF})f_i^2f_j + 2\Lambda_9^{FF}f_i^3f_j$	$x_1^{FF}f_i^2f_j + 2x_0^{FF}f_i^3f_j$
A_iA_i, A_jA_l	$2\Lambda_4^{FF}f_if_jf_l + 2\Lambda_9^{FF}f_i^2f_jf_l$	$2x_0^{FF}f_i^2f_jf_l$
A_jA_l, A_iA_i	$2\Lambda_6^{FF}f_if_jf_l + 2\Lambda_9^{FF}f_i^2f_jf_l$	$2x_0^{FF}f_i^2f_jf_l$
A_iA_j, A_iA_j	$2\Lambda_7^{FF}f_if_j + \Lambda_8^{FF}f_if_j(f_i + f_j) + 4\Lambda_9^{FF}f_i^2f_j^2$	$2x_2^{FF}f_if_j + x_1^{FF}f_if_j(f_i + f_j) + 4x_0^{FF}f_i^2f_j^2$
A_iA_j, A_iA_k	$\Lambda_8^{FF}f_if_jf_k + 4\Lambda_9^{FF}f_i^2f_jf_k$	$x_1^{FF}f_if_jf_k + 4x_0^{FF}f_i^2f_jf_k$
A_iA_j, A_kA_l	$4\Lambda_9^{FF}f_if_jf_kf_l$	$4x_0^{FF}f_if_jf_kf_l$

assuming non-inbred individuals, for these three pedigrees the IBD partitions are $x_0^{FF} = x_2^{FF} = 0$ and $x_1^{FF} = 1$ (see Table 2). Since these three pedigrees have the same IBD partitions, we can say that they belong to the same kinship class, and that they are then indistinguishable from the analysis of unlinked X-markers. This means that, resorting just to unlinked X-chromosomal information, a pair of samples belonging to a duo 'paternal half-sisters' involved in a mass disaster, for example, is indistinguishable from a pair of samples related as 'mother–daughter'. Under the assumption of independence, the likelihood ratio (LR) between these two hypotheses is theoretically equal to 1, which means that both alternatives are equally likely from the genetic point of view. On the other hand, two 'full-sisters', for example, certainly share the paternal IBD X-alleles, and the maternal ones will be IBD with half of probability for each marker. Thus the X-IBD partitions for this pedigree are $x_0^{FF} = 0$, $x_1^{FF} = x_2^{FF} = \frac{1}{2}$ (see Table 2). This pedigree is the only one with such IBD partitions and, thus, is always theoretically distinguishable from any other alternative pedigree (Pinto *et al.*, 2011a).

Table 2: IBD X-partitions for some genealogies linking two females.

Genealogies	IBD X-patterns

Mother–daughter

$$x_2^{FF} = 0$$
$$x_1^{FF} = 1$$
$$x_0^{FF} = 0$$

Paternal half-sisters

Paternal grandmother–granddaughter

Full-sisters

$$x_2^{FF} = 1/2$$
$$x_1^{FF} = 1/2$$
$$x_0^{FF} = 0$$

Note: Genealogies with the same IBD probabilities belong to the same kinship class. Full-sisters is the only pedigree with those specific IBD probabilities. The solid and dashed arrows are associated with probabilities of 1 and ½, respectively, for the allelic transmission.

1.1.2. Female–male pair

For a female–male pair, there are four possible X-IBD patterns (which are reduced to two if the female is assumed as non-inbred) between and within (at female) their three alleles (see Figure 3). The joint genotypic algebraic expressions are presented at Table 3.

A duo 'full-brother–sister' shares a pair of IBD X-alleles (necessarily maternally inherited) with probability of ½ and then: $x_1^{FM} = x_0^{FM} = ½$, as well as the 'maternal half-brother–sister' duo (see Table 4). Note that for a pair of 'paternal half-brother–sister', the IBD probabilities

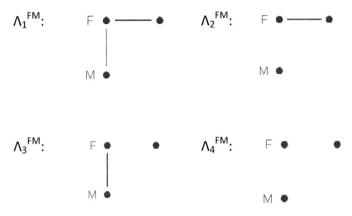

Figure 3:   Complete set of IBD measures for the X chromosome, considering a female F and a male M.

Table 3:   Joint genotypic probabilities for X-chromosome markers considering a female and a male and the IBD probabilities Λ_t^{FM}, $t = 1,...,4$, depicted in Figure 3.

Genotypes	Joint X-genotypic probabilities for a pair female/male	
	General	Non-inbred female
A_iA_i, A_i	$\Lambda_1^{FM}f_i + (\Lambda_2^{FM} + \Lambda_3^{FM})f_i^2 + \Lambda_4^{FM}f_i^3$	$x_1^{FM} f_i^2 + x_0^{FM} f_i^3$
A_iA_i, A_j	$\Lambda_2^{FM}f_if_j + \Lambda_4^{FM}f_i^2f_j$	$x_0^{FM} f_i^2f_j$
A_iA_j, A_i	$\Lambda_3^{FM}f_if_j + 2\Lambda_4^{FM} f_i^2f_j$	$x_1^{FM}f_if_j + 2x_0^{FM} f_i^2f_j$
A_iA_j, A_k	$2\Lambda_4^{FM}f_if_jf_k$	$2x_0^{FM}f_if_jf_k$

Note: The X-IBD probabilities x_t^{FM}, $t = 0, 1$, represent the probability of a pair non-inbred female–male sharing, respectively, none or one IBD X-allele.

Table 4: IBD X-partitions for some genealogies linking a female–male pair.

Genealogies	IBD X-patterns
Full brother–sister	$x_1^{FM} = \frac{1}{2}$ $x_0^{FM} = \frac{1}{2}$

| Maternal half-brother–sister | |

| Paternal half-brother–sister | $x_1^{FM} = 0$ $x_0^{FM} = 1$ |

Note: Genealogies with the same IBD probabilities belong to the same kinship class. The solid and dashed arrows are associated with probabilities of 1 and ½, respectively, for the allelic transmission.

are equal to $x_1^{FM} = 0$, $x_0^{FM} = 1$, as well as for unrelated individuals, since paternal X-transmission is interrupted at any 'father–son' transmission (see Table 4). This means that extra caution should be taken when X-chromosomal markers are used at situations where it is needed to discern unrelated individuals since, due to its mode of transmission, closely related individuals can be as unrelated from the X-chromosomal point of view.

1.1.3 Male–male pair

For a pair of males, there are two (trivial) X-IBD patterns between their two alleles (i.e. the alleles are IBD or not, see Figure 4). Note that, for obvious reasons, there are no inbred males in what concerns the X chromosome. The joint genotypic algebraic expressions are presented at Table 5.

Two 'full-brothers', for example, share with a half probability the (maternal) X-allele and, thus, $x_1^{MM} = x_0^{MM} = \frac{1}{2}$. On the other hand, a duo 'father–son' does not share IBD alleles and then $x_0^{MM} = 1$, $x_1^{MM} = 0$, as well as a duo 'paternal half-brothers' (see Table 6) or a pair of unrelated males. As for pairs female–male, when the aim is to discern related from unrelated individuals, the analysis of the X chromosome

Table 5:   Joint genotypic probabilities for X-chromosome markers considering two males and the IBD probabilities Λ_t^{MM}, $t = 1, 2$, depicted in Figure 4.

Genotypes	Joint X-genotypic probabilities for two males
A_i, A_i	$x_1^{MM} f_i + x_0^{MM} f_i^2$
A_i, A_j	$x_0^{MM} f_i f_j$

Note: For simplicity sake, we use the notation x_t^{MM}, $t = 0, 1$, representing the probability of two males sharing, respectively, none or one IBD X-allele.

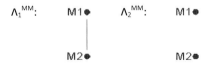

Figure 4:   Complete set of IBD measures for X chromosome, considering two males: M1 and M2.

Table 6: IBD X-partitions for some genealogies linking two males. Note that genealogies with the same IBD probabilities belong to the same kinship class.

Genealogies	IBD X-patterns
Full-brothers	$x_1^{MM} = \frac{1}{2}$ $x_0^{MM} = \frac{1}{2}$

| Father–son | $x_1^{FM} = 0$
$x_0^{FM} = 1$ |

Paternal half-brothers

Note: The solid and dashed arrows are associated with probabilities of 1 and ½, respectively, for the allelic transmission.

should be avoided due to the possibility of a father–son kinship within the linking pedigree. In these cases, the analysis of Y chromosome should be equated.

1.2 *Analyses of Larger Sets of Individuals*

The rationale behind the analysis of kinships linking more than a pair of individuals is entirely analogous to the one presented for the simplest case. In these scenarios, however, IBD patterns are established assuming the known relationships among individuals. As the number of individuals increases, also increases the complexity of the problem and, typically, computational tools are required to perform such complex analyses.

1.3 *Power of X-Chromosome Markers for Kinship Testing*

Traditionally, the utility or power of a marker (or set of markers) for kinship testing is measured through the probability of two random (unrelated) individuals having different genetic types: the so-called discrimination power or PD, or, alternatively, through the probability of two random (unrelated) individuals being excluded as being linked by a specific kinship accordingly with Mendelian rules of genetic transmission. When concerning paternity, this corresponds to the so-called exclusion power or PE, mean exclusion chance or paternal exclusion. Based in a somewhat historical reasoning these two parameters are, in fact, widely used in forensics, so much that they are, indeed, also known as "forensic parameters". The algebraic expressions for these statistics are presented next in the original formulation, denoting f_i the frequency of the ith allele from a total of n for a specific marker. All the statistics depend on the diversity and frequency of the marker alleles.

The power of discrimination is mainly related with stain analyses and the efficiency of the X-chromosomal markers depends, obviously, on the sex of the individuals.

For females' identification, the expected discrimination power is entirely analogous to the one expected for autosomes, since two alleles are also required to coincide at two random haplotypes. The algebraic expression for this statistic is given by (Desmarais *et al.*, 1998):

$$1 - 2\left(\sum_{i=1}^{n} f_i^2\right)^2 + \sum_{i=1}^{n} f_i^4. \tag{1}$$

On the other hand, X-chromosomal markers have lower power for the identification of males than autosomes, since two random haplotypes only have to coincide at one allele instead of at two. Nevertheless, of course that this statistic also depends on the diversity and allelic frequency of the markers and the algebraic expression is given by (Desmarais *et al.*, 1998):

$$1 - \sum_{i=1}^{n} f_i^2. \tag{2}$$

In what concerns the power of exclusion, formulae for autosomal markers were presented for both duos and trios (Ohno *et al.*, 1982). Equivalent expressions were later developed for X chromosomal markers assuming paternity testing with daughters (Desmarais *et al.*, 1998). If the mother is not available, the power of exclusion is given by the following algebraic expression:

$$1 - 2\sum_{i=1}^{n} f_i^2 + \sum_{i=1}^{n} f_i^3. \tag{3}$$

If the mother is available for testing, the power of exclusion is calculated through the following algebraic expression:

$$1 - \sum_{i=1}^{n} f_i^2 + \sum_{i=1}^{n} f_i^4 - \left(\sum_{i=1}^{n} f_i^2\right)^2. \tag{4}$$

Recently, it has been advocated that, since X-chromosomal markers are used for complex kinship cases when the alleged father is not available for testing, similar statistics for other kinship configurations, beyond paternity, in which it is possible to obtain Mendelian incompatibilities should be computed (Pinto *et al.*, 2013). For the case 'paternal half-sisters' when none of the mothers is available the algebraic formula is the same as for the motherless case of 'paternal grandmother–granddaughter':

$$\sum_{i=1}^{n} f_i^2(1-f_i)^2 + \sum_{i=1}^{n}\sum_{j=i+1}^{n} 2f_i f_j(1-f_i-f_j)^2. \tag{5}$$

As expected, the formula (5) is the same as the one for autosomal markers in paternity testing with duos, since all the cases comprise pairs of individuals with two alleles each, where the sharing of one pair of IBD alleles is mandatory and the only possibility.

For the case of 'paternal half-sisters', when one of the two mothers is available, the formula is the same as for the case 'paternal grandmother–granddaughter' when the mother is also available for testing:

$$\sum_{i=1}^{n} f_i(1-f_i+f_i^2)(1-f_i)^2 + \sum_{i=1}^{n-1}\sum_{j=i+1}^{n} f_i f_j(f_i+f_j)(1-f_i-f_j)^2. \tag{6}$$

Note that formula (6) is the same as for autosomal markers in paternity testing with trios. In fact, in all the cases it is questioned a relationship among two individuals, each one with two alleles, where the sharing of one pair of IBD alleles is the only possibility and the origin of half of the genetic configuration of the questioned child is known (through the undoubted mother).

Formulae for other cases (such as for 'full-sisters'–mother absent or not, and for 'paternal half-sisters' with both mothers available) are more complex and can be found at (Pinto *et al.*, 2013).

1.4 *Mutation Rates of X-Chromosomal Markers*

A mutation is a genetic phenomenon characterized by a change in the genome of somatic or germinal cells. In the case of germline mutation, an individual transmits to the offspring an allele not inherited parentally.

Indeed, mutations that occur in cells at the germinal line are susceptible of being transmitted to the offspring (in such cases a child can exhibit an allele different from any of their parents) and are those which are used to estimate the probability of mutational events relevant for kinship evaluation.

Mutation rates vary from one system to another, depending for instance on the type of markers and alleles and on the sex and age of the individuals. The very popular short tandem repeat markers (STRs) as well as larger repetitive motifs tend to be more prone to mutation than other, slower mutating loci (e.g. single nucleotide polymorphisms, SNPs), as well as males *vs.* females or older *vs.* younger individuals (Nachman and Crowell, 2000; Brinkmann *et al.*, 1998) (see however (Forster *et al.*, 2015), where no significant differences were found on mutation rates at teenager *vs.* ageing fathers). There is no evidence for the mechanism of mutation of X-markers to be different from that of autosomes or Y-markers, whose typical mutation rates are ~5 × 10^{-3} for STRs (see Nachman and Crowell, 2000, for example). Accordingly, in a large study considering 15 X-STRs, widely used in forensics, family data from several populations and more than 81,000 meiosis were analyzed and a mean mutation rate of 1.35 × 10^{-3} (95% CI, 1.1 × 10^{-3}–1.6 × 10^{-3}) was estimated (Diegoli *et al.*, 2014).

1.5 Haplotyping and Gametic Association

The immediate consequence of using syntenic loci (such as when several X-chromosomal markers are analyzed) is that the assumption of absence of gametic association is not generally met, which implies that the straightforward 'product rule', that allows the inclusion of any number of unassociated markers, cannot be applied. This association makes the likelihood calculations much more complex to compute, requiring the knowledge of parameters that are difficult to estimate accurately.

Broadly speaking, the two concepts responsible for the hardness of the statistical treatment of the genetic evidence provided by markers located on the X chromosome (or in other specific chromosome) are the concepts of linkage and of gametic association (or gametic phase disequilibrium).

Linkage is related with the physical location of the markers in the chromosome and can be defined as the absence of independent segregation of alleles at the considered loci, i.e. two alleles from different loci tend to be meiotically transmitted as a unit (with probability increasing with physical proximity). In fact, linkage between two loci can be expressed in terms of recombination fraction which is the probability of crossing over occurring between such regions of the chromosome. This genetic distance between loci is generally estimated from nuclear family data, and it is a parameter relating two loci, irrespectively of the involved allelic states.

On the other hand, the concept of gametic association (also known by the confusion prone designation of linkage disequilibrium, LD) is a population parameter (contrary to linkage) which can be defined by a non-random association of alleles at two or more loci in a specific population. Here it should be highlighted that, depending on the population under study, gametic association can exist between markers at different chromosomes or located far apart on the same chromosome (a fact particularly common in recently admixed populations). Conversely, closely linked markers do not necessarily show gametic association (see (O' Connor *et al.*, 2011; Wu *et al.*, 2014) for example).

A set of non-alleles (pairs, triplets, etc.) constitutes a haplotype, and when gametic association is found at the population haplotypic frequencies, rather than genotypic, are needed to be considered. In females, the X-chromosome specific haplotypes behave analogously as the autosomal counterparts and, resorting simply to the individual, it is not possible to discern which alleles were paternally or maternally inherited. A different situation exists, however, in males: either the haplotype harbors exactly (without recombination) the maternally transmitted haplotype or presents a 'null haplotype' in what concerns X-chromosomal evidence, corresponding to the Y chromosome.

The existence of gametic association is studied by comparing the observed haplotype frequencies with those expected based on allele data in the absence of association. If association is indeed observed, haplotypic frequencies can be established only from direct counting of population data, which implies that huge data sets are needed for accurate estimation of such parameters. Note that, in contrast to recombination fraction, any measure of gametic association is not a parameter relating loci, but alleles at these different loci, so that (with the single exception of a pair of bi-allelic loci), it is possible to find both gametic association and non-association between pairs of different alleles for the same loci.

Both recombination and mutation contribute to the reduction of gametic association. Thus, due to their moderately high mutation rate, STRs tend to exhibit weaker levels of gametic association than single nucleotide or insertion deletion polymorphisms. On the other hand, considering that X chromosomes only recombine in females, i.e. only two thirds of the chromosomal population are shuffled by recombination from one generation to the next, it is expected that the X chromosome will exhibit a greater degree of gametic association than the autosomal counterparts.

Szibor defined four linkage groups (see (Szibor, 2007) for a review), claiming that, when gametic association is found in the population, kinship analyses should be performed considering the individuals' haplotypes belonging to the respective linkage groups and treating them as four independent markers. Nevertheless, later findings (Tillmar *et al.*, 2008; Machado and Medina-Acosta, 2009) showed that some markers of the third and fourth linkage groups cannot, in fact, be regarded as independent.

Therefore, the treatment of the genetic information carried by the same recombining chromosome is a matter of great analytical and statistical complexity. This is particularly so when the pedigrees under consideration do not allow the inference of the haplotypic phase of the individuals. The number of possibilities which has to be considered for the calculations depends exponentially on the number of studied markers. Adding other sources of difficulty, such as the possibility of mutation for example, the treatment of such genetic information in a generalized framework becomes an extremely challenging problem with major importance in kinship testing.

2 X-Chromosomal Markers: Forensic Applications

X-chromosomal markers are particularly useful for kinship analyses with daughters when the alleged father is not available for testing. Here we will present some examples where X-chromosomal markers can complement, or even be the only solution, for the statistical treatment of genetic evidence.

Example 1

Consider that a geneticist is asked to weight the possibility of the female C to have the same father of her maternal sisters A and B. Under the hypothesis of full-sisterhood, females have to share at least the paternal X-allele while for autosomes incompatibilities are only found if more than four different alleles were observed. Powerful results are expected with the analysis of X-markers (see Figure 5).

Example 2

Consider that, after an abortion, female foetal material is collected for analysis. The woman has a mental disease and the possibility of incest is at stake. Some suspicions were raised that the mother was abused by her own father and brother. For the investigation, genetic material was collected from the woman and female foetus, and three hypotheses of kinship were considered: (a) the father is unrelated with the mother, (b) the father is also the father of the woman, and (c) the father is also the brother of the woman. Note that for hypothesis (a) the probability the child exhibits another allele is equal to the frequency of that allele in the population, for (b) and

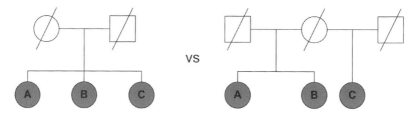

Figure 5: Genealogies involved in Example 1.

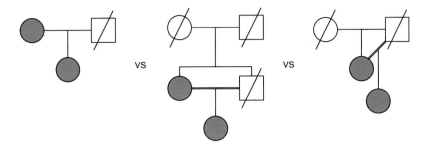

Figure 6:   Genealogies involved in Example 2.

(c) the same does not occur. Moreover, pedigree hypotheses (b) and (c) have the same autosomal IBD partitions associated and are, thus, indistinguishable by unlinked markers. This does not occur for X-chromosomal markers, since with a half probability it is expected that the mother will transmit a copy of the allele that foetus inherited paternally and, equally likely, it is expected both alleles of the foetus to be IBD relative to those of the mother (which transmitted the maternally inherited allele). On the other hand, for hypothesis (c), with one half probability the woman and the female foetus only share a pair of IBD alleles such as in the case of parents being unrelated (see Figure 6).

Example 3

In a shipwreck, three females (one mother and two daughters) disappeared at sea. Later, one female body was found and the only individual related with the three women that can be used for comparison in order to determine which female was (if, indeed, is one of the three) is the son of one of the two missing full-sisters. To test the hypothesis of maternity, powerful statistical results can be obtained with independent autosomes. Nevertheless, if maternity was not concluded, hypotheses 'grandmother–grandson' and 'aunt–nephew' should be tested. It is however proved that these two pedigrees (along with half-siblings) are indiscernible in the light of unlinked autosomes. In this case, the analysis of X chromosome is, indeed, crucial, since pedigrees only have different IBD partitions,

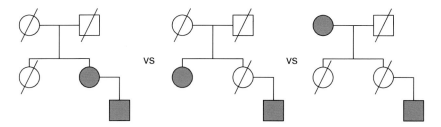

Figure 7: Genealogies involved in Example 3.

i.e. only are discernible, for such mode of transmission. Note that a duo maternal aunt–nephew has greater probability of sharing IBD X-alleles than a duo maternal grandmother–grandson since there is possibility of the aunt carrying the paternally inherited allele (see Figure 7).

3 Final Remarks

The use of X-chromosomal markers for kinship testing can be a powerful tool due to its dissimilar mode of transmission in males and females which implies: (a) the absence of randomness (unless mutation) in any link 'father–daughter', and (b) the loss of the X-chromosomal information in any link 'father–son'. In females, the X-chromosomal transmission occurs in the same manner as that for autosomal markers. This mode of genetic transmission leads to the same pedigree and has different measures of relatedness if analyzed from an autosomal or X-chromosomal point of view.

Generally, X-chromosomal markers are used as complementary information when inconclusive statistical results are reached with autosomal markers in complex kinship cases, but there are situations where their analysis is the only possible way to evaluate the involved pedigrees (cases where pedigrees belong to the same autosomal kinship class). Particularly powerful results are obtained when the kinships 'paternal grandmother–granddaughter' or 'paternal half-sisters' are involved, as well as in possibly incest kinship cases. Note that the possibility of two genetically close individuals who may be equated to unrelated (such as the case of 'father–son' or 'paternal half-brother–sister') cannot be seen as a drawback since it allows powerful conclusions when the alternative hypothesis is a pedigree with high probability of sharing IBD X-alleles.

Mainly due to their physically close location and lack of randomness from one generation to the next in, broadly speaking, one half of the cases, linkage and gametic association are major considerations for X-chromosomal markers. These features greatly increase the difficulty of computing kinship likelihoods. Great attention has been devoted to these topics by the scientific community but theoretical and computational developments are still needed to make possible, in a simplified and practical way, the management and computation of the data.

References

A. Bojesen, S. Juul and C. H. Gravholt. Prenatal and postnatal prevalence of Klinefelter syndrome: A national registry study. *The Journal of Clinical Endocrinology & Metabolism*, 88(2):622–626, 2003.

B. Brinkmann, M. Klintschar, F. Neuhuber, J. Huhne and B. Rolf. Mutation rate in human microsatellites: Influence of the structure and length of the tandem repeat. *The American Journal of Human Genetics*, 62(6):1408–1415, 1998.

D. Desmarais, Y. Zhong, R. Chakraborty, C. Perreault and L. Busque. Development of a highly polymorphic STR marker for identity testing purposes at the human androgen receptor gene (HUMARA). *Journal of Forensic Sciences*, 43(5):1046–1049, 1998.

T. M. Diegoli, A. Linacre, M. S. Schanfield and M. D. Coble. Mutation rates of 15 X chromosomal short tandem repeat markers. *International Journal of Legal Medicine*, 128(4):579–587, 2014.

M. D. C. Donaldson, E. J. Gault, K. W. Tan and D. B. Dunger. Optimising management in Turner syndrome: from infancy to adult transfer. *Archives of Disease in Childhood*, 91:513–520, 2006.

R. L. Fernando and M. Grossman. Genetic evaluation with autosomal and X-chromosomal inheritance. *Theoretical and Applied Genetics*, 80:75–80, 1990.

P. Forster, H. Carsten, B. Dunkelmann, M. Schürenkamp, H. Pfeiffer, F. Neuhuber and B. Brinkmann. Elevated germline mutation rate in teenage fathers. *Proceedings of the Royal Society B: Biological Sciences*, 282(1803), 2015.

M. Grossman and E. J. Eisen. Inbreeding, coancestry, and covariance between relatives for X-chromosomal loci. *Journal of Heredity*, 80(2):137–142, 1989.

M. Grossman and R. L. Fernando. Covariance between relatives for X-chromosomal loci in a population in disequilibrium. *Theoretical and Applied Genetics*, 77:311–319, 1989.

N. P. Iyer, D. F. Tucker, S. H. Roberts, M. Moselhi, M. Morgan and J. W. Matthes. Outcome of foetuses with Turner syndrome: A 10-year congenital anomaly register based study. *The Journal of Maternal-Fetal & Neonatal Medicine*, 25:68–73, 2012.

M. F. Karnis. Fertility, pregnancy, and medical management of Turner syndrome in the reproductive years. *Fertility and Sterility*, 98(4):787–791, 2012.

M. F. Lyon. Gene action in the X-chromosome of the mouse (Mus musculus L.). *Nature*, 190:372–373, 1961.

F. B. Machado and E. Medina-Acosta. Genetic map of human X-linked microsatellites used in forensic practice. *Forensic Science International: Genetics*, 3(3):202–204, 2009.

M. W. Nachman and S. L. Crowell. Estimate of the mutation rate per nucleotide in humans. *Genetics*, 156(1):297–304, 2000.

K. L. O'Connor, C. R. Hill, P. M. Vallone and J.M. Butler. Linkage disequilibrium analysis of D12S391 and vWA in U.S. population and paternity samples. *Forensic Science International: Genetics*, 5 (5):538–540, 2011.

Y. Ohno, I. M. Sebetan and S. Akaishi. A simple method for calculating the probability of excluding paternity with any number of codominant alleles. *Forensic Science International Genetics*, 19(1):93–98, 1982.

M. Otter, C. T. Schrander-Stumpel and L. M. Curfs. Triple X syndrome: A review of the literature. *European Journal of Human Genetics*, 18(3):265–271, 2010.

D. A. Paduch, A. Bolyakov P. Cohen and A. Travis. Reproduction in men with Klinefelter syndrome: The past, the present, and the future. *Seminars in Reproductive Medicine*, 27(2):137–148, 2009.

N. Pinto, P. V. Silva and A. Amorim. General derivation of the sets of pedigrees with the same kinship coefficients. *Human Heredity*, 70(3):194–204, 2010b.

N. Pinto, L. Gusmao and A. Amorim. X-chromosome markers in kinship testing: A generalisation of the IBD approach identifying situations where their contribution is crucial. *Forensic Science International Genetics,* 5(1):27–32, 2011a.

N. Pinto, P. V. Silva and A. Amorim. A general method to assess the utility of the X-chromosomal markers in kinship testing. *Forensic Science International Genetics,* 6:198–207, 2012d.

N. Pinto, L. Gusmão, T. Egeland and A. Amorim. Paternity exclusion power: Comparative behaviour of autosomal and X-chromosomal markers in standard and deficient cases with inbreeding. *Forensic Science International Genetics,* 7(2):290–295, 2013.

M. J. Schoemaker, A. J. Swerdlow, C. D. Higgins, A. F. Wright and P.A. Jacobs. Mortality in women with Turner syndrome in Great Britain: A national cohort study. *The Journal of Clinical Endocrinology & Metabolism,* 93:4735–4742, 2008.

C. A. Stratakis and O. M.Rennert. Turner syndrome: mMolecular and cytogenetics, dysmorphology, endocrine and other clinical manifestations and their management. Endocrinologist, 4:442–453, 1994.

R. Szibor. X-chromosomal markers: Past, present and future. *Forensic Science International: Genetics,* 1(2):93–99, 2007.

A. O. Tillmar, P. Mostad, T. Egeland, B. Lindblom, G. Holmlund and K. Montelius. Analysis of linkage and linkage disequilibrium for eight X-STR markers. *Forensic Science International: Genetics,* 3(1):37–41, 2008.

B. S. Weir, A. D. Anderson and A. B. Hepler. Genetic relatedness analysis: Modern data and new challenges. *Nature Reviews Genetics,* 7(10): 771–780, 2006.

W. Wu, H. Hao, Q. Liu, X. Han, Y. Wu, J. Cheng and D. Lu. Analysis of linkage and linkage disequilibrium for syntenic STRs on 12 chromosomes. *International Journal of Legal Medicine,* 128(5):735–739, 2014.

CHAPTER 11

Past, Present and Future of Forensic DNA Databases

C. P. (Kees) van der Beek

Netherlands Forensic Institute, DNA-database Department, PO Box 24044, 2490 AA The Hague, The Netherlands

1 Twenty Years of Forensic DNA Databases

Although there already were local DNA databases in the USA, the real development of national forensic DNA databases started in 1994 with the implementation and use of PCR-based multiplex STR typing systems. In that year, the former UK Forensic Science Service (FSS) launched its first multiplex STR typing system (Quad) consisting of the loci TH01, vWA, FES/FPS and F13A1 and Promega launched its CTT-Triplex consisting of the loci CSF1PO, TPOX and TH01. One year later, the FSS switched to the SGM-kit consisting of 6 loci + amelogenin. DNA profiles generated by these kits could easily be stored and compared and hence enabled the establishment of DNA databases.

In those days, we also saw the appearance of the first DNA laws because suspects could not be forced to take a DNA test as this was seen as a violation and breach of privacy. In 1994, the Netherlands and the USA approved their first DNA laws. These laws included the establishment of a DNA database. However, because of logistics, practical implementation took some time and did not happen until 1997 in the Netherlands and 1998 in the USA. The first national DNA database was established in the United Kingdom in 1995. Austria implemented its DNA database in 1997 and Germany followed in 1998.

The importance of DNA databases and their standardization to enable mutual comparison of DNA profiles was quickly recognized and in 1997 led the Council of the European Union to adopt a resolution (77/C 193/02) which called for the establishment of national DNA databases and the development of standards. Based on recommendations from the DNA Working Group of the European Network of Forensic Science Institutes (ENFSI) and formalized by means of EU Council resolution 2001/C 187/01 the European Standard Set of loci (ESS) became the standard for Europe in 2001. ESS originally consisted of 7 loci but was expanded to 12 loci in 2009 by Council resolution 2009/C 296/01. In the USA 13 STR-loci (Budowle *et al.*, 1988) were chosen by the FBI in 1997 to become the standard loci for the US CODIS National DNA database. In 2014, the FBI has expanded the CODIS core loci to 20 (Hares, 2015). In Figure 1, the present ESS and CODIS core loci are shown with the old standard loci in red.

Because the FBI also included the 5 new ESS loci in their new CODIS Core, all ESS loci are still part of the CODIS Core. An overview of other commonly used kits and loci can be found in the table of the ENFSI document on DNA database management[1] which is updated annually.

2 Basic DNA Database Principles

The main purpose of a forensic DNA database is to identify the donors of unknown crime related biological stains. So the database should contain profiles from both stains and known donors. For stains there are usually no legal inclusion restrictions but it is not

---

[1] http://www.enfsi.eu/sites/default/files/documents/enfsi_2014_document_on_dna-database_management_0.pdf.

Chromosome	Locus	ENFSI/European Union (ESS) Old	USA (CODIS core-loci) Old
1	D1S1656	+	+
2	D2S1338		+
2	TPOX		+
2	D2S441	+	+
3	D3S1358	+	+
4	FIBRA (FGA)	+	+
5	D5S818		+
5	CSF1PO		+
7	D7S820		+
8	D8S1179	+	+
10	D10S1248	+	+
11	TH01	+	+
12	vWA	+	+
12	D12S391	+	+
13	D13S317		+
16	D16S539		+
18	D18S51	+	+
19	D19S433		+
21	D21S11	+	+
22	D22S1045	+	+

Figure 1: Composition of the European Standard Set and the CODIS Core Loci.

very efficient to include stains from crimes of which the donors cannot be included in the DNA database. It depends on the law of a country if only convicted persons or also other type of crime associated persons like suspects and arrestees can be included in the DNA database. Other types of DNA profiles which may be included are (dead) victims of unsolved crimes and missing persons (if a crime is suspected). The reason for these inclusions is that matches with their profiles may assist in solving the crimes of which they are the victim. If for instance after some time a DNA profile from a blood stain found in a house matches a victim or a missing person, then people living in that house may know more about the fate of that victim or missing person.

Matches between DNA profiles of stains and DNA profiles of persons may occur after inclusion of a DNA profile of a stain if the person was already in the DNA database or after the inclusion of a DNA profile of a person if the stain was already in the DNA database. Sometimes, the latter happens only after many years and in those cases it may be difficult to find legally necessary additional evidence if the matching person has never been investigated before in relation to the crime. Matches between stains link crimes in which the same person has left his/her cell material. Especially in high volume crime cases (burglary, car theft, etc.), this can lead to big clusters of DNA profiles. If the DNA profiles of more than one person are found at a crime scene, some kind of cooperation may be assumed between these persons. If the DNA profile of one of these persons is found together with the DNA profile of a third person at another crime scene (and/or other traces), this information can be combined to visualize networks of crime scenes and criminals as shown in Figure 2.

3 Measuring the Success of a DNA Database

Matches between stains and persons identify people that may be involved in committing a crime. It is then up to the police to find the person and investigate his/her involvement in the crime and up to the judiciary to prosecute the person. Unfortunately, in most countries there is no feed-back of this process to the custodian of the DNA database, and hence there is no easy way to determine the contribution of a DNA database to the conviction of criminals and the solving of crimes. The only thing a custodian can do to show the effectiveness of the DNA database is to report the total number of matches that were found by means of the DNA database. Because a match between a stain and a person is equal to the identification of a possible suspect, politicians and policy makers may compare this way of identifying possible suspects to other ways the police have at their disposal to identify possible suspects. If DNA is the only thing that the police have found in an investigation of a crime, the DNA database is of course the only way to identify a possible suspect. By

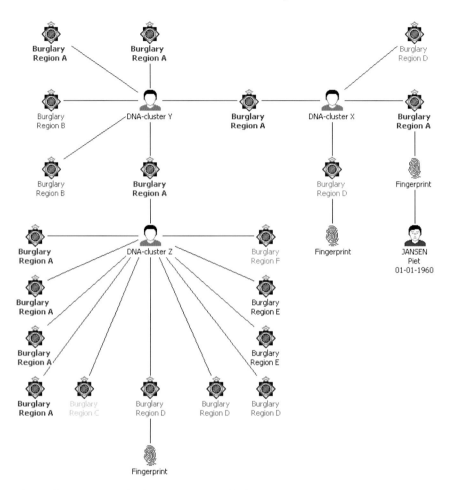

Figure 2: Three DNA clusters (X, Y, Z) linked by two crime scenes where DNA profiles from two clusters were found (X + Y and Y + Z) combined with two unidentified and one identified fingermark (from the ENFSI document on DNA-database management).

estimating the total (annual) costs of a running DNA database operation and dividing it by the number of stain to person matches, one can even calculate the cost of a DNA database derived identification and hence its efficiency as compared to other identification methods for possible suspects.

The efficiency of the DNA database itself can be measured by looking at two parameters:

- *The percentage of stains that matches a person.*
  This parameter sometimes is called the "hit-rate" and can be subdivided in a percentage of stains that immediately matches a person when they are added to the DNA database and a percentage of stains that matches a person after some time when the person is added to the DNA database. In the UK, the hit-rate was over 60% in the reporting year 2012/2013.[2] The hit-rate grows during the first 10–20 years after the establishment of a DNA database because many new criminally active persons are added in that period but then levels off because in theory all (or the vast majority) persons that can give matches are in the DNA database or are added to the DNA database. The hit-rate will then be determined by the percentage of stains that do not match a person because either they are not crime related or the matching person has not yet qualified for DNA database inclusion.

- *The percentage of persons that matches one or more stains.*
  This parameter indicates for which percentage of the persons in the DNA database the inclusion of their DNA profiles was a good investment. Unfortunately, it is not possible to reliably determine in advance which persons will give matches and which ones will not. That is why persons are added to the DNA database as a precaution. It is a one-time investment which will pay off if the person matches a stain.

The proper calculation of these parameters depends on the proper counting of numbers of profiles and matches. When DNA profiles of persons and/or stains are removed from the DNA database, historical data should be kept to enable to determine the number of profiles that were ever added to the DNA database. Also match counting requires attention. If two profiles have matched

---

[2]Annual Report UK National DNA-database 20122013, page 11, https://www.gov.uk/government/publications/national-dna-database-annual-report-2012-to-2013.

each other and a third profile matches these two profiles, three matches will be saved in the DNA database. If on successive dates X profiles match each other, the total number of saved matches is $(X-1)X/2$. For 10 matching profiles, this results in 45 saved matches. Because these numbers are not representative in relation to the number of cases involved, ENFSI has recommended that the number of matches should be equal to the number of matching profiles minus 1.[3] So a cluster of 10 matching profiles will be counted as 9 matches. This calculation, however, requires a proper administration of how many profiles have ever matched each other and can be done by giving all matching DNA profiles the same unique cluster number. Also, when a person profile is added to the DNA database and it matches nine stain profiles that have matched each other before, the original eight stain-to-stain matches should be removed from the statistics and replaced by 9 stain-to-person matches.

4 Preventing Errors

For obvious reasons, DNA profiles should be entered and stored correctly in a DNA database. Therefore, properly validated database software and automated ways of importing the profiles should be used. Manual entry of DNA profiles should be avoided or should be done by the double blind method (which the same manner as is used for entering a new password). Despite these measures, DNA profiles occasionally may contain errors as a result of:

* Allelic drop-ins or drop-outs.
* Allele calling errors.
* Primer binding site mutation differences between commercial kits.
* Mixture deconvolution errors made by DNA analysts.

As a result of such errors, matches may be missed (false negative matches or false exclusions). To find these errors, regular searches

---

[3] http://www.enfsi.eu/sites/default/files/documents/enfsi_dna_wg_terms_and_abbreviations_0.pdf.

should be conducted allowing one or more mismatches between two DNA profiles. The DNA profiles participating in such matches should then be investigated to find out if a mistake has been made during their production and/or processing. The acceptance of one mismatch is part of the default search configuration of the European countries which exchange DNA profiles under the terms of the EU-Prüm-Council-decisions.[4]

Another issue is adventitious or false positive matches (matches between profiles which come from different persons). When DNA databases become larger or when more DNA databases are searched like in European Union, the chance of finding adventitious matches increases, especially with partial and mixed profiles. In Europe where profiles in DNA databases are compared among countries, and (for political reasons) even matches on six loci may be returned, adventitious matches frequently occur. In the Netherlands, over 500 international six and seven locus matches were subjected to additional DNA testing to find out if the matches were adventitious hits or not. In addition, the Random Match Probability (RMP) of the matching loci was calculated (before the additional DNA testing). Six percent of the 7-locus matches and 62% of the 6-locus matches proved to be adventitious. In Figure 3, the RMPs of the matches are shown. As expected, there are no clear thresholds which determine if a six or seven locus match will be false positive or not. The only thing one can say is that until now six locus matches with an RMP less than 1 in 1 billion and seven locus matches with an RMP less than 1 in 10 billion have not yet found to be false positive. However this may change in the future because apart from the RMP, the expected number of adventitious matches in a certain time period also is dependent on the size(s) of the searched DNA database(s) and the number of searches in that period. Because more European DNA databases will be connected and all these DNA databases continue to grow, also the expected number of adventitious matches will increase. However, as long as custodians of DNA databases are aware of the phenomenon and take appropriate actions to prevent

---

[4]2008/615/JHA and 2008/616/JHA.

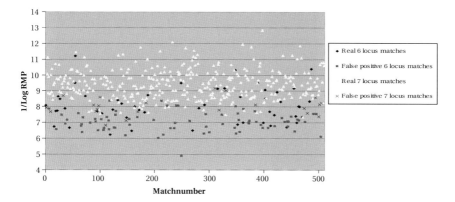

Figure 3: Random match probability (RMP) of real and false negative 6 and 7 locus matches obtained by the Dutch DNA-database team during the international exchange of DNA-profiles with other European countries.

the uninformed use of such matches, they can be processed. On the contrary, 62% false positive matches also mean 38% correct matches. It only takes some extra work to find them. So one may choose to further investigate such matches, only if they are stain-to-person matches and/or the stain comes from a more serious case.

5 Future Developments

Twenty years have passed since the growth of forensic DNA databases started. In the USA, all states are connected now to the NDIS level of CODIS. In the European Union (EU), however, there are still countries which do not have a DNA database and/or DNA database legislation in spite of the fact that in 2008 the former Treaty of Prüm was converted in EU-legislation which obliges each EU-member state to establish a DNA database and to enable automated searches by other member states. The main reason for this delay is that in a number of countries existing legislation had to be adjusted or new legislation had to be written. When this chapter was finalized (March 2016), 22 of the 28 EU-member states already were comparing DNA profiles with one or more other EU-member states. Apart from the 28 EU-member states Norway, Iceland, Switzerland and

Liechtenstein are allowed to join the Prüm operation and Norway and Iceland have already obtained permission from the EU to do so. So within a few years, the DNA databases of at least 30 European countries will be connected to each other and perhaps some of them also will be connected to the USA DNA database as the USA has signed Prüm-like treaties with several European countries as a condition for those countries to stay in the so-called Visa-Waiver-Program. These treaties are called PCSC-treaties (Prevention and Combatting Serious Crime).[5] However, to enable the implementation of the DNA part of these treaties, the Federal DNA act of 1994 has to be adjusted. Recently a proposal to adjust this act was sent to the House of Representatives but this proposal only deals with the introduction of Rapid DNA Technology.

The use of Rapid DNA technology will increase substantially in the coming years, especially in the USA where Rapid DNA machines are expected to appear in all booking stations of the police to enable them to quickly generate a DNA profile of arrestees and suspects and search these profiles to the national DNA database to see if there is (another) reason to keep the person in custody. As already mentioned in the previous paragraph, a proposal to change the Federal DNA act of 1994 has been sent to the House of Representatives to create the legal grounds for these plans. Next to this, a megaproject led by the FBI has started to implement the real time connection of these machines to the DNA database as well as the processes to verify if a person is already on the DNA database and if not, to generate a DNA profile and to process the match results.

Next generation sequencing (NGS) will be used as an adjunct to (or may even replace if and when it becomes cost effective) capillary electrophoresis (CE) as a technology to determine the alleles of STR DNA profiles. The present nomenclature of these alleles is based on the PCR-produced fragment length of the alleles. Both traditional sequencing and NGS have shown, however, that alleles of the same length may differ in their sequence, which from a genetic point of

---

[5] http://itlaw.wikia.com/wiki/Agreement_on_Preventing_and_Combating_ Serious_Crime.

view makes them different alleles (Zeng *et al.*, 2014; Warshauer *et al.*, 2015). When NGS becomes the preferred technology there may be several consequences:

- A new nomenclature will have to be developed and DNA database software programs (like CODIS) will have to be modified to allow the inclusion of the new alleles and ensure that the new nomenclature can "match" the nominal length allele nomenclature. Considerations on minimal nomenclature requirements for massively parallel sequencing of forensic STRs have recently been published by the DNA Commission of the International Society for Forensic Genetics (ISFG) (Parson *et al.*, 2016).
- The evidential value of DNA profiles will increase because Random Match Probabilities (RMP) will go down due to lower allele frequencies of alleles that are subdivided by different sequence variants. Familial searches in DNA databases usually result in many possible candidates most (or all) of which are false positives. If the RMP decreases, also the number possible candidates from a familial search will decrease which may reduce the need for additional autosomal and/or Y-chromosomal and/or mitochondrial DNA testing to eliminate the false positive matches.
- Mixtures will be easier to analyze because some loci will have more alleles than can be found with CE. The mixture shown in Figure 4 has three different compositions if determined by CE: 13/14 + 13/16 or 13/14 + 14/16 or 13/14 + 16/16. However if allele 14 shows a composition of 80% 14A + 20% 14B by NGS, then there is only one possibility to explain the mixture: 13/14A + 14B/16.

An additional advantage of NGS is that identical twins may be distinguished from each other because it can detect the rare somatic mutations that occur early after the human blastocyst has split in two and which are carried on into somatic tissue and the germ line (Weber-Lehman *et al.*, 2014). Until recently, identical twins could not be distinguished readily by their DNA profiles and many identical twins have escaped conviction because it could not be proven who committed the crime. Although, still costly NGS now makes it feasible to discriminate between identical twins.

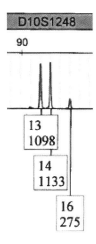

Figure 4:   Two person mixture at locus D10S1248.

Several programs (e.g. True Allele, STRmix, LRmix) have been developed to compare DNA profiles of reference samples with complex mixed profiles with possible allelic drop-ins and drop-outs and to calculate the likelihood ratio (LR) that the reference profile is included in the mixture. Work is in progress (Bleka *et al.*, 2013; Bright *et al.*, 2013) to adjust these programs to compare a complex mixed profile with all reference samples of a DNA database and to produce a shortlist of reference samples with the highest LR that the reference profile is included in the mixture. In this way, a list with names of possible contributors to the mixed profile can be obtained which can be used by the police to investigate if they may have been involved in the crime from which the complex mixed profile was obtained.

In conclusion, DNA databases have been a boon to assisting police by developing investigative leads and also have been used to exonerate individuals by pointing to other donors. Direct matching and indirect matching (i.e. familial searching) have helped solve many crimes where no suspect initially was identified. With continued developments in molecular biology, it is anticipated that more value can be gleaned from this valuable law enforcement asset.

References

Ø. Bleka, G. Dørum, H. Haned and P. Gill. Database extraction strategies for low-template evidence. *Forens. Sci. Int. Genet.*, 9:93–101, 2013.

J.-A. Bright, D. Taylor, J. Curran and J. Buckleton. Searching mixed DNA profiles directly against profile databases. *Forens. Sci. Int. Genet.*, 9:102–110, 2013.

B. Budowle *et al.* CODIS and PCR-based short tandem repeat loci: law enforcement tools. *Proceedings of the Second European Symposium on Human Identification*, Promega Corporation, Madison, WI, 73–88, 1988.

D. R. Hares. *Forensic Science International: Genetics*, Selection and implementation of expanded CODIS core loci in the United States, 17:33–34, 2015.

W. Parson *et al.* "http:/www.sciencedirect.com/science/article/pii/S18724973 16300096" \t "_blank" Massively parallel sequencing of forensic STRs: Considerations of the DNA commission of the International Society for Forensic Genetics (ISFG) on minimal nomenclature requirements. *Forens. Sci. Int. Genet.* 22:54, 2016.

D. H. Warshauer, J. L. King and B. Budowle. STRait Razor v2.0: The improved STR allele identification tool — razor. *Forens. Sci. Int. Genet.*, 14:182–186, 2015.

J. Weber-Lehman, E. Schilling, G. Gradl, C. Richter, J. Wiehler and B. Rolf. Finding the needle in the haystack: Differentiating "identical" twins in paternity testing and forensics by ultra-deep next generation sequencing. *Forens. Sci. Int. Genet.*, 9:42–46, 2014.

X. Zeng, J. L. King, M. Stoljarova, D. H. Warshauer, B. L. LaRue, A. Sajantila, J. Patel, D. R. Storts and B. Budowle. High sensitivity multiplex short tandem repeat loci analyses with massively parallel sequencing. *Forens. Sci. Int. Genet.*, 16C:38–47, 2014.

CHAPTER 12

The Y-Chromosome Haplotype Reference Database (YHRD) — Publicly Available Reference and Research Datasets for the Forensic Interpretation of Y-Chromosome STR Profiles

Lutz Roewer

Department of Forensic Genetics,
Institute of Legal Medicine and Forensic Sciences,
Charité — Universitätsmedizin Berlin, Germany

1 Introduction

Anyone who was involved in the development of the forensic Y chromosome short tandem repeat (STR) analysis would agree that this is an especially hard-won method. In contrast to autosomal STRs, the Y-chromosome haplotyping method is not routinely applicable to all kinds of forensic cases, but has shown its value mainly for sexually motivated crime where the minor male proportion of DNA mixtures frequently escapes standard analyses (Roewer, 2009; McDonald *et al.*, 2015). Only recently, the method has gained attention in the field of forensic intelligence, e.g. for prediction of deep-rooting geographic ancestry (Wetton *et al.*, 2005; Geppert *et al.*, 2010) and familial searching (Maguire *et al.*, 2013). Second, Y-STRs are not included in the standard marker set of police data-bases to which the majority of forensic labs have adjusted (and often restricted) their methodological spectrum. Third, the inter-pretation of a Y-STR profile match is different from autosomal markers where the match probability can be split into single-marker factors which are assumed not to be in linkage equilibrium (Caliebe *et al.*, 2015). Concepts which have been successfully developed in the early 90s for autosomal markers, namely the product rule, fail to work for Y-chromosome haplotypes each of which is a leaf at the human family tree, identical to some, similar to many, dissimilar to the most. Only mutation, not recombination or new assortment of variants in every new generation, creates the appreciable genetic dif-ferentiation among Y chromosomes. The variants are, however, not evenly distributed but are highly stratified among and within conti-nents. Geographic distance has a strong effect on the variance of Y haplotypes, but also residence patterns and linguistic affiliations. The genetic, demographic and cultural influences that have created a topology of tightly related, gradually radiating or sharply separated clusters of Y-chromosomal profiles, is not easy to disentangle. The freely available Y-Chromosome Haplotype Reference Database (YHRD) which is the subject of this chapter aims to contribute empirical data to decipher the Y-specific population differentiation and quantify its effects on the frequency estimation process.

At the very beginning of this project, the idea to deliver ade-quate statistical parameters for a whole chromosome aiming to qualify it as a standard DNA tool in forensic practice appeared in the best case as purely academic and was consequently regarded with trepidation by forensic practitioners. The argument was that statis-tics would not be necessary for a polymorphic DNA system which has relevance only for exclusions because its discriminative power, due to its inheritance mode, is too low to separate all male individu-als. However, in the middle of the 1990s, when a small group of European university institutes started an initiative to sample data to analyze the real proportions of shared/non-shared Y chromosome profiles consisting of the then available Y markers in a given population, the feedback was encouraging. For the first multicenter study, we received 3,825 haplotypes typed in 48 populations for up to 13 STRs (Kayser *et al.*, 1997). The accompanying article describing the population genetics aspects of Y chromosome inheritance provides first insights into the comparably large genetic distances between populations typed for YSTRs (de Knijff *et al.*, 1997), a phenomenon which has been better understood since then. Three years later, in June 2000, when the haplotype collections went online under the name YHRD (http://yhrd.org) the count increased to 18,050 haplotypes (Roewer *et al.*, 2001). Since then, the YHRD grows continuously and has now more than 143,000 haplotypes representing 940 populations from all continents (Willuweit and Roewer, 2015) (Figure 1). In geographic terms, about 39% of the YHRD samples are from Europe, 32% from Asia, 16% from South America, 6% from North America, 4% from Africa and 2% from Oceania/

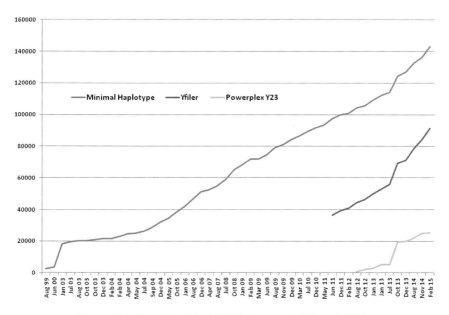

Figure 1:   Growth of the YHRD between 2000 and 2015.

Australia. With such a global database at hand, it can now be demonstrated that match probabilities for large marker sets are generally low and a probabilistic approach to allow an inclusion hypothesis is feasible. Accordingly, the Y-STR method grew out of its initial application as a sole exclusion tool and proved of value as a supplementary method in forensic identification cases. The YHRD is still a very active research project involving hundreds of researchers and forensic analysts around the world and is widely regarded to be the most comprehensive source of information of its kind. The principal function of the YHRD is the generation of frequency estimates for selected datasets and reference populations aiming to add evidentiary weight to a match of Y-STR profiles. The YHRD also provides standard reference datasets for use in the further development and evaluation of sensible and efficient methods for the match probability calculation.

2 Data Sources and Sampling Strategy

The database currently consists of five datasets. Datasets are collections of haplotypes which are defined for a certain set of Y-STR markers (see Table 1) and might therefore be part of other, bigger datasets. The sets available at YHRD are currently fixed and may change only with new database versions. Each result at YHRD is relative to the size and composition of the selected dataset. The most up-to-date commercial kits with 23 and 27 Y-STR markers represent two of the five datasets. Concerning the data sources, the YHRD relies on the decentralized sampling of reference populations by qualified forensic and academic institutions on all continents. Essential for this sampling strategy is the collaborative character relying on the engagement of individual laboratories to make their data accessible and comparable *via* a common internet platform and to agree upon a high standard of data quality (Purps *et al.*, 2014). The decentralized sampling strategy implies that each submitting group has to ascertain the sample population. This ascertainment includes informed consent documentation and proper definition of the samples using coordinates and ethnonyms.

Table 1: YHRD dataset compositions as of release 49 (February 2015).

Dataset	Y-STR markers	Number of haplotypes	Number of population samples	Number of national databases	Number of metapopulations
Minimal	DYS19, DYS389I, DYS389II, DYS390, DYS391, DYS392, DYS393, DYS385	143.044	940	128	33
Promega PowerPlex Y12	Minimal + DYS437, DYS438, DYS439	91.231	597	109	32
ThermoFisher Yfiler	PPY12 + DYS448, DYS456, DYS458, DYS635, YGATAH4	91.231	597	109	32
Promega PowerPlex Y23	Yfiler + DYS481, DYS533, DYS549, DYS570, DYS576, DYS643	25.499	179	55	28
ThermoFisher YfilerPlus	Yfiler + DYS576, DYS627, DYS460, DYS518, DYS570, DYS449, DYS481, DYF387S1, DYS533	2.071	16	10	10

Sample numbers depend on the size of the investigated population. Submitted studies should involve at least 200 randomly sampled individuals. Flexibility in the total sample number is possible with small size populations of forensic interest, such as minorities and small indigenous population groups (Carracedo *et al.*, 2014). Also requested is the publication of a manuscript which describes in detail the population(s) submitted to YHRD and contains the original data set. This manuscript is linked *via* an accession number to the respective database where the population sample can be searched. The names of the population samples chosen by the submitters need to follow a ternary code to provide a minimum of ancestry information: region, country (ethnic/linguistic group), e.g. Berlin, Germany (German). If sample populations are properly sampled and described, they can be merged into so-called metapopulations (MP). This category refers to geographically widespread populations which share a common recent genetic ancestry (ethnicity) which can be joined together. For example, Yoruba, Ibo, Tswana, Ahizi, Yacouba etc. belong to the Sub-Saharan MP; US American, Australian, Argentinean or South African Europeans as well as French, Spanish or Irish to the European MP; and Han, Hui and She to the Sino-Tibetan MP. The database supplies inventories of included populations that serve as guidance for the assignment of the relevant termini. The extent of homogeneity within a MP and the distance to others can be measured using the AMOVA algorithm by calculating genetic distances expressed by F_{ST} or R_{ST} values (http://yhrd.org/pages/tools/amova). It has been shown for an earlier edition of the YHRD with about 41,000 individuals typed for 9 markers in 339 population samples that the MP clustering is supported by the deeply structured haplotype data deposited in the database (Willuweit and Roewer, 2007). A more recent study comprising 19,630 23-loci haplotypes typed in 129 population samples indicates that with increasing numbers of Y-STRs included in a haplotype set, the genetic distances between MPs decreased monotonically but are not erased (Purps *et al.*, 2014).

The decentralized, non-systematical sampling strategy of the YHRD was sometimes criticized. While standards for the sample size and the sample quality are defined and studies which violate these requirements are rejected, the sampling strategy itself and the criteria for sample inclusion are not addressed explicitly. In fact, the YHRD currently accepts all population studies which fulfill the quantitative and qualitative criteria and where the accompanying articles include a satisfactory description of the sampling strategy. However, the database includes studies which explicitly exclude known relatives. Realistic frequency estimation however, whether it is based on naïve counting or on evolutionary modeling, relies on empirical data where unrelated and related men are included purely by chance. Extreme selection of unrelated men, e.g. by surname or haplotype filtering, distorts the population-specific haplotype distribution and could result in underrated frequency estimates. However, in the light of the huge denominator that YHRD has achieved, the error introduced by occasional violation of the principle of random sampling in certain studies (responsibility of the author) or fusion of samples of different sampling schemes (responsibility of the YHRD) tends to become smaller or negligible. However, it should be stressed here that the principle of random sampling should be followed for all YHRD projects which means that each individual is chosen randomly and entirely by chance, such that each individual has the same probability of being chosen at any stage during the sampling process, and each subset of individuals has the same probability of being chosen for the sample as any other subset (Starnes *et al.*, 2010). Another putative source of error is the repeated sampling of the same individuals in different studies. This error is minimized, because YHRD accepts studies on the same populations where overlaps cannot be excluded only after clearance of this issue by the authors. In summary, the YHRD is neither a dirty collection nor an ideal reference. Contributors, reviewers and curators take measures responsibly to improve its quality and thereby its forensic utility.

3 Quality Assessment

The quality assessment of submitted reference profiles is equally important as the sample size and sampling scheme for the use and acceptance of the database. Quality is especially important for those cases which are sent to trial and where the database was used as a source of information. Therefore, all institutions contributing haplotypes to the databases have to pass an obligate review to assess the quality of their data. For first submitters to YHRD also a QC test is mandatory, which includes five blind samples that have to be correctly typed for the submitted dataset. The QC results will be evaluated and certified by the YHRD curatorial board. Submitted population data for YHRD will be reviewed to find (i) typographical errors, (ii) mistaken nomenclature and (iii) systematic deviations to the core haplotype distributions of the MP or haplogroup. The database accepts no partial but only complete profiles which represent one of the five datasets. Because the use of commercial kits is the rule, the quality of the submissions is usually high. Errors are reported to the submitting laboratory and revisions replace former versions of the data collection. Once the lab has passed the QC and the data are evaluated, the lab receives an accession number for each submitted population sample. This accession number has to be included in the article, which will appear in one of the peer-reviewed forensic journals (e.g. *Forensic Science International: Genetics or International Journal of Legal Medicine*) as an announcement of population data. The editors of the forensic journals cooperate with the custodians of forensic population databases, e.g. YHRD, EMPOP or STRbASE, and have jointly issued guidelines for the publication of population data, which have to be followed by submitting authors. A recent study compared three disciplines (medical, evolutionary and forensic genetics) concerning the rates and policies of sharing human genetic variation data. The authors found that a significant higher proportion of primary data is made publicly available in forensic genetics than in medical genetics and that an important part of information is shared through online databases (Milia *et al.*, 2012).

4 Database Search Functions and Frequency Estimation Process

As new kits are including increasing number of Y-STR loci, it became inevitable to provide a fully electronic submission facility. The YHRD implemented a flexible Excel-, XML-, CSV-file upload mechanism. Users are able to use their GeneMapper (ThermoFisher, Foster City, USA) export files to conduct searches. All these measures help to avoid errors introduced by manual data transfer, which is of course possible as well. The default search for one selected dataset has two results, first the absolute number of observed matches and the relative frequency in the selected reference database (worldwide as default, MP or national databases can be added). This count has a corresponding confidence interval which is calculated using the Clopper–Pearson method (Clopper and Pearson, 1934). Secondly, the expected number of matches is provided. This category includes constant and variable estimators. Constant estimators are (i) the **augmented count** where the database is augmented by the targeted haplotype and (ii) the count with so-called **kappa (κ) inflation**. This method estimates the haplotype frequency by correcting the simple counting method using κ, with κ being the proportion of singletons (haplotypes that occur only once) in the dataset (Brenner, 2010). This estimate is given only when no matches are observed. Variable estimators, which give, in contrast to constant estimators, different estimates for each unobserved haplotype, are retrievable from three proposed methods all of which take the evolutionary distance between haplotypes into account. These methods are (i) the **surveying method** (Roewer *et al.*, 2000; Krawczak, 2001; Willuweit *et al.*, 2011), (ii) the **coalescence method** (Andersen *et al.*, 2013a) and (iii) the **discrete Laplace method** (Andersen *et al.*, 2013b, 2013c). Due to the still manageable computational demands, only the discrete Laplace estimation is currently included in the YHRD (for three datasets: minimal haplotype, Powerplex Y12, Yfiler).

The discrete Laplace (dL) distribution approximates properties of the Fisher–Wright model of evolution and can be used to estimate

Y-STR haplotype frequencies by modeling the frequency as a relation of the composition of the haplotype in question compared to each of the pre-calculated subpopulation centers (using the R packages disclapmix and fswim; see Andersen *et al.*, 2013c). This estimation method is available only for adequately sized MPs and datasets and in case of a worldwide dL estimation, the average of all nested MP estimations are given together with the one contributing the most. Figures 2 and 3 illustrate that constant estimators give the same frequency estimate for all unobserved haplotypes, whereas the three variable estimators provide values which are different for each haplotype. It is obvious that the constant estimators are bounded from below by the inverse of the database size and all values for different unobserved haplotypes are identical (with large error rates). In contrast, the variable estimators as the coalescence and the

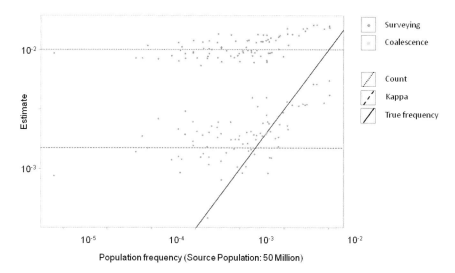

Figure 2: Match probability estimates (uncorrected count estimate, Brenner's estimate using kappa inflation, surveying estimate, coalescence-based) for singleton 7-loci haplotypes in a simulated population of 50 million, with a database size of $N = 100$ and a kappa proportion of singletons of $\kappa = 0.85$.

Note: Each point corresponds to one singleton haplotype. The solid line equates the estimated with the true match probability, i.e. the underlying population frequency (by courtesy of Mikkel Meyer Andersen, Department of Mathematical Sciences, Aalborg University, Denmark).

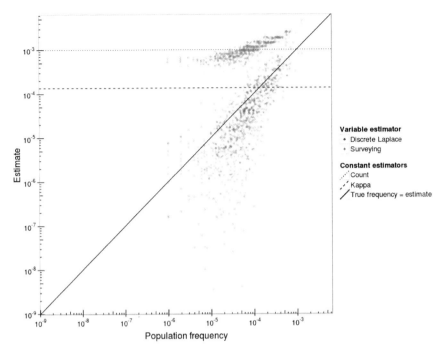

Figure 3: Match probability estimates (uncorrected count estimate, Brenner's estimate using kappa inflation, surveying estimate, discrete Laplace estimate) for singleton 7-loci haplotypes in a simulated population of 1 million, with a database size of $N = 1,000$ and a kappa proportion of singletons of $\kappa = 0.864$ (by courtesy of Mikkel Meyer Andersen, Department of Mathematical Sciences, Aalborg University, Denmark).

discrete Laplace approach give more realistic point estimates for each haplotype which better approximate the true frequency. In a much larger database, however, the number of singletons decreases and the constant estimators could provide values with a lower error rate than in this small simulation database. It is therefore of utmost importance to increase the size of reference databases which are used to assess the match probability. It is also important to sample haplotypes both in migrant populations (e.g. Australian or American Europeans) and in the source populations (e.g. European populations) to make an informed judgment on the occurrence and frequency of a certain haplotype. The YHRD follows this principle. On basis of nearly 1,000 different population studies, the user can build the most relevant reference database(s) for a given case. Tools implemented in the YHRD as Analysis of Molecular Variance & Multi-dimensional Scaling (**AMOVA & MDS**) can be of great help to uncover (sometimes unexpectedly) large or small genetic distances between populations. The algorithm allows clustering population samples on limits which are set by the analyst (e.g. based on the R_{ST} or F_{ST} value). All samples in which similarity index falls below a pre-defined threshold are clustered, and clusters can be used as reference MPs.

5 Ancestry Information

When adding the "Ancestry Information" feature to a result sheet for any targeted haplotype, the incremental minimal haplotype which is present in all sampled individuals is searched. If inspected with appropriate care and experience, this feature may produce some investigative leads on the ancestry of a trace donor. The following information is available:

Metapopulation frequency distribution: A graphical representation of the relative frequency of the minHT for each MP is given. A bolder font indicates a significantly higher relative frequency of the minimal haplotype in question. The YHRD currently comprises 33 MPs (Table 1), which are subject of changes if new samples arrive or variance analysis indicates a divergence of population groups.

Haplogroup assignment: Percentages of SNP-typed chromosomes are shown to which the target minimal haplotype matches. The graphic representation is a pie chart. All haplotypes without Y-SNP information will be mapped to the phylogenetic root "Y". Currently ~12% of the databased samples (more than 17,500 chromosomes) are typed for phylogenetic Y-SNPs. Each submitting laboratory is requested to provide the full list of analysed SNPs marked for the "ancestral" and "derived" state and use the minimal reference phylogeny for the human Y chromosome (www.phylotree.org/Y/tree/index.htm) to standardize the nomenclature and depict the local haplogroup frequencies (van Oven *et al.*, 2014).

National Database frequencies: For each match of the minimal haplotype, both the relative and the absolute frequencies in the national databases are given as a bar plot. Currently, the database includes 128 national databases. China, USA, Germany, Spain, Poland and Brazil are represented by more than 7,000 haplotypes.

Heat Map: A spatial projection of relative minimal haplotype frequency is given as an interactive world map, with each dot representing an individual sampling site. Non-matches are colored in blue, whereas red dots are those with at least one minimal haplotype match. An underlying heat map gradient in red is depicting sampling sites with high relative haplotype frequencies. Under the rubric "Resources", a heat map is provided for the relative frequency of haplogroups in different parts of the world.

Since the release, 51 ancestry information, including the heat map is also available for the 17-locus Yfiler format.

6 Forensic Tools

The YHRD is also a platform to calculate likelihood ratios (LRs) for different forensic scenarios (mixtures, kinship). The **Mixture analysis** tool is currently implemented (http://yhrd.org/pages/tools/mixture). It follows the first approach to identify the most likely contributors to a Y-STR mixture using count frequencies which was published about 10 years ago (Wolf *et al.*, 2005). Further approaches for calculating the probability of exclusion (PE) and/or likelihood ratio (LR) methods were published later (Ge *et al.*, 2010; Andersen *et al.*, 2015). The YHRD program followed the algorithm provided by the original work and calculates the LR of the donorship vs. the non-donorship of the suspect to the trace taking into account the known contributors and additional unknown contributors. To get started, the YHRD provides an example file with a two person mixture of 23-loci profiles with known suspect and another known contributor. The calculation jobs are queued and usually take less than a minute. If the haplotypes are not observed in the database, the count estimate of $1/(N+1)$ from the current database release is used. The result of the calculation is a verbal statement, in the example it reads: "Given the haplotypes above and that there is no additional unknown contributor, the likelihood of the donorship of the suspect is approximately 25,499 times more likely than the non-donorship".

7 Further Resources

The YHRD provides mutation rates for 27 STR loci which are included in the five datasets (http://yhrd.org/pages/resources/mutation_rates). The data are compiled from publications and unpublished studies received from contributors. Furthermore, the database presents the actual allele frequency distributions for all loci (http://yhrd.org/pages/resources/locus_information). Links direct the user to external databases where further information including sequence tagged sites can be retrieved (e.g. STRbase, UniSTS of the NCBI). The YHRD aims to build a comprehensive repository of Y-SNP data for forensic use which includes trees, markers, haplogroup designations and geographical information (http://yhrd.org/pages/resources/ysnps).

8 Summary

One of the great strengths of DNA typing is that it uses a statistical approach based on population genetics theory and empirical testing (Saks and Koehler, 2005). In the case of Y haplotypes which represent the extreme polymorphism of a single haploid locus, the probabilities of random matches across different reference populations can be derived from the YHRD database. The sheer amount of YHRD datasets of the highest forensic quality allows testing of new mathematical models to calculate the weight of evidence of a Y-STR haplotype match by means of likelihood principles. All proposed approaches with variable estimators (surveying, coalescence, discrete Laplace) have been tested using these reference data and will be further evaluated using new marker sets and even larger population samples. Because these methods are sensitive to population subdivision, the YHRD offers a program to calculate the genetic distance values between unrestricted numbers of population samples.

Since the YHRD is publicly available in the internet without restriction or registration, there is a permanent need for information and education. A great forum for education and discussion is the biannual Y-chromosome workshops where community databases such as the YHRD are discussed. This series started in 1996 in Berlin. The YHRD also provides screened tutorials, a manual, a FAQ section and lists of related publications. Full details on all submitted populations and their contributors guarantee that all authors are acknowledged for their work. The custodians of the database are committed to the maintenance of this database and will continue to improve its utility in the future.

Acknowledgments

The author would like to thank Mikkel Meyer Andersen, Michael Krawczak and Sascha Willuweit for helpful discussion and critical comments on an earlier version of this manuscript.

References

M. M. Andersen, A. Caliebe, A. Jochens, S. Willuweit and M. Krawczak. Estimating trace-suspect match probabilities for singleton Y-STR haplotypes using coalescent theory, *Forensic Sci. Int. Genet.*, 7(2):264–271, 2013a.

M. M. Andersen, P. S. Eriksen and N. Morling. The discrete Laplace exponential family and estimation of Y-STR haplotype frequencies, *J. Theor. Biol.*, 329:39–51, 2013b.

M. M. Andersen, P. S. Eriksen and N. Morling. A gentle introduction to the discrete Laplace method for estimating Y-STR haplotype frequencies, arXiv: 2013c, 1304.2129v4.

M. M. Andersen, P. S. Eriksen, H. S. Mogensen and Morling. Identifying the most likely contributors to a Y-STR mixture using the discrete Laplace method, *Forensic Sci. Int. Genet.*, 15:76–83, 2015.

C. H. Brenner. Fundamental problem of forensic mathematics — the evidential value of a rare haplotype, *Forensic Sci. Int. Genet.*, 4:281–291, 2010.

A. Caliebe, A. Jochens, S. Willuweit, L. Roewer and M. Krawczak. No short-cut solution to the problem of Y-STR match probability calculation, *Forensic Sci. Int. Genet.*, 15:69–75, 2015.

A. Carracedo, J. M. Butler, L. Gusmão, A. Linacre, W. Parson, L. Roewer and P. M. Schneider. Update of the guidelines for the publication of genetic population data, *Forensic Sci. Int. Genet.*, 10, A1–A2, 2014.

C. J. Clopper and E. S. Pearson. The use of confidence or fiducial limits illustrated in the case of the binomial, *Biometrika*, 26:404–413, 1934.

P. de Knijff, M. Kayser, A. Caglià, D. Corach, N. Fretwell, C. Gehrig, G. Graziosi, F. Heidorn, S. Herrmann, B. Herzog, M. Hidding, K. Honda, M. Jobling, M. Krawczak, K. Leim, S. Meuser, E. Meyer, W. Oesterreich, A. Pandya, W. Parson, G. Penacino, A. Perez-Lezaun, A. Piccinini, M. Prinz and L. Roewer. Chromosome Y microsatellites: population genetic and evolutionary aspects, *Int. J. Legal Med.*, 110(3):134–149, 1997.

J. Ge, B. Budowle and R. Chakraborty. Interpreting Y chromosome STR haplotype mixture, *Leg. Med. (Tokyo)*, 12(3):137–143, 2010.

M. Geppert, J. Rothe, M. Willuweit, M. Nagy and L. Roewer. Geographic origin of unknown DNA traces, *Rechtsmedizin*, 20, 270–274, 2010.

M. Kayser, A. Caglià, D. Corach, N. Fretwell, C. Gehrig, G. Graziosi, F. Heidorn, S. Herrmann, B. Herzog, M. Hidding, K. Honda, M. Jobling, M. Krawczak, K. Leim, S. Meuser, E. Meyer, W. Oesterreich, A. Pandya, W. Parson, G. Penacino, A. Perez-Lezaun, A. Piccinini, M. Prinz, C. Schmitt and L. Roewer. Evaluation of Y-chromosomal STRs: A multicenter study, *Int. J. Legal Med.*, 110(3):125–133, 141–149, 1997.

M. Krawczak. Forensic evaluation of Y-STR haplotype matches: A comment, *Forensic Sci. Int.*, 118(2–3):114–115, 2001.

C. N. Maguire, L. A. McCallum, C. Storey and J. P. Whitaker. Familial searching: A specialist forensic DNA profiling service utilising the National DNA Database® to identify unknown offenders via their relatives — The UK experience, *Forensic Sci. Int. Genet.*, 8:1–9, 2013.

A. McDonald, E. Jones, J. Lewis and P. O'Rourke. Y-STR analysis of digital and/or penile penetration cases with no detected spermatozoa, *Forensic Sci. Int. Genet.*, 15:84–89, 2015.

N. Milia, A. Congiu, P. Anagnostou, F. Montinaro, M. Capocasa, E. Sanna and G. Destro Bisol. Mine, yours, ours? Sharing data on human genetic variation, *PLoS One*, 7(6):e37552, 2012.

J. Purps, S. Siegert, S. Willuweit, M. Nagy, C. Alves, R. Salazar, S. M. Angustia, L. H. Santos, K. Anslinger, B. Bayer, Q. Ayub, W. Wei, Y. Xue, C. Tyler-Smith, M. B. Bafalluy, B. Martínez-Jarreta, B. Egyed, B. Balitzki, S. Tschumi, D. Ballard, D. S. Court, X. Barrantes, G. Bäßler, T. Wiest, B. Berger, H. Niederstätter, W. Parson, C. Davis, B. Budowle, H. Burri, U. Borer, C. Koller, E. F. Carvalho, P. M. Domingues, W. T. Chamoun, M. D. Coble, C. R. Hill, D. Corach, M. Caputo, M. E. D'Amato, S. Davison, R. Decorte, M. H. Larmuseau, C. Ottoni, O. Rickards, D. Lu, C. Jiang, T. Dobosz, A. Jonkisz, W. E. Frank, I. Furac, C. Gehrig, V. Castella, B. Grskovic, C. Haas, J. Wobst, G. Hadzic, K. Drobnic, K. Honda, Y. Hou, D. Zhou, Y. Li, S. Hu, S. Chen, U. D. Immel, R. Lessig, Z. Jakovski, T. Ilievska, A. E. Klann, C. C. García, P. de Knijff, T. Kraaijenbrink, A. Kondili, P. Miniati, M. Vouropoulou, L. Kovacevic, D. Marjanovic, I. Lindner, I. Mansour, M. Al-Azem, A. E. Andari, M. Marino, S. Furfuro, L. Locarno, P. Martín, G. M. Luque, A. Alonso, L. S. Miranda, H. Moreira, N. Mizuno, Y. Iwashima, R. S. Neto, T. L. Nogueira, R. Silva, M. Nastainczyk-Wulf, J. Edelmann, M. Kohl, S. Nie, X. Wang, B. Cheng, C. Núñez, M. M. Pancorbo, J. K. Olofsson, N. Morling, V. Onofri, A. Tagliabracci, H. Pamjav, A. Volgyi, G. Barany, R. Pawlowski, A. Maciejewska, S. Pelotti, W. Pepinski, M. Abreu-Glowacka, C. Phillips, J. Cárdenas, D. Rey-Gonzalez, A. Salas, F. Brisighelli, C. Capelli, U. Toscanini, A. Piccinini, M. Piglionica, S. L. Baldassarra, R. Ploski, M. Konarzewska, E. Jastrzebska, C. Robino, A. Sajantila, J. U. Palo, E. Guevara, J. Salvador, M. C. Ungria, J. J. Rodriguez, U. Schmidt, N. Schlauderer, P. Saukko, P. M. Schneider, M. Sirker, K. J. Shin, Y. N. Oh, I. Skitsa, A. Ampati, T. G. Smith, L. S. Calvit, V. Stenzl, T. Capal, A. Tillmar, H. Nilsson, S. Turrina, D. De Leo, A. Verzeletti, V. Cortellini, J. H. Wetton, G. M. Gwynne, M. A. Jobling, M. R. Whittle, D. R. Sumita, P. Wolańska-Nowak, R. Y. Yong, M. Krawczak, M. Nothnagel and L. Roewer. A global analysis of Y-chromosomal haplotype diversity for 23 STR loci, *Forensic Sci. Int. Genet.*, 12:12–23, 2014.

L. Roewer. Y chromosome STR typing in crime casework, *Forensic Sci. Med. Pathol.*, 5(2):77–84, 2009.

L. Roewer, M. Kayser, P. de Knijff, K. Anslinger, A. Betz, A. Caglià, D. Corach, S. Füredi, L. Henke, M. Hidding, H. J. Kärgel, R. Lessig, M. Nagy, V. L. Pascali, W. Parson, B. Rolf, C. Schmitt, R. Szibor, J. Teifel-Greding and M. Krawczak. A new method for the evaluation of matches in non-recombining genomes: application to Y-chromosomal short tandem repeat (STR) haplotypes in European males, *Forensic Sci. Int.*, 114(1):31–43, 2000.

L. Roewer, M. Krawczak, S. Willuweit, M. Nagy, C. Alves, A. Amorim, K. Anslinger, C. Augustin, A. Betz, E. Bosch, A. Cagliá, A. Carracedo, D. Corach, A. F. Dekairelle, T. Dobosz, B. M. Dupuy, S. Füredi, C. Gehrig, L. Gusmão, J. Henke, L. Henke, M. Hidding, C. Hohoff, B. Hoste, M. A. Jobling, H. J. Kärgel, P. de Knijff, R. Lessig, E. Liebeherr, M. Lorente, B. Martínez-Jarreta, P. Nievas, M. Nowak, W. Parson, V. L. Pascali, G. Penacino, R. Ploski, B. Rolf, A. Sala, U. Schmidt, C.Schmitt, P. M. Schneider, R. Szibor, J. Teifel-Greding and M. Kayser. Online reference database of European Y-chromosomal short tandem repeat (STR) haplotypes, *Forensic Sci. Int.*, 118(2–3):106–113, 2001.

M. J. Saks and J. J. Koehler. The coming paradigm shift in forensic identification science. *Science*, 309(5736):892–895, 2005.

D. S. Starnes, D. Yates and D. S. Moore. *The Practice of Statistics*, W. H. Freeman and Co., New York., 2010.

M. van Oven, A. Van Geystelen, M. Kayser, R. Decorte and M. H. Larmuseau. Seeing the wood for the trees: A minimal reference phylogeny for the human Y chromosome, *Hum. Mutat.*, 35(2):187–191, 2014.

J. H. Wetton, K. W. Tsang and H. Khan. Inferring the population of origin of DNA evidence within the UK by allele-specific hybridization of Y-SNPs, *Forensic Sci. Int.*, 152:45–53, 2005.

S. Willuweit and L. Roewer. The new Y Chromosome Haplotype Reference Database, *Forensic Sci. Int. Genet.*, 15:43–48, 2015.

S. Willuweit and L. Roewer. International Forensic Y Chromosome User Group. Y chromosome haplotype reference database (YHRD): Update, *Forensic Sci. Int. Genet.*, 1(2):83–87, 2007.

S. Willuweit, A. Caliebe, M. M. Andersen and L. Roewer. Y-STR Frequency Surveying Method: A critical reappraisal, *Forensic Sci. Int. Genet.*, 5(2):84–90, 2011.

A. Wolf, A. Caliebe, O. Junge and M. Krawczak. Forensic interpretation of Y-chromosomal DNA mixtures, *Forensic Sci. Int.*, 152(2–3):209–213, 2005.

CHAPTER 13

The Next State-of-the-Art Forensic Genetics Technology: Massively Parallel Sequencing

Bruce Budowle[*,†]*, Jennifer D. Churchill* *and Jonathan L. King*[*]

[*]*Institute of Applied Genetics, Department of Molecular and Medical Genetics, University of North Texas Health Science Center, 3500 Camp Bowie Blvd., Fort Worth, TX 76107, USA*
[†]*Center of Excellence in Genomic Medicine Research (CEGMR), King Abdulaziz University, Jeddah, Saudi Arabia*

1 Introduction

For over 25 years, the field of forensic science has embraced the use of molecular biology tools for its identity testing techniques and ability to characterize biological evidence (for examples see Berger *et al.*, 2012; Budowle and Eisenberg, 2007; Budowle and van Daal, 2008; Gomes *et al.*, 2012; Honda *et al.*, 1999; Hsieh *et al.*, 2003; Linacre and Tobe, 2011; Rasko *et al.*, 2011). The exploitation of the polymerase chain reaction (PCR) has enabled analysis of extremely minute quantities of DNA, and with concomitant detection methods, samples can be typed with a resolving power such that, in many cases, the number of potential contributors of an evidence sample can be reduced to only a few individuals (or to only one source).

The mainstay instrumentation of capillary electrophoresis (CE) permits detection of various fluorescently-labeled PCR products of genetic markers in an automated fashion. Moreover, with the implementation of quality assurance standards, these forensic molecular biology tools are very reliable because of well-defined validation requirements (SWGDAM, 2012).

The success of forensic DNA typing has led to further applications. One of the most notable has been developing investigative leads initially without a known suspect by implementation of DNA databases. Many countries have established DNA databanks that contain DNA profiles from convicted offenders, arrestees and forensic samples from unsolved cases (Budowle *et al.*, 1998; Martin *et al.*, 2001). These databases are designed to associate DNA profiles from individuals with those derived from forensic samples, link cases, or to identify missing persons. As an example, the U.S. databank — COmbined DNA Index System (CODIS) — as of October 2014 houses 11,219,527 offender profiles, 2,065,806 arrestee profiles and 590,079 forensic profiles and is relied upon routinely for developing meaningful investigative leads with 263,847 hits assisting in 252,272 investigations (CODIS, 2014).

Indeed, the DNA forensic field is quite mature (Budowle and van Daal, 2009). Given the current capabilities of forensic DNA typing, one might opine that for the foreseeable future there are few changes needed and only refinements will occur. After all, results can be obtained from as miniscule a sample as a single shed hair (Wilson *et al.*, 1995; Ottens *et al.*, 2013). However, sometimes a new technology can provide opportunities to improve substantially current practices and point to opportunities for advancement where previously the capabilities seemingly appeared to have reached the ultimate in application. That latest technology development is massively parallel sequencing (MPS). It holds promise to enable higher sample throughput with a larger set of genetic markers for characterization of biological evidence from humans, animals, plants and microbes, all leading to development of more investigative leads and greater opportunities to exclude those individuals that have been wrongly associated with biological evidence.

2 Gaps and Needs

Despite the field's maturity, there are a number of areas where MPS could enhance capabilities of forensic DNA analyses:

(1) The number of short tandem repeat (STR) loci, which are the primary genetic markers used in human identification, that can be multiplexed is limited to 20–30 loci (Flores *et al.*, 2014; Oostdik *et al.*, 2014; Thompson *et al.*, 2013). With CE-based analyses, the size of the amplicons labeled with the same fluorescent dye molecule at each locus must vary in order to assign alleles to the appropriate locus. This need for size variance limits the number of markers that can be multiplexed.

(2) Single nucleotide polymorphism (SNP) typing has not transferred readily to the CE. Attempts have been reported (Dixon *et al.*, 2005; Kidd *et al.*, 2006; Phillips *et al.*, 2007; Divne and Allen, 2005; Sanchez *et al.*, 2006; Edelmann *et al.*, 2009; Francez *et al.*, 2012; Li *et al.*, 2011), but the CE-based assays require substantial manipulation and often are not quantitative. Therefore, although SNPs offer the potential to analyze degraded samples more so than STRs and have a lower mutation rate, there has been little success in bringing SNPs and CE typing into the mainstream of forensic DNA analyses. Instead, insertion/deletions (indels) and insertion/nulls (innuls) are being sought as alternatives to SNPs (Budowle and van Daal, 2008; Edelmann *et al.*, 2009; Francez *et al.*, 2012; Li *et al.*, 2011; Pereira *et al.*, 2009; LaRue *et al.*, 2012a, 2012b).

(3) Only one marker type tends to be analyzed at a time, i.e. an STR kit generally allows typing of, for example, only autosomal STRs and a SNP kit allows typing of only SNPs. It is easy to envisage situations where multiple marker systems could be useful, such as kinship testing and familial searching, and analysis would be facilitated with combination marker kits (Ge *et al.*, 2014, 2012).

(4) Current sample throughput does not meet the increased demand of samples that confronts both case working and databasing

forensic laboratories. The reliance on offender, arrestees and forensic sample DNA databases continues to demand developments in automation and robust molecular assays. The number of reference samples from convicted felons, arrestees, detainees and missing persons continues to increase, and there is no indication of the demand subsiding.

(5) Because of the success of DNA profile searches for developing invaluable investigative leads, these DNA databases will increase in size and may generate additional information other than solely direct matching of DNA profiles for investigative leads, such as that which can be obtained by familial searching (Budowle, 2010; Ge *et al.*, 2011). An increased number of identity markers and lineage markers would facilitate familial searching and increase the number of viable investigative leads that could be developed using DNA databases. The sheer number of markers (and the inclusion of lineage based markers, i.e. Y STRs, Y SNPs and mtDNA) would provide more robust associations and reduce substantially candidate lists.

(6) Some analytical systems, such as sequencing mitochondrial DNA (mtDNA), are quite laborious, time consuming and expensive. Due to the demands of sequencing, only a small portion of forensic laboratories employ mtDNA sequencing. Thus, a valuable tool for analyzing low quantity and low quality biological evidence is not realized by the majority of forensic laboratories.

(7) Analysis of mixtures still is quite demanding (Budowle *et al.*, 2009; Gill *et al.*, 2012; Curran, 2008), and errors in interpretation arise far too often.

3 MPS

With the advent of accessible bench top high throughput sequencers (Quail *et al.*, 2012; Jünemann *et al.*, 2013), MPS, also termed next generation sequencing, can be considered an accessible technology for the application-oriented laboratory. MPS systems can overcome some of the limitations mentioned above and, combined with bioinformatics capabilities, offer a powerful tool to characterize forensic biological evidence (Budowle *et al.*, 2013a). There are a number of features that make MPS technology desirable for forensic genetic identification. Millions of sequencing reactions can be performed simultaneously in a single instrument run (Wetterstrand, 2013; Brenner *et al.*, 2000; Margulies *et al.*, 2005; Merriman and Rothberg, 2012; Metzker, 2010; Quail *et al.*, 2008; Shendure and Ji, 2008). With many copies sequenced at any targeted portion of the genome (known as depth of coverage or read depth), consensus sequence accuracy can be increased far beyond the per-read accuracy rate of any single molecule. With increased throughput, more markers and more samples can be analyzed simultaneously without sacrificing depth of coverage. Additionally, more complex samples (e.g. mixtures) may be analyzed at a greater depth of coverage resulting in better identification of alleles (and perhaps resulting in lower levels of allele drop out) as well as better deconvolution of contributing profiles. Barcoding (discussed in further detail below) allows multiple samples to be analyzed simultaneously. Size separation is no longer required for allele detection as it is with CE methods allowing a larger number of markers to be multiplexed together. Since separation by size is no longer needed, all amplicons can be similar in size and overall shorter in length than current constructs (Fordyce *et al.*, 2015; Zeng *et al.*, 2015). In fact, it is possible for the amplicon size of almost all STRs in a panel to be approximately 250 base pairs or less (Fordyce *et al.*, 2015). This size reduction could result in a more efficient PCR and a more robust assay for typing degraded samples. MPS systems enable detection of each DNA fragment/ molecule independently. Therefore, data can be generated over a wide dynamic range without a high signal amplicon product negatively impacting the signal of a low yield amplicon, which makes balance of amplicon signal in a multiplex less important. The same outcomes for STRs apply with SNPs and mtDNA sequencing. Additionally the whole mtDNA genome can be sequenced (Fordyce *et al.*, 2015; Zeng *et al.*, 2015; Gunnarsdottir *et al.*, 2011; Parson *et al.*, 2013; Mikkelsen *et al.*, 2014; King *et al.*, 2014; McElhoe *et al.*, 2014; Seo *et al.*, 2015), which in turn substantially increases the discrimination power of this marker system (King *et al.*, 2014). Therefore, MPS makes mtDNA sequencing a more desirable tool for typing low quantity samples.

MPS technologies promise to provide DNA sequencing data with unprecedented capacity and speed at a reduced cost. These features make the technology desirable for generating DNA profiles that may be uploaded into forensic offender, arrestee and family reference database files housed in DNA databases. Studies (Fordyce *et al.*, 2015; Zeng *et al.*, 2015; Churchill *et al.*, 2015) and the availability of commercial kits (such as Illumina ForenSeq Signature DNA Prep Kit (Illumina, San Diego, CA; and HID-Ion STR 10plex Panel; HID-Ion AmpliSeq™ Identity Panel; HID-Ion AmpliSeq™ Ancestry Panel (Thermo Fisher Scientific)) already demonstrate that autosomal STRs, Y-chromosome STRs, X-chromosome STRs, and human identity and ancestry informative SNPs can be typed simultaneously or in high capacity specific marker panels. Warshauer *et al.* (2013, 2015) and Budowle *et al.* (2013b) have described a capture-based panel with as many as 88 STRs (31 autosomal, 26 X chromosome, 31 Y chromosome) and 229 autosomal identity SNPs.

Several MPS platforms are available that provide substantial capacity in a reduced footprint. The primary benchtop MPS platforms include the MiSeq (Illumina), Ion Torrent Personal Genome Machine® (PGM) and Ion Proton™ System (Thermo Fisher Scientific), and the discontinued GS FLX system (Roche, Branford, CT). The Illumina NextSeq 500 system is the latest bench top platform to become commercially-available with 150 Gigabase throughput and simplified format, supporting the expectation that MPS throughput will continue to increase and cost will continue to decrease.

3.1 *Fundamental MPS Processes*

The fundamental steps for effective MPS workflow are extraction of DNA, library preparation, library amplification, sequencing and data analysis. Figure 1 shows the general workflow of MPS from DNA extraction through data analysis using the PGM platform as an example. Extraction of DNA is well established, and most current

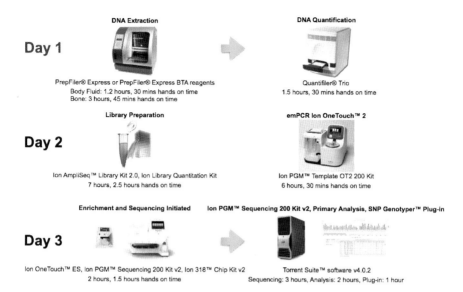

Figure 1: Illustration of the general workflow for MPS on one of the available commercial bench top platforms — the PGM. DNA extraction and quantitation are followed by library preparation, library amplification, sequencing and data analysis. *Source*: Thermo Fisher Scientific.

DNA extraction procedures provide DNA of sufficient purity for MPS. The amounts of input DNA range from < 1 ng to 225 ng. The larger amounts of input DNA are applicable to MPS for typing reference samples. The lower amounts of input DNA indicate that the same sensitivity of detection is possible with that of current methods of DNA analysis. The amount of DNA necessary for analysis is dictated by the library preparation method. For example, the Nextera Rapid Capture Custom Enrichment Kit (Illumina) requires approximately 50 ng (Illumina, 2013a) and Haloplex (Agilent, Santa Clara, CA) 225 ng (Agilent, 2013). The Nextera XT (Illumina) library preparation kit requires only 1 ng (Illumina, 2013b); however, this kit requires a PCR enrichment of relatively large size amplicons (>300 bp recommended). Studies such as those by Fordyce *et al.* (2015) and Zeng *et al.* (2015) demonstrated full and relatively balanced profiles can be obtained with DNA input amounts less than 250 pg making it possible to consider lower levels of input DNA within the realm of forensic analyses.

3.1.1 Library preparation

Library preparation, essentially, sets up targeted DNA fragments for sequence analysis (Hori *et al.*, 2007; Hodges *et al.*, 2007; Gnirke *et al.*, 2009; Kozarewa *et al.*, 2009; Syed *et al.*, 2009; Tewhey *et al.*, 2009; Mamanova *et al.*, 2010; Head *et al.*, 2014). Library preparation creates clones of many individual molecule fragments of DNA and adapters and other necessary short pieces of DNA are attached to facilitate the sequencing phase.

To meet sensitivity of detection with < 1 ng of input DNA, target enrichment is necessary. Target enrichment is obtained by a capture approach or by PCR. Capture approaches use specific probes to select only targets of interest from the genomic DNA in a sample. PCR-based methods, as with current forensic DNA typing methods, enrich targets by amplification using defined primers. PCR-based approaches offer greater sensitivity of detection, but require a great demand on primer design with a multiplex panel of markers. In contrast, a capture method requires more template DNA. While not impacting reference sample typing, a capture method generally would not provide the limit of detection necessary for most forensic analyses.

Examples of capture-based enrichment systems are the discontinued Illumina® TruSeq™ Custom Enrichment System and its replacement the Nextera Rapid Capture Custom Enrichment System. Using the Design Studio (Illumina), custom probes can be designed to target forensically-relevant markers (STRs, SNPs and Indels). Haloplex is another capture-based library preparation process (Agilent, 2013). This approach is a single-tube target amplification methodology that enables a large number of library samples to be prepared manually. The general process is: (1) restriction digest and denature the sample; (2) hybridize probes to targeted ends of the digested fragments; and (3) circularize and ligate the molecules and amplify the targets by PCR. PCR-based panels are available (or soon to be available) commercially for target enrichment and include the HID-Ion AmpliSeq™ Identity Panel, HID-Ion AmpliSeq™ Ancestry Panel, HID-Ion STR 10plex Panel, and the Illumina® ForenSeq™ DNA Signature Prep Kit.

The targeted fragments or PCR amplicons are size-selected for the range appropriate for downstream sequencing. Size selection removes undesired products that would consume sequencing reagents and negatively impact sequence coverage. Size selection is not a trivial part of the process. Indeed, selecting for fragments long enough to capture an entire allele of a large STR allele may result in loss of smaller sized alleles and undesired heterozygote imbalance or allele drop out. In contrast, selecting for smaller amplicons may result in loss of longer alleles and reduction in throughput of usable sequence data due to artifacts that were not removed consuming reagents. For example, Zeng *et al.* (2015) tested two methods for size selection: bead mixture (sample purification bead) and the MinElute PCR Purification Kit (Qiagen, Valencia, CA). Results showed that the MinElute PCR Purification Kit was equal at size selection based on alleles recovered, heterozygote allele coverage ratios and much better at total amount of amplified DNA recovered.

During the MPS process, it is sometimes necessary to fragment the DNA or amplicons. Fragmentation can be accomplished physically (typically by sonication), enzymatically (e.g. tagmentation (Syed *et al.*, 2009)), or by generating PCR amplicons (during enrichment) within a specified size range. With short PCR-generated amplicons, fragmentation may not be required. Finally, universal nucleotide sequences of known length are ligated to the 5′ and 3′ ends of the library fragments/amplicons, the most important being adapters and universal primer sequences that allow the library fragments to attach to a solid support for cloning and sequencing (Margulies *et al.*, 2005; Metzker, 2010; Van Tessell *et al.*, 2008).

Multiplexing by traditional forensic DNA analyses refers to the capability of analyzing a number of markers simultaneously for one sample. Because of the high throughput of MPS, multiplexing can be extended to simultaneous typing of many samples. Pooling of samples into one analysis has not been a practice in forensic DNA typing because each sample could not maintain its individuality during analysis. However, sample distinction can be achieved by barcoding using indexes which are short unique sequence tags attached to every fragment of a sample during library preparation.

This barcoding individualizes the pieces of DNA specific to each sample. After sequencing, the raw data can be demultiplexed bioinformatically based on the barcodes. While it is feasible to generate hundreds to thousands of barcodes, currently 12–384 different samples may be pooled (Knapp *et al.*, 2012; Hamady *et al.*, 2012).

3.1.2 Sequencing

Of the potential benchtop systems, the MiSeq and the PGM currently are the focus of forensic research and validation. Both platforms can yield reliable results. Each system employs a unique chemistry for generating sequence results. The MiSeq uses a solid phase amplification strategy where forward and reverse short length sequences are bound to the surface of a flow cell. The target DNA with reagents for amplification is washed over the flow cell (Quail *et al.*, 2008; Van Tessell *et al.*, 2008; Adessi *et al.*, 2000). Once the target DNA, with attached adapters complementary to the short sequences covalently bound on the flow cell, hybridizes, it is cloned through a process known as bridge amplification (Figure 2). The process generates millions of clusters (or clones) of target DNA fragments randomly distributed across the flow cell (Metzker, 2010; Shendure and Li, 2008; Adessi *et al.*, 2000; Fedurco *et al.*, 2006). The clusters are sequenced simultaneously using a sequencing-by-synthesis chemistry whereby in each cycle, the four different fluorescently-labeled nucleotides are added to the reaction in a similar strategy with that of terminator chemistry employed by Sanger sequencing (Sanger *et al.*, 1977; Turcatti *et al.*, 2008). When the appropriate complementary nucleotide is incorporated into the growing chain, its fluorescent tag is identified, and the sequence of each cluster is elucidated. The PGM uses semiconductor chip technology instead of a fluorescent dye and laser optics system, which have been the mainstay of forensic DNA typing strategies for many years. Instead of a flat solid phase flow cell for generating clusters, the PGM system uses a microbead and emulsion PCR (ePCR) to generate cloned target fragments for sequencing (Margulies *et al.*, 2005; Rothberg *et al.*, 2011; Merriman and Rotheberg, 2012). An individual fragment is attached to a

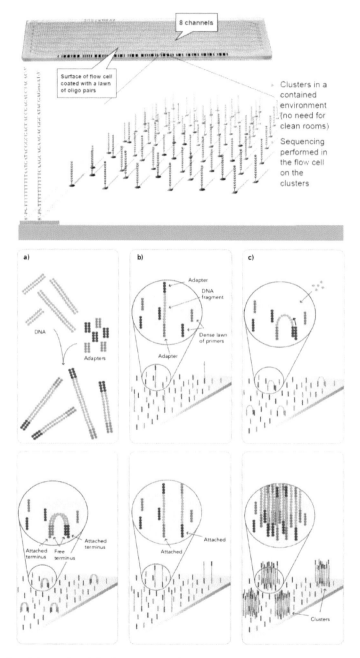

Figure 2: Schematic of the bridge amplification process taking place on a flow cell.
Source: Illumina, Inc.

Figure 3: The targeted amplicon is covalently attached to a microbead (called an Ion Sphere Particle by Ion Torrent) with a P1 adapter attached to the amplicon during library preparation.

Source: Thermo Fisher Scientific.

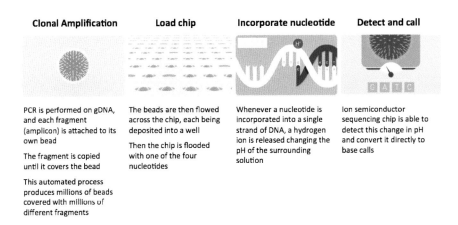

Clonal Amplification	Load chip	Incorporate nucleotide	Detect and call
PCR is performed on gDNA, and each fragment (amplicon) is attached to its own bead	The beads are then flowed across the chip, each being deposited into a well	Whenever a nucleotide is incorporated into a single strand of DNA, a hydrogen ion is released changing the pH of the surrounding solution	Ion semiconductor sequencing chip is able to detect this change in pH and convert it directly to base calls
The fragment is copied until it covers the bead	Then the chip is flooded with one of the four nucleotides		
This automated process produces millions of beads covered with millions of different fragments			

Figure 4: Illustration of the sequencing process on the PGM.

Source: Thermo Fisher Scientific.

microbead, facilitated by adapter sequences that have been covalently attached to the DNA fragments prior to ePCR (Figure 3). The single stranded DNA molecule is amplified within a micelle that contains all reagents necessary for generating sufficient clones for sequencing. The millions of beads each containing a separate clone are placed in wells in a sequencing chip. Using a sequence-by-synthesis strategy, nucleotides are sequentially washed over the chip and incorporation of a specific nucleotide into the growing chain is detected by a pH change when a proton is elicited (Fordyce *et al.*, 2015; Seo *et al.*, 2013, 2015) (Figure 4). Both the MiSeq and PGM strategies sequence millions of copies of targeted portions of the genome in a single reaction. While both platforms provide highly accurate base calling, the PGM methodology has more difficulties in accurately sequencing homopolymers compared with Illumina-based chemistry (Quail *et al.*, 2012; Loman *et al.*, 2012; Bragg *et al.*, 2013; Seo *et al.*, 2013), but new polymerases offer promise to reduce this problem (Vander Horn *et al.*, 2013). Both platforms offer read lengths up to 400 bases in length. While the read length will be a limitation for accommodating possibly the largest allele sizes for some STRs, this limitation is nominal. PCR primers can be repositioned to reduce the size of amplicons. On a practical level, some of the largest alleles (such as those in the FGA locus) sometimes are not detected due to lower amplification efficiency with current CE-based systems. Thus, the MPS performance of STR typing should be somewhat comparable with CE analyses for very large size alleles. Similar issues regarding interpretation will occur with MPS data as were confronted with CE-based typing methods.

3.1.3 Data analysis

The final major component of MPS is data analysis and interpretation of results, which has always been the most demanding part of forensic DNA analyses. Due to the massive amounts of generated data, bioinformatics is essential and critical to analyze the sequence data and answer forensic genetic questions using the processed data (Budowle *et al.*, 2014). Accuracy of identifying sequence variants (e.g. STR repeat regions and SNPs) may be dependent on a number of factors that include base calling and/or alignment, depth of sequence coverage, allele balance (allele coverage ratios), strand balance (each critical component being defined through validation studies), misincorporation rates and chemistry-specific issues. Quality metrics are generated during the analytical process and include quality scores for base calling, read-level quality control (to include trimming of low quality bases on fragment ends), alignment, GC content, depth of coverage, allele balance (allele coverage ratios), strand balance and variant calling (Budowle *et al.*, 2014).

Base calling is the identification of the specific nucleotide present at each position in each read and should be performed *via* instrument software. A quality threshold of base scoring is set with a Q score. A threshold of Q20 sets the minimum base call accuracy at 99% which translates into an incorrect base call per read at 1 in 100 and a Q30 score sets the accuracy at 99.9% which means an incorrect base call per read at 1 in 1,000 (Ewing and Green 1998). Depth of coverage or a minimum number of reads threshold will set limits of detection and stochastic effects parameters similar in principle to thresholds for CE-based analyses. Strand balance calculations determine the coverage contribution from both strands of the DNA. Allele balance calculations assess coverage obtained for both alleles in a heterozygote genotype and, thus, can evaluate the risk for allele drop-out and assist in mixture deconvolution. Strand balance and allele balance calculations may help assess the quality and accuracy of variant calls. Another component to consider for allele drop-out potential is read length.

There are a number of software tools that are needed to analyze sequence data. An example of the suite of tools that could be used in a single analysis is displayed in Figure 5.

Many of these same tools are within current commercial software dedicated to forensic marker panel systems, such as the HID SNP Genotyper Plugin and STR Genotyper Plugin (Thermo Fisher Scientific) and Universal Analysis Software (Illumina), which make the suite of tools appear seamless (i.e. in the background) to facilitate base calling.

Alignment involves arranging a read with a reference sequence and is similar in principle to mtDNA nomenclature strategies currently in place in the forensic community (Bandelt *et al.*, 2001; Parson *et al.*, 2004; Bandelt and Parson, 2008; Budowle *et al.*, 2010). Different alignment strategies can and do produce different results (Figure 6).

Differences in alignment will vary with software (Figure 7), and therefore, rules for alignment must be defined for consistency and traceability similar to those defined phylogenetically for mtDNA. Indeed, mtDNA sequence differences obtained from the same data

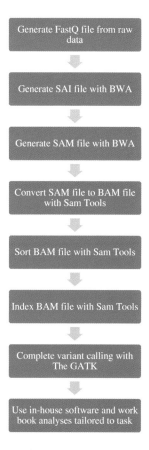

Figure 5:   Example of a bioinformatic pipeline for MPS data.

are well documented and often due to alignment strategy differences (Bandelt *et al.*, 2001; Parson *et al.*, 2004; Bandelt and Parson, 2008; Budowle *et al.*, 2010). King *et al.* (2014) developed mitoSAVE, an Excel-based workbook, to facilitate mtDNA variant designations in a semi-automated fashion and convert haplotypes to a standardized forensic format. There was a data analysis bottleneck in the process of extracting the information necessary to call mtDNA variants properly. Once familiar with the workflow, an analyst using mitoSAVE generated a haplotype from a Variant Call Format (VCF) file in less than one minute per sample. Thus, the automated variant

Option 1

AGCTCT-CCATGCATT   Reference sequence

AGCTCTCCCATGCATT Sample sequence

Option 2

AGCTCTCC-ATGCATT   Reference sequence

AGCTCTCCCATGCATT Sample sequence

Figure 6:   An illustration of two possible alignments with a reference sequence to describe the insertion in the sample sequence.

Note: These different alignments would result in a different haplotype nomenclature. Forensic community standards need to be part of alignment strategies for consistent haplotype nomenclature.

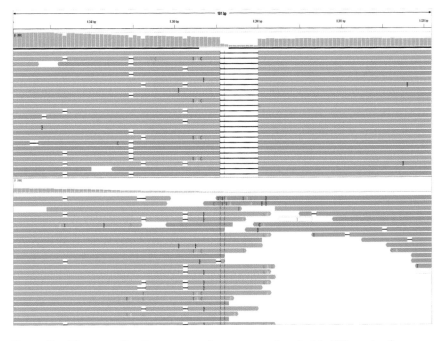

Figure 7:   The same FastQ sequence data were analyzed with different software.

Note: The top was aligned using TMAP, and the bottom was aligned using BWA. Distinct differences can be noted between the two alignment software.

reassignment and haplotype generation allowed for a much faster processing time and higher throughput concomitant with increased sample sequencing of MPS systems. Because accurate haplotypes are reliant on quality sequence data, users can set thresholds, review variants, and generate haplotypes in a more consistent manner than current MPS-related software allow. This level of control promotes accurate haplotype nomenclature and allows consistent haplotypes to be generated by different users.

Naming of STR alleles as nominal number of repeats from MPS data originally was attempted with an alignment strategy (Bornman *et al.*, 2012). However, this approach requires prior knowledge of allelic sequence information. As a result, those alleles for which there are no sequence data and novel alleles or allelic variants may not be detected. Warshauer *et al.* (2013, 2015) and Van Este *et al.* (2015a, 2015b) created more practical and efficient STR allele calling software to increase the chances of detecting allele sequence data. To convert sequence data to the legacy nomenclature of STR alleles, Warshauer *et al.* (2013, 2015) developed software named STRait Razor (the STR allele identification tool — Razor). STRait Razor is a Linux-based Perl script that detects STR alleles by identifying the unique leading and trailing flanking region(s) surrounding the repeat(s) of each STR locus. Then, all sequence data surrounding the repeat region are removed, such that only the repeat units sequence remains. Alleles are called by comparing the length of the repeat unit region with known allele lengths. For example, a repeat sequence length of 40 bases would be translated into a 10 allele for a tetranucleotide repeat locus. The total counts (i.e. reads) of each allele at each locus are ordered and stored in an output file for further analysis and comparison with other samples. Van Este *et al.* (2015a, 2015b) developed My-Forensic-Loci-queries (MyFLq) for analysis of MPS data, which performs in a somewhat similar fashion as STRait Razor. Instead of relying initially on the flanking region for locus read identification, reads are assigned to a locus based on the PCR primer sequences that define the amplicon for that locus. The MyFLq framework uses a MySQL reference allele database and

Table 1: An example of sequence variants seen for allele 13 in the STR marker D8S1179 in a sample of only 12 individuals (Churchill *et al.*, 2015).

Sequence
TATCTATCT**G**TCT**A**TCTATCTATCTATCTATCTATCTATCTATCTATCTATC
TATCTATCT**ATCT**G**TCT**A**TCTATCTATCTATCTATCTATCTATCTATCTATC
TATCTATCT**G**TCT**A**TCTATCTATCTATCTATCTATCTATCTATCTATCTATC
TATCTATCT**A**TCT**A**TCTATCTATCTATCTATCTATCTATCTATCTATCTATC
TATCTATCT**G**TCT**A**TCTATCTATCTATCTATCTATCTATCTATCTATCTATC

Note: The variants are bolded.

automatically determines the target regions using python scripts to compare MPS sequences against the known allele database. This software can be applied to STR and SNP data. Both MyFLq and Strait Razor software generate STR allele nomenclature that is concordant with length-based allele detection offered by CE methods. These software programs are capable of analyzing repeat motifs ranging from simple to complex, and they are less confounded by unexpected sequence variation within repeats. In addition to an allele designated by the number of repeats, intra-allelic sequence variants are detected which provide additional benefits of increased diversity for some loci and the potential to deconvolve mixtures better when such SNPs are present (Table 1). The commercial software described above now incorporate similar approaches for STR allele calling from MPS data. These software tools will improve the ability to identify STR alleles in such massive data sets; but unless they are designed well will have a potential for missing some alleles and induce pseudoallele drop out.

4 Potential Applications

There are many applications that can be envisioned with MPS. They range from traditional human identification approaches to novel leads based on the phenotype of the unknown sample contributor to characterization of microbes that may be used in an act of bioterrorism. Not all possibilities can be explained herein. However, some are likely to have immediate impact, and others are near term for coming to fruition. A few examples are given below to provide insight on the state-of-the-art of MPS applications and what may be expected as immediate fruitful outcomes.

4.1 *Databasing*

The FBI Laboratory's Combined DNA Index System (CODIS) has become the premier DNA database tool, particularly in North America as well as a number of countries around the world, to assist in developing investigative leads (Budowle *et al.*, 1998). DNA profiles from offenders, arrestees, forensic evidence, missing persons, unidentified human remains and biological relatives of missing persons are housed within CODIS, and these data assist in making associations of forensic biological evidence in traditional casework and in missing and unidentified persons cases. The 13 core CODIS loci are: CSF1PO, FGA, TH01, TPOX, vWA, D3S1358, D5S818, D7S820, D8S1179, D13S317, D16S359, D18S51, and D21S11 (Budowle *et al.*, 1998). Hares (2012a, 2012b), representing the position of the FBI, recommended that the core 13 STR loci for CODIS should be changed and augmented. Initially, the FBI advocated 20 STR loci (24 total if a second panel of four additional STRs is considered) and settled on 22 loci to serve potentially as the new CODIS panel of markers. Ge *et al.* (2014, 2012) suggested that there were additional factors and applications beyond that which Hares (2012a, 2012b) relied upon for selecting a core set of markers. The alternate viewpoint was that the loci selected should be driven by the demands of casework, i.e. loci should be selected based on performance with degraded and inhibited samples, be more versatile for a variety of search strategies, or be the best for developing additional investigative leads. Thus, there are differences of opinion on how to proceed on core marker selection (Ge *et al.*, 2012, 2014). However, the high throughput capabilities of MPS can render the marker selection debate moot. It is entirely possible that all forensically-relevant identified autosomal STRs, such as the 24 STR loci initially advocated by Hares (2012a, 2012b) and beyond, a set of Y STRs and X STRs, and SNPs (comprising hundreds of markers and more if desired) can be typed simultaneously. Since sequence data are completely compatible with the nominal STR allele calls resident in current DNA databases, conversion to MPS generated STR data should not be an impediment with regard to comparison with existing data. Any new expanded marker panel can readily contain a country's core set of STRs, and therefore, new reference profiles can be fully linked to legacy data. In addition, depending on the laboratory's mission, needs, type of samples, etc., a subset of the most efficient markers fit for the purpose (e.g. SNPs for highly degraded samples) could be typed on casework and be compared with the reference samples that would be comprehensively typed. Even if another laboratory used an entirely different set of markers for typing forensic evidence (perhaps because the core set did not provide useful data and as long as the markers are a subset of the MPS-generated large panel of markers) an analyst may still be able to link the profile to the more comprehensively typed reference sample. The implications are that fully typed reference samples would allow linking partial data from disparate cases that may have been analyzed with different data sets, thus increasing the investigative lead potential of DNA typing.

The feasibility of comprehensive marker panels for analyzing DNA from reference samples has been described by Budowle *et al.* (2013b) who demonstrated a capture-based panel with 88 STRs (31 autosomal, 26 X chromosome, 31 Y chromosome) and 229 autosomal identity SNPs can be typed with 50 ng input DNA. The autosomal STRs are all those included in the suite of commercial kits produced by the two US manufacturers and some reported in use in China (Collins *et al.*, 2004; Krenke *et al.*, 2002; Budowle *et al.*, 2011; AmpFlSTR® Kit Product Portfolio; Promega Corporation STR Analysis Kits). The Y STRs are those included in all the commercial kits produced by the two US manufacturers (Thompson *et al.*, 2013; Mulero *et al.*, 2006; Krenke *et al.*, 2005; Davis *et al.*, 2013) and those reported by Hedmann *et al.* (2011). The X STRs are derived from the forensic science literature (Inturri *et al.*, 2011; Li *et al.*, 2011; Liu *et al.*, 2011; Luo *et al.*, 2011; Nakamura and Minaguchi, 2010; Pasino *et al.*, 2011). The SNPs best suited for human identity testing can be found at http://alfred.med.yale.edu/alfred/snpSets.asp and are described in the literature (Dixon *et al.*, 2005; Sanchez *et al.*, 2006; Kidd *et al.*, 2011; Kosoy *et al.*, 2010; Pakstis *et al.*, 2007, 2010; Phillips *et al.*, 2007; Vallone *et al.*, 2005). This number of markers requires only a few thousand bases of genomic real estate to be sequenced. Thus, given the throughput of each MPS benchtop platform, it is conceivable that at least 100 individuals can be sequenced at approximately 100X coverage in one multiplex reaction.

More recently, manufacturers have developed a number of either commercially available or soon to be available kits produced for forensic human identification. The ForenSeq panel provides primers for 59 STRs (including 27 autosomal STRs, 8 X-STRs, and 24 Y-STRs), 95 identity informative SNPs, 56 ancestry informative SNPs, and 22 phenotypic informative SNPs. The HID-Ion AmpliSeq™ Identity Panel enables typing of 90 autosomal identity informative SNPs and 34 upper clade Y-chromosome SNPs and the HID-Ion AmpliSeq™ Ancestry Panel permits typing of 165 autosomal ancestry informative SNPs. These PCR-based enrichment kits expand large panel analyzes for typing more limited quantity samples and make it possible to analyze samples with the same sensitivity of detection of CE-based methods.

4.2 SNP Typing

SNPs are another class of genetic markers that have held promise for forensic analyses (Budowle and van Daal, 2008; Kidd *et al.*, 2006; Phillips *et al.*, 2007; Sanchez *et al.*, 2006), but they have not been used widely to date. SNPs are base substitutions, insertions, or deletions that occur at single positions in the genome of any organism. Most SNPs are bi-allelic and, thus, are not as informative on a per-locus basis as are the forensically-selected STR loci. Yet, there is a wealth of genetic information that can be tapped since approximately 85% of human variation is derived from SNPs (Cooper *et al.*, 1985; Holden,

2002; Wang *et al.*, 1998). The SNPs for forensic analyses can be divided into five categories (Budowle and van Daal, 2008):

- Identity informative SNPs — for individualization; require high heterozygosity and a low coefficient of inbreeding (F_{ST}) (i.e. low population heterogeneity). They provide genetic information to differentiate people in a similar fashion to that of STRs.
- Lineage informative SNPs — for individualization and kinship; sets of tightly linked SNPs that function as haplotype markers; Lineage markers can be SNPs residing in haploblocks (Ge *et al.*, 2010), SNPs residing on the X and Y chromosomes, and the mitochondrial genome.
- Ancestry informative SNPs — for establishing high probability of an individual's biogeographical ancestry or to indirectly infer some phenotypic characteristics; require low heterozygosity and high F_{ST} values.
- Phenotype informative SNPs — for establishing high probability that an individual has a particular phenotypic characteristic, such as skin color, hair color, or eye color.
- Molecular Autopsy SNPs — for establishing cause and manner of death due to adverse reaction to drugs, stress, or other factors.

These SNPs now can be analyzed more effectively by MPS (such as with the commercial kits described above) and provide novel investigative lead data not previously done easily by CE-based systems. As an example, Churchill *et al.* (2015) recently described a blind test to assess the capability of the PGM system to sequence forensically-relevant genetic marker panels (i.e. HID-Ion AmpliSeq™ Identity Panel, HID-Ion AmpliSeq™ Ancestry Panel, HID-Ion STR 10plex Panel) and the whole mitochondrial genome to characterize 12 unknown samples for ancestry and possible relatedness. The samples were provided by a third party (from the Green Mountain DNA Conference) for blinded genetic analysis. The mitochondrial genome was analyzed as described previously (Seo *et al.*, 2015). Completeness of genetic profiles, depth of coverage, strand balance

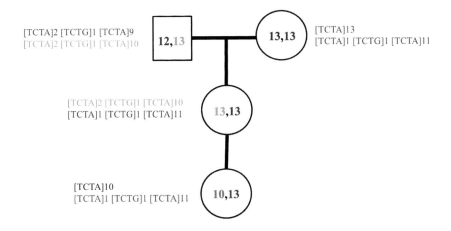

Figure 8:   Pedigree determined for 4 individuals out of the 12 blind samples.

Note: The STR profile data alone provided a likelihood ratio (LR) of 300 million times more likely to observe the genetic data if the four individuals are related vs. they are four unrelated individuals. With only the SNP data, a combined LR of 3.34 E46 was generated (Churchill *et al.*, 2015).

and allele balance were evaluated as informative metrics for the quality and reliability of the data produced, and all metrics demonstrated high performance. The SNP genotypes were used to identify sex, potential paternal lineage relationships and population ancestry, and in combination with STR genotypes and mitochondrial genome data were able to establish a kinship among four of the sample donors (Figure 8). Within this pedigree, the D8S1179 locus 13 allele displayed three intra repeat sequence variants. Such variation can aid in familial analysis of unknown individuals and may facilitate family reconstruction missing person cases. All results from analysis of the 12 genomic samples were consistent with sample information subsequently provided by the sample providers. The relatively easy identification of intra-STR allele SNPs offers the potential for increased discrimination power and improvement in mixture analysis when analyzing biological evidence. The promising nature of these results warrant full validation studies of these PGM systems and continued development of tools for data analysis.

4.3 *Mitochondrial Genome Sequencing*

Mitochondria are subcellular organelles that contain an extrachromosomal genome separate and distinct from the nuclear genome. The mtDNA genome encodes 13 polypeptides of approximately 80 protein subunits involved in oxidative phosphorylation, in addition to two ribosomal RNAs and 22 transfer RNAs. Due to the higher copy number per cell compared with nuclear markers, mtDNA sequencing is sought for characterization of challenged samples such as bones, single hair shafts, and teeth (Wilson *et al.*, 1995; Budowle *et al.*, 2003). Sanger *et al.* (1977) sequencing, which is based on separation and fluorescent detection by CE, is the standard method for sequencing mtDNA in the forensic laboratory. However, the ~16,569 nucleotide long mitochondrial genome is not feasibly sequenced in a practical manner with this technology. Therefore, sequencing focuses on a subset of the genome within the non-coding region, which are two hypervariable regions (hypervariable region 1 (HV1) and hypervariable region 2 (HV2)). These two regions are of interest for human identity testing because a concentration of variation among individuals is found within these regions. While Sanger sequencing has been the standard method for mtDNA sequencing of forensic samples for two decades, the current mtDNA typing protocols are labor intensive, time consuming and relatively costly. Far more discrimination power could be attained by expanding genetic interrogation to the entire mitochondrial genome. A number of studies have shown that stream-lined whole mitochondrial genome sequencing can be achieved, and far higher discrimination power can be obtained than possible by sequencing only HV1 and HV2 (Parson *et al.*, 2013; Mikkelsen *et al.*, 2014; King *et al.*, 2014; McElhoe *et al.*, 2014; Seo *et al.*, 2015). Seo *et al.* (2015) sequenced 24 mitochondrial genomes with the PGM and demonstrated that whole genome sequencing is highly reliable. Depth of coverage variation and strand bias were limited and did not impact reliability of variant calls. On the MiSeq, King *et al.* (2014) sequenced the whole mitochondrial genome and generated haplotypes for 283 individuals with high depth of coverage and limited strand bias.

With these studies, the distribution of variants across the entire mitochondrial genome was described, and of the total variation contained within the mitochondrial genome, more than two-thirds resided in the untapped coding region. A substantial increase in haplotype (or genetic) diversity and random match probability was obtained over traditional mtDNA sequencing. Additionally, better haplogroup assignment was achievable. Sequence data generated on the PGM and the MiSeq systems were highly concordant except for the number of Cs in homopolymers around nucleotide positions 310 and 16189, which are not used currently for forensic identifications generated using Sanger-based methods (SWGDAM, 2013). Parson *et al.* (2013) also demonstrated that sequencing results with the PGM were reliable and highly concordant with those obtained by Sanger sequencing. The overall data supported that the entire mitochondrial genome is capable of being sequenced reliably and at much lower costs with both MPS platforms than that of Sanger sequencing and should be pursued for application in forensics.

It should be noted that most MPS studies of the mitochondrial genome are based on PCR-enrichment methods using long PCR generating two amplicons ~8.5kb in length (Gunnarsdottir *et al.*, 2011; Parson *et al.*, 2013; Fendt *et al.*, 2009). With highly degraded DNA, long PCR is not practical. Multiplexed short amplicons that span the entire mitochondrial genome are better suited for forensic analyses. A number of studies have described shorter amplicons of varying length (ranging from 800 to 3,000 bases in length) for whole genome mitochondrial DNA sequencing (Levin *et al.*, 2003; Palanichamy *et al.*, 2004; Rieder *et al.*, 1998; Taylor *et al.*, 2001). Davis *et al.* (2015) demonstrated that short amplicon typing of mtDNA is highly informative, and less than 1 ng of DNA can produce reliable results. Eighteen buccal samples from different individuals; blood, buccal and hair samples from an additional five individuals; and four casework bones previously analyzed by Sanger methodology were sequenced with MPS on the MiSeq. Hypervariable regions I and II were amplified and sequenced, and complete concordance was obtained for all base calls. Heteroplasmy, which is similar in nature to mixtures, was better resolved. These results supported that mixture interpretation can be addressed better with MPS than by Sanger sequencing. With high coverage and similar depth of coverage, representation of the DNA of contributors will be observed better. Stochastic effects may be overcome to a degree by devoting more coverage per sample.

Concordance testing, when feasible, provides information on reliability of results. With current technologies, such testing would be a time-consuming, arduous task which is impractical and cost prohibitive. However, cross laboratory testing on the same and different MPS platforms can be instructive on the potential robustness of such systems. A 7-sample exchange with Walther Parson's laboratory (Institute of Legal Medicine, Innsbruck Medical University, Innsbruck, Austria) produced concordant results. The Innsbruck data were generated using Sanger sequencing as well as on the PGM, and the data at UNTHSC were generated on both the MiSeq and PGM. The data were concordant at all SNP variants (excluding comparisons at homopolymeric stretches), which further supports reliability of both systems. Interestingly, two of the exchanged samples each had an example of point heteroplasmy which was concordant between the MPS methods. The quantitative assessment between laboratories and different MPS systems (PGM in Innsbruck and PGM and MiSeq in UNTHSC, respectively) was very similar. For position 195 Y (T/C) in one sample and position 234 R (A/G) in another sample, the relative contributions of the heteroplasmic variants between laboratories were 0.67C/0.33T, 0.74C/0.26T, 0.71C/0.29T, and 0.54A/0.26G, 0.53A/0.47G, 0.51A/0.49G, respectively. These concordant results support the reliability of sequence results obtained by the methodologies described herein.

The results supported that mtDNA sequencing will enhance forensic analyses. Indeed, it would have been impossible to generate the same amount of data with a Sanger sequencing protocol (routinely used in forensic laboratories), and the quantitative nature of MPS data allowed for better definition of heteroplasmy. Moreover, with MPS, the technology for mtDNA sequencing essentially is the same as that for other markers; there should not be a substantial additional technical learning curve for a different marker system.

4.4 Mixtures

Typing of STR alleles by MPS provides the traditional length of the allele but also allows for discovery of intra-allele sequence variants, thereby increasing the power of discrimination. Since MPS determines the exact sequence of each allele, SNPs residing within a repeat or in the flanking area can be recorded. These intra-STR SNPs offer greater resolving power when analyzing mixtures both qualitatively and quantitatively (Fordyce *et al.*, 2015; Zeng *et al.*, 2015; Churchill *et al.*, 2015). Intra-allelic variants detected by MPS have been reported for the loci D3S1358, D8S1179, vWA, D21S11 and D2S1338. Figure 9

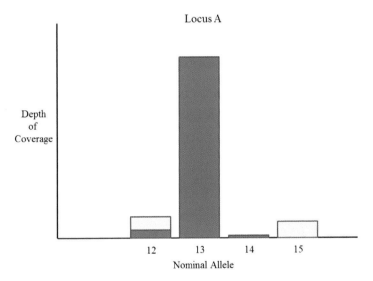

Figure 9: A pictorial representation of a two-person mixture in the format of CE-generated STR data.

Note: The major is blue and the minor is gray. The major is a 13,13 homozygote, and the minor is a 12,15 heterozygote. There is a minor stutter product at allele position 12 and a plus stutter product at allele position 14 from the major contributor. The minor contributor's allele 12 resides in the same position as the minus stutter product of the major contributor. In such scenarios, interpretation can become complicated in deconvoluting the minor contributor type. However, in this example, the 13 allele and its stutter product contain a SNP that is different than that of the 12 allele from the minor contributor. The allele contributions are color coded to demonstrate the ability of intra-allelic SNP data to determine the contributors and the quantity of their contribution with shared alleles.

shows an example of a mixture where interpretation potentially could be better facilitated due to the presence of intra-STR allele SNPs (e.g. providing better determination of stutter vs. a minor contributor).

4.5 *Differentiating Identical Twins*

The general dogma in forensic DNA analyses is that monozygotic twins are genetically identical. In cases where one of the identical twins cannot be excluded based on forensic DNA analyses, the other twin is also included as a potential contributor. However, it has been well known for many years that there are genetic differences between monozygotic twins due to the accumulation of somatic mutations (Bruder *et al.*, 2008; Kondos *et al.*, 2002; Li *et al.*, 2014; Machin, 1996; Razzaghian *et al.*, 2010; Vavlamudi *et al.*, 2010; Krawczak *et al.*, 2012; Ye *et al.*, 2013; Weber-Lehhmann *et al.*, 2014), but there was no readily facile way to locate the few somatic variants that would be different between the twins and, in turn, use those variants to determine the twin that was the source of the forensic biological evidence. Now, the throughput power of MPS will enable identification of somatic SNP variants in a straight forward manner.

Recently, Weber-Lehmann *et al.* (2014) using the 600 gigabase throughput Illumina HiSeq 2000 platform (although not one of the bench top systems) and standard sequencing chemistry demonstrated that it is feasible to identify somatic differences between twins. Five SNPs were identified that distinguished the twins. The five SNP variants of one of the twins were observed in his son. Four of five SNPs detected in the twin father's buccal cell DNA were observed in his sperm DNA (ectodermal tissues). One of the SNPs was detected in both sperm and blood DNA. Lastly, one SNP was observed solely in sperm DNA. These findings support that the SNPs that arise after twins separate may be able to distinguish the twins genetically and associate forensic evidence with a particular twin with a high degree of confidence. Of course, there are factors that impact the uncertainty of any results such as how early in development a SNP arises, the rarity of a SNP (which could infer a low mutation rate), the depth of coverage, and whether any or how many reads show the alternate SNP state in the associated twin.

5 Concluding Remark

The use of MPS and a large battery of genetic markers likely will raise concerns about privacy, what markers should be placed in DNA databases and on general human rights (Budowle and van Daal, 2008). As all these issues are important, the application of large marker panels for human identification purposes should be based on informed decisions and potential realistic concerns regarding the violation of the privacy of individuals. STRs, identity informative SNPs, and SNPs within the lineage chromosomes provide little or no predictive value (Budowle and van Daal, 2008). However, the possible linkage to a disease gene might be a criterion to consider regarding privacy with ancestry informative SNPs. Yet, the predictive power of these SNPs likely is to be low and thus pose little privacy concern of their use as information placed in a DNA database or in an investigation. However, some analyses should be performed on ancestry informative SNPs to determine if there is a substantial privacy risk with any ancestry informative SNPs that would be part of a panel. Lastly, it is unlikely that MPS will be used routinely to sequence the entire genome of an individual(s) because it would compromise throughput, not be cost effective, and, most importantly, not be particularly useful for human identification purposes. Thus, genetic information, such as disease causing genes, will not be collected. However, the identification of somatic SNPs for differentiating identical twins opens the door on access to potential genetic privacy information. While the SNPs that distinguish the twins may pose little privacy concern, the access to all of the genome of an individual could be an issue. Policies should be developed to address how such whole genome data (or specific genes), if generated, should be handled and disclosed to maintain the privacy of individuals, which our society cherishes. Balance must be struck between the usefulness of genetic identity tools, such as MPS, to help solve cases and exclude those falsely associated with biological evidence vs.

the rights and privacy of the individual. With the advent of MPS into the forensic science arena, these issues will be raised in the not too distant future.

Acknowledgments

We would like to express our deep thanks to Illumina, Inc. and Thermo Fisher Scientific for kindly providing some figures for this chapter.

References

C. Adessi, G. Matton, G. Ayala, G. Turcatti, J. J. Mermod, P. Mayer and E. Kawashima. Solid phase DNA amplification: characterisation of primer attachment and amplification mechanisms, *Nucleic Acids Res.*, 28(20):E87, 2000.

Agilent. HaloPlex Target Enrichment System-ILM. 2013. http://www. chem.agilent.com/Library/usermanuals/Public/G9900-90001.pdf.

H.-J. Bandelt, P. Lahermo, M. Richards and V. Macaulay. Detecting errors in mtDNA data by phylogenetic analysis, *Int. J. Leg. Med.*, 115:64–69, 2001.

H.-J. Bandelt and W. Parson. Consistent treatment of length variants in the human mtDNA control region: a reappraisal, *Int. J. Leg. Med.*, 122:11–21, 2008.

C. Berger, B. Berger and W. Parson W. Sequence analysis of the canine mitochondrial DNA control region from shed hair samples in criminal investigations, *Methods Mol. Biol.*, 830:331–348, 2012.

L. M. Bragg, G. Stone, M. K. Butler, P. Hugenholtz and G. W. Tyson. Shining a light on dark sequencing: characterising errors in Ion Torrent PGM data, *PLoS Comput. Biol.*, 9(4):e1003031, 2013.

S. Brenner, S. R. Williams, E. H. Vermaas, T. Storck, K. Moon, C. McCollum, J. I. Mao, S. Luo, J. J. Kirchner, S. Eletr, R. B. DuBridge, T. Burcham and G. Albrecht. *In vitro* cloning of complex mixtures of DNA on microbeads: physical separation of differentially expressed cDNAs, *Proc. Natl. Acad. Sci. USA*, 97(4):1665–1670, 2000.

C. E. Bruder, A. Piotrowski, A. A. Gijsbers, R. Andersson, S. Erickson, Diaz de T. Ståhl, U. Menzel, J. Sandgren, von D. Tell, A. Poplawski, M. Crowley, C. Crasto, EC. Partridge, H. Tiwari, D. B. Allison,

J. Komorowski, G. J. van Ommen, DI. Boomsma, N. L. Pedersen, den J. T. Dunnen, K. Wirdefeldt and J. P. Dumanski. Phenotypically concordant and discordant monozygotic twins display different DNA copy-number-variation profiles, *Am. J. Hum. Genet.*, 82:763–771, 2008.

B. Budowle, N. D. Connell, A. Bielecka-Oder, R. R. Colwell, C. R. Corbett, J. Fletcher, M. Forsman, D. R. Kadavy, A. Markotic, S. A. Morse, R. S. Murch, A. Sajantila, S. E. Schmedes, K. L. Ternus, S. D. Turner and S. Minot. Validation of high throughput sequencing and microbial forensics applications, *BMC Invest. Genet.* 5:9, 2014.

B. Budowle and A. J. Eisenberg. Forensic Genetics, in D. L. Rimoin, J. M. Connor, R. E. Pyeritz and B. R. Korf (eds.), *Emery and Rimoin's Principles and Practice of Medical Genetics*, 5th edn., Vol. 1, pp. 501–517. Elsevier, Philadelphia, 2007.

B. Budowle. Familial searching: extending the investigative lead potential of DNA typing, Profiles in DNA, 13(2):2010, Available at:. www.promega.com/profiles/1302/1302_07.html.

D. M. Bornman, M. E. Hester, J. M. Schuetter, M. D. Kasoji, A. Minard-Smith, C. A. Barden, S. C. Nelson, G. D. Godbold, C. H. Baker, B. Yang, J. E. Walther, I. E. Tornes, P. S. Yan, B. Rodriguez, R. Bundschuh, M. I. Dickens, B. A. Young and S. A. Faith. Short-read, high-throughput sequencing technology for STR genotyping, *Biotechniques*, 1–6, 2012.

B. Budowle, M. W. Allard, M. R. Wilson and R. Chakraborty. Forensics and mitochondrial DNA: Applications, debates and foundations, *Ann. Rev. Genomics Hum. Genetics*, 4:119–141, 2003.

B. Budowle, J. Ge, R. Chakraborty, A. J. Eisenberg, R. Green, J. Mulero, R. Lagace and L. Hennessy. Population genetic analyses of the NGM STR loci, *Int. J. Leg. Med.*, 125:101–109, 2011.

B. Budowle, A. J. Onorato, T. F. Callaghan A. Della. Manna, A. M. Gross, R. A. Guerrieri, J. C. Luttman and D. L. McClure. Mixture interpretation: defining the relevant features for guidelines for the assessment of mixed DNA profiles in forensic casework, *J. Forens. Sci.*, 54:810–821, 2009.

B. Budowle, T. R. Moretti, S. J. Niezgoda and B. L. Brown. CODIS and PCR-based short tandem repeat loci: Law enforcement tools, In: *Second European Symposium on Human Identification 1998*, Promega Corporation, Madison, Wisconsin, pp. 73–88, 1998.

B. Budowle, D. Polanskey, C. L. Fisher, B. K. Den, Hartog, R. B. Kepler and J. W. Elling. Automated alignment and nomenclature for consistent treatment of polymorphisms in the human mitochondrial DNA control region, *J. Forensic Sci.*, 55(5):1190–1195, 2010.

B. Budowle, S. Schmedes and R. S. Murch. The microbial forensics pathway for use of massively-parallel sequencing technologies, *The science and applications of microbial genomics.* Institute of Medicine, Washington, DC, The National Academies Press, pp. 117–133, 2013a.

B. Budowle and A. van Daal. Forensically relevant SNP classes, *Biotechniques,* 44:603–610, 2008.

B. Budowle, D. H. Warshauer, S. B. Seo, J. L. King, C. Davis and B. LaRue. Massively parallel sequencing provides comprehensive multiplex capabilities, *Forensic Sci. Int. Genet. Suppl. Ser.,* 4:e334–e335, 2013b.

B. Budowle and A. van Daal. Extracting evidence from forensic DNA analyses: future molecular biology directions, *BioTechniques,* 46(5):339–350, 2009.

J. D. Churchill, J. Chang, J. Ge, N. Rajagopalan, R. Lagacé, W. Liao, J. L. King and B. Budowle. Blind study evaluation of the Ion PGM™ System for use in human identity DNA typing, *Croat. Med. J.,* (submitted), 2015.

CODIS. http://www.fbi.gov/about-us/lab/biometric-analysis/codis/ndis-statistics, 2014.

D. N. Cooper, B. A. Smith, H. J. Cooke, S. Niemann and J. Schmidtke. An estimate of unique DNA sequence heterozygosity in the human genome, *Hum. Genet.,* 69:201–205, 1985.

P. J. Collins, LK. Hennessy, C. S. Leibelt, R. K. Roby, D. J. Reeder and P. A. Foxall. Developmental validation of a single-tube amplification of the 13 CODIS loci, D2S1338, D19S433, and amelogenin: The AmpFlSTR® Indentifiler® PCR Amplification Kit, *J. Forensic Sci.,* 49(6):1265–1277, 2004.

J. M. Curran. A MCMC method for resolving two person mixtures, *Science and Justice,* 48:168–177, 2008.

C. Davis, J. Ge, C. Sprecher, A. Chidambaram, J. Thompson, M. Ewing, P. Fulmer, D. Rabbach, D. Storts and B. Budowle. Prototype PowerPlex® Y23 System: A Concordance Study, *Forensic Sci. Int. Genet.,* 7(1):204–208, 2013.

C. Davis, D. Peters, D. Warshauer, J. King and B. Budowle. Sequencing the hypervariable regions of human mitochondrial DNA using massively parallel sequencing: Improved methods for DNA samples encountered in forensic testing, *Leg. Med.,* 2015 (in press).

A.-M. Divne and M. Allen. A DNA microarray system for forensic SNP analysis, *Forensic Sci. Int.,* 154(2–3), 111–121, 2005.

L. A. Dixon, C. M. Murray, E. J. Archer, A. E. Dobbins, P. Koumi and P. Gill. Validation of a 21-locus autosomal SNP multiplex for forensic identification purposes, *Forensic Sci. Int.,* 154(1):62–77, 2005.

J. Edelmann, S. Hering, C. Augustin and R. Szibor. Indel polymorphisms — an additional set of markers on the X-chromosome, *Forensic Sci. Int. Genet. Suppl. Ser.*, 2(1):510–512, 2009.

B. Ewing and P. Green. Base-calling of automated sequencer traces using phred. II. Error probabilities, *Genome Res.*, 8:186–194, 1998.

M. Fedurco, A. Romieu, S. Williams, I. Lawrence and G. Turcatti. BTA, a novel reagent for DNA attachment on glass and efficient generation of solid-phase amplified DNA colonies, *Nucleic Acids Res.*, 34(3):e22, 2006.

L. Fendt, B. Zimmermann, M. Daniaux and W. Parson. Sequencing strategy for the whole mitochondrial genome resulting in high quality sequences, *BMC Genomics*, 10:139, 2009.

S. K. Flores, J. Sun, J. King and B. Budowle. Validation of the GlobalFiler™ Express PCR Amplification Kit for the direct amplification of single-source DNA samples on a high-throughput automated workflow, *Forens. Sci. Int. Genet.*, 10:33–39, 2014.

S. L. Fordyce, H. S. Mogensen, C. Børsting, R. E. Lagacé, C. W. Chang, N. Rajagopalan and N. Morling. Second-generation sequencing of forensic STRs using the Ion Torrent™ HID STR 10-plex and the Ion PGM™, *Forensic Sci. Int. Genet.*, 14:132–140, 2015.

P. A. Francez, E. M. Ribeiro-Rodrigues and S. E. dos Santos. Allelic frequencies and statistical data obtained from 48 AIM INDEL loci in an admixed population from the Brazilian Amazon, *Forensic Sci Int. Genet.*, 6(1):132–135, 2012.

J. Ge, B. Budowle, J. V. Planz and R. Chakraborty. Haplotype block: A new type of forensic DNA marker, *Int. J. Leg. Med.*, 124(5):353–361, 2010.

J. Ge, R. Chakraborty, A. Eisenberg and B. Budowle. Comparisons of the familial DNA database searching policies, *J. Forensic Sci.*, 56(6):1448–1456, 2011.

J. Ge, A. Eisenberg and B. Budowle. Developing criteria and data to determine best options for expanding the core CODIS loci, *BMC Investig. Genet.*, 3:1, 2012.

J. Ge, H. Sun, H. Li, C. Liu, J. Yan and B. Budowle. Future directions of forensic DNA databases, Croatian Med. J., 55:163–166, 2014.

P. Gill, L. Gusmão, H. Haned, W. R. Mayr, N. Morling, W. Parson, L. Prieto, M. Prinz, H. Schneider, P. M. Schneider and B. S. Weir. DNA commission of the International Society of Forensic Genetics: Recommendations on the evaluation of STR typing results that may include drop-out and/or drop-in using probabilistic methods, *Forensic Sci. Int. Genet.*, 6(6):679–688, 2012.

C. Gomes, M. Magalhães, C. Alves, A. Amorim, N. Pinto and L. Gusmão. Comparative evaluation of alternative batteries of genetic markers to complement autosomal STRs in kinship investigations: Autosomal indels vs. X-chromosome STRs, *Int J. Legal Med.*, 126(6):917–921, 2012.

A. Gnirke, A. Melnikov, J. Maguire, P. Rogov, E. M. LeProust, W. Brockman, T. Fennell, G. Giannoukos, S. Fisher, C. Russ, S. Gabriel, D. B. Jaffe, E. S. Lander and C. Nusbaum. Solution hybrid selection with ultra-long oligonucleotides for massively parallel targeted sequencing, *Nat. Biotechnol.*, 27:182–189, 2009.

E. D. Gunnarsdottir, M. Li, M. Bauchet, K. Finstermeier and M. Stoneking. High-through- put sequencing of complete human mtDNA genomes from the Philippines, *Genome Res.*, 21:1–11, 2011.

M. Hamady, J. J. Walker, J. K. Harris, N. J. Gold and R. Knight. Error-correcting barcoded primers allow hundreds of samples to be pyrosequenced in multiplex. *Nat. Methods*, 5:235–237, 2012.

D. R. Hares. Addendum to expanding the CODIS core loci in the United States, *Forensic Sci. Int. Genet.*, 6:e135, 2012a.

D. R. Hares. Expanding the CODIS Core Loci in the United States, *Forensic Sci. Int. Genet.*, 6:e52–e54, 2012b.

S. R. Head, H. K. Komori, S. A. LaMere, T. Whisenant, Van F. Nieuwerburgh, D. R. Salomon and P. Ordoukhanian. Library construction for next-generation sequencing: overviews and challenges, *Biotechniques*, 56(2):61–68, 2014.

M. Hedman, A. M. Neuvonen, A. Sajantila and J. U. Palo. Dissecting the Finnish male uniformity: The value of additional Y-STR loci, *Forensic Sci. Int. Genet.*, 5(3):199–201, 2011.

E. Hodges, Z. Xuan, V. Balija, M. Kramer, M. N. Molla, S. W. Smith, C. M. Middle, M. J. Rodesch, T. J. Albert, G. J. Hannon and W. R. McCombie. Genome-wide in situ exon capture for selective resequencing, *Nat. Genet.*, 39:1522–1527, 2007.

A. L. Holden. The SNP consortium: Summary of a private consortium effort to develop an applied map of the human genome, *BioTechniques*, 32, S22–S26, 2002.

K. Honda, L. Roewer and P. de Knijff. Male DNA typing from 25-year-old vaginal swabs using Y chromosomal STR polymorphisms in a retrial request case, *J. Forensic Sci.*, 44(4):868–872, 1999.

M. Hori, H. Fukano and Y. Suzuki. Uniform amplification of multiple DNAs by PCR. emulsion, *Biochem. Biophys. Res. Commun.*, 352:323–328, 2007.

H. M. Hsieh, R. J. Hou, L. C. Tsai, C. S. Wei, S. W. Liu, L. H. Huang, Y. C. Kuo, A. Linacre and J. C. Lee. A highly polymorphic STR locus in Cannabis sativa, *Forensic Sci. Int.*, 131(1):53–58, 2003.

Illumina. Nextera Rapid Capture Custom Enrichment Kit. 2013a. http://www.illumina.com/products/nextera-rapid-capture-custom-enrichment-kit.html.

Illumina. Nextera XT DNA Sample Preparation Kit. 2013b. http://www.illumina.com/products/nextera_xt_dna_sample_prep_kit.ilmn.

S. Inturri, S. Menegon, A. Amoroso, C. Torre and C. Robino. Linkage and linkage disequilibrium analysis of X-STRs in Italian families, *Forensic Sci. Int. Genet.*, 5:152–154, 2011.

S. Jünemann, F. J. Sedlazeck, K. Prior, A. Albersmeier, U. John, J. Kalinowski, A. Mellmann, A. Goesmann, A. von Haeseler, J. Stoye and D. Harmsen. Updating benchtop sequencing performance comparison, *Nat. Biotechnol.*, 31:294–296, 2013.

J. R. Kidd, F. R. Friedlaender, W. C. Speed, A. J. Pakstis, De La F. M. Vega and K. K. Kidd. Analyses of a set of 128 ancestry informative single-nucleotide polymorphisms in a global set of 119 population samples, *BMC Invest. Genet.*, 2(1):1, 2011.

K. K. Kidd, A. J. Pakstis, W. C. Speed, E. L. Grigorenko, S. L. B. Kajuna, N. J. Karoma, S. Kungulilo, J.-J. Kim, R.-.B Lu, A. Odunsi, F. Okonofua, J. Parnas, L. O. Schulz, O. V. Zhukova and J. R. Kidd. Developing a SNP panel for forensic identification of individuals, *Forensic Sci Int.*, 164(1):20–32, 2006.

J. L. King, B. L. LaRue, N. Novroski, M. Stoljarova, S. B. Seo, X. Zeng, D. Warshauer, C. Davis, W. Parson, A. Sajantila and B. Budowle. High-quality and high-throughput massively parallel sequencing of the human mitochondrial genome using the Illumina MiSeq, *Forensic Sci. Int. Genet.*, 12:128–135, 2014.

J. L. King, A. Sajantila and B. Budowle. mitoSAVE: mitochondrial sequencing analysis of variants in excel, *Forensic Sci. Genet. Int.*, 12:122–125, 2014.

M. Knapp, M. Stiller and M. Meyer. Generating barcoded libraries for multiplex high-throughput sequencing, *Methods Mol. Biol.*, 840:155–170, 2012.

S. Kondo, B. C. Schutte, R. J. Richardson, B. C. Bjork, A. S. Knight, Y. Watanabe, E. Howard, de R. L. Lima, S. Daack-Hirsch, A. Sander, D. M. McDonald-McGinn, EH. Zackai, E. J. Lammer, A. S. Aylsworth, H. H. Ardinger, A. C. Lidral, B. R. Pober, L. Moreno, M. Arcos-Burgos, C. Valencia, C. Houdayer, M. Bahuau, D. Moretti-Ferreira, A. Richieri-Costa, M. J. Dixon and J. C Murray. Mutations in IRF6 cause Van der

Woude and popliteal pterygium Syndromes, *Nat. Genet.*, 32:285–289, 2002.

R. Kosoy, R. Nassir, C. Tian, P. A. White, L. M. Butler, G. Silva, R. Kittles, M. E. Alarcon-Riquelme, P. K. Gregersen, J. W. Belmont, De La F. M. Vega and M. F. Seldin. Ancestry informative marker sets for determining continental origin and admixture proportions in common populations in America, *Hum. Mutat.*, 30:69–78, 2010.

I. Kozarewa, Z. Ning, M. A. Quail, M. J. Sanders, M. Berriman and D. J. Turner. Amplification-free Illumina sequencing-library preparation facilitates improved mapping and assembly of (G+C)-biased genomes, *Nat. Methods*, 6:291–295, 2009.

M. Krawczak, D. N. Cooper, F. Fändrich, W. Engel and J. Schmidtke. How to distinguish genetically between an alleged father and his monozygotic twin: a thought experiment, *Forensic Sci. Int. Genet.*, 6:129–130, 2012.

B. E. Krenke, A. Tereba, S. J. Anderson, E. Buel, S. Culhane, C. J. Finis, C. S. Tomsey, J. M. Zachetti, A. Masibay, D. R. Rabbach, E. A. Amiott and C. J. Sprecher. Validation of a 16-locus fluorescent multiplex system, *J. Forensic Sci.*, 47(4):773–785, 2002.

B. E. Krenke, L. Viculis, M. L. Richard, M. Prinz, S. C. Milne, C. Ladd, A. M. Gross, T. Gornall, J. R. H. Frappier, A. J. Eisenberg, C. Barna, X. G. Aranda, M. S. Adamowicz and B. Budowle. Validation of a male-specific, 12-locus fluorescent Short Tandem Repeat (STR) multiplex, *Forensic Sci. Int.*, 148(1):1–14, 2005.

B. L. LaRue, J. Ge, J. L. King and B. Budowle. A validation study of the Qiagen Investigator DIPplex® Kit; an INDEL based assay for human identification, *Int. J. Leg. Med.*, 126(4):533–540, 2012a.

B. L. LaRue, S. K. Sinha, A. H. Montgomery, R. Thompson, L. Klaskala, J. Ge, J. King, M. Turnbough and B. Budowle. INNULs, a new strategy for human identification based on retrotransposable elements, *Hum. Hered.*, 74(1):27–35, 2012b.

B. C. Levin, K. A. Holland, D. K. Hancock, M. Coble, T. J. Parsons, L. J. Kienker, D. W. Williams, M. Jones and K. L. Richie. Comparison of the complete mtDNA genome sequences of human cell lines — HL-60 and GM10742A — from individuals with pro-myelocytic leukemia and leber hereditary optic neuropathy, respectively and the inclusion of HL-60 in the NIST human mitochondrial DNA standard reference material — SRM 2392-I, *Mitochondrion*, 2:387–400, 2003.

life Technologies AmpFlSTR® Kit Product Portfolio. http:/www.thermo fisher.com/us/en/home/industrial/human-identification/ampflstr-kit.html, accessed March 6, 2016

A. Linacre and S. S. Tobe. An overview to the investigative approach to species testing in wildlife forensic science, *BMC Investig. Genet.*, 2(1):2, 2011.

C. Li, T. Ma, S. Zhao, S. Zhang, J. Xu, Z. Zhao, L. Jin and S. Li. Development of 11 X-STR loci typing system and genetic analysis in Tibetan and Northern Han populations from China, *Int. J. Leg. Med.*, 125:753–756, 2011.

R. Li, A. Montpetit, M. Rousseau, S. Y. Wu, C. M. Greenwood, T. D. Spector, M. Pollak, C. Polychronakos and J. B. Richards. Somatic point mutations occurring early in development: a monozygotic twin study, *J. Med. Genet.*, 51(1):28–34, 2014.

Q. Liu, D. Lu, X. Li, H. Zhao, J. Zhang, Y. Lai and Y. Chen. Development of the nine X-STR loci typing system and genetic analysis in three nationality populations from China, *Int. J. Leg. Med.*, 125:51–58, 2011.

C. Li, S. Zhao, S. Zhang, L. Li, Y. Liu, J. Chen and J. Xue. Genetic polymorphism of 29 highly informative InDel markers for forensic use in the Chinese Han population, *Forensic Sci. Int. Genet.*, 5(1):e27–e30, 2011.

N. J. Loman, R. V. Misra, T. J. Dallman, C. Constantinidou, S. E. Gharbia, J. Wain and M. J. Pallen. Performance comparison of benchtop high-throughput sequencing platforms, *Nat. Biotech.* 30:434–439, 2012.

H. Luo, Y. Ye, Y. Wang, W. Liang, L. Yun, M. Liao, J. Yan, J. Wu, Y. Li and Y. Hou. Characteristics of eight X-STR loci for forensic purposes in the Chinese population, *Int. J. Leg. Med.*, 125:127–131, 2011.

G. A. Machin. Some causes of genotypic and phenotypic discordance in monozygotic twin pairs, *Am. J. Med. Genet.*, 61:216–228, 1996.

L. Mamanova, A. J. Coffey, C. E. Scott, I. Kozarewa, E. H. Turner, A. Kumar, E. Howard, J. Shendure and D. J. Turner. Target-enrichment strategies for next-generation sequencing, *Nat. Methods*, 7:111–118, 2010.

M. Margulies, M. Egholm, W. E. Altman, S. Attiya, J. S. Bader, L. A. Bemben, J. Berka, M. S. Braverman, Y. J. Chen, Z. Chen, S. B. Dewell, L. Du, J. M. Fierro, X. V. Gomes, B. C. Godwin, W. He, S. Helgesen, C. H. Ho, G. P. Irzyk, S. C. Jando, M. L. Alenquer, T. P. Jarvie, K. B. Jirage, J. B. Kim, J. R. Knight, J. R. Lanza, J. H. Leamon, S. M. Lefkowitz, M. Lei, J. Li, K. L. Lohman, H. Lu, V. B. Makhijani, K. E. McDade, M. P. McKenna, E. W. Myers, E. Nickerson, J. R. Nobile, R. Plant, B. P. Puc, M. T. Ronan, G. T. Roth, G. J. Sarkis, J. F. Simons,

J. W. Simpson, M. Srinivasan, K. R. Tartaro, A. Tomasz, K. A. Vogt, G. A. Volkmer, S. H. Wang, Y. Wang, M. P. Weiner, P. Yu, R. F. Begley and J. M. Rothberg. Genome sequencing in microfabricated high-density picolitre reactors, *Nature*, 437(7057):376–380, 2005.

P. D. Martin, H. Schmitter and P. M. Schneider. A brief history of the formation of DNA databases in forensic science within Europe, *Forens. Sci. Int.*, 119(2):225–231, 2001.

J. A. McElhoe, M. M. Holland, K. D. Makova, M. S. Su, I. M. Paul, C. H. Baker, S. A. Faith and B. Young. Development and assessment of an optimized next-generation DNA sequencing approach for the mtgenome using the Illumina MiSeq, *Forensic Sci. Int. Genet.*, 13:20–29, 2014.

B. Merriman and J. M. Rothberg. Progress in ion torrent semiconductor chip based sequencing, *Electrophoresis*, 33(23):3397–3417, 2012.

M. L. Metzker. Sequencing technologies — the next generation, Nature Reviews Genetics, 11(1):31–46, 2010.

M. Mikkelsen, R. F. Hansen, A. J. Hansen and N. Morling. Massively parallel pyrose-quencing 454 methodology of the mitochondrial genome in forensic genetics, *Forensic Sci. Int. Genet.*, 12:30–37, 2014.

J. Mulero, C. Chang, L. Calandro, R. Green, Y. Li, C. Johnson and L. Hennessy. Development and validation of the AmpFiSTR Yfiler PCR Amplification Kit: a male specific, single amplification 17 Y-STR multiplex system, *J. Forensic Sci.*, 51(1):64–75, 2006.

Y. Nakamura and K. Minaguchi. Sixteen X-chromosomal STRs in two octaplex PCRs in Japanese population and development of 15-locus multiplex PCR system, *Int. J. Leg. Med.*, 124:405–414, 2010.

K. Oostdik, K. Lenz, J. Nye, K. Schelling, D. Yet, S. Bruski, J. Strong, C. Buchanan, J. Sutton, J. Linner, N. Frazier, H. Young, L. Matthies, A. Sage, J. Hahn, R. Wells, N. Williams, M. Price, J. Koehler, M. Staples, K. L. Swango, C. Hill, K. Oyerly, W. Duke, L. Katzilierakis, M. G. Ensenberger, J. M. Bourdeau, C. J. Sprecher, B. Krenke and D. R. Storts. Developmental validation of the PowerPlex® Fusion System for analysis of casework and reference samples: A 24-locus multiplex for new database standards, *Forensic Sci. Int. Genet.*, 12:69–76, 2014.

R. Ottens, D. Taylor, D. Abarno and A. Linacre. Successful direct amplification of nuclear markers from a single hair follicle, *Forensic Sci. Med. Pathol.*, 9(2):238–243, 2013.

A. J. Pakstis, W. C. Speed, R. Fang, F. C. L. Hyland, M. R. Furtado, J. R. Kidd and K. K. Kidd. SNPs for a universal individual identification panel, *Human Genetics*, 127:315–324, 2010.

A. J. Pakstis, W. C. Speed, J. R. Kidd and Kidd K. K. Candidate SNPs for a universal individual identification panel, *Human Genetics*, 121:305–317, 2007.

M. G. Palanichamy, C. Sun, S. Agrawal, H. J. Bandelt, Q. P. Kong, F. Khan, C. Y. Wang, T. K. Chaudhuri, V. Palla and Y. P. Zhang. Phylogeny of mitochondrial DNA macrohaplogroup N in India, based on complete sequencing: implications for the peopling of South Asia, *Am. J. Hum. Genet.*, 75:966–978, 2004.

W. Parson, A. Brandstätter, A. Alonso, N. Brandt, B. Brinkmann, A. Carracedo, D. Corach, O. Froment, I. Furac, T. Grzybowski, K. Hedberg, C. Keyser-Tracqui, T. Kupiec, S. Lutz-Bonengel, B. Mevag, R. Ploski, H. Schmitter, P. Schneider, D. Syndercombe-Court, E. Sørensen, H. Thew, G. Tully and R. Scheithauer. The EDNAP mitochondrial DNA population database (EMPOP) collaborative exercises: organisation, results and perspectives, *Forensic Sci. Int.*, 139:215–226, 2004.

S. Pasino, S. Caratti, Del M. Pero, A. Santovito, C. Torre and Robino C. . Allele and haplotype diversity of X-chromosomal STRs in Ivory Coast, *Int. J. Leg. Med.*, 125:749–752, 2011.

W. Parson, C. Strobl, G. Huber, B. Zimmermann, S. M. Gomes, L. Souto, L. Fendt, R. Delport, R. Langit, S. Wootton, R. Lagacé and J. Irwin.). Evaluation of next generation mtGenome sequencing using the Ion Torrent Personal Genome Machine (PGM), *Forensic Sci. Int. Genet.*, 7:543–549, 2013.

R. Pereira, C. Phillips, C. Alves, A. Amorim, Á. Carracedo and L. Gusmão. Insertion/deletion polymorphisms: a multiplex assay and forensic applications, *Forensic Sci. Int. Genet. Suppl. Ser.*, 2(1):513–515, 2009.

C. Phillips, R. Fang, D. Ballard, M. Fondevila, C. Harrison, F. Hyland, E. Musgrave-Brown, C. Proff, E. Ramos-Luis, B. Sobrino, A. Carracedo, M. R. Furtado, D. S. Court and P. M. Schneider. Evaluation of the Genplex SNP typing system and a 49plex forensic marker panel, *Forensic Sci Int. Genet.*, 1(2):180–185, 2007.

C. Phillips, A. Salas, J. J. Sánchez, M. Fondevila, A. Gómez-Tato, J. Álvarez-Dios, M. Calaza, M. Casares de Cal, D. Ballard, M. V. Lareu and A. Carracedo. The SNPforID Consortium. Inferring ancestral origin using a single multiplex assay of ancestry-informative marker SNPs, *Forensic Sci. Int. Genet.*, 1:273–280, 2007.

Promega Corporation STR Analysis Kits. http://worldwide.promega.com/products/genetic-identity/str-amplification/, accessed March 6, 2016.

M. A. Quail, M. Smith, P. Coupland, T. D. Otto, S. R. Harris, T. R. Connor, A. Bertoni, HP. Swerdlow and Y. Gu. A tale of three next generation sequencing platforms: Comparison of Ion Torrent, Pacific Biosciences and Illumina MiSeq sequencers, *BMC Genomics*, 13:341, 2012.

M. A. Quail, I. Kozarewa, F. Smith, A. Scally, PJ. Stephens, R. Durbin, H. Swerdlow and D. J. Turner. A large genome center's improvements to the Illumina sequencing system, *Nature Methods*, 5:1005–1010, 2008.

M. A. Quail, M. Smith, P. Coupland, T. D. Otto, S. R. Harris, T. R. Connor, A. Bertoni, H. P. Swerdlow and Y. Gu. A tale of three next generation sequencing platforms: comparison of Ion Torrent, Pacific Biosciences and Illumina MiSeq sequencers, *BMC Genomics*, 13:341, 2012.

D. A. Rasko, P. L. Worsham, T. G. Abshire, S. T. Stanley, J. D. Bannan, M. R. Wilson, R. J. Langham, R. S. Decker, L. Jiang, T. D. Read, A. M. Phillippy, S. L. Salzberg, M. Pop, M. N. Van Ert, L. J. Kenefic, P. S. Keim, C. M. Fraser-Liggett and J. Ravel. Bacillus anthracis comparative genome analysis in support of the Amerithrax investigation, *Proc. Natl. Acad. Sci. USA*, 108(12):5027–5032, 2011.

H. R. Razzaghian, M. H. Shahi, L. A. Forsberg, de T. D. Ståhl, D. Absher, N. Dahl, M. P. Westerman and J. P. Dumanski. Somatic mosaicism for chromosome X and Y aneuploidies in monozygotic twins heterozygous fo r sickle cell disease mutation, *Am. J. Med. Genet.*, 52A, 2595–2598, 2010.

M. J. Rieder, S. L. Taylor, V. O. Tobe and D. A. Nickerson. Automating the identification of DNA variations using quality-based fluorescence resequencing: Analysis of the human mitochondrial genome, *Nucleic Acids Res.*, 26:967–973, 1998.

J. M. Rothberg, W. Hinz, T. M. Rearick, J. Schultz, W. Mileski, M. Davey, J. H. Leamon, K. Johnson, M. J. Milgrew, M. Edwards, J. Hoon, J. F. Simons, D. Marran, J. W. Myers, J. F. Davidson, A. Branting, J. R. Nobile, B. P. Puc, D. Light, T. A. Clark, M. Huber, J. T. Branciforte, I. B. Stoner, S. E. Cawley, M. Lyons, Y. Fu, N. Homer, M. Sedova, X. Miao, B. Reed, J. Sabina, E. Feierstein, M. Schorn, M. Alanjary, E. Dimalanta, D. Dressman, R. Kasinskas, T. Sokolsky, J. A. Fidanza, E. Namsaraev, K. J. McKernan, A. Williams, G. T. Roth and J. Bustillo. An integrated semiconductor device enabling non-optical genome sequencing, *Nature*, 475:348–352, 2011.

J. J. Sanchez, C. Phillips, C. Børsting, K. Balogh, M. Bogus, M. Fondevila, C. D. Harrison, E. Musgrave-Brown, A. Salas, D. Syndercombe-Court, P. M. Schneider, A. Carracedo and N. Morling. A multiplex assay with 52 single nucleotide polymorphisms for human identification, *Electrophoresis*, 27(9):1713–1724, 2006.

F. Sanger, S. Nicklen and A. R. Coulson. DNA sequencing with chain-terminating inhibitors, *Proc. Natl. Acad. Sci. USA*, 74(12):5463–5467, 1977.

Scientific Working Group on DNA Analysis Methods. Interpretation Guidelines for Mitochondrial DNA Analysis by Forensic DNA Testing Laboratories. 2013. http://media.wix.com/ugd/4344b0_c5e20877c02f 403c9ba16770e8d41937.pdf, accessed March 6, 2016.

Scientific Working Group on DNA Analysis Methods Validation Guidelines for DNA Analysis Methods, 2012. At: http://media.wix.com/ugd/ 4344b0_cbc27d16dcb64fd88cb36ab2a2a25e4c.pdf, accessed March 6, 2016.

S. B. Seo, J. King, D. Warshauer, C. Davis, J. Ge and B. Budowle. Single nucleotide polymorphism typing with massively parallel sequencing for human identification, *Int. J. Leg. Med.*, 127(6):1079–1086, 2013.

S. B. Seo, X. Zeng, J. L. King, B. L. Larue, M. Assidi, M. H. Al-Qahtani, A. Sajantila and B. Budowle. Underlying data for sequencing the mitochondrial genome with the massively parallel sequencing platform Ion Torrent™ PGM™, *BMC Genomics*, 2015 (in press).

J. Shendure and H. Ji. Next-generation DNA sequencing, *Nature Biotechnology*, 26(10):1135–1145, 2008.

F. Syed, H. Gruenwald and N. Caruccio. Next-generation sequencing library preparation: simultaneous fragmentation and tagging using *in vitro* transposition, *Nat. Methods*, 2009. Available at http://www. nature.com/nmeth/journal/v6/n11/full/nmeth.f.272.html, accessed March 6, 2016.

R. W. Taylor, G. A. Taylor, S. E. Durham and D. M. Turnbull. The determination of complete human mitochondrial DNA sequences in single cells: implications for the study of somatic mitochondrial DNA point mutations, *Nucleic Acids Res*, 29:e74, 2001.

R. Tewhey, J. B. Warner, M. Nakano, B. Libby, M. Medkova, P. H. David, S. K. Kotsopoulos, M. L. Samuels, J. B. Hutchison, JW. Larson, E. J. Topol, M. P. Weiner, O. Harismendy, J. Olson, D. R. Link and K. A. Frazer. Microdroplet-based PCR enrichment for large-scale targeted sequencing. *Nat. Biotechnol.*, 27:1025–1031, 2009.

J. M. Thompson, M. M. Ewing, W. E. Frank, J. J. Pogemiller, C. A. Nolde, D. J. Koehler, A. M. Shaffer, D. R. Rabbach, P. M. Fulmer, C. J. Sprecher and D. R. Storts. Developmental validation of the PowerPlex® Y23

System: A single multiplex Y-STR analysis system for casework and database samples, *Forensic Sci. Int. Genet.*, 7:240–250, 2013.

G. Turcatti, A. Romieu, M. Fedurco, A. P. Tairim. A new class of cleavable fluorescent nucleotides: synthesis and optimization as reversible terminators for DNA sequencing by synthesis, *Nucleic Acids Res.*, 36(4):e25, 2008.

L. Vadlamudi, L. M. Dibbens, K. M. Lawrence, X. Iona, J. M. McMahon, W. Murrell, A. Mackay-Sim, I. E. Scheffer and S. F. Berkovic. Timing of de novo mutagenesis–a twin study of sodium-channel mutations, *N. Engl. J. Med.*, 363(14):1335–1340, 2010.

P. M. Vallone, A. E. Decker and J. M. Butler. Allele frequencies for 70 autosomal SNP loci with U.S. Caucasian, African-American and Hispanic samples, *Forensic Sci. Int.*, 149:279–286, 2005.

C. P. Van Tassell, T. P. Smith, L. K. Matukumalli, J. F. Taylor, R. D. Schnabel, C. T. Lawley, C. D. Haudenschild, S. S. Moore, W. C. Warren and T. S. Sonstegard. SNP discovery and allele frequency estimation by deep sequencing of reduced representation libraries, *Nat. Meth.*, 5:247–252, 2008.

P. B. Vander Horn, A. Kraltcheva, G. Luo, M. Landes, S. Chen, K. Heinemann, T. Nikiforov, J. Shirley, E. Tozer and D. Mazur. The Ion PGM™ Hi-Q™ Sequencing Polymerase: Reducing Systematic Error, Increasing Accuracy and Improving Read-length, 2013. http://www.ashg. org/2014meeting/abstracts/fulltext/f140121252.htm, accessed March 6, 2016.

C. Van Neste, M. Vandewoestyne, W. Van Criekinge, D. Deforce and F. Van Nieuwerburgh. My-Forensic-Loci-queries (MyFLq) framework for analysis of forensic STR data generated by massive parallel sequencing, *Forens. Sci. Int. Genet.*, 2015 (in press).

C. Van Neste, Y. Gansemans, D. De Coninck, D. Van Hoofstat, W. Van Criekinge, D. Deforce and F. Van Nieuwerburgh. Forensic massively parallel sequencing data analysis tool: Implementation of MyFLq as a standalone web- and Illumina BaseSpace®-application, *Forensic Sci. Int. Genet.*, 2015 (in press).

D. H. Warshauer, D. Lin, K. Hari, R. Jain, C. Davis, B. LaRue, J. King and B. Budowle. STRait Razor: A length-based forensic STR allele-calling tool for use with second generation sequencing data, *Forens. Sci. Int. Genet.*, 7:409–417, 2013.

D. H. Warshauer, J. L. King and B. Budowle. STRait Razor v2.0: the improved STR allele identification tool — razor, *Forens. Sci. Int. Genet.*, 14:182–186, 2015.

D. G. Wang, J. B. Fan, C. J. Siao, A. Berno, P. Young, R. Sapolsky, G. Ghandour, N. Perkins, E. Winchester, J. Spencer, L. Kruglyak, L. Stein, L. Hsie, T. Topaloglou, E. Hubbell, E. Robinson, M. Mittmann, M. S. Morris, N. Shen, D. Kilburn, J. Rioux, C. Nusbaum, S. Rozen, T. J. Hudson, R. Lipshutz, M. Chee and E. S. Lander. Large scale identification, mapping and genotyping of single-nucleotide polymorphisms in the human genome, *Science*, 280:1077–1082, 1998.

J. Weber-Lehmann, E. Schilling, G. Gradl, D. C. Richter, J. Wiehler and B. Rolf. Finding the needle in the haystack: Differentiating 'identical' twins in paternity testing and forensics by ultra-deep next generation sequencing, *Forensic Sci. Int. Genet.*, 9:42–46, 2014.

K. S. Wetterstrand. DNA Sequencing Costs: Data from the NHGRI Large-Scale Genome Sequencing Program, 2013. Available at: https://www.genome.gov/sequencingcosts/.

M. R. Wilson, D. Polanskey, J. Butler, J. A. DiZinno, J. Replogle and B. Budowle. Extraction, PCR amplification, and sequencing of mitochondrial DNA from human hair shafts, *BioTechniques*, 18:662–669, 1995.

K. Ye, M. Beekman, E. W. Lameijer, Y. Zhang, M. H. Moed, van den E. B. Akker, J. Deelen, J. J. Houwing Duistermaat, D. Kremer, S. Y. Anvar, J. F. Laros, D. Jones, K. Raine, B. Blackburne, S. Potluri, Q. Long, V. Guryev, van der R. Breggen, R. G. Westendorp, P. A. 't Hoen, J. den Dunnen, G. J. van Ommen, G. Willemsen, S. J. Pitts, D. R. Cox, Z. Ning, D. I. Boomsma and P. E. Slagboom. Aging as accelerated accumulation of somatic variants: whole-genome sequencing of centenarian and middle-aged monozygotic twin pairs. *Twin Research and Human Genetics*, 16(6):1026–1032, 2013.

X. Zeng, J. L. King, M. Stoljarova, D. H. Warshauer, B. L. LaRue, A. Sajantila, J. Patel, D. R. Storts and B. Budowle. High sensitivity multiplex short tandem repeat loci analyses with massively parallel sequencing, *Forens. Sci. Int. Genet.*, 2015 (in press).

CHAPTER 14

Massively Parallel Mitochondrial DNA Sequencing in Forensic Genetics: Principles and Opportunities

Jodi A. Irwin[*], *Rebecca S. Just*[*] *and Walther Parson*[†,‡]

[*]*FBI Laboratory, Quantico, VA, USA*
[†]*Institute of Legal Medicine, Medical University of Innsbruck, Innsbruck, Austria*
[‡]*Forensic Science Program, The Pennsylvania State University, University Park, PA, USA*

1 Introduction

Let us consider a hypothetical, albeit realistic forensic case in, say, Italy. Police collect evidence from a crime scene at which hair samples are the only source of biological evidence. Nuclear DNA typing does not produce useful results for the identification of the hair donor(s), and sequence analysis of the mitochondrial DNA (mtDNA) control region (CR) yields the same result in all analyzed samples. The CR haplotype — 16519C 263G 315.1C — is the most common sequence observed in Europe ($\approx$3%) ((Parson *et al.*, 1998), for example, www.empop.org). As part of the investigation, the police identify a suspect who shares this CR haplotype. As a result, he cannot be excluded as a potential donor of the hair samples. However, because of the frequency of the profile, the statistical strength of the non-exclusion is somewhat low.

This scenario represents the current, commonly employed approach to mtDNA analysis based on conventional Sanger-based sequencing of the approximately 1,100 base pair CR. Additional testing of mtDNA variation outside the CR is currently legally restricted in some jurisdictions, and is generally infeasible with standard Sanger-based protocols anyway. However, as we will describe in this chapter, massively parallel sequencing (MPS) of the entire mitochondrial genome (mtGenome) is technically feasible from forensic samples, even from minute quantities of mtDNA isolated from commonly encountered evidentiary specimens such as hair shafts (Parson *et al.*, 2015). This, combined with the fact that a variety of studies have shown that individuals who share common CR haplotypes — as in the case above — can routinely be distinguished based on information outside of the control region (Coble *et al.*, 2004; Bodner *et al.*, 2015), suggests that complete mtGenome sequencing by MPS is likely to greatly expand the utility of mtDNA analysis in forensic casework.

2 Massively Parallel Sequencing — The Next Generation

The emergence of extremely high-throughput sequencing platforms a decade ago has permanently transformed the landscape of genetic data generation. The development of MPS technology was primarily driven by large-scale sequencing projects (Margulies *et al.*, 2005). Indeed, sequencing of entire organismal genomes, which forms the basis of high profile endeavors such as the 1000 Genomes Project (Abecasis *et al.*, 2010) and the Neanderthal Genome Project (Green *et al.*, 2010), is clearly one of the most powerful applications of MPS. Yet these methods, which produce large quantities of sequence data at very low cost compared to Sanger sequencing, are now being applied to both large and small-scale questions across numerous scientific disciplines. In the field of forensics, investigations into MPS for both nuclear DNA and mitochondrial DNA typing are well underway (Holland *et al.*, 2011; Irwin *et al.*, 2011; Loreille *et al.*, 2011; Bornman *et al.*, 2012; Van Neste *et al.*, 2012; Rockenbauer *et al.*, 2014; Weber-Lehmann *et al.*, 2014; Bintz *et al.*, 2014; Parson *et al.*, 2013; Scheible *et al.*, 2014; King *et al.*, 2014; McElhoe *et al.*, 2014; Mikkelsen *et al.*, 2014; Davis *et al.*, 2015; Parson *et al.*, 2015; Fordyce *et al.*, 2015; Zeng *et al.*, 2015; for instance). However, the technology has not yet been widely tested for practical casework application. In this section, we discuss the MPS strategies and methods employed in various disciplines for mitochondrial DNA data generation, and address these approaches as they relate to current forensic practice and anticipated forensic application.

Across a number of genetic disciplines, mtGenome data have been fairly easily recovered by a variety of MPS techniques, including shotgun genomic libraries of high quality samples, and even hybridization-enriched libraries targeting other markers (e.g. the human exome; Picardi and Pesole, 2012; Diroma *et al.*, 2014; Ye *et al.*, 2014a). However, the most straightforward and cost-effective means of developing mtDNA sequences are targeted methods designed specifically for mtDNA. These approaches exploit the high throughput capacity of MPS to develop data at high depths of coverage for tens or hundreds of individuals, and numerous studies have demonstrated the clear utility of MPS for this purpose (Gunnarsdottir *et al.*, 2011; Barbieri *et al.*, 2012; Duggan *et al.*, 2013, 2014; Delfin *et al.*, 2014; Lippold *et al.*, 2014; Rebolledo-Jaramillo *et al.*, 2014; Skonieczna *et al.*, 2015; Naue *et al.*, 2015; Li *et al.*, 2015; and others). The throughput and sensitivity of the technology not only result in far more efficient and cost-effective data production than can be achieved *via* Sanger sequencing, but also permit comprehensive examinations of molecular and population genetic features of the molecule that were previously not possible. In addition, the completely different paradigm for sequence data generation has facilitated the development of novel laboratory processes that circumvent some of the key limitations of Sanger workflows for the types of low quality/quantity samples to which mtDNA analysis is often applied. Though originally designed specifically for mtDNA recovery (Briggs *et al.*, 2009; Maricic *et al.*, 2010), these MPS approaches have now found widespread utility for other markers as well (Carpenter *et al.*, 2013; Enk *et al.*, 2014; Der Sarkissian *et al.*, 2015).

The single greatest potential benefit of MPS for mtDNA sequencing in forensics is, without question, the recovery of more information — complete mtGenomes, in fact — from all types of samples. There has been significant interest over the past decade in non-CR mtDNA data and the additional discriminatory power that it may bring to mtDNA testing in forensics. Valuable data and assays have resulted from these efforts (Coble *et al.*, 2004; Vallone *et al.*, 2004; Divne *et al.*, 2005; Kline *et al.*, 2005; Brandstatter *et al.*, 2006; Grignani *et al.*, 2006; Alvarez-Iglesias *et al.*, 2007; Andreasson *et al.*, 2007; Nelson *et al.*, 2007; Parson and Bandelt, 2007; Kohnemann *et al.*, 2008; Just *et al.*, 2009; for instance). However, it is only recently that population-based studies have clearly demonstrated what has long been suspected: complete mtGenome data significantly improve the discriminatory power of mtDNA testing. In a recent study examining inter-individual variation among randomly sampled persons from across the United States, HVS-I and HVS-II information provided resolution of 64–76% of the sampled haplotypes (depending on population) and CR data increased those values to 74–80%. However, complete mtGenome data permitted nearly full resolution in the three populations studied (94% in Hispanics, 98.5% in Caucasians and 98.8% in African–Americans; (Just *et al.*, 2014b). Similarly, an examination of three smaller population samples from Texas demonstrated mtDNA lineage resolution ranging from 85% to 93% when only HVS-I/HVS-II profiles were considered, but almost complete discrimination (98–100%) when variation across the full mtGenome was considered (King *et al.*, 2014).

Even if these marked increases in resolution and discriminatory power among randomly sampled individuals had been well-understood over the past decade, the substantial technical and cost barriers to developing such data would still have precluded routine mtGenome sequencing in forensic casework. Traditional Sanger-based workflows targeting just the highly variable 1.1 kbp mtDNA CR have generally required, depending on sample quality, between 2 and 10 amplicons (Wilson *et al.*, 1995; Gabriel *et al.*, 2001; Eichmann and Parson, 2008; Berger and Parson, 2009), often in independent polymerase chain reactions (PCRs). Amplification has then been followed by at least two sequencing reactions per PCR product. Thus, between 12 and 20 independent sequencing reactions have historically been required to develop complete CR haplotypes to the highest-quality forensic standards. To span the entire mtGenome *via* Sanger sequencing, the most reliable and robust protocols require upwards of 96 sequencing reactions per sample (Coble *et al.*, 2004; Fendt *et al.*, 2009). Further complicating matters, mtDNA data are primarily sought in forensics when the genetic material is severely limited and/or compromised (e.g. hair and calcified tissue specimens), and thus the acquisition of sequence data is nearly always dependent on the recovery of numerous small amplicons. There simply is not enough evidentiary material in most forensic cases to support amplification and Sanger sequencing of the entire mtGenome. Given this required level of effort, expense and sample material, it is not surprising that mtDNA examinations in forensics and other disciplines have historically refrained from sequencing of the entire molecule.

With MPS, the landscape of what is possible in the forensic context changes significantly. Large-scale mtGenome sequencing projects that were previously infeasible — or at best extremely expensive — are now possible. In addition, a number of benchtop, medium through-put MPS instruments designed specifically for smaller laboratories are available from a host of vendors. In other disciplines, these developments have brought large-scale sequencing capabilities to even the smallest of laboratories, leading to a so-called "democratization" of DNA sequencing (Shendure and Ji, 2008). A similar democratization is almost certain to take place in forensics; and among the many changes that are expected to come with MPS is the significant expansion of mtDNA application and utility. MtDNA analysis will no longer be the niche DNA subdiscipline restricted primarily to large well-funded laboratories that it has been in the past. Instead, even small forensic laboratories will have the resources and opportunity to perform, and take full advantage of, mtDNA testing.

2.1 Complete mtGenome Sequencing from High Quality Samples

While mtDNA testing in forensic casework has historically been driven by sample quality, with mtDNA data sought largely in those cases for which sample material will not yield probative nuclear DNA profiles, mtDNA data are also extremely helpful for missing persons investigations, disaster victim identification, and immigration and intelligence applications that do not necessarily involve low quality and quantity specimens. These latter cases benefit from the uniparental inheritance of the marker and its utility in clarifying extended familial relationships. mtDNA data can often offer significant information when (i) autosomal short tandem repeats (STRs) alone provide little or no evidence of relatedness, when (ii) high kinship indices are encountered in searches of large databases (and may therefore be adventitious rather than "true" hits), and when (iii) specific hypotheses of relatedness (e.g. maternal) are in question.

In a MPS framework, the recovery of complete mtGenomes from these types of high-quality samples is, technically speaking, quite straightforward. A litany of assays and approaches for MPS-based mtGenome sequencing have been published over the past 5 or so years, primarily in other disciplines for studies of mitochondrial disease and/or the association of mitochondrial DNA variants with other disorders. Though these approaches have been developed with other applications in mind, the assays themselves and many aspects of MPS data analysis and interpretation translate directly to forensics.

The vast majority of published assays for high-quality samples employ long-range PCR enrichment of the mtDNA genome. Amplification is then followed by mechanical or enzymatic shearing, MPS library preparation and, finally, sequencing. A number of amplification approaches have been described. However, in most assays, two amplicons of approximately 9 kb in size are used (Fendt *et al.*, 2009; He *et al.*, 2010; Ye *et al.*, 2014b; Clarke *et al.*, 2014). These 2-amplicon long-range PCR approaches have also been the most widely tested for potential forensic application (Parson *et al.*, 2013, 2015; King *et al.*, 2014; Mikkelsen *et al.*, 2014; McElhoe *et al.*, 2014); yet, other approaches employing between one and 8 amplicons have also been described (Vancampenhout *et al.*, 2014; Gardner *et al.*, 2015). Theoretically, any PCR amplification strategy would be feasible for full mtGenome enrichment provided the final data quality (which is heavily influenced by every step of the upstream process — including library preparation and the selected sequencing chemistry/platform) is adequate. Because the use of fewer amplification products tends to simplify MPS library preparation and data analysis, as well as reduce overall costs, long-range PCR is desirable for routine high-throughput production of mtGenomes. However, other practical considerations related to the logistics and costs of casework implementation, to include required reagents and reagent quality control, will ultimately need to be factored in. To the best of our knowledge, no studies thus far have systematically compared different PCR enrichment approaches in terms of their effect on final mtDNA data quality or the anticipated true cost of routine use in mtDNA casework.

Following generation, MPS-based mtGenome data are routinely assessed by a number of features. These include Phred quality score (Q-score), depth and uniformity of coverage, and strand bias. These features are generally evaluated both across the mtGenome to gain an overall view of data quality, as well as at the specific sites identified in an alignment as either variants or mixtures relative to the revised Cambridge reference sequence (rCRS, Andrews *et al.*, 1999).

Q-scores are commonly employed at various stages of the MPS data analysis process to ensure data quality. Originally developed for Sanger-based sequence data to provide a reliable measure of sequencing accuracy that could be used to automate data analysis and minimize the need for human data review, Q-scores historically found their greatest use in large-scale Sanger sequencing projects (e.g. Lander *et al.*, 2001). In Sanger-based forensic mtDNA testing, however, they have rarely been employed. Because raw Sanger electropherograms and alignments are routinely scrutinized base-by-base by multiple DNA analysts, there has simply been no need to incorporate quality scores in the overall forensic mtDNA process. However, with the thousands upon thousands of reads generated in a given MPS experiment, it is simply not feasible to manually review every base generated for a given sample or MPS run. Thus, in a MPS framework, Q-scores serve the very purpose for which Sanger-based Phred scores were originally intended.

While Q-scores most commonly refer to the probability that a given base has been miscalled, they are now also used to describe read quality, read mapping quality and consensus base quality. Reads generally must meet minimum Q-score requirements just to make it through to the alignment and mapping stage. Aligned reads are often further culled by how well they map, with those reads of low mapping quality generally removed from downstream variant calling processes (Templeton *et al.*, 2013; Samuels *et al.*, 2013). Finally, consensus variants are routinely called only when the Q-scores of the component bases meet a particular minimum (Gardner *et al.*, 2015). At each of these stages, a Q-score of 30 or greater, which reflects an error in one out of every 1,000 bases (or an incorrectly mapped read one of every 1,000 mapped reads, for example) is a commonly employed metric. This type of Q-score based data filtering and analysis is widely used in MPS applications. However, Q-scores are particularly valuable in mtDNA workflows where point and length heteroplasmy — features specific to the molecule — can affect base, read and mapping qualities. Reads with Q-scores greater than 30 generally comprise the vast majority of MPS data produced from PCR-enriched mtDNA libraries (McElhoe *et al.*, 2014; Parson *et al.*, 2015), and variant and read mapping quality score requirements of > Q30 have been successfully employed to call variants from difficult sample libraries as well (Templeton *et al.*, 2013; Samuels *et al.*, 2013; Parson *et al.*, 2015). That said, Q-scores as low as 20 have also been shown to produce reliable mtDNA results (Mikkelsen *et al.*, 2014).

When considering read coverage across the molecule, depth and uniformity are plainly influenced by the amplification strategy itself. Although coverage patterns are quite reproducible even between high and low quality samples when the same amplification strategy is used, different PCR enrichment methods generate distinctly different patterns. For example, when coverage maps from three studies employing different amplification strategies but similar library preparation and sequencing methods are compared, variable patterns are observed (see King *et al.*, 2014, Figure 1; Parson *et al.*, 2015, Figure 3; McElhoe *et al.*, 2014, Figure 3). These PCR-induced differences tend to be even further exacerbated by downstream library preparation (shearing methods, primarily), MPS sequencing chemistry and final data handling (Vancampenhout *et al.*, 2014), due to particular biases at each step of the process. In fact, data handling is very likely to be one of the greatest factors in variability. Read filtering, trimming and alignment parameters, together with variant calling parameters — which are all generally dependent on base quality score — undoubtedly affect mtGenome data assembly and therefore coverage.

Despite coverage differences that can be attributed to different steps of the process, it is also the case that many of the same data features emerge regardless of the workflow. For example, reduced coverage around polycytosine stretches at positions 309 and 573 is common across nearly all studies. This is typically understood to be the result of known issues with the sequencing and, perhaps even more so, alignment of homopolymer regions (Parson *et al.*, 2013, 2015; King *et al.*, 2014; Seo *et al.*, 2015). In addition, when studies employing a standard enzymatic shearing and tagmentation approach with different PCR-enrichment strategies are compared, a few particular regions of reduced coverage are quite reproducible (King *et al.*, 2014; McElhoe *et al.*, 2014). The reasons underlying consistently low coverage in these regions are not entirely clear. High and low GC content may account for some regions of high and low read coverage, respectively (Aird *et al.*, 2011; Ekblom *et al.*, 2014). Yet, analyses of GC content in human mtGenome studies specifically have failed to offer sufficient evidence (McElhoe *et al.*,

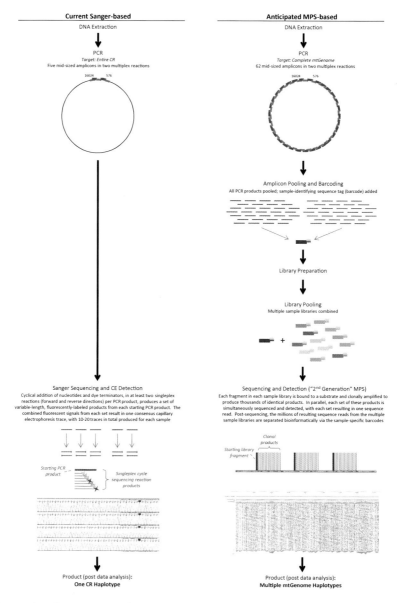

Figure 1: Comparison of current Sanger and anticipated MPS mtDNA data generation workflows.

Note: These example Sanger (CR) and MPS (mtGenome) workflows are based on the multiplex PCR approaches described in Eichmann and Parson (2008) and Parson *et al.* (2015), respectively, and would be suitable for the aged, degraded forensic specimens to which mtDNA typing is often applied.

2014; Clarke *et al.*, 2014). These conflicting indications may be due to differences in the PCR and library preparation protocols that would tend to exacerbate or minimize the coverage differences due to GC content (Aird *et al.*, 2011). Another possibility is that these regions, due to their particular sequence composition, are more prone to base misincorporation during sequencing. An excess of such sequencing errors would lead to reads with low quality scores, which may in turn either be filtered prior to assembly or pass filter but not assemble due to an excess of differences from the reference (i.e. baseline sequencing errors or misincorporation errors resulting from DNA damage (Nakamura *et al.*, 2011; Parks and Lambert, 2015)). In either case, the errors would ultimately result in reduced coverage. A specific area of low coverage around position 3500 in the mtGenome has been observed in multiple recent studies (King *et al.*, 2014; McElhoe *et al.*, 2014; Parson *et al.*, 2015). Interestingly, an early MPS-based examination of mtDNA heteroplasmy that employed mechanical rather than enzymatic shearing of a PCR-enriched library reported 3492 as an error hotspot (Li *et al.*, 2010), and data from a hybridization (rather than PCR) protocol for mtDNA enrichment displayed a coverage dip in the same area (see Maricic *et al.*, 2010, Figure 2). The fact that this specific low coverage region is observed regardless of enrichment and library preparation method, together with the fact that 3492 has been identified as an error hotspot, may point to context-dependent sequencing error as the explanation for this particular region of low coverage. It is important to note, however, that all of these examinations used a sequencing-by-synthesis MPS platform, and that sequencing error hotspots have not only been associated with specific sites and genomes, but also specific sequencing platforms (Li and Stoneking, 2012).

Thus far, in those studies for which mtDNA data generated *via* Sanger technology have been available for direct comparison, the final haplotypes produced *via* MPS have been consistent with the benchmark Sanger haplotypes, with only two exceptions: the detection of low level point heteroplasmies, and the alignment and number of insertions and deletions (Parson *et al.*, 2015; King *et al.*,

2014; Davis *et al.*, 2015; Skonieczna *et al.*, 2015). In the case of heteroplasmy detection, it is expected — and has indeed been shown — that MPS is more sensitive to low level variants. Some authors have suggested that low-level heteroplasmy, mixtures and nuclear pseudogenes may be detectable at levels at or below 1% with adequate coverage (Guo *et al.*, 2012; Bintz *et al.*, 2014; Rebolledo-Jaramillo *et al.*, 2014; Li *et al.*, 2015). Yet, reliable MPS detection thresholds for given depths of coverage and data quality have yet to be firmly established (Just *et al.*, 2014a).

Alignment of indels is a slightly different matter. Guidelines for the alignment of indel regions of the mtGenome in Sanger-based data have been put forth by both the International Society of Forensic Genetics (ISFG, (Parson *et al.*, 2014)) and the U.S. Scientific Working Group on DNA Methods (SWGDAM, 2013). However, with MPS data, the alignment of reads assembled to the reference typically cannot be adjusted or manually manipulated. As a result, MPS alignment algorithms that do not uniformly handle indels often create artificial discrepancies between Sanger and MPS haplotypes (Goto *et al.*, 2011; Parson *et al.*, 2015). The presence of length heteroplasmy in some indel regions further complicates the issue (Just *et al.*, 2015b). Proper alignment of indels in MPS-based data will hopefully be a matter of incorporating the Sanger-based guidelines into forensic-specific alignment algorithms, perhaps in combination with bioinformatic translation of the haplotypes post-secondary analysis (King *et al.*, 2014).

Another feature used to broadly assess the quality of MPS data is strand bias. When used in the context of MPS, strand bias most commonly refers to differential read coverage in one direction vs. the other. This is also known as unbalanced strand mapping. On a finer level, the term also captures more specific differences between the complementary reads at any given position. These fine scale strand biases often contribute to alignment issues that, in turn, directly impact the broad scale biases in strand coverage. Systematic sequencing errors in MPS data have been shown to exhibit bias (Nakamura *et al.*, 2011; Meacham *et al.*, 2011; Minoche *et al.*, 2011; Li and Stoneking, 2012; Schirmer *et al.*, 2015). That is, a given error is more likely to occur in one strand than the other. Flaherty *et al.*, (2012) showed that while error rates between reads on the same strand can be highly correlated, error rates between forward and reverse strands generally cannot. This is not unlike current Sanger sequencing technology where sequencing artifacts manifest differently in forward and reverse strands. In both cases, the cause of unidirectional base misincorporation is likely the result of a number of factors, including localized sequence motif, base composition, sequence context, base pair stacking, and secondary structure of the single-stranded molecules (Parker *et al.*, 1995, 1996; Li *et al.*, 2010; Nakamura *et al.*, 2011; Ross *et al.*, 2013; Minoche *et al.*, 2011).

As a result of these biases, and for the same reasons that both forward and reverse strand sequence information is sought with Sanger-based data, balanced complementary strand coverage is also desirable with MPS data. Relatively even forward and reverse coverage mitigates the chance that sequencing errors/artifacts may be identified as true variants (false positives), and serves as a general indication that sequencing problems are absent for the region (Nakamura *et al.*, 2011). Broadly speaking, a balance of forward and reverse reads over any given position provides greater confidence that the authentic haplotype is reflected in the consensus. Thus, along with read coverage and quality score, strand bias is an additional feature of MPS data that can and should be considered in evaluating read, variant and overall quality (McElroy *et al.*, 2013 and references therein, Guo *et al.*, 2012; Bull *et al.*, 2011).

Though efforts to better characterize and understand critical features of MPS workflows and the resulting quality of data produced are still underway in forensics, carefully considered informatics pipelines that establish particular standards with respect to read coverage, strand balance, and read/base quality score have already been shown to be robust (Li *et al.*, 2010; King *et al.*, 2014; Rebolledo-Jaramillo *et al.*, 2014; Parson *et al.*, 2015; Skonieczna *et al.*, 2015; Li *et al.*, 2015). As a result, the rather straightforward methods for mtGenome production from non-compromised specimens are likely to be more extensively used to elucidate population histories

(Barbieri *et al.*, 2012; Duggan *et al.*, 2013, 2014; Delfin *et al.*, 2014; Lippold *et al.*, 2014; for example), further characterize mtGenome population variation (Gunnarsdottir *et al.*, 2011; King *et al.*, 2014) and develop mtGenome reference population datasets for forensic application (King *et al.*, 2014). Such studies from high quality samples will form the necessary body of MPS data required to better understand and define key aspects of MPS workflows and data (e.g. signal: noise ratios, depth of coverage, sensitivity) that factor heavily into the development of data analysis and interpretation guidelines appropriate for forensic application.

2.2 Complete mtGenome Sequencing from Low Quality Samples

Given that the vast majority of MPS methods now available for mtGenome sequencing center on high quality samples, it is somewhat ironic that many of the earliest studies describing MPS-developed mtDNA data actually came from ancient DNA (aDNA) laboratories targeting mtDNA for its many benefits with the lowest DNA quality specimens (Gilbert *et al.*, 2007; Briggs *et al.*, 2009; Stiller *et al.*, 2009; Knapp and Hofreiter, 2010). MPS brought completely new capability to a DNA studies. The earliest MPS-based ancient DNA studies employed shotgun sequencing approaches for the recovery of complete genome (nuclear and mitochondrial) information. Although poor sample quality and extremely low endogenous DNA content relative to microbial DNA contaminants made these studies extremely expensive, inefficient and time consuming, they provided clear evidence that MPS offered opportunities with the most damaged DNA that simply did not exist otherwise. As soon as this potential was established, it was not long before novel MPS methods were designed to more efficiently and constructively recover large quantities of targeted, endogenous DNA from the lowest quality samples (Knapp and Hofreiter, 2010).

In the context of forensic DNA testing, "low quality" is a fairly broad term. It often refers to any sample that is challenging to amplify with routine assays and protocols. Here, the term "low quality" is used to describe specimens in which the DNA has been significantly altered or damaged in one way or another. The most obvious and routinely encountered form of damage in forensic specimens is DNA fragmentation or degradation (Figure 1). However, it is often the case that individual bases are missing or modified as well. Any sample subjected to environmental, chemical or other insults may exhibit these features. In the worst of these cases, the endogenous DNA will be so fragmented that templates long enough for targeted PCR are no longer present, and thus PCR fails outright.

Because the size of mtDNA amplicons that can be targeted in any given situation is strictly correlated to the state of preservation of the DNA in a specimen, standard Sanger-based mtDNA laboratory workflows become ever more complicated, costly and labor-intensive as sample quality decreases. With decreasing DNA quality, the size of recoverable amplicons diminishes and the number of amplicons required to yield probative data increases. Furthermore, there are lower limits to the size of an amplicon that can be effectively sequenced with Sanger technology. Amplicons smaller than 70 or 80 bp yield only 20–30 bases of usable sequence even under the best of circumstances, and for DNA fragmented beyond that size range, creative methods that artificially extend the length of the amplicon in order to improve the quantity of sequence data recovered are required (Big Dye® Direct, Applied Biosystems, Foster City, CA; Binladen *et al.*, 2007; O. Loreille, personal communication). Regardless of these inventive approaches, there is little question that limitations of standard PCR-enrichment/Sanger sequencing workflows greatly restrict the ease of recovering complete mtGenome data from the lowest quality specimens.

In situations for which PCR-enrichment approaches prove challenging, target enrichment based on hybridization capture has been shown to be particularly effective in recovering data for the full mtGenome when paired with MPS. These methods, which rely on the use of mtGenome-specific probes to capture mtDNA fragments from a DNA extract, have been employed to develop complete mtGenome haplotypes from ancient and modern specimens alike (Briggs *et al.*, 2009; Krause *et al.*, 2010; Maricic *et al.*, 2010; Templeton *et al.*, 2013; Meyer *et al.*, 2014; for example). The fact that DNA fragments of any size can be recovered *via* hybridization makes this approach especially appealing for samples that fail to yield amplification products with targeted PCR. Unfortunately, there are some drawbacks. First and foremost, enrichment is not as efficient as targeted PCR. Final mapped read percentages are often reported as being between 60% and 90% (Enk *et al.*, 2014; Parla *et al.*, 2011; mycroarray.com); however, many studies, and particularly those performed on highly degraded and heavily microbially contaminated samples, report enrichment efficiencies much lower (Enk *et al.*, 2013; Carpenter *et al.*, 2013; Briggs *et al.*, 2009; Loreille *et al.*, 2011; Avila-Arcos *et al.*, 2011). The effectiveness of enrichment seems to be at least partially dependent on the ratio of target to non-target DNA in the extract. Libraries with a high proportion of target DNA in the sample already (e.g. pristine samples or other samples resistant to degradation and contamination, such as hair) tend to yield higher percentages of on-target reads following enrichment, but a lower degree of enrichment overall than low quality samples. Libraries with a low quantity of target DNA, on the other hand, show a higher degree of enrichment (e.g. from 0.3% pre-enrichment to 20% post-enrichment, or a 70-fold increase) but a final percentage of on-target reads that is generally much lower overall (Carpenter *et al.*, 2013; Enk *et al.*, 2013). In these cases, numerous off-target fragments are carried over in the final library, producing a large (if not majority) number of off-target reads in the final data.

Hybridization enriched libraries also tend to reflect more non-specifically captured fragments than libraries enriched *via* other methods (Li and Stoneking, 2012). That is, targets similar in sequence to the fragments of interest, and therefore similar to the probes, are more readily captured in these workflows. A relevant example is the recovery of mtGenome-specific sequences from 1000 Genomes Project whole exome data. Although the early-design probes were intended to target nuclear DNA exclusively, "contaminant" mtDNA sequences similar to the NUMT-targeted probes were captured as well (Picardi and Pesole, 2012). In MPS data from high quality specimens, identification at the data analysis step of non-specifically captured large pseudogenes or intact contaminant molecules may not be too difficult, and bioinformatic methods and tools to flag such sequences can be implemented (Li and Stoneking, 2012; Bintz *et al.*, 2014; Li *et al.*, 2015). But in MPS data, from compromised specimens where the DNA of interest is highly fragmented, distinguishing non-specific targets from the authentic DNA sequence is likely to be complicated by both short read lengths as well as damage-induced sequencing errors that may impact read mapping (Schubert *et al.*, 2012).

Despite these drawbacks, hybridization enrichment is the only option for samples harboring DNA too fragmented for PCR enrichment. In addition, hybridization enrichment may be preferable to PCR enrichment under particular circumstances. For instance, when the DNA of interest is just partially degraded but can only be recovered together with more intact, non-target contaminant molecules, hybridization capture may be preferable to PCR enrichment. Where PCR enrichment might favor the larger, intact contaminant molecules as a result of amplicon size, hybridization-based enrichment — which imposes no size restrictions — may improve the recovery of short authentic DNA molecules relative to the larger contaminants. Regardless, it seems clear that the lower limit of sample quality from which probative data can be recovered will expand as a result of these types of assays (Loreille *et al.*, 2011); and thus it is reasonable to expect that samples of lower and lower quality will be submitted to forensic laboratories as the success of hybridization capture on previously intractable specimens is realized.

Though hybridization capture will clearly present opportunities to DNA type samples that have been recalcitrant with previous Sanger-based methods (Loreille *et al.*, 2011; Templeton *et al.*, 2013), it is likely that PCR enrichment will be the methodology most commonly employed in forensic mtDNA casework in the near term. Most routine mtDNA cases (e.g. hair and unidentified human remains) yield DNA fragments amenable to targeted PCR (i.e. > 100 bp), and NGS multiplex approaches to both control region and mtGenome data generation have already been developed (Parson *et al.*, 2015). PCR-based enrichment is also straightforward and efficient in terms of the laboratory workflow and the data recovered, with nearly 100% of the reads from PCR-enriched libraries mapping to target. Finally, because PCR-based approaches to mtDNA typing are the historical standard, a smaller shift in laboratory practices, reagents and instrumentation will be required in the transition to MPS. It is possible, however, that over time, and particularly if probative data continue to be recovered from lower and lower quality specimens, hybridization methods may prove to have broader utility in forensic DNA investigations. Capture can be designed to simultaneously enrich for the entire mtGenome as well as various nuclear DNA markers of forensic interest without the need to optimize large PCR-based multiplexes (Hancock-Hanser *et al.*, 2013), and the fact that capture methods can be uniformly applied regardless of DNA quality would likely streamline laboratory workflows.

Aside from its quite significant benefits in terms of raw data recovery from the most difficult specimens, MPS also brings other advantages to the analysis of degraded and low quality DNA. Sequencing errors and artifacts that result from damaged DNA templates are routinely encountered in data from the most compromised specimens (Hofreiter *et al.*, 2001; Stiller *et al.*, 2006; Gilbert *et al.*, 2007). Such errors can manifest as complete base substitutions (if the misincorporation occurs during the early cycles of the PCR), but are more often observed as mixed bases.

A number of strategies have been employed in Sanger-based workflows to detect and resolve misincorporation errors. These include replicate extractions and/or amplifications, as well as overlapping sequence data from different amplicons. Because misincorporation artifacts are difficult to reproduce due to the random nature of their occurrence in the first place, replicate testing often resolves the issue. Conventional molecular cloning — a time-consuming and labor intensive process — has also historically been used to identify and characterize damage. Positions that manifest as mixed bases in Sanger data can be further resolved at the molecular level through cloning. Cloning has also been used to discern damaged authentic DNA molecules from undamaged contaminants, which tend to exhibit fewer misincorporation errors (Meyer *et al.*, 2014).

In a MPS framework, replicate testing will still be of value when targeted PCR is used for enrichment, as only replicate extractions and/or amplifications can reveal some of the more pronounced stochastic effects of the PCR process. When it comes to characterizing the nature of the damage and further resolving authentic from contaminant molecules, however, MPS data are perfectly suited. Because MPS reads are developed and presented at the level of single molecules, fine-scale insights into DNA quality and damage can be directly assessed from the data. MPS is, in essence, cloning on an extremely large scale. As such, the types of questions and data quality control checks that were previously addressed *via* conventional molecular cloning on a relatively limited scale can be directly, and comprehensively, addressed by MPS. In fact, MPS is now used quite regularly and effectively for this purpose (Ginolhac *et al.*, 2011; Skoglund *et al.*, 2014; Meyer *et al.*, 2014).

Given the fine-scale differences in data between high and low quality specimens, data handling that specifically addresses the characteristics of damaged fragments is likely to be useful. For instance, analysis parameters that only consider unique reads (those with different start and end points) should reduce the effects of damage in final MPS derived haplotypes. Data filters that eliminate clonal reads serve as a measure against stochastic effects in the library amplification that can lead to overrepresentation of artifacts and errors in the final data. Such filters are routinely employed in ancient DNA applications, and are very likely to be of use for forensic testing of low quality specimens as well. In addition, it has been shown that a greater number of sequencing errors occur towards the ends of reads. For high quality samples, this is due primarily to deteriorating data quality as the sequencing reaction progresses. For low-quality samples, the cause is a bit more complicated. The sequencing process is of course a factor, but errors at read extremities (both 5' and 3') are also, if not more so, due to more extensive base misincorporation in the single-stranded overhangs of damaged fragments (Briggs *et al.*, 2007). To minimize the complications that such errors may present, more aggressive read trimming or a requirement that sequence variants be confirmed by mid-read data could also be implemented (Skoglund *et al.*, 2014). Bioinformatic filtering, based on comparison of sample data to sequences from high-quality population specimens produced using the same protocols, to reduce the impact of systematic sequencing errors (Bansal *et al.*, 2010; Li and Stoneking, 2012; Li *et al.*, 2015) may also have utility.

2.3 Mixtures

Another area in which MPS is likely to have a significant impact in mitochondrial DNA analysis is in the resolution of mixed samples. Historically, mixtures of mtDNA sequences have generally not been reported or considered due to the difficulty of interpreting mixed Sanger sequence data. Major and minor components may be evident in Sanger electropherograms, but because dye terminator base incorporation is not necessarily uniform by base or sequence motif, the apparent major and/or minor component bases cannot necessarily be associated with each other. Without knowledge of the phasing of bases at mixed sites, sequences of the component haplotypes cannot be definitively established. While this ambiguity can be handled by considering and reporting all possible haplotype combinations (Melton *et al.*, 2012), most laboratories simply elect not to interpret or report mixtures. In either case, mixed data significantly restrict the value of mtDNA analysis — either by limiting the types of cases and samples for which mtDNA testing can offer probative data or by limiting the value of the mtDNA evidence in those cases for which all possible component haplotypes are reported.

In theory, sequence variants associated with well-defined mtDNA lineages can be used to establish the haplotypic backgrounds of mixed sequences (Bandelt *et al.*, 1999, 2002; Just *et al.*, 2014a) and allow for some level of mixture deconvolution with just Sanger electropherograms. Unfortunately, the approach is not altogether straightforward. For one, recognition of haplogroup specific variants and motifs requires extensive understanding of, and familiarity with, the human mtDNA phylogeny. Additionally, mixed bases that are not associated with a particular lineage — that is, so-called private mutations among the contributing individuals — cannot be confidently associated to one haplotype or another. Mixed contributor situations are also further complicated by authentic heteroplasmies, as well as DNA damage in the case of compromised specimens.

Laboratory-based approaches for dealing with mixtures in the current Sanger-based forensic mtDNA testing framework do exist. However, they have either entailed data production and analysis workflows that further complicate the already labor intensive mtDNA sequencing process, or they produce data that are an overall net reduction of information, and therefore resolution, in the end. For instance, denaturing high performance liquid chromatography (DHPLC) has been shown to be quite effective in separating components of a mixed samples following PCR amplification, provided the haplotypes differ at a sufficient number of sites (Danielson *et al.*, 2007; LaBerge *et al.*, 2003). However, the sequence specific fractionation of the mixture must still be followed by mtDNA sequencing to gather any probative data. Thus, another step is added to the overall mtDNA typing process. Similarly, while mass spectrometry has been shown to be useful in resolving mitochondrial DNA mixtures, the final data from a standard mass spec workflow leads to an overall loss of resolution on the whole (Eduardoff *et al.*, 2013).

MPS stands to change the feasibility and ease of analyzing mixed mtDNA sequences/samples. Though very little work has been performed on this topic specifically in the context of forensic mtDNA analysis, the data required to deconvolute mixed sequences are the precise output of the MPS process. In the same way that MPS has been successfully used to discern damaged and heteroplasmic sequences (Ginolhac *et al.*, 2011; Skoglund *et al.*, 2014; Meyer *et al.*, 2014; Rebolledo-Jaramillo *et al.*, 2014; Li *et al.*, 2015), a number of studies have demonstrated the principle of employing MPS to discern the component haplotypes of "mixed" sequence data. In these cases, the "mixtures" resolved by MPS have comprised authentic mtDNA amplicons and their nuclear-mitochondrial pseudogene counterparts (Bintz *et al.*, 2014), endogenous degraded molecules and modern contaminants (Meyer *et al.*, 2014) and constructed mixtures of multiple individuals (Holland *et al.*, 2011; Kim *et al.*, 2015). MPS approaches to mixture deconvolution are not subject to any of the disadvantages of the non-MPS methods. In other words, no additional steps in the overall mtDNA sequencing workflow are required, and since the resulting data are in fact sequence data, no information is lost in the process of identifying and characterizing the component haplotypes. The complexity of mtDNA mixture deconvolution *via* MPS will no doubt depend on the similarity of the component haplotypes, and the extent of fragmentation, damage and misincorporation. Nevertheless, given the granularity of MPS data in terms of its explicit presentation of the component molecules, as well as the preliminary studies demonstrating the value of MPS in the detection of mixtures, pseudogenes and authentic heteroplasmy, it seems very likely that some measure of mtDNA mixture deconvolution will be possible. This is clearly an area that would benefit from future research, as mtDNA mixture deconvolution would expand the range of samples, and therefore cases, for which mtDNA data would prove useful.

3 Conclusions and Future Perspectives

Though the largest technical and cost barriers to developing mtGenome data from both high and low quality samples have largely been overcome, additional work is required to further define data development and data analysis parameters appropriate for routine mitochondrial DNA sequencing in forensics. Despite early concerns that MPS may not be suitable for forensic application (Bandelt and Salas, 2012), it has become increasingly clear that MPS — when applied properly with robust and reliable laboratory assays and well tested data analysis pipelines — is not just well suited, but is perhaps even better suited than Sanger-based approaches for forensic mtDNA applications.

The forensic community would nevertheless be wise to move forward systematically. A number of non-forensic studies based on MPS-developed mitochondrial DNA sequence data have already been shown to harbor errors resulting from sample mix-up and contamination (Bandelt and Salas, 2009; Just *et al.*, 2014a, 2015a; Skonieczna *et al.*, 2015). Continued testing of MPS laboratory protocols and data analysis workflows, further characterization of MPS developed mtGenome data, and general expansion of the foundation of basic knowledge that will be required to apply MPS in forensic casework are still needed. To that end, recently available mtGenome data developed *via* Sanger technology and according to strict forensic data generation and analysis guidelines (Just *et al.*, 2015b) can serve as a quality benchmark against which new MPS developed mtGenome datasets may be measured. Established high quality MPS data can then provide the foundation from which robust MPS data production and analysis guidelines can be developed for forensics.

In support of these forensic data quality requirements, the European DNA Profiling Group (EDNAP; www.ednap.org) has advanced a concept for forensic mtDNA reference population databases that is based on provision of only the highest quality mtDNA data in an open, freely accessible format (Parson *et al.*, 2004). This database, EMPOP (www.empop.org), which is freely available *via* the internet, was originally designed for Sanger-based control region data, but can currently accommodate MPS mtGenome data as well. As of August 2015, EMPOP houses 26,127 high quality control region profiles against which query profiles may be searched. The EMPOP search engine is based on a string searching algorithm that compares query and database sequences in alignment-free format and therefore eliminates search biases resulting from mtDNA notation based on direct comparison to the rCRS (Bandelt and Parson, 2008; Röck *et al.*, 2011). EMPOP additionally provides a variety of software tools that allow users to perform independent quality control of mtDNA datasets (Parson and Dür, 2007; Zimmermann *et al.*, 2011, 2014). For all datasets intended for upload into the searchable EMPOP database, EMPOP scientists also perform comprehensive review. This confirmatory review ensures that only the highest quality data are made publicly available in the database to not only the forensic, but also the broader scientific, community. EMPOP's emphasis on data quality has led editors of the leading forensic genetic journals (*Forensic Science International Genetics, International*

Journal of Legal Medicine) to require that mtDNA population datasets be quality-controlled *via* EMPOP prior to manuscript submission (Carracedo *et al.*, 2014; Parson and Roewer, 2010).

Given the emergence of mtGenome MPS, EMPOP has initiated substantial changes to the basic infrastructure of the database, and the data storage and search capabilities in particular. Not only is EMPOP being optimized to handle the larger quantities of data and more complicated searches that go hand-in-hand with mtGenome sequencing, but also search parameters designed specifically for mtDNA coding region features are being added. An option that permits the exclusion of coding region mutational hotspots in a search (an option that was established and extensively used for control region queries) will be implemented. In addition, and again in line with EMPOP features available for control region queries, both direct matches to as well as nearest neighbors of a queried mtGenome sequence will be displayed in the search results. The haplogroup status of the given mtDNA haplotypes will also be provided in the newest release of the software, with the haplogroup assignments supported by a maximum likelihood based algorithm (Röck *et al.*, 2013). All of these features will be available in version (V3) of the database released in December 2015.

The direct near-term benefits of mtDNA testing *via* NGS seem clear (increased discriminatory power, decreased testing costs, mixture deconvolution). However, given the broader technological advancements that will come with MPS, it may also be the case that mtDNA will be used more routinely in forensic DNA casework moving forward — even when STR profiles are recoverable. MPS removes one of the last practical barriers to routine mtDNA data production in a forensic setting. MtDNA typing has historically required the application of laboratory configurations, laboratory processes, and data analysis tools and strategies entirely distinct from those used for nuclear DNA typing. With MPS, mtDNA and nuclear DNA typing will entail highly similar or even identical workflows, virtually eliminating the cost and logistical differences in data production for the different marker types. In fact, commercial assays and data analysis packages designed specifically for forensics are now available, and a number of these assays are specifically designed to simultaneously recover data from both nuclear and mtDNA genomes.

Though data from multiple marker systems will not be needed in all situations (direct comparisons between evidence when full STR profiles are recovered, for instance), some common scenarios are likely to benefit greatly from concurrent development of nuclear and mtDNA data. Cases involving touch or low DNA template samples — those that have traditionally been addressed with a "Low Template" or "Low Copy Number" approach to autosomal STR typing and which often yield only poor, partial STR profiles — would clearly benefit from the addition of mtGenome information. The low random match probability (RMP) of mtGenome information is equivalent to the combined RMP of 2–3 STR loci (using an average RMP of 0.04 for any given autosomal STR locus). Similarly, in those criminal, missing persons, mass disaster or other investigations where kinship and relatedness are in question, mtDNA data will continue to offer substantial additional resolution. Finally, the availability of data from multiple markers should assist in determining the number of persons represented in mixed contributor samples, with mtDNA information potentially distinguishing individuals unresolvable by limited STR data alone.

On a larger and longer-term scale, mtDNA data (and complete mtGenomes to be specific) recovered from more evidentiary samples could very well lead to more crime to crime and missing persons comparisons in DNA databases. Generally speaking, and in order to prevent adventitious hits, STR profiles must meet minimum requirements for database upload. In cases for which that minimum is not met, profiles cannot be uploaded and searched. The addition of full mtGenome data to otherwise insufficient STR profiles, however, could reduce the chance of adventitious hits by serving as an additional filter for returned candidate associations.

The final, and perhaps greatest, barrier to the near-term implementation of full mtGenome sequencing in forensic practice concerns the medico-legal-ethics implications of retrieving genetic data with potential medical significance. The community has touched briefly on this topic in the past with regard to typing greater portions of the mtGenome (Coble *et al.*, 2004, 2006; Budowle *et al.*, 2005; Irwin *et al.*, 2011), but further examination of the pertinent issues is needed urgently. A small number of mtDNA coding region mutations have long been confirmed as disease-associated (for instance, with Leber Hereditary Optic (Erickson, 1972; Wallace *et al.*, 1988) and Leigh disease (Adams *et al.*, 1997), and many others have been suspected (see the extensive list at http://www.mitomap. org (Kogelnik *et al.*, 1996)). Yet, while the incidental recovery of information with medical significance in the course of identity testing is clearly not desirable, a risk-benefit analysis may well determine that the greater good achieved by complete mtGenome sequencing is worth the effort that will be required to establish new policies and systems for protecting privacy in forensic mtDNA practice.

Genetic privacy and several related socio-ethical issues are increasingly matters of examination in relation to the societal benefits of DNA-based human identification efforts and crime resolution (Williams and Johnson, 2004; Asplen 2004; Caenazzo *et al.*, 2013; Cox and Jones, 2014; Scully, 2014; Haimes and Toom, 2014; Penchaszadeh, 2015). In the broader genetics testing and research communities as well, very similar questions regarding the handling of genetic information in the "genomic era" have become a subject of intense focus (Presidential Commission, 2012, 2013; McEwen *et al.*, 2013; Knoppers *et al.*, 2013; Green *et al.*, 2013; van El *et al.*, 2013; Capps *et al.*, 2013; Paltoo *et al.*, 2014; Nuffield Council, 2015; for example). It is possible that some clear best-practice models may emerge from those discussions that could be adopted — or, more likely, adapted — for forensic practice.

In many ways, the safeguards that already exist for forensic genetic database profiles used for criminal justice purposes mirror those that are being implemented in the medical community to protect sensitive health information while enabling broader use of genetic data for research purposes. For instance, the current data sharing policy for the National Institutes of Health (NIH) in the

United States includes: stringent requirements for data acceptance; de-identification of the stored genetic data; strict and multi-level access controls for not only the data (from an individual or in aggregate) but also any personally identifiable information (PII); and variable limitations on use of the data depending on their origin and the intent of the investigation (Paltoo *et al.*, 2014). Though forensic typing of genetic markers is likely to remain highly targeted, even if the full mtGenome were routinely sequenced for some sample types in the future, the scope of the health privacy challenges faced in forensics seems to fall well within those in the medical research community where genome-wide association studies have long been the norm and whole exome or complete genome sequencing is poised to become relatively commonplace (McEwan *et al.*, 2013). Thus, several of the strategies proposed by bioethicists and implemented as policy in some biomedical settings (McEwan *et al.*, 2013; Paltoo *et al.*, 2014; Capps *et al.*, 2013) might be considered for any future forensic databases that may contain data with potential medical relevance. These include:

(1) Formalized and funded oversight committees, composed of both scientific and non-scientific experts, that (a) develop and enforce policies for data protection, data use, and data reporting, and (b) regularly review policies and procedures in light of both data usage and technological advances,

(2) Education and training to organizations/institutions that participate in use of the database (whether by submission or query) and

(3) Public education and transparency regarding policies, procedures, safeguards, policy violations (if any occur), and societal benefits.

With mtGenome assays and mtGenome datasets now available for validation and implementation in forensic casework, it seems that the primary technical obstacles to achieving the full potential of mtDNA testing have been surmounted. What now stands in the way of its realization in the forensic context is appropriate policy for employing complete mtGenome data in human identification cases. The United States Scientific Working Group on DNA Methods (SWGDAM) has recently fostered a discussion among stakeholders both internal and external to the forensic genetics community to address responsible handling of potentially sensitive data, the advancement of public understanding regarding risks/benefits of mtGenome typing, and approaches to fostering public dialogue and trust (SWGDAM January 2015 Semi-Annual Report, swgdam.org). Others are also recognizing and promoting the need for coordinated interdisciplinary dialogue to address these matters (Hunt, 2015). If these and other bioethical/legal considerations can be effectively addressed, and if cost, throughput, sample consumption, ease of recovery and ease of analysis are no longer restrictions to the development of complete mtDNA data, there would seem to be little downside to expanded mtDNA typing in forensic casework — only benefit.

Acknowledgments

The authors would like to thank Odile Loreille for discussion, Thomas Callaghan and Constance Fisher for manuscript review, and Gabriela Huber and Mayra Eduardoff for their help with the figure. This work received funding from the Austrian Science Fund (FWF) (P22880-B12) and TR L397, as well as by the European Union Seventh Framework Programme (FP7/2007–2013) under grant agreement no. 285487 (EUROFORGEN-NoE). Names of commercial manufacturers are provided for identification purposes only, and inclusion does not imply endorsement of the manufacturer or its products or services by the FBI. The opinions or assertions presented herein are the private views of the authors and should not be construed as official or as reflecting the official policy or position of the Department of Justice, the Federal Bureau of Investigation, or the US Government.

References

G. R. Abecasis, D. Altshuler, A. Auton, L. D. Brooks, R. M. Durbin, R. A. Gibbs, M. E. Hurles and G. A. Mcvean. A map of human genome variation from population-scale sequencing. *Nature*, 467:1061–1073, 2010.

P. L. Adams, R. N. Lightowlers and D. M. Turnbull. Molecular analysis of cytochrome c oxidase deficiency in Leighs syndrome. *Ann Neurol*, 41:268–270, 1997.

D. Aird, M. G. Ross, W. S. Chen, M. Danielsson, T. Fennell, C. Russ, D. B. Jaffe, C. Nusbaum and A. Gnirke. Analyzing and minimizing PCR amplification bias in Illumina sequencing libraries. *Genome Biol*, 12:R18, 2011.

V. Alvarez-Iglesias, J. C. Jaime, A. Carracedo and A. Salas. Coding region mitochondrial DNA SNPs: targeting East Asian and Native American haplogroups. *Forensic Sci Int Genet*, 1:44–55, 2007.

H. Andreasson, M. Nilsson, H. Styrman, U. Pettersson and M. Allen. Forensic mitochondrial coding region analysis for increased discrimination using pyrosequencing technology. *Forensic Sci Int Genet*, 1:35–43, 2007.

R. M. Andrews, I. Kubacka, P. F. Chinnery, R. N. Lightowlers, D. M. Turnbull and N. Howell. Reanalysis and revision of the Cambridge reference sequence for human mitochondrial DNA. *Nat Genet*, 23:147, 1999.

C. H. Asplen, American Society of Law, Medicine and Ethics Report: The Non-Forensic Use of Biological Samples Taken for Forensic Purposes: An International Perspective, American Society of Law, Medicine and Ethics; Boston, MA, pp. 1–24, 2004.

M. C. Avila-Arcos, E. Cappellini, J. A. Romero-Navarro, N. Wales, J. V. Moreno-Mayar, M. Rasmussen, S. L. Fordyce, R. Montiel, J. P. Vielle-Calzada, E. Willerslev and M. T. Gilbert. Application and comparison of large-scale solution-based DNA capture-enrichment methods on ancient DNA. *Sci Rep*, 1:74, 2011.

H. J. Bandelt and W. Parson. Consistent treatment of length variants in the human mtDNA control region: A reappraisal. *Int J Legal Med*, 122:11–21, 2008.

H. J. Bandelt, P. Forster and A. Rohl. Median-joining networks for inferring intraspecific phylogenies. *Mol Biol Evol*, 16:37–48, 1999.

H. J. Bandelt, L. Quintana-Murci, A. Salas and V. Macaulay. The fingerprint of phantom mutations in mitochondrial DNA data. *Am J Hum Genet*, 71:1150–1160, 2002.

H. J. Bandelt and A. Salas. Contamination and sample mix-up can best explain some patterns of mtDNA instabilities in buccal cells and oral squamous cell carcinoma. *BMC Cancer*, 9:113, 2009.

H. J. Bandelt and A. Salas. Current next generation sequencing technology may not meet forensic standards. *Forensic Sci Int Genet*, 6:143–145, 2012.

V. Bansal, O. Harismendy, R. Tewhey, S. S. Murray, N. J. Schork, E. J. Topol and K. A. Frazer. Accurate detection and genotyping of SNPs utilizing population sequencing data. *Genome Res*, 20:537–545, 2010.

C. Barbieri, M. Whitten, K. Beyer, H. Schreiber, M. Li and B. Pakendorf. Contrasting maternal and paternal histories in the linguistic context of Burkina Faso. *Mol Biol Evol*, 29:1213–23, 2012.

C. Berger and W. Parson. Mini-midi-mito: Adapting the amplification and sequencing strategy of mtDNA to the degradation state of crime scene samples. *Forensic Sci Int Genet*, 3:149–153, 2009.

J. Binladen, M. T. Gilbert, P. F. Campos and E. Willerslev. 5'-tailed sequencing primers improve sequencing quality of PCR products. *Biotechniques*, 42:174–176, 2007.

B. J. Bintz, G. B. Dixon and M. R. Wilson. Simultaneous detection of human mitochondrial DNA and nuclear-inserted mitochondrial-origin sequences (NumtS) using forensic mtDNA amplification strategies and pyrosequencing technology. *J Forensic Sci*, 59:1064–1073, 2014.

M. Bodner, A. Iuvaro, C. Strobl, S. Nagl, G. Huber, S. Pelotti, D. Pettener, D. Luiselli and W. Parson. Helena, the hidden beauty: Resolving the most common West Eurasian mtDNA control region haplotype by massively parallel sequencing an Italian population sample. *Forensic Sci Int Genet*, 15:21–26, 2015.

D. M. Bornman, M. E. Hester, J. M. Schuetter, M. D. Kasoji, A. Minard-Smith, C. A. Barden, S. C. Nelson, G. D. Godbold, C. H. Baker, B. Yang, J. E. Walther, I. E. Tornes, P. S. Yan, B. Rodriguez, R. Bundschuh, M. L. Dickens, B. A. Young and S. A. Faith. Short-read, high-throughput sequencing technology for STR genotyping. *Biotech Rapid Dispatches*, 1–6, 2012.

A. Brandstatter, A. Salas, H. Niederstatter, C. Gassner, A. Carracedo and W. Parson. Dissection of mitochondrial superhaplogroup H using coding region SNPs. *Electrophoresis*, 27:2541–2550, 2006.

A. W. Briggs, J. M. Good, R. E. Green, J. Krause, T. Maricic, U. Stenzel and S. Paabo. Primer extension capture: Targeted sequence retrieval from heavily degraded DNA sources. *J Vis Exp*, 31:1573, 2009.

A. W. Briggs, U. Stenzel, P. L. Johnson, R. E. Green, J. Kelso, K. Prufer, M. Meyer, J. Krause, M. T. Ronan, M. Lachmann and S. Paabo. Patterns of damage in genomic DNA sequences from a Neandertal. *Proc Natl Acad Sci USA*, 104:14616–14621, 2007.

B. Budowle, U. Gyllensten, R. Chakraborty and M. Allen. Forensic analysis of the mitochondrial coding region and association to disease. *Int J Legal Med*, 119:314–315, 2005.

R. A. Bull, F. Luciani, K. Mcelroy, S. Gaudieri, S. T. Pham, A. Chopra, B. Cameron, L. Maher, G. J. Dore, P. A. White and A. R. Lloyd. Sequential bottlenecks drive viral evolution in early acute hepatitis C virus infection. *PLoS Pathog*, 7:e1002243, 2011.

L. Caenazzo, P. Tozzo and D. Rodriguez. Ethical issues in DNA identification of human biological material from mass disasters. *Prehosp Disaster Med*, 28:393–396, 2013.

B. Capps. Defining variables of access to UK Biobank: the public interest and the public good. Law, Innovation and Technology 5(1):113–139, 2013.

M. L. Carpenter, J. D. Buenrostro, C. Valdiosera, H. Schroeder, M. E. Allentoft, M. Sikora, M. Rasmussen, S. Gravel, S. Guillen, G. Nekhrizov, K. Leshtakov, D. Dimitrova, N. Theodossiev, D. Pettener, D. Luiselli, K. Sandoval, A. Moreno-Estrada, Y. Li, J. Wang, M. T. Gilbert, E. Willerslev, W. J. Greenleaf and C. D. Bustamante. Pulling out the 1%: Whole-genome capture for the targeted enrichment of ancient DNA sequencing libraries. *Am J Hum Genet*, 93:852–864, 2013.

A. Carracedo, J. M. Butler, L. Gusmao, A. Linacre, W. Parson, L. Roewer and P. M. Schneider. Update of the guidelines for the publication of genetic population data. *Forensic Sci Int Genet*, 10:A1–A2, 2014.

A. C. Clarke, S. Prost, J. A. Stanton, W. T. White, M. E. Kaplan, E. A. Matisoo-Smith and C. Genographic. From cheek swabs to consensus sequences: An A to Z protocol for high-throughput DNA sequencing of complete human mtGenomes. *BMC Genomics*, 15:68, 2014.

M. D. Coble, R. S. Just, J. E. O'callaghan, I. H. Letmanyi, C. T. Peterson, J. A. Irwin and T. J. Parsons. Single nucleotide polymorphisms over the entire mtDNA genome that increase the power of forensic testing in Caucasians. *Int J Legal Med*, 118:137–146, 2004.

M. D. Coble, P. M. Vallone, R. S. Just, T. M. Diegoli, B. C. Smith and T. J. Parsons. Effective strategies for forensic analysis in the mitochondrial DNA coding region. *Int J Legal Med*, 120:27–32, 2006.

M. Cox and P. Jones. Ethical considerations in the use of DNA as a contribution toward the determination of identification in historic cases: Considerations from the Western front. *New Genet. Soc.*, 33: 295–312, 2014.

P. B. Danielson, H. Y. Sun, T. Melton and R. Kristinsson. Resolving mtDNA mixtures by denaturing high-performance liquid chromatography and linkage phase determination. *Forensic Sci Int Genet*, 1:148–153, 2007.

C. Davis, D. Peters, D. Warshauer, J. King and B. Budowle. Sequencing the hypervariable regions of human mitochondrial DNA using massively parallel sequencing: Enhanced data acquisition for DNA samples encountered in forensic testing. *Leg Med (Tokyo)*, 17:123–127, 2015.

F. Delfin, A. Min-Shan Ko, M. Li, E. D. Gunnarsdottir, K. A. Tabbada, J. M. Salvador, G. C. Calacal, M. S. Sagum, F. A. Datar, S. G. Padilla, M. C. De Ungria and M. Stoneking. Complete mtDNA genomes of Filipino ethnolinguistic groups: A melting pot of recent and ancient lineages in the Asia-Pacific region. *Eur J Hum Genet*, 22:228–237, 2014.

C. Der Sarkissian, M. E. Allentoft, M. C. Avila-Arcos, R. Barnett, P. F. Campos, E. Cappellini, L. Ermini, R. Fernandez, R. Da Fonseca, A. Ginolhac, A. J. Hansen, H. Jonsson, T. Korneliussen, A. Margaryan, M. D. Martin, J. V. Moreno-Mayar, M. Raghavan, M. Rasmussen, M. S. Velasco, H. Schroeder, M. Schubert, A. Seguin-Orlando, N. Wales, M. T. Gilbert, E. Willerslev and L. Orlando. Ancient genomics. *Philos Trans R Soc Lond B Biol Sci*, 370:20130387, 2015.

M. A. Diroma, C. Calabrese, D. Simone, M. Santorsola, F. M. Calabrese, G. Gasparre and M. Attimonelli. Extraction and annotation of human mtGenomes from 1000 Genomes Whole Exome Sequencing data. *BMC Genomics*, 15(3):S2, 2014.

A. M. Divne, M. Nilsson, C. Calloway, R. Reynolds, H. Erlich and M. Allen. Forensic casework analysis using the HVI/HVII mtDNA linear array assay. *J Forensic Sci*, 50:548–554, 2005.

A. T. Duggan, M. Whitten, V. Wiebe, M. Crawford, A. Butthof, V. Spitsyn, S. Makarov, I. Novgorodov, V. Osakovsky and B. Pakendorf. Investigating the prehistory of Tungusic peoples of Siberia and the Amur-Ussuri region with complete mtDNA genome sequences and Y-chromosomal markers. *PLoS One*, 8:e83570, 2013.

A. T. Duggan, B. Evans, F. R. Friedlaender, J. S. Friedlaender, G. Koki, D. A. Merriwether, M. Kayser and M. Stoneking. Maternal history of

Oceania from complete mtDNA genomes: contrasting ancient diversity with recent homogenization due to the Austronesian expansion. *Am J Hum Genet*, 94:721–733, 2014.

M. Eduardoff, G. Huber, B. Bayer, D. Schmid, K. Anslinger, T. Gobel, B. Zimmermann, P. M. Schneider, A. W. Rock and W. Parson. Mass spectrometric base composition profiling: Implications for forensic mtDNA databasing. *Forensic Sci Int Genet*, 7:587–592, 2013.

C. Eichmann and W. Parson. 'Mitominis': multiplex PCR analysis of reduced size amplicons for compound sequence analysis of the entire mtDNA control region in highly degraded samples. *Int J Legal Med*, 122:385–388, 2008.

R. Ekblom, L. Smeds and H. Ellegren. Patterns of sequencing coverage bias revealed by ultra-deep sequencing of vertebrate mitochondria. *BMC Genomics*, 15:467, 2014.

J. Enk, J. M. Rouillard and H. Poinar. Quantitative PCR as a predictor of aligned ancient DNA read counts following targeted enrichment. *Biotechniques*, 55:300–309, 2013.

J. M. Enk, A. M. Devault, M. Kuch, Y. E. Murgha, J. M. Rouillard and H. N. Poinar. Ancient whole genome enrichment using baits built from modern DNA. *Mol Biol Evol*, 31:1292–1294, 2014.

R. P. Erickson. Leber's optic atrophy, a possible example of maternal inheritance. *Am J Hum Genet*, 24:348–349, 1972.

L. Fendt, B. Zimmermann, M. Daniaux and W. Parson. Sequencing strategy for the whole mtGenome resulting in high quality sequences. *BMC Genomics*, 10:139, 2009.

P. Flaherty, G. Natsoulis, O. Muralidharan, M. Winters, J. Buenrostro, J. Bell, S. Brown, M. Holodniy, N. Zhang and H. P. Ji. Ultrasensitive detection of rare mutations using next-generation targeted resequencing. *Nucleic Acids Res*, 40:e2, 2012.

S. L. Fordyce, H. S. Mogensen, C. Borsting, R. E. Lagace, C. W. Chang, N. Rajagopalan and N. Morling. Second-generation sequencing of forensic STRs using the Ion Torrent HID STR 10-plex and the Ion PGM. *Forensic Sci Int Genet*, 14:132–140, 2015.

M. N. Gabriel, E. F. Huffine, J. H. Ryan, M. M. Holland and T. J. Parsons. Improved MtDNA sequence analysis of forensic remains using a "mini-primer set" amplification strategy. *J Forensic Sci*, 46:247–253, 2001.

K. Gardner, B. A. Payne, R. Horvath and P. F. Chinnery. Use of stereotypical mutational motifs to define resolution limits for the ultra-deep resequencing of mitochondrial DNA. *Eur J Hum Genet*, 23:413–415, 2015.

M. T. Gilbert, L. P. Tomsho, S. Rendulic, M. Packard, D. I. Drautz, A. Sher, A. Tikhonov, L. Dalen, T. Kuznetsova, P. Kosintsev, P. F. Campos, T. Higham, M. J. Collins, A. S. Wilson, F. Shidlovskiy, B. Buigues, P. G. Ericson, M. Germonpre, A. Gotherstrom, P. Iacumin, V. Nikolaev, M. Nowak-Kemp, E. Willerslev, J. R. Knight, G. P. Irzyk, C. S. Perbost, K. M. Fredrikson, T. T. Harkins, S. Sheridan, W. Miller and S. C. Schuster. Whole-genome shotgun sequencing of mitochondria from ancient hair shafts. *Science,* 317:1927–1930, 2007.

A. Ginolhac, M. Rasmussen, M. T. Gilbert, E. Willerslev and L. Orlando. mapDamage: testing for damage patterns in ancient DNA sequences. *Bioinformatics,* 27:2153–2155, 2011.

H. Goto, B. Dickins, E. Afgan, I. M. Paul, J. Taylor, K. D. Makova and A. Nekrutenko. Dynamics of mitochondrial heteroplasmy in three families investigated via a repeatable re-sequencing study. *Genome Biol,* 12:R59, 2011.

R. E. Green, J. Krause, A. W. Briggs, T. Maricic, U. Stenzel, M. Kircher, N. Patterson, H. Li, W. Zhai, M. H. Fritz, N. F. Hansen, E. Y. Durand, A. S. Malaspinas, J. D. Jensen, T. Marques-bonet, C. Alkan, K. Prufer, M. Meyer, H. A. Burbano, J. M. Good, R. Schultz, A. Aximu-Petri, A. Butthof, B. Hober, B. Hoffner, M. Siegemund, A. Weihmann, C. Nusbaum, E. S. Lander, C. Russ, N. Novod, J. Affourtit, M. Egholm, C. Verna, P. Rudan, D. Brajkovic, Z. Kucan, I. Gusic, V. B. Doronichev, L. V. Golovanova, C. Lalueza-Fox, M. De la rasilla, J. Fortea, A. Rosas, R. W. Schmitz, P. L. Johnson, E. E. Eichler, D. Falush, E. Birney, J. C. Mullikin, M. Slatkin, R. Nielsen, J. Kelso, M. Lachmann, D. Reich and S. Paabo. A draft sequence of the Neandertal genome. *Science,* 328:710–722, 2010.

R. C. Green, J. S. Berg, W. W. Grody, S. S. Kalia, B. R. Korf, C. L. Martin, A. L. Mcguire, R. L. Nussbaum, J. M. O'daniel, K. E. Ormond, H. L. Rehm, M. S. Watson, M. S. Williams, L. G. Biesecker, American College of Medical, G. and Genomics. ACMG recommendations for reporting of incidental findings in clinical exome and genome sequencing. *Genet Med,* 15:565–574, 2013.

P. Grignani, G. Peloso, A. Achilli, C. Turchi, A. Tagliabracci, M. Alu, G. Beduschi, U. Ricci, L. Giunti, C. Robino, S. Gino and C. Previdere. Subtyping mtDNA haplogroup H by SNaPshot minisequencing and its application in forensic individual identification. *Int J Legal Med,* 120:151–156, 2006.

E. D. Gunnarsdottir, M. Li, M. Bauchet, K. Finstermeier and M. Stoneking. High-throughput sequencing of complete human mtDNA genomes from the Philippines. *Genome Res*, 21:1–11, 2011.

Y. Guo, Q. Cai, D. C. Samuels, F. Ye, J. Long, C. I. Li, J. F. Winther, E. J. Tawn, M. Stovall, P. Lahteenmaki, N. Malila, S. Levy, C. Shaffer, Y. Shyr, X. O. Shu and J. D. Boice Jr. The use of next generation sequencing technology to study the effect of radiation therapy on mitochondrial DNA mutation. *Mutat Res*, 744:154–160, 2012.

A. Haimes and V. Toom. Hidden in full sight: Kinship, science and the law in the aftermath of the Srebrenica genocide. *New Genet.Soc.*, 33:277–294, 2014.

B. L. Hancock-Hanser, A. Frey, M. S. Leslie, P. H. Dutton, F. I. Archer and P. A. Morin. Targeted multiplex next-generation sequencing: advances in techniques of mitochondrial and nuclear DNA sequencing for population genomics. *Mol Ecol Resour*, 13:254–268, 2013.

Y. He, J. Wu, D. C. Dressman, C. Iacobuzio-Donahue, S. D. Markowitz, V. E. Velculescu, L. A. Diaz, Jr. K. W. Kinzler, B. Vogelstein and N. Papadopoulos. Heteroplasmic mitochondrial DNA mutations in normal and tumour cells. *Nature*, 464:610–614, 2010.

M. Hofreiter, V. Jaenicke, D. Serre, A. Von haeseler and S. Paabo. DNA sequences from multiple amplifications reveal artifacts induced by cytosine deamination in ancient DNA. *Nucleic Acids Res*, 29:4793–4799, 2001.

M. M. Holland, M. R. Mcquillan and K. A. O'hanlon. Second generation sequencing allows for mtDNA mixture deconvolution and high resolution detection of heteroplasmy. *Croat Med J*, 52:299–313, 2011.

T. Hunt, Next-Gen is now: legal implications and strategic preparation for massively parallel DNA sequencing in forensic science. American Academy of Forensic Sciences Meeting, February 16–21, 2015 Orlando.

J. A. Irwin, W. Parson, M. D. Coble and R. S. Just. mtGenome reference population databases and the future of forensic mtDNA analysis. *Forensic Sci Int Genet*, 5:222–225, 2011.

R. S. Just, M. D. Leney, S. M. Barritt, C. W. Los, B. C. Smith, T. D. Holland and T. J. Parsons. The use of mitochondrial DNA single nucleotide polymorphisms to assist in the resolution of three challenging forensic cases. *J Forensic Sci*, 54:887–891, 2009.

R. S. Just, J. A. Irwin and W. Parson. Questioning the prevalence and reliability of human mitochondrial DNA heteroplasmy from massively parallel sequencing data. *Proc Natl Acad Sci USA*, 111:E4546–E4547, 2014a.

R. S. Just, M. K. Scheible, S. A. Fast, K. Sturk-Andreaggi, J. L. Higginbotham, E. A. Lyons, J. M. Bush, M. A. Peck, J. D. Ring, T. M. Diegoli, A. W. Rock, G. E. Huber, S. Nagl, C. Strobl, B. Zimmermann, W. Parson and J. A. Irwin. Development of forensic-quality full mtGenome haplotypes: success rates with low template specimens. *Forensic Sci Int Genet*, 10:73–79, 2014b.

R. Just, J. Irwin and W. Parson. Mitochondrial DNA heteroplasmy in the emerging field of massively parallel sequencing. *Forensic Science International Genetics* (in press), 2015a.

R. S. Just, M. K. Scheible, S. A. Fast, K. Sturk-Andreaggi, A. W. Rock, J. M. Bush, J. L. Higginbotham, M. A. Peck, J. D. Ring, G. E. Huber, C. Xavier, C. Strobl, E. A. Lyons, T. M. Diegoli, M. Bodner, L. Fendt, P. Kralj, S. Nagl, D. Niederwieser, B. Zimmermann, W. Parson and J. A. Irwin. Full mtGenome reference data: Development and characterization of 588 forensic-quality haplotypes representing three U.S. populations. *Forensic Sci Int Genet*, 14:141–155, 2015b.

H. Kim, H. A. Erlich, C. D. Calloway. Analysis of mixtures using next generation sequencing of mitochondrial DNA hypervariable regions. *Croat Med J*, 56:208–217, 2015.

J. L. King, B. L. Larue, N. M. Novroski, M. Stoljarova, S. B. Seo, X. Zeng, D. H. Warshauer, C. P. Davis, W. Parson, A. Sajantila and B. Budowle. High-quality and high-throughput massively parallel sequencing of the human mtGenome using the Illumina MiSeq. *Forensic Sci Int Genet*, 12:128–135, 2014.

J. L. King, A. Sajantila and B. Budowle. mitoSAVE: mitochondrial sequence analysis of variants in Excel. *Forensic Sci Int Genet*, 12:122–125, 2014.

M. C. Kline, P. M. Vallone, J. W. Redman, D. L. Duewer, C. D. Calloway and J. M. Butler. Mitochondrial DNA typing screens with control region and coding region SNPs. *J Forensic Sci*, 50:377–385, 2005.

M. Knapp, and M. Hofreiter. Next Generation Sequencing of Ancient DNA: Requirements, Strategies and Perspectives. *Genes (Basel)*, 1:227–243, 2010.

B. M. Knoppers, A. Thorogood and R. Chadwick. The Human Genome Organisation: towards next-generation ethics. *Genome Med*, 5, 38, 2013.

A. M. Kogelnik, M. T. Lott, M. D. Brown, S. B. Navathe and D. C. Wallace. Mitomap: a human mtGenome database. *Nucleic Acids Res*, 24:177–179, 1996.

S. Kohnemann, U. Sibbing, H. Pfeiffer and C. Hohoff. A rapid mtDNA assay of 22 SNPs in one multiplex reaction increases the power of forensic testing in European Caucasians. *Int J Legal Med*, 122:517–523, 2008.

J. Krause, Q. Fu, J. M. Good, B. Viola, M. V. Shunkov, A. P. Derevianko and S. Paabo. The complete mitochondrial DNA genome of an unknown hominin from southern Siberia. *Nature*, 464:894–897, 2010.

G. S. Laberge, R. J. Shelton and P. B. Danielson. Forensic utility of mitochondrial DNA analysis based on denaturing high-performance liquid chromatography. *Croat Med J*, 44:281–288, 2003.

E. S. Lander, L. M. Linton, B. Birren, C. Nusbaum, M. C. Zody, J. Baldwin, K. Devon, K. Dewar, M. Doyle, W. Fitzhugh, R. Funke, D. Gage, K. Harris, A. Heaford, J. Howland, L. Kann, J. Lehoczky, R. Levine, P. Mcewan, K. Mckernan, J. Meldrim, J. P. Mesirov, C. Miranda, W. Morris, J. Naylor, C. Raymond, M. Rosetti, R. Santos, A. Sheridan, C. Sougnez, N. Stange-Thomann, N. Stojanovic, A. Subramanian, D. Wyman, J. Rogers, J. Sulston, R. Ainscough, S. Beck, D. Bentley, J. Burton, C. Clee, N. Carter, A. Coulson, R. Deadman, P. Deloukas, A. Dunham, I. Dunham, R. Durbin, L. French, D. Grafham, S. Gregory, T. Hubbard, S. Humphray, A. Hunt, M. Jones, C. Lloyd, A. Mcmurray, L. Matthews, S. Mercer, S. Milne, J. C. Mullikin, A. Mungall, R. Plumb, M. Ross, R. Shownkeen, S. Sims, R. H. Waterston, R. K. Wilson, L. W. Hillier, J. D. Mcpherson, M. A. Marra, E. R. Mardis, L. A. Fulton, A. T. Chinwalla, K. H. Pepin, W. R. Gish, S. L. Chissoe, M. C. Wendl, K. D. Delehaunty, T. L. Miner, A. Delehaunty, J. B. Kramer, L. L. Cook, R. S. Fulton, D. L. Johnson, P. J. Minx, S. W. Clifton, T. Hawkins, E. Branscomb, P. Predki, P. Richardson, S. Wenning, T. Slezak, N. Doggett, J. F. Cheng, A. Olsen, S. Lucas, C. Elkin, E. Uberbacher, M. Frazier *et al.* Initial sequencing and analysis of the human genome. *Nature*, 409:860–921, 2001.

M. Li, A. Schonberg, M. Schaefer, R. Schroeder, I. Nasidze and M. Stoneking. Detecting heteroplasmy from high-throughput sequencing of complete human mitochondrial DNA genomes. *Am J Hum Genet*, 87:237–249, 2010.

M. Li and M. Stoneking. A new approach for detecting low-level mutations in next-generation sequence data. *Genome Biol*, 13:R34, 2012.

M. Li, R. Schroder, S. Ni, B. Madea and M. Stoneking. Extensive tissue-related and allele-related mtDNA heteroplasmy suggests positive selection for somatic mutations. *Proc Natl Acad Sci USA*, 112:2491–2496, 2015.

S. Lippold, H. Xu, A. Ko, M. Li, G. Renaud, A. Butthof, R. Schroder and M. Stoneking. Human paternal and maternal demographic histories:

insights from high-resolution Y chromosome and mtDNA sequences. *Investig Genet,* 5:13, 2014.

O. Loreille, H. Koshinsky, V. Y. Fofanov, J. A. Irwin. Application of next generation sequencing technologies to the identification of highly degraded unknown soldiers' remains. *Forensic Sci. Int. Genet. Suppl. Ser.* e540–e541, 2011.

M. Margulies, M. Egholm, W. E. Altman, S. Attiya, J. S. Bader, L. A. Bemben, J. Berka, M. S. Braverman, Y. J. Chen, Z. Chen, S. B. Dewell, L. Du, J. M. Fierro, X. V. Gomes, B. C. Godwin, W. He, S. Helgesen, C. H. Ho, G. P. Irzyk, S. C. Jando, M. L. Alenquer, T. P. Jarvie, K. B. Jirage, J. B. Kim, J. R. Knight, J. R. Lanza, J. H. Leamon, S. M. Lefkowitz, M. Lei, J. Li, K. L. Lohman, H. Lu, V. B. Makhijani, K. E. Mcdade, M. P. Mckenna, E. W. Myers, E. Nickerson, J. R. Nobile, R. Plant, B. P. Puc, M. T. Ronan, G. T. Roth, G. J. Sarkis, J. F. Simons, J. W. Simpson, M. Srinivasan, K. R. Tartaro, A. Tomasz, K. A. Vogt, G. A. Volkmer, S. H. Wang, Y. Wang, M. P. Weiner, P. Yu, R. F. Begley and J. M. Rothberg. Genome sequencing in microfabricated high-density picolitre reactors. *Nature,* 437:376–380, 2005.

T. Maricic, M. Whitten and S. Paabo. Multiplexed DNA sequence capture of mtGenomes using PCR products. *PLoS One,* 5:e14004, 2010.

J. A. Mcelhoe, M. M. Holland, K. D. Makova, M. S. Su, I. M. Paul, C. H. Baker, S. A. Faith and B. Young. Development and assessment of an optimized next-generation DNA sequencing approach for the mtgenome using the Illumina MiSeq. *Forensic Sci Int Genet,* 13:20–29, 2014.

K. Mcelroy, O. Zagordi, R. Bull, F. Luciani and N. Beerenwinkel. Accurate single nucleotide variant detection in viral populations by combining probabilistic clustering with a statistical test of strand bias. *BMC Genomics,* 14:501, 2013.

J. E. Mcewen, J. T. Boyer and K. Y. Sun. Evolving approaches to the ethical management of genomic data. *Trends Genet,* 29:375–382, 2013.

F. Meacham, D. Boffelli, J. Dhahbi, D. I. Martin, M. Singer and L. Pachter. Identification and correction of systematic error in high-throughput sequence data. *BMC Bioinformatics,* 12:451, 2011.

T. Melton, C. Holland and M. Holland. Forensic mitochondrial DNA analysis: Current practice and future potential. *Forensic Sci Rev,* 24:22, 2012.

M. Meyer, Q. Fu, A. Aximu-Petri, I. Glocke, B. Nickel, J. L. Arsuaga, I. Martinez, A. Gracia, J. M. De castro, E. Carbonell and S. Paabo.

A mtGenome sequence of a hominin from Sima de los Huesos. *Nature*, 505:403–406, 2014.

M. Mikkelsen, R. Frank-Hansen, A. J. Hansen and N. Morling. Massively parallel pyrosequencing of the mtGenome with the 454 methodology in forensic genetics. *Forensic Sci Int Genet*, 12:30–37, 2014.

A. E. Minoche, J. C. Dohm and H. Himmelbauer. Evaluation of genomic high-throughput sequencing data generated on Illumina HiSeq and genome analyzer systems. *Genome Biol*, 12:R112, 2011.

K. Nakamura, T. Oshima, T. Morimoto, S. Ikeda, H. Yoshikawa, Y. Shiwa, S. Ishikawa, M. C. Linak, A. Hirai, H. Takahashi, M. Altaf-Ul-Amin, N. Ogasawara and S. Kanaya. Sequence-specific error profile of Illumina sequencers. *Nucleic Acids Res*, 39:e90, 2011.

J. Naue, S. Horer, T. Sanger, C. Strobl, P. Hatzer-Grubwieser, W. Parson and S. Lutz-Bonengel. Evidence for frequent and tissue-specific sequence heteroplasmy in human mitochondrial DNA. *Mitochondrion*, 20:82–94, 2015.

T. M. Nelson, R. S. Just, O. Loreille, M. S. Schanfield and D. Podini. Development of a multiplex single base extension assay for mitochondrial DNA haplogroup typing. *Croat Med J*, 48:460–472, 2007.

Nuffield Council on Bioethics. The collection, linking and use of data in biomedical research and health care: Ethical issues. Nuffield Council on Bioethics, London, England, 2015, pp. 1–198.

D. N. Paltoo, L. L. Rodriguez, M. Feolo, E. Gillanders, E. M. Ramos, J. L. Rutter, S. Sherry, V. O. Wang, A. Bailey, R. Baker, M. Caulder, E. L. Harris, K. Langlais, H. Leeds, E. Luetkemeier, T. Paine, T. Roomian, K. Tryka, A. Patterson, E. D. Green and National Institutes of Health Genomic Data Sharing Governance, C. Data use under the NIH GWAS data sharing policy and future directions. *Nat Genet*, 46:934–938, 2014.

L. T. Parker, Q. Deng, H. Zakeri, C. Carlson, D. A. Nickerson and P. Y. Kwok. Peak height variations in automated sequencing of PCR products using Taq dye-terminator chemistry. *Biotechniques*, 19:116–121, 1995.

L. T. Parker, H. Zakeri, Q. Deng, S. Spurgeon, P. Y. Kwok and D. A. Nickerson. AmpliTaq DNA polymerase, FS dye-terminator sequencing: analysis of peak height patterns. *Biotechniques*, 21:694–699, 1996.

M. Parks and D. Lambert. Impacts of low coverage depths and post-mortem DNA damage on variant calling: a simulation study. *BMC Genomics*, 16:19, 2015.

J. S. Parla, I. Iossifov, I. Grabill, M. S. Spector, M. Kramer and W. R. Mccombie. A comparative analysis of exome capture. *Genome Biol*, 12:R97, 2011.

W. Parson and H. J. Bandelt. Extended guidelines for mtDNA typing of population data in forensic science. *Forensic Sci Int Genet*, 1:13–19, 2007.

W. Parson, A. Brandstatter, A. Alonso, N. Brandt, B. Brinkmann, A. Carracedo, D. Corach, O. Froment, I. Furac, T. Grzybowski, K. Hedberg, C. Keyser-Tracqui, T. Kupiec, S. Lutz-Bonengel, B. Mevag, R. Ploski, H. Schmitter, P. Schneider, D. Syndercombe-Court, E. Sorensen, H. Thew, G. Tully and R. Scheithauer. The EDNAP mitochondrial DNA population database (EMPOP) collaborative exercises: Organisation, results and perspectives. *Forensic Sci Int*, 139:215–226, 2004.

W. Parson and A. Dur. Empop — a forensic mtDNA database. *Forensic Sci Int Genet*, 1:88–92, 2007.

W. Parson, L. Gusmao, D. R. Hares, J. A. Irwin, W. R. Mayr, N. Morling, E. Pokorak, M. Prinz, A. Salas, P. M. Schneider and T. J. Parsons. DNA Commission of the International Society for Forensic Genetics: revised and extended guidelines for mitochondrial DNA typing. *Forensic Sci Int Genet*, 13:134–142, 2014.

W. Parson, G. Huber, L. Moreno, M. B. Madel, M. D. Brandhagen, S. Nagl, C. Xavier, M. Eduardoff, T. C. Callaghan and J. A. Irwin. Massively parallel sequencing of complete mtGenomes from hair shaft samples. *Forensic Sci Int Genet*, 15:8–15, 2015.

W. Parson, T. J. Parsons, R. Scheithauer and M. M. Holland. Population data for 101 Austrian Caucasian mitochondrial DNA d-loop sequences: application of mtDNA sequence analysis to a forensic case. *Int J Legal Med*, 111:124–132, 1998.

W. Parson and L. Roewer. Publication of population data of linearly inherited DNA markers in the International Journal of Legal Medicine. *Int J Legal Med*, 124:505–509, 2010.

W. Parson, C. Strobl, G. Huber, B. Zimmermann, S. M. Gomes, L. Souto, L. Fendt, R. Delport, R. Langit, S. Wootton, R. Lagace and J. Irwin. Evaluation of next generation mtGenome sequencing using the Ion Torrent Personal Genome Machine (PGM). *Forensic Sci Int Genet*, 7:543–549, 2013.

V. B. Penchaszadeh. Ethical, legal and social issues in restoring genetic identity after forced disappearance and suppression of identity in Argentina. *J Community Genet*, 6:207–213, 2015.

E. Picardi and G. Pesole. MtGenomes gleaned from human whole-exome sequencing. *Nat Methods*, 9:523–524, 2012.

Presidential Commission for the Study of Bioethical Issues, Privacy and progress in whole genome sequencing, Washington, DC, 2012, pp. 1–140.

Presidential Commission for the Study of Bioethical Issues, Anticipate and Communicate: Ethical Management of Incidental and Secondary Findings in the Clinical, Research and Direct-to-Consumer Contexts, Washington, DC, 2013, pp. 1–146.

B. Rebolledo-Jaramillo, M. S. Su, N. Stoler, J. A. Mcelhoe, B. Dickins, D. Blankenberg, T. S. Korneliussen, F. Chiaromonte, R. Nielsen, M. M. Holland, I. M. Paul, A. Nekrutenko and K. D. Makova. Maternal age effect and severe germ-line bottleneck in the inheritance of human mitochondrial DNA. *Proc Natl Acad Sci USA*, 111:15474–15479, 2014.

A. Rock, J. Irwin, A. Dur, T. Parsons and W. Parson. SAM: String-based sequence search algorithm for mitochondrial DNA database queries. *Forensic Sci Int Genet*, 5:126–132, 2011.

A. W. Rock, A. Dur, M. Van oven and W. Parson. Concept for estimating mitochondrial DNA haplogroups using a maximum likelihood approach (EMMA). *Forensic Sci Int Genet*, 7:601–609, 2013.

E. Rockenbauer, S. Hansen, M. Mikkelsen, C. Borsting and N. Morling. Characterization of mutations and sequence variants in the D21S11 locus by next generation sequencing. *Forensic Sci Int Genet*, 8:68–72, 2014.

M. G. Ross, C. Russ, M. Costello, A. Hollinger, N. J. Lennon, R. Hegarty, C. Nusbaum and D. B. Jaffe. Characterizing and measuring bias in sequence data. *Genome Biol*, 14:R51, 2013.

D. C. Samuels, C. Li, B. Li, Z. Song, E. Torstenson, H. Boyd clay, A. Rokas, T. A. Thornton-Wells, J. H. Moore, T. M. Hughes, R. D. Hoffman, J. L. Haines, D. G. Murdock, D. P. Mortlock and S. M. Williams. Recurrent tissue-specific mtDNA mutations are common in humans. *PLoS Genet*, 9:e1003929, 2013.

M. Scheible, O. Loreille, R. Just and J. Irwin. Short tandem repeat typing on the 454 platform: Strategies and considerations for targeted sequencing of common forensic markers. *Forensic Sci Int Genet*, 12:107–119, 2014.

M. Schirmer, U. Z. Ijaz, R. D'amore, N. Hall, W. T. Sloan and C. Quince. Insight into biases and sequencing errors for amplicon sequencing with the Illumina MiSeq platform. *Nucleic Acids Res*, 43:e37, 2015.

M. Schubert, A. Ginolhac, S. Lindgreen, J. F. Thompson, K. A. Al-Rasheid, E. Willerslev, A. Krogh and L. Orlando. Improving ancient DNA read mapping against modern reference genomes. *BMC Genomics*, 13:178, 2012.

J. L. Scully. Naming the dead: DNA-based identification of historical remains as an act of care. *New Genet Soc*, 33:313–332, 2014.

S. B. Seo, X. Zeng, J. L. King, B. L. Larue, M. Assidi, M. H. Al-Qahtani, A. Sajantila and B. Budowle. Underlying Data for Sequencing the MtGenome with the Massively Parallel Sequencing Platform Ion Torrent PGM. *BMC Genomics*, 16(1):S4, 2015.

J. Shendure and H. Ji. Next-generation DNA sequencing. *Nat Biotechnol*, 26:1135–1145, 2008.

P. Skoglund, B. H. Northoff, M. V. Shunkov, A. P. Derevianko, S. Paabo, J. Krause and M. Jakobsson. Separating endogenous ancient DNA from modern day contamination in a Siberian Neandertal. *Proc Natl Acad Sci USA*, 111:2229–2234, 2014.

K. Skonieczna, B. Malyarchuk, A. Jawien, A. Marszalek, Z. Banaszkiewicz, P. Jarmocik, M. Borcz, P. Bala and T. Grzybowski. Heteroplasmic substitutions in the entire mtGenomes of human colon cells detected by ultra-deep 454 sequencing. *Forensic Sci Int Genet*, 15:16–20, 2015.

M. Stiller, R. E. Green, M. Ronan, J. F. Simons, L. Du, W. He, M. Egholm, J. M. Rothberg, S. G. Keates, N. D. Ovodov, E. E. Antipina, G. F. Baryshnikov, Y. V. Kuzmin, A. A. Vasilevski, G. E. Wuenschell, Termini, J. M. Hofreiter, V. Jaenicke-Despres and S. Paabo. Patterns of nucleotide misincorporations during enzymatic amplification and direct large-scale sequencing of ancient DNA. *Proc Natl Acad Sci USA*, 103:13578–13584, 2006.

M. Stiller, M. Knapp, U. Stenzel, M. Hofreiter and M. Meyer. Direct multiplex sequencing (DMPS) — a novel method for targeted high-throughput sequencing of ancient and highly degraded DNA. *Genome Res*, 19:1843–1848, 2009.

Swgdam, Scientific Working Group on DNA Analysis Methods. Interpretation Guidelines for Mitochondrial DNA Analysis by Forensic DNA Testing Laboratories, 2013.

J. E. Templeton, P. M. Brotherton, B. Llamas, J. Soubrier, W. Haak, A. Cooper and J. J. Austin. DNA capture and next-generation sequencing can recover whole mtGenomes from highly degraded samples for human identification. *Investig Genet*, 4:26, 2013.

P. M. Vallone, R. S. Just, M. D. Coble, J. M. Butler and T. J. Parsons. A multiplex allele-specific primer extension assay for forensically informative SNPs distributed throughout the mtGenome. *Int J Legal Med*, 118:147–157, 2004.

C. G. Van el, M. C. Cornel, P. Borry, R. J. Hastings, F. Fellmann, S. V. Hodgson, H. C. Howard, A. Cambon-Thomsen, B. M. Knoppers, H. Meijers-Heijboer, H. Scheffer, L. Tranebjaerg, W. Dondorp, G. M. De Wert, E. Public and Professional Policy, C. Whole-genome sequencing in health care. Recommendations of the European Society of Human Genetics. *Eur J Hum Genet*, 21(1):S1–S5, 2013.

C. Van Neste, F. Van Nieuwerburgh, D. Van Hoofstat and D. Deforce. Forensic STR analysis using massive parallel sequencing. *Forensic Sci Int Genet*, 6:810–818, 2012.

K. Vancampenhout, B. Caljon, C. Spits, K. Stouffs, A. Jonckheere, L. De Meirleir, W. Lissens, A. Vanlander, J. Smet, B. De paepe, R. Van coster and S. Seneca. A bumpy ride on the diagnostic bench of massive parallel sequencing, the case of the mtGenome. *PLoS One*, 9:e112950, 2014.

D. C. Wallace, G. Singh, M. T. Lott, J. A. Hodge, T. G. Schurr, A. M. Lezza, L. J. Elsas, 2nd and E. K. Nikoskelainen. Mitochondrial DNA mutation associated with Leber's hereditary optic neuropathy. *Science*, 242:1427–1430, 1988.

J. Weber-Lehmann, E. Schilling, G. Gradl, D. C. Richter, J. Wiehler and B. Rolf. Finding the needle in the haystack: differentiating "identical" twins in paternity testing and forensics by ultra-deep next generation sequencing. *Forensic Sci Int Genet*, 9:42–46, 2014.

R. Williams and P. Johnson. Inclusiveness, effectiveness and intrusiveness: issues in the developing uses of DNA profiling in support of criminal investigations. *J Law Med Ethics*, 33:545–558, 2004.

M. R. Wilson, J. A. Dizinno, D. Polanskey, J. Replogle and B. Budowle. Validation of mitochondrial DNA sequencing for forensic casework analysis. *Int J Legal Med*, 108:68–74, 1995.

F. Ye, D. C. Samuels, T. Clark and Y. Guo. High-throughput sequencing in mitochondrial DNA research. *Mitochondrion*, 17:157–163, 2014a.

K. Ye, J. Lu, F. Ma, A. Keinan and Z. Gu. Extensive pathogenicity of mitochondrial heteroplasmy in healthy human individuals. *Proc Natl Acad Sci USA*, 111:10654–10659, 2014b.

X. Zeng, J. L. King, M. Stoljarova, D. H. Warshauer, B. L. Larue, A. Sajantila, J. Patel, D. R. Storts and B. Budowle. High sensitivity multiplex short tandem repeat loci analyses with massively parallel sequencing. *Forensic Sci Int Genet*, 16:38–47, 2015.

B. Zimmermann, A. Rock, G. Huber, T. Kramer, P. M. Schneider and W. Parson. Application of a west Eurasian-specific filter for quasi-median network analysis: Sharpening the blade for mtDNA error detection. *Forensic Sci Int Genet*, 5:133–137, 2011.

B. Zimmermann, A. W. Rock, A. Dur and W. Parson. Improved visibility of character conflicts in quasi-median networks with the Empop NETWORK SOFTWARE. *Croat Med J*, 55:115–120, 2014.

CHAPTER 15

DNA and Missing Persons Identification: Practice, Progress and Perspectives

Thomas J. Parsons and René L. M. Huel

*International Commission on Missing Persons, Sarajevo,
Bosnia and Herzegovina*

1 Introduction

Modern DNA testing is unparalleled in its ability to provide essentially definitive evidence of individual identification in a scientifically validated and objective manner as set out, for example, in the 2009 National Research Council report on forensic science (NRC, 2009). The range of genetic systems available for analysis now provides the forensic scientist with a flexible arsenal to address missing persons cases from a wide variety of contexts and characteristics. Autosomal short tandem repeat (STR) loci are now targeted by large, highly sensitive commercial multiplex kits; mitochondrial DNA (mtDNA) sequence analysis permits access to the most highly degraded samples and the ability to compare questioned samples to even distant maternal relatives; Y-chromosome STRs permit tracing along patrilineages; single nucleotide polymorphism (SNP) assays can, in larger numbers, rival or exceed the power of discrimination of STRs and/or provide ancestry and phenotypic traits; and X-chromosomal STRs permit a unique ability to resolve special classes of kinship cases.

The fact that persons go missing with their fate and/or identity unknown has been a serious challenge posed to society, individuals and families throughout human history. In today's world, untallied but vast numbers of individuals go missing as a result of natural disaster, transportation incidents, terrorism, armed conflict, human rights violations, war crimes, routine crime, organized crime, human trafficking and economic or political migration. Modern techniques, including and especially DNA analysis, have recently permitted the fate/identity of the missing to be clarified in many instances and on a scale never previously possible.

Depending on the context under which people go missing, lack of resolution of fate or identity can have broad reaching societal effects or at the very least have profound impact on the family of each of the missing. In the case of missing persons that result from armed conflict, human rights violations, acts of terrorism, or criminal enterprise such as human trafficking, the identification of the missing has implications in possible criminal or war crimes prosecutions. Additionally, scientifically conclusive resolution of the fate of missing persons through the identification of their remains often has critical implications for families accessing funds/pensions or other compensation and legal rights. When applied on a large scale, there can be a profound impact on societal healing and accountability of states.

Large-scale identification of the missing can provide a scientifically accurate account of events. In politically charged environments, where persons "disappear" as a consequence of systematic human rights violations or crimes against humanity, evidence of victim identity through an irrefutable scientific approach constrains the ability to deny or twist facts, or to rewrite history. Precise information is critical to the prevention of myth building and the denial of atrocities committed. Scientific evidence is critical to families seeking justice and is essential for governments seeking to restore the confidence of their citizens in state institutions (Rauchfuss and Schmolze, 2008).

DNA techniques have been applied to the identification of missing persons spanning a wide range of circumstances, many of which overlap in categorization. Disaster Victim Identification (DVI) has been a major area of DNA application and refers to events involving natural disasters, transportation accidents, terrorism or conflict, either separately or in combination. "Routine" missing persons cases have been referred to as a "silent mass disaster" (Ritter, 2007) with virtually every country experiencing high numbers of reported missing persons on the one hand, and large numbers of unidentified bodies/humans remains in the custody of authorities such as coroners, law enforcement or medical examiners. A huge and increasing problem of the missing is posed by large-scale human migration under dangerous conditions often leading to large numbers of deaths. Every year vast numbers of individuals flee economic hardship, armed conflict, ethnic persecution, or violent threat due to organized crime. Related to this is the issue of human trafficking, as migrants or other vulnerable individuals fall prey to criminal enterprise, and become missing either due to death, or as the "living missing" with undocumented whereabouts as a result of such things as involuntary servitude/slavery, sexual exploitation, or illegal adoption.

This chapter will not attempt to comprehensively review the very diverse field of DNA of identification of missing persons and the innumerable instances where it has been applied, but aims to highlight particular topics and specific case/project examples selected to exemplify the primary features and challenges of such work, instances of notable success or impact on the development of the field, and the range of technical components involved.

2 Historical Cases and Prominent Cases of Missing Persons

One of the most highly publicized areas of DNA investigation into the identity of deceased individuals relates to the authentication of human remains suspected or claimed to be of famous historical figures. More than a dozen of such cases have been reported in the scientific literature or sometimes only in the popular press: Josef

Mengele (Jeffreys *et al.*, 1992), Jesse James (Stone *et al.*, 2001), children of Thomas Jefferson (Foster *et al.*, 1998), Christopher Columbus (Alvarez-Cubero *et al.*, 2012) and King Richard III (King *et al.*, 2014a) to name a few. These cases are almost always outside of the realm of active criminal investigations, and often involve university researchers, rather than being conducted solely by forensic criminalistics laboratories. The techniques involved in these cases span the gamut of modern forensic DNA testing methods, and in some instances the cases have served as showcases for emerging techniques. On the flip side, some of these academic investigations have lacked the rigor normally associated with forensics and/or the results have been touted in the press in the absence of publication in peer-reviewed scientific journals (for example: Edwards, 2014; Connor, 2014).

One of the first important historical missing persons cases to use DNA was the identification of the Nazi SS Officer Joseph Mengele (Jeffreys *et al.*, 1992), whose presumed body had been exhumed six years after death in Brazil. The Mengele case and a previous murder victim case by the same group (Hagelberg *et al.*, 1991) were notable as an early demonstration of the ability to recover authentic human DNA from degraded human bone, the successful PCR amplification of microsatellite loci from degraded bone, and the use of kinship comparisons to establish identity (Mengele was identified through comparison to his son and wife's DNA, and the murder victim to her parents'). Such early forensic cases were considered extensions of the field of ancient DNA analysis, where the authenticity of results received much scrutiny with regard to contamination, especially for work involving humans. Criteria for authenticity of results in the forensic arena are largely adopted from the ancient DNA field, with the requirement for carefully separated laboratory environments for contamination avoidance, separation of pre- and post-PCR rooms, controls, replication of results, and adherence to the expectation that smaller DNA fragments predominate (see, e.g. Cooper and Poinar, 2000).

Undoubtedly one of the most formative of all historical DNA case investigations is that of Tsar Nicholas Romanov II and his family.

This was a DNA case that unfolded in multiple acts over the course of 15 years. In 1918, the Soviets executed Tsar Nicholas II, his wife Tsarina Alexandra and his five children, but the location of their bodies was unknown, fueling widespread speculation regarding their fate. In 1991, remains suspected of being the Romanov family and their retinue were unearthed. DNA testing was performed by Peter Gill and Russian collaborator Pavel Ivanov at the Forensic Science Service in the UK, with remarkable results at that time for such old, degraded skeletal remains (Gill *et al.*, 1994). Results were obtained for five nuclear autosomal loci that demonstrated the sex of the skeletons and indicated familial relationships among the remains consistent with them including the Tsar and Tsarina, and three of their daughters.

However, when mtDNA analysis was used to compare profiles to distant maternal relatives of the Tsar, and the Tsarina and the children, confirmation of the identities was complicated by a "mismatch" at one position between the Tsar and reference individuals separated by multiple generations. The bones from the Tsar showed a heteroplasmic mixture of C and T, while the references showed only T. mtDNA analysis at that time was becoming widely used for identification cases from old bones, and this case served to highlight a (then) poorly characterized but quite significant complication in mtDNA testing: that an individual's mtDNA "type" is actually a population of molecules with a high mutation rate, with sequence variants subject to a comparatively high degree of intra-individual and inter-generational variation due developmental and germ line transmission (Wilson *et al.*, 1997; Gocke *et al.*, 1998; Parsons *et al.*, 1997).

The incompletely explained "discrepancy" in the mtDNA matching of the Tsar was used as leverage in the politically contentious debate on the fate of the Romanovs, but was solved when mtDNA sequences were obtained from the Tsar's brother Georgji Romanov (Ivanov *et al.*, 1996), who was shown also to be heteroplasmic at the position in question. The instance of heteroplasmy, then, went from a discrepancy to an additional shared rare genetic characteristic highly supportive of identity. Despite that, there were continued ever more far-fetched counter arguments, some invoking uncharacterized conspiracy theories and/or picking on isolated elements of the case-work while conspicuously overlooking the whole results (Zhivotovsky, 1999; Knight *et al.*, 2004). While these attacks were convincingly debunked (Hofreiter *et al.*, 2004; Gill and Hagelberg, 2004), it is with the final round of the story that the identities of the Romanovs appear to finally be settled. Modern de-mineralization bone DNA extraction techniques (Loreille *et al.*, 2007) permitted full multiplex STR profiles to be recovered from the Romanov skeletons, including new recoveries of the two children missing from the original excavation, with full reproduction of the mtDNA results as well (Coble *et al.*, 2009).

Lineage markers, such as those residing on mtDNA and the Y chromosome, often play a predominant role in historical cases, as the family reference samples available are usually separated by many generations. It can be difficult to find reliable living reference individuals based on genealogical records. Another approach to obtaining reference samples in historical cases is to exhume closer relatives of the subject individual from their supposedly known graves. This approach has been employed in the case of investigations of the skull of Mozart and the skeletal remains of German poets Goethe and Schiller. While as yet unpublished in the scientific literature (however, see the German language book by Parson, 2014), a very strong cautionary lesson comes through efforts to date, where the marked historical graves selected as references often do not themselves contain the individuals they are supposed to contain.

The recent case of British King Richard III (died 1485; King *et al.*, 2014a) highlights the strengths and weaknesses of lineage markers for distant genealogical comparisons, and illustrates some of the most modern DNA techniques that are now being brought to bear on missing persons casework. Skeletal remains suspected to come from Richard III were excavated from a car park in Leicester, England. Using a combination of Sanger sequencing and Next Generation Sequencing (NGS) on the Life Technologies Ion Torrent instrument, the entire mtDNA genome was sequenced from skeletal remains suspected to come from Richard III, and from two living maternal relatives separated from Richard III by 19 and 21 generations. An exact match over the entire mtDNA genome to a sequence not seen previously in any forensic database provided very strong evidence in support of the hypothesis of identity, but highlights the dependence of the strength of mtDNA data on the size and representation of existing databases.

Y-chromosome SNPs and STRs were obtained from both hybrid capture/NGS and standard CE-based STR multiplex testing, but indicated an exclusion in comparison to supposed reference samples from the paternal line of Richard III. For the hypothesis of identity to stand, a non-paternity event somewhere within 19 generations of the lineage would have to have occurred, which the authors convincingly argue would not be particularly unlikely.

The recent development of hair and eye color predictive DNA tests (Walsh *et al.*, 2011, 2013) has been suggested as a significant tool to provide clues in missing persons investigations and was applied in the case of King Richard III, with a prediction of blue eyes and blond hair resulting from NGS-based sequencing. Unfortunately, definitive records of the hair and eye color for Richard III do not exist, although the predicted results were consistent with one historical painting, if allowance is made for blond hair changing to brown over the course of aging. Such difficulties, together with the low discrimination power at the population level suggest that such phenotypic trait predictive DNA tests will be of value in missing persons cases only where it is possible to expend substantial investigative effort to direct the case toward the more definitive DNA tests of identity.

The published DNA investigations of both the Romanovs and King Richard III are notable for their well-reasoned presentation of the DNA results within a Bayesian framework for interpretation of the significance of the results. The Romanov papers (Gill and Hagelberg, 1994; Ivanov *et al.*, 1996) address the issue of mtDNA intergenerational mutation rate in a likelihood ratio (LR) framework. The Bayesian treatment of the Richard III study additionally considers estimates of non-paternity rates in a way that would be generally useful in dealing with this common issue in missing persons casework. Moreover, the latter study includes a Bayesian evaluation of the non-DNA evidence in the case relating to circumstantial evidence and anthropological observations, to which the DNA LRs may be directly combined. While exact values relating to the frequency of various conditions/characteristics and prior probabilities were not precisely known, nor would they be generally, the calculations are well-framed with regard to conservative bounds. Similar approaches have been proposed elsewhere for non-DNA evidence (Steadman *et al.*, 2006). Such a quantitative framework that allows integration of DNA evidence into an overall quantitative evaluation should serve as an aspirational model for multidisciplinary forensic investigations of missing persons.

3 mtDNA from Post-Conflict Skeletal Remains

In the early 1990's, the US Department of Defence established the US Armed Forces DNA Identification Laboratory (AFDIL) within the Office of the Armed Forces Medical Examiner, with a mission to ensure the identification of US military service personnel killed in the line of duty. For deaths in present-day duty, a highly efficient DNA identification system was established through direct matching, based on the mandatory collection of blood sample cards from all active duty military personnel. By having blood reference cards readily available for profiling and comparison, STR typing could be conducted in cases where personnel were killed or missing, providing a rapid and essentially certain means of identification. Established in 1993, the Armed Forces Repository of Specimen Samples for the Identification of Remains (AFRSSIR) contains samples not only of military personnel but other at-risk government agency and contractor personnel. As of 2012, AFRSSIR contains more than 6.5 million blood-stain cards (Mehlman and Li, 2014).

However, it is in the area of post-conflict identification of skeletal remains where the greatest effort and innovation has occurred over the last two decades. AFDIL's early and on-going effort in this area focused on unidentified skeletal remains from the Vietnam War (Holland *et al.*, 1993; Edson *et al.*, 2004). Most cases were recovered after decades of exposure to a hot, humid environment of SE Asia, causing the DNA to be fragmented to small size and in low copy number. Like most other cases of degraded skeletal remains at the time, the Vietnam War remains were considered in the realm of mtDNA testing, where the relatively high copy number of mtDNA provided a key advantage for testing success and the ability to compare to distant maternal relatives abetted the process of reference sample collection.

The resources made available for the identification of US missing in action (MIA's) contributed greatly to the maturation of forensic mtDNA testing, particularly from skeletal remains. A minimum of two maternal relatives per case was sought, and comparisons among many cases gave rise to many observations of heteroplasmic sequence variation within individuals (as in Tsar Nicholas) and differential segregation of heteroplasmic ratios between maternal relatives, sometimes manifesting as fixed differences in sequences at an unexpectedly high rate (Parsons *et al.*, 1997). As mtDNA testing in missing persons casework became widely applied, it was necessary to address some of the biggest obstacles to practical application and interpretation of results such as basic questions of mtDNA biology, population genetic variation, and the size and representation of population databases (e.g. Holland and Parsons, 1999; Tully *et al.*, 2000; Irwin *et al.*, 2007, 2009). Moreover, mtDNA casework from highly degraded skeletal remains was an area that early-on explored the limit of low copy number (LCN) typing, with high PCR cycle number amplifications, and a formidable challenge of contamination with exogenous, high copy number mtDNA. Missing persons casework contributed greatly to establishing the norms of the field for forensic mtDNA analysis (Carracedo *et al.*, 2000; Parson *et al.*, 2014).

Identity testing of aged, degraded bones for many years was considered primarily a realm for mtDNA analysis, but the limitations of mtDNA are substantial for application on a large scale. First of all, mtDNA is not a stand-alone identifier and is only useful in concert with substantial additional identification information. In most cases, as generally with AFDIL's work on Vietnam MIA's, mtDNA was used to confirm or refute pre-existing hypotheses of identity derived from other evidence, or to discriminate amongst a small number of possible identities (i.e. within a "closed" population of victims) (Just *et al.*, 2009).

Over the years with the improvement of bone DNA extraction methods (Yang *et al.*, 1998; Alonso *et al.*, 2001; Rohland and Hofreiter, 2007; Loreille *et al.*, 2007; Rohland *et al.*, 2010) and increasingly sensitive commercial multiplex STR kits, the strength of nuclear loci and combined genetic systems have been used in selected case investigations to effect identifications of missing U.S. service personnel (Irwin *et al.*, 2007; Sturk *et al.*, 2009). Nuclear STR testing on skeletal remains has been successful in other post war contexts as well (e.g. Marjanovic *et al.*, 2009; Pajnic *et al.*, 2012).

4 Large Scale Post-Conflict DNA Identifications in the Western Balkans

A major transition in the area of post-conflict missing persons DNA identification is marked by the work of the International Commission on Missing Persons (ICMP) in its development of a "DNA-led" system of identification to address the ~40,000 persons missing in the countries of the Western Balkans following the armed conflict in the region in the 1990's (Huffine *et al.*, 2001). The ICMP was established in 1996 with the mandate to secure the co-operation of governments and other authorities in locating and identifying persons missing as a result of conflicts, human rights abuses, disasters, organized violence and other causes and to assist them in doing so. ICMP also supports the work of other organizations in their efforts, encourages public involvement in its activities and contributes to the development of appropriate expressions of commemoration and tribute to the missing (www.icmp.int).

The territorial conflicts in the Western Balkans in the 1990's were characterized not only by battlefield deaths among combatants, but in the forced displacement and killing of large numbers of civilians in what became known as "ethnic cleansing." Global attention was paid to perceived atrocities during the conflict, and in 1993 the United Nations established a special International Criminal Tribunal for the Western Balkans (ICTY) to investigate and prosecute individuals on four categories of offences: grave breaches of the 1949 Geneva conventions, violations of the laws or customs of war, genocide and crimes against humanity (see www.icty.org). Soon after the cessation of hostilities as a result of 1995 Dayton Accords, teams of ICTY investigators including pathologists, forensic anthropologists and forensic archaeologists conducted excavations and exhumations of human remains from mass graves (and a wide range of other types of sites) in an effort to document and prosecute crimes. Many thousands of cases were recovered and examined, but the ICTY process did not include provision for large-scale victim identification (Vollen, 2001). This situation created an urgent social need for identifications, and identifying the missing was one of the technical elements that the ICMP took on, in addition to taking over from the ICTY extensive technical support to national authorities in archaeology, anthropology and pathology (for a detailed account of the ICMP's role and the overall context of the missing in Bosnia and Herzegovina, see Sarkin *et al.*, 2014).

At the time the ICMP undertook its identification program, the prevailing model for the use of DNA for identification for post-conflict or other human rights violations was as a tool to confirm or refute pre-existing hypotheses of identity derived from other investigations. Limitations of this approach were soon starkly evident in the context of the Western Balkans, given the very large number of missing persons, the skeletonized nature of the remains, and the general lack of medical or dental records for distinctive identifying information. After struggling with traditional approaches for several years and making few identifications, the decision was made to attempt a program of autosomal nuclear DNA testing on skeletal remains, with "blind" kinship matching to large databases of STR profiles from families of the missing, conducted on a very large, regional scale (Huffine *et al.*, 2001). In this approach, the initial indications of identification come from highly certain DNA matches, which then trigger multi-disciplinary analyses for final confirmation of identification.

The ICMP DNA-led model proved highly effective for establishing the scientific basis for identification on a large scale, based on three successful foundations: a high success rate for obtaining autosomal

STRs from degraded bone samples (ranging over the course of the project from 5 years to 20 years postmortem), a successful outreach program to acquire multiple family reference samples for missing individuals (collected as blood stains on cards), and informatics capabilities for kinship matching within and between large databases of postmortem and family DNA profiles. As an example, for victims related to the Srebrenica mass killing, the number of identifications using DNA jumped from 52 in 2001 to 516 in 2002 with the adoption of the DNA-led approach.

The primary DNA database for the Western Balkans has been established with the PowerPlex16 STR multiplex (Promega Corporation, Madison, WI, USA), and at the time of this writing consists of 41,483 postmortem DNA profiles (21,446 unique DNA profiles), 91,699 family reference profiles representing 29,784 individuals; with high certainty DNA matches having been made for 17,910 unique individuals with an additional 18,507 DNA reports re-associating unlinked skeletal elements (the ICMP maintains an On-Line Inquiry Center on its web site where up to date information on progress in various projects is charted).

The ICMP's DNA identification system has been subject to constant improvement through the years. Improvements in DNA extraction and amplification efficiency over time (Davoren *et al.*, 2007; Amory *et al.*, 2012) have largely kept pace with increasing degradation of DNA in the samples. Large DNA testing sample sizes of various bone types have provided a knowledge base of the highly variable relative preservation of DNA in different skeletal elements (Milos *et al.*, 2007; Hines *et al.*, 2014). The concordance of these results with other studies (Edson *et al.*, 2004; Mundorff and Davoren, 2014; Pinhasi *et al.*, 2015) now provides a quite complete picture of optimal skeletal DNA sampling protocols (Hines *et al.*, 2014).

Many of the skeletal remains worked on by the ICMP come from secondary mass graves, where the bodies having first been buried in primary mass graves were later exhumed and transferred to new secondary graves. This practice was a common occurrence in one of the ICMP's largest sub-projects, relating to the systematic killing of ~8,000 Muslim men and boys associated with the fall of UN Safe Area

Srebrenica to Bosnian Serb forces in July, 1995 (Vollen, 2001; Sarkin *et al.*, 2014; Brown, 2006). Bodies were originally buried by perpetrators in very large mass graves (some containing on the order of 1,000 individuals), but after several months, the perpetrators removed them by heavy machinery and deposited them in over 90 clandestine secondary graves spread widely throughout the remote countryside of Eastern Bosnia. In the process, the remains became fragmented and commingled, sometimes to a very large extent, greatly complicating the identification challenge (Sarkin *et al.*, 2014).

Body parts of the same individual were frequently recovered as numerous separate cases, and in many instances from different secondary graves. The vast scale of the event caused anthropological re-association of the remains to be of limited utility, even as expert anthropological case examination became all the more necessary to properly separate out distinct sets of morphologically associated skeletal elements. DNA testing has therefore been widely used for re-association as well as family matching. For a time, a custom designed mini-amplicon STR multiplex with 7 loci was used specifically for re-association purposes, but this approach was abandoned as it was found that a higher number of loci were useful in distinguishing between closely related victims (Parsons *et al.*, 2007). At the time of this writing, the ICMP has issued DNA identification Match Reports on 6,833 individuals reported as missing from the 1995 Srebrenica event, and 10,269 DNA re-association Reports.

DNA identification is often used to resolve the fate of missing persons and, in the case of murder victims, can come to be involved in the criminal trials of the perpetrators. Nowhere is this more pronounced than with the role that the ICMP's DNA evidence has played in war crimes trials at the ICTY in The Hague. Altogether, ICMP's DNA evidence has played a role in five major ICTY indictments, with the ICMP providing the ICTY with a total listing of over 15,000 DNA Match Reports. Two cases are ongoing at the time of this writing: that of former Bosnian Serb President Radovan Karadzic, and his former General Ratko Mladic, with indictments for both including charges of genocide, crimes against humanity, and violations of the laws and customs of war (www.icty.org). DNA evidence presented at these trials related not only to large numbers of individual identifications, but the hundreds of DNA re-association linkages between various primary and secondary graves were taken to have great relevance to the large scale pattern of activity taken in the construction of the graves with the apparent intent to conceal evidence of the crime.

DNA identifications relating to armed conflict and human rights abuses are sometimes referred to as a "humanitarian" undertaking (ICRC, 2013) but the present example serves to underscore the importance of maintaining a high degree of forensic rigor, as cases can be pivotal to criminal prosecutions and the desire of families for access to justice, in addition to knowledge of the fate of the missing. In this regard, the ICMP has since 2007 maintained internationally recognized ISO 17025 accreditation of its DNA testing and matching procedures. Particular challenges have been faced with regard to the provision of DNA evidence in ICTY trials, as the sheer volume of DNA case files is too high to permit meaningful counter examination in its entirety, and, more importantly, the genetic and other private information of the victims and their families can be provided by the ICMP only upon consent of family members. Upon request of defense in the Karadzic trial, the ICMP obtained consent from a large number of family members to permit full case file disclosure on a random, representative sample of 295 DNA identification cases.

5 DNA Matching in Large Scale Missing Persons Applications

Large scale DNA identification projects require advanced DNA comparison software capable of direct matching between postmortem samples, direct matching between postmortem samples and direct reference samples, and kinship matching between postmortem samples and family references. There are an increasing number of sophisticated software packages available from commercial, academic or government sources. Some of the more widely used software packages include DNA•VIEW (Brenner, 1997), Bonaparte (van Dongen *et al.*, 2011; Slooten, 2011), Familias (Kling *et al.*, 2014), CODIS 6.0 (Bradford *et al.*, 2011) and M-FISYS (Cash *et al.*,

2003; Garcia *et al.*, 2009). Other kinship programs have been developed either in-house or by manufacturers as part of larger laboratory suites of software (for a comprehensive review of available software see http://www.cstl.nist.gov/strbase/kinship.htm). For DNA matching, the ICMP employs a hybrid system of rapid database screening based on in-house custom software, and the commercial software package DNA·VIEW. Elements of this system will be described to illustrate the issues that are generally encountered.

In order to maximize objectivity and avoid perception of bias, ICMP samples are immediately assigned bar codes and progress through DNA testing and initial screening for re-association and family matching without any identifying or case specific information. When a new postmortem profile is uploaded to the database, two sets of automated pair wise comparisons are standardly performed: between it and all other postmortem profiles for direct matching, and between it in all family reference profiles, with an output that is a ranked list of pair wise calculated parentage indexes and sibling indexes. The pair wise comparisons run very quickly, which is an important consideration for databases of this size. For kinship, once candidate pair wise matches are found to a family for a particular missing person, the software imports all family reference profiles for that missing person into the DNA·VIEW program for full kinship analysis.

Rather than pair wise screening, some software packages instead perform pedigree screening on the entire database as a first step. This is computationally much more intensive and can be slow for large databases. A more significant disadvantage of pedigree screening, though, is the chance for missing matches in cases involving non-paternity or other problems with the recorded relationships amongst the families involved. Most programs have a useful "pedigree validation" feature that checks the feasibility of the reference relationships before matching is performed, but sometimes problems are only evident when the postmortem profile is included in the calculation. For example, if a missing person has as references a mother and two reported full siblings, but the missing person is in fact a half sibling to the references, a pedigree screen can miss this family association, calculating an exclusion based on stated relationships. The ICMP's pair wise search approach on the other hand will show elevated kinship statistics on these references individually. The pair wise approach with some regularity detects such family associations where follow-on steps to resolve the relationship issues enable identifications to be finalized. On the flip side, pair wise screens have the potential to miss matches in the uncommon cases where the kinship indices individually are not high enough to stand out from adventitious matches, but the LRs for the entire pedigree are in fact strong enough to indicate a match. To account for this, the ICMP periodically performs pedigree screens on unmatched profiles using features of DNA·VIEW. To avoid missing matches, it is optimal to employ both pedigree and pair wise screening capabilities.

Dealing with adventitious matches (elevated match statistics that result from chance similarities rather than genuine relationship) is one of the biggest challenges for DNA matching amongst large databases (Brenner and Weir, 2003; Alonso *et al.*, 2005; Birus *et al.*, 2003). In practice, thresholds are normally applied in the evaluation and reporting of matching to deal with adventitious matches and to take into account the size of the event (Budowle *et al.*, 2011; Biesecker *et al.*, 2005). The primary output of DNA matching comparisons is a LR indicating the relative probability of the DNA evidence under two hypotheses. In missing persons cases, the relevant hypotheses are generally (but not always) that the DNA profile in question comes from the missing person vs. that it comes from an unrelated missing person. In the Bayesian approach, the significance of a DNA comparison is product of the DNA LR and the prior probability of the identification in question, with the prior probability being independent of the DNA evidence. While final identifications may consider the evidence and prior probabilities from any number of disciplines (as in the case of Richard III, King *et al.*, 2014a) from the standpoint of a laboratory evaluating and reporting DNA matches, it is usually the case that prior probabilities are best taken as the number of individuals missing from an event, or a simple modification thereof (for example, the number of missing females, given that sex is indicated by the DNA test). In this way, database calculations can be conservatively evaluated on an event-wide basis, without the need for case specific information or the input from other disciplines, which are not the purview of the DNA laboratory.

At the ICMP, the standard threshold for issuing a kinship DNA match report is a posterior probability of 99.95%, with prior probability defined by the number of individuals missing from an event or well-defined sub-event (such as the Srebrenica mass killing). Prior probabilities may be decreased during the course of a project, as individuals become identified with known DNA profiles and the number of still missing persons decreases. Because of the potential for recovery of partial profiles from remains, and the variability in the number and type of family references available for a given missing person, it is not uncommon to detect possible or probable relatedness that nevertheless falls below the match report threshold. Such below threshold possible matches trigger an attempt to acquire more information: if possible, additional reference samples are sought, additional extractions or amplifications may be attempted to fill in a partial profile, or additional genetic systems are targeted.

To increase the DNA LR, or rule out the possibility of relatedness, the PP16 STR profiles from the case may be augmented by additional autosomal STR testing and lineage markers (Y-STR and mtDNA) used when applicable to the case. Testing a case with PowerPlex ESX17 kit (Promega Corporation) provides the potential for recovery of 8 additional loci with that of the PP16 kit, and in cases of actual relatedness increases the LR on average by a factor of 10,000 (unpublished). Lineage markers are likewise quite useful, but are limited in potential significance by the size of available reference population databases. When the ICMP Match Reports include lineage markers, the LRs are listed separately for the autosomal vs. lineage markers, and a combined value based on multiplying the LRs is also reported, the latter consistent with recent recommendations (Parson *et al.*, 2014; Gjertson *et al.*, 2007; Prinz *et al.*, 2007, SWGDAM, 2014).

The concept of setting a 99.95% DNA match report threshold based only on the number of missing persons is that the ICMP, in this case, considers this a reasonable level of certainty for missing persons identification, that is, a 1 in 2000 possibility that the match is adventitious. The DNA match report alone should not serve as the basis for identification, but as a trigger for consideration of all additional information in the case, both contextually and including results from other scientific disciplines. Even if this information does not provide additional quantitative evidence in support of the identification, as a quality control measure cases must be examined for any discrepancies. Discrepancies can arise from many causes such as mislabeling of samples submitted to the DNA laboratory, sample switches in the laboratory processing, or issues involving related missing persons (for example, failure to report a closely related missing person whose remains may be mistakenly matched in absence of this information). Such problems should be rare, and their potential obviously calls for a high level of forensic quality assurance overall, but inter-disciplinary concordance is a key component of for reliability of the identification process. As such, the DNA laboratory must be prepared for an efficient ability to coordinate with other disciplines and a mechanism for investigating and resolving discrepancies.

The ICMP also employs mechanisms for engaging other disciplines to resolve cases that, despite exhaustive effort, do not meet the DNA match threshold. Cases with significantly elevated kinship statistics are communicated to the responsible pathologist or anthropologist with a potential name association. Generally the DNA LR is not communicated, but simply an indication that this identity should perhaps be evaluated. If non-DNA evidence is taken to significantly encourage this hypothesis of identity, a DNA "Statistical Comparison Report" is issued to indicate the DNA evidence. Care should be taken in such a process to maintain objectivity as best as possible. The significance of contextual and other non-DNA evidence can be subject to a higher degree of subjective interpretation. Communication of DNA results may sway evaluation, and the process runs the risk of over-interpretation of mere "consistency," instead of evaluating whether the evidence truly supports the hypothesis of identity vs. non-relatedness.

The common occurrence of related victims in large scale events requires the evaluation of different hypotheses than the standard "related vs. unrelated." In fact, for same sex siblings with only parents as references, the DNA evidence cannot distinguish between the siblings, and at the ICMP, DNA matches are issued in both names. Logical consistency suggests that the threshold for distinguishing between related victims should be the same as for single identifications. In a case, say, of missing father and son, the LR indicating relatedness to the family vs. unrelated may be astronomical, but could favor the identity of one over the other by a much lesser extent (depending on references available in the case). In such a case, the ICMP will issue a Match Report only in the name of one family member only if the LR between the two hypotheses of identity exceeds 2,000 (consistent with 99.95%). Otherwise, the DNA Match Report contains information alerting the pathologist that the alternative identity of the relatives should be considered.

As a general issue, relatedness among victims can cause great complexities in evaluation and reporting, with the need to sometimes consider many alternative scenarios. Software that permits relative evaluation of alternative hypotheses in one analysis, such as the Bayesian Calculator function in DNA·VIEW, can be very helpful, but does not substitute for a high degree of expertize and experience in navigating evaluation in such cases. In cases involving multiple victims of the same family, the DNA profiles from identified victims can be used as reference profiles in the identification of their missing relatives. However, this case should be conducted only when the first identification does not involve DNA data relating to the other missing family members, to avoid the application of circular logic in making serial identifications that are not, in fact, independent. In the general case, simultaneous rather than serial calculations are needed to properly evaluate the DNA evidence in cases of multiple missing relatives (Brenner, 2006).

6 DNA in Disaster Victim Identification (DVI)

Certainly one of the predominant areas for the application of DNA testing to missing persons is that of DVI, or as sometimes referred to, mass fatality identification (MFI). In addressing this topic, we encounter the issue of defining what a "disaster" or a "mass fatality" is. A disaster can have many causes, ranging from transportation accidents, fires, extreme weather events (such as hurricanes, typhoons and tornados), earthquakes, or human-caused events many of which are considered as "terrorism" or other crimes. With this wide range of size and nature of event, DNA testing in such instances to date has been so widespread and numerous as to defy any attempt to list them. There is no accepted definition of the number of victims that constitute a "mass" fatality, but from the standpoint of the DNA laboratory, hallmarks of a mass fatality are when the normal processing flow of the lab is disrupted with regard to throughput and/or time urgency, and there is a need to conduct DNA screening and matching within a sizable event database of reference and victim profiles.

Taken over the range of experience and application, the use of DNA in DVI spans virtually every aspect or variation that is encountered in any missing persons DNA effort. Accordingly, the many published or disseminated guidelines, recommendations or reviews stand as rich resource to be accessed for laboratories planning missing persons DNA applications generally (Prinz *et al.*, 2007; Budowle *et al.*, 2005; Weedn and Baum, 2011; Lee *et al.*, 2008; Lessig *et al.*, 2011; Sozer *et al.*, 2010; NIJ, 2005; Sozer, 2014).

The efforts undertaken by and in support of the New York City Office of the Chief Medical Examiner (OCME) in response to the 9/11 attack on the World Trade Center (WTC) towers were seminal in the development of DNA application to DVI. The extreme fragmentation of the remains meant that DNA would be the only possible form of identification in almost all of the cases, and the high heat and much extended duration of the recovery process caused great difficulties for DNA testing. Moreover, an announcement was made to the public in the early days after the attack that every piece of human remains would be identified. This set in motion what has clearly been by far the most expensive DVI effort ever undertaken.

In the immediate aftermath of the event, the National Institute of Justice (NIJ) convened a Kinship and Data Analysis Panel

(KADAP) of experts in forensic DNA, statistical genetics and informatics to assist the OCME in the complex DNA identification effort (Biesecker *et al.*, 2005). The KADAP provided recommendations and guidance on dealing with the daunting task at a time when there was an urgent demand for identifications, but still many unknowns about the magnitude of the task, and much uncharted territory with regard to such a large and complex undertaking. A key question posed to the KADAP by Robert Schaller (then heading the OCME Forensic Biology Department) at the outset was: What level of DNA matching certainty should be required to constitute an identification, and how is such certainty calculated? This was an "open" DVI event, meaning that it was unknown with precision who was missing, and what the number of victims was. Initial considerations based on various reports used a nominal value of 5,000 as the number of missing, and established an event-related prior probability for DNA matches as 1/5,000 (using kinship, or direct matching in the case of antemortem biological samples from the victims themselves). An early *ad hoc* decision was made for direct matching LR threshold of 10^{10}, reflecting an extremely conservative perspective of permitting not more than a 1/1,000 chance of a single erroneous identification within 1,000 such identified victims (Brenner and Weir, 2003). In contrast, kinship matches were later required to have a lower and more practical LR threshold of 3×10^6.

The WTC response brought a spotlight to the complex issues of large scale DNA identification in DVI, including the need for integrated management planning in advance of major events. It is now established wisdom that reacting only after an event has occurred will inevitably cause great difficulties, resulting in increased cost, delay, management stress and detrimental public impact. A rich resource of published articles have sprung from the WTC work and lessons learned, including statistics and bioinformatics (Brenner and Weir, 2003; Cash *et al.*, 2003), practical DNA testing approaches (Budimlija *et al.*, 2003; Holland *et al.*, 2003; Biesecker *et al.*, 2005) and anthropological examination and sampling for DNA (Mundorff *et al.*, 2014, Mundorff and Davoren, 2014). The KADAP produced an extensive "lessons learned" document stemming from the 9/11

DNA experiences that stands as one of the most comprehensive existing resources on the use of DNA in DVI, including integration with overall incident management, DNA input into the family assistance process, expectation management, DNA laboratory planning and best practice, identification reconciliation and quality control (NIJ, 2006). Quality control of information on the missing and reference samples collected from multiple public agencies was a serious problem for the identification effort, and this issue is addressed also in respect to the DNA identification response to Hurricane Katrina (Donkervoort *et al.*, 2008). As of July, 2015, the total number of reported missing persons from the WTC is 2,753, of which 1,640 (60%) have been identified; 21,906 body parts were recovered, 14,202 of which have been re-associated by DNA (NYC OCME, personal communication).

Another seminal DVI event that provided extreme challenges and resulted in important lessons learned was that of the SE Asian tsunami that resulted from a severe undersea earthquake on December 26, 2004. The tsunami resulted in the death of an estimated 280,000 people (Lay *et al.*, 2006; INTERPOL, 2010), from 13 countries, the hardest hit being Indonesia suffering ~160,000 (INTERPOL, 2010) dead and Sri Lanka with over 38,000 (Steinlechner *et al.*, 2006). The only country that received major internationally-supported DVI response was Thailand with a final tally of 5,395, of which ~2,400 were foreign nationals from 36 different countries (INTERPOL, 2010). A central challenge in this event was coordination of DVI teams consisting of 2,000 persons from 31 countries (INTERPOL, 2010; Lessig *et al.*, 2006) whose primary initial priority was to identify and repatriate citizens of their countries. Different teams accustomed to working to different standards and different protocols created a chaotic situation, and gave rise to an urgent need for centralized management. Moreover, country-specific repatriation goals have an inherent paradox: since it is generally not possible to identify an individual as a citizen of a specific country without identifying the victim as an individual, country-specific approaches do not work. In response, a Thai Tsunami victim identification (TTVI) management structure was eventually established with much assistance from INTERPOL, under the general jurisdiction of the Thailand Royal Police, overseeing an Executive Committee made up of numerous Thai and international representatives with INTERPOL as Secretariat (INTERPOL, 2010).

After initial *ad hoc* identifications by local authorities based on a variety of traditional methods, 3,684 remaining unidentified victims were subjects of the long term TTVI operation (Pong-Rack Sribanditmongkol, personal communication). The following over-arching tenets were adopted: "every victim would be treated equally without prejudice" and "that the INTERPOL DVI process would be the agreed method to deliver the identity of all victims" (INTERPOL, 2010). While the DVI teams involved brought a high degree of expertize in multiple forensic identification disciplines, effective mechanisms had to be put into place on the fly. For Western victims with comparatively good medical and dental records, many dental identifications were made quickly and easily (James, 2005; Schuller-Gotzburg and Suchanek, 2007). In contrast, there was no standing capacity or organized strategy to support DNA identification, and a variety of laboratories with varying levels of expertize in forensic testing of degraded DNA became involved in an uncoordinated manner that produced few early identifications (INTERPOL, 2010; Lessig *et al.*, 2006), although not all initial efforts were ineffective (Steinlechner *et al.*, 2006). The comparatively ineffective application of DNA testing in the early months of the TTVI response contributed to some criticism of DNA as tool of primary importance in DVI (New Scientist, 2005), in comparison to odontological or friction ridge methods.

The initial problems with the implementation of the DNA portion of the identification process included lack of competent labs with high throughput capabilities (Lessig *et al.*, 2006), poor sampling protocols (INTERPOL, 2010; Lessig *et al.*, 2006), and complications by commercial interests (Lessig *et al.*, 2006) delayed the proper use of DNA in the identification process until May–June of 2005. In May of 2005, the ICMP's offer of assistance for DNA identification was taken up by the TTVI and began STR profiling of bone and tooth samples in a high throughput manner (INTERPOL,

2010). ICMP donated its DNA matching software to the project, and ICMP staff were deployed to the TTVI center in Phuket to conduct matching. DNA match reports mounted steadily thereafter, with the now "degraded" bone samples yielding a 96% STR success rate overall (out of 1,819 bone samples tested by ICMP). Fingerprints and odontology indeed played a major role in identifications, but a combination of identifiers was sought whenever possible. The ICMP issued DNA match reports on 802 individuals, allowing for multiple modes of identification in many cases. Moreover, DNA played a greatly disproportionate role in the identification of two groups of victims. In the end, DNA was the primary identification mode for 54% of Thai nationals and > 50% of the children under 19 years of age — both groups being comparatively deficient in antemortem dental or fingerprint records (Pong-Rack Sribanditmongkol, personal communication).

Through the action of its DVI Standing Committee and DVI Steering Group, INTERPOL (www.interpol.int) plays a prominent role in defining standards and organizational protocols in DVI, which are delineated in the INTERPOL DVI Guidelines (INTERPOL, 2013). Seeking to enhance standing mechanisms for preparedness as a result of lessons learned from the 2004 tsunami, in 2007 and again in 2014 INTERPOL and ICMP have established standing agreements for cooperation in DVI to enable, among other things, a rapid and effective DNA identification response. The ICMP also regularly participates in INTERPOL Response Team (IRT) deployments that are conducted at the invitation of affected countries, to assess needs and provide recommendations in DVI events. As a result of one IRT, the ICMP DNA identification standing capacity was brought into operation to assist with DVI from 2008 Typhoon Frank in the Philippines. In this event, the ferry Princess of the Stars capsized with the loss of some 1,200 persons. Within less than two weeks, training of local authorities and provision of forms and family reference DNA collection kits put into place effective operations that, combined with STR profiling from 559 bone samples at a greater than 97% success rate, resulted in 456 individuals identified by DNA.

Given that mass fatalities where DVI is applied may be caused by criminal human activity such as terrorism, DNA methods can play a role not only in identification *per se*, but in criminal investigation and prosecution as well. This fact can give rise to complications with regard to jurisdiction and institutional responsibility, but again highlights that as a general issue DVI efforts should be approached in the context of applicable rule of law rather than as "humanitarian" undertakings, with appropriate forensic rigor to support justice mechanisms. In terrorist attacks, often involving highly fragmented human remains where DNA plays an especially predominant role, a perpetrator(s) is often among the deceased. This situation puts DNA DVI into an investigatory role, where a process of elimination comes into play in determining post-mortem DNA profiles that cannot be attributed to the reported missing persons (e.g. Sudoyo *et al.*, 2008). It is likely that reference samples for the perpetrator(s) will not be available, or become available only much later in the investigation. In such cases, biogeographical ancestry information inherent in DNA has been assessed to provide clues as to the origin or identity of the perpetrator(s) as in the case of 9/11 Flight 93 (crashed in rural Pennsylvania), the 9/11 Flight 77 (crashed into the Pentagon) (Edson *et al.*, 2004), and the 2004 "11-M" Madrid bombing attack (Phillips *et al.*, 2009).

7 "Routine" Missing Persons

While public attention on DVI is often focused on missing persons related to distinct catastrophic events, a program sponsored by the US National Institute of Justice emphasizes that the issue of persons who go missing on a day-to-day basis can be considered as a "silent mass disaster" (Ritter, 2007). The US National Missing Person DNA Database (NMPDD) is operated by the Federal Bureau of Investigation (FBI) as part of the National DNA Index System (NDIS). Specified laboratories in the US, such as the University of North Texas Center for Human Identification, the California Department of Justice Jan Bashinski Laboratory, and the forensic science division of the Minnesota Bureau of Criminal Apprehension can upload genetic profiles from either family members or from the remains of the missing. The testing of both post mortem and *ante mortems* samples is supported by funding from the National Institute of Justice. Samples are tested not only for autosomal markers but for lineage, both Y chromosome and mtDNA, markers also. General guidelines for the use of DNA in missing persons and specific operational procedures for searching missing persons and reference profiles within the NDIS system using CODIS software have been published by the Scientific Working Group on DNA Analysis Methods (SWGDAM) (SWGDAM, 2014).

Other countries around the world maintain or are in the process of adopting legislation that allows for the creation of national missing persons databases. According to the European Network of Forensic Science Institutes (ENFSI) DNA Working Group 13 countries in Europe hold missing persons databases (http://www.enfsi. eu/sites/default/files/documents/enfsi_2014_document_on_dna-database_management_0.pdf). One of the main drawbacks with National DNA databases is that, there is little legislation and few effective mechanisms/programs to permit searching across borders. This limitation continues despite the magnitude of and severity of the issue of cross-border missing. The International Organization on Migration (IOM) has estimated that between the months of January and September 2014, a total of 4,077 migrant border-related fatalities (Brian and Laczko, 2014) The majority (3,072) occurred in the Mediterranean, followed by East Africa (251) and the Mexico/ US border (230).

The INTERPOL DNA Gateway that member countries can use to internationally search DNA profiles in criminal investigations, also has provisions to store and search DNA profiles from unidentified bodies and compare them to missing persons' DNA profiles. So far, over 50 countries have submitted DNA profiles from missing persons and/or unidentified bodies and have contributed to solving international missing persons cases. The program has mainly relied on direct matching between unidentified remains and *antemortem* profiles of the missing, but INTERPOL has begun to extend the program to permit kinship matching with family reference profiles.

8 DNA and the Living Missing

Databases for DNA kinship matching hold great promise for the re-unification of living persons, particularly with regard to children who are separated from their families, as a result of e.g. example armed conflict, migration or trafficking. The Argentinean organization Abuelas de Plaza de Mayo has a long standing program for searching for children missing after their parents were forcibly disappeared by the military regime between 1976 and 1983 (Penchaszadeh, 1997). DNA comparisons across generations have been used to assist in resolution of particular cases. The Asociación ProBusqueda (http://www.probusqueda.org.sv/) similarly seeks children taken by armed forces in during the 1980–1992 civil war in El Salvador. Many of these children are thought to have been taken for adoption by military personnel in El Salvador, or sent for adoption to other countries, particularly the USA. ProBusqueda has taken a full scale DNA database matching approach in cooperation with the California-based Alliance of Forensic Scientists for Human Rights and Humanitarian Investigations, the Berkeley Human Rights Center, and the ICMP. At the time of this writing, ProBusqueda has received 953 reported cases, 422 of which have been resolved with linking children (now grown) to their biological families (ProBusqueda, personal communication). The ProBusqueda database now contains 1,172 family reference DNA profiles and DNA profiles from 281 individuals who are seeking to find their biological families.

DNA-PROKIDS is a multi-institutional program targeting the international issue of cross-border trafficking of children, with an emphasis on Latin America. The program was founded by the University of Granada Genetic Identification Laboratory now partners with the University of North Texas Center for Human Identification (UNTCHI) (Alvarez-Cubero *et al.*, 2012; Kim and Katsanis, 2013). As of 2012, DNA-PROKIDS has been able to reunite more than 330 children with the biological parents (Alvarez-Cubero *et al.*, 2012; Kim and Katsanis, 2013), with updated figures on the UNTCHI website (https://www.unthsc.edu/graduate-school-of-biomedical-sciences/molecular-and-medical-genetics/about-2/dna-prokids-fact-sheet/) listing a current database of 11,000 DNA samples from 15 countries, and 724 children returned to families.

DNA testing and establishment of effective databases has the potential to play an important role in combating human trafficking (e.g. Katsanis *et al.*, 2014). Prostitution and other sexual exploitation, forced labor, servitude, slavery, illegal immigration, adoption fraud and removal of organs for sale are activities involving trafficking where establishing identity and kinship through DNA can resolve cases and reunite families. This need for identification is particularly true in the case of children, whose identity upon recovery years later may be impossible to establish in other ways. For example, calls have been sounded for DNA collection and comparison efforts to reunite girls abducted by the Nigerian group Boko Harem (Sheridan, 2014). Individuals or populations at high risk for violent death or enforced disappearance could have samples taken proactively to aid in subsequent identification, investigation and prosecution. Such a program has been initiated for sex workers as part of the Dallas Prostitution Diversion Initiative, to aid in criminal homicide investigations (Kim and Katsanis, 2013, 2014).

9 Future Perspectives

The burgeoning field of NGS or massively parallel sequencing (MPS) in application to forensic genetics will have a strong impact on DNA identification of missing persons. It is beyond the scope of this article to review the rapidly developing MPS methodologies and their applications, however recent publications in forensic genetics indicate great potential (King *et al.*, 2014a, 2014b; Seo *et al.*, 2013; Gettings *et al.*, 2015; Borsting and Morling, 2015). With regard to missing persons applications, the field of forensic genetics would benefit the most from capitalizing on the strength of MPS to, in combination, make great strides in the following areas: recovery of genetic information from highly degraded samples, greatly expand the accessible loci to permit kinship matching to distant relatives (see e.g. Huff *et al.*, 2011), and develop multiplexing and other work flow/informatics optimization to greatly decrease the price per sample.

We will see in the following paragraph that some of the greatest limitations in the use of DNA for missing persons come not from technical aspects of DNA testing. Nonetheless, the cost per DNA test in forensics is a technical issue that does define a principle limitation in missing persons applications. Since its inception, MPS has decreased the cost of DNA sequencing in genomics and clinical diagnostics by many orders of magnitude (Wetterstrand, 2015), and there must be MPS approaches that can be developed in human identity and kinship testing that will also permit major changes in the cost of identifying the missing by DNA.

DNA databases and kinship matching capabilities have a profound potential for identifying the missing and returning them to their families, whether as deceased victims or as reunited living persons. At the same time, these DNA data can serve as potent evidence in the prosecution of some of humanity's most heinous crimes, such as mass killings, forced disappearance and human trafficking. However, this potential is far from realized. There are primary challenges in the lack of international and inter-institutional mechanisms to link the missing and their families across borders, to ensure genetic privacy, to safeguard the security of vulnerable families and populations who report missing persons, and to address overlapping concerns of medical ethics in the incidental findings that may result from forensic genetic data (Katsanis *et al.*, 2014). To be effective, DNA databases must be linked to other types of data on the missing and their families, so there must be effective informatics tools that can span these data categories. Importantly, these tools must be accessible both to affected populations for registration of the missing and provision of relevant information and to the agencies working to resolve the cases, while at the same time affording effective data protection. The ICMP has developed an integrated Identification Data Management System (iDMS) with a developing Online Inquiry Center (http://www.icmp.int/fdmsweb/index.php?w=intro) to fill this need.

Many questions remain regarding the policies, data sharing practices and agencies/institutions that can provide information access, operational effectiveness (including DNA) and protection. These critical issues were a central theme of a Forum convened by the ICMP in 2013 entitled "The Missing: An Agenda for the Future" (ICMP, 2014a). For DNA and missing persons databases, substantial challenges exist for defining involvement of various types of institutions from the standpoint of such issues as public trust, data security, centralized effectiveness and high standards of forensic rigor and accountability. In this regard, the ICMP in its sole mission to address global issues of the missing, has recently been awarded the status of an International Organization (ICMP, 2014b) with internationally sanctioned privileges and immunities that are intended to provide powerful advantages in navigating the issues of international and inter-institutional database security and connectivity.

References

A. Alonso, S. Andelinovic, P. Martin, D. Sutlovic, I. Erceg, E. Huffine, L. Fernandex de Simon, C. Albarran, M. Definis-Gojanovic, A. Fernandez-Rodrigues, P. Garcia, I. Drmic, B. Rezic, S. Kuret, M. Sancho and D. Primorac. DNA typing from skeletal remains: Evaluation of multiplex and megaplex STR systems on DNA isolated from bone and teeth samples. *Croatian Medical Journal*, 42(3):260–266, 2001.

A. Alonso, P. Martin, C. Albarran, P. Garcia, L. Fernandez de Simon, M. Jesus Iturralde, A. Fernandez-Rodriguez, I. Atienza, J. Capilla, J. García-Hirschfeld, P. Martinez, G. Vallejo, O. García, E. García, E. P. Real, D. Alvarez, A. Leon and M. Sancho. Challenges of DNA profiling in mass disaster investigations. *Croatian Medical Journal*, 46(4): 540–548, 2005.

M. J. Alvarez-Cubero, M. Saiz, L. J. Martinez-Gonzalez, J. C. Alvarez, A. J. Eisenberg, B. Budowle and J. A. Lorente. Genetic identification of missing persons: DNA analysis of human remains and compromised samples. *Pathobiology*, 79:228–238, 2012.

S. Amory, R. Huel, A. Bilic, O. Loreille and T. J. Parsons. Automatable full demineralization DNA extraction procedure from degraded skeletal remains. *Forensic Science International: Genetics*, 6:398–406, 2012.

L. G. Biesecker, J. E. Bailey-Wilson, J. Ballantyne, H. Baum, F. R. Bieber, C. Brenner, B. Budowle, J. M. Butler, G. Carmody, P. M. Conneally,

B. Duceman, A. Eisenberg, L. Forman, K. K. Kidd, B. Leclair, S. Niezgoda, T. J. Parsons, E. Pugh, R. Shaler, S. T. Sherry, A. Sozer and A. Walsh. DNA identifications after the 9/11 World Trade Center attack. *Science*, 310:1122–1123, 2005.

I. Birus, M. Marcikic, D. Lauc, S. Dzijan and G. Lauc. How high should paternity index be for reliable identification of war victims by DNA typing? *Croatian Medical Journal*, 44(3):322–326, 2003.

C. Borsting and N. Morling. Next generation sequencing and its application in forensic genetics. *Forensic Science International: Genetics*, 18:78–89, 2015. http://dx.doi.org/10.1016/j.fsigen.2015.02.002, accessed September 13, 2015.

L. Bradford, J. Heal, J. Anderson, N. Faragher, K. Duval and S. Lalonde. Disaster victim investigation recommendations from two simulated mass disaster scenarios utilized for user acceptance testing CODIS 6.0, *Forensic Science International: Genetics*, 5:291–296, 2011.

C. Brenner. Symbolic kinship program. *Genetics*, 145:535–542, 1997.

C. H. Brenner and B. S. Weir. Issues and strategies in the DNA identifications of the World Trade Center victims. *Theoretical Population Biology*, 63:173–178, 2003.

C. H. Brenner. Some mathematical problems in the DNA identification of the victims of the 2004 tsunami and similar mass fatalities. *Forensic Science International*, 157:172–180, 2006.

T. Brian and F. Laczko. *Fatal Journeys. Tracking Lives Lost During Migration.* IOM, Geneva, 2014. http://publications.iom.int/bookstore/free/FatalJourneys_CountingtheUncounted.pdf, accessed September 13, 2015.

A. G. Brown. The use of forensic botany and geology in war crimes investigations in NE Bosnia. *Forensic Science International*, 163:204–210, 2006.

Z. M. Budimlija, M. K. Prinz, A. Zelson-Mundorff, J. Wiersema, E. Bartelink, G. MacKinnon, B. L. Nazzaruolo, S. M. Estacio, M. J. Hennessey and R. C. Shaler. World Trade Center human identification project: Experiences with individual body identification cases. *Croatian Medical Journal*, 44(3):259–263, 2003.

B. Budowle, F. R. Bieber and A. J. Eisenberg. *Legal Medicine*, 7:230–243, 2005.

B. Budowle, J. Ge, R. Chakraborty and H. Gill-King, Use of prior odds for missing persons identifications. *Investigative Genetics*, 2:15, 2011.

A. Carracedo, W. Bar, P. Lincoln, W. Mayr, N. Morling, B. Olaisen, P. Schneider, B. Budowle, P. Gill, M. Holland, G. Yully and M. Wilson.

DNA commission of the International Society for Forensic Genetics: guidelines for mitochondrial DNA typing. *Forensic Science International*, 110:79–85, 2000.

H. D. Cash, J. W. Hoyle and A. J. Sutton. Development under extreme conditions: Forensic bioinformatics in the wake of the World Trade Center disaster. *Pacific Symposium on Biocomputing*, 8:638–653, 2003.

M. D. Coble, O. M. Loreille, M. J. Wadhams, S. M. Edson, K. Maynard, C. E. Meyer, H. Niederstatter, C. Berger, B. Berger, A. B. Falsetti, P. Gill, W. Parson and L. N. Finelli. Mystery solved: the identification of the two missing Romanov children using DNA analysis. *PLoS ONE*, 4(3): e4838, 2009.

S. Connor. *Jack the Ripper: Scientist who claims to have identified notorious killer has 'made serious DNA error'. The Independent.* 19 October, 2014. http://www. independent.co.uk/news/science/jack-the-ripper-id-hinges-on-a-decimal-point-as-scientists-flag-up-dna-error-in-book-that-claims-to-identify-the-whitechapel-killer-9804325.html, accessed August 04, 2015.

A. Cooper and H. N. Poinar. Ancient DNA: Do it right or not at all. *Science*, 289(5482):1139, 2000.

J. Davoren, D. Vanek, R. Konjhodzic, J. Crew, E. Huffine and T. J. Parsons. Highly effective DNA extraction method for nuclear short tandem repeat testing of skeletal remains from mass graves. *Croatian Medical Journal*, 48:478–485, 2007.

S. Donkervoort, S. M. Dolan, M. Beckwith, T. P. Northrup and A. Sozer. Enhancing accurate data collection in mass fatality kinship identifications: Lessons learned from Hurricane Katrina. *Forensic Science International: Genetics*, 2:354–362, 2008.

S. M. Edson, J. P. Ross, M. D. Coble, T. J. Parsons and S. M. Barritt. Naming the dead — Confronting the realities of rapid identification of degraded skeletal remains. *Forensic Science Review*, 16:63–90, 2004.

R. Edwards. *Naming Jack the Ripper*. Lyons Press, Guilford CT, USA, 2014.

E. A. Foster, M. A. Jobling, P. G. Taylor, P. de Knijff, R. Mieremet, T. Zerjal and C. Tyler-Smith. Jefferson fathered slave's last child. *Nature*, 396:27–28, 1998.

M. Garcia, L. Martinez, M. Stephensen, J. Crews and F. Piccerelli. Analysis of complex kinship cases for human identification of civil war victims in Guatemala using M-FISys software. *Forensic Science International: Genetics Supplemental*, 2:250–252.

K. Gettings, K. M. Kiesler and P. M. Vallone. Performance of a next generation sequencing SNP assay on degraded DNA. *Forensic Science*

International: Genetics, 19:1–9, 2015. http://dx.doi.org/10.1016/j.fsigen. 2015.04.010.

P. Gill, P. L. Ivanov, C. Kimpton, R. Piercy, N. Benson, G. Tully, I. Evett, E. Hagelberg and K. Sullivan. Identification of the remains of the Romanov family by DNA analysis. *Nature Genetics*, 6:130–135, 1994.

P. Gill and E. Hagelberg. Ongoing controversy over Romanov remains. *Science*, 306:408–409, 2004.

D. W. Gjertson, C. H. Brenner, M. P. Baur, A. Carracedo, F. Guidet, J. A. Luque, R. Lessig, W. R. Mayr, V. L. Pascali, M. Prinz, P. M. Schneider and N. Morling. ISFG: Recommendations on biostatistics in paternity testing. *Forensic Science International: Genetics*, 1:223–231, 2007.

C. D. Gocke, F. A. Benko and P. K. Rogan. Transmission of mitochondrial DNA heteroplasmy in normal pedigrees. *Human Genetics*, 102:182–186, 1998.

E. Hagelberg, I. C. Gray and A. J. Jeffreys. Identification of the skeletal remains of a murder victim by DNA analysis. *Nature*, 352:427–429, 1991.

D. Z. C. Hines, M. Vennemeyer, S. Amory, R. L. M. Huel, I. Hanson, C. Katzmarzyk and T. J. Parsons. Prioritized sampling of bone and teeth for DNA analysis in commingled cases. In B. J. Adams and J. E. Byrd (eds.), *Commingled Human Remains: Methods in Recovery, Analysis, and Identification*, pp. 275–305. Academic Press, Oxford, 2014.

M. Hofreiter, O. Loreille, D. Ferriola and T. J. Parsons. Ongoing controversy over Romanov remains. *Science*, 306:407–408, 2004.

M. M. Holland, D. L. Fisher, L. G. Mitchell, W. C. Rodriguez, J. J. Canik, C. R. Merril and V. W. Weedn. Mitochondrial DNA sequence analysis of human skeletal remains: Identification of remains from the Vietnam War. *Journal of Forensic Science*, 38(3):542–553, 1993.

M. H. Holland, C. A. Cave, C. A. Holland and T. W. Bille. Development of a quality, high throughput DNA analysis procedure for skeletal samples to assist with the identification of victims from the World Trade Center attacks. *Croatian Medical Journal*, 44(3):264–272, 2003.

C. D. Huff, D. J. Witherspoon, T. S. Simonson, J. Xing, W. S. Watkins, Y. Zhang, T. M. Tuohy, D. W. Neklason, R. W. Burt, S. L. Guthery, W. R. Woodward and L. B. Jorde. Maximum-likelihood estimation of recent shared ancestry (ERSA). *Genome Research*, 21(5):768–774, 2011. http://www.genome.org/cgi/doi/10.1101/gr.115972.110.

E. Huffine, J. Crews, B. Kennedy, K. Bomberger and A. Zinbo. Mass identification of persons missing from the break-up of the Former Yugoslavia:

Structure, function, and role of the International Commission on Missing Persons. *Croatian Medical Journal*, 42(3):271–275, 2001.

International Commission on Missing Persons (ICMP). *The Missing — An Agenda for the Future: Conference Report*. The Hague, The Netherlands, 2014a (20 May, 2014). http://www.icmp.int/wp-content/uploads/2014/07/conferencereporteng.pdf, accessed September 13, 2015.

International Commission on Missing Persons (ICMP). *ICMP established as International Organization in its own right*, 2014b. (Press Release, 15 December, 2015). http://www.icmp.int/news/icmp-established-as-international-organization-in-its-own-right/, accessed September 13, 2015.

International Committee of the Red Cross (ICRC). *Forensic science and humanitarian action*, 2013. https://www.icrc.org/eng/assets/files/publications/icrc-002-4156.pdf, accessed September 13, 2015.

INTERPOL. *INTERPOL disaster victim identification guide*, 2013. http://www.interpol.int/Media/Files/INTERPOL-Expertise/DVI/DVI-Guide-new-version-2013, accessed August 04, 2015.

INTERPOL. *INTERPOL Tsunami Evaluation Working Group. The DVI response to the South East Asian Tsunami between December 2004 and February 2006*, 2010. http://www.interpol.int/Media/Files/INTERPOL-Expertise/DVI/INTERPOL-Tsunami-Evaluation-Working-Group, accessed August 05, 2015.

J. A. Irwin, M. D. Leney, O. Loreille, S. M. Barritt, A. F. Christensen, T. D. Holland, B. C. Smith and T. J. Parsons. Application of low copy number STR typing to the identification of aged, skeletal remains. *Journal of Forensic Science*, 52(6):1322–1327, 2007.

J. A. Irwin, J. L. Saunier, K. M. Strouss, K. S. Sturk, T. M. Diegoli, A. Brandstätter, W. Parson and T. J. Parsons. Investigation of point heteroplasmy in the mitochondrial DNA control region: A synthesis of observations from over 5000 global population samples. *Journal of Molecular Evolution*, 68:516–527, 2009.

P. L. Ivanov, M. J. Wadhams, R. K. Roby, M. M. Holland, V. W. Weedn and T. J. Parsons. Mitochondrial DNA sequence heteroplasmy in the Grand Duke of Russia Georgij Romanov establishes the authenticity of the remains of Tsar Nicholas II. *Nature Genetics*, 12(4):417–420, 1996.

H. James. Thai tsunami victim identification overview to date. *Journal of Forensic Odonto-stomatology*, 23(1):1–18, 2005

A. J. Jeffreys, M. J. Allen, E. Hagelberg and A. Sonnberg. Identification of the skeletal remains of Josef Mengele by DNA analysis. *Forensic Science International*, 56:65–76, 1992.

R. S. Just, M. D. Leney, S. M. Barritt, C. W. Los, B. C. Smith, T. D. Holland and T. J. Parsons. The use of mtDNA SNPs to assist in the resolution of three challenging forensic cases. *Journal of Forensic Sciences*, 54:887–891, 2009.

S. H. Katsanis and J. Kim. DNA in Immigration and Human Trafficking. In D. Primorac and M. Schanfield (eds.), *Forensic DNA Applications: An Interdisciplinary Perspective*, pp. 537–554. CRC Press, Boca Raton, Florida, 2014.

S. H. Katsanis, J. Kim, M. A. Minear, S. Chandrasekharan and J. K. Wagner. Preliminary perspectives on DNA collection in anti-human trafficking efforts. *Recent Advances in DNA and Gene Sequences*, 8(2):78–90, 2014.

J. Kim and S. H. Katsanis. Brave new world of human-rights DNA collection. *Trends in Genetics*, 29(6):329–332, 2013. http://dx.doi.org/10.1016/j.tig.2013.04.002, accessed July 4, 2013.

T. E. King, G. G. Fortes, P. Balaresque, M. G. Thomas, D. Balding, P. Delser Maisano, R. Neumann, W. Parson, M. Knapp, S. Walsh, L. Tonasso, J. Holt, M. Kayser, J. Appleby, P. Forster, D. Ekserdjian, M. Hofreiter and K. Schürer. Identification of the remains of King Richard III. *Nature Communications*, 5:5631, 2014a.

J. L. King, B. L. LaRue, N. M. Novroski, M. Stoljarova, S. B. Seo, X. Zeng, D. H. Warshauer, C. P. Davis, W. Parson, A. Sajantila and B. Budowle High-quality and high-throughput massively parallel sequencing of the human mitochondrial genome using the Illumina MiSeq. *Forensic Science International: Genetics*, 12:128–135, 2014b. http://dx.doi.org/10.1016/j.fsigen.2014.06.001, accessed September 14, 2015.

D. Kling, A. O. Tillmar and T. Egeland. Familias 3 — Extensions and new functionality. *Forensic Science International: Genetics*, 13:121–127, 2014. http://dx.doi.org/10.1016/j.fsigen.2014.07.004, accessed August 10, 2015.

A. Knight, L. A. Zhivotovsky, D. H. Kass, D. E. Litwin, L. D. Green, P. S. White and J. L. Mountain. Molecular, forensic and haplotypic inconsistencies regarding the identity of the Ekaterinburg remains. *Annals of Human Biology*, 31(2):129–138, 2004.

J. Lee, P. Scott, D. Carroll, C. Eckhoff, S. Harbison, V. Lentile, R. Goetz, J. W. Scheffer, P. Stringer and G. Turbett. Recommendations for DNA laboratories supporting disaster victim identification (DVI) operations — Australian and New Zealand consensus on ISFG recommendations. *Forensic Science International: Genetics*, 3:54–56, 2008.

R. Lessig, J. Edelmann, L. Aspinall, P. Krumm, I. Bastisch, P. Wiegand, C. Hohoff, M. Steinlechner and L. Roewer. German standards for forensic molecular genetics investigations in cases of mass disaster victim identification (DVI). *Forensic Science International: Genetics*, 5:247–248, 2011. http://www.ncbi.nlm.nih.gov/pubmed/20457065.

O. M. Loreille, T. M. Diegoli, J. A. Irwin, M. D. Coble and T. J. Parsons. High efficiency DNA extraction from bone by total demineralization. *Forensic Science International: Genetics*, 1:191–195, 2007.

T. Lay, H. Kanamori, C. J. Ammon, M. Nettles, S. N. Ward, R. C. Aster, S. L. Beck, S. L. Bilek, M. R. Brudzinski, R. Butler, H. R. DeShon, G. Ekstrom, K. Satake and S. Sipkin. The great Sumatra-Andaman earthquake of 26 December 2004. *Science*, 308:1127–1133, 2005.

R. Lessig, C. Grundmann, F. Dahlmann, K. Rotzscher, J. Edelmann and P. M. Schneider. Tsunami 2004 — a review of one year of continuous forensic medical work for victim identification. *EXCLI Journal*, 5: 128–139, 2006.

D. Marjanovic, A. Durmic-Pasic, L. Kovacevic, J. Avdic, M. Dzehverovic, S. Haveric, J. Ramic, M. B. Kalamujic, L. L. Bilela, V. Skaro, P. Projic, K. Bajrovic, K. Drobnic, J. Davoren and D. Primorac. Identification of skeletal remains of communist armed forces victims during and after World War II: Combined Y-chromosome short tandem repeat (STR) and MiniSTR approach. *Croatian Medical Journal*, 50:296–304, 2009.

M. J. Mehlman and T. Y. Li. Ethical, legal, social, and policy issues in the use of genomic technology by the U.S. military. *Journal of Law and the Biosciences*, 1(3):244–280, 2014.

A. Milos, A. Selmanovic, L. Smajlovic, R. L. M. Huel, C. Katzmarzyk, A. Rizvic and T. J. Parsons. Success rates of nuclear short tandem repeat typing from different skeletal remains. *Croatian Medical Journal*, 48:486–493, 2007.

A. Mundorff and J. M. Davoren. Examination of DNA yield rates for different skeletal elements at increasing post mortem intervals. *Forensic Science International: Genetics*, 8:55–63, 2014. http://dx.doi.org/10.1016/j.fsigen.2013.08.001.

A. Z. Mundorff, R. Shaler, E. T. Bieschke and E. Mar-Cash. Marrying anthropology and DNA: Essential for solving complex commingling problems in cases of extreme fragmentation. In B. J. Adams and J. E. Byrd (eds.), *Commingled Human Remains: Methods in Recovery, Analysis and Identification*, Academic Press, Oxford, pp. 257–273, 2014.

New Scientist. *Dental records beat DNA in tsunami IDs. newscientist.com*, 2005. https://www.newscientist.com/article/mg18725163-900-dental-records-beat-dna-in-tsunami-ids/, accessed August 31, 2015.

National Institute of Justice (NIJ). *Mass fatality incidents: A guide for human forensic identification.* U.S. Department of Justice, Washington, 2005. https://www.ncjrs.gov/pdffiles1/nij/199758.pdf, accessed August 04, 2015.

National Institute of Justice (NIJ). *Lessons learned from 9/11: DNA identification in mass fatality incidents.* U.S. Department of Justice, Washington, 2006. https://www.ncjrs.gov/pdffiles1/nij/214781.pdf, accessed August 04, 2015.

National Research Council (NRC), Committee on Identifying the Needs of the Forensic Sciences Community. *Strengthening Forensic Science in the United States: A Path Forward.* The National Academies Press, D. C. Washington. https://www.ncjrs.gov/pdffiles1/nij/grants/228091.pdf, accessed September 13, 2015.

I. Z. Pajnic, B. G. Pogorelc, J. Balazic, T. Zupanc and B. Stefanic. Highly efficient nuclear DNA typing of World War II skeletal remains using three new autosomal short tandem repeat amplification kits with extended European standard set of loci. *Croatian Medical Journal,* 53:17–23, 2012.

W. Parson. *Irgendwann kommt alles an licht,* Ecowin. Benevento Publishing, Salzburg, Austria, 2014.

W. Parson, L. Gusmao, D. R. Hares, J. A. Irwin, W. R. Mayr. N. Morling, E. Pokorak, M. Prinz, A. Salas, P. M. Schneider and T. J. Parsons. DNA commission of the International Society for Forensic Genetics: Revised and extended guidelines for mitochondrial DNA typing. *Forensic Science International: Genetics,* 13:134–142, 2014. http://dx.doi.org/10.1016/j.fsigen.2014.07.010

T. J. Parsons, D. S. Muniec, K. Sullivan, N. Woodyatt, R. Alliston-Greiner, M. R. Wilson, D. L. Berry, D. L. Holland, V. W. Weedn, P. Gill and M. H. Holland. A high observed substitution rate in the human mitochondrial DNA control region. *Nature Genetics,* 15:363–368, 1997.

T. J. Parsons, R. Huel, J. Davoren, C. Katzmarzyk, A. Milos, A. Selmanovic, L. Smajlovic, M. D. Coble and A. Rizvic. Application of novel "mini-amplicon" STR multiplexes to high volume casework on degraded skeletal remains. *Forensic Science International: Genetics,* 1:175–179, 2007.

V. B. Penchaszadeh. Genetic identification of children of the disappeared in Argentina. *Journal of the American Medical Women's Association,* 52(1): 16–21, 1997.

C. Phillips, L. Prieto, M. Fondevila, A. Salas, A. Gomez-Tato, J. Alvarez-Dios, A. Alonso, A. Blanco-Verea, M. Brion, M. Montesino, A. Carrecedo and M. V. Lareau. Ancestry Analysis in the 11-M Madrid Bomb Attack Investigation. *PLoS ONE,* 4(8):e6583, 2009.

R. Pinhasi, D. Fernandes, K. Sirak, M. Novak, S. Connell, S. Alpaslan-Roodenberg, F. Gerritsen, V. Moiseyev, A. Gromov, P. Raczky,

A. Anders, M. Pietrusewsky, G. Rollefson, M. Jovanovic, H. Trinhhoang, G. Bar-Oz, M. Oxenham, H. Matsumura and M. Hofreiter. Optimal ancient DNA yields from the inner ear part of the human petrous bone. *PLoS ONE*, 10(6):e0129102, 2015.

M. Prinz, A. Carracedo, W. R. Mayr, N. Morling, T. J. Parsons, A. Sajatila, R. Scheithauer, H. Schmitter and P. M. Schneider. DNA commission of the International Society for Forensic Genetics (ISFG): Recommendations regarding the role of forensic genetics for disaster victim identification (DVI). *Forensic Science International: Genetics*, 1:3–12, 2007.

N. Rohland and M. Hofreiter. Comparison and optimization of ancient DNA extraction. *BioTechniques*, 42:343–352, 2007.

N. Rohlan, H. Siedel and M. Hofreiter. A rapid column-based ancient DNA extraction method for increased sample throughput. *Molecular Ecology Resources*, 10:677–683, 2010.

N. Ritter. Missing persons and unidentified remains: The Nation's silent mass disaster. *NIJ Journal*, 256:2–7, 2007.

J. Sarkin, L. Lettelfield, M. Matthews and R. Kosalka. *Bosnia and Herzegovina. Missing persons from the armed conflicts of the 1990s: A stocktaking.* International Commission on Missing Persons (ICMP), Sarajevo, 2014. http://www.ic-mp.org/wp-content/uploads/2014/12/Stocktaking Report_ENG_web.pdf, accessed September 13, 2015.

P. Schuller-Gotzburg and J. Suchanek. Forensic odontologists successfully identify tsunami victims in Phuket, Thailand. *Forensic Science International*, 171:204–207, 2007.

Scientific Working Group on DNA Analysis Methods (SWGDAM). *Missing Persons Casework Guidelines*, 2014. http://www.swgdam. org/#!publications/c1mix, accessed September 13, 2015.

S. B. Seo, J. L. King, D. H. Warshauer, C. P. Davis, J. Ge and B. Budowle. Single nucleotide polymorphism typing with massively parallel sequencing for human identification. *International Journal of Legal Medicine*, 127:1079–1086, 2013.

K. Sheridan. *How DNA forensics could identify lost Nigerian girls*, 2014. http://phys.org/news/2014-05-dna-forensics-lost-nigerian-girls.html, accessed September 13, 2015.

K. Slooten. Validation of DNA-based identification software by computation of pedigree likelihood ratios. *Forensic Science International: Genetics*, 4:308–315, 2011.

M. Sozer, M. Baird, M. Beckwith, B. Harmon, D. Lee, G. Riley and S. Schmitt. *Guidelines for Mass Fatality DNA Identification Operations.* American Association of Blood Banks (AABB), Bethesda, MD, 2010. https://www.aabb.org/programs/disasterresponse/Documents/aabbdnamassfatalityguidelines.pdf, accessed August 04, 2015.

A. C. Sozer. *DNA Analysis for Missing Person Identification in Mass Fatalities.* CRC Press, Boca Raton, Florida, 2014.

D. W. Steadman, B. J. Adams and L. W. Konigsberg. Statistical basis for positive identification in forensic anthropology. *American Journal of Physical Anthropology*, 131(1):15–26, 2006.

M. Steinlechner, W. Parson, W. Rabl, P. Grubwieser and R. Scheithauer. Tsunami-disaster: DNA typing of Sri Lanka victim samples and related AM matching procedures. *International Congress Series*, 1288:741–743, 2006.

A. C. Stone, J. E. Starrs and M. Stoneking. Mitochondrial DNA analysis of the presumptive remains of Jesse James. *Forensic Science International*, 46(1):173–176, 2001.

K. A. Sturk, M. D. Coble, S. M. Barritt and J. A. Irwin. Evaluation of modified Yfiler amplification strategy for compromised samples. *Croatian Medical Journal*, 50:228–238, 2009.

H. Sudoyo, P. T. Widodo, H. Suryadi, Y. S. Lie, D. Safari, A. Widjajanto, D. A. Kadarmo, S. Hidayat and S. Marzuki. DNA analysis in perpetrator identification of terrorism-related disaster: Suicide bombing of the Australian Embassy in Jakarta 2004. *Forensic Science International: Genetics*, 2:231–237, 2008.

L. A. Tully, T. J. Parsons, R. J. Steighner, M. M. Holland, M. A. Marino and V. L. Prenger. A Sensitive DGGE Assay Reveals a High Frequency of Heteroplasmy in Hypervariable Region One of the Human Mitochondrial DNA Control Region. *American Journal of Human Genetics*, 67:432–443, 2000.

C. J. van Dongen, K. Slooten, M. Slagter, W. Burgers and W. Wiegerinck. Bonaparte: Application of new software for missing persons program. *Forensic Science International: Genetics, Supplemental Series*, 3:e119–e120, 2011.

L. Vollen. All that remains: Identifying the victims of the Srebrenica massacre. *Cambridge Quarterly of Healthcare Ethics*, 10(3):336–340, 2001.

S. Walsh, F. Liu, K. N. Ballantyne, M. van Oven, O. Lao and M. Kayser. IrisPlex: A sensitive DNA tool for accurate prediction of blue and brown eye colour in the absence of ancestry information. *Forensic Science International: Genetics*, 5:170–180, 2011.

S. Walsh, F. Liu, A. Wollstein, L. Kavatsi, A. Ralf, A. Kosiniak-Kamysz, W. Branicki and M. Kayser. The HIrisPlex system for simultaneous prediction of hair and eye colour from DNA. *Forensic Science International: Genetics*, 7:98–115, 2013. http://dx.doi.org/10.1016/j.fsigen.2012.07.005, accessed August 4, 2015.

V. W. Weedn and H. J. Baum. DNA identification in mass fatality incidents. *The American Journal of Forensic Medicine and Pathology*, 32(4):393–397, 2011.

K. A. Wetterstrand. *DNA Sequencing Costs: Data from the NHGRI Genome Sequencing Program (GSP)*, 2015. www.genome.gov/sequencingcosts, accessed September 15, 2015.

M. R. Wilson, D. Polanskey, J. Replogle, J. A. DiZinno and B. Budowle. A family exhibiting heteroplasmy in the human mitochondrial DNA control region reveals both somatic mosaicism and pronounced segregation of mitotypes. *Human Genetics*, 100:167–171, 1997.

D. Y. Yang, B. Eng, J. S. Waye, J. C. Dudar and S. S. Suanders. Technical note: Improved DNA extraction from ancient bones using silica-based spin columns. *American Journal of Physical Anthropology*, 105:539–543, 1998.

L. A. Zhivotovsky. Recognition of the remains of Tsar Nicholas II and his family: A case of premature identification? *Annals of Human Biology*, 26(6):569–577, 1999.

CHAPTER 16

Molecular Autopsy

Antti Sajantila*,†and Bruce Budowle†,‡

*Department of Forensic Medicine, University of Helsinki,
Helsinki, Finland
†Department of Molecular and Medical Genetics,
Institute of Applied Genetics,
University of North Texas Health Science Center, Fort Worth, TX, USA
‡Center of Excellence in Genomic Medicine Research (CEGMR),
King Abdulaziz University, Jeddah, Saudi Arabia

1 Introduction

Autopsy (from the Greek word autopsia; to see with one's own eyes), also known as a post-mortem (PM) examination, necropsy, *autopsia cadaverum* or obduction, is a classical method to investigate the sequence of events and their causes, which lead to the death of an individual. In this type of investigation, two concepts are important to understand and treat separately, i.e. the cause of death (CoD) and the manner of death (MoD). For international standardization, the World Health Organization (WHO) has defined CoD as the (a) disease or trauma that initiated the train of morbid events leading directly to death or (b) the circumstances of the accident of violence that produced the fatal injury. MoD is defined as the way or circumstances that led to the CoD. The WHO also created a classification system, the International Classification of Diseases, which is designed to endorse comparisons in the collection, processing, classification and presentation of mortality statistics at an international level (Ruzicka and Lopez, 1990, Lozano *et al.*, 2012, Murray and Lopez, 1996, Chugh *et al.*, 2008).

Most natural deaths belong to the realm of clinicians, and if an autopsy is needed, it is performed by the hospital pathologist, in many countries with the permission of the next-of-kin. These autopsies focus on the correlation of findings with the clinical records, i.e. when clinical data do not allow unequivocal determination of the CoD or when treating medical doctors wish to further understand the pathology and mechanism of a disease, its unexpected development, or curious outcome of the treatment in natural deaths. Ultimately, hospital autopsies serve as an additional quality measure of medical treatment and have an educational purpose for clinicians and medical students. The rate of clinical autopsies has declined in the recent decade (Start *et al.*, 1993) due to development of clinical laboratory and imaging techniques (Dirnhofer *et al.*, 2006), although concern has been expressed about this trend (Lugli *et al.*, 1999, Beer, 2000). An exception to the declining trend has been described in a recent report on the autopsy rate in China (Zhu *et al.*, 2014).

The overall objective of the autopsy is to serve the immediate family or other relatives, the physicians, general public, medical education, and medical and public health research. In addition, medico-legal autopsy was developed for law enforcement and judicial purposes to find details that help determine the causes and mechanisms in unnatural deaths, i.e. death not due to a disease, and where MoD is suspected to be due to accident, homicide or suicide.

Medico-legal autopsies are needed in deaths that are associated with violent acts, and specifically to reconstruct the chain of events in such crimes. In accidental deaths, the medico-legal autopsy aids in establishing whether the death mechanism was indeed a trauma. Suicidal deaths may be associated with a common medico-legal autopsy substance, and the data obtained from these cases generate a unique perspective for various studies of suicide (Ylijoki-Sorensen *et al.*, 2014a; Vuorio *et al.*, 2014; Laukkala *et al.*, 2014), including prevention (Haw and Hawton, 2015). In addition, deaths in custody (Wangmo *et al.*, 2014), military or police service (Tiesman *et al.*, 2010), and in medical institutions or medical care (Madea *et al.*, 2009; Madea and Preuss, 2009) are of special medico-legal interest, and may reveal important data for public security and welfare. In some countries, medico-legal autopsies may be performed to investigate if the CoD in a single case could influence public health, insurance policies or occupational regulations (Tiesman *et al.*, 2010; Turnbull *et al.*, 2015). Finally, medico-legal autopsy may initiate identification of human remains.

Apart from suspected violent, accidental or suicidal deaths medico-legal autopsies are performed when deaths are natural, but occur suddenly and unexpectedly or the deceased has not been under medical care. Even if unnatural deaths are the primary purview of forensic pathology, natural diseases are frequently revealed as underlying CoD after an autopsy.

The rate of medico-legal autopsies vary from country to country reflecting legislation and traditions (Rajs and Jakobsson, 1985; Saukko, 1995; Nordrum *et al.*, 1998; Schmeling *et al.*, 2009; Ylijoki-Sorensen *et al.*, 2014a, 2014b). Although the benefits of autopsies for society are obvious (Beer, 2000), classical autopsy work has been criticized, and some have advocated replacement of classical autopsy with imaging techniques (Bolliger and Thali, 2015). However, PM investigations can, when appropriately archived and analyzed, reveal patterns and trends that can be helpful for decision-makers for implementing preventive actions and developing health policies.

In a small proportion of medico-legal autopsies no CoD, and thus no MoD, can be established even after a thorough investigation has occurred including death scene investigation, evaluation of medical history, macroscopic autopsy and ancillary tests (e.g. histology, toxicology, biochemistry and imaging). These cases are known as negative autopsies (Lawler, 1990; Cohle and Sampson, 2001). Another challenge in medico-legal autopsies work is cases where the CoD can be established, but the MoD remains unclear, for example, sometimes it is impossible to distinguish between intentional and unintended intoxication (suicide *vs.* accident, respectively) (Rockett *et al.*, 2015).

Some of these negative autopsies may be deciphered with the arrival of molecular autopsy (Ackerman *et al.*, 1999a, 1999b, 2001a, 2001b). Elucidating genetic signatures may present an explanation for CoD and MoD, and the advent of advanced molecular biology techniques holds promise for applying successfully molecular genetic analyses in PM diagnostics.

It should be noted that no clear definition exists for molecular autopsy. Molecular autopsy in some regards is not a novel approach used by the pathologist or medical examiner. Indeed, one could submit that e.g. biochemistry and toxicology, which have been used routinely for many years, make use of molecular analyses. However, molecular autopsy has mostly been related to DNA diagnostics used in a PM setting, and therefore we suggest that other terms, such as genetic or laboratory autopsy, may be applied. Herein, we describe molecular autopsy as a discipline of analyses that relies on genetic-based typing to help determine CoD and/or MoD. Clearly, the field of molecular autopsy is still in its infancy and molecular biology technology and biomarkers will contribute to the maturation of the field. Given the advances in genetic typing that range from determining the primary sequence of a DNA target to expression of genes (i.e. epigenetic control) and analyses related to the metabolome, it may be prudent to consider molecular autopsy as "omics" autopsy. It is expected in the not too distant future that tools will be developed to facilitate omics autopsies and provide greater opportunities to reduce the number of negative autopsies that occur currently. However, we will refer to the concept as molecular autopsy herein for consistency with the scientific literature.

2 Molecular Autopsy

The revolution of genetic testing as part of "the autopsy in the age of molecular biology" was foreseen by Dr. Charles S. Davidson 50 years ago (Davidson, 1965). However, it took until more recent years for molecular autopsy to become a reality with genomic discoveries of genes related to arrhythmic channelopathies (Curran *et al.*, 1995; Keating, 1995) and myocardiopathies (Geisterfer-Lowrance *et al.*, 1990; Thierfelder *et al.*, 1994). A pivotal change in the use of the molecular autopsy was brought to the scientific arena by a series of publications from the Mayo Clinic, where carefully selected cases of death after near-drowning were convincingly shown to be due inherited genetic variants associated with LQTS (long QT syndrome) (Ackerman *et al.*, 1999a, 1999b). The authors also coined the term "molecular autopsy" (Ackerman *et al.*, 2001b). Subsequently, more genetic studies were published, confirming and expanding on earlier findings (Lunetta *et al.*, 2002, 2003; Tester and Ackerman, 2005; Tester *et al.*, 2005). Later, similar techniques were applied to other sudden unexplained deaths (SUDs), such as sudden infant death syndrome (SIDS) (Ackerman *et al.*, 2001a; Arnestad *et al.*, 2007). These early studies showed that at least for some of the previously troublesome negative autopsies there was a molecular mechanism that could explain some SUDs.

The genetic signatures that impact SUDs are often referred to as mutations or variants and the terms are used interchangeably. Strictly speaking mutations should be a change in an allele or locus during transmission from parent to offspring or a change somatically in an allele in a cell in a tissue. Mutations can occur at single nucleotide position or on a localized or large portion of the genome. Variants, on the other hand, should refer to the different allele states of those loci that exist in the population (and are inherited unchanged from parent to offspring).

The majority of negative autopsies where the use of molecular autopsy has made breakthroughs has been deaths that were described as sudden cardiac deaths, but did not show any pathological-anatomical changes to assist in making a diagnosis as to the CoD. There are also other classes of deaths where molecular autopsy techniques can be informative, such as deep venous thrombosis and related pulmonary embolism, ruptures of aortic wall aneurysms, and intracranial hemorrhage. In addition, molecular autopsies have shown to be useful in understanding toxic deaths, where individual genetic variation can cause fatal adverse drug reactions (ADRs), even with normal drug dosages.

Negative autopsies are vexing challenges for medical examiners. Recent examples of molecular autopsies have demonstrated that the mysteries surrounding SUDs can be unraveled by identifying genetic variations that can result in or predispose an apparently healthy individual to sudden death (Di Paolo *et al.*, 2004). Understanding the genetic components of the common diseases, coupled with the use of molecular genetic testing, is becoming an increasingly important tool in medical examiners' armamentarium in determining CoD or contributing factors to death. In addition, the ability to establish a genetic cause as the basis of the CoD may help to avoid a recurring tragedy within a family and encourage the family members, who may be at similar risk, to seek genetic counseling.

3 Sudden Unexpected Death

In older adults (> 40 yrs), natural deaths often are associated with diseases affecting the cardiovascular system, such as coronary artery atherosclerosis, hypertensive heart disease, and pulmonary thromboembolism, all of which are readily observed in an autopsy. In contrast, in young adults (< 40 yrs), unexplained deaths, which are described as sudden cardiac deaths (SCDs) is reported in high frequencies, ranging from 40 to 100 deaths per 1,00,000 persons (Chugh *et al.*, 2008; Farioli *et al.*, 2015), although large variation approximately from 4% to 65% exist in such estimations in different studies (Table 1). Since SCDs occur in such cases of apparently healthy individuals, they have no previous symptoms, and are therefore not under medical care. Therefore, there is little if any medical history related to these SUDs, and a full medico-legal autopsy is of utmost importance. Principally any developmental anomaly, degenerative or acute disease in the valvular, vascular, myocardial or pericardial parts in the cardiac system can cause SCD. In some cases, which are described as SCD, no structural pathological change in the myocardium can be found (Cohle and Sampson, 2001; Chugh *et al.*, 2000, 2008). In infants and children, in addition to cardiac arrhyth-

Table 1: Prevalence of negative autopsies or SUDs (sudden unexplained deaths) in various studies.

Prevalence (%)	N	Age group (Yrs)	Population	Reference
4.4	270	> 20	USA (Minnesota)	Chugh *et al.* (2000)
17.7	107	1–35	Spanish	Morentin *et al.* (2003)
19.7	690	14–40	USA (Maryland)	Burke *et al.* (1991)
20.0	100	1–40	Italy (Lazio region)	di Gioia *et al.* (2006)
21.0	181	15–35	Swedish	Wisten *et al.* (2002)
27.8	273	≤ 35	Italy (Veneto region)	Corrado *et al.* (2001)
28.9	469	1–35	Danish	Winkel *et al.* (2011)
29.0	241	5–35	Australia (Sydney)	Puranik *et al.* (2005)
31.1	193	≤ 35	Australia (Sydney)	Doolan *et al.* (2004)
34.9	126	18–35	USA (military recruits)	Eckart *et al.* (2004)
64.6	223	≤ 35	UK (throughout country)	Fabre and Sheppard (2006)

mias associated with structurally normal or abnormal hearts (Ilina *et al.*, 2011), developmentally related diseases may present, such as metabolic disorders (Scalais *et al.*, 2015) and sudden unexplained death in epilepsy (Berg *et al.*, 2013).

Yet, genetic predisposition to some of these SCDs has been identified. The most common monogenic diseases, having well-established mutation spectrum, that cause SCDs, are summarized below.

3.1 Sudden Cardiac Deaths

3.1.1 Familial hypercholesterolemia

Familial hypercholesterolemia (FH) (Muller, 1938; Goldstein and Brown, 1973; Brown and Goldstein, 1976a, 1976b) (Müller, 1938) is among the most common group of single-gene diseases having an average worldwide prevalence of heterozygous patients of 1 in 500 (Goldstein *et al.*, 1983). Three genes are known to be involved in the phenotype of FH: low-density lipoprotein-receptor (LDLR), apolipoprotein B (APOB) and proprotein convertase subtilisin/ kexin type 9 (PCSK9) (Besseling *et al.*, 2015). Although the FH phenotype is highly variable, the variants in these genes result in increased levels of LDL-cholesterol (LDLC) and consequent premature coronary heart disease (CHD) (Hovingh *et al.*, 2013). If heterozygous males with FH are not treated, CHD typically manifests during the fourth decade of life, and in female patients a decade later (Besseling *et al.*, 2015; Hovingh *et al.*, 2013). Homozygous individuals, on the other hand, have major CHD events as early as in their 20s (Goldstein and Brown, 2001, Rader *et al.*, 2003). As expected, stat in treatment has drastically changed the premature occlusive CHD events, including death (Baigent *et al.*, 2010).

SCD in a case of a 26 year-old young adult due to FH has been reported based on PM cholesterol measurement (Leadbeatter and Stansbie, 1984). But PM biochemical cholesterol measurement has constraints, and DNA diagnostics would be desirable in a PM setting. Although > 1,000 mutations exist in the LDL receptor gene for FH (Leigh *et al.*, 2008), DNA level screening can be particularly cost-effective in populations, that particularly have only a handful of founder genes. Indeed, molecular autopsy screening of such founder mutations in young men (< 50 yrs) suffering from SCD has been reported, showing that FH mutations that were not diagnosed during life can be found in medico-legal autopsies (Vuorio *et al.*, 1999).

3.1.2 Cardiomyopathies

Cardiomyopathies are a wide category of diseases of the myocardium, classified according to morphological findings, in which the most common forms are hypertrophic cardiomyopathy (HCM), dilated cardiomyopathy (DCM), and arrhythmogenic right ventricular cardiomyopathy (ARVC). Also rare forms of cardiomyopathies are known such as restrictive cardiomyopathy (RCM) and left ventricular non-compaction cardiomyopathy (LVNCCM). Cardiomyopathies often have characteristic macroscopic alterations, some accompanied with characteristic features visible under light microscopy (Grant and

Evans, 2009; Watkins *et al.*, 2011), although PM changes often can hamper proper observations and diagnosis.

Patients with cardiomyopathies are at risk of irreversible arrhythmic events that lead to cardiac failure and death, unless electrically reversed. The clinical problem is that fatal arrhythmias can occur without previous symptoms, and diagnosis typically is made only at autopsy. Since the cardiac conduction system can be affected without structural changes in the myocardium, the effect may not become obvious even at the autopsy. Lack of gross anatomic or microscopic changes can be found in children with developing heart cardiomyopathies (Tester and Ackerman, 2009). In addition, cardiomyopathies can be single disease entities or a part of a genetic syndrome (Bonne *et al.*, 2000).

Cardiomyopathies are genetically heterogeneous; each cardiomyopathy is caused by multiple genes, and various rare variants are found in those genes (Watkins *et al.*, 2011). Molecular diagnostics is further complicated in that the same genes and mutations can be responsible for different cardiomyopathies (Figure 1). For instance, the MYH7 gene is responsible for all three types of cardiomyopathies: hypertrophic, dilated and left ventricular non-compaction (Klaassen *et al.*, 2008). In addition, genotype–phenotype correlation in cardiomyopathies is complicated by genetic and allelic heterogeneity, genetic and environmental modifier effects, and variable penetrance and expression. Nevertheless, molecular testing of candidate genes responsible for cardiomyopathies are especially useful when structural changes are subtle or absent, and thus do not meet classic morphological diagnosis.

Hypertrophic cardiomyopathy. The first cardiomyopathy to be characterized on a molecular level was HCM, an autosomal dominant disease with unexplained hypertrophy of the left ventricle (gross anatomy), and characteristic disarray in the myocardial fibers (histology). The genetic defect was described 35 years ago as a missense mutation in the beta-cardiac myosin heavy chain gene HCM (Geisterfer-Lowrance *et al.*, 1990). Later, it was established that HCM is a genetic disorder resulting from pathogenic mutations in several

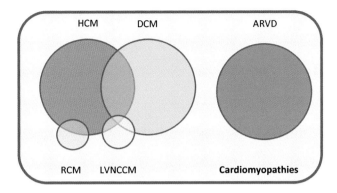

Figure 1:   Relationship of cardiomyopathies and their genetic characteristics. The major cardiomyopathy forms HCM and DCM at times can have a similar genetic basis, while ARVC (arrhythmogenic right ventricular cardiomyopathy) has an entirely different genetic and mutational spectrum. RCM (restrictive cardiomyopathy) is caused by many common genes and mutations with HCM, while LVNCCM (left ventricular non-compaction cardiomyopathy) is a heterogeneous mixture; patients can have genetic aspects similar to HCM and DCM.

genes encoding or processing sarcomere proteins. Thus, it also has been coined as the disease of the sarcomere (Thierfelder *et al.*, 1994).

Dilated cardiomyopathy. An assembly of factors can lead to DCM, such as inflammatory sequel (e.g. viral myocarditis), exposure to cardiac toxins (e.g. medications, alcohols, illicit drugs), metabolic disease, or genetic defects. Pathological and histological changes in the DCM include left ventricular dilatation, myocyte death, and myocardial fibrosis. Familial form of the disease arises in 20–48% of patients (Taylor *et al.*, 2006). The most common mode of inheritance is autosomal dominant transmission, although autosomal recessive and X-linked forms have been described (Jefferies *et al.* 2010). Over 40 genes have been identified to cause DCM, encoding two major subgroups of proteins cytoskeletal and sarcomeric proteins. However, unlike HCM, mutations in the DCM genes encode components of a wide variety of cellular compartments and pathways. DCM is sometimes inherited with other phenotypes, namely cardiac conduction disorder or non-cardiac sensorineural hearing loss. In children, DCM can be caused by disrupted mito-chondrial function and metabolic abnormalities (Jefferies and Towbin, 2010).

Arrhythmogenic right ventricular cardiomyopathy. Under light micros-copy, ARVC shows inflammatory and fibrofatty infiltration of the right ventricle, and in some cases, gross anatomic changes may be observed. ARVC is a familial disease with an autosomal dominant mode of inheritance in about half of the cases (Watkins *et al.*, 2011). This disease has been known to cause SUDs in young people (Thiene *et al.*, 1988). The genes that cause ARCV are those encod-ing desmosomal proteins (desmoplakin, plakoglobin, plakophilin 2, desmoglein 2, and desmocollin 2) (Sen-Chowdhry *et al.*, 2007). Most of the mutations in these genes are insertions, deletions or nonsense mutations, which tend to cause premature truncation of the trans-lated proteins. Two non-desmosomal genes have been implicated in ARVC: one for transforming growth factor $\beta3$ (TGF-$\beta3$) and the other for transmembrane protein 43 (Lombardi and Marian, 2011). The alterations in desmosomal encoding genes also have been found in two related autosomal recessive disorders, Naxos disease and Carvajal syndrome. These data suggest that more genes are involved in the development of ARVC.

For practical medico-legal autopsy, molecular autopsies of car-diomyopathies are far from the routine work of the medical examiner or pathologist, and more research is clearly needed to make full use of this important capability. An example of such work was presented by Larsen *et al.* (2012), who characterized muta-tional spectrum of pathogenic mutations in a SCD cohort of deceased aged 0–40 yrs. The study subjects were suspected of hav-ing died from HCM, DHC or ARVC. Nine of the 41 cases had a rare sequence variant in the MYBPC3, MYH7, LMNA, PKP2 or TMEM43 genes, of which 4 cases (9.8%) were pathogenic. The data in Larsen *et al.* (2012) show that molecular autopsies of SCD in the young can reveal exact underlying molecular changes at least in some cases where the structural abnormality leads the diagnostic procedure PM.

3.1.3 Cardiac channelopathies

Arrhythmic cardiac diseases are long known to be inherited and to cause SCDs, but the genetic architecture of several conduction system defects has only recently been characterized. In fact, it was the investigation of genes encoding cell membrane ion-channels and associated proteins (genetic channelopathies) in SUDs, classified as negative autopsies, which led to the concept of the molecular autopsy.

Functional defects in the cardiac conduction system (i.e. proteins needed for conduction of electrical impulse in the myocytes) cause irregularities in the heart rhythm. In the most severe situations those arrhythmic events can cause SCDs in the absence of any macroscopically or microscopically detectable structural changes. The inherited forms of these defects are now known to be due to variants in certain genes. The functionally different alleles encode proteins involved in the ion channels in the myocardium which cause a potential irreversible imbalance of ionic current and a momentous change in the action potential leading to ventricular fibrillation and death.

Each of the cardiac channelopathies shows a characteristic change in an electrocardiogram (ECG) (Cerrone and Priori, 2011). However, often young adults and children have not had an ECG and thus remain uninformed of potential risks. Since the first description in 1995 (Curran *et al.*, 1995; Keating, 1995), a number of channelopathies have been characterized. These findings have contributed substantially to unraveling cases of SUDs in young individuals and are now known to be caused by distinct heritable arrhythmic conditions, such as long QT syndrome (LQTS), the short QT syndrome (SQTS), Brugada syndrome (BrS) and catecholaminergic polymorphic ventricular tachycardia (CPVT) (Cerrone and Priori, 2011). The genes associated with these disorders are known to be partially overlapping (Figure 2). It is estimated that 10–15% of SIDS cases are due to variants in the heritable channelopathy genes (Arnestad *et al.*, 2007; Ackerman *et al.*, 2001a; Millat *et al.*, 2009). At the molecular level, channelopathies are caused either by abnormal functions of the cardiac ion channels (Na+, K+,

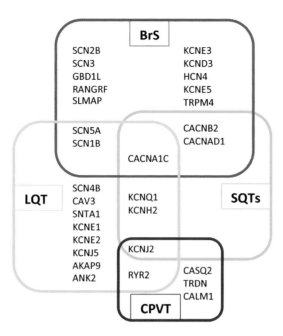

Figure 2: A schematic diagram of the relationships between cardiac channelopathies and the genes causing the clinical disorders and the risks for SCDs (sudden cardiac deaths)/SUDs (sudden unexplained deaths). LQTs = long QT syndrome, SQTs = short QT syndrome, BrS = Brugada syndrome, CPVT = catecholinergic polymorphic ventricular tachycardia.

and Ca2+), or protein processing. Genes encoding for most of the cardiac ion channels and associated proteins have been mapped and cloned (Cerrone and Priori, 2011).

Molecular autopsy by typing variants in these genes is the only means of revealing the exact CoD, since there are no signs in the myocardium, or elsewhere, to be found by a PM investigation. Therefore, SUD often is the only indication of possible channelopathies in apparently healthy individuals.

3.2 *Other Sudden Unexpected Deaths*

3.2.1 Deep venous thrombosis and pulmonary embolism

Fatal pulmonary embolism (PE) is typically a result of a massive blood clot blocking pulmonary arteries or its large branches, which causes hemodynamic collapse or infarct of the corresponding pulmonary lobe. Fatal PE is associated with deep venous thromboembolism (VTE), although VTE is not always noted in the autopsy. German pathologist Rudolf Virchow (Bagot and Arya, 2008) described three predisposing factors associated with most deaths caused by PE: vascular injury, stasis and hypercoagulability (Kumar *et al.*, 2010). VTE is a multifactorial disease and accounts for approximately 100,000 deaths annually in the United States (Heit *et al.*, 1999). The genetic risk for VTE and consequently PE include mutations in factor V Leiden and prothrombin, deficiencies of antithrombin, proteins C and S, and other factors in the coagulation cascade (Favaloro and Lippi, 2011).

Population based differences often are observed with a number of diseases or disorders. A recent report of a large cohortof fatal PE showed that the victims of fatal VTE-PE are predominately Blacks, and they died at an earlier age compared with Whites (Tang *et al.*, 2011). Consistent with other studies, Blacks were less likely to be carriers of the common VTE-associated variants found in Whites (Tang *et al.*, 2011). Thus, ethnicity seems to play a significant role in fatal PE, though the mechanism is unknown. Such differences can be attributed to genetics and environmental factors. The more heterogeneous the disease is, the more difficult it is to determine CoD.

3.2.2 Aortic aneurysm rupture

A common type of a SUD in an elderly individual is a rupture of the aorta followed by fatal haemorrhaging. Symptoms often are sudden with severe abdominal pain and collapse. An autopsy typically reveals a large volume hemorrhage in the abdominal cavity and an aneurysm in the aortic wall. Risk factors in such cases include atherosclerotic development in the aorta. Aortic dissection and rupture can take place in individuals with genetic disorders of collagen formation, such as Marfan syndrome (McKusick, 1991) and Ehlers–Danlos syndrome type IV (Beighton, 1968). In medico-legal autopsies these disorders are rare, but well established, and mutation screening for FBN1 (Dietz *et al.*, 1991) and COL3A1 genes (Schwarze *et al.*, 1997) can be useful in determining the underlying CoD.

4 Pharmacogenomics and Molecular Autopsy

Although favism and an adverse reaction have been known for millennia, pharmacogenetics (PGt) can be traced to the 1950s, when it was realized that the primaquine (an antimalarial drug) caused intravascular hemolysis in about 10% of African–Americans, but the adverse effect was rarely observed in Caucasians (Hockwald *et al.*, 1952). A deficiency of glucose-6-phosphate dehydrogenase was the cause of the reaction (Carson *et al.*, 1956). Soon after it became apparent that there were individual differences in response to drug therapy, the field of PGt was born to elucidate the underlying genetic components.

Pharmacogenetics (PGt)/pharmacogenomics (PGx) combine pharmacology with genetics with an expectation of better personalized prediction of drug response. When an individual is prescribed a therapeutic drug, there are three outcomes: the drug helps the patient in the intended way, there is no effect with the drug, or an adverse reaction can occur by exposure to the drug. Better healthcare can be achieved by determining how an individual will respond to exposure of a drug and especially the latter two outcomes should be avoided. The focus of PGt/PGx is on individual inherited variation that impacts drug response. The disciplines basically elucidate, on a molecular level, the known concept of "responders" and "nonresponders" to drug treatment. The practical aim in PGt and PGx is to assist practitioners in prescribing individually tailored medications for best response and concomitantly to minimize adverse reactions to drugs that may be administered by a physician. PGt and PGx have exploded as a field in the last decade because of the impact on personalized (or precision) medicine. This increase in PGx is illustrated, e.g. with the number of articles published in the last few years. In PubMed using the keyword PGx and PGx reviews, 18,046 and 6,243 hits, respectively, were observed and the words forensic genetics and forensic genetics reviews listed 9,347 and 664 articles, respectively (August 2015). Due to the extensive interest and potential of PGt/PGx, the U.S. Department of Health and Human Services Food and Drug Administration has published Definitions for

Genomic Biomarkers, Pharmacogenomics, Pharmacogenetics, Genomic Data and Sample Coding Categories. PGx is defined as the study of variations of DNA and RNA characteristics as related to drug response, and PGt, a subset of PGx, is defined as the study of variations in DNA sequence as related to drug response. Illicit drug response also falls under the same concerns about adverse reactions and the genetic causes of response may assist in CoD and MoD in a criminal investigation.

4.1 *Adverse Drug Reactions and Medico-Legal Interest*

ADR is defined as an unintended response to a drug occurring at a conventional dose and used for disease in prophylaxis, diagnosis, therapy, or for modification of physiological functions (WHO, factsheet No. 293). Although the efficacy of drugs for human use is scrutinized in clinical trials, more than half of the ADRs are detected after the drugs are on the market (Moore *et al.*, 1998). In the clinical setting, ADRs are difficult to identify and report. ADRs are divided into six categories (type A–F reactions) according to severity (Pirmohamed *et al.*, 1998, Edwards and Aronson, 2000). Understandably, the number of reported ADRs depends on many factors. Mild ADRs are not necessarily realized, and fatalities are not always associated with ADRs. There are also differences of practice in reporting ADRs among medical institutions. These differences affect the gathering and analysis of information, and thus, many events may remain underreported. Despite the difficulties of collating systematic data, medical and pharmaceutical societies try to compare ADRs of different drugs and to manage them in large databases (see, e.g. www.who-umc.org/).

Lazarou *et al.* (1998) found an overall incidence of fatal ADRs which is 0.32% among U.S. hospital inpatients. Similarly, Ebbesen *et al.*, (2001) studied prospectively 13,992 Scandinavian patients and estimated the incidence of fatal ADR to be 0.95%, and Pirmohamed *et al.* (2004) observed 0.15–2.3% ADR lethality for hospital admissions in 18,820 patients. These studies suggest that suspected ADR-related deaths should be investigated using PGt and PGx knowledge in molecular autopsies (Musshoff *et al.*, 2010; Sajantila *et al.*, 2010). Based on some meta-studies on fatal ADRs, this phenomenon could be of great medico-legal interest.

4.2 Forensic Toxicology

In order to establish drug related deaths or to investigate potential ADRs as a CoD, the auxiliary test of choice traditionally is forensic toxicological screening. The objective of PM forensic toxicology in general is to analyze drugs and poisons or any other toxic agent in cadavers for medico-legal purposes. Information is attained by developing and evaluating analytical methods and instrumentation for such screening (Ojanpera *et al.*, 2012), compiling of fatal and control concentrations in PM samples (Druid and Holmgren, 1997), establishing comparisons of drug concentrations in PM samples to that of therapeutic concentrations (Launiainen and Ojanpera, 2014), and studying the PM effects on the findings (Pounder and Jones, 1990). These studies are necessary for the interpretation of the results in the PM and medico-legal context (Koski *et al.*, 2005). Also *ante mortem* parameters, such as compliance, adherence, and other behavioral habits are of importance in medico-legal interpretation. For example, borrowing and sharing of drugs, enhancement of the effect of illicit drugs with prescription drugs of medication (Petersen *et al.*, 2008, Vuori *et al.*, 2003), and co-use of prescription drugs with over-the-counter drugs or abuse of prescribed drugs often can be deduced from medico-legal autopsy reports.

In addition, another typical factor of modern society is reflected in the tendency of polypharmacy. Knowledge of alcohol-drug combinations and drug–drug interactions in forensic toxicology interpretation is necessary (Koski *et al.*, 2003; Launiainen *et al.*, 2011; Jones *et al.*, 2011). These data can be translated to clinics for treatment or diagnosis (Launiainen *et al.*, 2010). Interpretation of forensic toxicology results can be particularly challenging in the investigation of CoD and MoD in cases of unclear intoxications. Problems can appear, e.g. in establishing MoD as a suicide or an accident (Rockett *et al.*, 2015).

4.3 PM Pharmacogenetics — A Combination of PM Toxicology and Genetics

The underlying cause of the response observed in toxicology screens can be helpful in medico-legal CoD investigations. PGt can support the medico-legal CoD investigation and needs to be integrated with forensic pathology and toxicology. The investigation should accumulate data from pathophysiology of the diseased; the pharmacological history, including prescription drugs and any habitual use of illicit drugs; and concentrations of all drugs and their relevant metabolites in the PM blood. These data then can be utilized when considering the relevant individual allelic variants of genes and the genetic pathways related to the drugs found in a toxicology screen. Indeed, demonstrative cases have been described (Koren *et al.*, 2006), and some promising data have been published (Table 2).

PM PGt interpretations in the CoD investigation should consider the fact that an individual's pathophysiology affects drug efficacy (the ability of a drug to produce the desired therapeutic effect) and depends also on the genetic variation spectrum. These additional factors include developmental stage (e.g. age and sex), physiological (e.g. mental and physical stress, hormonal changes, seasonal and circadian factors) and environmental factors (e.g. diet, exposure to environmental toxins, use of alcohol and drugs), and diseases or specific conditions (e.g. diabetes, obesity, gut microbiology). Genotype-to-phenotype translation is crucial for effective clinical application of PGt/PGx. Few guidelines exist for genotype–drug dosage relationship (Roots *et al.*, 2004; Stehle *et al.*, 2008), but using solely the easily available and manageable genomic data, the prediction of the phenotype from the genotype has challenges (Haufroid and Hantson, 2015; Kirchheiner, 2008). However, PM studies can be useful in divulging genotype–phenotype relationships, and thus contribute to personalized medicine. However, due to the multifold data in a PM investigation, interpretation guidelines cannot easily be put forward, and the field needs substantial research.

Table 2: Post-mortem pharmacogenetic analysis in some medico-legal cases, listed by drugs, drug classes and gene(s).

Drug	Drug class	Gene	Reference
Fluoxetine	Antidepressant	CYP2D6	Sallee *et al.* (2000)
Doxepine	Antidepressant	CYP2D6	Koski *et al.* (2007)
		CYP2C19	
Oxycodone	Analgesic (opioid)	CYP2D6	Jannetto *et al.* (2002)
Methadone	Dependence (withdrawal)	CYP2D6	Wong *et al.* (2003)
Codeine	Analgesic (opioid)	CYP2D6	Gasche *et al.* (2004)
Fentanyl	Anesthetic/Analgesic	CYP3A	Jin *et al.* (2005)
Amitriptyline	Antidepressant	CYP2D6	Koski *et al.* (2006)
		CYP2C19	
Hydrocodon	Analgesic/Antitussive (opioid)	CYP2D6	Madadi *et al.* (2010)
Digoxin	Cardiac glycoside	ABCB1	Neuvonen *et al.* (2011)
Morphine	Analgesic (opioid)	CYP2D6	Andresen *et al.* (2013)
/codeine		CYP2C19	
Codeine	Analgesic (opioid)	CYP2D6	Lam *et al.* (2014)
		UGT2B7	
		ABCB1	
		OPRM1	
		COMT	

In a medico-legal setting, it would be ideal to have a catalogue of the drugs typically found in forensic toxicological screening and the genetic variants that affect metabolic pathways. Practically, it would be helpful to make a distinction genetically between the classical poor metabolizer and ultra-rapid metabolizer phenotypes (Druid *et al.*, 1999; Levo *et al.*, 2003). Indeed, convincing examples exist in the use of PGt methodology in medico-legal cases. The examples are cases or case series with deceased psychiatric patients and use of opioid analgesics. The cases describe the suicide-or-accident/suicide-or-homicide dilemma, which is a great challenge in medico-legal autopsies. They also represent good examples of using genotyping of poor metabolizer and ultra-rapid metabolizer phenotypes to determine whether drug exposure may have had an impact on CoD.

One of the first case-reports utilizing the concept of a PM PGt approach was published by Sallee *et al.* (2000). The authors reported a fatal drug intoxication of a 9-year-old boy who was treated with fluoxetine because of behavioral problems. A high concentration of fluoxetine and its major active metabolite norfluoxetine were found by a forensic toxicology screen and prompted a PM PGt investigation. The genetic analysis revealed a completely defective cytochrome P450 (CYP) 2D6 gene, resulting in a poor ability to metabolize fluoxetine. Similarly, CYP genotyping in PM CoD investigation has been used to assist interpretation of PM toxicology results in unexpected deaths related to the use of oxycodone (Jannetto *et al.*, 2002), methadone (Wong *et al.*, 2003) and fentanyl (Jin *et al.*, 2005). Indeed, PM PGt has focused predominately on genetic variation at CYP enzymes in relation to drug intoxications and metabolism, although many other proteins are involved in ADRs.

Ultra-rapid drug metabolism has been reported with fatal ADRs. The fatality in such cases is due to the conversion of a prodrug into an active and potentially toxic metabolite via an enhanced enzymatic reaction. An illustrative and eye-opening case was published by Koren *et al.* (2006), who described an analysis of the CYP2D6 gene related to a death investigation of a two-week old neonate. PM analysis revealed morphine intoxication as the CoD. Based on this CoD, the investigation would have focused on infanticide and/or child abuse. However, the mother was given codeine for pain relief after an episiotomy while giving birth. Using the knowledge that codeine is O-demethylated to morphine in a reaction catalyzed by CYP2D6 enzyme, a PM PGt analysis was attempted. The test revealed that the mother had a duplication of the CYP2D6 gene which explained an increased metabolism of codeine to morphine, and resultant high morphine concentration in the mother's bottled breast-milk. The child died by consuming breast-milk with high concentrations of morphine. The case turned from a suspected infanticide or medical misconduct to an unfortunate, but accidental death. The case also changed the FDA's recommendation on use of codeine products for nursing mothers (http://www.fda.gov/Drugs/DrugSafety/PostmarketDrugSafetyInformationforPatientsand Providers/ucm124889.htm).

Another interesting study related to medico-legal autopsies was described by Ahlner *et al.* (2010). The authors analyzed violent suicides and natural deaths and found that the CYP2D6 gene with ≥ 2 copies occurred ≥ 10 times more often in the suicide group than in the group of natural deaths. Although the mechanism in which CYP2D6 is triggering suicides is unknown, this study should be of interest for practitioners, who treat individuals at risk of suicide. In addition, other cases and case series studies have been published showing the extending application of PM PGt. A collection of reports using PGt analyses in medico-legal autopsies is presented in Table 2.

Principally, any gene involved in the absorption, distribution, metabolism (see cases described above) or excretion of the drugs can have an effect on the outcome of the intended drug treatment. This group of genes has collectively been termed ADME, although the terms LADME (L for liberation) or ADMET (or ADME-tox) (for toxic reactions) have been applied as well. The ADME genes form the largest and best known group of pharmacogenetic factors currently known. Their principal function is to protect us against harmful foreign compounds, which we ingest or which are medically administered into our bodies. The potential harmful compounds are removed in three reactions modification (phase I), conjugation (phase II) and excretion (phase III).

Absorption determines the drugs' bioavailability and depends on the administration of the drugs. Many factors, such as drug's solubility, gastric emptying time, intestinal transit time, stability in the intestine, and ability to permeate the intestinal wall can have an effect to the extent to which a drug is absorbed after oral administration. Therefore, some drugs need to be administered e.g. *via* blood or inhaled. Distribution of the drug is defined as the transfer of a drug from one body compartment to another (e.g. blood–brain barrier). Distribution of drugs is affected e.g. by differences in blood flow rates in different parts of the body, and molecular size and polarity of the drugs, as well as binding to the proteins in serum. As a drug enters a body, it is metabolized, and new compounds (metabolites) are formed. Depending on the drug, either the parental drug or its metabolite(s) is active. In the final phase, the drug, and its metabolites are excreted from the body, mostly *via* urine, bile and feces or lungs. If this phase is not complete, accumulation of foreign substances can adversely affect normal metabolism. As a number of ADME genes are well known, there is an abundance of target genes that can be studied for medico-legal applications. A list of some of the ADME genes are given in Table 3.

5 Future Directions

While many advances have been made, the field of molecular autopsy can still be considered in its infancy. A real benefit of the use of genetic data in medico-legal autopsies will be realized only when a battery of genes and all their variants can be analyzed cost-effectively. A new era is now on the horizon with the advent of high throughput DNA sequencing technology, i.e. massively parallel sequencing (MPS), also coined as next-generation sequencing. MPS already has shown promise for use in forensics for identification work (Parson *et al.*, 2013; King *et al.*, 2014; Mikkelsen *et al.*, 2014; Seo *et al.*, 2013; Seo *et al.*, 2015; Zeng *et al.*, 2015; Warshauer *et al.*, 2015)

It should be obvious that MPS enables detection of all variants within a gene(s) and thus is less biased than typing only known (or most common) single nucleotide polymorphisms (SNPs) associated with functional allelic variants of a gene(s). Results from recent studies suggest that MPS could be a very informative investigative tool for illuminating the role of pathogenetic variants cases of SCD (Campuzano *et al.*, 2014; Hertz *et al.*, 2015).

Santori *et al.* (2015) investigated the involvement of subtle cardiac conditions, detected only *via* molecular autopsy, in 41 cases of SUDs in infants and young children. The authors used MPS to study 86 sudden cardiac death-related genes and intensive *in silico* analyzes in order to prioritize the putative pathogenic variants and found 63 variants located in cardiomyopathy genes in 35 cases. In a recent

Table 3: Examples of genes, their full names and their basic roles in the ADME–system (absorption, distribution, metabolism or excretion).

Gene	Full gene name	Class
ABCB1	ATP-binding cassette, sub-family B (MDR/TAP), member 1	Transporter
ABCC2	ATP-binding cassette, sub-family C (CFTR/MRP), member 2	Transporter
ABCG2	ATP-binding cassette, sub-family G (WHITE), member 2	Transporter
CYP1A1	Cytochrome P450, family 1, subfamily A, polypeptide 1	Phase I
CYP1A2	Cytochrome P450, family 1, subfamily A, polypeptide 2	Phase I
CYP2A6	Cytochrome P450, family 2, subfamily A, polypeptide 6	Phase I
CYP2B6	Cytochrome P450, family 2, subfamily B, polypeptide 6	Phase I
CYP2C19	Cytochrome P450, family 2, subfamily C, polypeptide 19	Phase I
CYP2C8	Cytochrome P450, family 2, subfamily C, polypeptide 8	Phase I
CYP2C9	Cytochrome P450, family 2, subfamily C, polypeptide 9	Phase I
CYP2D6	Cytochrome P450, family 2, subfamily D, polypeptide 6	Phase I
CYP2E1	Cytochrome P450, family 2, subfamily E, polypeptide 1	Phase I
CYP3A4	Cytochrome P450, family 3, subfamily A, polypeptide 4	Phase I
CYP3A5	Cytochrome P450, family 3, subfamily A, polypeptide 5	Phase I
DPYD	Dihydropyrimidine dehydrogenase	Phase I
GSTM1	Glutathione S-transferase M1	Phase II
GSTP1	Glutathione S-transferase pi	Phase II
GSTT1	Glutathione S-transferase theta 1	Phase II
NAT1	N-acetyltransferase 1 (arylamine N-acetyltransferase)	Phase II
NAT2	N-acetyltransferase 2 (arylamine N-acetyltransferase)	Phase II
SLC15A2	Solute carrier family 15 (H+/peptide transporter), member 2	Transporter
SLC22A1	Solute carrier family 22 (organic cation transporter), member 1	Transporter
SLC22A2	Solute carrier family 22 (organic cation transporter), member 2	Transporter
SLC22A6	Solute carrier family 22 (organic anion transporter), member 6	Transporter
SLCO1B1	Solute carrier organic anion transporter family, member 1B1	Transporter
SLCO1B3	Solute carrier organic anion transporter family, member 1B3	Transporter
SULT1A1	Sulfotransferase family, cytosolic, 1A, phenol-preferring, member 1	Phase II
TPMT	Thiopurine S-methyltransferase,	Phase II
UGT1A1	UDP glucuronosyltransferase 1 family, polypeptide A1	Phase II
UGT2B15	UDP glucuronosyltransferase 2 family, polypeptide B15	Phase II
UGT2B17	UDP glucuronosyltransferase 2 family, polypeptide B17	Phase II
UGT2B7	UDP glucuronosyltransferase 2 family, polypeptide B7	Phase II

study, Hertz *et al.* (2015) evaluated the use of MPS in molecular autopsies performed in association of SUD/SCD cases. They estimated the frequency of pathogenic variants by analyzing 34 genes known to be involved in SUDs and found a likely pathogenic mutation in three out of 15 (20%) of their cases. Also Brion *et al.* (2014) validated MPS for identifying inherited arrhythmogenias for medico-legal CoD investigations by studying 28 genes known to be associated with those disorders in 53 SCDs. In the analysis, 46 possible variants in 31 cases were found. Using bioinformatic tools, they found 13 variants in 11 cases likely to be pathogenic. By combining bioinformatic methods for pathogenicity inference, pathogenic variants are indeed found, at least for some otherwise unexplained SUDs/SCDs. These studies support that MPS allows much better detection and more accurate diagnosis.

6 Conclusion

Molecular autopsy is not yet a routine part of the medico-legal CoD investigation, but it is expected to become an integrated component in the near future for cases of SUD. Indeed, it should be considered an integral part of a PM investigation, especially in SUDs and SCDs. An incorporation of this relatively new technology needs a change in the mind-set of the medical examiner and society as a whole, so that a multi-disciplinary approach can be realized. The benefits of molecular autopsies for autopsy negative cases are obvious; genetic analyses will decrease the number of undetermined CoDs and MoDs. But, molecular autopsy also may clear cases where the forensic pathologist cannot discern whether the MoD was suicide or accident, e.g. in intoxication cases (Rockett *et al.*, 2015). More generally, the mechanisms underlying previously unknown deaths can be better understood. The greatest challenge to acceptance and use is translating genetic information, combined with traditional medico-legal data, to predict the phenotype for deducing CoD.

As the PGt/PGx field is rapidly moving forward in the clinical world, the data from clinical PGt/PGx can be expected to translate to the medico-legal CoD investigation. However, studies in the molecular autopsy may in turn support diagnostics in the clinical setting. It is obvious for ethical and conduct reasons that humans are not subjected to testing of illicit drugs. However, since some individuals expose themselves to such drugs, data can be collected during a molecular autopsy. Subsequently, the samples and the data can be utilized for scientific studies that may shed invaluable light on reactions to certain drugs, and that may prove useful in the clinical setting for translating genotype to phenotype predictions.

Apart from technical development and biological (mutational) findings, other important issues need to be addressed before molecular autopsies can fully be utilized in the routine medico-legal autopsies. The same genetic information that can be used to determine CoD may be applied to the evaluation of the risks for SUDs or serious ADRs in other family members. Thus, the medico-legal autopsy needs guidance for reporting the results (Sajantila and Budowle, 2015) and genetic counseling for families, which perhaps may be the best outcome of the molecular autopsy.

References

M. J. Ackerman, B. L. Siu, W. Q. Sturner, D. J. Tester, C. R. Valdivia, J .C. Makielski and J. A. Towbin. Postmortem molecular analysis of SCN5A defects in sudden infant death syndrome. *JAMA*, 286:2264–2269, 2001a.

J. M. Ackerman, D. J. Tester and D. J. Driscoll. Molecular autopsy of sudden unexplained death in the young. *Am J Forensic Med Pathol*, 22:105–111, 2001b.

M. J. Ackerman, D. J. Tester and C. J. Porter. Swimming, a gene-specific arrhythmogenic trigger for inherited long QT syndrome. *Mayo Clin Proc*, 74:1088–1094, 1999a.

M. J. Ackerman, D. J. Tester, C. J. Porter and W. D. Edwards. Molecular diagnosis of the inherited long-QT syndrome in a woman who died after near-drowning. *N Engl J Med*, 341:1121–1125, 1999b.

J. Ahlner, A. L. Zackrisson, B. Lindblom and L. Bertilsson. CYP2D6, serotonin and suicide. *Pharmacogenomics*, 11:903–905, 2010.

A. Andresen, C. Augustin and T. Streichert. Toxicogenetics–cytochrome P450 microarray analysis in forensic cases focusing on morphine/codeine and diazepam. *Int J Legal Med*, 127: 395–404, 2013.

M. Arnestad, L. Crotti, T. O. Rognum, R. Insolia, M. Pedrazzini, C. Ferrandi, A. Vege, D. W. Wang, T. E. Rhodes, A. L. George, Jr. and P. J. Schwartz. Prevalence of long-QT syndrome gene variants in sudden infant death syndrome. *Circulation,* 115:361–367, 2007.

C. N. Bagot and R. Arya. Virchow and his triad: a question of attribution. *Br J Haematol,* 143:180–190, 2008.

C. Baigent, L. Blackwell, J. Emberson, L. E. Holland, C. Reith, N. Bhala, R. Peto, E. H. Barnes, A. Keech, J. Simes and R. Collins. Efficacy and safety of more intensive lowering of LDL cholesterol: a meta-analysis of data from 170,000 participants in 26 randomised trials. *Lancet,* 376:1670–1681, 2010.

J. H. Beer. High necropsy rates: just a ritualistic mantra? *Lancet,* 355, 934, 2000.

P. Beighton. Lethal complications of the Ehlers-Danlos syndrome. *Br Med J,* 3:656–659, 1968.

A. T. Berg, K. Nickels, E. C. Wirrell, A. T. Geerts, P. M. Callenbach, W. F. Arts, C. Rios, P. R. Camfield and C. S. Camfield. Mortality risks in new-onset childhood epilepsy. *Pediatrics,* 132:124–131, 2013.

J. Besseling, B. Sjouke and J. J. Kastelein. Screening and treatment of familial hypercholesterolemia — Lessons from the past and opportunities for the future (based on the Anitschkow Lecture 2014). *Atherosclerosis,* 241:597–606, 2015.

S. A. Bolliger and M. J. Thali. Imaging and virtual autopsy: looking back and forward. *Philos Trans R Soc Lond B Biol Sci,* 370:2015.

S. Bonne, J. Van Hengel and F. Van Roy. Assignment of the plakophilin-2 gene (PKP2) and a plakophilin-2 pseudogene (PKP2P1) to human chromosome bands 12p11 and 12p13, respectively, by *in situ* hybridization. *Cytogenet Cell Genet,* 88:286–287, 2000.

M. Brion, A. Blanco-Verea, B. Sobrino, M. Santori, R. Gil, E. Ramos-Luis, M. Martinez, J. Amigo and A. Carracedo. Next generation sequencing challenges in the analysis of cardiac sudden death due to arrhythmogenic disorders. *Electrophoresis,* 35:3111–3116, 2014.

M. S. Brown and J. L. Goldstein. Familial hypercholesterolemia: A genetic defect in the low-density lipoprotein receptor. *N Engl J Med,* 294:1386–1390, 1976a.

M. S. Brown and J. L. Goldstein. Receptor-mediated control of cholesterol metabolism. *Science,* 191:150–154, 1976b.

A.P. Burke, A. A. Farb, R. Virmani, J. Goodin and J.E. Smialek. Sports-related and non-sports-related sudden cardiac death in young adults, *Am Heart J,* 121:568–575, 1991.

O. Campuzano, C. Allegue, S. Partemi, A. Iglesias, A. Oliva and R. Brugada. Negative autopsy and sudden cardiac death. *Int J Legal Med,* 128:599–606, 2014.

P. E. Carson, C. L. Flanagan, C. E. Ickes and A. S. Alving. Enzymatic deficiency in primaquine-sensitive erythrocytes. *Science,* 124:484–485, 1956.

M. Cerrone and S. G. Priori. Genetics of sudden death: focus on inherited channelopathies. *Eur Heart J,* 32:2109–2118, 2011.

S. S. Chugh, K. L. Kelly and J. L. Titus. Sudden cardiac death with apparently normal heart. *Circulation,* 102:649–654, 2000.

S. S. Chugh, K. Reinier, C. Teodorescu, A. Evanado, E. Kehr, M. Al Samara, R. Mariani, K. Gunson and J. Jui. Epidemiology of sudden cardiac death: clinical and research implications. *Prog Cardiovasc Dis,* 51: 213–228, 2008.

S. D. Cohle and B. A. Sampson. The negative autopsy: sudden cardiac death or other? *Cardiovasc Pathol,* 10:219–222, 2001.

D. Corrado, C. Basso and G. Thiene. Sudden cardiac death in young people with apparently normal heart. *Cardiovasc Res,* 50:399–408, 2001.

M. E. Curran, I. Splawski, K. W. Timothy, G. M. Vincent, E. D. Green and M. T. Keating. A molecular basis for cardiac arrhythmia: HERG mutations cause long QT syndrome. *Cell,* 80:795–803, 1995.

C. S. Davidson. The Autopsy in the Age of Molecular Biology. *JAMA,* 193:813–814, 1965.

M. Di Paolo, D. Luchini, R. Bloise and S. G. Priori. Postmortem molecular analysis in victims of sudden unexplained death. *Am J Forensic Med Pathol,* 25:182–184, 2004.

H. C. Dietz, G. R. Cutting, R. E. Pyeritz, C. L. Maslen, L. Y. Sakai, G. M. Corson, E. G. Puffenberger, A. Hamosh, E. J. Nanthakumar, S. M. Curristin *et al.*, Marfan syndrome caused by a recurrent de novo missense mutation in the fibrillin gene. *Nature,* 352:337–339, 1991.

C. R. di Gioia, C. Autore, D.M. Romeo, C. Ciallella, M. R. Aromatario, A. Lopez, E. Pagannone, C. Giordano, P. Gallo and G. d'Amati. Sudden cardiac death in younger adults: autopsy diagnosis as a tool for preventive medicine, *Hum Pathol,* 37:794–801, 2006.

R. Dirnhofer, C. Jackowski, P. Vock, K. Potter and M. J. Thali. Virtopsy: minimally invasive, imaging-guided virtual autopsy. *Radiographics,* 26:1305–1333, 2006.

A. Doolan, N. Langlois and C. Semsarian. Causes of sudden cardiac death in young Australians. *Med J Aust,* 180:110–112, 2004.

H. Druid and P. Holmgren. A compilation of fatal and control concentrations of drugs in postmortem femoral blood. *J Forensic Sci,* 42:79–87, 1997.

H. Druid, P. Holmgren, B. Carlsson and J. Ahlner. Cytochrome P450 2D6 (CYP2D6) genotyping on postmortem blood as a supplementary tool for interpretation of forensic toxicological results. *Forensic Sci Int*, 99:25–34, 1999.

J. Ebbesen, I. Buajordet, J. Erikssen, O. Brors, T. Hilberg, H. Svaar and L. Sandvik. Drug-related deaths in a department of internal medicine. *Arch Intern Med*, 161:2317–2323, 2001.

R. E. Eckart, S. L. Scoville, C. L. Campbell, E. A. Shry, K. C. Stajduhar, R. N. Potter, L. A. Pearse and R. Virmani. Sudden death in young adults: a 25-year review of autopsies in military recruits. *Ann Intern Med*, 141:829–834, 2004.

I. R. Edwards and J. K. Aronson. Adverse drug reactions: definitions, diagnosis and management. *Lancet*, 356:1255–1259, 2000.

A. Farioli, C. A. Christophi, C. C. Quarta and S. N. Kales. Incidence of sudden cardiac death in a young active population. *J Am Heart Assoc*, 4: e001818, 2015.

A. Fabre and M. N. Sheppard. Sudden adult death syndrome and other non-ischaemic causes of sudden cardiac death. *Heart*, 92:316–320, 2006.

E. J. Favaloro and G. Lippi. Coagulation update: what's new in hemostasis testing? *Thromb Res*, 127 Suppl 2, S13–S16, 2011.

Y. Gasche, Y. Daali, M. Fathi, A. Chiappe, S. Cottini, P. Dayer and J. Desmeules.Codeine intoxication associated with ultrarapid CYP2D6 metabolism. *N Engl J Med*, 351:2827–2831, 2004.

A. A. Geisterfer-Lowrance, S. Kass, G. Tanigawa, H. P. Vosberg, W. Mckenna, C. E. Seidman and J. G. Seidman. A molecular basis for familial hypertrophic cardiomyopathy: A beta cardiac myosin heavy chain gene missense mutation. *Cell*, 62:999–1006, 1990.

J. L. Goldstein and M. S. Brown. Familial hypercholesterolemia: identification of a defect in the regulation of 3-hydroxy-3-methylglutaryl coenzyme A reductase activity associated with overproduction of cholesterol. *Proc Natl Acad Sci U S A*, 70:2804–2808, 1973.

J. L. Goldstein and M. S. Brown. Molecular medicine. The cholesterol quartet. *Science*, 292:1310–1312, 2001.

J. L. Goldstein, T. Kita and M. S. Brown. Defective lipoprotein receptors and atherosclerosis. Lessons from an animal counterpart of familial hypercholesterolemia. *N Engl J Med*, 309:288–296, 1983.

E. K. Grant and M. J. Evans. Cardiac findings in fetal and pediatric autopsies: a five-year retrospective review. *Pediatr Dev Pathol*, 12:103–110, 2009.

V. Haufroid and P. Hantson. CYP2D6 genetic polymorphisms and their relevance for poisoning due to amfetamines, opioid analgesics and antidepressants. *Clin Toxicol (Phila)*, 53:501–510, 2015.

C. Haw and K. Hawton. Suicide and Self-Harm by Drowning: A Review of the Literature. *Arch Suicide Res*, 11:1–18, 2015.

J. A. Heit, M. D. Silverstein, D. N. Mohr, T. M. Petterson, W. M. O'Fallon and L. J. Melton. Predictors of survival after deep vein thrombosis and pulmonary embolism: a population-based, cohort study. *Arch Intern Med*, 159:445–453, 1999.

C. L. Hertz, S. L. Christiansen, L. Ferrero-Miliani, S. L. Fordyce, M. Dahl, A. G. Holst, G. L. Ottesen, R. Frank-Hansen, H. Bundgaard and N. Morling. Next-generation sequencing of 34 genes in sudden unexplained death victims in forensics and in patients with channelopathic cardiac diseases. *Int J Legal Med*, 129:793–800, 2015.

R. S. Hockwald, J. Arnold, C. B. Clayman and A. S. Alving. Toxicity of primaquine in Negroes. *J Am Med Assoc*, 149:1568–1570, 1952.

G. K. Hovingh, M. H. Davidson, J. J. Kastelein and A. M. O'Connor. Diagnosis and treatment of familial hypercholesterolaemia. *Eur Heart J*, 34:962–971, 2013.

M. V. Ilina, C. A. Kepron, G. P. Taylor, D. G. Perrin, P. F. Kantor and G. R. Somers. Undiagnosed heart disease leading to sudden unexpected death in childhood: a retrospective study. *Pediatrics*, 128: e513–e520, 2011.

P. J. Jannetto, S. H. Wong, S. B. Gock, E. Laleli-Sahin, B. C. Schur and J. M. Jentzen. Pharmacogenomics as molecular autopsy for postmortem forensic toxicology: genotyping cytochrome P450 2D6 for oxycodone cases. *J Anal Toxicol*, 26:438–447, 2002.

J. L. Jefferies and J. A. Towbin. Dilated cardiomyopathy. *Lancet*, 375:752–762, 2010.

M. Jin, S. B. Gock, P. J. Jannetto, J. M. Jentzen and S. H. Wong. Pharmacogenomics as molecular autopsy for forensic toxicology: genotyping cytochrome P450 3A4*1B and 3A5*3 for 25 fentanyl cases. *J Anal Toxicol*, 29:590–598, 2005.

A. W. Jones, F. C. Kugelberg, A. Holmgren and J. Ahlner. Drug poisoning deaths in Sweden show a predominance of ethanol in mono-intoxications, adverse drug-alcohol interactions and poly-drug use. *Forensic Sci Int*, 206:43–51, 2011.

M. T. Keating. Molecular genetics of long QT syndrome. *Soc Gen Physiol Ser*, 50:53–60, 1995.

J. L. King, B. L. Larue, N. M. Novroski, M. Stoljarova, S. B. Seo, X. Zeng, D. H. Warshauer, C. P. Davis, W. Parson, A. Sajantila and B. Budowle. High-quality and high-throughput massively parallel sequencing of the human mitochondrial genome using the Illumina MiSeq. *Forensic Sci Int Genet,* 12:128–135, 2014.

J. Kirchheiner. CYP2D6 phenotype prediction from genotype: which system is the best? *Clin Pharmacol Ther,* 83:225–227, 2008.

S. Klaassen, S. Probst, E. Oechslin, B. Gerull, G. Krings, P. Schuler, M. Greutmann, D. Hurlimann, M. Yegitbasi, L. Pons, M. Gramlich, J. D. Drenckhahn, A. Heuser, F. Berger, R. Jenni and L. Thierfelder. Mutations in sarcomere protein genes in left ventricular noncompaction. *Circulation,* 117:2893–2901, 2008.

G. Koren, J. Cairns, D. Chitayat, A. Gaedigk and S. J. Leeder. Pharmacogenetics of morphine poisoning in a breastfed neonate of a codeine-prescribed mother. *Lancet,* 368:704, 2006.

A. Koski, I. Ojanpera and E. Vuori. Interaction of alcohol and drugs in fatal poisonings. *Hum Exp Toxicol,* 22:281–287, 2003.

A. Koski, E. Vuori and I. Ojanpera. Relation of postmortem blood alcohol and drug concentrations in fatal poisonings involving amitriptyline, propoxyphene and promazine. *Hum Exp Toxicol,* 24:389–396, 2005.

A. Koski, J. Sistonen, I. Ojanperä, M. Gergov, E. Vuori and A. Sajantila. CYP2D6 and CYP2C19 genotypes and amitriptyline metabolite ratios in a series of medicolegal autopsies. *Forensic Sci Int,* 158:177–183, 2006.

A. Koski, I. Ojanpera, J. Sistonen, E. Vuori and A. Sajantila. A fatal doxepin poisoning associated with a defective CYP2D6 genotype. *Am J Forensic Med Pathol,* 28(3):259–61, 2007.

D. R. Kumar, E. Hanlin, I. Glurich, J. J. Mazza and S. H. Yale. Virchow's contribution to the understanding of thrombosis and cellular biology. *Clin Med Res,* 8:168–172, 2010.

J. Lam, K. L. Woodall, P. Solbeck, C. J. Ross, B. C. Carleton, M. R. Hayden, G. Koren and P. Madadi. Codeine-related deaths: The role of pharmacogenetics and drug interactions. *Forensic Sci Int,* 239:50–56, 2014.

M. K. Larsen, P. H. Nissen, K. E. Berge, T. P. Leren, I. B. Kristensen, H. K. Jensen and J. Banner. Molecular autopsy in young sudden cardiac death victims with suspected cardiomyopathy. *Forensic Sci Int,* 219: 33–38, 2012.

T. Laukkala, T. Partonen, M. Marttunen and M. Henriksson. Suicides among military conscripts between 1991–2007 in Finland–a descriptive replication study. *Nord J Psychiatry,* 68:270–274, 2014.

T. Launiainen and I. Ojanpera. Drug concentrations in post-mortem femoral blood compared with therapeutic concentrations in plasma. *Drug Test Anal,* 6:308–316, 2014.

T. Launiainen, I. Rasanen, E. Vuori and I. Ojanpera. Fatal venlafaxine poisonings are associated with a high prevalence of drug interactions. *Int J Legal Med,* 125:349–358, 2011.

T. Launiainen, A. Sajantila, I. Rasanen, E. Vuori and I. Ojanpera. Adverse interaction of warfarin and paracetamol: evidence from a post-mortem study. *Eur J Clin Pharmacol,* 66:97–103, 2010.

W. Lawler. The negative coroner's necropsy: a personal approach and consideration of difficulties. *J Clin Pathol,* 43:977–980, 1990.

J. Lazarou, B. H. Pomeranz and P. N. Corey. Incidence of adverse drug reactions in hospitalized patients: a meta-analysis of prospective studies. *JAMA,* 279:1200–1205, 1998.

S. Leadbeatter and D. Stansbie. Postmortem diagnosis of familial hypercholesterolaemia. *Br Med J (Clin Res Ed),* 289:1656, 1984.

S. E. Leigh, A. H. Foster, R. A. Whittall, C. S. Hubbart and S. E. Humphries. Update and analysis of the University College London low density lipoprotein receptor familial hypercholesterolemia database. *Ann Hum Genet,* 72:485–498, 2008.

A. Levo, A. Koski, I. Ojanpera, E. Vuori and A. Sajantila. Post-mortem SNP analysis of CYP2D6 gene reveals correlation between genotype and opioid drug (tramadol) metabolite ratios in blood. *Forensic Sci Int,* 135:9–15, 2003.

R. Lombardi and A. J. Marian. Molecular genetics and pathogenesis of arrhythmogenic right ventricular cardiomyopathy: a disease of cardiac stem cells. *Pediatr Cardiol,* 32:360–365, 2011.

R. Lozano, M. Naghavi, K. Foreman, S. Lim, K. Shibuya, V. Aboyans, J. Abraham, T. Adair, R. Aggarwal, S. Y. Ahn, M. Alvarado, H. R. Anderson, L. M. Anderson, K. G. Andrews, C. Atkinson, L. M. Baddour, S. Barker-Collo, D. H. Bartels, M. L. Bell, E. J. Benjamin, D. Bennett, K. Bhalla, B. Bikbov, A. Bin Abdulhak, G. Birbeck, F. Blyth, I. Bolliger, S. Boufous, C. Bucello, M. Burch, P. Burney, J. Carapetis, H. Chen, D. Chou, S. S. Chugh, L. E. Coffeng, S. D. Colan, S. Colquhoun, K. E. Colson, J. Condon, M. D. L. Connor, T. Cooper, M. Corriere, M. Cortinovis, K. C. De Vaccaro, W. Couser, B. C. Cowie, M. H. Criqui, M. Cross, K. C. Dabhadkar, N. Dahodwala, D. De Leo, L. Degenhardt, A. Delossantos, J. Denenberg, D. C. Des Jarlais, S. D. Dharmaratne, E. R. Dorsey, T. Driscoll, H. Duber, B. Ebel, P. J. Erwin, P. Espindola,

M. Ezzati, V. Feigin, A. D. Flaxman, M. H. Forouzanfar, F. G. Fowkes, R. Franklin, M. Fransen, M. K. Freeman, S. E. Gabriel, E. Gakidou, F. Gaspari, R. F. Gillum, D. Gonzalez-Medina, Y. A. Halasa, D. Haring, J. E. Harrison, R. Havmoeller, R. J. Hay, B. Hoen, P. J. Hotez, D. Hoy, K. H. Jacobsen, S. L. James, R. Jasrasaria, S. Jayaraman, N. Johns, G. Karthikeyan, N. Kassebaum, A. Keren, J. P. Khoo, L. M. Knowlton, O. Kobusingye, A. Koranteng, R. Krishnamurthi, M. Lipnick, S. E. Lipshultz, S. L. Ohno, *et al.* Global and regional mortality from 235 causes of death for 20 age groups in 1990 and 2010: a systematic analysis for the Global Burden of Disease Study 2010. *Lancet,* 380:2095–2128, 2012.

A. Lugli, M. Anabitarte and J. H. Beer. Effect of simple interventions on necropsy rate when active informed consent is required. *Lancet,* 354:1391, 1999.

P. Lunetta, A. Levo, P. J. Laitinen, H. Fodstad, K. Kontula and A. Sajantila. Molecular screening of selected long QT syndrome (LQTS) mutations in 165 consecutive bodies found in water. *Int J Legal Med,* 117:115–117, 2003.

P. Lunetta, A. Levo, A. Mannikko, A. Penttila and A. Sajantila. Death in bathtub revisited with molecular genetics: a victim with suicidal traits and a LQTS gene mutation. *Forensic Sci Int,* 130:122–124, 2002.

P. Madadi, D. Hildebrandt, I. Y. Gong, U. I. Schwarz, C. Ciszkowski, C. J. Ross, J. Sistonen, B. C. Carleton, M. R. Hayden, A. E. Lauwers and G. Koren. Fatal hydrocodone overdose in a child: pharmacogenetics and drug interactions. *Pediatrics,* 126:e986–e989, 2010.

B. Madea, F. Musshoff and J. Preuss. Medical negligence in drug associated deaths. *Forensic Sci Int,* 190:67–73, 2009.

B. Madea and J. Preuss. Medical malpractice as reflected by the forensic evaluation of 4450 autopsies. *Forensic Sci Int,* 190:5866, 2009.

V. A. Mckusick. The defect in Marfan syndrome. *Nature,* 352:279–281, 1991.

M. Mikkelsen, R. Frank-Hansen, A. J. Hansen and N. Morling. Massively parallel pyrosequencing of the mitochondrial genome with the 454 methodology in forensic genetics. *Forensic Sci Int Genet,* 12:30–37, 2014.

G. Millat, B. Kugener, P. Chevalier, M. Chahine, H. Huang, D. Malicier, C. Rodriguez-Lafrasse and R. Rousson. Contribution of long-QT syndrome genetic variants in sudden infant death syndrome. *Pediatr Cardiol,* 30:502–509, 2009.

B. Morentin, M.P. Suárez-Mier and B. Aguilera. Sudden unexplained death among persons 1–35 years old. *Forensic Sci Int,* 135:213-217, 2003.

N. Moore, D. Lecointre, C. Noblet and M. Mabille. Frequency and cost of serious adverse drug reactions in a department of general medicine. *Br J Clin Pharmacol,* 45:301–8, 1998.

C. Muller. Xanthoma, hypercholesterolemia, angina pectoris. *Acta Med Scandinav.* 95:75, 1938.

C. J. Murray and A. D. Lopez. Evidence-based health policy–lessons from the Global Burden of Disease Study. *Science,* 274:740–743, 1996.

F. Musshoff, U. M. Stamer and B. Madea. Pharmacogenetics and forensic toxicology. *Forensic Sci Int,* 203:53–62, 2010.

A. M. Neuvonen, J. U. Palo and A. Sajantila. Post-mortem ABCB1 genotyping reveals an elevated toxicity for female digoxin users. *Int J Legal Med,* 125: 265–269, 2011.

I. Nordrum, T. J. Eide and L. Jorgensen. Medicolegal autopsies of violent deaths in northern Norway 1972–1992. *Forensic Sci Int,* 92:39–48, 1998.

I. Ojanpera, M. Kolmonen and A. Pelander. Current use of high-resolution mass spectrometry in drug screening relevant to clinical and forensic toxicology and doping control. *Anal Bioanal Chem,* 403:1203–1220, 2012.

W. Parson, C. Strobl, G. Huber, B. Zimmermann, S. M. Gomes, L. Souto, L. Fendt, R. Delport, R. Langit, S. Wootton, R. Lagace and J. Irwin. Evaluation of next generation mtGenome sequencing using the Ion Torrent Personal Genome Machine (PGM). *Forensic Sci Int Genet,* 7:543–549, 2013.

E. E. Petersen, S. A. Rasmussen, K. L. Daniel, M. M. Yazdy and M. A. Honein. Prescription medication borrowing and sharing among women of reproductive age. *J Womens Health (Larchmt),* 17:1073–1080, 2008.

M. Pirmohamed, A. M. Breckenridge, N. R. Kitteringham and B. K. Park. Adverse drug reactions. *BMJ,* 316:1295–1298, 1998.

M. Pirmohamed, S. James, S. Meakin, C. Green, A. K. Scott, T. J. Walley, K. Farrar, B. K. Park and A. M. Breckenridge. Adverse drug reactions as cause of admission to hospital: prospective analysis of 18 820 patients. *BMJ,* 329:15–19, 2004.

D. J. Pounder and G. R. Jones. Post-mortem drug redistribution–a toxicological nightmare. *Forensic Sci Int,* 45:253–263, 1990, 2003.

R. Puranik, C. K. Chow, J. A. Duflou, M. J. Kilborn and M. A. McGuire. Sudden death in the young. *Heart Rhythm,* 2:1277–1282, 2005.

D. J. Rader, J. Cohen and H. H. Hobbs. Monogenic hypercholesterolemia: new insights in pathogenesis and treatment. *J Clin Invest,* 111:1795–1803.

J. Rajs and S. W. Jakobsson. Cause of death in persons aged between 15 and 50 years in the community of Stockholm. A forensic-pathologic and statistical study. *Forensic Sci Int,* 29:21326, 1985.

I. R. Rockett, G. R. Hobbs, D. Wu, H. Jia, K. B. Nolte, G. S. Smith, S. L. Putnam and E. D. Caine. Variable Classification of Drug-Intoxication suicides across US States: A partial artifact of forensics? *PLoS One,* 10: e0135296, 2015.

I. Roots, T. Gerloff, C. Meisel, J. Kirchheiner, M. Goldammer, R. Kaiser, G. Laschinski, J. Brockmoller, I. Cascorbi, U. Kleeberg and A. G. Hildebrandt. Pharmacogenetics-based new therapeutic concepts. *Drug Metab Rev,* 36:617–638, 2004.

L. T. Ruzicka and A. D. Lopez. The use of cause-of-death statistics for health situation assessment: national and international experiences. *World Health Stat Q,* 43:249–258, 1990.

A. Sajantila, J. U. Palo, I. Ojanpera, C. Davis and B. Budowle. Pharmacogenetics in medico-legal context. *Forensic Sci Int,* 203:44–52, 2010.

A. Sajantila and B. Budowle. Postmortem medicolegal genetic diagnostics also require reporting guidance. *Eur J Hum Genet,* 24:329–330, 2016.

F. R. Sallee, C. L. Devane and R. E. Ferrell. Fluoxetine-related death in a child with cytochrome P-450 2D6 genetic deficiency. *J Child Adolesc Psychopharmacol,* 10:27–34, 2000.

M. Santori, A. Blanco-Verea, R. Gil, J. Cortis, K. Becker, P. M. Schneider, A. Carracedo and M. Brion. Broad-based molecular autopsy: a potential tool to investigate the involvement of subtle cardiac conditions in sudden unexpected death in infancy and early childhood. *Arch Dis Child,* 100:952–956, 2015.

P. Saukko. Medicolegal investigative system and sudden death in Scandinavia. *Nihon Hoigaku Zasshi,* 49:458–465, 1995.

E. Scalais, J. Bottu, R. J. Wanders, S. Ferdinandusse, H. R. Waterham and L. De Meirleir. Familial very long chain acyl-CoA dehydrogenase deficiency as a cause of neonatal sudden infant death: improved survival by prompt diagnosis. *Am J Med Genet A,* 167A:211–214, 2015.

A. Schmeling, G. Geserick and I. Wirth. [Medico-legal autopsies in Berlin from 1999 to 2003]. *Arch Kriminol,* 224:158–167, 2009.

U. Schwarze, J. A. Goldstein and P. H. Byers. Splicing defects in the COL3A1 gene: marked preference for 5′ (donor) spice-site mutations in patients with exon-skipping mutations and Ehlers-Danlos syndrome type IV. *Am J Hum Genet,* 61:1276–1286, 1997.

S. Sen-Chowdhry, P. Syrris, D. Ward, A. Asimaki, E. Sevdalis and W. J. Mckenna. Clinical and genetic characterization of families with arrhythmogenic right ventricular dysplasia/cardiomyopathy provides novel insights into patterns of disease expression. *Circulation,* 115: 1710–1720, 2007.

S. B. Seo, J. L. King, D. H. Warshauer, C. P. Davis, J. Ge and B. Budowle. Single nucleotide polymorphism typing with massively parallel sequencing for human identification. *Int J Legal Med*, 127:1079–1086, 2013.

S. B. Seo, X. Zeng, J. L. King, B. L. Larue, M. Assidi, M. H. Al-Qahtani, A. Sajantila and B. Budowle. Underlying Data for Sequencing the Mitochondrial Genome with the Massively Parallel Sequencing Platform Ion Torrent PGM. *BMC Genomics*, 16 Suppl 1:S4, 2015.

R. D. Start, T. A. Mcculloch, E. W. Benbow, I. Lauder and J. C. Underwood. Clinical necropsy rates during the 1980s: the continued decline. *J Pathol*, 171:63–66, 1993.

S. Stehle, J. Kirchheiner, A. Lazar and U. Fuhr. Pharmacogenetics of oral anticoagulants: a basis for dose individualization. *Clin Pharmacokinet*, 47:565–594, 2008.

Y. Tang, B. Sampson, S. Pack, K. Shah, S. Yon Um, D. Wang, T. Wang and M. Prinz. Ethnic differences in out-of-hospital fatal pulmonary embolism. *Circulation*, 123:2219–2225, 2011.

M. R. Taylor, E. Carniel and L. Mestroni. Cardiomyopathy, familial dilated. *Orphanet J Rare Dis*, 1:27, 2006.

D. J. Tester and M. J. Ackerman. Sudden infant death syndrome: how significant are the cardiac channelopathies? *Cardiovasc Res*, 67:388–396, 2005.

D. J. Tester and M. J. Ackerman. Cardiomyopathic and channelopathic causes of sudden unexplained death in infants and children. *Annu Rev Med*, 60:69–84, 2009.

D. J. Tester, L. J. Kopplin, W. Creighton, A. P. Burke and M. J. Ackerman. Pathogenesis of unexplained drowning: new insights from a molecular autopsy. *Mayo Clin Proc*, 80:596–600, 2005.

G. Thiene, A. Nava, D. Corrado, L. Rossi and N. Pennelli. Right ventricular cardiomyopathy and sudden death in young people. *N Engl J Med*, 318:129–133, 1988.

L. Thierfelder, H. Watkins, C. Macrae, R. Lamas, W. Mckenna, H. P. Vosberg, J. G. Seidman and C. E. Seidman. Alpha-tropomyosin and cardiac troponin T mutations cause familial hypertrophic cardiomyopathy: A disease of the sarcomere. *Cell*, 77:701–712, 1994.

H. M. Tiesman, S. A. Hendricks, J. L. Bell and H. A. Amandus. Eleven years of occupational mortality in law enforcement: The census of fatal occupational injuries, 1992-2002. *Am J Ind Med*, 53:940–949, 2010.

A. Turnbull, M. Osborn and N. Nicholas. Hospital autopsy: Endangered or extinct? *J Clin Pathol*, 68:601–604, 2015.

T. Wangmo, G. Ruiz, J. Sinclair, P. Mangin and B. S. Elger. The investigation of deaths in custody: A qualitative analysis of problems and prospects. *J Forensic Leg Med*, 25:30–37, 2014.

D. H. Warshauer, J. D. Churchill, N. Novroski, J. L. King and B. Budowle. Novel Y-chromosome Short Tandem Repeat Variants Detected Through the Use of Massively Parallel Sequencing. *Genomics Proteomics Bioinformatics*, 13:250–257, 2015.

H. Watkins, H. Ashrafian and C. Redwood. Inherited cardiomyopathies. *N Engl J Med*, 364:1643–1656, 2011.

B. G. Winkel, A. G. Holst, J. Theilade, I. B. Kristensen, J. L. Thomsen, G. L. Ottesen, H. Bundgaard, J. H. Svendsen, S. Haunsø and J. Tfelt-Hansen. Nationwide study of sudden cardiac death in persons aged 1–35 years. *Eur Heart J*, 32:983–990, 2011.

A. Wisten, H. Forsberg, P. Krantz and T. Messner. Sudden cardiac death in 15–35-year olds in Sweden during 1992–1999, *J Intern Med*, 252:529–536, 2002.

S. H. Wong, M. A. Wagner, J. M. Jentzen, C. Schur, J. Bjerke, S. B. Gock and C. C. Chang. Pharmacogenomics as an aspect of molecular autopsy for forensic pathology/toxicology: does genotyping CYP 2D6 serve as an adjunct for certifying methadone toxicity? *J Forensic Sci*, 48:1406–1415, 2003.

E. Vuori, J. A. Henry, I. Ojanpera, R. Nieminen, T. Savolainen, P. Wahlsten and M. Jantti. Death following ingestion of MDMA (ecstasy) and moclobemide. *Addiction*, 98:365–368, 2003.

A. Vuorio, T. Laukkala, P. Navathe, B. Budowle, A. Eyre and A. Sajantila. Aircraft-Assisted Pilot Suicides: Lessons to be Learned. *Aviat Space Environ Med*, 85:841–846, 2014.

A. F. Vuorio, K. Kontula, H. Turtola and A. Sajantila. Post mortem molecularly defined familial hypercholesterolemia and sudden cardiac death of young men. *Forensic Sci Int*, 106:87–92, 1999.

S. Ylijoki-Sorensen, J. L. Boldsen, L. W. Boel, H. Boggild, K. Lalu and A. Sajantila. Autopsy rate in suicide is low among elderly in Denmark compared with Finland. *Forensic Sci Int*, 244:158–165, 2014a.

S. Ylijoki-Sorensen, A. Sajantila, K. Lalu, H. Boggild, J. L. Boldsen and L. W. Boel. Coding ill-defined and unknown cause of death is 13 times more frequent in Denmark than in Finland. *Forensic Sci Int*, 244:289–294, 2014b.

X. Zeng, J. L. King, M. Stoljarova, D. H. Warshauer, B. L. Larue, A. Sajantila, J. Patel, D. R. Storts and B. Budowle. High sensitivity multiplex short tandem repeat loci analyses with massively parallel sequencing. *Forensic Sci Int Genet,* 16:38–47, 2015.

K. Zhu, H. Feng, Y. Xu, Z. Mao, W. Zhang, J. Chen, L. Ma, M. Chen, Q. Shi and S. Zhang. An analysis of 60 years of autopsy data from Zhejiang university in Hangzhou, China. *PLoS One,* 9:e112500, 2014.

CHAPTER 17

Predicting Human Appearance from DNA for Forensic Investigations

Susan Walsh* and Manfred Kayser†

*Department of Biology, Indiana University–Purdue University Indianapolis (IUPUI), Indianapolis, IN, USA
†*Department of Genetic Identification, Erasmus MC University Medical Center Rotterdam, Rotterdam, The Netherlands*

1 Forensic Motivations for DNA Prediction of Human Appearance Traits

When the word DNA is mentioned in relation to forensics, the general understanding of its use is immediately associated with a 'match' in a criminal DNA database, or a match with the profile of a suspect, to any human material found at a crime scene. However, left with reality, many cases are not so cut and dry resulting in no match in a criminal DNA database, or with any of the case suspect(s) not included in the database. Forensic DNA profiling, which typically analyses sets of highly variable short tandem repeat (STR) polymorphisms, works completely comparatively i.e. matching (or not) the DNA profile obtained from crime scene material with that of a person whose DNA profile is already known to the investigating authorities. Consequently, the current forensic use of DNA does not allow identification of individuals who are completely unknown to the investigators. DNA in all its glory, over the last 30 years since its original conception by Sir Alec Jeffreys in the early 1980's, was thought to be useless for identifying the source of the evidence without such a match i.e. for sample providers whose DNA profile is not already known to the authorities.

More recently, familial searching *via* DNA profiles has started to be used, depending on a country's legal framework, to help identify an unknown individual using his/her close family relatives whose DNA profile already is known to the investigators. This approach involves searching through a criminal DNA database, or databases established as part of DNA mass screenings, for partial matches of the DNA profile obtained from the crime scene material. Depending on the degree of profile similarities, this approach may indicate family relatives of the unknown sample donor, providing leads in the investigation to eventually trace the donor of the sample and, subsequently identify the individual by complete profile matching. However, familial search using autosomal DNA profiles with the currently applied number of STRs only works for close family members such as siblings or parents, but not for any more distant relatives. The reason for this is that the DNA profiles become more and more different as the opportunity for recombination events increases with the number of meiosis having occurred between the related individuals within a family. Ultimately, if close family members of the unknown sample donor are not in the forensic DNA database or are unknown with their DNA profile otherwise, a familial search using DNA is non-informative.

In such cases, where DNA profiling has been deemed non-informative because the DNA profiles of the sample donor or his/her close relatives are unknown to the authorities, another potential investigative lead could be an eyewitness report. Descriptions of externally visible appearance traits of the putative sample donor seen by a witness at, or near, the crime scene, at the known or expected time the crime occurred, could at least provide some clues as to what the individual who likely left the sample may look like, and potentially lead to identification. In such cases, phantom images based on the eye witness report are prepared by forensic artists, and shared with the public to hope that the resemblance with the true person will provide reported hints on their identification, which ultimately will be followed-up by DNA profiling. However, human eyewitnesses are not always available and if so their testimonies are not always reliable because of personal biases and/or environmental conditions impacting detailed observations and/or memory issues etc.

Hence, a blending of these two approaches, DNA with its objective nature, and physical appearance description with its value to provide investigative leads, is the niche of forensic DNA phenotyping (FDP). FDP is the production of a 'biological witness' from crime scene DNA (alternatively other biomarkers extractable from human forensic stains). FDP thus provides the most statistically probable physical appearance description of the crime scene sample donor from evidence DNA, based on genetic information that directly or indirectly determines human appearance. Twin studies have confirmed the notion that appearance traits have a strong heritability. From the very fact that monozygotic twins, who share almost 100% of the DNA sequence, resemble each other in their appearance traits to a very large degree (especially at younger ages when environmental effects that can cause appearance differentiation have not yet accumulated), it can be concluded that appearance must be coded in our DNA to a large extent. Thus, in principle, DNA is the most reliable 'witness' tool for physical appearance, if only the appropriate DNA markers, i.e. those that directly or indirectly determine our appearance, are identified and made available for FDP purposes.

Until the day individual-specific facial appearance can be predicted accurately and reliably from crime scene stains (which is not expected in the near future, see below), FDP will not replace STR profiling; it will simply serve as an additional tool in the investigative process in an effort to narrow down the very large list of potential suspects in cases without any known suspect. The physical characterization can work alone or in concert with many other (non-DNA) tools used in the run of an investigation to locate potential suspects and deliver them for STR profile matching for potential individual identification. For the time being, the role of FDP is in guiding investigators in suspect-less cases towards a particular subset of individuals who match the appearance trait information predicted from the evidence DNA. The then identified potential suspect(s) will eventually be assessed *via* conventional STR profiling for crime scene sample DNA matching and final individual identification, or in case of no DNA match being observed for exclusion. Likewise, FDP can serve as an exclusionary tool in a large group of suspects that require STR profiling, i.e. it can be performed to assess what physical appearance traits the crime scene sample donor does *not* fit, i.e. a black haired, brown eyed prediction from the crime scene DNA is highly unlikely to be the source from a blond-haired, blue-eyed potential suspect. In the current days of pressure on investigators to save time and money, this can be a useful addition to support police work. FDP can particularly provide potential leads to cold cases that have been waiting decades, or may never be considered for the STR profile match in the, by than enlarged database, or with a newly traced suspect in the re-investigated case. Moreover, FDP can provide leads in missing person identification, including disaster victim identification cases, particularly those cases where DNA profile matches with *antemortem* reference samples, or informative partial matches with putative relatives are not available, and where body parts available for DNA analysis do not display appearance information such as bones or teeth.

One argument usually drawn against FDP is the possibility of faking appearance traits. Obviously, appearance can be artificially altered as hair can be dyed, colored contacts can be used, wrinkles can be treated with botox, and an entire face can be altered *via* plastic surgery. However, it is generally known for more than 100 years that wearing gloves avoids leaving physical fingerprints. And still, individual identification *via* physical fingerprints remains a successful approach because so many perpetrators do not wear gloves. Clearly, changing appearance traits involves a good deal of more planning and organization than simply wearing gloves. Hence, we cannot see that faked appearance will become a practical hurdle for FDP in many cases.

It is important to differentiate the overall notion of appearance DNA prediction i.e. FDP in its strict sense, from DNA inference of bio-geographic ancestry sometimes lumped into FDP. Although both techniques are invaluable in DNA investigative intelligence work to find unknown donors, that may eventually lead to individual identification from a sample through STR profile matching, the DNA inference of bio-geographic ancestry does not always portray the visual physical appearance of an individual e.g. due to genetic admixture. Therefore, appearance should not be simply inferred from a DNA ancestry result, and inferring bio-geographic ancestry from results of DNA-based appearance testing strongly depends on the geographic distribution of the appearance trait involved. Instead, ancestry-informative DNA markers, which can be involved in geographically restricted appearance traits, but do not have to be, shall be used for bio-geographic ancestry DNA testing. Likewise, DNA markers directly or indirectly involved in appearance determination, which can serve as an ancestry marker in case the appearance trait is of restricted geographic distribution, shall be used for appearance DNA testing. Hence, both applications typically involve different DNA marker sets that have to be identified *via* dedicated research.

In terms of laboratory analyses, appearance-predictive DNA testing, quite like bio-geographic ancestry DNA testing, will be performed post-STR profiling, i.e. in cases where no STR match is obtained. While STR profiling generates the necessary information required to search a criminal DNA database, it also relays information regarding the DNA quantity of the sample, (in case no DNA-based quantification analysis is done) whether it is single source or a mixture (an accurate phenotyping result typically cannot be obtained from DNA mixtures of different individuals), and if it is of good quality or possibly degraded. Having this information prior to running the DNA phenotyping assays ensures the result will be optimal for phenotyping analyses in the prediction models, and will produce the most reliable physical appearance prediction result.

In the following, we will concentrate on FDP in its strict sense i.e. appearance prediction from DNA for forensic purposes. For ancestry inference from DNA for forensic purposes, we refer the reader to a separate chapter.

2 Current Standing of Forensic DNA Phenotyping

The discipline of FDP is a young one and has only recently, over the last five years, gained momentum as a tool in forensic casework, depending on a country's legal framework. Although some appearance genes (mostly for pigmentation traits) were known before, this hot topic for forensic geneticists was mostly made feasible after genome-wide genotyping technologies and statistical data analysis methodologies for mapping genes of common traits, initially applied to common diseases, started to be used successfully for normal (i.e. not disease related) appearance traits. Through candidate gene studies, and especially genome-wide association studies, genes involved in some appearance traits were identified, and subsequently the predictive power of the identified statistically significantly associated DNA markers (usually single nucleotide polymorphisms, SNPs) was established, which provided the basis for FDP tool development and FDP applications in forensic routine. Still, our current understanding of the genetic basis of human physical appearance is largely incomplete, perhaps with the exception of pigmentation (see below). The genetic basis of human appearance is complex, with many genes contributing to the respective appearance phenotypes together with the influence of non-genetic environmental factors that differ in their extent between different appearance traits. Understating the genetic basis of polygenic externally visible characteristics (EVC's) is certainly a surmountable task with continued research, but it will take some time to assess which multifactorial traits are possible, and which are not, to reliably predict a personalized 'DNA mugshot'. Depending on the necessary research funding and efforts, this capability will come with time and persistence. After all 'Rome was not built in a day', and it is expected that with continuing fundamental research on human appearance genetics, new DNA markers and new traits will be added to the physical appearance trait prediction repertoire.

The biggest hurdle so far (apart from dedicated research funding), when considering the use of large numbers of SNPs typically accessed *via* microarrays (and in the future more likely *via* exome or whole genome sequencing data), is the vast numbers of individuals required to find EVC genes *via* genome-wide association studies (GWAS) because of their small effect size. Consequently sample sizes needed can easily be thousands or tens of thousands, even hundreds of thousands, depending on the degree of genetic complexity of the trait. Only by combining research group resources can there be a way forward. International consortia, such as the Genetic Investigation of Anthropometric Traits (GIANT) Consortium and the International Visible Trait Genetics (VisiGen) Consortium, have been instrumental in this regard. This research in turn will allow the unveiling of predictive DNA markers from these vast trait-associative SNP lists, and eventually allow development of tools for practical FDP applications. Of all human externally visible characteristics, pigmentation — particularly of the eye (iris) and hair, currently are the genetically most completely understood appearance traits already allowing practical FDP (see next chapter), while for all other physical appearance traits, more fundamental research into the underlying genes and predictive DNA markers is needed.

3 DNA Prediction of Pigmentation Traits

3.1 *Eye Color*

Since 2003, there have been several key studies (Frudakis *et al.*, 2007; Sulem *et al.*, 2007; Sturm *et al.*, 2008; Eiberg *et al.*, 2008; Kayser *et al.*, 2008) using candidate gene and GWAS approaches to identify genes involved in human eye color variation such as *SLC24A4*, *KITLG*, *6p25.3*, *TYR*, *OCA2-HERC2*, *MC1R* and *TYR* to name a few. In 2009, the first comprehensive DNA prediction study on eye color was performed by Liu *et al.* (2009). The authors assessed 37 SNPs from eight pigmentation genes for their eye color predictive capabilities on > 6,100 Dutch Europeans. The exploratory analyses revealed that 24 of these SNPs from eight genes were the most predictive for eye color. To produce a reliable prediction model, the model training set consisted of > 3,800 individuals and was tested for its performance on > 2,300 independent samples (not involved in the training set) to reveal area under the receiver operating curve (AUC) prediction accuracy values of 0.93 for brown and 0.91 for blue eye color. An AUC of 1.0 reflects completely accurate prediction, i.e. the prediction in every individual tested is correct. However, intermediate color was considerably more difficult to resolve with those 24 particular SNPs at a value of 0.73. In fact, this study also revealed that using just six of the top SNPs from six different genes, i.e. *HERC2*-rs12913832, *OCA2*-rs1800407, *SLC24A4*-rs12896399, *SLC45A2*-rs16891982, *TYR*-rs1393350 and *IRF4*-rs12203592), provided similarly high AUC accuracy values as all 24 markers, with the added advantage of performing less SNP genotyping.

Realizing that the prediction of an eye color phenotype was entirely possible from a genotype, additional groups began investigating how well certain SNPs performed in the prediction of eye color and other pigment traits. In parallel to Liu *et al.* (2009), Valenzuela *et al.* (2010) tested 75 SNPs from 24 pigmentation candidate genes for their eye, hair and skin color prediction capabilities on > 780 European and non-European individuals. A three SNP combination of *HERC2*-rs12913832, *SLC45A2*-rs16891982 and *SLC24A5*-rs1426654 provided R^2 correlation values of 76.45% using categorical eye color from multiple linear regression modelling, with the majority of the correlation coming from *HERC2* rs12913832 (74.8%). The choice in SNPs for this combination could have been hampered by the inclusion of multiple European and non-European populations, as it does pose difficulty in separating out ancestry effects from true phenotypic effects, certainly in the case of eye color only being variable in individuals originating from Europe and neighboring regions. Further investigations (Branicki *et al.*, 2011; Lamason *et al.*, 2005) revealed that *SLC24A5*-rs1426654 is unlikely to be involved in eye (and hair) color variation. Investigating eye color in Danish Europeans, Mengel-From *et al.* (2009) also confirmed the accuracy of using *HERC2*-rs12913832, together with two other *HERC2* SNPs rs1129038 and rs11636232 that are known to be in strong linkage disequilibrium (LD) with rs12913832, and *OCA2*-rs1800407 on 400 individuals. They illustrated, using this 4-SNP profile, that dark eye color can be predicted with likelihood ratios (LRs) of up to 29.3 for dark eye color and up to 10.7 for light eye color.

In 2010/2011, Walsh *et al.* (2011a) described the IrisPlex test system for eye color prediction from DNA consisting of a genotyping assay and a statistical prediction model. The IrisPlex multiplex assay contains the six most informative eye color predicting SNPs from Liu *et al.* (2009). The IrisPlex prediction model parameters were obtained from Liu *et al.* (2009) and combined into an interactive and easy-to-use excel sheet that provides categorical eye color probabilities from user input SNP genotypes. To drive consistency and establish validity among working forensic laboratories, the forensic developmental validation study of the IrisPlex assay was published in 2011 demonstrating the assay's full compatibility with SWGDAM guidelines (2012), a necessary requirement for forensic casework (Walsh *et al.*, 2011b). The IrisPlex assay is highly sensitive, delivering complete 6-SNP profiles down to about 30 pg input DNA (Walsh *et al.*, 2011b). To further assess the performance of the IrisPlex system, the prediction of eye color was performed on > 940 worldwide DNA samples (Walsh *et al.*, 2011a). The predicted eye color outcomes conformed to general knowledge that eye color variation is restricted to Europe and its immediate surrounding areas, and distant regions such as East Asia, Africa, Oceania and from Native Americans only display (and only predicting using IrisPlex) the brown eye phenotype (Walsh *et al.*, 2011a). These results strongly support that the IrisPlex system predicts eye color in a reliable way without the need of prior biogeographic ancestry DNA testing. Additional testing on the performance of the prediction model on > 3,800 Europeans from seven countries was performed and published in 2011/12 (Walsh *et al.*, 2012). The AUC values achieved in this pan-European study were even higher than established before with the IrisPlex markers (0.96 for blue and brown, respectively) (Lui *et al.*, 2009), which the authors attributed to the use of more accurate phenotype data in the pan-European set (Walsh *et al.*, 2012).

In 2014 (Walsh *et al.*, 2014), an enhanced IrisPlex prediction model for eye color was introduced (and available online; http://www.erasmusmc.nl/fmb/resources/Irisplex_HIrisPlex/) and is based on > 9,100 individuals from eight parts of Europe that achieved AUCs of 0.95 for brown, 0.94 for blue, and 0.74 for intermediate eye color. This set is currently the largest used online prediction parameter database for a human physical appearance trait. When this enhanced model was assessed on an independent set of about 120 Polish individuals, not included in model building or model validation, performance accuracies of 84% were achieved; or 93% when only brown and blue prediction was assessed and the intermediate category was not included (Walsh *et al.*, 2014). More recently, the IrisPlex assay was tested by the European DNA Profiling Group (EDNAP) of the International Society for Forensic Genetics (ISFG) in a multi-center exercise involving > 20 laboratories with various levels of application experience (including novices), and was described as being easy to implement and highly reliable (Chaitanya *et al.*, 2014). Figure 1 displays eye images of 12 individuals together with their DNA predicted eye color using the enhanced IrisPlex model.

In order to ensure the most up-to-date system or tool is in place, it is necessary for research groups to question or compare different techniques, technologies, or choice of SNPs when designing prediction tools and revealing alternative assessments, e.g. different populations. In terms of eye color DNA prediction tools, other SNP sets with partially overlapping markers have been proposed by different groups. Spichenok *et al.* (2011) set the SNP component of their eye color prediction tool to consist of *HERC2*-rs12193832, *IRF4*-rs12203592, *SLC45A2*-rs16891982, *OCA2*-rs1545397, *ASIP*-rs6119471, and *MC1R*-rs885479, of which the former three are in common with IrisPlex. The choice of these SNPs and their associated prediction design was ascertained from > 550 European and non-European samples, a scenario that is best suited to avoid, if possible,

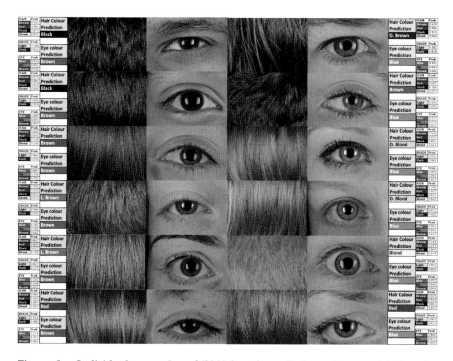

Figure 1: Individual examples of DNA-based prediction of eye and hair color using the HIrisPlex system.

Note: Categorical eye and hair color probabilities obtained from the HIrisPlex genotypes using the enhanced IrisPlex model for eye color and the enhanced HIrisPlex model for hair color are shown for 12 individuals together with the finally concluded eye and hair color category, and eye and hair images of the individuals predicted to allow visual comparisonv between HIrisPlex-predicted and observed eye and hair colors. The figure is organized into two sets of 6 individuals; on the left (brown-eyed) and right (blue-eyed) ordered according to their HIrisPlex predicted eye colors. Note that observed eye (nor hair) color phenotypes were not considered in the ordering of the individual eye (and hair) pictures. Hair images display natural non-dyed hair colors. Guides on how to reach the finally concluded eye and hair color predictions from the obtained probabilities can be found in previous IrisPlex and HIrisPlex publications (Walsh *et al.*, 2011a, 2011b, 2014, 2013).

population stratification effects, when dealing with a trait that is restricted to a certain population, such as eye color is to Europeans (and people from neighboring regions). While the MC1R gene is well-known for having a strong effect on light skin color, freckles and red hair seen in Europeans, the inclusion of a SNP from the

MC1R gene may not be useful, as almost all previous (and subsequent) studies have not observed any effect on eye color variation. As a follow up by the group, Pneuman *et al.* (2012) tried to directly compare prediction outcomes of the Spichenok *et al.* system with the IrisPlex system. However, such comparison is expected to be difficult, as there is a definitional difference between the two approaches. The prediction outcomes from the IrisPlex system have a final prediction result based on highest probability value for that category, i.e. blue, brown or intermediate eye color as established from a statistical model based on thousands of individuals. The outcomes of the Spichenok *et al.* prediction approach are obtained from an *ad hoc* multi-step classification procedure with the main preliminary step producing "non-blue" and "non-brown" predictions, an outcome that does not produce a statistical estimation. This "non-color" prediction may be difficult to interpret, but also makes a direct comparison with other color probability prediction approaches, such as those of the IrisPlex system, problematic in terms of accuracy. Research in New Zealand into eye color prediction tested 19 SNPs from 10 genes on a small sample of 101 New Zealanders of European and non-European origin (Allwood and Harbison, 2013). A set of four SNPs was chosen to provide the most accurate prediction values of 89% for blue and 94% for brown eye color using a similar classification tree model. The SNPs in question consist of all IrisPlex SNPs, apart from *HERC2*-rs12913832 where they used a SNP in strong LD — *HERC2*-rs1129038.

In an effort to improve the prediction of the intermediate category, an area where the researchers involved with the IrisPlex system development admit that it needs improvement, Ruiz *et al.* (2013) described an eye color test based on 37 SNPs that were tested in > 410 Europeans. Based on 13 SNPs, including all 6 IrisPlex SNPs, they revealed an AUC increase from 0.756 to 0.816 for the intermediate category and slight improvements for brown from 0.978 to 0.990 and blue from 0.986 to 0.999 AUC, relative to IrisPlex in the same samples (Walsh *et al.*, 2012). The set specifically emphasizes the inclusion of SNPs in strong LD with *HERC2*-rs12913832 such as *HERC2*-rs1129038, *HERC2*-rs7182877 and *HERC2*-rs1667394, stating their independent addition to prediction accuracy value benefits the prediction of green-eyed phenotypes in particular Ruiz *et al.*, (2013). However, Freire-Aradas *et al.* (2014) recently showed that the inclusion of *HERC2*-rs1129038 may overestimate intermediate (green-hazel) eye color prediction at least when performed on samples in the Americas, Middle-East and West Asia as they reported seeing higher than expected intermediate predictions where IrisPlex had predicted brown as rather expected in individuals from this region; unfortunately there were no eye color phenotypes available to substantiate their findings. It seems to be the case that further investigation into the SNPs surrounding the most predictive SNP for eye color within the *HERC2* region as well as SNPs in LD located within the affected neighboring *OCA2* region would be beneficial to eye color prediction research in general and in particular the elucidation of the more difficult non-blue, non-brown eye color associated SNPs.

Recently, it has been shown (Freire-Aradas *et al.*, 2014; Dembinski and Picard, 2014) that non-European populations that have experienced European admixture in their population history, and therefore express eye color variation, may display more difficult genotype prediction profiles, perhaps due to their increased number of derived alleles. For instance, Dembinski and Picard (2014) analyzed the 6 IrisPlex SNPs in 200 US Americans and applied the IrisPlex prediction model to reveal high rates of correct predictions for blue eye color (95% using an 0.7 and 0.5 probability threshold), while brown eye color predictions were considerably less accurate (76% and 88% with the 0.7 and 0.5 threshold, respectively). A more in depth look at European-admixed populations in the future, and possibly the addition of such individuals into the prediction model, may correct these deviations in prediction accuracy for brown eye color. However, for the intermediate color categories, we believe fundamental research is needed to find the particular SNPs/genes associated with colors such as green.

The ultimate future for eye color prediction lies in the shifting from categorical prediction to predicting continuous or quantitative eye color. In reality, color cannot simply be put into box definitions — blue, brown, or non-blue, non-brown, as is currently done with all available eye color DNA prediction systems. The nature of eye color between the two extremes of blue and brown leaves this intermediary color space the most difficult to predict and therefore more fundamental research needs to be performed by redefining the colors and finding more SNP/gene associations with these quantitatively-defined color values. Rather than providing a verbal cue as to what eye color category was ascertained in an FDP application, an individualized color prediction from DNA resulting into a color print out or reference color number will allow investigators to follow with less interpretative difficulties associated with categorical predictions. This research change in direction has already begun by Liu *et al.* (2010) exemplifying that a GWAS on continuous eye color obtained from high-resolution digital eye images in thousands of individuals allows the identification of additional genes that remained elusive in previous gene search studies using categorical eye color phenotypes; Other research groups too have begun to look into quantitative eye color more specifically (Andersen *et al.*, 2013; Pietroni *et al.*, 2014).

3.2 Hair Color

A DNA test for hair color prediction, red hair in particular, was one of the earliest prediction tests available as described by Grimes *et al.* (2001) in 2001. The test included 12 DNA variants from the *MC1R* gene used to determine whether an individual had red hair or not, and revealed an accuracy of 96%, albeit in a small study. In 2007, a DNA prediction test for all hair color categories was made available by Sulem *et al.* (2007). The authors used just two *MC1R* SNPs, rs1805008 and rs1805007, to first predict red hair; if red was predicted with an > 0.5 probability, the resulting 70% of individuals did show signs of the red hair phenotype. Subsequently, to predict other hair colors by omitting red hair determination, they assessed SNPs from six regions, most notably *SLC24A4*-rs12896399, *HERC2*-rs1667394 and *KITLG*-rs12821256, but the predictions of black, brown and blond hair color were less accurate compared to predictions for red hair. In 2010, Valenzuela *et al.* (2010) reported a trio of SNPs

(*SLC45A2*-rs16891982, *SLC24A5*-rs1426654 and *HERC2*-rs12913832) to achieve correlation (R^2) values of up to 76.3% between observed and DNA-predicted hair color. In 2011, similar to the systematic eye color prediction study by Liu *et al.* (2009), Branicki *et al.* (2011) assessed 46 SNPs from 13 genes previously associated with hair color to reveal an optimised model consisting of 22 SNPs from 11 genes that achieved AUC values of 0.93 for red, 0.87 for black, 0.82 for brown and 0.81 for blond on a test set of 385 Polish Europeans. In an assessment of the contribution of *SLC24A5*-rs1426654 to hair color prediction, several groups (Branicki *et al.*, 2011; Lamason *et al.*, 2005; Soejima and Koda, 2007) could not replicate the findings Valenzuela *et al.* (2010) obtained likely because of their multi-ethnic study design (see notion above for eye color). A possible reason for the likely ancestry effect of *SLC24A5*-rs1426654 picked-up as hair (and eye) color effect by Valenzuela *et al.* (2010) is its involvement in skin color variation having an inter- (and intra)-continental distribution pattern (see below in next section).

Similar to eye color prediction, the need for a hair color DNA prediction system in forensic casework was deemed necessary, and the first one to predict all hair color categories, including shade, was developed and published by Walsh *et al.* (2013). The SNP content of this system, termed HIrisPlex, was based on the SNP prediction rankings established earlier by Branicki *et al.* (2011). The HIrisPlex system includes a single multiplex genotyping assay for 24 eye and hair color predicting DNA markers (including all six from IrisPlex), and two prediction models, one for eye (IrisPlex parameters) and one for hair color. The 24 HIrisPlex DNA markers include 10 SNPs and 1 indel from *MC1R* (Y152OCH, N29insA, rs1805006, rs11547464, rs1805007, rs1805008, rs1805009, rs1805005, rs2228479, rs1110400 and rs885479) allowing the prediction of red hair color, as well as two SNPs each of *SLC45A2* (rs28777 and rs16891982), *SLC24A4* (rs2402130 and rs12896399) and *TYR* (rs1042602 and rs1393350), as well as one SNP each of *KITLG* (rs12821256), *EXOC2* (rs4959270), *IRF4* (rs12203592), *OCA2* (rs1800407), *HERC2* (rs12913832), *ASIP/PIGU* (rs2378249) and *TYRP1* (rs683) for predicting the other (non-red) hair color categories. Twenty-two SNPs, i.e. all but two IrisPlex

SNPs (*TYR*-rs1393350 and *SLC24A4*-rs12896399), are used for model-based hair color prediction, while the six IrisPlex SNPs are used for eye color prediction. An assessment of >1,500 individuals from three regions of Europe was performed where 80% ($n = 1243$) were used to train the hair color prediction model, and 20% ($n = 308$) were used to test the models performance. In conjunction with the probabilities produced by the prediction model, there is a hair color prediction guide that utilizes specific thresholds and incorporates hair color shade to the prediction. The individual-based prediction accuracies employing the prediction-guided approach on average were 69.5% for blond, 78.5% for brown, 80% for red and 87.5% for black hair color.

To further assess the system's suitability for forensic casework, in 2014, the forensic developmental validation study was performed with the HIrisPlex assay, demonstrating that it meets SWGDAM guidelines (2014). An assessment of the high sensitivity of the HIrisPlex assay has proven that complete 24-SNP profiles can be produced in quantities as low as 60 pg input DNA. This study also includes an increased model training set of >1,600 individuals (SWGDAM, 2014) with AUC prediction accuracies of 0.92 for red, 0.85 for black, 0.81 for blond, and 0.75 for brown hair color. Upon assessment of 120 Polish individuals set aside for model testing, the enhanced HIrisPlex hair color prediction model performed on average with an accuracy level of 73% across all hair colors. Furthermore, a freely accessible online prediction tool was introduced and is considered the phenotypic prediction model currently available for the prediction of eye and hair color from DNA. It allows the probability estimation of both partial and complete HIrisPlex profiles and can be found at http://www.erasmusmc.nl/fmb/resources/Irisplex_HIrisPlex/. Figure 1 provides examples of HIrisPlex-based eye and hair color DNA prediction outcomes together with the respective eye and hair photos showing the observed colors in 12 example individuals.

As emphasized previously, additional fundamental research into understanding the mechanisms or processes involved in age-related hair color changes, and adding this knowledge to a prediction model shall improve hair color prediction accuracy (Walsh *et al.*, 2013). This idea of age-related changes affecting HIrisPlex predictions is supported by data in 157 Irish individuals for which information on age-related hair color change information was collected and non-died non-grey hair images were available (Walsh *et al.*, 2013). Of the 157 individuals, 8 were phenotypically classified as blond, were also blond as children and were predicted correctly as blond by the HIrisPlex system. Fourteen individuals that were predicted blond by the HIrisPlex system with a high probability ($p > 0.7$), did not display adult blond hair but more light brown to black shades. However, all 14 were noted to display lighter hair colors such as blond as a child. Age dependent hair color darkening occurs in some but not all individuals and needs to be fully understood before hair color DNA prediction accuracies, particularly for blond and brown typically are involved in the change with age, can improve. Also, the loss of hair pigment or hair greying/whitening would be a valid addition to FDP; however, the current genetic knowledge on age-dependent hair color loss is very limited and needs to be substantially improved before DNA predictive markers and tools can be developed. Such a FDP tool would be especially informative when combined with DNA-based age tests, which are starting to become available (see below).

Likewise with eye color, hair color prediction performed by the HIrisPlex system on worldwide DNA samples suggests that it performs accurately independent of bio-geographic ancestry (Walsh *et al.*, 2013), although no hair color phenotypes were available to definitively prove this point. Notably, there is one region far away from Europe where blond hair is also found (without European admixture), namely in the Pacific, albeit in much lower frequency than in Europeans. It has been established that R93C, a functional SNP in *TYRP1,* is highly associated with blond hair in Pacific Islanders, where it accounted for 46.4% of blond hair color in the study population (Draus-Barini *et al.*, 2013). This SNP marks an independent mutation in the *TYRP1* gene that is not involved in the expression of blond hair in Europeans, while other *TYRP1* SNPs such as rs683 are involved. Therefore, R93C was not included in the HIrisPlex system, while rs683 is included.

The HIrisPlex system has been applied to DNA samples extracted from old and ancient bones and teeth (Draus-Barini *et al.*, 2013), demonstrating its suitability in degraded DNA analysis. Of the 26 DNA extracts from bones and teeth between 1 and about 800 years of post-mortem age, 23 yielded complete 24-SNP HIrisPlex profiles (Draus-Barini *et al.*, 2013). In 2014, eye and hair color prediction markers that make up the HIrisPlex system were sequenced by King *et al.* (2014) on DNA obtained from skeletal remains that were later confirmed *via* living relatives (among other evidence) as belonging to King Richard III of England (1452–1485). By using the IrisPlex and HIrisPlex models, a prediction probability of 96% for blue eye color together with a 77% blond hair probability enabled the authors to link the most accurate posthumous painting portrait to the dead king (King *et al.*, 2014).

As already stipulated for the future of eye color research, hair color research and prediction from DNA eventually needs to move from the simple categorical levels, which simplify hair color phenotyping, to the continuous or quantitative level it biologically represents. By doing so, the level of detail DNA-based hair color prediction can increase and reduce putative police interpretative issues by avoiding verbal category statements as test outcomes in the final report to the police.

3.3 Skin Color

Skin color is the final trait to be added to the pigmentation DNA prediction repertoire in humans. However, until now there has been less genetic knowledge and data available for skin color variation in comparison to eye and hair color, in particular its DNA-based prediction. Factors that include the global distribution of skin color variation make it more difficult to identify genes involved in skin color in comparison to eye and hair color, which have a more restricted European distribution in its total phenotypic variation allowing successful genes searches using Europeans. Skin color however, displays its maximum phenotypic variation among individuals from different continental regions, which can not simply be pooled in the gene search due to expected high rates of false positives, because there are many more genes with differences between continental groups than those involved in skin color. Therefore, GWAS studies on skin color were performed solely within continental groups such as Europeans (Sulem *et al.*, 2007; Han *et al.*, 2008; Jacobs *et al.*, 2013) or within Asians (Stokowski *et al.*, 2007), but within continental groups skin color variation is limited. Therefore it is more difficult to gain a comprehensive understanding of the genetic factors determining skin color variation and thus finding an optimal set of DNA markers that allow prediction of skin color in its entire range both between and within continental groups.

Some attempts towards skin color prediction from DNA were performed, but their outcomes are limited. In 2010, Spichenok *et al.* (2011), described a 7-SNP set (that was used to predict eye color) to infer a skin color prediction of 'not white' and 'not dark', reporting only three errors among 398 predictions. Although for 28% of the tested samples, no prediction was obtained due to inconclusive outcomes, Pneuman *et al.* (2012) verified this 7-SNP set on an independent cohort of > 250 individuals reporting 1% error and 19% inconclusive outcomes. Hart *et al.* (2013) using 6 of the 7 SNPs (excluding *IRF4*-rs12203592), reported no errors, although 38% were inconclusive in a > 200 additional test set. Although all tests displayed little to no error, the inconclusive prediction formed the bulk of the prediction outcomes, which can be a significant drawback towards the use of an *ad hoc* prediction approach. Care must be taken with interpretation of such a "no-color"-based prediction outcome (see above for eye color) as well as the lack in detail at the prediction outcomes in Europeans, where all were deemed by the authors as 'white' ignoring existing skin color variation among them.

In 2014, the most comprehensive skin color prediction study was published by Maronas *et al.* (2014). The group investigated 59 SNPs previously associated with skin, eye and hair color in > 280 individuals from European and non-European individuals based on questionnaire ascertained data and skin reflectance measurements. Twenty-nine SNPs were identified as the most correlated with skin color variation in the sample set used and then were assessed for their predictive capabilities. The authors suggested an optimal set of 10 SNPs (*SLC45A2*-rs16891982, *SLC24A5*-rs1426654, *KITLG*-rs10777129, *ASIP*-rs6058017, *TYRP1*-rs1408799, *OCA2*-rs1448484, *SLC45A2*-rs13289, *SLC24A4*-rs2402130, *TPCN2*-rs3829241 and *ASIP*-rs6119471) for which they reported AUC prediction values of 0.999 for white, 0.966 for black and 0.803 for intermediate skin color from 118 individuals used for validation. Due to such small numbers that may not represent a large spectrum of possible skin color variation, additional data from more populations shall further assess the capability of this skin color prediction SNP set, as well as additional SNPs not tested by these authors. The authors also revealed the integration of their skin color predictive tool into the '*snipper*' suite platform available online at http://mathgene.usc.es/snipper/skinclassifier.html.

Finally, as already emphasized in eye and hair color prediction, skin color research into the best predictive markers available to be used on a worldwide panel of individuals needs to move towards the more biological continuous or quantitative spectrum of color for more accurate prediction outcomes.

4 Appearance Traits that May be Predictable from DNA in the Near or Distant Future

Apart from pigmentation, there are currently no more DNA prediction tests available for any other physical appearance traits (with the exception of age if considered a physical trait) due to limited knowledge of their genetic bases and the consequent lack of sufficient predictive DNA markers that cover enough of the respective phenotypic variation. Clearly, more fundamental research needs to be applied to the traits listed below for finding more genes and predictive DNA markers. It is believed that some traits, such as male baldness, shall be available in the near future and maybe considered the next additions to come for FDP applications. However, other traits, such as facial morphology, will require substantial fundamental research to understand the underlying highly complex genetics, particularly because of the (almost) individualized nature of the human face.

4.1 *Body Height*

Body height currently is the most genetically studied human physical trait because it was and still is used as a model in common trait gene mapping in humans. This is possible because height is collected as additional phenotype in many cohort studies established for mapping various human disease genes. Therefore, delving into the understanding of height genetics was one of the first major EVC's investigated *via* large GWAS. In 2010 (Lango *et al.*, 2010), the international GIANT (Genetics of Anthropomorphic Traits) Consortium published at that time the largest GWAS on body height, which included >183,000 individuals and identified SNPs in approximately 180 genetic loci across the genome that displayed statistically significant height association. However, these 180 genetic loci only explained about 10% of height variation within the study cohort whereas it has been estimated from twin studies that the heritability of height is about 80%. It was estimated that > 480,000 individuals would be needed to identify about 650 significantly associated height genetic loci to even explain just 15% of height variance (Lango *et al.*, 2010). In 2014 (Wood *et al.*, 2014), GIANT published a follow-up GWAS on body height involving 250,000 individuals, found about 700 significant height-associated SNPs, which explained about 15% of height variation in the study subjects. These findings illustrate that many thousands of SNPs will likely be needed to explain all of the 80% heritable height variation.

In 2009, the first DNA prediction study on height was performed by Aulchenko *et al.* (2009) and achieved an AUC value of 0.65 only (where AUC of 0.5 reflects random prediction) in predicting the tallest 5% of individuals from a Dutch European cohort. The test included 54 height-associated SNPs known at the time. More recently, Liu *et al.* (2014) tried to improve this accuracy value using the power of 180 genetic loci with significant association to normal height variation identified by the GIANT consortium (Lango *et al.*, 2010). In an effort to try to predict extremely tall stature, they used 770 extremely tall individuals in addition with > 9,500 Dutch Europeans of normal height variation and reported an AUC value of 0.75 based on the 180 GIANT height SNPs. Clearly, many more predictive SNPs need to be identified before extreme tall stature can be predicted from DNA with an accuracy high enough for practical FDP applications, and many more for accurately predicting DNA normal body height.

4.2 Hair Loss and Hair Structure

To date, a few GWAS studies have been published that investigated early-onset androgenetic alopecia (AGA) or male pattern baldness, the most common form of hair loss in humans. In 2012 (Li *et al.*, 2012), the largest GWAS on AGA including > 12,800 Europeans identified 8 genetic loci with genome-wide significant associations — *TARDBP, HDAC4, HDAC9, AUTS2, 17q21.31* and *SETBP1*, were newly identified and *PAX1/FOXA2* and *AR/EDA2R* were replicated from previous studies (Hillmer *et al.*, 2008). The locus *AR/EDA2R* contained the most strongly associated SNPs and is located on the X chromosome. This finding substantiates why AGA typically is more associated with males and links some of the genetic risk for baldness with inheritance from a male's maternal grandfather. A recent study (Heilmann *et al.*, 2013) found four additional regions; 2q35, 3q25.1, 5q33.3 and 12p12.1 associated with the AGA phenotype. Using 8 baldness-associated SNPs, Li *et al.* (2012) calculated a genotype risk score, and from this they could establish whether individuals belonged to a six-fold increase in risk group for early onset AGA. Early onset female pattern hair loss (FPHL) shares some similarities with AGA in terms of underlying genetic loci (*AR* and *EDA2R* genes); however, many genes known from AGA are not replicated in the female form of baldness, leaving it certainly an area that requires more investigation. An important point to note is that our current genetic knowledge on male hair loss is largely driven by studies performed on patients displaying early onset forms of AGA and it is not clear whether these genes similarly explain the natural late onset forms of baldness, while both would be interesting for FDP purposes. Future studies into the association of non-disease related late-onset baldness may cast better light on the predictability of this EVC for FDP.

In terms of hair morphology, only three genes have been found to date. In 2008, Fujimoto *et al.* (2008a) investigated hair morphology in an Asian population, and identified *EDAR* as the main gene associated with Asian hair thickness. This finding was confirmed in other studies on humans (Fujimoto *et al.*, 2008b) and functional work in mice (Kamberov *et al.*, 2013). A year later (Fujimoto *et al.*, 2009), Fujimoto *et al.* suggested another gene, *FGFR2*, to be involved in Asian hair thickness. Also in 2009, Medland *et al.* (2009) published a GWAS on hair morphology in Australian Europeans and found the *TCHH* gene to be significantly associated with European straight hair, explaining 6% of variance in the population studied, most notably rs11803731 representing a coding, non-synonymous variant in exon 3 of the *TCHH* gene. An increase in the proportion of *TCHH*-rs11803731 T-alleles has a direct correlation with the straight hair phenotype. As the derived minor T-allele was fully present in Europe and surrounding regions, but absent from East Asia, Oceania, Sub-Saharan Africa and in Native Americans, the authors proposed it arose in Europe and may have been driven to the frequencies observed today by sexual selection *via* mate choice preferences (Frost *et al.*, 2006). The authors also investigated the 170 candidate genes suggested by Fujimoto *et al.* (2009), including *EDAR* and *FGFR2*, but besides *TCHH*, could only report a strong association for *WNT10A* (Medland *et al.*, 2009). Additional research into the highly variable nature of hair structure within Europeans, but also other groups such as Africans, may prove more beneficial to elucidate the causative genes useful for straight, wavy, curly and frizzy hair, which would be vital to include in a DNA-based physical appearance prediction tool.

4.3 *Chronological Age*

Most physical appearance traits are affected by chronological age, this is a natural phenomenon, and therefore it is favorable to have an age predictive DNA tool for both, predicting age from forensic stains by itself and to improve the FDP outcome of those DNA predicted appearance traits that largely vary with age, such as baldness. In 2010, Zubakov *et al.* (2010), utilized knowledge on T-cell decreases with age, including the T-cell DNA rearrangement sjTREC. A quantitative DNA test was introduced that achieved AUC prediction capabilities between 0.88 and 0.97 for four age groups separated into 20 year categories. This category-based approach proved more effective as precise age estimation by this single DNA test was more limited — R^2 of 0.835 (SE 8.9 years). More recently, investigations into the methylation status of DNA sites (so called CpG's) have been deemed more favorable to estimate age. This field of epigenetics has delivered many promising CpG candidate markers for age prediction. For example, Bocklandt *et al.* (2011) highlighted three sites at promoter regions of the genes *EDARADD*, *TOM1L1* and *NPTX2*. A combination of two CpG markers could explain about 73% of age variance, and the ability to predict individual age was narrowed to an accuracy of about 5 years. Three alternative CpG sites were highlighted by Garagnani *et al.* (2012), genes *ELOVL2*, *FHL2* and *PENK*, of which *ELOVL2* appeared to be the most promising with a Spearman's correlation coefficient of 0.92. Weidner *et al.* (2014), examined > 100 CpG sites that were correlated with chronological age and reported a mean absolute deviation in age of only 3.34 years with a high R^2 correction of 0.98. They also introduced a freely available online calculator for epigenetic aging signatures, which can be found at http://www.molcell. rwth-aachen.de/epigenetic-aging-signature/.

There are many theories behind the usefulness of DNA methylation patterns for chronological age prediction as different researchers view them as more associated with biological or cell type aging, which may largely be affected by an individual's disease status. Therefore, it is essential to fully validate and substantiate these findings on large cohorts of healthy and non-healthy individuals to fully understand their true role in chronological age. At this moment, the available knowledge suggests that DNA methylation provides the most promising molecular markers for age prediction. In terms of prediction capabilities of DNA methylation markers, Yi *et al.* (2014) reported a correlation between predicted age from eight loci and observed age as $R^2 = 0.828$, although the sample size was quite low, only 65 individuals, while the marker identification set was even lower, only 10 young and 10 old individuals, with no marker validation or involvement in biological age being performed. Recently, Zbiec-Piekarska *et al.* (2015) was able to provide better data evidence by focussing on DNA methylation in the *ELOVL2* gene, reporting the age prediction using two CpGs of $R^2 = 0.859$ from blood samples of > 300 individuals aged between 2 and 75 years of age. Upon evaluation of their model on 124 additional samples, an R^2 of 0.866 was reported with on average 68.5% correct group category-predictions (0–19, 20–39, 40–59 and 60–80 years of age). *ELOVL2* methylation has now been reported in several independent studies (Garagnani *et al.*, 2012; Zbieć-Piekarska *et al.*, 2015; Hannum *et al.*, 2013; Johansson *et al.*, 2013; Florath *et al.*, 2014) suggesting it to be one of the most promising molecular markers currently available for human age estimation.

4.4 *Facial Morphology*

Fundamental research on the composition of human facial morphology is few and far between, there are less than a handful of publications on this area to date. Consequently, the human face certainly is not yet a possible inclusion into the FDP portfolio. That is not to say that in years to come with research into finding the genes that determine normal facial variation and identifying enough predictive DNA markers, we eventually will get there. But for now, individual-specific facial prediction from DNA seems far away. Only since 2012 have systematic studies begun on the investigation into the genetic determination of human facial morphology. Liu *et al.* (2012), performing a GWAS with replication on almost

10,000 Europeans identified five genes *PAX3, PRDM16, TP63, C5orf50* and *COL17A1* with genome-wide significant association to several facial distances, which were assessed through automated facial landmarking of 3D magnetic resonance images (MRIs) of the head and 2D portrait pictures for replication. Three of the five genes had been previously implicated in craniofacial development and disease. The *PAX3* association, that was found to influence the position of the nasion, also was found in a parallel study by Paternoster *et al.* (2012) to be significantly associated in Europeans. Notably, Paternoster *et al.* (2012) used children, while Liu *et al.* (2012) used elderly people, and both highlighted the *PAX3* genes to be involved in the nasion. Notably, these two studies currently represent the only systematic investigations into genes involved in human facial shapes. Both studies also demonstrated that genetic effects on the studies facial distances were small. As this can be expected for all facial traits, large numbers of genes/DNA variants are expected to explain facial morphology. For instance, the SNP rs17447439 in the *TP63* gene, reported to have the largest effect in the study by Liu *et al.* (2012), could only infer a reduction in eye-to-eye distance of approximately 0.9 mm (heterozygote) or 1.8 mm (homozygote) opposite to the wild-type genotype, where about 20 mm total eye-to-eye distance variation was observed in the study population.

Recently, Claes *et al.* (2014a) employed a more complex approach to facial phenotyping, and instead of the genome-wide approach used SNPs from craniofacial candidate genes particularly selected to have large frequency differences between populations. The authors reported a set of 24 SNPs from 20 genes claimed to be useful for facial morphology prediction. In a subsequent study, Claes *et al.* (2014b), while using the same data, emphasized that sex and genetic ancestry provided most of the DNA-based facial composites needed, while the effect of the 24 'facial' SNPs was marginal (e.g. only 1% increase in accuracy). However, the statistical approach and selection of candidate genes used by Claes *et al.* were criticized (Hallgrimsson *et al.*, 2014). Nevertheless, this method has gained a lot of press recently because of a US-based company advertising for the ability to produce general facial images of suspects using this approach (http://www.nytimes.com/2015/02/24/science/ building-face-and-a-case-on-dna.html). Based on the presented underlying science (Claes *et al.*, 2014a, 2014b), this approach is unlikely to be reliable.

In reality, we are just at the very beginning of understanding which genes determine normal facial variation and quite far from assessing markers for their predictive capabilities for practical FDP usage. Maybe one day, a search through DMV or passport records will lead police to a suspect through DNA-based facial morphology prediction, but it certainly is not near term application.

5 Issues with Future Directions of Forensic DNA Phenotyping

As described throughout this chapter, FDP has made great strides but still has a long way to go. Its potential, however, has been unleashed. Now, time, dedication and funding are needed to capture more complete genetic information determining human appearance to deliver the needed DNA markers allowing to predict human appearance with its many traits accurately and reliably. Ultimately, including them all into a practical FDP toolbox that can be used for individualized physical appearance prediction for forensic intelligence purposes is the goal. This desire leads us to the technological advances needed for parallel genotyping of large numbers of SNPs from low quality and low quantity DNA as confronted in forensic analyses where SNP microarrays typically fail. In this respect, we are right at the forefront of studies on the multiplexing capabilities of large numbers of targeted SNPs via massive parallel sequencing (MPS) or next generation sequencing (NGS) technologies for instance using Life Technologies Ion Torrent Personal Genome Machine or Illumina's forensic platform the MiSeq FGx system. It already has been demonstrated that more than 500 Y-chromosomal SNPs can be successfully combined in a targeted manner *via* a single run using the Ion Torrent Personal Genome Machine (Ralf *et al.*, 2015). Furthermore, a recent proof-of-principle study demonstrated that multilocus STR-based individual identification and multilocus mRNA-based tissue identification can be combined in a single run via targeted NGS (Zubakov *et al.*, 2015), and more combinations for other purposes, including appearance and biogeographic ancestry DNA prediction are expected soon. These technological developments are very promising and come prudently with the discovery of more and appearance (likewise ancestry) informative SNPs. Now is the time to prepare for this development, both scientifically, societally and legally. In the end, one single test outcome may surely identify any forensic sample donor without the current burden of comparative DNA profiling that is unable to identify unknown persons. In the future, non-comparative individual identification through individualized facial reconstruction from forensic DNA samples is the ultimate goal, making criminal DNA (profile) databases a thing of the past.

Acknowledgments

The authors thank all colleagues working in the field of genetic exploration and DNA prediction of human appearance for their achievements, those they cited here and others they were unable to cite due to space constraints. MK's original work on appearance genetics and DNA prediction is funded by Erasmus University Medical Center, Rotterdam and has been previously supported by funds provided by the Netherlands Genomics Initiative/Netherlands Organization for Scientific Research (NWO) within the framework of the Forensic Genomics Consortium Netherlands (FGCN) and the Netherlands Consortium of Healthy Ageing (NCHA), as well as by previous funds from the Netherlands Forensic Institute (NFI). SW's original work on Forensic DNA Phenotyping is supported by Indiana University–Purdue University Indianapolis (IUPUI) and the US National Institute of Justice.

References

J. S. Allwood and S. Harbison. SNP model development for the prediction of eye colour in New Zealand. *Forensic Sci Int: Gene*, 7(4):444–452, 2013.

J. D. Andersen, P. Johansen, S. Harder, S. R. Christoffersen, M. C. Delgado, S. T. Henriksen *et al.* Genetic analyses of the human eye colours using a novel objective method for eye colour classification. *Forensic Sci Int Genet*, 7(5):508–515, 2013.

Y. S. Aulchenko, M. V. Struchalin, N. M. Belonogova, T. I. Axenovich, M. N. Weedon, A. Hofman *et al.* Predicting human height by Victorian and genomic methods. *Eur J Hum Genet*, 17(8):1070–1075, 2009.

S. Bocklandt, W. Lin, M. E. Sehl, F. J. Sánchez, J. S. Sinsheimer, S. Horvath and E. Vilain. Epigenetic Predictor of Age. *PLoS ONE*, 6(6):e14821, 2011.

W. Branicki, F. Liu, K. van Duijn, J. Draus-Barini, E. Pospiech, S. Walsh *et al.* Model-based prediction of human hair color using DNA variants. *Hum Genet*, 129:443–454, 2011.

L. Chaitanya, S. Walsh, J. D. Andersen, R. Ansell, K. Ballantyne, D. Ballard *et al.* Collaborative EDNAP exercise on the IrisPlex system for DNA-based prediction of human eye colour. *Forensic Sci Int: Genet*, 11: 241–251, 2014.

P. Claes, D. K. Liberton, K. Daniels, K. M. Rosana, E. E. Quillen, L. N. Pearson *et al.* Modeling 3D Facial Shape from DNA. *PLoS Genet*, 10(3):e1004224, 2014a.

P. Claes, H. Hill and M. D. Shriver. Toward DNA-based facial composites: Preliminary results and validation. *Forensic Sci Int: Genet*, 13:208–216, 2014b.

G. M. Dembinski and C. J. Picard. Evaluation of the IrisPlex DNA-based eye color prediction assay in a United States population. *Forensic Sci Int Gene*, 9:111–117, 2014.

J. Draus-Barini, S. Walsh, E. Pospiech, T. Kupiec, H. Glab, W. Branicki and M. Kayser. Bona fide colour: DNA prediction of human eye and hair colour from ancient and contemporary skeletal remains. *Investigative Genetics*, 4(1):3, 2013.

H. Eiberg, J. Troelsen, M. Nielsen, A. Mikkelsen, J. Mengel-From, K. Kjaer and L. Hansen. Blue eye color in humans may be caused by a perfectly associated founder mutation in a regulatory element located within the *HERC2* gene inhibiting *OCA2* expression. *Human Genetics*, 123(2): 177–187, 2008.

I. Florath, K. Butterbach, H. Müller, M. Bewerunge-Hudler and H. Brenner, Cross-sectional and longitudinal changes in DNA methylation with age: An epigenome-wide analysis revealing over 60 novel age-associated CpG sites. *Human Molecular Genetics*, 23(5):1186–1201, 2014.

A. Freire-Aradas, Y. Ruiz, C. Phillips, O. Maroñas, J. Söchtig, A. G. Tato *et al.* Exploring iris colour prediction and ancestry inference in admixed populations of South America. *Forensic Sci Int Genet*, 13:3–9, 2014.

P. Frost. European hair and eye color. *Evolution and Human Behavior*, 27(2):85–103, 2006.

T. Frudakis, T. Terravainen and M. Thomas, Multilocus *OCA2* genotypes specify human iris colors. *Human Genetics*, 122(3–4):311–326, 2007.

A. Fujimoto, R. Kimura, J. Ohashi, K. Omi, R. Yuliwulandari, L. Batubara *et al.* A scan for genetic determinants of human hair morphology: *EDAR* is associated with Asian hair thickness. *Human Molecular Genetics*, 17(6):835–843, 2008a.

A. Fujimoto, J. Ohashi, N. Nishida, T. Miyagawa, Y. Morishita, T. Tsunoda *et al.* A replication study confirmed the *EDAR* gene to be a major contributor to population differentiation regarding head hair thickness in Asia. *Human Genetics*, 124(2):179–185, 2008b.

A. Fujimoto, N. Nishida, R. Kimura, T. Miyagawa, R. Yuliwulandari, L. Batubara *et al. FGFR2* is associated with hair thickness in Asian populations. *J Hum Genet*, 54(8):461–465, 2009.

P. Garagnani, M. G. Bacalini, C. Pirazzini, D. Gori, C. Giuliani, D. Mari *et al.* Methylation of *ELOVL2* gene as a new epigenetic marker of age. Aging Cell, 11(6):1132–1134, 2012.

E. A. Grimes, P. J. Noake, L. Dixon and A. Urquhart. Sequence polymorphism in the human melanocortin 1 receptor gene as an indicator of the red hair phenotype. *Forensic Sci Int*, 122(2,Äi3):124–129, 2001.

G. Hannum, J. Guinney, L. Zhao, L. Zhang, G. Hughes, S. Sadda *et al.* Genome-wide Methylation Profiles Reveal Quantitative Views of Human Aging Rates. *Molecular Cell*, 49(2):359–367, 2013.

J. Han, P. Kraft, H. Nan, Q. Guo, C. Chen, A. Qureshi *et al.*, A Genome-wide association study identifies novel alleles associated with hair color and skin pigmentation. *PLoS Genet*, 4(5):e1000074, 2008.

B. Hallgrimsson, W. Mio, R. S. Marcucio and R. Spritz. Let's Face It — Complex Traits Are Just Not That Simple. *PLoS Genet*, 10(11): e1004724, 2014.

K. L. Hart, S. L. Kimura, V. Mushailov, Z. M. Budimlija, M. Prinz and E. Wurmbach. Improved eye- and skin-color prediction based on 8 SNPs. *Cro Med J*, 54(3):248–256, 2013.

S. Heilmann, A. K. Kiefer, N. Fricker, D. Drichel, A. M. Hillmer, C. Herold *et al.* Androgenetic Alopecia: Identification of Four Genetic Risk Loci and Evidence for the Contribution of *WNT* Signaling to Its Etiology. *J Invest Dermatol*, 133(6):1489–1496, 2013.

A. M. Hillmer, F. F. Brockschmidt, S. Hanneken, S. Eigelshoven, M. Steffens, A. Flaquer *et al.* Susceptibility variants for male-pattern baldness on chromosome 20p11. *Nat Genet*, 40(11):1279–1281, 2008.

L. Jacobs, A. Wollstein, O. Lao, A. Hofman, C. Klaver, A. Uitterlinden *et al.* Comprehensive candidate gene study highlights *UGT1A* and *BNC2* as new genes determining continuous skin color variation in Europeans. *Human Genetics*, 132(2):147–158, 2013.

Å. Johansson, S. Enroth and U. Gyllensten, Continuous Aging of the Human DNA Methylome Throughout the Human Lifespan. *PLoS ONE*, 8(6):e67378, 2013.

Y. G. Kamberov, S. Wang, J. Tan, P. Gerbault, A. Wark, L. Tan *et al.* Modeling Recent Human Evolution in Mice by Expression of a Selected *EDAR* Variant. *Cell*, 152(4):691–702, 2013.

M. Kayser, F. Liu, A. Janssens, F. Rivadeneira, O. Lao, K. van Duijn *et al.* Three genome-wide association studies and a linkage analysis identify *HERC2* as a human iris color gene. *Am J Hum Genet*, 82:411–423, 2008.

E. E. Kenny, N. J. Timpson, M. Sikora, M.-C. Yee, A. Moreno-Estrada, C. Eng *et al.* Melanesian Blond Hair Is Caused by an Amino Acid Change in *TYRP1*. *Science*, 336(6081):554, 2012.

T. E. King, G. G. Fortes, P. Balaresque, M. G. Thomas, D. Balding, P. M. Delser *et al.* Identification of the remains of King Richard III. *Nat Commun*, 5, 2014.

R. L. Lamason, M.-A. P. K. Mohideen, J. R. Mest, A. C. Wong, H. L. Norton, M. C. Aros *et al.* *SLC24A5*, a Putative Cation Exchanger, Affects Pigmentation in Zebrafish and Humans. *Science*, 310(5755):1782–1786, 2005.

H. Lango Allen, K. Estrada, G. Lettre, S. I. Berndt, M. N. Weedon, F. Rivadeneira *et al.* Hundreds of variants clustered in genomic loci and biological pathways affect human height. *Nature*, 467(7317):832–838, 2010.

R. Li, F. F. Brockschmidt, A. K. Kiefer, H. Stefansson, D. R. Nyholt, K. Song *et al.* Six Novel Susceptibility Loci for Early-Onset Androgenetic Alopecia and Their Unexpected Association with Common Diseases. *PLoS Genet*, 8(5):e1002746, 2012.

F. Liu, K. van Duijn, J. Vingerling, A. Hofman, A. Uitterlinden, A. Janssens and M. Kayser. Eye color and the prediction of complex phenotypes from genotypes. *Curr Biol*, 19:192–193, 2009.

F. Liu, A. E. Hendriks, A. Ralf, A. Boot, E. Benyi, L. Sävendahl *et al.* Common DNA variants predict tall stature in Europeans. *Human Genetics*, 133(5):587–597, 2014.

F. Liu, F. van der Lijn, C. Schurmann, G. Zhu, M. M. Chakravarty, P. G. Hysi *et al.* A Genome-wide association study identifies five loci influencing facial morphology in europeans. *PLoS Genet*, 8(9):e1002932, 2012.

F. Liu, A. Wollstein, P. G. Hysi, G. A. Ankra-Badu, T. D. Spector, D. Park *et al.* Digital Quantification of Human Eye Color Highlights Genetic Association of Three New Loci. *PLoS Genet*, 6(5):e1000934, 2010.

O. Maroñas, C. Phillips, J. Söchtig, A. Gomez-Tato, R. Cruz, J. Alvarez-Dios *et al.* Development of a forensic skin colour predictive test. *Forensic Sci Int Genet*, 13:34–44, 2014.

S. E. Medland, D. R. Nyholt, J. N. Painter, B. P. McEvoy, A. F. McRae, G. Zhu *et al.* Common Variants in the Trichohyalin Gene Are Associated with Straight Hair in Europeans. *Am J Human Genet*, 85(5):750–755, 2009.

J. Mengel-From, T. Wong, N. Morling, J. Rees and I. Jackson. Genetic determinants of hair and eye colours in the Scottish and Danish populations. *BMC Genetics*, 10(1):88, 2009.

L. Paternoster, Alexei I. Zhurov, Arshed M. Toma, John P. Kemp, B. St. Pourcain, Nicholas J. Timpson *et al.*, Genome-wide association study of three-dimensional facial morphology identifies a variant in *PAX3* associated with nasion position. *Am J Human Genet*, 90(3):478–485, 2012.

C. Pietroni, J. D. Andersen, P. Johansen, M. M. Andersen, S. Harder, R. Paulsen *et al.* The effect of gender on eye colour variation in European populations and an evaluation of the IrisPlex prediction model. *Forensic Sci Int: Genet*, 11:1–6, 2014.

A. Pneuman, Z. M. Budimlija, T. Caragine, M. Prinz and E. Wurmbach. Verification of eye and skin color predictors in various populations. *Legal Medicine*, 14(2):78–83, 2012.

A. Ralf, M. van Oven, K. Zhong and M. Kayser. Simultaneous analysis of hundreds of Y-chromosomal SNPs for high-resolution paternal lineage classification using targeted semiconductor sequencing. *Human Mutation*, 36(1):151–159, 2015.

Y. Ruiz, C. Phillips, A. Gomez-Tato, J. Alvarez-Dios, M. Casares de Cal, R. Cruz *et al.* Further development of forensic eye color predictive tests. *Forensic Sci Int Genet*, 7:28–40, 2013.

Scientific Working Group on DNA Analysis Methods. Revised Validation Guidelines for DNA Analysis Methods. Accepted 2012 (Available from http://media.wix.com/ugd/4344b0_cbc27d16dcb64fd88cb36a-b2a2a25e4c.pdf).

M. Soejima and Y. Koda, Population differences of two coding SNPs in pigmentation-related genes *SLC24A5* and *SLC45A2*. *Int J Legal Med*, 121(1):36–39, 2007.

O. Spichenok, Z. Budimlija, A. Mitchell, A. Jenny, L. Kovacevic, D. Marjanovic *et al.* Prediction of eye and skin color in diverse populations using seven SNPs. *Forensic Sci Int Genet*, 5:472–478, 2011.

P. Sulem, D. Gudbjartsson, S. Stacey, A. Helgason, T. Rafnar, K. Magnusson *et al.* Genetic determinants of hair, eye and skin pigmentation in Europeans. *Nat Genet*, 39:1443–1452, 2007.

R. P. Stokowski, P. V. K. Pant, T. Dadd, A. Fereday, D. A. Hinds, C. Jarman *et al.* A Genomewide Association Study of Skin Pigmentation in a South Asian Population. *Am J Human Genet*, 81(6):1119–1132, 2007.

R. A. Sturm, D. L. Duffy, Z. Z. Zhao, F. P. N. Leite, M. S. Stark, K. Nicholas Hayward *et al.* A Single SNP in an Evolutionary Conserved Region within Intron 86 of the *HERC2* Gene Determines Human Blue-Brown Eye Color. *The American Journal of Human Genetics*, 82(2):424–431, 2008.

R. K. Valenzuela, M. S. Henderson, M. H. Walsh, N. A. Garrison, J. T. Kelch, O. Cohen-Barak *et al.* Predicting Phenotype from Genotype: Normal Pigmentation. *Journal of Forensic Sciences*, 55(2):315–322, 2010.

S. Walsh, F. Liu, K. Ballantyne, M. van Oven, O. Lao and M. Kayser. IrisPlex: A sensitive DNA tool for accurate prediction of blue and brown eye colour in the absence of ancestry information. *Forensic Sci Int Genet*, 5: 170–180, 2011a.

S. Walsh, A. Lindenbergh, S. Zuniga, T. Sijen, P. de Knijff, M. Kayser and K. Ballantyne. Developmental validation of the IrisPlex system: Determination of blue and brown iris colour for forensic intelligence. *Forensic Sci Int Genet*, 5:464–471, 2011b.

S. Walsh, A. Wollstein, F. Liu, U. Chakravarthy, M. Rahu, J. Seland *et al.* DNA-based eye colour prediction across Europe with the IrisPlex system. *Forensic Sci Int Genet*, 6:330–340, 2012.

S. Walsh, L. Chaitanya, L. Clarisse, L. Wirken, J. Draus-Barini, L. Kovatsi *et al.* Developmental validation of the HIrisPlex system: DNA-based eye and hair colour prediction for forensic and anthropological usage. *Forensic Sci Int: Genet*, 9:150–161, 2014.

S. Walsh, F. Liu, A. Wollstein, L. Kovatsi, A. Ralf, A. Kosiniak-Kamysz *et al.* The HIrisPlex system for simultaneous prediction of hair and eye colour from DNA. *Forensic Sci Int Genet*, 7:98–115, 2013.

C. I. Weidner, Q. Lin, C. M. Koch, L. Eisele, F. Beier, P. Ziegler *et al.* Aging of blood can be tracked by DNA methylation changes at just three CpG sites. *Genome Biology*, 15(2):R24–R24, 2014.

A. R. Wood, T. Esko, J. Yang, S. Vedantam, T. H. Pers, S. Gustafsson *et al.*, Defining the role of common variation in the genomic and biological architecture of adult human height. *Nat Genet*, 46(11):1173–1186, 2014.

S. H. Yi, L. C. Xu, K. Mei, R. Z. Yang and D. X. Huang. Isolation and identification of age-related DNA methylation markers for forensic age-prediction. *Forensic Sci Int: Genet*, 11:117–125, 2014.

R. Zbieć-Piekarska, M. Spólnicka, T. Kupiec, Ż. Makowska, A. Spas, A. Parys-Proszek *et al.* Examination of DNA methylation status of the *ELOVL2* marker may be useful for human age prediction in forensic science. *Forensic Sci Int: Genet*, 14:161–167, 2015.

D. Zubakov, I. Kokmeijer, A. Ralf, N. Rajagopalan, L. Calandro, S. Wootton, R. Langit, C. Chang, R. Lagace and M. Kayser. Towards simultaneous individual and tissue identification: A proof-of-principle study on parallel sequencing of STRs, amelogenin, and mRNAs with the Ion Torrent PGM. *Forensic Sci. Int: Genet*, 17:122–128, 2015.

D. Zubakov, F. Liu, M. C. van Zelm, J. Vermeulen, B. A. Oostra, C. M. van Duijn *et al.* Estimating human age from T-cell DNA rearrangements. *Current Biology*, 20(22): R970-R971, 2010.

CHAPTER 18

Wildlife Forensic Science

Adrian Linacre* and Sherryn A. Ciavaglia*,†

*School of Biological Sciences, Flinders University, Adelaide, Australia
†Forensic Science SA, 21 Divett Place, Adelaide

1 Scope of Wildlife Crime

Wildlife crime is a world-wide phenomenon attracting massive financial gain to those that partake of this illegal activity. The scale is unknown as much crime originates in poorly-developed countries where there are limited enforcement capabilities and the end products are sold in financially rich countries often far removed from the original source. The outcome for the country of origin is the destruction of habitats, the extinction of many native and too often endemic animal and plant species, and the loss of much biodiversity. If a country values its biodiversity, then it is essential that there is investigation of alleged wildlife crime and prevention of future illegal activities by bringing to justice those organized syndicates that gain financially from this illegal trade. The latest estimate of wildlife crime is around USD32 billion per year, but this does not include the trade in illegally logged timber (~USD4 billion) and illegal fishing (~USD17 billion). This cost compares to an estimate of USD55 billion for the heroin trade (Johnson *et al.*, 2014) (see Figure 1). These figures are mere estimates as the scale of the trade is extremely

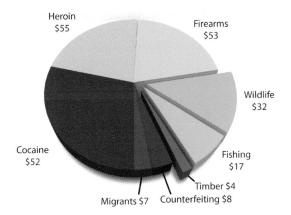

Figure 1: Approximate value in billion USD for the financial gain from a range of illegal activities. The total financial gain from wildlife includes illegal fishing and illegal logging.

hard to quantify as so much of it goes undetected. Given that the international trade in wildlife crime is second only to controlled narcotics, it might be expected that there are well-developed standard operating procedures to investigate such alleged activities and processes in place to enforce national legislation. This infrastructure is rarely the case, with few accredited forensic laboratories undertaking such cases; rather the entire focus in these laboratories is on crimes against humans and their property.

Contrary to this absence of mainstream forensic science laboratories undertaking alleged wildlife crime investigations, there is much public interest in the protection of wildlife. Testimony to this interest is societies such as the World Wildlife Fund and the International Fund for Animal Welfare, which receive substantial public support. Within the forensic community, there is a developing interest in non-human DNA typing as reflected by recent reviews on the subject (Johnson *et al.*, 2014; Iyengar, 2014; Tobe and Linacre, 2010; Wilson-Wilde *et al.*, 2010; Ogden, 2010) and publishers commissioning text books in this discipline (Linacre and Tobe, 2013; Hawk, 2012). The need to encourage best practice is reflected by papers on quality control and standardization of techniques such as a Commission by the International Society for Forensic Genetics (ISFG) (Linacre, 2010), a report by the International Society for Animal Genetics (Budowle *et al.*, 2005) and a workshop at the 25th Congress of the ISFG in September 2013 in Melbourne. There is also the recent (2009) establishment of the Society for Wildlife Forensic Science (SWFS), which publishes standards in forensic practice, aids in distributing proficiency tests and operates a certification process developed through a Scientific Working Group for Wildlife Forensic Sciences (SWGWILD) (Hawk, 2012). Other examples of proficiency tests of non-human animal species include those of dogs (van Asch *et al.*, 2009).

The type of animal or plant material that is traded illegally is exceptionally wide-ranging and can include: invertebrates through to orchids, living or dead whole organisms; skins, pelts, teeth (ivory) and horn; and highly processed materials such as ointments, potions and 'medicines'. In the case of a whole organism, the identification of the species could be undertaken by a competent morphologist who can provide an expert opinion. Morphological analysis includes the identification of a species through the examination of: hair and feather; shells and horn; flowers and pollen; and skulls and teeth. Only rarely are there sufficient morphological characteristics to be able to determine the unknown sample to species-level, rather it is often only possible to place an unknown sample into a taxonomic family or genus. While noting that microscopy and morphological comparisons are appropriate identification methods in certain circumstances, this book chapter is aimed at describing the identification of unknown material using DNA-based methods.

2 Legislation and Enforcement

Before discussing the DNA-based methods, it may be useful to consider two high profile examples of trade in wildlife products. These examples illustrate the complexity of the legislation, which creates the requirement to develop tests that can help to enforce such convoluted legislation.

2.1 *Ivory*

Ivory provides an example where both legal and illegal trade exists. For instance, ivory from the mammoth may be traded legally, as this species is already extinct and there is no rationale (and hence legislation) to protect an extinct species. It is however the case that ivory is often deliberately labelled as coming from a mammoth even though it is from a species for which trade is illegal. What appears to be an anomaly is an instance in Thailand, where it is currently legal to purchase ivory from domestic Asian elephants (*Elephas maximus*), whereas the sale of ivory from African elephants (*Loxodonta africana*) is prohibited under Thai law. The tusks from these two species can normally be distinguished by morphological comparison and hence can resolve any possible transgression of national legislation in Thailand. This situation is an oddity of legislation at a national level, as the international trade of ivory from the Asian elephant is illegal in any country that is a signature to the Convention on International Trade in Endangered Species of Flora and Fauna (CITES) (www.cites.org), which includes Thailand.

In countries such as the USA, there are restrictions and exceptions to the trade and ownership of ivory depending on: (i) the species from which the ivory originates (narwhal, walrus, hippopotamus, or elephant for example), (ii) whether it is carved or not and (iii) when it was collected. The species from which the ivory was removed can be determined by sectioning the item and examining the inner portions using microscopy; this is a skilful task and to the untrained eye such identification is not easy. The onus of proof of legality now required in the US (since 2014) is such that persons wishing to trade any ivory must be able to prove that it is legal; this is converse to the presumption of innocence enshrined in most legal systems.

2.2 Timber

The burden of proof of legality also is placed on the importation and trade of timber products in many countries, with the aim of trying to stop massive deforestation resulting from illegal logging.

Since amendments to the US Lacey Act were passed in May 2008, it is now illegal to import, export, transport, sell, receive, acquire, or purchase in interstate or international commerce any plant (with some limited exceptions), taken or traded in violation of the laws of the US, a US State, or relevant foreign law. The onus is on the trader to exhibit due care and ensure that they comply with the due diligence system (DDS). This revision aims to minimize the risk of illegal wood entering supply chains.

The Australian Government has passed the Illegal Logging Prohibition Act 2012, which stipulates as an offence the importation into Australia of illegally logged timber and any associated product; this restriction includes processing of domestic raw timbers which have been logged illegally. The legislation carries with it significant penalties if found guilty; breaching this offence carries a maximum penalty of five years imprisonment, plus fines of USD85,000 for an individual and USD425,000 for a corporation. Forfeiture of timber products also applies if the perpetrator is found guilty of having imported or processed illegally logged timber knowingly, intentionally or recklessly. In addition, on November 30, 2014, the Illegal Logging Prohibition Amendment Regulation 2013 took effect. This Regulation requires importers of regulated timber products and domestic processors of raw logs to have a DDS in place.

The European Union Timber Regulation (EUTR) prohibits the placing of illegally harvested timber on the European market and requires companies placing legal timber or timber products (both imported and domestic) to implement a DDS. Companies trading wood products within the EU are responsible for keeping records of their suppliers and customers to allow these samples to be traced to the point of felling. The EUTR also affects companies outside of the EU with the aim of safeguarding products that might be imported into the EU further down the supply chain. This Regulation covers a broad range of timber products including solid wood products, flooring, plywood, pulp and paper.

Enforcement of these Acts and Regulations requires identification of the tree species from which the wood originated, potentially linking pieces of timber to each other and/or to a particular stump, and to where in the world the wood grew before being felled. DNA typing can play a key role in addressing both species identification and genetic assignment to both a tree and geographical provenance.

3 Scope of Wildlife Forensic Science

The ivory and timber examples illustrate scenarios where forensic science can play a role in: (i) identifying the species present, as this is relevant to legal restrictions; (ii) linking two or more samples to a specific individual and to determine the size of any seizure; and (iii) determining the most likely geographical location from where the sample originated.

Questions which can now be asked of DNA, and answered, include the following:

Is this sample from a legally protected species? The process of reporting on the species present is now a relatively routine practice and uses many standard procedures that allow the work to be accepted by a court.

Is this sample from a specific member of a legally protected species? Linking one piece of tissue to another by DNA typing uses methods analogous to those used in human identification. Crucial differences lie in the biology of the species (e.g. is it polygamous and does it migrate) and in the evaluation of any matching DNA profiles (e.g. whether the population is highly inbred).

Is this sample from a specific population or geographical region? Assigning a sample to a particular discrete population is becoming increasingly important and more frequently requested. High profile examples include the determination of poaching hotspots and common areas where illegal logging occurs. Population assignment has been used largely for investigative purposes and is currently in the early stages of validation.

3.1 *Species Testing*

The identification of a species from a single source sample has become a routine wildlife forensic analysis technique. There are published primers for many loci on the mitochondrial and chloroplast genomes that amplify a section of DNA that has sufficient polymorphic content to give confidence in a species assignment.

The ability to obtain a sufficient quantity of DNA from hairs, furs, pelts and horns has improved with the availability of commercial DNA extraction kits. Shells and ivory (which are essentially large teeth) suffer the same challenges associated with extracting DNA from bone and teeth in the human arena (Lee *et al.*, 2009; Hsieh *et al.*, 2006; Lo *et al.*, 2006). The isolation of DNA from wood and processed timber is far from easy, including problems involving co-extraction of components that inhibit DNA amplification. While there are some commercial kits for plant DNA extraction, many who work on these types of samples still use their own extraction buffers and revert to an organic extraction protocol as the most efficient means of isolating DNA (Allen *et al.*, 2006).

The benefit of working on mitochondrial DNA (mtDNA) is that there is a much greater copy number present in comparison to nuclear markers. In human mtDNA typing, this advantage can have consequences; specialist laboratory equipment and protocols are needed to minimize the chance of sample contamination by the operator and other exogenous human DNA present at low levels within the laboratory. Contamination by the analyst is less of an issue in wildlife forensic science, as human mtDNA is rarely the target of examinations. Provided reference materials are physically separated from case samples and standard clean laboratory procedures are applied, then contamination is less of an issue when working on non-human DNA.

There remains no standard mitochondrial locus that is used by all laboratories for species testing. This target variation is hardly surprising as mitochondrial loci have different evolutionary rates and the timelines separating members within different types of organisms can vary. Thus, different loci are likely to be useful for species identification in insect, crustacean, fish, amphibian, avian and mammalian species. The mitochondrial loci used most commonly in wildlife forensic science are the cytochrome b (cyt *b*) (Hsieh *et al.*, 2006, 2001, 2003; Lee *et al.*, 2006) and cytochrome oxidase 1 genes (COI) (Dawnay *et al.*, 2007; Hebert *et al.*, 2003a; Hebert *et al.*, 2003a, 2003b, 2004; Ivanova *et al.*, 2012). Both of these loci are highly represented on the online DNA repository (GenBank) and certainly for animal species testing they are a crucial advantage. Green plant species identification uses two loci on the chloroplast genome called *rbcL* and *matK* (Kress *et al.*, 2005), and again there is extensive coverage on GenBank. The ability to compare an unknown DNA sequence from a seized sample to a trusted set of reference DNA sequences is essential in forensic wildlife investigations. GenBank offers an extensive and ever increasing library of DNA sequences and remains a tremendous source of genetic information. Those who rely on GenBank also are cognizant of the fact that errors exist with a few DNA sequences assigned to the wrong species (Bidartondo *et al.*, 2008; Forster, 2003; Harris, 2003; Longo *et al.*, 2011). The Barcode of Life organization (www.boldsystems.org) has addressed these errors in part by only registering DNA sequences which have been verified, typically by supplying morphological or non-genetic data at the time of up-load to the databank. This step towards minimizing errors is welcome, although the databank only includes data from the COI, *rbcL* and *matK* loci, with no plans to extend the repertoire to other valuable loci.

Primers that are 'universal' to all species are published for a range of loci, including the three loci adopted by BOLD and cyt *b*, allowing amplification of sections of either mtDNA or chloroplast DNA in the absence of species-specific DNA sequence knowledge (Hsieh *et al.*, 2001; Parson *et al.*, 2000; Pääbo *et al.*, 1988). The user of these universal primers needs to be aware that they may not be a perfect match to their target species, due to potential polymorphic DNA bases in the primer region. Additionally, it should be noted that mammalian universal primers also will bind to human DNA. Amplification of human and non-human DNA will generate PCR products of the same size at either the cyt *b* or COI locus and hence there is no means to identify any contamination until the DNA sequence is examined. If there is knowledge of the DNA sequence for a particular species, then a species-specific primer can be designed to work in tandem with a universal primer to produce a product of an expected size (Tobe and Linacre, 2008a, 2008b).

If a DNA sequence on GenBank matches a sequence generated from a seized sample, then what can be reported? In line with other areas of forensic genetics, the ideal outcome would be to provide a match probability, i.e. the chance of obtaining the same data if the DNA came from a member of a different species. It is not possible to provide a numerical response with species testing but equally it is not good practice to give a definitive statement that the DNA came from a particular species to the exclusion of all others; as it is not possible to type every member belonging to every species. By considering the DNA data as a likelihood ratio (LR), two alternate scenarios can be compared. These would be: the probability that the unknown sample is from a particular species given the sequence data, compared to the probability that the unknown comes from another species and happens to match by chance given the same sequence data. Currently, any report is based on the amount of sequence used (commonly ~400 bp of cyt *b* or 648 bp of COI) and the similarity of match to a specific species along with the similarity to the next closest genetic species. For a more comprehensive discussion on statements and reporting, see Chapter 6 of reference (Linacre and Tobe, 2013) but an example is shown below.

> "A DNA sequence was obtained from sample X and found to match reference sequence Y with a similarity of 99% over 402 DNA bases. These are the data expected if sample X comes from species Y. These are not the data expected if sample X comes from a species other than species Y. If sample X does not come from species Y then these DNA sequences must match by chance. This chance can only be considered likely if there is a greater than expected inter-species variation or if the DNA sequence comes from a species yet to be recorded."

Confidence in a species identification result also can be increased if the unknown DNA sequence is compared by way of a phylogenetic tree to reference samples of the suspected species obtained from an online databank such as GenBank. A phylogenetic tree illustrates not only the similarity of DNA sequences to one another, but also the relationships among all the species included, according to the locus used. If no representative of the actual species exists on GenBank, then such a tree also will illustrate the similarity to the next most closely related species that is listed (such

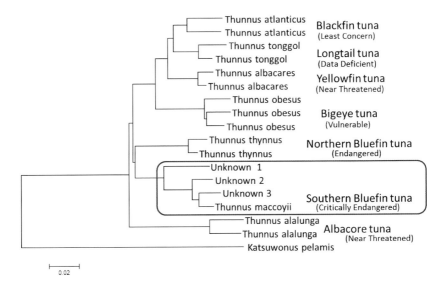

Figure 2: An example of placing unknown, or questioned, DNA sequence on a phylogenetic tree. This is adapted from a real case where three unknown samples are shown to group with a protected species of tuna. The other tuna DNA sequences were obtained from GenBank.

as members of the same genus). In such an instance, the unknown will group with the members of a known genus — this may be highly useful if all members of this genus are CITES listed such as the members of the *Alisterus* genus (King parrots). An example of placing a questioned DNA sequence in a phylogenetic tree, in this case a DNA sequence from a piece of tissue suspected as being a protected tuna species, is shown in Figure 2.

3.2 Genetic Assignment to an Individual

This book contains information on the use of both autosomal and sex chromosome linked short tandem repeat (STR) loci used in human identification. Almost all DNA profiling for human identification uses kits from a commercial supplier to ensure quality and reproducibility of the data. The kits may seem expensive, but much research and validation testing have been performed prior to their release. Many who conduct human identification using such kits will give little thought to: how the STR loci were characterized; how the loci were placed into a multiplex that routinely amplifies alleles with balanced peak heights across the different loci; and how the multiplex kit allows for standardized genotype designation by comparison to a comprehensive allelic ladder. The results are robust, generating reproducible genotypes that can be presented in a criminal or civil case with general acceptance. The wealth of scientific knowledge underpinning STR typing for human identification is such that it is regarded as the 'Gold Standard' in the forensic science report of the US National Academy of Sciences (National Research Council, 2009). Multiplex amplifications available for species other than humans are those developed for domestic or commercial species such as dogs (Berger *et al.*, 2008; Kanthaswamy *et al.*, 2009; van Asch *et al.*, 2009), cats (Coomber *et al.*, 2007; Menotti-Raymond *et al.*, 1997, 1999, 2005, 2012), horses (Dimsoski, 2003; van de Goor *et al.*, 2010), cows (van de Goor *et al.*, 2009) and pigs (Lin *et al.*, 2014); these systems are very rarely available from commercial suppliers as the demand is too low. Wildlife forensic science may encounter many more species for which there is limited genetic knowledge.

Iconic species such as the brown bear (Andreassen *et al.*, 2012), African and Asian elephant (Wasser *et al.*, 2004), Black and White rhino (Harper *et al.*, 2013), chimpanzee (Ely *et al.*, 1998; Lazaruk *et al.*, 2001) and the extant subspecies of tiger (Singh *et al.*, 2004) have recently had STR loci developed for use in wildlife forensic science, along with other species such as the European badger (Dawnay *et al.*, 2008), wolf (van Asch *et al.*, 2010), deer (Szabolcsi *et al.*, 2008) and a few plant species such as cannabis (Hsieh *et al.*, 2003) and agar wood (Eurlings *et al.*, 2010). Some high profile avian species such as birds of prey (Dawnay *et al.*, 2009), pigeons (Chun-Lee *et al.*, 2007) and cockatoos (White *et al.*, 2012) also have been examined for STR loci. However, the number of species for which there is accessible and useful genetic data is very small in comparison to the large number of protected species that are encountered in wildlife forensic science.

An initial question is '*how to find an STR locus for a new species*'. The original human STR loci were identified by serendipity, as they were within an intron of a gene of interest (e.g. vWA in intron 40 of the von Willebrand Factor gene or TH01 found in intron 1 of the tyrosine hydrolase gene). Many of the STR loci used originally in human identification were isolated by this chance discovery. Much more recently, additional STR loci incorporated into commercial kits were located *via* the decoding of the entire human genome (McPherson *et al.*, 2001). The original STR loci used in wildlife studies came from one of three methods: either (1) serendipity where a repeat sequence was noted within an intron; (2) the genomic DNA was cleaved with a restriction enzyme, cloned into bacteria, the bacterial cultures screened using an oligonucleotide containing a random 4 base repeat sequence, and clones with a positive response to the oligonucleotide then sequenced; or (3) more simply (if available), knowledge from a closely related species was used in the hope that the primers would cross-react. This latter approach was used to develop tiger STR loci (Singh *et al.*, 2004) by applying primer sets designed for the domestic cat (Menotti-Raymond *et al.*, 2005).

The advent of High Throughput DNA sequencing (HTS) has made the process of finding potential STR loci much easier. This ease still depends on access to specialized equipment and sufficient funding to pay for the cost of whole genome sequencing; this cost is falling rapidly but still is sizeable for many laboratories. Once the whole genome data are obtained, there is a software available for detecting the short repetitive DNA sequences characteristic of STR loci (for example Micro-Checker (Van Oosterhout *et al.*, 2004)). Di-nucleotide repeats are the most common form of STRs within eukaryotic genomes, but suffer greatly from increased stutters and artefacts in the amplification. As adopted by the human identification community, tetra-nucleotide repeats are recommended for wildlife forensic science (Linacre *et al.*, 2010). Many developmental steps follow the identification of a putative repetitive sequence. The first step is to identify potential primer sequences that will amplify the target locus (software such as Primer3 can aid with the design). Typing members of the population/species with the primers and recording the allelic range will determine whether the locus is polymorphic. A number of alleles need to be sequenced to determine variation between alleles at the sequence level. Sequence data may assist in determining whether the STR motif type is simple, compound or complex. Normally with HTS, a large number (> 50) of potential STR loci can be identified initially. The marker set then is reduced after screening for polymorphic content, by removal of loci exhibiting low allelic diversity. The final marker set represents possible loci for which primers are redesigned to fit into a multiplex for standard capillary electrophoresis-based typing. A gap must exist between previously identified allelic ranges of neighboring loci to ensure that there is no subsequent overlap of alleles belonging to the two loci that would complicate allelic designation. An example of a multiplex assay plan is shown in Figure 3. A fluorescent tag must be added to one of the primers for visualization by capillary electrophoresis. The multiplex needs to be tested for heterozygote balance, stutter heights and potential null alleles. Basic validation testing must be undertaken using steps such as: specificity testing, to ensure the primers react with the species (or members of a genus) for which they were designed; sensitivity to determine the limit of detection and optimal amount of starting template DNA; stability tests to ensure that the targets defined by the primers are robust after environmental insult; followed by reproducibility studies to determine variation due to separation by capillary electrophoresis.

It is a standard practice to compare unknown STR alleles to an allelic ladder to allow standardization of genotyping using a program

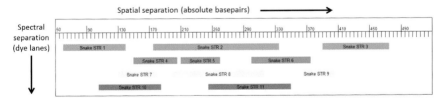

Figure 3: An example of developing an STR multiplex. Colored bars denote allelic size ranges of each STR locus. Typing multiple individuals has shown that alleles fall within the size ranges shown at each locus. Note the gap between the ranges of neighboring loci. Colors correspond to fluorescent label of primer set. The markers shown in this example are part of a forensic STR multiplex assay development project for carpet pythons.

such as Genemapper™. The creation of an allelic ladder requires sampling many members of the population, with the aim of representing the most common alleles within the ladder — this amount of sampling can be an issue if the population, or number of surviving members of the species, is small. These steps provide a flavor of the amount of work required to develop an STR multiplex for a species. It is substantial and requires much time and resources for a species that might be encountered relatively infrequently in forensic investigations. The development of a STR multiplex where full validation has been undertaken is for domestic dogs (Berger *et al.*, 2008). Readers should look at this reference by Berger *et al.* (2008) to understand the steps needed to develop and ultimately publish a novel multiplex. Consideration should be given to the fact that dog hairs are encountered frequently in forensic investigations relating to an offence against a human rather than wildlife. There is therefore a rationale for a multiplex to be developed for this non-human species. It is worth considering the work required for a species that is encountered for the first time and may not be encountered again in the foreseeable future.

Given that a number of polymorphic STR loci have been characterized, what would be the significance of a match between an unknown sample and a reference profile at all alleles detected? This estimation only can be addressed through the development of an allele frequency database. Typically a minimum of 100–200 individuals is sampled to determine the occurrence of an allele within the population. Many of the species encountered in wildlife forensic science are endangered and the populations may be small in the first instance, therefore finding 100 'unrelated' individuals may be problematic. Having constructed a database, the typical tests of departure from Hardy–Weinberg Equilibrium (HWE) are performed. These include a test for homozygosity, as well as an indication of the probability that an allele seen in two different members of the population is identical by descent, rather than by chance (i.e. they have a recent common ancestor). Small, isolated populations are anticipated to exhibit loci with much higher numbers of homozygotes than larger out-breeding populations, and also much allele sharing within sub-populations. Kinship factors (F_{ST} or θ) of 0.0625 are not uncommon in small wildlife populations; which assumes all members of the population are second cousins. This value compares with a kinship factor of 0.01 that is applied to large human populations and 0.03 to smaller isolated human populations (Buckelton *et al.*, 2005). Fisher's Exact Test is a standard test applied in human identification and should be used in non-human species.

It is essential to determine if any of the loci are genetically linked. If the chromosomal locations of the loci are not known, then genetic linkage can be assessed by studying inheritance patterns across generations and performing standard linkage tests (Hedrick, 2005).

If STR loci have been characterized comprehensively as described, then (and only then) it will be possible to perform genetic testing using the product rule. The product rule assumes that all STR loci in the multiplex are inherited independently. Multiplication of the genotype frequencies assesses the probability that an unknown sample comes from a known individual compared to the probability that it comes from any other member of the population. The appropriate equation is the same as that used in human identification, which incorporates a θ value, and reported as a LR. The wording of any report or statement should adopt the same approach as used for human identification. Typically the wording would be:

> *"A DNA profile from sample X was found to match reference sample Y at all loci tested. These are the data expected if sample X came from reference sample Y rather than coming from any other member of the species. If sample X did not come from reference sample Y then it must match by chance. It is estimated that the results are x times more likely under the hypothesis that sample X comes from reference sample Y than under the hypothesis of coming from an unrelated member of the same species."*

3.3 *Geographical or Population Assignment*

It may be that a seized sample could be linked to a particular population or geographical region. The information about provenance can demonstrate whether a crime has, or has not, been committed.

An example is the scenario where a fish has allegedly been harvested from an area where the species can be caught legally, but is suspected to have actually been caught illegally in a protected no-fishing zone. Further examples include: the provenance of timber from specific sustainable forests, rather than unregulated illegal logging; aiding in determining hot spots of elephant poaching for the illegal ivory trade; and determining which sub-species is present within a sample. This determination is particularly important when one species, or sub-species, warrants protection and the other does not.

Tigers are an example of the latter scenario, as there are four recognized sub-species of tiger in the wild; the Sumatran tiger (*Panthera tigris sumatrae*), the Bengal tiger (*P. t. tigris*), the Indo-Chinese tiger (*P. t. corbetti*), and the Siberian tiger (*P. t. altica*). There are minor differences within the mitochondrial genome between these sub-species that can be used to confidently distinguish the sub-species (Kitpipit *et al.*, 2012a). As these sub-species do not overlap in their current geographic range, sub-species and hence geographical provenance can be reported based on the sequences in their mitochondrial genome (Kitpipit *et al.*, 2012b). Although all sub-species of tiger are protected, it may be that geographical information adds an extra level to the criminal allegations.

Discrete populations that are geographically separated but members of the same species, such as current tiger populations, are ideal for population assignment. Such separation is rarely the case, and two or more populations may overlap, leading to the possibility of false positive assignment to a particular population. The genetic marker(s) chosen is important, as sub-populations of the same species may be recently separated and only show variation due to genetic drift in loci where there is no selection. The non-coding D-loop within the mitochondrial genome is an option for recently separated populations. Sequence analysis of this locus was applied to the Chinese sika deer, *Cervus nippon*, which is classified into four sub-species (Wu *et al.*, 2005). Populations of this deer species were decimated due to illegal hunting to supply the traditional medicine trade. The result is two sub-species that no longer exist in the wild, but only in captivity where they are bred in large numbers for supposed medicinal use. The remaining two sub-species that survive in the wild are critically endangered and protected by Chinese law. To enforce this conservation legislation, a method to discriminate one of the wild subspecies from one of the domesticated subspecies was developed based on variation in the D-loop sequence.

A number of single nucleotide polymorphisms (SNPs) have been developed to distinguish between salmon species for the prosecution of illegal fishing in the NW Pacific (Withler *et al.*, 2004). Large databases have been established for populations of these salmon (Seeb *et al.*, 2007), but applications are currently limited for endangered species where data are difficult to collect.

The software package STRUCTURE was developed for assignment of an unknown sample to a particular population (Manel *et al.*, 2002; Pritchard *et al.*, 2000). An excellent overview of this software can be found in (Porras-Hurtado *et al.*, 2013). This software uses a Bayesian approach to compare genetic data coming from one population with that coming from any other population. Necessarily, the software relies on data for the chosen population. The end point is a probability of assignment to a population. An example of a report from this type of study might be:

> *"A DNA profile from sample X was found to match references from population Y. These are the data expected if sample X came from a member of population Y rather than coming from any other population for which there are data. If sample X did not come from a member of population Y then it must match by chance. It is estimated that the chance that sample X comes from member of population Y is greater than Z."*

4 Conclusion

The need to investigate and enforce legislation to tackle the illegal trade in wildlife and wildlife related products is ever increasing. A dedicated few laboratories offer assistance, with far fewer gaining accreditation for their processes. Determining the species-origin of an unknown item remains the most commonly requested type of laboratory analysis. The ability to identify a population from which a seized item most likely originated is gaining increasing interest as an investigative tool. Many of the methods used in forensic wildlife investigations were developed originally for conservation biology purposes. They therefore need to demonstrate adherence to the high standards required by the forensic genetic community and the criminal justice system. In the future wildlife forensic science, and in particular the application of DNA-based methods to this area of forensic science, will be considered as valuable and as reliable as any other mainstream forensic discipline.

References

G. C. Allen, M. A. Flores-Vergara, S. Krasynanski, S. Kumar and W. F. Thompson. A modified protocol for rapid DNA isolation from plant tissues using cetyltrimethylammonium bromide. *Nature Protocols*, 1:2320–2325, 2006.

R. Andreassen, J. Schregel, A. Kopatz, C. Tobiassen, P. M. Knappskog, S. B. Hagen, *et al.* A forensic DNA profiling system for Northern European brown bears (Ursus arctos). *Forensic Science International-Genetics*, 6:798–809, 2012.

B. Berger, C. Eichmann and W. Parson. Forensic Canine STR Analysis. In Coyle H, editor. *Nonhuman DNA typing*. Boca Raton: CRC Press; 2008.

M. I. Bidartondo, T. D. Bruns, M. Blackwell, I. Edwards, A. F. S. Taylor, T. Horton, *et al.* Preserving accuracy in GenBank. *Science*, 319:1616, 2008.

J. Buckelton, C. M. Triggs and S. J. Walsh. *Forensic DNA Evidence Evaluation*. Boca Raton: CRC Press; 2005.

B. Budowle, P. Garofano, A. Hellman, M. Ketchum, S. Kanthaswamy, W. Parson, *et al.* Recommendations for animal DNA forensic and identity testing. *International Journal of Legal Medicine*, 119:295–302, 2005.

J. Chun-Lee, L. C. Tsai, Y. Y. Kuan, W. H. Chien, K. T. Chang, C. H. Wu, *et al.* Racing pigeon identification using STR and chromo-helicase DNA binding gene markers. Electrophoresis, 28:4274–4281, 2007.

N. Coomber, V. A. David, S. J. O'Brien and M. Menotti-Raymond. Validation of a short tandem repeat multiplex typing system for genetic individualization of domestic cat samples. *Croatian Medical Journal*, 48:547–555, 2007.

H. Coyle. *Nonhuman DNA Typing. International Forensic Science and Investigation Series*. Boca Raton: CRC Press; 2008.

N. Dawnay, R. Ogden, R. McEwing, G. R. Carvalho and R. S. Thorpe. Validation of the barcoding gene COI for use in forensic genetic species identification. *Forensic Science International*,173:1–6, 2007.

N. Dawnay, R. Ogden, R. S. Thorpe, L. C. Pope, D. A. Dawson and R. McEwing. A forensic STR profiling system for the Eurasian badger: A framework for developing profiling systems for wildlife species. *Forensic Science International-Genetics*, 2:47–53, 2008.

N. Dawnay, R. Ogden, J. H. Wetton, R. S. Thorpe and R. McEwing. Genetic data from 28 STR loci for forensic individual identification and parentage analyses in 6 bird of prey species. *Forensic Sci Int Genet*, 3:e63–e69, 2009.

P. Dimsoski. Development of a 17-plex microsatellite polymerase chain reaction kit for genotyping horses. *Croatian Medical Journal*, 44:332–335, 2003.

J. J. Ely, D. L. Gonzalez, A. Reeves-Daniel and W. H. Stone. Individual identification and paternity determination in chimpanzees (Pantroglodytes) using human short tandem repeat (STR) markers. *International Journal of Primatology*, 19:255–271, 1998.

M. C. M. Eurlings, H. H. van Beek and B. Gravendeel. Polymorphic microsatellites for forensic identification of agarwood (Aquilaria crassna). *Forensic Science International*, 197:30–34, 2010.

P. Forster. To Err is Human. *Annals of Human Genetics*, 67:2–4, 2003.

C. K. Harper, G. J. Vermeulen, A. B. Clarke, J. I. De Wet and A. J. Guthrie. Extraction of nuclear DNA from rhinoceros horn and characterization of DNA profiling systems for white (Ceratotherium simum) and black (Diceros bicornis) rhinoceros. *Forensic Science International: Genetics*, 7:428–433, 2013.

D. J. Harris. Can you bank on GenBank? Trends in Ecology and Evolution,18:317–319, 2003.

D. Hawk. Society for Wildife Forensic Science. In: J. Huffman, J. Wallace, editors. *Wildlife Forensics*. Chichester, UK: Wiley-Blackwell, p. 15–34, 2012.

D. Hawk. *Wildlife Forensics: Methods and Applications*. Wiley-Blackwell, 2012.

P. D. N. Hebert, A. Cywinska, S. L. Ball and J. R. DeWaard. Biological identifications through DNA barcodes. *Proceedings of the Royal Society B-Biological Sciences* ,270:313–321, 2003.

P. D. N. Hebert, S. Ratnasingham and J. R. de Waard. Barcoding animal life: cytochrome c oxidase subunit 1 divergences among closely related species. *Proceedings of the Royal Society of London Series B: Biological Sciences*, 270:S96–S99, 2003.

P. D. N. Hebert, M. Y. Stoeckle, T. S. Zemlak and C. M. Francis. Identification of birds through DNA barcodes. *PLoS Biology*, 2:1657–1663, 2004.

P. W. Hedrick. Genetics of Populations. Sudbury: Jones and Bartlett, 2005.

H.-M. Hsieh, H.-L. Chiang, L.-C. Tsai, S.-Y. Lai, N.-E. Huang, A. Linacre, *et al.* Cytochrome b gene for species identification of the conservation animals. *Forensic Science International*, 122:7–18, 2001.

H. M. Hsieh, R. J. Hou, L. C. Tsai, C. S. Wei, S. W. Liu, L. H. Huang, *et al.* A highly polymorphic STR locus in Cannabis sativa. *Forensic Science International*, 131:53–58, 2003.

H.-M. Hsieh, L.-H. Huang, L.-C. Tsai, Y.-C. Kuo, H.-H. Meng, A. Linacre, *et al.* Species identification of rhinoceros horns using the cytochrome b gene. Forensic Science International, 136:1–11, 2003.

H. M. Hsieh, L. H. Huang, L. C. Tsai, C. L. Liu, Y. C. Kuo, C. T. Hsiao, *et al.* Species identification of Kachuga tecta using the cytochrome b gene. *Journal of Forensic Sciences*, 51:52–56, 2006.

N. V. Ivanova, E. L. Clare and A. V. Borisenko. DNA barcoding in mammals. *Methods In Molecular Biology* (Clifton, NJ), 858:153–182, 2012.

A. Iyengar. Forensic DNA analysis for animal protection and biodiversity conservation: A review. *Journal for Nature Conservation*. 22:195–205, 2014.

R. N. Johnson, L. Wilson-Wilde and A. Linacre. Current and future directions of DNA in wildlife forensic science. *Forensic Science International: Genetics*, 10:1–11, 2014.

S. Kanthaswamy, B. K. Tom, A. M. Mattila, E. Johnston, M. Dayton, J. Kinaga, *et al.* Canine Population Data Generated from a Multiplex STR Kit for Use in Forensic Casework. *Journal of Forensic Sciences*, 54: 829-40, 2009.

T. Kitpipit and A. Linacre. The complete mitochondrial genome analysis of the tiger (Panthera tigris). *Molecular Biology Reports*, 39:5745–5754, 2012.

T. Kitpipit, S. S. Tobe, A. C. Kitchener, P. Gill and A. Linacre. The development and validation of a single SNaPshot multiplex for tiger species and subspecies identification-Implications for forensic purposes. *Forensic Science International: Genetics*,6:250–257, 2012.

W. J. Kress, K.J. Wurdack, E. A. Zimmer, L. A. Weigt and D. H. Janzen. Use of DNA barcodes to identify flowering plants. *Proceedings of the National Academy of Sciences of the United States of America*, 102:8369–8374, 2005.

K. Lazaruk, J. Wallin, C. Holt, T. Nguyen and P. S. Walsh. Sequence variation in humans and other primates at six short tandem repeat loci used in forensic identity testing. *Forensic Science International*,119:1–10, 2001.

J. Lee, H. M. Hsieh, L. H. Huang, Y. C. Kuo, J. H. Wu, S. C. Chin, *et al.* Ivory identification by DNA profiling of cytochrome b gene. *International Journal of Legal Medicine*, 123:117–21, 2009.

J. C. I. Lee, L. C. Tsai, C. Y. Yang, C. L. Liu, L. H. Huang, A. Linacre, *et al.* DNA profiling of shahtoosh. *Electrophoresis*, 27:3359–3362, 2006.

Y. C. Lin, H. M. Hsieh, J. C. I. Lee, C. T. Hsiao, D. Y. Lin, A. Linacre, *et al.* Establishing a DNA identification system for pigs (Sus scrofa) using a multiplex STR amplification. *Forensic Science International: Genetics*, 9:12–19, 2014.

A. Linacre, L. Gusmão, W. Hecht, A. P. Hellmann, W. R. Mayr, W. Parson, *et al.* ISFG: Recommendations regarding the use of non-human (animal) DNA in forensic genetic investigations. *Forensic Science International Genetics*. 2010.

A. M. Linacre and S. S. Tobe. *Wildlife DNA Analysis*. Chichester, UK: John Wilely & Sons, 2013.

C. F. Lo, Y. R. Lin, H. C. Chang and J. H. Lin. Identification of turtle shell and its preparations by PCR-DNA sequencing method. *Journal of Food and Drug Analysis*, 14:153–158, 2006.

M. S. Longo, M. J. O'Neill and R. J. O'Neill. Abundant human DNA contamination identified in non-primate genome databases. *PLoS ONE*, 6, 2011.

S. Manel, P. Berthier and G. Luikart. Detecting wildlife poaching: Identifying the origin of individuals with Bayesian assignment tests and multilocus genotypes. *Conservation Biology*, 16:650–659, 2002.

J. D. McPherson, M. Marra, L. Hillier, RH. Waterston, A. Chinwalla, J. Wallis, *et al.* A physical map of the human genome. *Nature*, 409:934–941, 2001.

M. MenottiRaymond, V. A. David, J. C. Stephens, L. A. Lyons and S. J. Obrien. Genetic individualization of domestic cats using feline STR loci for forensic applications. *Journal of Forensic Sciences*, 42:1039–1051, 1997.

M. Menotti-Raymond, V. A. David, B. S. Weir and S. J. O'Brien. A Population Genetic Database of Cat Breeds Developed in Coordination with a Domestic Cat STR Multiplex. *Journal of Forensic Sciences*, 57:596–601, 2012.

M. A. Menotti-Raymond, V. A. David, L. A. Lyons, A. A. Schaffer, J. F. Tomlin, M. K. Hutton, *et al.* A genetic linkage map of microsatellites in the domestic cat (Felis catus). Genomics, 57:9–23, 1999.

M. A. Menotti-Raymond, V. A. David and S. J. O'Brien. STR-Based Forensic Analysis of Felid Samples from Domstic and Exotic Cats. In: HM. Coyle, editor. *Nonhuman DNA Typing*. Boca Raton: CRC Press, 2008.

M. A. Menotti-Raymond, V. A. David, L. L. Wachter, J. M. Butler and S. J. O'Brien. An STIR forensic typing system for genetic individualization of domestic cat (Felis catus) samples. *Journal of Forensic Sciences*, 50: 1061–1070, 2005.

National Research Council of the National Academies. *Strengthening Forensic Science in the United States: A Path Forward.* Washington D.C.: National Academies Press, 2009

R. Ogden. Forensic science, genetics and wildlife biology: getting the right mix for a wildlife DNA forensics lab. *Forensic Science Medicine and Pathology,* 6:172–179, 2010.

S. Pääbo, J. A. Gifford and A. C. Wilson. Mitochondrial DNA sequences from a 7000-year old brain. *Nucleic Acids Research,* 16:9775–9787, 1988.

W. Parson, K. Pegoraro, H. Niederstatter, M. Foger and M. Steinlechner. Species identification by means of the cytochrome b gene. *International Journal of Legal Medicine,* 114:23–28, 2000.

L. Porras-Hurtado, Y. Ruiz, C. Santos, C. Phillips, Á. Carracedo and M. Lareu. An overview of STRUCTURE: Applications, parameter settings and supporting software. *Frontiers in Genetics,* 4, 2013.

J. K. Pritchard, M. Stephens and P. Donnelly. Inference of population structure using multilocus genotype data. *Genetics,* 155:945–959, 2000.

L. W. Seeb, A. Antonovich, M. A. Banks, T. D. Beacham, M. R. Bellinger, S. M. Blankenship, *et al.* Development of a standardized DNA database for chinook salmon. *Fisheries,* 32:540–552, 2007.

A. Singh, A. Gaur, K. Shailaja, B. S. Bala and L. Singh. Novel microsatellite (STR) marker for forensic identification of big cats in India. *Forensic Science International,* 141:143–147, 2004.

Strengthening Forensic Science in the United States: A Path Forward. Washington, DC: National Academies Press, 2009.

Z. Szabolcsi, B. Egyed, P. Zenke, A. Borsy, Z. Pádár, L. Zöldág, *et al.* Genetic identification of red deer using autosomal STR markers. *Forensic Science International: Genetics Supplement Series,* 1:623–624, 2008.

S. S. Tobe and A. Linacre. A method to identify a large number of mammalian species in the UK from trace samples and mixtures without the use of sequencing. *Forensic Science International: Genetics Supplement Series,* 1: 625–627, 2008.

S. S. Tobe and A. Linacre. DNA typing in wildlife crime: recent developments in species identification. *Forensic Science Medicine and Pathology,* 6:195–206, 2010.

S. S. Tobe and A. M. T. Linacre. A multiplex assay to identify 18 European mammal species from mixtures using the mitochondrial cytochrome b gene. *Electrophoresis,* 29:340–347, 2008.

B. van Asch, C. Albarran, A. Alonso, R. Angulo, C. Alves, E. Betancor, *et al.* Forensic analysis of dog (Canis lupus familiaris) mitochondrial DNA sequences: An inter-laboratory study of the GEP-ISFG working group. *Forensic Science International: Genetics*, 4:49–54, 2009.

B. van Asch, C. Alves, L. Gusmao, V. Pereira, F. Pereira and A. Amorim. A new autosomal STR nineplex for canine identification and parentage testing. *Electrophoresis*, 30:417–423, 2009.

B. van Asch, C. Alves, L. Santos, R. Pinheiro, F. Pereira, L. Gusmao, *et al.* Genetic profiles and sex identification of found-dead wolves determined by the use of an 11-loci PCR multiplex. *Forensic Science International-Genetics*, 4:68–72, 2010.

L. H. P. van de Goor, H. Panneman and W. A. van Haeringen. A proposal for standardization in forensic equine DNA typing: allele nomenclature for 17 equine-specific STR loci. *Animal Genetics*, 41:122–127, 2010.

L. H. P. van de Goor, H. Panneman and W. A. van Haeringen. A proposal for standardization in forensic bovine DNA typing: allele nomenclature of 16 cattle-specific short tandem repeat loci. *Animal Genetics*, 40:630–636, 2009.

C. Van Oosterhout, W. F. Hutchinson, D. P. M. Wills and P. Shipley. MICRO-CHECKER: Software for identifying and correcting genotyping errors in microsatellite data. *Molecular Ecology Notes*, 4:535–538, 2004.

S. K. Wasser, A. M. Shedlock, K. Comstock, E. A. Ostrander, B. Mutayoba and M. Stephens. Assigning African elephant DNA to geographic region of origin: Applications to the ivory trade. *Proceedings of the National Academy of Sciences of the United States of America*, 101:14847–14852, 2004.

N. E. White, R. Dawson, M. L. Coghlan, S. R. Tridico, P. R. Mawson, J. Haile, *et al.* Application of STR markers in wildlife forensic casework involving Australian black-cockatoos (Calyptorhynchus spp.). *Forensic Science International: Genetics*, 6:664–670, 2012.

L. Wilson-Wilde, J. Norman, J. Robertson, S. Sarre and A. Georges. Current issues in species identification for forensic science and the validity of using the cytochrome oxidase I (COI) gene. *Forensic Science Medicine and Pathology*, 6:233–241, 2010.

R. E. Withler, J. R. Candy, T. D. Beacham and K. M. Miller. Forensic DNA analysis of Pacific salmonid samples for species and stock identification. *Environmental Biology of Fishes*, 69:275–285, 2004.

H. Wu, Q. H. Wan, S. G. Fang and S. Y. Zhang. Application of mitochondrial DNA sequence analysis in the forensic identification of Chinese sika deer subspecies. *Forensic Science International*, 148:101–105, 2005.

CHAPTER 19

The Application of Forensic Animal DNA Analysis in Criminal and Civil Investigations

Robert Oldt[*], *Jillian Ng*[*] *and Sree Kanthaswamy*[†,‡,§]

[*]*Molecular Anthropology Laboratory,*
University of California, Davis, CA, USA
[†]*School of Mathematical and Natural Sciences,*
New College of Interdisciplinary Arts and Sciences
[‡]*Arizona State University (ASU)*
Glendale, AZ, USA
[§]*sree.kanthaswamy@asu.edu*

Recognition of human DNA analysis as an indispensable tool in forensic investigation has opened new avenues for non-human genetic analyses. Of the forensic specialties, animal DNA analysis stands as a fairly recent but powerful field. Animal forensic genetics is defined as "the application of relevant genetic techniques and theory to legal matters, or enforcement issues, concerning animal biological material" (International Society for Animal Genetics, 2008).

The advancement of animal forensic genetics has been two-fold. On one level, being able to have reliable animal models is a major support to human forensic study. By analyzing genetic variation in these animals, researchers are able to explore relevant genetic concepts while developing procedures and tools for human application. For example, DNA left at crime scenes is often low quality; experimenting on animal samples can provide better extraction and amplification measures (Dayton *et al.*, 2009). Variable components of our genome, such as single nucleotide polymorphisms (SNPs) and microsatellites, are similarly present in animals, allowing for the development of identification methods and computational programs based on these variations.

The second and most explicit success in animal forensic genetics has been the direct use of animal samples in forensic investigations. Both of these steps have always developed in parallel with each other rather than one preceding the other. This topic is multi-faceted ranging from animal trade, issues of food composition, cases of human-on-animal and animal-on-human violence, and use of animal biological material to place a suspect at a crime scene. Of the two divisions of forensic animal DNA analysis, this one forms the core of the field and will be the main focus of this chapter.

1 Animals in Forensic Investigations

Even before the acceleration of DNA analysis, animal forensics was a burgeoning field in forensics. Animals deposit a variety of biological material into their environment which can be used in legal proceedings (D'Andrea *et al.*, 1998). In the US, 40 million households have at least one cat and 57 million households have a dog (American Pet Products Association, 2014). These numbers are comparable to the population of over 60 million pet cats and dogs living in the EU (FEDIAF The European Pet Food Industry, 2012). Locard's Exchange Principle dictates that an individual at a crime scene will exchange physical materials with the surroundings (James *et al.*, 2003). This Principle, taken with the fact that animal hair and dander is one of the most commonly recovered types of trace evidence, makes animal biological material invaluable for forensic analyses as long as the animal evidence can be identified and separated from human biological evidence (Halverson and Basten, 2005; Smalling *et al.*, 2010).

Before molecular-based techniques, such as DNA and proteins, entered the animal forensics arena, scientists relied on the morphological characteristics of samples to determine their animal origin. However, the usefulness of samples was constricted as the methods could only identify the sample down to the species level, and at times the breed level (Peabody *et al.*, 1983). Even the first molecular approaches to animal identification, such as isoelectric focusing of keratin in hair samples, only provided species identification (Carracedo *et al.*, 1987). For maximum utility, samples need to be traced to an individual animal.

2 Animal Genetic Individualization

The capability to individualize animals for forensic purposes established itself almost as soon as human DNA fingerprinting using variable number tandem repeats (VNTRs) for forensic investigations (Jeffreys *et al.*, 1985). As part of this process, oligonucleotide probes were designed to target genomic regions that demonstrate high levels of variability. The variability included a differing number of tandem repeats as well as the presence, absence and identity of SNPs. Just as humans could be identified to the individual level using this strategy, so could animals. Introduction of the same probes to animal DNA yielded similarly useful multilocus results that were individual-specific (Jeffreys and Morton, 1987). As the technology and field of animal DNA science improved, specialized species-specific markers were developed for companion animals such as dogs and cats, as well as a variety of domestic and wild animals (Menotti-Raymond *et al.*, 2005; van de Goor *et al.*, 2011a, 2011b; Ogden *et al.*, 2012).

Similar to humans, expanded genetic profiling of animals has resulted in allele frequency reference databases (Kanthaswamy *et al.*, 2009; van de Goor *et al.*, 2011b; Menotti-Raymond *et al.*, 2012; Wictum *et al.*, 2013). Allele and haplotype frequencies were determined by examining the variability in nuclear and mitochondrial DNA (Smalling *et al.*, 2010). The growth and maintenance of these information banks enable robust random match probability calculations that are essential for forensic analyses. Databases of allele information also have allowed researchers to conveniently categorize animals by species and breed, generate evolutionary relationships between populations and species, and to study biodiversity and animal trade (Kanthaswamy *et al.*, 2009; van de Goor *et al.*, 2011b; Menotti-Raymond *et al.*, 2012; Wictum *et al.*, 2013).

3 Using Nuclear DNA

For individualization, nuclear DNA (nuDNA) is the preferred genomic medium since its abundance of non-coding DNA can accumulate variability due to low selective-constraints. Variations, including insertions and deletions (indels), SNPs and repetitive elements, are frequently different from individual-to-individual even with the higher degree of inbreeding that occurs with most domestic animals. Therefore, markers designed targeting these variations as highly discriminatory and of great utility for forensic analyses (University of North Texas Center for Human Identification, 2007).

Of all the types of genetic variants, microsatellites or STRs have proven to be the most useful for individual identification. In addition, STR loci can be used to test inheritance patterns and linkage. Successful markers are pooled together and amplified in a premixed primer kit, simplifying amplification and sample processing. While some animals, such as dogs (Wictum *et al.*, 2013), cats (Menotti-Raymond *et al.*, 2005), cattle (Thermo Scientific Bovine Genotypes Panel 3.1) and horses (Thermo Scientific Equine Genotypes Panel 1.1), have commercially available DNA typing kits, there are still many species for which there is little STR loci characterization. In these cases, STR loci must be identified, analyzed and assessed for forensic applications prior to use in accordance with the Scientific Working Group on DNA Analysis Methods (2012) guidelines.

While having developed alongside similar forensic genetic techniques such as STRs, SNPs and mitochondrial DNA (mtDNA) in humans, there are still some significant differences between human and animal genetic applications. Though both human and animal identification analyses utilize STR markers, different repeat motifs are targeted in animal DNA testing; human analyses rely primarily on tetranucleotide repeats while dinucleotide repeats are often used with animals (Budowle *et al.*, 2005). Despite being problematic with issues such as increased stutter peaks (Carracedo and Lareu, 1998), dinucleotide STRs are most commonly isolated and recommended for animal use by the International Society of Animal Genetics (van de Goor *et al.*, 2009; Andreassen *et al.*, 2012). For example, dinucleotide repeats are the predominant class of STRs in equine species (Chen *et al.*, 2010) and they also have been shown to be more effective in typing samples such as hair and feces due to their shorter amplicon sizes (Taberlet *et al.*, 1996).

Animals kept in captivity or sold commercially can be genotyped to build an allele frequency database of sufficient size. Clearly, this task can be difficult for rare or endangered species where population size is limited. In such cases, unrelated individual animals can be sampled and genotyped and shared alleles assumed to be identical-by-descent. To appropriately estimate the degree of genetic relatedness between any two individuals in a population, a kinship factor can be used to account for population structure. Population sub-structuring can be determined by calculating FST, which estimates differentiation by comparing a subgroup's genetic variance to the variance of the entire population (Wright, 1951, 1978; Holsinger and Weir, 2009). For limited size populations, a high-relatedness level should be assumed for these groups as allele frequencies can be skewed due to inbreeding and differentiation (Johnson *et al.*, 2014).

4 Using Mitochondrial DNA

While nuDNA (nuclear DNA) methods allow for easier individual identification of a species, mtDNA is best suited for speciation and investigations where nuDNA is too degraded for adequate characterization. Additionally, mtDNA is a powerful tool in wildlife investigations. While nuDNA for many wild species is relatively uncharacterized, mtDNA has been frequently studied for species assignment purposes (Tobe and Linacre, 2008; Johnson *et al.*, 2014).

The two markers often targeted in animal mtDNA analysis are cytochrome oxidase B (CYTB) and cytochrome c oxidase I (*COX1* or *COI*), two genes integral to the mitochondrial electron transport chain (Hsieh *et al.*, 2001; Dawnay *et al.*, 2007). Though both markers are useful in species testing, there is debate as to which locus is better. Recent research suggests that CYTB offers higher informational value in a smaller fragment, making it more useful for trace animal samples (Tobe *et al.*, 2009). On the other hand, *COI* is the preferred locus of the Barcode for Life Consortium for species identification and biodiversity preservation (Hebert *et al.*, 2003b). Also of note is the mitochondrial D-loop (also often referred to as the "control region"): the hypervariable, non-coding region of mtDNA that allows for more precise identification beyond the species level. This region is used to establish haplotypes in humans and can similarly be used for breed and subpopulation identification in animals (Pun *et al.*, 2009).

Whereas nuDNA relies on STRs for identification, mtDNA utilizes SNPs for speciation and to a limited degree lineage analyses. Individual species have been shown to contain SNPs that are species-specific (Kitpipit *et al.*, 2012). Such SNPs are found by aligning sequences from multiple species and searching for a novel nucleotide difference at each position (Figure 1). SNPs are highly informative and can be used to create phylogenetic trees that illustrate species relatedness and differentiation. Due to its taxonomic usefulness, a wealth of mitochondrial data already exists that can be used for forensic investigations. For instance, the GenBank database (Benson *et al.*, 2013) allows for the alignment of large amounts of mtDNA sequences

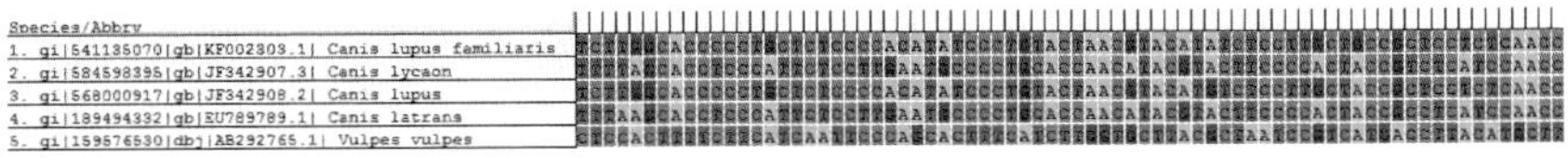

Figure 1: Individual canid species including *Canis lupus familiaris* (domestic dog), *C. lycaon* (Eastern wolf), *C. lupus* (Grey wolf), *C. latrans* (coyote) and *Vulpes vulpes* (fox) exhibit mtDNA SNPs that are species-specific.

Note: Alignment and phylogenetic analyses were performed using MEGA v5.2 (Tamura *et al.*, 2011).

and for the search of species specific SNPs. However, there may be a lack of information on wild and exotic species compared to animals used as livestock, companion animals, or research models.

In comparison to nuDNA and the hypervariable region within the mtDNA, most regions of the mitochondrial genome are highly conserved across species and mutations in mitochondrial genes are often fatal. Because of this conservation, universal primers have been designed that work on ostensibly any animal (Tobe and Linacre, 2008), making mtDNA primer selection much less work-intensive. As primer selection is often challenging and time-consuming, having universal primers is vital for the fast turn-around of analysis of collected evidence.

Similar to human studies, mtDNA can be useful when analyzing highly degraded samples such as wildlife samples in particular, which suffer from low nuclear DNA amplification (Holland, 2001). A common example of mtDNA compensating for the lack of nuDNA is in hair samples. Often, animal hair left at a crime scene was not plucked but shed naturally. Plucked hair samples have roots or hair follicles containing keratinocytes that contain nuDNA while shed hairs, i.e. telogenic or non-growing hairs, tend not to have follicular material, making shed hair unlikely to yield full nuclear profiles. Non-plucked hair, however, has mitochondria that can be used to generate mtDNA profiles for speciation but not individualization (Angleby and Savolainen, 2005; Roberts and Calloway, 2007).

Besides the inability to individualize a sample, other potential limitations prevent animal mtDNA from precisely and confidently matching a sample to its source. The human mtDNA control region, though only rarely able to identify an individual, is excellent for haplotype analysis. In forensic investigations where only mtDNA is recovered, the haplotype may be specific enough to generate a relatively high random match probability score typically limited by reference database size (van Oven and Kayser, 2009). In animals, using haplotypes for forensic analyses can be much more difficult since domestic animals, like cats and dogs, have fewer haplotypes and many animals share the same haplotype (Wetton *et al.*, 2003). Therefore, the technique's usefulness is limited — although in a small amount of cases, such as Westerfield *vs.* Superior Court (2002), animal haplotyping was key to securing a verdict.

5 Animal DNA Recommendations

The International Society for Forensic Genetics (ISFG) lists 13 recommendations for working with animal DNA in a forensic setting (Linacre *et al.*, 2011).

1. Procedures for sample collection should remain consistent regardless of sample purpose.
2. Reference samples should be from a known, validated source (a 'voucher specimen') if possible.
3. Loci choice should be chosen based on the potential to place an unknown sample correctly in a phylogeny.
4. The primer-binding sequence in the genome must be reported.
5. New primer sets should be tested for inter- and intra-species specificity. These tests should take sensitivity and reproducibility into account.
6. Primers should be published in the public domain.
7. Tetranucleotide STRs are favored for identification purposes when possible.
8. Allelic ladders are necessary when working with STRs so that alleles are properly called. The number of repeats is reported, not the total number of base pairs.
9. Mutation probabilities should be estimated where there is genetic inconsistency at one or more loci.
10. Enough individuals should be sampled to establish confident allele frequency estimates.
11. Allele frequencies need to be calculated with the use of a kinship factor.
12. To evaluate evidence significance, a match likelihood ratio (LR) is the recommended method.

13. The laboratory should be properly accredited for routine animal DNA use.

6 Applications of Animal Forensic Genetics

One of the first cases where animal DNA was applied to solve a case involved the illegal purchasing of cattle in the Basque Country, a region in the western Pyrenees between France and Spain. Six blood samples were submitted for genetic analysis, which were three samples from the suspected stolen animals and three from their alleged mothers. Analysis of four loci resulted in maternal matches for each of the animals, which was sufficient to support that the animals were stolen (Beamonte *et al.*, 1995).

Arguably the most famous animal DNA case is that of Snowball the cat, which was the first to use animal DNA to solve a human-on-human crime. In 1994, on Prince Edward Island in eastern Canada, the body of a woman was found in a shallow grave. The authorities also found a bloody leather jacket that was used to cover the body. The jacket was believed to belong to the deceased's husband, the main suspect of the case. While the blood could be traced to the deceased woman, the actual ownership of the jacket could not be deduced. In addition to blood, white hairs were found in the jacket and were discovered to have originated from a cat. Though the suspect did not have a cat, his parents, whom he had been living with, owned a white cat named Snowball. Snowball's blood was analyzed and compared to the hair samples found in the jacket. The samples matched perfectly at the 10 dinucleotide STR loci tested, concretely linking the suspect to the crime and resulting in his conviction (Menotti-Raymond *et al.*, 1997). Since these early undertakings, animal genetics has branched out to assist in multiple forensic specialties.

7 Biodiversity Efforts and Food Regulation

The end goal of these nuclear and mitochondrial DNA methods is to enable a fast and confident match of an evidentiary sample to a reference sample. Once enough samples of a species or subgroup are analyzed, databases can be established that support matching a sample profile to an existing profile or calculate random match probabilities from the stored allele frequencies. This database development makes large-scale handling of species information possible. The capability of matching genetic material to prior collected data is essential for monitoring animal populations and conservation efforts, ensuring proper food regulations, and cataloguing the wealth of Earth's organismal diversity.

The grey wolf is considered an endangered species in almost every one of its natural territories. One of these territories is Yellowstone National Park, which has not had a wolf pack since 1926. In 1995, 31 individuals were reintroduced to the area as part of a restoration project (Smith *et al.*, 2011). The population was characterized at 26 STR markers for a decade to monitor genetic diversity. These data can be used to explore the impact of behavioral patterns and to monitor inbreeding. At the end of the reintroduction period, the population contained high diversity, low inbreeding and pronounced population expansion. Even though there is a high chance of in-pack breeding, the researchers found that the wolves avoided inbreeding by having the males disperse to mate with non-related females in other packs. Currently, the grey wolf population in Yellowstone is one of the most diverse wolf populations in the world (Vonholdt *et al.*, 2008).

In 2013, the United Kingdom was at the center of an international food scandal concerning unlabeled horsemeat. While horsemeat is safe to consume, the scandal raised many questions about how we regulate what is in our food. At one point, unlabeled horsemeat was found in almost 5% of beef products in Europe (European Commission, 2013). The European Union used species-specific quantitative real-time PCR targeting species-informative mtDNA to identify the species present in various meat products (European Union Reference Laboratory for Animal Proteins in feedstuffs, 2013). Since then, multiple companies have pledged to genetically test their meats to ensure their composition and proper labeling (York, 2013; BBC News, 2015).

The Consortium for the Barcode of Life is an international project that supports species identification, quantification and regulation through DNA "barcoding" of mtDNA (Hebert *et al.*, 2003a). The goal of the project is to have a well-maintained database of species mtDNA information so that any sample can be matched to a species. This capability has applications with the food industry (as discussed above) and biodiversity assessments. The initiative uses the *CO1* gene as its standard locus in each species (Hebert *et al.*, 2003b).

8 Human-on-Animal and Animal-on-Human Violence

Another avenue of animal forensics is using DNA markers to identify individual animals that are directly involved in crimes. This type of crime can either be violence directed at an animal or an attack on a human by an animal. In these cases, DNA can be extracted from biological evidence, such as saliva, blood, or hair, and be used to identify an individual animal or link an animal to a crime scene, victim, or suspect (Tsuji *et al.*, 2008; American Society for the Prevention of Cruelty to Animals (ASPCA), 2011; Bond, 2013).

Dog-on-human attacks are very common — about 4.5 million bite injuries occur per year in the US with 885,000 needing medical attention and 238 resulting in death (Centers for Disease Control and Prevention, 2003; Gilchrist *et al.*, 2008; American Society of Plastic Surgeons, 2012). The first use of animal DNA extracted from around a bite wound was introduced in a pit bull-mauling case in 1999. When the neighbors of the victim denied their pit bull's culpability, salivary DNA was extracted from the victim's clothing and compared to the pit bull's DNA. Profile comparisons consisting of alleles from 10 nuDNA STR markers matched at all loci between the two samples, providing the confidence required to link the neighbor's dog to the crime and resulting in the conviction of the neighbors (Eichmann *et al.*, 2004). Similar strategies have been applied to other cases involving owners of violent dogs (Padar *et al.*, 2002).

While animals are often the cause of human–animal violence, animals also can be victims as well. One particularly violent example of human-on-animal cruelty was a case of animal abuse in 2001. A nursing mother llama was found dead after being sodomized and beaten with a broken golf club and its cria alive but permanently blinded. DNA samples collected from the golf club and surrounding foliage matched the DNA profiles of the llamas, establishing the golf club as the murder weapon. One suspect, who denied any direct involvement in the crime after his partner was implicated, had a small blood spot on his shirt that, when profiled, placed him at the scene with probable participation in the act. Both perpetrators were convicted and served jail time (Quioco, 2001).

9 Using Animal DNA in Human Cases

The most appealing application of animal DNA in forensic investigation is the potential to tie a person to the scene where the crime was committed. In the early 2000s, a bouncer in the United Kingdom was stabbed to death outside of the pub where he worked. A blood trail that led away from the body was found to be canine in origin and not human. A man who was previously barred from the pub and known to own a dog was a prime suspect in this case. Samples from the blood trail and references from the suspect's dog were shipped to the University of California, Davis Veterinary Genetics Laboratory for analysis. DNA was extracted from the blood and the STR data matched the profile of the suspect's dog. It was later revealed that after being denied entry, the suspect stabbed the bouncer and wounded his own dog in the struggle (Agronis, 2002).

Of note is a criminal case, operating under the same principles as above, where nuclear DNA was inadequate and called for the use of mtDNA. In the case Westerfield *vs.* Superior Court (2002), a seven-year-old girl was kidnapped and murdered. One main piece of evidence in the case was dog hair that was found in the suspect's dryer vent and the victim had a pet dog while the suspect did not. A nuDNA STR profile could not be generated, so mtDNA was analyzed instead. The control region of the sample mtDNA was amplified and the haplotype that was found only occurred in 9% of dogs, including the victim's dog. This evidence was used to link Westerfield to the crime and secure a conviction (Westerfield *vs.* Superior Court, 2002).

10 Growing Challenges in the Field

Increasing interest in animal DNA use in forensics has proportional increases in challenges that the field of forensics must address or the specialty will remain underutilized. A major concern is the accreditation and growth of animal forensic labs. Most labs that analyze forensic animal samples do so infrequently and often do not have procedures for handling or processing evidentiary samples. These labs were established for general animal genetic testing and are not accredited for forensic services nor are the analysts trained or certified to conduct forensic tests. Accreditation for any laboratory is expensive and time-consuming, something that is not feasible for smaller labs and not worth the effort for labs that rarely analyze forensic samples. Moreover, there are few trained researchers who can make sense of animal evidence when it is often overwhelmed by non-evidence. These difficulties cause animal DNA analyses to be requested less frequently, which results in laboratories being reluctant to obtain accreditation and fewer certified experts in the field (Budowle *et al.*, 2005; Scharnhorst and Kanthaswamy, 2011).

As the field of animal forensics is not as developed as the "gold standard" human forensics, it is less accepted in the scientific community (Lynch, 2003) and runs the risk that evidence will not be found admissible in court. Animal DNA kits and genetic databases are are still lagging their human counterparts, which confirms how underdeveloped the field is currently. While databases exist for animals such as cats and dogs, they may not contain enough representative samples for robust forensic analyses. As laboratories continue to genetically profile animals following the ISFG recommendations, these databases will improve, which in turn will improve the forensic application of animal DNA analyses and the entire field of animal forensics.

References

A. Agronis. The blood wasn't human. *UC Davis Magazine*, 19: 2002.

American Pet Products Association. APPA releases 2013–14 National Pet Owners Survey. 2014. http://www.petfoodindustry.com/articles/3515-appa-releases-2013-14-national-pet-owners-survey, accessed March 6, 2016.

American Society for the Prevention of Cruelty to Animals (ASPCA). ASPCA announces first uses of DNA in trials of NYC animal cruelty cases. 2011. https://www.aspca.org/about-us/press-releases/aspca-announces-first-uses-dna-trials-nyc-animal-cruelty-cases, accessed March 6, 2016.

American Society of Plastic Surgeons. Plastic Surgery Statistics Report. 2012. http://www.plasticsurgery.org/Documents/news-resources/statistics/2012-Plastic-Surgery-Statistics/full-plastic-surgery-statistics-report.pdf, accessed March 6, 2016.

R. Andreassen, J. Schregel, A. Kopatz, C. Tobiassen, P. M. Knappskog, S. B. Hagen, O. Kleven, M. Schneider, I. Kojola, J. Aspi, A. Rykov, K. F. Tirronen, P. I. Danilov and H. G. Eiken. A forensic DNA profiling system for Northern European brown bears (Ursus arctos). *Forensic Sci Int Genet*, 6:798–809, 2012.

H. Angleby and P. Savolainen. Forensic informativity of domestic dog mtDNA control region sequences. *Forensic Sci Int*, 154:99–110, 2005.

BBC News. DNA meat tests: Ireland's growing appetite for food chain checks. 2015. http://www.bbc.com/news/world-europe-31504213, accessed March 6, 2016.

D. Beamonte, A. Guerra, B. Ruiz and J. Alemany. Microsatellite DNA polymorphism analysis in a case of an illegal cattle purchase. *J Forensic Sci*, 40:692–694, 1995.

D. A. Benson, M. Cavanaugh, K. Clark, I. Karsch-Mizrachi, D. J. Lipman, J. Ostell and E. W. Sayers. GenBank. *Nucleic Acids Res*, 41:D36–D42, 2013.

A. Bond. DNA from a cat snares killer after its hair was found on victim's dismembered body. 2013. http://www.dailymail.co.uk/news/article-2392724/Cat-DNA-helps-convict-killer-David-Hilder-hair-victim-David-Guys-dismembered-body.html, accessed March 6, 2016.

B. Budowle, P. Garofano, A. Hellman, M. Ketchum, S. Kanthaswamy, W. Parson, W. van Haeringen, S. Fain and T. Broad. Recommendations for animal DNA forensic and identity testing. *Int J Legal Med*, 119:295–302, 2005.

A. Carracedo and M. V. Lareu. Development of new STRs for forensic case-work: criteria for selection, sequencing and population data and forensic validation. In *The Ninth International Symposium on Human Identification*, pp. 89–107, Orlando, CA, 1998.

A. Carracedo, J. M. Prieto, L. Concheiro and J. Estefania. Isoelectric focusing patterns of some mammalian keratins. *J Forensic Sci*, 32:93–99, 1987.

Centers for Disease Control and Prevention. Nonfatal dog bite-related injuries treated in hospital emergency departments — United States, 2001. *Morbidity and Mortality Weekly Report*, 52:605–610, 2003.

J. W. Chen, C. E. Uboh, L. R. Soma, X. Li, F. Guan, Y. You and Y. Liu. Determining the source of equine bloodstains by dinucleotide repeats. *J Forensic Sci*, 55:1610–1614, 2010.

F. D'Andrea, F. Fridez and R. Coquoz. Preliminary experiments on the transfer of animal hair during simulated criminal behavior. *J Forensic Sci*, 43:1257–1258, 1998.

N. Dawnay, R. Ogden, R. McEwing, G. R. Carvalho and R. S. Thorpe. Validation of the barcoding gene COI for use in forensic genetic species identification. *Forensic Sci Int*, 173:1–6, 2007.

M. Dayton, M. T. Koskinen, B. K. Tom, A. M. Mattila, E. Johnston, J. Halverson, D. Fantin, S. DeNise, B. Budowle, D. G. Smith and S. Kanthaswamy. Developmental validation of short tandem repeat reagent kit for forensic DNA profiling of canine biological material. *Croat Med J*, 50:268–285, 2009.

C. Eichmann, B. Berger, M. Reinhold, M. Lutz and W. Parson. Canine-specific STR typing of saliva traces on dog bite wounds. *Int J Legal Med*, 118:337–342, 2004.

European Commission. Commission publishes European test results on horse DNA and Phenylbutazone: no food safety issues but tougher penalties to apply in the future to fraudulent labelling. 2013. http://europa.eu/rapid/press-release_IP-13-331_en.htm, accessed March 6, 2016.

European Union Reference Laboratory for Animal Proteins in feedstuffs Detection of horse DNA using real-time PCR, EURL-AP recommended protocol. 2013. http://www.innofoodsee.eu/downloads/protocol_detection_horse_dna_using.pdf, accessed March 6, 2016.

FEDIAF The European Pet Food Industry. Facts and figures. 2012. http://www.fediaf.org/facts-figures/.

J. Gilchrist, J. J. Sacks, D. White and M. J. Kresnow. Dog bites: Still a problem? *Inj Prev*, 14:296–301, 2008.

J. L. Halverson and C. Basten. Forensic DNA identification of animal-derived trace evidence: Tools for linking victims and suspects. *Croat Med J,* 46:598–605, 2005.

P. D. Hebert, A. Cywinska, S. L. Ball and J. R. deWaard. Biological identifications through DNA barcodes. *Proc Biol Sci,* 270:313–321, 2003a.

P. D. Hebert, S. Ratnasingham and J. R. deWaard. Barcoding animal life: Cytochrome c oxidase subunit 1 divergences among closely related species. *Proc Biol Sci,* 270(1):S96–S99, 2003b.

M. M. Holland. 2001. Molecular Analysis of the Human Mitochondrial DNA Control Region for Forensic Identity Testing. In *Current Protocols in Human Genetics.* John Wiley and Sons, Inc., New Jersey.

K. E. Holsinger and B. S. Weir. Genetics in geographically structured populations: Defining, estimating and interpreting FST. *Nat Rev Genet,* 10:639–650, 2009.

H. M. Hsieh, H. L. Chiang, L. C. Tsai, S. Y. Lai, N. E. Huang, A. Linacre and J. C. Lee. Cytochrome b gene for species identification of the conservation animals. *Forensic Sci Int,* 122:7–18, 2001.

International Society for Animal Genetics. Animal Forensic Workshop. In *ISAG Conference,* Amsterdam, the Netherlands, 2008.

S. James, J. J. Nordby and S. Bell. *Forensic Science: An Introduction to Scientific and Investigative Techniques.* CRC Press, Boca Raton, FL, 2003.

A. J. Jeffreys and D. B. Morton. DNA fingerprints of dogs and cats. *Anim Genet,* 18:1–15, 1987.

A. J. Jeffreys, V. Wilson and S. L. Thein. Hypervariable /'minisatellite/' regions in human DNA. *Nature,* 314:67–73, 1985.

R. N. Johnson, L. Wilson-Wilde and A. Linacre. Current and future directions of DNA in wildlife forensic science. *Forensic Sci Int Genet,* 10:1–11, 2014.

S. Kanthaswamy, B. K. Tom, A. M. Mattila, E. Johnston, M. Dayton, J. Kinaga, B. J. Erickson, J. Halverson, D. Fantin, S. DeNise, A. Kou, V. Malladi, J. Satkoski, B. Budowle, D. G. Smith and M. T. Koskinen. Canine population data generated from a multiplex STR kit for use in forensic casework. *J Forensic Sci,* 54:829–840, 2009.

T. Kitpipit, S. S. Tobe, A. C. Kitchener, P. Gill and A. Linacre. The development and validation of a single SNaPshot multiplex for tiger species and subspecies identification–implications for forensic purposes. *Forensic Sci Int Genet,* 6:250–257, 2012.

A. Linacre, L. Gusmao, W. Hecht, A. P. Hellmann, W. R. Mayr, W. Parson, M. Prinz, P. M. Schneider and N. Morling. ISFG: Recommendations regarding the use of non-human (animal) DNA in forensic genetic investigations. *Forensic Sci Int Genet*, 5:501–505, 2011.

M. Lynch. God's signature: DNA profiling, the new gold standard in forensic science. *Endeavour*, 27:93–97, 2003.

M. A. Menotti-Raymond, V. A. David, B. S. Weir and S. J. O'Brien. A population genetic database of cat breeds developed in coordination with a domestic cat STR multiplex. *J Forensic Sci*, 57:596–601, 2012.

M. A. Menotti-Raymond, V. A. David and S. J. O'Brien. Pet cat hair implicates murder suspect. *Nature*, 386:774, 1997.

M. A. Menotti-Raymond, V. A. David, L. L. Wachter, J. M. Butler and S. J. O'Brien. An STR forensic typing system for genetic individualization of domestic cat (*Felis catus*) samples. *J Forensic Sci*, 50:1061–1070, 2005.

R. Ogden, R. J. Mellanby, D. Clements, A. G. Gow, R. Powell and R. McEwing. Genetic data from 15 STR loci for forensic individual identification and parentage analyses in UK domestic dogs (*Canis lupus familiaris*). *Forensic Sci Int Genet*, 6:e63–e65, 2012.

Z. Padar, B. Egyed, K. Kontadakis, S. Furedi, J. Woller, L. Zoldag and S. Fekete. Canine STR analyses in forensic practice. Observation of a possible mutation in a dog hair. *Int J Legal Med*, 116:286–288, 2002.

A. J. Peabody, R. J. Oxborough, P. E. Cage and I. W. Evett. The discrimination of cat and dog hairs. *J Forensic Sci Soc*, 23:121–129, 1983.

K. M. Pun, C. Albrecht, V. Castella and L. Fumagalli. Species identification in mammals from mixed biological samples based on mitochondrial DNA control region length polymorphism. *Electrophoresis*, 30:1008–1014, 2009.

E. Quioco. Animal cruelty case expands. 2001. http://www.sptimes. com/News/030201/TampaBay/Animal_cruelty_case_e.shtml, accessed March 6, 2016.

K. A. Roberts and C. Calloway. Mitochondrial DNA amplification success rate as a function of hair morphology. *J Forensic Sci*, 52:40–47, 2007.

G. Scharnhorst and S. Kanthaswamy. An assessment of scientific and technical aspects of closed investigations of canine forensics DNA — case series from the University of California, Davis, USA. *Croat Med J*, 52:280–292, 2011.

Scientific Working Group on DNA Analysis Methods (SWGDAM). Validation guidelines for DNA analysis methods. 2012. http://media. wix.com/ugd/4344b0_cbc27d16dcb64fd88cb36ab2a2a25e4c.pdf, accessed March 6, 2016.

B. B. Smalling, J. A. Satkoski, B. K. Tom, W. Y. Szeto, B. J.-A. Erickson, T. F. Spear, D. G. Smith, B. Budowle, K. M. Webb, M. Allard and S. Kanthaswamy. The significance of regional and mixed breed canine mtDNA databases in forensic science. *Bentham Open-Open Forensic Science Journal*, 3:22–32, 2010.

D. Smith, D. Stahler, E. Stahler, M. Metz, R. McIntyre, J. Irving, R. Raymond, C. Anton, R. Kindermann and N. Bowersock. Yellowstone wolf project annual report. 2011. http://www.nps.gov/yell/learn/nature/upload/Wolf_AR_2011.pdf, accessed March 6, 2016.

P. Taberlet, S. Griffin, B. Goossens, S. Questiau, V. Manceau, N. Escaravage, L. P. Waits and J. Bouvet. Reliable genotyping of samples with very low DNA quantities using PCR. *Nucleic Acids Research*, 24:3189–3194, 1996.

K. Tamura, D. Peterson, N. Peterson, G. Stecher, M. Nei and S. Kumar. MEGA5: molecular evolutionary genetics analysis using maximum likelihood, evolutionary distance and maximum parsimony methods. *Mol Biol Evol*, 28:2731–2739, 2011.

S. S. Tobe, A. Kitchener and A. Linacre. Cytochrome b or cytochrome c oxidase subunit I for mammalian species identification — An answer to the debate. *Forensic Sci Int Genet Suppl Series*, 2:306–307, 2009.

S. S. Tobe and A. M. Linacre. A technique for the quantification of human and non-human mammalian mitochondrial DNA copy number in forensic and other mixtures. *Forensic Sci Int Genet*, 2:249–256, 2008.

A. Tsuji, A. Ishiko, H. Kimura, M. Nurimoto, K. Kudo and N. Ikeda. Unusual death of a baby: A dog attack and confirmation using human and canine STRs. *Int J Legal Med*, 122:59–62, 2008.

University of North Texas Center for Human Identification. DNA defined. 2007. https://hsc.unt.edu/departments/pathology_anatomy/dna/Forensics/Defined/Defined.cfm, accessed March 6, 2016.

L. H. van de Goor, M. T. Koskinen and W. A. van Haeringen, Population studies of 16 bovine STR loci for forensic purposes. *Int J Legal Med*, 125:111–119, 2011a.

L. H. van de Goor, H. Panneman and W. A. van Haeringen. A proposal for standardization in forensic bovine DNA typing: Allele nomenclature of 16 cattle-specific short tandem repeat loci. *Anim Genet*, 40:630–636, 2009.

L. H. van de Goor, W. A. van Haeringen and J. A. Lenstra. Population studies of 17 equine STR for forensic and phylogenetic analysis. *Anim Genet*, 42:627–633, 2011b.

M. van Oven and M. Kayser. Updated comprehensive phylogenetic tree of global human mitochondrial DNA variation. *Hum Mutat*, 30:E386–E394, 2009.

B. M. Vonholdt, D. R. Stahler, D. W. Smith, D. A. Earl, J. P. Pollinger and R. K. Wayne. The genealogy and genetic viability of reintroduced Yellowstone grey wolves. *Mol Ecol*, 17:252–274, 2008.

V. Westerfield, Superior Court 98 Cal. App. 4th 145, 2002.

J. H. Wetton, J. E. Higgs, A. C. Spriggs, C. A. Roney, C. S. Tsang and A. P. Foster. Mitochondrial profiling of dog hairs. *Forensic Sci Int*, 133:235–241, 2003.

E. Wictum, T. Kun, C. Lindquist, J. Malvick, D. Vankan and B. Sacks. Developmental validation of DogFiler, a novel multiplex for canine DNA profiling in forensic casework. *Forensic Sci Int Genet*, 7:82–91, 2013.

S. Wright. The genetical structure of populations. *Ann Eugen*, 15:323–354, 1951

S. Wright. *Evolution and the genetics of populations, Vol. 4: Variability within and among natural populations.* University of Chicago Press, Chicago, IL, 1978.

E. B. York. McDonald's, BK step up DNA tests on beef in Europe. In *Chicago Tribune*, 2013, http://articles.chicagotribune.com/2013-02-27/business/chi-mcdonalds-calls-for-supplemental-beef-testing-in-europe-20130227_1_dna-tests-horse-meat-diego-beamonte, accessed March 6, 2016.

CHAPTER 20

Applications of DNA-Based Methods in Food Forensics

Ricardo Araújo[,†], Filipe Pereira[‡] and Barbara van Asch[†,§]*

[*]*Instituto de Investigação e Inovação em Saúde,*
Universidade do Porto, Portugal
[†]*Instituto de Patologia e Imunologia Molecular da*
Universidade do Porto (IPATIMUP),
Rua Dr. Roberto Frias, s/n, 4200-465 Porto, Portugal
[‡]*Interdisciplinary Centre of Marine and Environmental Research*
(CIIMAR/CIMAR), University of Porto,
Rua dos Bragas 289, Porto 4050-123, Portugal
[§]*Department of Genetics, Stellenbosch University,*
Private Bag X1, Matieland 7602, South Africa

1 Introduction

Economical fraud, disloyal competition among producers and the violation of the rights of consumers to make informed choices has stimulated growing interest in authentication and certification of food, feed and ingredients (Woolfe and Primrose, 2004; Mafra *et al.*, 2008). This chapter aims at providing an overview of some current applications of food testing to the non-specialist who is well versed on forensic genetics methodologies. It should be read as an introduction to a vast area of research that has proposed many strategies to investigate the biological composition of food products with regards to species, variety or cultivar and geographic origin. It is our hope that this summary will motivate analysts and researchers alike to the challenges of this important theme.

2 Olive Oil

Olive oil and other vegetable oils have become increasingly popular as they may contribute to the prevention of serious health conditions such as coronary disease. Olive oil also is important as one of the most valuable food products in the Mediterranean region where a millenary production and consumption tradition remains deeply engrained in daily life until today. In recent years, the European Union (EU) has developed efforts to protect the 'liquid gold' from profitable adulteration (e.g. addition of lower value vegetable oils), and fraudulent description (e.g. geographical origin, cultivars and the production methods). Generally, monovarietal olive oils labeled with the EU Protected Designation of Origin (PDO) and Protected Geographical Indication (PGI) reach premium prices and are potentially vulnerable to fraudulent practices (Kiritsakis and Christie, 2000). Olive oil adulterants such as hazelnut, almond, maize, palm and sunflower oils have been identified by chemical methods (Frankel, 2010) but research has shown that the presence of hazelnut and almond oils in olive oil could not be detected in percentages lower than or equal to 5% (Christopoulou *et al.*, 2004). Chromatography and spectroscopy also are amongst the most commonly proposed technologies for cultivar authenticity assessment (Luykx and van Ruth, 2008). However, the chemical composition of olive oil varies greatly and depends on the growing area's environmental conditions and cultivation strategies, thus rendering the use of chemical markers not valuable for this purpose.

DNA-based markers have been increasingly investigated because they are independent from environmental fluctuations and cultivation techniques (Costa *et al.*, 2012). Although DNA recovery from olive oil samples may present a challenge, several studies have evidenced successful extraction, amplification and cultivar discrimination using Amplified Fragment Length Polymorphism (AFLP), Random Amplified Polymorphic DNA (RAPD), SSR (Simple Sequence Repeat), Inter Simple Sequence Repeat (ISSR) and Single Nucleotide Polymorphism (SNP)-based analysis and real-time PCR (Muzzalupo and Perri, 2002; Busconi *et al.*, 2003; Nikoloudakis *et al.*, 2003; Breton *et al.*, 2004; Fernando de la Torre *et al.*, 2004; Pasqualone *et al.*, 2004; Reale *et al.*, 2006; Consolandi *et al.*, 2007; Muzzalupo *et al.*, 2007; Martins-Lopes *et al.*, 2008; Giménez *et al.*, 2010; Vietina *et al.*, 2011; Bazakos *et al.*, 2012). However, caution should be exercised in DNA-based cultivar identification of olive oils using leaf reference profiles since non-maternal alleles were observed in embryos (stone) and the paste obtained by crushing whole fruits, and the resulting oil (Doveri *et al.*, 2006). The olive tree being an allogamous wind-pollinated species, DNA profiles from olive oil are likely to represent a composite profile of the maternal alleles juxtaposed with alleles contributed by various pollen donors. Future developments with regards to DNA extraction methods and genotyping technology will contribute to the increased use of DNA profiling for assessing the biological composition and origin of premium olive oils (see reviews Mafra *et al.*, 2008; Agrimonti *et al.*, 2011; Costa *et al.*, 2012).

3 Wine and Grapevines

Wine, as an alcoholic beverage produced from grapes, is one of the most well-prized food products in the world and it has an important social and economic significance in many regions. Information regarding cultivar, cultivation area, and year of production contribute to intrinsic and perceived wine quality worldwide. Wine legislation in the EU regulates origin and geographical indications, traditional terms and labeling and presentation of wine. Since 2011, wine quality categories in the EU are separated into PDO and PGI.

Cultivar information, although not mandatory by European law, has become an important aspect of the commercial value of wines in a highly competitive market environment. Accurate cultivar identification upstream and downstream of the production is increasingly becoming a distinguishing factor that benefits consumers and compliant producers. Ampelographic, chemical and biochemical methods have allowed for the identification and characterization of grapevine cultivars with regard to the geographical area of production, albeit with the limitations that result from cultivation, climate and environmental variation.

Genetic identification of grapevine cultivars is particularly relevant for single variety wines that must contain at least 85% of the stated variety. The development of DNA-based strategies for grapevine cultivar identification has resulted in many studies that have mainly focused on nuclear STR analyses (see review (Santos *et al.*, 2014)), although some effort has recently been dedicated to SNP-based methodologies (Lijavetzky *et al.*, 2007; Cabezas *et al.*, 2011; Di Genova *et al.*, 2014). Currently, a set of six specific dinucleotide STRs widely used by many laboratories is recommended by the European Vitis Database (www.eu-vitis.de) for grapevine profiling (This *et al.*, 2004). The resulting STR profiles are given in estimated fragment length with the associated difficulties for data compilation and comparison (e.g. lack of allele standardization based on the number of repeats, absence of allelic ladder), additionally to the problems derived from the scoring of dinucleotide alleles (e.g. the presence of stuttering peaks) in a forensic context. More recently, a set of tetranucleotide STR markers for grapevine identification was presented along with a dataset of grapevine genetic profiles. The authors also provided the first database of grapevine genotypes with alleles given in terms of the number of repeated units, thus allowing for direct intra and inter-laboratory comparisons (Cipriani *et al.*, 2008; Cipriani *et al.*, 2010). These studies have shown that, in addition to the selection of adequate DNA markers for grapevine cultivar identification, the construction and curation of databases of grapevine profiles are far from being a simple task. In fact, the complex pattern of synonyms (different names for the same cultivar) and homonyms (different cultivars identified under the same name) generated throughout centuries of propagations, exchange and dispersion is still far from being resolved to general consensus.

DNA recovery from finished wine has also been a difficult task. Experimental wine must (freshly pressed grape juices including fruit skins and seeds) have been successfully profiled, although the subsequent decanting, clarification and filtration steps are probably responsible for negative DNA extraction, and inhibitors and low-quality DNA for hampering PCR (Faria *et al.*, 2000; Siret *et al.*, 2000; Garcia-Beneytez *et al.*, 2002; Siret *et al.*, 2002; Baleiras-Couto and Eiras-Dias, 2006; Harta *et al.*, 2010). For genetic profiling in finished wine to become widely used, it is necessary that some effort is directed towards the development of new approaches for DNA recovery from this complex matrix.

In addition to wines, other grape and grape-derived products may contain a high degree of inaccuracy with regard to the information provided to the consumer, as evidenced in a survey of commercial table grapes and raisins in Austria. This study revealed that approximately 30% of the market fruit was mislabeled in terms of the cultivar (Sefc *et al.*, 1998) and clearly illustrates the need for better identification of grapes and grape-derived products.

4 Honey

Honey quality and characteristics are closely associated with the botanical provenance of nectar, pollen and honeydew available for production and the climate and environmental conditions of the area of origin (Stolzenbach *et al.*, 2011). The main honey varieties that can be marketed in the EU fall under labelling requirements that must indicate the floral origin, physicochemical properties, organoleptic characteristics and regional provenance (Directive, 2000). Physicochemical properties such as pH, conductivity, sugar, aminoacids, vitamins and minerals and organoleptic parameters can be determined by well-established analytical methods. Geographic origin is less straightforward but can be inferred by microscopic analysis of the spectrum of pollen residues to determine the botanical composition of honey. This technique, known as melissopalynology, is time-consuming, requires significant expertize and the interpretation of the results is often challenging.

Recent research has focused on DNA-based tools to identify the botanical composition of honey. The methodologies include primers and probes designed to recognize specific plant species (Laube *et al.*, 2010), and DNA barcoding (i.e. taxon identification using a standardized DNA region) approaches using DNA markers such as nuclear 18S rDNA (Olivieri *et al.*, 2012) and the plastid trnL gene (Valentini *et al.*, 2010), as illustrated in Figure 1. In this

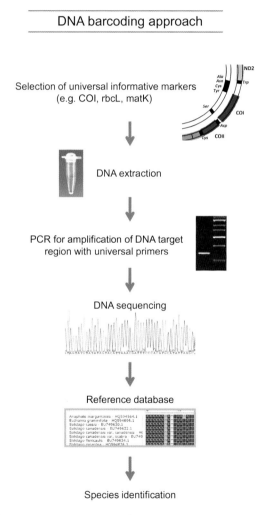

Figure 1: Schematic representation of the DNA barcoding approach for species identification.

strategy, the species present in mixture matrices are determined by comparing sequences of the same target DNA region with a reference database (Casiraghi *et al.*, 2010; Galimberti *et al.*, 2013). As in other phyla, the selection of universal informative markers is crucial to identify and differentiate among closely related taxa in complex unknown matrices (Sandionigia *et al.*, 2012). The Plant Working Group of the Consortium for the Barcode of Life (CBOL; http://www.barcoding.si.edu/plant_working_group. html) proposed the plastid coding regions rbcL and matK as core barcodes for botanical identification, and additional regions, such as trnH-psbA and ITS2, could be used to analyze closely related taxa (Hollingsworth *et al.*, 2011). A recent study aimed at evaluating the usefulness of a 'DNA-barcoding' strategy for determining the botanical composition of honey concluded that this approach is a valid alternative to mellisopalynological analyses for the purpose of honey traceability because although all samples contained a mixture of common plants, the presence of at least one endemic plant allowed to connect a particular honey to a particular region (Bruni *et al.*, 2015). However, the authors recommended that this approach should be combined with next generation sequencing of vast collections of samples, including complex food matrices, so that more species present in trace amounts can be identified (Park *et al.*, 2012). Although the DNA-barcoding approach is promising in the long run, to date this technique does not allow for the quantification of the biological composition of complex matrices, which is a serious disadvantage because European guidelines demand an accurate quantitative description to certify the quality and designation of honey. Another problem currently impeding the determination of the biological origin of honey is the absence of a general consensus regarding plant barcoding regions, due to their variable identification performances amongst different plant groups (Cowan and Fay, 2012). Lastly, the constitution of well-populated databases of DNA-barcoding references sequences for local flora in important honey-producing regions is mandatory.

5 Mushrooms

In the food forensics context, DNA-based rapid identification of edible macro fungi offers a wide array of potential applications, such as the detection of illicit hallucinogenic mushrooms (Lee *et al.*, 2000; Nugent and Saville, 2004). Another source of concern is that the consumption of 'wild' (i.e. uncultivated, field collected) edible fungi requires expert identification skills to avoid accidental poisoning due to confusion with toxic species with similar morphology. Serious health damage and even lethal intoxication occur frequently in all world regions, including Europe, America and Asia. The great majority of casualties is attributed to species belonging to the genus Amanita, particularly the death cap (*Amanita phalloides*) (Berger and Guss, 2005). A recent study presented the development of a genetic test for the detection of deadly poisonous European species of the genus Amanita, namely *A. phalloides, A. virosa* and *A. verna* using direct PCR amplification and sequencing of a nuclear ribosomal DNA (rDNA) fragment. The authors were able to successfully detect the targeted species in a variety of samples, including raw, fried, digested mushrooms and fecal specimens (Gausterer *et al.*, 2014). Another study focused on the identification of 15 fragments of dried commercial porcini originating in China by sequencing the full ITS region of the nuclear ribosomal DNA (nrDNA) (Dentinger and Suz, 2014). The authors reported the finding of three unnamed species corresponding to lineages that, although previously reported in phylogenetic analyses, had never been formally named or described at the time. These results clearly show that identification and monitoring of edible fungi in food products are still at the preliminary stages of development. Another study described a real-time PCR method based on the survey of ITS1 and ITS2 fragments for the detection of *Amanita phalloides, Lepiota cristata, Lepiota brunneoincarnata* and *Inocybe asterospora,* the four poisonous mushroom species most commonly responsible for human intoxication in Italy (Epis *et al.*, 2010). The authors tested the methodology for specificity and sensitivity in cooked mushroom samples and gastric aspirates and demonstrated that it performs well for the identification of species in samples that have lost the original morphological characteristics through processing, cooking or digestion. A similar species-specific real-time PCR methodology has been developed in the context of poisonous mushrooms from Japan (*Omphalotus japonicas, Entoloma rhodopolius, Tricholoma ustale* and *Clitocybe acromelalga*), although the authors have not tested fecal or gastric samples (Maeta *et al.*, 2008). Another potential application of genetic fungi identification is the assessment of authenticity of well-prized European black truffle (*Tuber melanosporum*). A DNA-based methodology for the identification of *T. melanosporum* from fruitbodies and inoculum was developed using direct PCR of a fragment of the rDNA ITS with species-specific primers (Bonito 2009). The lack of standard guidelines for certifying the quality of truffles, inocula and truffle-inoculated materials had been previously discussed and efforts have been developed for the genetic identification of *T. indicum*, the Asian black truffle that is fraudulently commercialized as *T. melanosporum* and *T. Brumale* (Douet *et al.*, 2004).

6 Dairy Products

The identification of the species present in dairy products is important for certification of authenticity and for the verification of compulsory production specifications, such as those defined for traditional products by the European PDO, PGI and Traditional Specialty Guaranteed (TSG) standards. In this context, especially premium cheeses with European designation of origin are vulnerable to adulteration by replacement or omission of high-value ingredients in the manufacturing process with the objective of attaining economic gain. In this case, the quality and identity of the products are compromised, as well as the consumer's right to make informed choices based on accurate descriptions of food composition. Previous studies focusing on the biological composition of commercial dairy products in several countries and world regions (Italy, Spain, Portugal, the Czech Republic, Poland, Croatia, Egypt, Taiwan, China, India and Pakistan) showed that non-conformity with the alleged composition in terms of species is a global and widespread problem (Bottero *et al.*, 2003; Di Pinto *et al.*, 2004; Feligini *et al.*, 2005; Cheng *et al.*, 2006; Maskova and Paulickova, 2006; Díaz *et al.*, 2007; Kotowicz *et al.*, 2007; Lopparelli *et al.*, 2007; Mafra *et al.*, 2007; Reale *et al.*, 2008; Darwish *et al.*, 2009; Cottenet *et al.*, 2011).

DNA-based methods for species identification are particularly useful for the analysis of commercial dairy products. DNA derived from animal somatic cells is theoretically retrievable from all dairy products, even after thermal treatment and other types of processing (e.g. pasteurization, ultra-high-temperature (UHT) treatment, rennet and acid coagulation, dehydration, fermentation, ripening, smoking). Secondly, since dairy products are widely manufactured from goat, sheep, cow and water buffalo milk, it is very unlikely that DNA from other species is incorporated in the production. Thus, the targets for genetic species identification are restricted to only four different mammals. Although low concentrations of DNA in suboptimal conditions are to be expected in dairy products, the problem can be minimized by the use of mitochondrial DNA (mtDNA) as a PCR target, with the advantage that the high mutation rate of this marker allows for discrimination among closely related species. In the past decade, several works have proposed methods based on species-specific PCR followed by electrophoresis for investigating the composition of dairy products in terms of the contributing species, with an important part focusing on the detection of cow in buffalo milk and cheese (Rea *et al.*, 2001; Bottero *et al.*, 2002; Di Pinto *et al.*, 2004; Feligini *et al.*, 2005; Lopez-Calleja *et al.*, 2005; Darwish *et al.*, 2009; De *et al.*, 2011) and in goat and sheep products (Mafra *et al.*, 2004; Cheng *et al.*, 2006; Kotowicz *et al.*, 2007; Lopparelli *et al.*, 2007; Mafra *et al.*, 2007), and also the presence of goat in sheep products (Lopez-Calleja *et al.*, 2007). These methods have the disadvantage of not including the simultaneous detection of the most important four dairy species (goat, sheep, cow and buffalo). As an example, a recent methodology (Goncalves *et al.*, 2012) allows for the simultaneous detection of all four species based on a single multiplex PCR targeting short (< 200 bp) species-specific

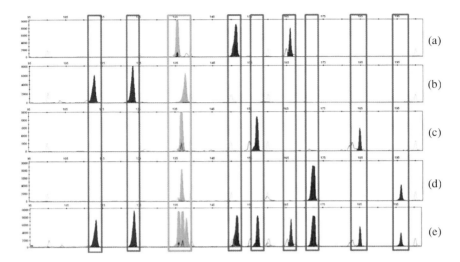

Figure 2: Electrophoretic profiles representative of reference DNA samples of (a) cow, (b) goat, (c) sheep, (d) buffalo and (e) an allelic ladder composed by a DNA mixture (1:1:1:1) of the four species, as obtained using the ABI 3130 xl sequencing platform. PCR amplifications were performed in multiplex using nine pairs of primers resulting in species-specific fragments (blue) and conserved fragments (green).

mtDNA regions (Figure 2). The multiplex includes an internal control for DNA extraction, and it is flexible in terms of the post-PCR electrophoresis and fragment-size detection method. The multiplex PCR allows for the amplification of two species-specific fixed-size fragments per species and one mammalian-specific fragment that acts as an internal control. The sensitivity was estimated to be at least 1% (v/v) milk mixtures in both alternative electrophoretic methods for fragment size detection (ABI 3130 XL sequencer and the QIAxcel system). A market survey of dairy products associated with the same study revealed a significant level of discrepancy between the declared and the actual compositions in terms of the contributing species. This finding clearly shows that the control of the authenticity of dairy products, especially traditional European cheeses, is far from being a futile activity.

7 Food Microbiology and Health Safety

Food microbiology evaluates quality and safety of food samples in order to prevent health problems and diseases related to food consumption. For example, milk and its derived products are an important food segment of which consumers are particularly aware. Therefore, food laboratories under stringent guidelines routinely verify microbial load present indairy samples attesting its safety and compliance to official regulations. The presence of particular bacterial species may be largely associated to food deterioration and represent an increased risk for public and animal health. The presence of microorganisms, e.g. *Salmonella enterica, Listeria monocytogenes* or *Campylobacter jejuni* in food samples can cause serious health complications and be occasionally associated to fatal diseases (Mammina *et al.*, 2009; Hauser *et al.*, 2010; Sheppard *et al.*, 2010; Zou *et al.*, 2012). Other micro-organisms can be present in food samples under certain limits, and there are very heterogenic species, for example *Escherichia coli* which may present highly pathogenic strains, such as O157:H7, with just a few cells being sufficient to cause serious illness (Ateba and Mbewe, 2013).

Food deterioration or contamination can be caused accidently by environmental factors but occasionally human intervention also is reported. The characterization, analysis of evidence and final validation that are used for the description of an intentional act of biocrime represents the main target of microbial forensics. One of the most demanding efforts in such an investigation is to confirm strain origin and identify the person and/or the motifs behind such crime (Budowle *et al.*, 2005). Some cases of use and release of microbial agents as bioweapons in order to perpetrate murder or injury against people already have been described. Intentionality is difficult to attest based on epidemiological and molecular data analyses but major advances have been made in this field during the last decade. One of the most studied cases reports to 1996 in Dallas, Texas, USA. A criminal act involving *Shigella dysenteriae* type 2 and food contamination affected 12 people in St. Paul Medical Centre hospital. Molecular tests confirmed later that the micro-organisms isolated from stool samples (from nine patients), uneaten muffins and a stock collection from a medical laboratory were indistinguishable by pulsed-field gel electrophoresis (PFGE) analysis (Kolavic *et al.*, 1997). The criminal investigation focused on a laboratory technician who was later found guilty of several felony assaults (intentional infection by pathogenic organism) and falsification of laboratory documents. Another relevant case was related to consecutive outbreaks of cyclosporiasis caused by contaminated Guatemalan raspberries in USA and Canada, from 1996 to 1998 (Herwaldt and Ackers, 1997; Herwaldt and Beach, 1999). These cases alerted to the continuous need of attention to food products coming from some countries and showed how fragile heath and legal systems can be in the case of an intentional biological attack. Epidemiology studies remain extremely relevant to understand the frequency of certain diseases in our communities. Such studies must be regularly performed, as updated epidemiological values might work as important references for identification of disease outbreaks and community disturbances.

8 Tracing Transmission, Identity and Authenticity

Microbial profiling and community characterization are important issues for microbial forensics. Biogeographic patterns can be described for some bacterial and fungal species and their value is huge for large-scale genotyping and strain tracing studies, authenticity of products and comparison of microbial populations. Genetically isolated populations are more susceptible to local adaptation due to stressful environmental conditions. Endemic (i.e. geographically delimited strains) might occur and be a consequence of adaptation to places or regions. In fact, some microbial strains may be better adapted than others to specific environments, as previously described (Fulthorpe *et al.*, 1998; Cho and Tiedje, 2000; Rodrigues *et al.*, 2009).

Microbial adaptations can be helpful for studying transmission, trace the origin of pathogenic organisms and prevent the spread of such strains. This ability is relevant to ensure food quality and safety and to distinguish among microbial strains, as proved by several studies. In Germany, similar *S. enterica* multiresistant isolates from the Saintpaul clonal line were found widespread in live turkeys and derived products (Beutlich *et al.*, 2010), and the serovar 4,[5],12:i: was isolated from pig, pork meat and human samples evidencing transmission along the food chain (Hauser *et al.*, 2010). Other cases of food associated diseases have been reported worldwide by employing molecular tests particularly PFGE. This molecular strategy is practical and cost effective in small collections of isolates and employs restriction enzymes to fraction microbial DNA that is then submitted to electrophoresis in agarose gels in order to generate molecular fingerprints (Figure 3 shows representative examples). Similar isolates tend to present similar fingerprint or PFGE profile while distinct isolates will generate distinct profiles. The PFGE profile of 80 isolates confirmed the *Salmonella enteritidis* strain was responsible for an outbreak in the USA due to consumption of contaminated eggs (Zou *et al.*, 2012). Local and international transmission of *Campylobacter* genotypes have been proved based on host-associated lineages among food animal species (Sheppard *et al.*, 2010). Cases also have been described of locally restricted microorganism associated with food deterioration. Microbial fingerprinting studies showed as association between strains of *Listeria* spp. and the

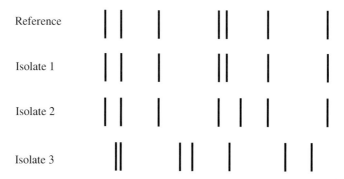

Figure 3: Representative example of pulse filed gel electrophoresis (PFGE) profiles of four bacterial isolates. Isolate 1 is similar to the reference, isolate 2 is closely related and isolate 3 shows a very distinct PFGE profile.

locally produced meat by a specific manufacturing plant (Syne *et al.*, 2011). In addition, specific types of *C. jejuni* were described in New Zealand due to its geographical isolation and its uniquely structured poultry industry (Mullner *et al.*, 2010).

Phytopathogens also are relevant, and more attention has been given to the transport of microbes from region to region and between different countries. Other forensic tests have been developed for detection of specific quarantine microorganisms. One example is *Phymatotrichopsis omnivore*, a soil-borne fungus that causes significant crop losses on cotton, alfalfa and other dicot crops in south-western United States and northern Mexico and limiting crop growth in contaminated soils. A rapid and sensitive real-time quantitative PCR method has been recently proposed for the detection of *P. omnivore* in plant materials by targeting the genes encoding for rRNA ITSs, beta-tubulin and the second-largest subunit of RNA polymerase II (Arif *et al.*, 2013).

Microbial communities also can be tested for certification and authenticity of local produced products. Major differences in the metabolic profiles and microbial communities were found in Fiore Sardo cheeses, a traditional Italian raw ewe's milk cheese certified as Protected Designation of Origin (Piras *et al.*, 2013); high genetic heterogeneity was detected in *Lactobacillus* populations of Piedmont hard cheese made of raw milk without thermal treatment or addition of industrial starter (Bautista-Gallego *et al.*, 2014). Molecular fingerprinting of *Candida zeylanoides* isolated in Sardinia from goat's milk showed very distinct patterns compared to isolates from other origins (Fadda *et al.*, 2010).

The range of potential application of microbial data in forensics is huge and new directions and challenges are being faced today. For example, the community structure of skin-associated bacteria can be used to differentiate objects handled by different individuals, such as computer keys and computer mice (Fierer *et al.*, 2010). There is such a high degree of inter-individual variability in skin-associated bacterial communities that personalized microbial communities can represent the starting point for the development of a unique forensic approach. A common and a variable group of fungi also can be found in the oral cavity which is responsible for great inter-individual variability but consistent intra-individual stability over time among individuals (Monteiro-da-Silva *et al.*, 2014). Even identical twins showed substantially different microbial communities (Turnbaugh *et al.*, 2009), suggesting once again that the genomes of microbial communities can be more useful for identification than our own human genomes or at least can be used as a complementary approach in forensic studies. The microbiome projects conducted all over the world have revealed interesting insights into human diversity and its interaction with the surrounding environment (Cox *et al.*, 2013). There is no doubt that many aspects of human well being may be influenced by our associated and dynamic microbiota.

9 Next Generation of Forensic Tools and its Role for Food Quality and Safety

Molecular tools have brought considerable advances to food microbiology. The characterization of full microbial communities is now possible due to the next generation of molecular tools, and the value of such information is huge. Several non-cultivable bacteria have been described over the last years but the role of such microorganisms still needs to be fully understood (Yeung, 2012). These technologies have considerable impact on food microbiology for revealing new microorganisms as well as they can largely improve the sensitivity and specificity of diagnostic tools and facilitate the identification of microbes responsible for food associated diseases. It is urgent to understand the interaction between microorganisms, communities of microorganisms (belonging or not to the same species) and spread of microbial strains, particularly ones with increased pathogenicity or resistance. Controls, recommendations and validation guidelines should be constantly updated and made available for laboratory and scientific communities, particularly regarding the topics of food safety and public health.

The era of second and third generation massive sequencing analyses arrived and the amount of data being generated is huge.

Further technologies applied to food microbiology will certainly enable simultaneous detection, identification and molecular characterization of complex communities existing in food samples. Extensive databases and software for data analyses remain urgently needed in order to facilitate the interpretation of genomic data and communication among laboratories and researchers. Importantly, the success of previous molecular tools in microbiology has been largely associated with the facility to deposit, compare and share data among laboratories.

References

C. M. Agrimonti, M. Vietina *et al.* The use of food genomics to ensure the traceability of olive oil. *Trends in Food Science & Technology*, 22(5):237–244, 2011.

M. Arif, J. Fletcher *et al.* Development of a rapid, sensitive, and field-deployable razor ex BioDetection system and quantitative PCR assay for detection of Phymatotrichopsis omnivora using multiple gene targets. *Applied and Environmental Microbiology*, 79(7):2312–2320, 2013.

C. N. Ateba and M. Mbewe. Determination of the genetic similarities of fingerprints from Escherichia coli O157:H7 isolated from different sources in the North West Province, South Africa using ISR, BOXAIR and REP-PCR analysis. *Microbiological Research*, 168(7):438–446, 2013.

M. M. Baleiras-Couto and J. E. Eiras-Dias. Detection and identification of grape varieties in must and wine using nuclear and chloroplast microsatellite markers. *Analytica Chimica Acta*, 563(1–2):283–291, 2006.

J. Bautista-Gallego, V. Alessandria *et al.* Diversity and functional characterization of Lactobacillus spp. isolated throughout the ripening of a hard cheese. *International Journal of Food Microbiology*, 181:60–66, 2014.

C. Bazakos, A. O. Dulger *et al.* A SNP-based PCR-RFLP capillary electrophoresis analysis for the identification of the varietal origin of olive oils. *Food Chemistry*, 134(4):2411–2418, 2012.

K. J. Berger and D. A. Guss. Mycotoxins revisited: Part I. *Journal of Emergency Medicine*, 28(1):53–62, 2005.

J. Beutlich, I. Rodriguez *et al.* A predominant multidrug-resistant Salmonella enterica serovar Saintpaul clonal line in German turkey and related food products. *Applied and Environmental Microbiology*, 76(11):3657–3667, 2010.

G. Bonito. Fast DNA-based identification of the black truffle Tuber melanosporum with direct PCR and species-specific primers. *FEMS Microbiology Letters*, 301(2):171–175, 2009.

M. T. Bottero, T. Civera *et al.* Identification of cow's milk in "buffalo" cheese by duplex polymerase chain reaction. *Journal of Food Protection*, 65(2):362–366, 2002.

M. T. Bottero, T. Civera *et al.* A multiplex polymerase chain reaction for the identification of cows', goats' and sheep's milk in dairy products. *International Dairy Journal*, 13(4):277–282, 2003.

C. Breton, D. Claux *et al.* Comparative study of methods for DNA preparation from olive oil samples to identify cultivar SSR alleles in commercial oil samples: possible forensic applications. *Journal of Agricultural and Food Chemistry*, 52(3):531–537, 2004.

I. Bruni, A. Galimberti *et al.* A DNA barcoding approach to identify plant species in multiflower honey. *Food Chemistry*, 170:308–315.

B. Budowle, R. Murch *et al.* Microbial forensics: the next forensic challenge. *International Journal of Legal Medicine*, 119(6):317–330, 2005.

M. Busconi, C. Foroni *et al.* DNA extraction from olive oil and its use in the identification of the production cultivar. *Food Chemistry*, 83(1):127–134, 2003.

J. A. Cabezas, J. Ibanez *et al.* A 48 SNP set for grapevine cultivar identification. *BMC Plant Biology*, 11:153, 2011.

M. Casiraghi, M. Labra *et al.* DNA barcoding: a six-question tour to improve users' awareness about the method. *Briefings in Bioinformatics*, 11(4):440–453, 2010.

H.-H. Cheng, Y.-H. Cheng *et al.* Investigation of goats' milk adulteration with cows' milk by PCR. *Asian–Australasian Journal of Animal Sciences*, 19(10):1503–1507, 2006.

Y. H. Cheng, S. D. Chen *et al.* Investigation of goats' milk adulteration with cows' milk by PCR. *Asian-Australasian Journal of Animal Sciences*, 19(10):1503–1507, 2006.

J. C. Cho and J. M. Tiedje. Biogeography and degree of endemicity of fluorescent Pseudomonas strains in soil. *Applied and Environmental Microbiology*, 66(12):5548–5556, 2000.

E. Christopoulou, M. Lazaraki *et al.* Effectiveness of determinations of fatty acids and triglycerides for the detection of adulteration of olive oils with vegetable oils. *Food Chemistry*, 84(3):463–474, 2004.

G. Cipriani, M. T. Marrazzo *et al.* A set of microsatellite markers with long core repeat optimized for grape (Vitis spp.) genotyping. *BMC Plant Biology*, 8:127, 2008.

G. Cipriani, A. Spadotto *et al.* The SSR-based molecular profile of 1005 grapevine (Vitis vinifera; L.) accessions uncovers new synonymy and parentages, and reveals a large admixture amongst varieties of different geographic origin. *TAG Theoretical and Applied Genetics*, 121(8):1569–1585, 2010.

C. Consolandi, L. Palmieri *et al.* Olive variety identification by ligation detection reaction in a universal array format. *Journal of Biotechnology*, 129(3):565–574, 2007.

J. Costa, I. Mafra *et al.* Advances in vegetable oil authentication by DNA-based markers. *Trends in Food Science & Technology*, 26(1):43–55, 2012.

G. Cottenet, C. Blancpain *et al.* Simultaneous detection of cow and buffalo species in milk from China, India, and Pakistan using multiplex real-time PCR. *Journal of Dairy Science*, 94(8):3787–3793, 2011.

R. S. Cowan and M. F. Fay. Challenges in the DNA barcoding of plant material. *Methods in Molecular Biology*, (862):23–33, 2012.

M. J. Cox, W. O. Cookson *et al.* Sequencing the human microbiome in health and disease. *Human Molecular Genetics*, 22(R1):R88–R94, 2013.

S. F. Darwish, H. A. Allam *et al.* Evaluation of PCR Assay for Detection of Cow's Milk in Water Buffalo's Milk. *World Applied Sciences Journal*, 7(4):461–467, 2009.

S. De, B. Brahma *et al.* Simplex and duplex PCR assays for species specific identification of cattle and buffalo milk and cheese. *Food Control*, 22(5):690–696, 2011.

B. T. Dentinger and L. M. Suz. What's for dinner? Undescribed species of porcini in a commercial packet. *PeerJ*, 2:e570, 2014.

A. Di Genova, A. M. Almeida *et al.* Whole genome comparison between table and wine grapes reveals a comprehensive catalog of structural variants. *BMC Plant Biology*, 14:7, 2014.

A. Di Pinto, M. C. Conversano *et al.* Detection of cow milk in buffalo "Mozzarella" by polymerase chain reaction (PCR) assay. *Journal of Food Quality*, 27:428–435, 2004.

I. L.-C. Díaz, I. G. Alonso *et al.* Application of a polymerase chain reaction to detect adulteration of ovine cheeses with caprine milk. *European Food Research and Technology*, 225(3–4):345–349, 2007.

C. Directive. Proposal for a Council Directive relating to honey-DENLEG/2000/10. Brussels, 18 May, 2000.

J. P. Douet, M. Castroviejo *et al.* Rapid molecular typing of Tuber melanosporum, T. brumale and T. indicum from tree seedlings and canned truffles. *Analytical and Bioanalytical Chemistry*, 379(4):668–673, 2004.

S. Doveri, D. M. O'Sullivan *et al.* Non-concordance between genetic profiles of olive oil and fruit: a cautionary note to the use of DNA markers for provenance testing. *Journal of Agricultural and Food Chemistry,* 54(24):9221–9226.

S. Epis, C. Matinato *et al.* Molecular detection of poisonous mushrooms in different matrices. *Mycologia,* 102(3):747–754, 2010.

M. E. Fadda, S. Viale *et al.* Characterization of yeast population and molecular fingerprinting of Candida zeylanoides isolated from goat's milk collected in Sardinia. *International Journal of Food Microbiology,* 136(3):376–380, 2010.

M. A. Faria, R. Magalhaes *et al.* Vitis vinifera must varietal authentication using microsatellite DNA analysis (SSR). *Journal of Agricultural and Food Chemistry,* 48(4):1096–1100, 2000.

M. Feligini, I. Bonizzi *et al.* Detection of adulteration in Italian Mozzarella cheese using mitochondrial DNA templates as biomarkers. *Food Technology and Biotechnology,* 43(1):91–95, 2005.

F. Fernando de la Torre, R. Bautista *et al.* Isolation of DNA from olive oil and oil sediments: application in oil fingerprinting. *Food, Agriculture & Environment,* 2(1):84–89, 2004.

N. Fierer, C. L. Lauber *et al.* Forensic identification using skin bacterial communities. *Proceedings of the National Academy of Sciences,* 107(14):6477–6481, 2010.

E. N. Frankel. Chemistry of extra virgin olive oil: adulteration, oxidative stability, and antioxidants. *Journal of Agricultural and Food Chemistry,* 58(10):5991–6006, 2010.

R. R. Fulthorpe, A. N. Rhodes *et al.* High levels of endemicity apparent in 3-chlorobenzoate degrading soil bacteria. Applied and Environmental Microbiology, (64):1620–1627, 1998.

A. Galimberti, F. De Mattia *et al.* DNA barcoding as a new tool for food traceability. *Food Research International,* 50(1):55–63, 2013.

E. Garcia-Beneytez, M. V. Moreno-Arribas *et al.* Application of a DNA analysis method for the cultivar identification of grape musts and experimental and commercial wines of Vitis vinifera L. using microsatellite markers. *Journal of Agricultural and Food Chemistry,* 50(21):6090–6096, 2002.

C. Gausterer, M. Penker *et al.* Rapid genetic detection of ingested Amanita phalloides. *Forensic Science International: Genetics,* 9:66–71, 2014.

M. J. Giménez, F. Pistón *et al.* Application of real-time PCR on the development of molecular markers and to evaluate critical aspects for olive oil authentication. *Food Chemistry*, 118(2):482–487, 2010.

J. Goncalves, F. Pereira *et al.* New method for the simultaneous identification of cow, sheep, goat, and water buffalo in dairy products by analysis of short species-specific mitochondrial DNA targets. *Journal of Agricultural and Food Chemistry*, 60(42):10480–10485, 2012.

M. Harta, D. Pamfil *et al.* Identification of Romanian Vitis vinifera L. Cultivars in Must Using Nuclear Microsatellite Markers. *Bulletin of University of Agricultural Sciences and Veterinary Medicine Cluj-Napoca. Horticulture*, 67(1):198–203, 2010.

E. Hauser, E. Tietze *et al.* Pork contaminated with Salmonella enterica serovar 4,[5],12:i:-, an emerging health risk for humans. *Applied and Environmental Microbiology*, 76(14):4601–4610, 2010.

B. L. Herwaldt and M. L. Ackers. An outbreak in 1996 of cyclosporiasis associated with imported raspberries. The Cyclospora Working Group. *The New England Journal of Medicine*, 336(22):1548–1556, 1997.

B. L. Herwaldt and M. J. Beach. The return of Cyclospora in 1997: Another outbreak of cyclosporiasis in North America associated with imported raspberries. Cyclospora Working Group. *Annals of Internal Medicine*, 130(3):210–220, 1999.

P. M. Hollings worth, S. W. Graham *et al.* Choosing and using a plant DNA barcode. *PLoS One*, 6(5):e19254, 2011.

K. Kiritsakis and W. W. Christie. Analysis of edible oils. Handbook of Oive Oil. Aspen Publishers, R. A. L. John. Gaithersburg (USA), 129–151, 2000.

S. A. Kolavic, A. Kimura *et al.* An outbreak of Shigella dysenteriae type 2 among laboratory workers due to intentional food contamination. *The Journal of the American Medical Association*, 278(5):396–398, 1997.

M. Kotowicz, E. Adamczyk *et al.* Application of a duplex-PCR for detection of cows' milk in goats' milk. *Annals of Agricultural and Environmental Medicine*, 14(2):215–218, 2007.

I. Laube, H. Hird *et al.* Development of primer and probe sets for the detection of plant species in honey. *Food Chemistry*, 118(4):979–986, 2010.

J. C.-I. Lee, M. Cole *et al.* Identification of hallucinogenic fungi from the genera Psilocybe and Panaeolus by amplified fragment length polymorphism. *Electrophoresis*, 21(8):1484–1487, 2000.

D. Lijavetzky, J. A. Cabezas *et al.* High throughput SNP discovery and genotyping in grapevine (Vitis vinifera L.) by combining a re-sequencing approach and SNPlex technology. *BMC Genomics,* 8:424, 2007.

I. Lopez-Calleja, I. G. Alonso *et al.* PCR detection of cows' milk in water buffalo milk and mozzarella cheese. *International Dairy Journal,* 15(11):1122–1129, 2005.

I. Lopez-Calleja, I. Gonzalez *et al.* Application of a polymerase chain reaction to detect adulteration of ovine cheeses with caprine milk. *European Food Research and Technology,* 225:345–349, 2007.

R. M. Lopparelli, B. Cardazzo *et al.* Real-time TaqMan polymerase chain reaction detection and quantification of cow DNA in pure water buffalo mozzarella cheese: method validation and its application on commercial samples. *Journal of Agricultural and Food Chemistry,* 55(9):3429–3434, 2007.

D. M. A. M. Luykx and S. M. van Ruth. An overview of analytical methods for determining the geographical origin of food products. *Food Chemistry,* 107(2):897–911, 2008.

K. Maeta, T. Ochi *et al.* Rapid species identification of cooked poisonous mushrooms by using real-time PCR. *Applied and Environmental Microbiology,* 74(10):3306–3309, 2008.

I. Mafra, I. M. Ferreira *et al.* A novel approach to the quantification of bovine milk in ovine cheeses using a duplex polymerase chain reaction method. *Journal of Agricultural and Food Chemistry,* 52(16):4943–4947, 2004.

I. Mafra, I. M. Ferreira *et al.* Food authentication by PCR-based methods. *European Food Research and Technology,* 227(3):649–665, 2008.

I. Mafra, A. Roxo *et al.* A duplex polymerase chain reaction for the quantitative detection of cows' milk in goats' milk cheese. *International Dairy Journal,* 17(9):1132–1138, 2007.

C. Mammina, A. Aleo *et al.* Characterization of Listeria monocytogenes isolates from human listeriosis cases in Italy. *Journal of Clinical Microbiology,* 47(9):2925–2930, 2009.

P. Martins-Lopes, S. Gomes *et al.* DNA Markers for Portuguese Olive Oil Fingerprinting. *Journal of Agricultural and Food Chemistry,* 56(24):11786–11791, 2008.

E. Maskova and I. Paulickova. PCR-based detection of cow's milk in goat and sheep cheeses marketed in the Czech Republic. *Czech Journal of Food Sciences,* 24(3):127–132, 2006.

F. Monteiro-da-Silva, R. Araújo *et al.* Interindividual variability and intraindividual stability of oral fungal microbiota over time. *Medical Mycology*, 52(5):498–505, 2014.

P. Mullner, J. M. Collins-Emerson *et al.* Molecular epidemiology of Campylobacter jejuni in a geographically isolated country with a uniquely structured poultry industry. *Applied and Environmental Microbiology*, 76(7):2145–2154, 2010.

I. Muzzalupo, M. Pellegrino *et al.* Detection of DNA in virgin olive oils extracted from destoned fruits. *European Food Research and Technology*, 224(4):469–475, 2007.

I. Muzzalupo and E. Perri. Recovery and characterisation of DNA from virgin olive oil. *European Food Research and Technology*, 214(6):528–531, 2002.

N. Nikoloudakis, G. Banilas *et al.* Discrimination and genetic diversity among cultivated olives of Greece using RAPD markers. *Journal of the American Society for Horticultural Science*, 128(5):741–746, 2003.

K. G. Nugent and B. J. Saville. Forensic analysis of hallucinogenic fungi: a DNA-based approach. *Forensic Science International*, 140(2–3):147–157, 2004.

C. Olivieri, I. Marota *et al.* Tracking Plant, Fungal, and Bacterial DNA in Honey Specimens*. *Journal of Forensic Sciences*, 57(1):222–227, 2012.

J. Park, S. Lee *et al.* Comparative study between Next Generation Sequencing Technique and identification of microarray for Species Identification within blended food products. *BioChip Journal*, 6(4):354–361, 2012.

A. Pasqualone, C. Montemurro *et al.* Identification of Virgin Olive Oil from Different Cultivars by Analysis of DNA Microsatellites. *Journal of Agricultural and Food Chemistry*, 52(5):1068–1071, 2004.

C. Piras, F. Cesare Marincola *et al.* A NMR metabolomics study of the ripening process of the Fiore Sardo cheese produced with autochthonous adjunct cultures. *Food Chemistry*, 141(3):2137–2147, 2013.

S. Rea, K. Chikuni *et al.* Use of duplex polymerase chain reaction (duplex-PCR) technique to identify bovine and water buffalo milk used in making mozzarella cheese. *Journal of Dairy Research*, 68(4):689–698, 2001.

S. Reale, A. Campanella *et al.* A novel method for species identification in milk and milk-based products. *Journal of Dairy Research*, 75(1):107–112, 2008.

S. Reale, S. Doveri *et al.* SNP-based markers for discriminating olive (Olea europaea L.) cultivars. *Genome / National Research Council Canada = Genome / Conseil national de Recherches Canada*, 49(9):1193–1205, 2006.

D. F. Rodrigues, E. da C Jesus *et al.* Biogeography of two cold-adapted genera: Psychrobacter and Exiguobacterium. *The ISME Journal*, 3(6):658–665, 2009.

A. Sandionigia, A. Galimbertia *et al.* Analytical approaches for DNA barcoding data — how to find a way for plants? *Plant Biosystems*, 146(4):805–813, 2012.

S. Santos, M. Oliveira *et al.* A forensic perspective on the genetic identification of grapevine (Vitis vinifera L.) varieties using STR markers. *Electrophoresis*, 35(21–22):3201–3207, 2014.

K. M. Sefc, S. Guggenberger *et al.* Genetic analysis of grape berries and raisins using microsatellite markers. *Vitis*, 37(3):123–125, 1998.

S. K. Sheppard, F. Colles *et al.* Host association of Campylobacter genotypes transcends geographic variation. *Applied and Environmental Microbiology*, 76(15):5269–5277, 2010.

R. Siret, J. M. Boursiquot *et al.* (2000). Toward the authentication of varietal wines by the analysis of grape (Vitis vinifera L.) residual DNA in must and wine using microsatellite markers. *Journal of Agricultural and Food Chemistry*, 48(10):5035–5040, 2000.

R. Siret, O. Gigaud *et al.* Analysis of grape Vitis vinifera L. DNA in must mixtures and experimental mixed wines using microsatellite markers. *Journal of Agricultural and Food Chemistry*, 50(13):3822–3827, 2002.

S. Stolzenbach, D. V. Byrne *et al.* Sensory local uniqueness of Danish honeys. *Food Research International*, 44(9):2766–2774, 2011.

S. M. Syne, A. Ramsubhag *et al.* Occurrence and genetic relatedness of Listeria spp. in two brands of locally processed ready-to-eat meats in Trinidad. *Epidemiology and infection*, 139(5):718–727, 2011.

P. This, A. Jung *et al.* Development of a standard set of microsatellite reference alleles for identification of grape cultivars. *Theoretical and Applied Genetics*, 109(7):1448–1458, 2004.

P. J. Turnbaugh, M. Hamady *et al.* A core gut microbiome in obese and lean twins. *Nature*, 457(7228):480–484, 2009.

A. Valentini, C. Miquel *et al.* DNA barcoding for honey biodiversity. *Diversity*, 2(4):610–661, 2010.

M. Vietina, C. Agrimonti *et al.* Applicability of SSR markers to the traceability of monovarietal olive oils. *Journal of the Science of Food and Agriculture*, 91(8):1381–1391, 2011.

M. Woolfe and S. Primrose. Food forensics: using DNA technology to combat misdescription and fraud. *Trends in Biotechnology*, 22(5):222–226, 2004.

M. Yeung. ADSA Foundation Scholar Award: Trends in culture-independent methods for assessing dairy food quality and safety: Emerging metagenomic tools. *Journal of Dairy Science*, 95(12):6831–6842, 2012.

M. Zou, S. Keelara *et al.* Molecular characterization of Salmonella enterica serotype Enteritidis isolates from humans by antimicrobial resistance, virulence genes, and pulsed-field gel electrophoresis. *Foodborne Pathogens and Disease*, 9(3):232–238, 2012.

CHAPTER 21

Forensic Botany

Kayla Baylor and Heather Miller Coyle

Forensic Science Department,
Henry C. Lee College of Criminal Justice & Forensic Sciences,
University of New Haven, 300 Boston Post Road,
West Haven, CT 06516, USA

1 Introduction

Plants are monitored as they are transported between countries for a variety of reasons. In agricultural import or export, they are monitored for quality and quantity for tax purposes and to insure they are of correct identity (Espinoza *et al.*, 2014; Liu *et al.*, 2013; Moya *et al.*, 2013; Gathier *et al.*, 2013; Sajeva *et al.*, 2013; Lancaster and Espinoza, 2012; Xiang *et al.*, 2011; Lahaye *et al.*, 2008). CITES.org is a website that monitors trends for reported and unreported trade of many types of species and exotics. The Convention on International Trade in Endangered species of Wild Fauna and Flora (CITES) is an agreement between governments to prevent illegal trade in species that if over harvested will become endangered or extinct (Barrett *et al.*, 2010; Kite *et al.*, 2010; Roberts and Solow, 2008). For plants, these species primarily fall into two major categories: those for illicit drug trade and those for illicit collection. Two monitored plant species discussed here are cycads and wild orchids. Wild orchids in Nepal, for example, are protected under The Forest Act (1993), Forest Regulations (1995) and an all-inclusive protection provided by amendment to these policies in 2001. Despite these policies, the Nepalese government on April 14, 2008 published notification allowing for collection of wild orchids for trade. Absence of clear policy and lack of enforcement has led to a rise in illegal trade of wild orchids from this region. Wild orchids are primarily collected and used for flora culture or medicinal purposes (Rokaya *et al.*, 2014; Subedi *et al.*, 2013). Medicinal purposes vary widely and the orchids are ground to a paste, mixed with a liquid such as honey or milk and applied to burns and fractured bones or consumed as a tonic. Average price for Nepalese orchids is USD 1.5–2.5 per pot (7.5–10 pots, 1 kg) but rare species can bring up to 1,300 USD per kg for certain Asian markets. This is a difficult market for monitoring since the issue originates from a traditional medicine health care system for the country and produces substantial income for families who practice subsistence agriculture.

Cycads with the exception of a few species such as sago palm, are extremely rare and are on the CITES Appendix I list which bans any international trade. CITES Appendix II lists plants that may be traded but only with a legal export permit certifying that the plant was artificially propagated and not taken from the wild (www.CITES.org). The sago palm is readily found in garden shops in Florida and Southern California and is a common landscaping species. Rare species of cycad, however, are being purchased by plant collectors who enjoy the cycad as a piece of Jurassic history where after surviving approximately 250 million years; some species are now endangered or extinct (Kessler, 2005). In the desire to save and possess, the effect of humans in the past 100 years due to over collection and destruction of habitat has decimated the world's cycad population. The financial incentive is high for smugglers as locals can be paid as little as two dollars per day but a rare species once smuggled in to the US, can fetch as much as USD 50,000 per plant. In fact, in August 2014, thieves stole 24 cycads; most were the critically endangered cycad *Encephalartos latifrons,* and two cycads, *Encephalartos caffer.* These rare species are indigenous to South Africa according to a spokesperson with the South African National Biodiversity Institute (Sanbi). The estimated combined plant and animal illegal international trade is thought to be between six and ten million dollars annually. For both of these plants, orchids and cycads, there has been extensive molecular biological analysis of genetic diversity in populations as well as genome sequencing to carefully characterize existing populations for evolutionary studies and conservation biology (Yang *et al.*, 2013; Tsai *et al.*, 2008; Cai *et al.*, 2015; Bogler and Francisco-Ortega, 2004; Feng *et al.*, 2014; The Plant Genomics Consortium, 2015).

2 Genetics

2.1 *Population Genetics*

Biodiversity is the genetic term for variation in an organisms DNA and allows for the accumulation of differences between individuals within the same population. These differences can be used to classify a plant specimen to a major group (species), subgroup (subspecies) and sometimes uniqueness if sufficient genetic differences are detected within a population to assess the sample as unique. The selection of a region of an organism's genome is typically based on an initial survey of a plant population for variation with a panel of genetic markers; if sufficient variation is present in the population, it is a useful region or marker to track genetic diversity. If sufficient regions or markers are tested, then classification can be made with a high degree of statistical and scientific certainty. Even if a level of uniqueness cannot be fully achieved and classification to a species level is the limit, exclusions are still informative.

Biodiversity is studied for academic purposes and for species preservation for conservation biology and breeding programs. If a species becomes too genetically uniform, it may be susceptible to large scale disease and other inbreeding effects (Pekkala *et al.*, 2014). Inbreeding effect refers to a population deriving from a small founder group or a larger isolated group that continually breeds within its own group to the point of its own genetic detriment

(Vinson *et al.*, 2015). Inbreeding in humans can be due to social or cultural reasons where individuals prefer to marry and bear children within their own populations (e.g. Amish) (Seboun *et al.*, 2005; van der Walt *et al.*, 2005). This is the basis for reporting forensic genetic statistics for random match probabilities for different human populations as Caucasian, Black, Asian and Hispanic in forensic human identification. Studies on allele frequencies show that there are differences based on origin or ethnicity between these human population groups and therefore, statistically, these populations are not combined when calculating random match probabilities or likelihood ratios (LRs). The same concept holds true for plant species and common genetics can be used with appropriate marker systems to show an association back to an original founder population for geographic sourcing (Shirley *et al.*, 2013; Allgeier *et al.*, 2011). This method for sourcing is especially useful if the original populations are highly inbred as is common with plant seed stocks since breeders intentionally back-cross into their own genetic lines to maintain uniformity of traits such as disease resistance, grain yield or flower morphology (Placido *et al.*, 2013). In this manner, traditional plant breeders can optimize a plant for the positive attributes and alter one feature at a time to improve flower color for example. Within a population, occasional genetic mutations occur and if the mutation results in the positive attribute, the mutant plant is back-crossed into the founder seed line to incorporate the new genetic trait. Certain plant species are more prone to genetic mutations that alter ploidy or chromosome number, which in humans would be commonly lethal or interferes with sexual reproduction but in plants is tolerated (Liu *et al.*, 2015; Gross and Schiestl, 2015; Scholes and Paige, 2015). Wheat, orchids and marijuana are good examples of highly tolerated increases in ploidy that yield genetically positive results over time through breeding programs (Yang *et al.*, 2014; Bagheri and Mansouri, 2015; Pinheiro *et al.*, 2010; Zonneveld, 2012) (Table 1). In general, increased ploidy leads to increased production in biosynthetic pathways and larger flower and leaf morphology which are often considered more desirable in flora culture.

Table 1: Common ploidy levels in wild and cultivated plant populations where N is the haploid condition. Ploidy reference: $2N$ (diploid), $4N$ (tetraploid), $6N$ (hexaploid).

Genus species	Wild ploidy	Cultivated ploidy
Wheat	$2N$	$2N, 4N, 6N$
Marijuana	$2N$	$2N, 4N$
Orchid	$2N$	$2N, 4N$
Cycad	$2N$	$2N, 4N, 6N$

2.2 Plant BioProjects

There are an estimated number of 400,000 plant species in our global world. In 1997, The World Conservation Union (IUCN) listed 34,000 as threatened species out of the 60,000 evaluated or approximately 50% of the plant species in their study (Brummitt *et al.*, 2015). Other estimates are similar and range from 25% to 50% of all plants in the world that are threatened by lack of genetic diversity and number either through rarity in nature, limited geography for natural habitat, or over harvesting to the point of rarity. The plants that are most significantly studied for information on whole genomes and transcriptomes are those that are our edible grains and provide a foundation for each countries agronomic business and food supply (Table 2). These primarily include corn, wheat, sorghum and rice. The National Center for Biotechnology Information (NCBI) plant registry for genome sequencing and transcriptome sequencing projects is a good resource for identifying whole plant genome sequencing programs as most are listed at the site due to the national sequence repository (NCBI).

3 Methods for Classification

3.1 Morphology

Orchids
Orchids are angiosperms or flowering land plants. Within the angiosperms, a total of 377 orchid species belonging to 100 genera are

Table 2:   Genome projects listed in NCBI BioProject.

Latin name	Common name	Project location
Camellia sinensis	Tea	State Key Laboratory of Tea Plant Biology and Utilization
Triticum aestivum	Bread Wheat	University of Minnesota
Fragaria vesca subsp americana	Woodland Strawberry	Anhui Agricultural University
Oryza sativa japonica	Rice	University of Arkansas
Arabidopsis thaliana	Mouse Ear Cress	Max Planck Institute for Plant Breeding Research
Sorghum bicolor	Sorghum	National Institute of Agrobiological Sciences
Solanum lycopersicum	Tomato	Michigan State University
Cannabis sativa	Marijuana	University of Toronto

reported from Nepal alone. Due to a traditional plant, medicinal culture and lack of modern health care facilities, the orchid is still used medicinally by approximately 80% of its population (Bharal *et al.*, 2014; Paul *et al.*, 2013). Orchids are primarily identified by the flower morphology so if flowering cannot be induced, then DNA barcoding is used to identify to the species level (Figure 1). It appears that orchids have some antibiotic and pain relief properties as majority use is for skin burns, fractured and dislocated bones, headache, fever and wounds. Medicinal genera include *Acampe, Aerides, Coelogyne, Crepidium, Dactylorhiza, Dendrobium, Gastrodia, Eulophia, Flickingeria, Otochilus, Pholidota, Satyrium* and *Vanda.*

Cycads
Belonging to the approximately 1,000 species of gymnosperms or seed-bearing vascular plants, are the conifers, cycads and the gingko. For accuracy in naming, a consortium between the Royal Botanic Gardens, Kew and Missouri Botanical Garden has created "The Plant List" that provides the accepted Latin name for most species, the synonyms by which many plants are known and the unresolved names by which some species are referred to (The Plant List). The

Dendrobium Orchid. (*source:* http://naturalgarden.org/dendrobium-orchids)

Satyrium Orchid. (*source:* http://pacificbulbsociety.org/pbswiki/index.php/Satyrium)

Acampe Orchid. (*source:* http://www.rv-orchidworks.com/orchidtalk/orchids-other-genera-bloom/20103-acampe-praemorsa.html)

Flickingeria Orchid. (*source:* http://www.orchidspecies.com/flickscopa.htm)

Figure 1:   Examples of floral morphology of various orchid genera.

Plant List includes over a million scientific plant names to species rank, of which 298,900 are accepted species names. For example, searching under the keyword *Encephalartos,* a genus of cycad native to Africa, yielded a total of 148 characterized plant records from The Plant List database with provenance. These types of resources are useful as known reference databases for species identification by morphology and DNA barcoding (Figure 2).

Figure 2: A member of the Cycadales (http://www.adonline.id.au/plantevol/tour/seed-plants).

3.2 *Molecular Methods*

Common DNA markers for classification of plants are listed in Table 3 (Hollingsworth, 2011; Parks *et al.*, 2009). These genetic markers (rbcL, matK, ITS and trn) are common ones used to barcode and delineate evolutionary trends in gene inheritance for plant lineages but are also useful for forensic classification schemes. Fine mapping of genetic differences in lineages is performed by DNA sequencing and is used in forensic applications for haplotype grouping of populations and often for species identification (Hollingsworth, 2011; Parks *et al.*, 2009). Within the DNA sequences of these different amplification products of genetic marker regions are single base variations (SNPs) and indels (insertion–deletions) that have been identified through sequence alignment of common regions between different samples of the same species. Sequence differences that hold true within a species can be used to classify to the species level within DNA databases when comparing sequences of the same region across species. In the NCBI SNP database (dbSNP), there are 38, 282, 603 recorded SNPs, primarily in plant

Table 3: Common biomarkers used alone or in combination for classification in plant phylogenies.

Abbreviation	Genetic locus information	Genome
rbcL	Ribulose-bisphosphate carboxylase, large subunit	Plastid region, well-characterized, frequent component of a barcode system for high level species discrimination, less variable than other plant markers but universal amplification across species
trnH-psbA	Transfer RNA series (trnH) — chloroplast genome (psbA)	93% amplification across land plants, high level of species discrimination, but sequencing difficulty in obtaining bidirectional traces make this marker challenging
matK	Chloroplast maturase K gene	Plastid region, rapidly evolving, high level of discrimination between species but not all species amplify with common PCR primers
ITS	Internal transcribed spacer region	Non-functional RNA spacer sequence

species of agricultural significance (*Zea mays* (corn), *Oryza sativa* (rice), and *Arabidopsis thaliana* (cress)). In this manner, DNA databases can be mined for information regarding potential for unique markers based on hyper-variability using a bioinformatics approach.

For orchids, in the year 2014, the first whole genome of *Phalaenopsis equestris,* a parent of many commercial breeding programs was sequenced (Cai *et al.,* 2015; *Science Daily*). This orchid species also holds a second claim to fame as being also the first plant with a CAM (Crassulacean Acid Metabolism) biosynthetic pathway to be completely sequenced. Evidence of gene duplication, transposable elements and expanded and highly diverse MADS-box genes were identified. This sequencing project known as Orchid Genome Project (an international collaboration between Tsinghua University and The National Orchid Conservation Center in China as well as other collaborators in Chengkong University, Taiwan; Ghent

University, Belgium; and Institute of Botany of CAS, China) was a first step in establishing a benchmark for exploring existing orchid genetic diversity as the high levels of illegal collection are decimating the natural populations globally. The gene duplication events are tracked by comparison of homologous genes in other plant systems and some loss in CAM genes in the orchid lineage could explain the current CAM biosynthetic pathway for photosynthesis observed in current *Phalaenopsis*. The transposable elements would account for the expanded intron length in orchids which is on average 2,922 base pairs in length, much larger than for other plants that have been genome sequenced. MADS-box genes regulate floral development and the expanded diversity in the MADS-box C and D classes, B class of AP3 and AGL6 class genes likely contribute to the extremely diverse size and shapes of flowers observed in orchids. Once assembled, the *Phalaenopsis* genome was found to contain 29, 431 potential protein encoding regions and these will be further studied to elucidate function and may identify the compounds with antibiotic-like properties observed for some orchid species.

For cycads, the Plant Genomics Consortium (Cold Spring Harbor Laboratory, New York University, American Museum of Natural History) is using a comparative genomics approach by constructing cDNA libraries and examining expressed sequence tags (ESTs) to compare development of both vegetative and reproductive tissues for select taxa (Feng *et al.*, 2014; Cycad and Gymnosperm Project). Since cycads are ancient plant species, there is interest in determining how gene structure and function changed during evolution to create angiosperms, higher order flowering plants as well as for conservation studies of restricted natural populations of cycads. Interestingly, cycads are also being studied for potential medicinal value and neurotoxic compounds such as beta methyl-amino-L-alanine (BMAA) which was discovered by accident to be a non-proteinogenic amino acid produced by cyanobacteria that reside in the roots of the cycad (Vyas and Weiss, 2009; Holtcamp, 2012). BMAA was first identified in 1967 in cycad trees from Guam and was also identified from seeds that were part of the diet of afflicted populations with ALS/Parkinsonism dementia complex.

The role of BMAA is hypothesized to mimic a neurotransmitter, glutamate, thus over-stimulating the glutamate neurotransmitter in human neurons and additional studies show this substance acts in three ways to degenerate neurons: non-cell autonomous death, excitotoxicity and by mitochondrial dysfunction (Holtcamp, 2012).

In summary, these are just two examples of plants that are highly trafficked plant species that are being monitored by CITES and are being investigated for genetic diversity for conservation biology programs as well as for potential medicinal value (Uzuner *et al.*, 2012; Fan *et al.*, 2012; Chen *et al.*, 2012). A large number of genetic study and deep-sequencing programs include identification of plant and animal DNA found in traditional Chinese medicines (TCMs) and are part of a quality control program for the herbal markets for heavy metals and plant toxins that have been identified in some TCMs. Undeclared or misidentified ingredients in TCMs can pose health concerns including plant toxins, heavy metals, allergens and pharmaceutically active ingredients of undetermined concentrations. One excellent example for potential public safety issues is described in (Coghlan *et al.*, 2012) such as the misidentification of *Aristolochia* for *Stephania* in the 1990's which led to more than a hundred women to suffer kidney failure and for some, urinary tract cancer. While many of our best medicines such as aspirin (identified in 1763, willow tree) and taxol (identified in 1962, Pacific yew) have originated from plant species, there are obviously more yet to be discovered and studied for best practices, therapy and dosages. Protection of natural plant populations and monitoring by CITES is a key as that is the wild reservoir for genetic diversity that must be maintained to some level or loss of diversity and inbreeding effects can eliminate these useful plant populations.

References

L. Allgeier, J. Hemenway, N. Shirley, T. LaNier and H. Coyle. Field testing of collection cards for *Cannabis sativa* samples with a single hexanucleotide DNA marker. *Journal of Forensic Sciences*, 56(5):1245–1249, 2011.

M. Bagheri and H. Mansouri. Effect of induced polyploidy on some biochemical parameters in *Cannabis sativa L. Applied Biochemistry and Biotechnology*, 175(5):2366–2375, 2015.

M. Barrett, J. Brown, M. Morikawa, J. Labat and A. Yoder. Conservation. CITES designation for endangered rosewood in Madagascar. *Science*, 328:1109–1110, 2010.

A. Bharal, M. Kashyap, V. Kumar Sohpal and J. Kaur Sembi. Evaluation of antimicrobial properties of terrestrial orchids (collected from Northern Himalayas) against certain human pathogens. *International Journal of Bioassays*, 3(6):3036–3039, 2014.

D. Bogler and J. Francisco-Ortega. Molecular systematic studies in Cycads: evidence from the trnL intron and ITS2 rDNA sequences. *The Botanical Review*, 70(2):260–273, 2004.

N. Brummitt, S. Bachman, E. Aletrari, H. Chadburn, J. Griffiths-Lee, M. Lutz, J. Moat, M. Rivers, M. Syfert and E. Nic Lughadha. The sampled red list index for plants, Phase II: Ground-truthing specimen-based conservation assessments. *Philosophical Transactions of the Royal Society of London, B: Biological Sciences*, 370(1662):20140015, 2015.

R. Chen, J. Dong, X. Cui, W. Wang, A. Yasmeen, Y. Deng, X. Zeng and Z. Tang. DNA based identification of medicinal materials in Chinese patent medicines. *Scientific Reports*, 2(958):1–5, 2012.

M. Coghlan, J. Haile, J. Houston, D. Murray, N. White, P. Moolhuijzen, M. Bellgard and M. Bunce. Deep sequencing of plant and animal DNA contained within traditional Chinese medicines reveals legality issues and health safety concerns. PLoS Genetics, 8(4):1–11, 2012.

J. Cai, X. Liu, K. Vanneste, S. Proost, W.-C. Tsai, K.-W. Liu, L.-J. Chen, Y. He, Q. Xu, C. Bian, Z. Zheng, F. Sun, W. Liu, Y.-Y. Hsiao, Z.-J. Pan, C.-C. Hsu, Y.-P. Yang, Y.-C. Hsu, Y.-C. Chuang, A. Dievart, J.-F. Dufayard, X. Xu, J.-Y. Wang, J. Wang, X.-J. Xiao, X.-M. Zhao, R. Du, G.-Q. Zhang, M. Wang, Y.-Y. Su, G.-C. Xie, G.-H. Liu, L.-Q. Li, L.-Q. Huang, Y.-B. Luo, H.-H. Chen, Y. Van de Peer and Z.-J. Liu. The genome sequence of the orchid *Phalaenopsis equestris. Nature Genetics*, 47:65–72, 2015.

Cycad and Gymnosperm Genomic Project — The Plant Genomics Consortium. http://sciweb.nybg.org/science2/GenomicsLab.asp.html, accessed March 10, 2015.

Cycad and Gymnosperm Genomics Project. http://sciweb.nybg.org, accessed March 10, 2015.

E. Espinoza, C. Lancaster, N. Kreitals, M. Hata, R. Cody and R. Blanchette. Distinguishing wild from cultivated agarwood (*Aquilaria* spp.) using direct analysis in real time and time of-flight mass spectrometry. *Rapid Communications in Mass Spectrometry*, 28(3):281–289, 2014.

T.-P. Fan, G. Deal, H.-L. Koo, D. Rees, H. Sun, S. Chen, J.-H. Dou, V. Makarov, O. Pozharitskaya, A. Shikov, Shik Y. Kim, Y.-T. Huang, Y. Shiun Chang, W. Jia, A. Dias, V. Chi-woon Wong and K. Chan. Future development of global regulations of Chinese herbal products. *Journal of Ethnopharmacology*, 140:568–586, 2012.

X. Feng, Y. Wang and X. Gong. Genetic diversity, genetic structure and demographic history of *Cycas simplicipinna* (Cycadaceae) assessed by DNA sequences and SSR markers. *BMC Plant Biology*, 14:187–203, 2004.

G. Gathier, T. van der Niet, T. Peelen, R. van Vugt, M. Eurlings and B. Gravendeel. Forensic identification of CITES protected slimming cactus (*Hoodia*) using DNA barcoding. *Journal of Forensic Science*, 58(6):1467–1471, 2013.

K. Gross and F. Schiestl. Are tetraploids more successful? Floral signals, reproductive success and floral isolation in mixed-ploidy populations of a terrestrial orchid. *Annals of Botany*, 115(2):263–273, 2015.

P. Hollingsworth, S. Graham and D. Little. Choosing and using a plant DNA barcode. *PLoS ONE*, 6(5):1–13, 2011.

W. Holtcamp. The emerging science of BMAA. *Environmental Health Perspectives*, 120(3):A110–A117, 2012.

L. Kessler. The Cult of the Cycads. http://www.nytimes.com/2005/08/28/magazine/28CYCADS.html?pagewanted=print, accessed March 19, 2015.

G. Kite, P. Green, N. Veitch, M. Groves, P. Gasson and M. Simmonds. Dalnigrin, aneoflavonoid marker for the identification of Brazilian rosewood (*Dalbergia nigra*) in CITES enforcement. *Phytochemistry*, 71(10):1122–1131, 2010.

R. Lahaye, M. van der Bank, D. Bogarin, J. Warner, F. Pupulin, G. Gigot, O. Maurin, S. Duthoit, T. Barraclough and V. Savolainen. DNA barcoding the floras of biodiversity hotspots. *Proceedings of the National Academy of Sciences USA*, 105(8):2923–2928, 2008.

C. Lancaster and E. Espinoza. Analysis of select *Dalbergia* and trade timber using direct analysis in real time and time-of-flight mass spectrometry for CITES enforcement. *Rapid Communications in Mass Spectrometry*, 26(9):1147–1156, 2012.

Y. Liu, S. Ahmed and C. Long. Ethnobotanical survey of cooling herbal drinks from southern China. *Journal of Ethnobiology and Ethnomedicine*, 9:82, 2013.

Y. Liu, D. Li, L. Yan and H. Huang. The microgeographical patterns of morphological and molecular variation of a mixed ploidy population in the species complex. *Actinidia chinensis*. *PLoS One*, 10(2):e0117596, 2015.

R. Moya, M. Wiemann and C. Olivares. Identification of endangered or threatened Costa Rican tree species by wood anatomy and fluorescence activity. *Revista de Biología Tropical*, 61(3):1133–1156, 2013.

National Center for Biotechnology Information (NCBI). http://www.ncbi.nlm.nih.gov, accessed March 19, 2015.

M. Parks, R. Cronn and A. Liston. Increasing phylogenetic resolution at low taxonomic levels using massively parallel sequencing of chloroplast genomes. *BMC Biology*, 7:84, 2009.

M. Patton. Genetic studies in the Amish community. *Annals of Human Biology*, 32(2):163–167, 2005.

P. Paul, A. Chowdhury, D. Nath and M. Kanti Bhattacharjee. Antimicrobial efficacy of orchid extracts as potential inhibitors of antibiotic resistant strains of *Escherichia coli*. *Asian Journal of Pharmaceutical and Clinical Research*, 6(3):108–111, 2013.

N. Pekkala, K. Knott, J. Kotiaho, K. Nissinen and M. Puurtinen. The effect of inbreeding rate on fitness, inbreeding depression and heterosis over a range of inbreeding coefficients. *Evolutionary Applications*, 7(9):1107–1119, 2014.

F. Pinheiro, F. De Barros, C. Palma-Silva, D. Meyer, M. Fay, R. Suzuki, C. Lexer and S. Cozzolino. Hybridization and introgression across different ploidy levels in the Neotropical orchids *Epidendrum fulgens* and *E. puniceoluteum* (Orchidaceae). *Molecular Ecology*, 19(18):3981–3994, 2010.

D. Placido, M. Campbell, J. Folsom, X. Cui, G. Kruger, P. Baenziger and H. Walia. Introgression of novel traits from a wild wheat relative improves drought adaptation in wheat. *Plant Physiology*, 161(4):1806–1819, 2013.

Research SEA. Scientists completed the first orchid whole genome sequencing. Science Daily. http://www.sciencedaily.com, accessed March 10, 2015.

D. Roberts and A. Solow. The effect of the Convention on International Trade in Endangered Species on scientific collections. *Proceedings of the Royal Society B: Biological Sciences*, 275:987–989, 2008.

M. Rokaya, Y. Uprety, R. Poudel, B. Timsina, Z. Münzbergová, H. Asselin, A. Tiwari, S. Shrestha and S. Sigdel. Traditional uses of medicinal plants in gastrointestinal disorders in Nepal. *Journal of Ethnopharmacology*, 158PA:221–229, 2014.

M. Sajeva, C. Augugliaro, M. Smith and E Oddo. Regulating Internet trade in CITES species. *Conservation Biology*, 27(2):429–430, 2013.

E. Seboun, A. Lemainque and C. Jackson. Amish brittle hair syndrome gene maps to 7p14.1. *American Journal of Medical Genetics Part A*, 134(3):290–294, 2005.

D. Scholes and K. Paige. Plasticity in ploidy: A generalized response to stress. *Trends in Plant Science*, 20(3):165–175, 2015.

N. Shirley, L. Allgeier, T. Lanier and H. Coyle. Analysis of the NMI01 marker for a population database of cannabis seeds. *Journal of Forensic Sciences*, 58(1):S176–S182, 2013.

A. Subedi, B. Kunwar, Y. Choi, Y. Dai, T. van Andel, R. Chaudhary, H. de Boer and B. Gravendeel. Collection and trade of wild-harvested orchids in Nepal. *Journal of Ethnobiology and Ethnomedicine*, 9(1):64, 2013.

The Plant List. http://www.theplantlist.org, accessed March 21, 2015.

W.-C. Tsai, Y.-Y. Hsiao, Z.-J. Pan, C.-C. Hsu, Y.-P. Yang, W.-H. Chen and H.-H. Chen. Molecular biology of orchid flowers: With emphasis on *Phalaenopsis*. *Advances in Botanical Research*, 47:100–135, 2008.

H. Uzuner, R. Bauer, T.-P. Fan, D. Guo, A. Dias, H. El-Nezami, T. Efferth, E. Williamson, M. Heinrich, N. Robinson, P. Hylands, B. Hendry, Y.-C. Cheng and Q. Xu. Traditional Chinese medicine research in the post-genomic era: Good practice, priorities, challenges and opportunities. *Journal of Ethnopharmacology*, 140:458–468, 2012.

J. van der Walt, W. Scott, S. Slifer, P. Gaskell, E. Martin, K. Welsh-Bohmer, M. Creason, A. Crunk, D. Fuzzell, L. McFarland, C. Kroner, C. Jackson, J. Haines and M. Pericak-Vance. Maternal lineages and Alzheimer disease risk in the Old Order Amish. *Human Genetics*, 118(1):115–122, 2005.

C. Vinson, M. Kanashiro, S. Harris and D. Boshier. Impacts of selective logging on inbreeding and gene flow in two Amazonian timber species with contrasting ecological and reproductive characteristics. *Molecular Ecology*, 24(1):38–53, 2015.

K. Vyas and J. Weiss. BMAA — An unusual cyanobacterial neurotoxin. *Amyotrophic Lateral Sclerosis*, 2:50–55, 2009.

X. Xiang, H. Hu, W. Wang and X. Jin. DNA barcoding of the recently evolved genus Holcoglossum (*Orchidaceae: Aeridinae*):A test of DNA barcode candidates. *Molecular Ecology Resources*, 11(6):1012–1021, 2011.

J.-B. Yang, M. Tang, H.-T. Li, Z.-R. Zhang and D.-Z. Li. Complete chloroplast genome of the genus, *Cymbidium*, lights into species identification, phylogenetic implications and population genetic analyses. *BMC Evolutionary Biology*, 13:84–96, 2013.

C. Yang, L. Zhao, H. Zhang, Z. Yang, H. Wang, S. Wen, C. Zhang, S. Rustgi, D. von Wettstein and B. Liu. Evolution of physiological responses to salt stress in hexaploid wheat. *Proceedings of National Academy of Science USA*, 111(32):11882–11887, 2014.

B. Zonneveld. Genome sizes for all genera of Cycadales. *Plant Biology* (Stuttgart), 14(1):253–256, 2012.

CHAPTER 22

Genetic and Genomic Methods of Microbial Taxonomic Assignment

Marc W. Allard,* Mark Wilson† and Eric W. Brown*

*Food and Drug Administration, Office of Regulatory Science, Division of Microbiology, HFS-712, 5100 Paint Branch Parkway, College Park, MD 20740, USA
†Forensic Science Program, 325 Natural Science Bldg, Western Carolina University, Cullowhee, NC 28723, USA

1 Microbial Forensics

Microbial forensics is a relatively new scientific discipline dedicated to analyzing evidence for attribution purposes from a bioterrorism act, a biocrime, or an inadvertent micro-organism/toxin release. Some essential elements of this new discipline have long been growing in scope and capabilities. Epidemiologists, particularly those in public health fields, have used very similar forensic practices for decades to identify causative agents and the etiology of a disease or the source of a food borne outbreak. The goal of microbial forensics is very similar. A combination of diverse disciplines is exploited to analyze this kind of evidence, including biology, epidemiology, microbiology, medicine, physiology, chemistry, physics, statistics, population genetics and computer science. However,

DNA sequencing improvements and the wealth of data that this technology now easily provides renders it a central scientific method in this growing field (Breeze *et al.*, 2005).

A good example of microbial forensics in practice as applied to a case scenario is the set of analyses that were performed in response to the 2001 anthrax letter attacks. In that case, very diverse and numerous scientific disciplines were brought together in an attempt to identify the source of the evidence and/or the perpetrator of the crime. All of the above-mentioned disciplines were involved, including high-resolution imaging and elemental composition techniques, carbon-dating and traditional forensic techniques such as trace evidence analysis and the chemical analysis of inks and dyes.

2 Taxonomic Concepts

Taxonomy is the classification and identification of things. It is most frequently used for the identification and classification of organisms, and as all living things have genomes, then genomic taxonomy is the comparative use of the genomes of organisms to classify and characterize them. A taxonomist job is to survey the natural diversity present among organisms and use that variation to determine what is unique to each living thing and use the differences between them as the basis of a classification. Natural diversity is hierarchical due to the evolutionary relationships of all living things. Taxonomists have long used the phenotypic diversity present among life to create keys that list and compare specific characteristics of organisms to identify and classify them. So mammals have hair, and birds have feathers, and one then follows the key and examines the organism at hand to determine what kind of thing it is. Genomic taxonomy is no different conceptually but differs in using genome characteristics rather than phenotypic characters to identify and classify organisms. It is worthy to note that taxonomy is not limited to species identification but to all levels of organization across the great tree of life. Because life evolved in a nested hierarchical manner, we know that every branch on the tree has some characteristics that distinguish it from another. The cataloging of all of these changes is still going on in the great museums of the world and numerous applications have arisen where people want to know what kind of living thing they have. The hard work of taxonomists is to build databases of the natural variation, both genetic and morphological, for all of the living things. Once the variation is described and cataloged, then a phylogeny is built that is based on the characters that define each branch of the tree. For genetics and genomics, the characters are sequences collected from various organisms. Many of the earlier genetic databases used indirect methods to assess sequence diversity such as short tandem repeats (STRs), and pulse field gel electrophosesis (PFGE) which catalogued fragment sizes that are based on nucleotide sequence differences.

2.1 *Current Techniques Used for Taxonomic Identification*

The best systematic methods are able to place every character onto the phylogenetic tree, so that one can see the character evolution that has occurred for each and every character. Parsimony methods are excellent at determining the simplest explanation of the data and the character evolution of each change on the phylogenetic tree, thus providing this detailed information for keys (Kitching *et al.*, 1998). By looking at the tree and the characters that fall on the different branches, one is able to determine which characters define each lineage. Knowing the characters that define each lineage is very useful as this provides an essential key for identifying unknowns. If your unknown sample has the same characters that place it to a specific branch on the tree, then you can be certain that you have identified your sample correctly (Farris, 1970, 1988; Fitch, 1971, 1988, reviewed in Wilson and Allard, 2004). Also, once you have identified which specific characters are unique to a lineage of interest, it is relatively easy to design a rapid test to only screen for the specific character that defines the group rather than conduct a more expensive test that collects the entire genome. For example, using knowledge of what is genetically unique to *Salmonella* has allowed investigators to design PCR tests to identify when *Salmonella* is present in a contaminated food.

2.2 Taxonomic Assignment via Matching

Earlier methods of taxonomy did not use an evolutionary approach but rather just used matching criteria to a set of curated and validated knowns. It is relatively easy to identify samples that are an exact match to a known and many different kinds of statistical matching methods can do this. The most commonly used match of genetic sequence data is a BLAST search at the National Center for Biotechnology information at the National Library of medicine (http://blast.ncbi.nlm.nih.gov/Blast.cgi). Using BLAST you can upload any sequence collected and compare it to all of the data in the NCBI database to determine which sequence is the closest genetic match to your data in the database. For many applications, this is a useful approach. It is best to look at the next best match as well or even the best 3–4 matches to see if they are in agreement as to the taxonomic assignment based on a BLAST result (Figure 1).

But what do you do if there is not a perfect match, due to some genetic changes in the particular unknown sample that you are trying to characterize? It can be difficult to determine whether the nucleotide changes are unique to your sample, or are genetic reversals, or independent gains of the substitution, and how many differences are enough to say that you have found something new. It is best understood through phylogenetic analysis for one can determine the importance of the characters that distinguish your sample from others (Hennig, 1966; Farris, 1970; Fitch, 1971; reviewed in Hillis *et al.*,

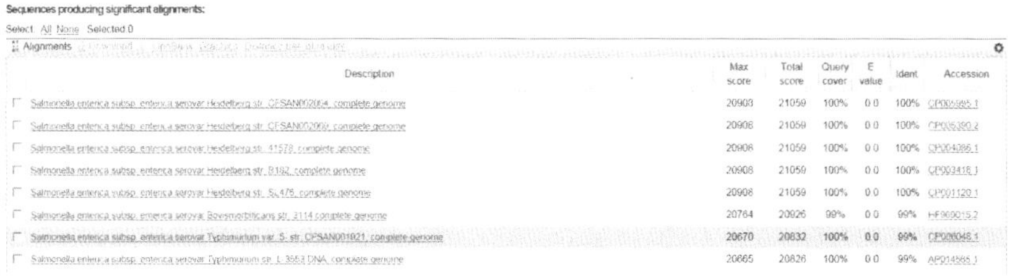

Sequences producing significant alignments:

Select: All None Selected 0

Alignments

Description	Max score	Total score	Query cover	E value	Ident	Accession
Salmonella enterica subsp. enterica serovar Heidelberg str. CFSAN002064, complete genome	20903	21059	100%	0.0	100%	CP005995.1
Salmonella enterica subsp. enterica serovar Heidelberg str. CFSAN002069, complete genome	20908	21059	100%	0.0	100%	CP006390.2
Salmonella enterica subsp. enterica serovar Heidelberg str. 41578, complete genome	20908	21059	100%	0.0	100%	CP004086.1
Salmonella enterica subsp. enterica serovar Heidelberg str. B182, complete genome	20908	21059	100%	0.0	100%	CP003416.1
Salmonella enterica subsp. enterica serovar Heidelberg str. SL476, complete genome	20908	21059	100%	0.0	100%	CP001120.1
Salmonella enterica subsp. enterica serovar Bovismorbificans str. 3114 complete genome	20764	20926	99%	0.0	99%	HF969015.2
Salmonella enterica subsp. enterica serovar Typhimurium var. 5- str. CFSAN001921, complete genome	20670	20832	100%	0.0	99%	CP006048.1
Salmonella enterica subsp. enterica serovar Typhimurium str. L-3553 DNA, complete genome	20665	20826	100%	0.0	99%	AP014565.1

Figure 1: Results for sequences producing significant alignments.

Note: BLAST report generated from submitting an unknown bacterial sequence to the Standard Nucleotide BLAST portal at http://blast.ncbi.nlm.nih.gov/Blast.cgi?PROGRAM=blastn&PAGE_TYPE=BlastSearch&LINK_LOC=blasthome.

1993; Allard *et al.*, 2002; Wilson *et al.*, 2013). Another common problem is what if you get multiple equally good matches to your unknown? For many databases based on one gene fragment, it is possible that all strains of the same species may all have an identical match. In this case, you should only report the taxonomic assignment to the highest level of classification that is shared among the matches, or list all possible matches and report the ambiguity in determining which the closest match is. For example, in Figure 1, there are multiple matches to *S.* Heidelberg so this is the correct level of identification based on the sequence used in the BLAST search.

Non-human taxonomy is also conducted by numerous federal and state agencies and these include rapid genetic characterizations of other species the commercial production of which the government regulates. A common approach used falls under the technology termed bar-coding, which is the databasing and use of a genetic identifier (e.g. barcode) to rapidly identify an organism without relying on the phenotypic characteristics of the organism. Several of the strengths that proponents advance for bar-coding is that non-specialists can do these simple genetic sequencing tests without detailed knowledge of the phenotypic diversity present in an organism. Also, in some cases, the organism has been modified and is not easily recognizable like meat from game or fish fillets and thus genetic tests can be applied as long as DNA is still present in the sample. To work effectively, the barcode database needs to be made up of properly identified known samples with genetic sequence for a target molecule that exhibits sufficient variation to cover all of the diversity for the organisms that the application wishes to identify. An example of a forensic database using bar-coding is the DNA based use for the identification of seafood (see http://www.fda.gov/Food/FoodScience Research/DNASeafoodIdentification/). The FDA's interest in the taxonomy of fish is based on the need to determine whether this food source is safe, wholesome and properly labeled. The seafood identification database leverages the existing database for the barcode of life (BOL) and the FISH-BOL which is a database of a piece of sequence from the mitochondrial DNA (mtDNA) cytochrome c oxidase subunit I gene (CO1). The database is made up of curated fish specimens that a trained icthyologist has identified and collected a matching genetic sample. When unknown fish fillets are genetically identified, the unknown samples COI sequence is compared against the known seafood sequences present in this barcode database. Numerous other similar and or related databases are used to identify endangered species for use by the Department of Natural Resources (DNR), insect identifications for both the U.S. Department of Agriculture (USDA) and the Department of Defense (DOD), and botany samples in supplements (FDA) to name a few. Literally any living organism could be characterized in this way if there is a specific application and need for rapid characterization and identification of the group. The process is to gather hundreds of knowns from past collections, sequence a particular genetic target and maintain the results in a database for comparison to unknowns. Many metagenomics applications of describing all species present in an environmental sample use a 16s rRNA database called Greengenes for taxonomic assignment of PCR products (DeSantis *et al.*, 2006; Ottesen *et al.*, 2013). There have been numerous attempts to come up with global markers, including ribosomal genes (e.g. 16S, 23S), micro-satellites such as enterobacterial repetitive intergenic consensus (ERIC) sequences and other repeats, (Sharples and Lloyd, 1990; Wilson and Sharp, 2006; Wise *et al.*, 2008), and variable house-keeping genes, called multiple locus sequence typing (MLST).

2.3   *Taxonomic Characterization Using MLST Approaches*

As the diversity of organisms sampled for forensic analysis grows, so does the knowledge of what sort of genetic variation should be expected within and between species. Also, for some applications, a single gene is not sufficient information to taxonomically classify the organism to the level required for the particular application. This is especially true for closely related taxa or taxonomy at the subspecies or subtype level, where more than one gene is generally required to separate kinds. The initial decision is to choose the appropriate genetic region(s) to sequence to be able to assess the genetic variation present across the available taxa, and to obtain enough genetic variation so that all of the individuals can be genetically identified and sorted into their respective lineages. One weakness of MLST is choosing which genes to add to the database. The historical process has often been a trial and error affair as new taxa may have unknown levels of genetic variation at a particular locus. Hence, numerous loci may need to be examined and collected. Another limitation of MLST methods arises when each allele is coded and numbered and then the simple allele counts are used for determining relatedness. This approach ignores the nature of the genetic substitutions (single nucleotide polymorphisms, SNPs) that define the alleles. Generally, when an MLST database is reduced to allele calls, then the loss of the underlying SNP information can often reduce the ability to genetically distinguish all types. SNP-based approaches to taxonomic assignment that retain the information of the particular change have higher resolution and discrimination than the MLST allelic approach. Depending on the particular application, this may not be a limitation if full separation and resolution of all types is not required. Currently, based on capillary sequencing approaches, it was recommended that one collect 7–15 different genetic regions and to use genes that were not linked to one another so that there were independent lines of evidence supporting the relationships among taxa. Microbiologists often use MLST for bacterial identifications (http://pubmlst.org/). Many tree of life taxonomic studies combine several independent lines of genetic evidence, along with the morphological data, to determine the phylogenetic placement of the taxa sampled. This strategy is known as total evidence or simultaneous analysis. The advantage is that by combining all of the evidence, one is likely to more accurately determine the evolutionary relationships among closely related taxa. The question of why the use of all of the evidence is the best strategy to solve complex evolutionary problems has been discussed numerous times (Kluge, 1989; Allard and Carpenter, 1996; Nixon and Carpenter, 1996).

A recent advance in MLST approaches is the application of whole genome sequencing. By collecting the genome of an organism, one can generate many more sequences allowing one to expand the MLST approach to thousands of genes as opposed to 10 or so.

This expansion of capturing more of the genetic diversity within an organism greatly expands the resolution and ability to distinguish among types. Nonetheless the more data included in a molecular taxonomy, the better the resolution, as any reduction of the total genome is a loss of information. A subset of genome sequencing which incorporates the MLST approach is known as whole genome MLST (wgMLST). A full genome approach to taxonomy attempts to analyze all of the genes present in the genomes of organisms and also includes the presence and absence of genes, duplications and genomic rearrangements (Read *et al.*, 2003). In wgMLST, a large pre-determined subset of genes is used in the comparison, while non-coding segments and rearrangements are ignored. In the case, for instance, where mobile elements or other transient markers (i.e. plasmids or phages) provide additional attribution to a strain, it would seem imperative to include all of the data in order to capture such diversity. Comparison of the complete genomes among taxa will have the highest resolution in discriminating among kinds.

Genetic databases, whether based on single genes, multiple genes or complete genomes, share common issues that must be addressed when building a database. For example, how transparent and readily accessible is the data? Who can add new data to the database, and who will curate the data when misidentifications arise? How is curation documented? Two beneficial considerations are long-term support and full public access to all of the data. Equally important is the quality of the metadata associated with the sequence data. The greater the quality present in the metadata, the more applicability the data will have to support additional applications. Open data means full transparency of the data, and reproducibility of the results requires full transparency of the data analysis methods that interpret the results.

2.4 *Variation within a Group can Affect Taxonomic Assignment Interpretation*

Forensic databases have used genetics and taxonomy for casework for some time, though most methods of analysis have relied on finding an exact match between a piece of unknown evidence and a known sample. Most genetic characters examined to date for forensics of vertebrates does not change within an individual or even over the organism's lifetime. Thus, it is reasonable to accept matches as the criteria for the identification of a sample. An example of a forensic application using a genetic match is the CODIS database for mtDNA sequences from evidence of hair, bones and teeth. This database is used to match DNA sequence from a human to a database of convicted felons to see if they are repeat offenders and have left genetic evidence at another crime scene. With mtDNA, a single mismatch is considered inconclusive, and two mismatches between samples is considered an exclusion, according to current protocol and scientifically based on what is known about mtDNA molecular evolution (Budowle *et al.*, 2003).

Longitudinal studies that determine how much variation arises over a short period of time greatly assists in the interpretation of sequence data in a forensic context. This sort of data exploration is also necessary for determining intra-individual variation. Because matching criteria in a forensic case are correctly viewed as two or more samples clustering in the same lineage, the issue of mutation rate within lineages becomes relevant. For bacterial and viral investigations, one will need to know, at least in an approximate way, how much variation arises over a few generations, so that a reasonable assessment as to whether the samples in question are from the same individual or a close relative can be made (Allard *et al.*, 2012). This should also include natural variation as well as variation introduced in culturing techniques. Strictly speaking, after assessing the population's genetic variation and after some longitudinal studies, where the same organism is sampled over a known period of time, one will likely identify the most variable genetic sites that change rapidly over a taxon's lifetime. This will have to be tempered with comparisons of unrelated individuals that will have a distinctly different variation compared to closely related taxa. The actual levels of variation and the sites that vary will be species-specific, reflecting the evolutionary history of the species, and will likely vary among the different species of interest.

Understanding the genetic variation among and within organisms will require careful sampling of vetted material and then generating databases that capture the variation. Forensic applications have long relied on high quality databases for all of the material found as evidence, not just the genetic data. Once known samples are made available to the public, they can be compared independently on a regular basis, and in this way the database is continually checked and rechecked for consistency and accuracy. Usually, this either requires some controls and limitations on who can add genetic information to the database so that only qualified individuals are adding information to the database. The identities of the individuals adding information are recorded so that one can better assess potential errors in the database. The risks associated with a fully open database mean that some lower quality data may enter into the database. The benefit of an open model is that more people can add data to the database, which then grows at a faster pace and expands with a greater diversity as input is coming from a broader base. The current open model for databases is to maximize uploading and availability of the data. As long as the data and methods are validated, the judicial system is satisfied that rigorous science is applied. Other, more closed models, could be envisioned for sensitive data such as select agents for biosecurity purposes or for private applications.

Besides the issues of data entry and data availability, one must also make some decisions about the available format or formats that will be made available in the constructed database. The national genetic database GenBank (http://www.ncbi.nlm.nih.gov/genbank/) is the most common model of how data are made available. This typically includes a full data entry including all of the metadata details of an organism, including when and where they came from as well as who did the sampling and where the voucher of the specimen is housed, and whether the data are published. Additionally, a FASTA format is available and downloadable. For genomic levels of data, the current standard is the SRA format at the NCBI (http://www.ncbi.nlm.nih.gov/sra).

A sequence analysis pipeline is another useful resource but with any analysis a clear description of the software and analyses conducted should be included. Transparency of data analysis is critical as different software and data analysis approaches may lead to some disagreements between database results and interpretation. While this is not often the case, investigators need to understand how software differences affect interpretation, and only vetted and validated data analysis pipelines should be used for regulatory and forensic decision-making. For example, while specific investigators may have differing opinions as to which alignment method is the most reproducible and which exhibits the properties that should be used in conjunction with a particular database, an open and transparent process is best suited for understanding how specific software affects interpretation. By requiring transparency for data analysis, the system is open to review and improvements. By developing validated databases of known results, anyone with a new software approach can check their data analysis pipeline to see if they can get the correct interpretation faster than an older software approach. For genomic methods, many software programs are improving at a rapid rate and new software is being developed daily. See Pettengill *et al.*, 2014 for an example of a comparative genomic data analysis pipeline that is publicly available.

2.5 *Phylogenetic Approaches to Taxonomic Assignment*

Another issue is that different species evolve at different rates and some have different levels of recombination that may rearrange the genomes. These higher levels of genetic diversity are particularly true for viruses and bacterial samples, as both of these entities are rapidly evolving and can change from one generation to another. Thus, the time between a sample being collected during an investigation and another known sample collected for comparison in a case can be many generations apart in an organism's life, while for most higher organism investigations there are either direct comparisons or at most one generation removed comparisons performed. For bacteria and viruses, there are often some genetic differences between the samples under comparison. Hence, forensic analysis of genetic data not only had to accommodate identical matches, but also had to consider closely related samples. This issue of increased variability also applies to kinship analyses of higher organisms when an attempt is made to match the unknown to a relative. Common cases of kinship analysis occur when there is no direct sample to compare against the body in question so the unknown is compared to a sibling or a parent to assist in identification, such as might be involved with identifications at mass grave sites. Another forensic application is for the identification of an historical figure by comparing samples to a known living descendant. Taxonomic methods, which determine the lineage to which an organism belongs, have become a regular systematic tool to support forensic investigations.

Systematic methods are the best way to determine from which lineage a genetic sample belongs. For some rapidly evolving organisms like bacteria and viruses, it is unlikely that one will find an identical match between samples and much more likely that they will find a few unique substitutions that define each type. For less rapidly evolving organisms like eukaryotes, one needs to either collect genes that have evolved more quickly or collect more data to discover variable genetic difference to use in a phylogenetic analysis. The more specific an identification that is needed for the application, the more data one needs to collect. One example is to collect the entire genome of the mitochondrial DNA (mtDNA, Webb and Allard, 2009b) for forensic identification of dogs as opposed to just the D-loop of the mtDNA (Gundry *et al.*, 2007; Himmelberger *et al.*, 2008; Webb and Allard, 2009a). A larger eukaryotic genomic database can be found at the NISC Comparative Sequencing Program of which the ENCODE consortium was one of the earlier large databases from which mammalian genomic diversity and phylogenies were constructed (Prasad *et al.*, 2008). More recently, partial genomes of eukaryotes have been obtained by sequencing RNA to collect only the expressed genes, thus reducing the costs of sequencing the genome to only its transcriptome (Riesgo *et al.*, 2012). To date, most forensic databases have not yet adopted a genomics approach. Nonetheless, it is no longer a requirement that the samples be genetically identical. This is a topic that is not new to forensics but this concept still needs repeating in cases so that one can understand the reasoning for a phylogenetic interpretation. It is not enough just to describe the phylogenetic clustering of the sample in comparison to other samples. Good forensic interpretation should also include the level of variation that has been observed for the particular taxa, the specific evidence for the clustering pattern, and the level of support that has been discovered for this pattern of variation. Questions that arise in a phylogenetic analysis include what is the best phylogenetic match to the unknown sample, how significant is this cluster pattern, and how certain are the investigators that this is a significant or actionable match (Wilson *et al.*, 2013).

Evidence of genetic diversity among viruses and bacteria are relatively new in forensic practice. However, a genome is just additional genetic data, and is not conceptually different from evidence obtained from a single gene. In all cases, the context of the diversity must be assessed using validated methods. The most common cases of phylogenetic clustering in virus cases are of HIV samples. An early virus case using comparative genetics came from a dentist and several of his patients that were infected with HIV. The combined analysis of the dentist, his purported victim and unrelated HIV isolates clearly showed that the patient's samples belonged to the same HIV lineage as the dentist's, and also, to place the association in a context, that none of the unrelated individuals were associated with the dentist's HIV strain (Ou *et al.*, 1992). This example documents several important strategies for presenting phylogenetic methods in an investigation.

To make a convincing case that samples belong to the same cluster, it is always recommended that the analysis include numerous examples that are not related to the case. It is relatively easy to focus on a particular lineage by excluding some of the more closely related samples from the analysis. The stronger the case is tested by unrelated outside samples the stronger is the evidence when they cluster together. This will be particularly important as single gene databases grow to full genome databases. With a full genome of an organism there will typically not be a genetically identical match as the more data that are analyzed the more likely is the chance that some part of the genome has changed over time. Since all organisms will show some small differences, it is thus necessary to rigorously test the hypothesis that the cluster is directly related. To alleviate this potential bias, it is important to include all of the samples, including those that are most closely related to the evidentiary material, in the combined analysis to test the phylogenetic results (Allard *et al.*, 2013).

The exact phylogenetic method used to compare samples should be a published method that has been used by the scientific community. Most phylogenetic software analysis packages have been published numerous times in peer reviewed journals, so most methods would qualify as having been tested by the scientific community. This includes maximum likelihood, parsimony, neighbor-joining and Bayesian methods. We have made the case in an earlier review (Wilson *et al.*, 2013) why maximum parsimony methods are the preferred choice of phylogenetic techniques for forensic casework and for microbial forensics. Other broad reviews of phylogenetic methods also exist (Hillis *et al.*, 1996; Kitching *et al.*, 1998; Page and Holmes, 2009).

3 Phenotypic Characterization of Unknowns Using Gene Presence

In the quest to improve taxonomic assignment, many single gene systems are being developed into multiple gene systems. More recently, the goals are not just to improve the resolution of the taxonomic placement by adding more genes, but also to provide predictions of phenotype as an additional level of characterization. For bacteria, one important phenotype is antimicrobial resistance and an assessment of the possible presence of known virulence gene complexes. Note that the strategy for adding phenotypic prediction has some important differences to strict taxonomic assignment. For increasing the number of genes using an MLST approach, it was considered important to make sure that genes were not closely linked genetically so that one was assessing a broader portion of the genome and not being unduly influenced by horizontal gene transfer or recombination events. But with phenotypic characterization, the opposite is true, in that we seek certainty that the phenotypic markers are directly linked to the same organism. This is especially true when screening mixed environmental samples. If multiple organisms, are present in an environmental sample, one will want to know which species also has the markers for antimicrobial resistance. Hence linkage to that trait within a mixed population is desired. For example, in the screening of shiga-toxin producing *E. coli* (STEC), it is important to know which of the virulence factors go with which of the serotypes. This is because, for some pathogens, the presence of one of the stx gene markers is not associated with virulence, but only when both stx1 and stx2 markers are present in the same serotype is the isolate considered as especially dangerous. In a mixed environmental sample, there may be several pathogens present in the sample, and it is important to know whether the different kinds each carry their own virulence marker or whether one of the kinds carries both markers in the same strain. In the former case, the bacteria are less likely to be virulent and thus a more limited response is warranted. Linkage is difficult to establish when screening mixed environmental samples, so this is mostly performed on pure samples cultured from the mixture.

Another common feature of many taxonomic databases is that they are governed by a standardizing body which decides whether or not a new methodology is valid, accurate and reproducible. Some governing bodies may decide whether the new methods should be approved for adoption into the forensic community. They also may advise as to how to integrate a new method into the existing standard operating procedures (SOPs) and databases. This can be rather complicated, as there are many existing SOPs that describe how to handle evidence. Often, there are existing constraints on the organization of the forensic laboratory as well, and these constraints will affect adoption of new methods, especially if the new methods disrupt the older ones. All of this may affect when and how a particular sample is collected for casework, but it should have little effect on building a genetic database for a particular organism. Organizational bodies such as the International Association of Food Protection (IAFP) and the International Organization for Standardization (ISO) have recently added specialty groups in the use of genetics and genomics for taxonomic assessment. These groups may also assist in organizing blind testing, for validation, and or certification of laboratories that wish to be approved for the new procedures of molecular taxonomic assignment. The standardization of tests for genetic interpretation is an important part of harmonizing approaches so that forensic methods are accepted worldwide.

4 GenomeTrakr Network and Database of Foodborne Pathogens

Foodborne pathogens and their detection at the Food and Drug Administration (FDA) have many similarities to the methods of microbial forensics in other departments and agencies. The FDA, along with other state and federal partners, is tasked with identifying the species, sub-species and serotypes when microbial outbreaks occur from food sources. These agencies try to determine the source of the biological agent or agents, and are under pressure to accomplish this task in a rapid and accurate manner. The primary goal is to interpret the data quickly, but also not allow false negatives to occur. It is becoming a common practice for these agencies to rely more and more on comparative genomics methods (Read *et al.*, 2003; Wilson *et al.*, 2013). With the rise of new methods of DNA sequencing that are highly processive, it is now cost effective to sequence the entire genome of bacteria and viruses.

FDA has created and applied, in real-time regulatory use, a U.S.-based open-source whole genome sequencing (WGS) integrated network of state, federal, academic, international and commercial partners. The network, known as "GenomeTrakr", represents the first of its kind distributed genomic food shield for detecting and tracing foodborne outbreak pathogens back to their source. The GenomeTrakr Network is only two years old and is already leading investigations of outbreaks of foodborne illnesses. Some of these illnesses result in compliance actions with more accurate and rapid recalls of contaminated foods, as well as more effective monitoring of preventive practices in the food manufacturing environment. The genomic information guides investigators to specific food products, processing sites, and farm sources of pathogen outbreaks, providing valuable insight into the origin of the contaminated food.

This capability is important considering the limited number of FDA food inspectors and the global nature of the food supply. Sample collection and sequence cataloging from food production sites can help monitor compliance with FDA's rules on safe food-handling practices and enhance preventive controls for food safety.

WGS analysis of microbial pathogens is now supplanting traditional microbiological analytics with rapid single data output summaries for antimicrobial resistance profiling, detection of high risk virulence profiles, and general identification strategies that supersede serological, phenotypic, and classical culture-based testing for taxonomic assignment. This ORA/FERN GenomeTrakr network (Figure 2) serves to provide a national, rapid and fully accessible sentinel surveillance system for pathogen trace back and antimicrobial drug resistance characterization, which is critical for an effective public health response to bacterial outbreaks.

FDA-CFSAN has deployed GenomeTrakr to fully exploit WGS to promote food safety. This involves the creation of a centralized database containing microbial sequence and sample metadata to increase the likelihood that sequences obtained from current outbreaks will match

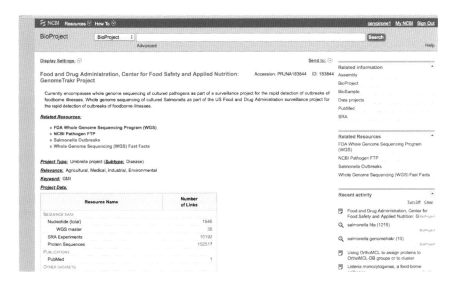

Figure 2: GenomeTrakr web page for *Salmonella*.

to historical ones. This database is public, meaning that anyone in the world can freely contribute and obtain information from it. Some information in the metadata may be withheld from public release by individual organizations due to concerns about the public release of proprietary information. Metadata describe the sample (sampling location, food or environmental source, host, date of isolation), and the isolated specimen (serotype, pathotype). The quality of the metadata connected to a sequence greatly expands the utility of the sequence, enabling FDA and other partners to track the origin of pathogen reservoirs and discover specific geographic regions that may harbor unique pathogen types.

This public approach provides useful data to industry and academic partners, as well as any federal or international agency that wishes to add value to the collected data. The current GenomeTrakr database contains roughly 11,000 *Salmonella* and 2,000 *Listeria* isolates, and is growing at roughly 850 new draft genomes per month, or a new pathogen draft genome every hour. New phylogenetic trees showing emerging clustering patterns and relatedness are produced daily by NCBI and are publicly accessible. Regulatory offices at FDA are using WGS and the GenomeTrakr to discover new contamination events on a monthly basis, with additional requests for whole genome sequencing expanding. This is primarily due to the high-resolution of this tool and the ability to provide insight into the causes of outbreaks, risks and compliance-monitoring.

The GenomeTrakr and other similar databases represent rich repositories from which to obtain genetic polymorphisms for the many serovars collected, and a foundation from which to determine the next set of genetic targets to be used for the rapid identification and characterization of unknown pathogens. Many different scientific groups are building similar genomic data sets to determine where the natural variation exists between the different species and serotypes. It is likely that these databases will continue to expand in size in the next few years as genome sequencing becomes cheaper and the technology advances. Once variable positions are determined among the genomes, most of the SNP detection technologies can take advantage of this information through the redesign of old targets as well as design of new targets. The SNP detection methods

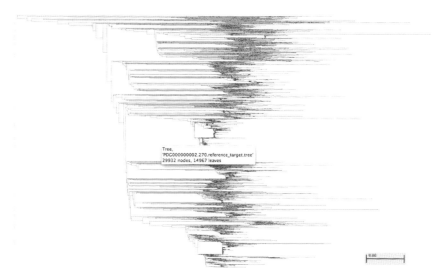

Figure 3:   GenomeTrakr large tree including all *Salmonella* in database.

for the identification of the presence of pathogens will be largely used as screening tools for surveying large numbers of samples in laboratories that test raw fresh produce such as peppers, tomatoes, spinach, and lettuce coming into the food supply from foreign and domestic sources. The growing trend for many department of health laboratories is to have two aspects of surveillance in place. First the laboratories conduct rapid screening for species identification for the presence of a pathogen in foods, often using SNP detection for surveillance. If a known pathogen tests positive in a food sample, then isolates are cultured, and this is followed by comparative genomics for source tracking of the pathogenic strain (Figure 3). The combination of these two testing phases is rapidly becoming the model for microbial forensics taxonomic assignment, and will determine how the contaminant entered the food supply chain. This general approach is being utilized, is rapidly becoming the model for microbial forensics taxonomic assignment, whether this is occurring in the Health and Human services, Departments of Justice, Homeland security or Defense. The availability of open government databases is also increasingly becoming the norm, so that industry, academia and our foreign and domestic partners can all add value and help realize the goal of rapid identification and trace back of pathogens.

As more laboratories obtain the robotic technologies to rapidly handle and genetically type more samples, genomic pathogen databases will grow exponentially. This capability will expand the requirements of the computer systems needed to collect and analyze the data. Many genomics laboratories have relied on a centralized approach using clusters of computers to store and to analyze this deluge of data. Currently, much of the software that is available is highly specialized, requiring some programming skills of the investigator. Recent advances in software to support the genomic sequencing technology are creating more turnkey solutions so that non-specialists can rapidly analyze and interpret their results. Software is also moving toward smaller local analysis of a portion of the data so that distributed laboratories can conduct local and independent investigations. This, along with publicly available centralized solutions, will allow more people to make forensic decisions locally, or to query centralized databases that are able to analyze the data faster and more globally. Currently, it is easier to collect the data than it is to process and interpret it, but hopefully this is changing as software is developed to enhance the capability of the user to fully understand the data and make informed decisions based on it.

Good taxonomic identification requires an understanding of which genetic characters define each group of interest. In this context, building a phylogeny is just the means to an end. Once the relationships among all of the organisms are known, it is possible to define all of the groups and thus also all of the characters that define them (Figure 4). The first step is determining the phylogeny and finding the genetic markers that can distinguish between all of the various species, serotypes and cultures of the numerous pathogens. These genetic markers do not have to be special but rather they only need to discriminate in a predictable and reliable manner. Almost any kind of genetic variant could fill this role. The advances in identifying novel genetic markers make it possible to not only discriminate the lineage of the pathogen, but also to determine the genetic determinants of virulence. This includes sequencing plasmids that carry drug resistance and pathogenicity (Chen *et al.*, 2013; Hoffman *et al.*,

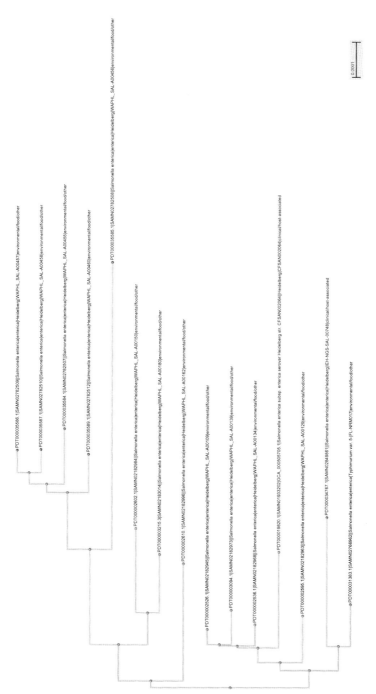

Figure 4:   Zoomed in portion of S. Heidelberg phylogeny showing close relationship among several isolates.

2014); or regions of the genome that code for H and O antigens that allow the pathogen to invade the host (Fitzgerald *et al.*, 2007). The logic behind sequencing and learning the function of genes is that many organisms seem to gain their pathogenicity or virulence through horizontal gene transfer of mobile genetic elements (Mirold *et al.*, 2001; Boyd and Brussow, 2002; Chen *et al.*, 2013; Hoffman *et al.*, 2014), thus some have argued that one should follow the genes that confer pathogenicity rather than markers of the lineages that are currently pathogenic. It seems prudent to do both as there will always be continuing evolution, genetic rearrangements, and horizontal gene transfer which do not follow the rules of strict lineage sorting. Moreover, it should be recalled that WGS information, for public health application, is often taken in context of other observations made during outbreak investigation, whether they be epidemiologic or surveillance-based.

Acknowledgments

The use of trade, firm, or corporation names in this publication (or page) is for the information and convenience of the reader. Such use does not constitute an official endorsement or approval by the United States Food and Drug administration of any product or service to the exclusion of others that may be suitable.

References

M. W. Allard and J. M. Carpenter. On weighting and congruence. *Cladistics*, 12:183–198, 1996.

M. W. Allard, M. Wilson, K. Miller, K. Monson and B. Budowle. Characterization of the Caucasian haplogroups present in the SWGDAM forensic mtDNA data set for 1771 human control region sequences. *Journal of Forensic Sciences*, 47:1215–1223, 2002.

M. W. Allard, Y. Luo, E. Strain, C. Li, C. E. Keys, I. Son, R. Stones, S. M. Musser and E. W. Brown. High resolution clustering of *Salmonella enterica* serovar montevideo strains using a next-generation sequencing approach. *BMC Genomics*, 13:32, 2012.

M. W. Allard, Y. Luo, E. Strain, J. Pettengill, R. Timme, C. Wang, C. Li, C. E. Keys, J. Zheng Robert Stones, M. R. Wilson, S. M. Musser and E. W. Brown. On the evolutionary history, population genetics and diversity among isolates of *Salmonella* Enteritidis PFGE pattern JEGX01.0004. *PLoS ONE*, 8(1):e55254, 2013.

E. F. Boyd and H. Brussow. Common themes among bacteriophage encoded virulence factors and diversity among the bacteriophages involved. *Trends in Microbiology*, 10:521–529, 2002.

R. G. Breeze, Bruce Budowle and S. E. Schutzer (eds.). *Microbial Forensics.* Elsevier Press, Amsterdam, 2005.

B. Budowle, M. W. Allard, M. R. Wilson and R. Chakraborty. Forensic mitochondrial DNA: Applications, Debates and Foundations. *Annual review of Genomics and Human Genetics*, 4:119–143, 2003.

B. Budowle, M. R. Wilson and M. W. Allard. Characterization of heteroplasmy and hypervariable sites in HVI: Critique of D'Eustachio's interpretations. *Forensic Science International*, 130:68–70, 2002.

B. Budowle, C. L. Fisher, D. Polanskey, B. K. D. Hartog, R. B. Kepler and J. W. Elling. Stabilizing mtDNA sequence nomenclature with an operationally efficient approach. *Forensic Science International: Genetics Supplement Series*, 1(1):671–673, 2008.

Y. Chen, S. Mukherjee, M. Hoffmann, M. L Kotewicz, S. Young, J. Abbott, Y. Luo, M. K. Davidson, M. Allard, P. McDermott and S. Zhao. Whole-Genome Sequencing of Gentamicin-Resistant Campylobacter coli Isolated from U.S. Retail Meats Reveals Novel Plasmid-Mediated Aminoglycoside Resistance Genes. *Antimicrobial Agents and Chemotherapy*, 57(11):5398–5405, 2013.

T. Z. DeSantis, P. Hugenholtz, N. Larsen, M. Rojas, E. L. Brodie, K. Keller, T. Huber, D. Dalevi, P. Hu and G. L. Andersen. Greengenes, a Chimera-Checked 16S rRNA gene database and workbench compatible with ARB. *Applied and Environmental Microbiology*, 72:5069–5072, 2006.

J. Farris. Methods for computing Wagner trees. *Systematic Zoology*, 19:83–92, 1970.

J. Farris. Hennig86, ver. 1.5. Program and Documentation, Distributed by the Author. Port Jefferson Station, NY, 1988.

W. Fitch. Toward defining the course of evolution: Minimal change for a specific tree topology. *Systematic Zoology*, 20:406–416, 1971.

R. Gundry, M. W. Allard, D. Foran, T. Moretti, R. Honeycutt and M. Wilson. Mitochondrial DNA analysis of the Domestic Dog: Control region variation within and between breeds. *Journal of Forensic Sciences*, 52:562–572, 2007.

W. Hennig. *Phylogenetic Systematics.* University of Illinois Press, Urbana, 1966.

D. M. Hillis, M. W. Allard and M. M. Miyamoto. Analysis of DNA sequence data: Phylogenetic inference, the practical issues. In E. A. Zimmer, T. J. White, R. L. Cann and A. C. Wilson (eds.), *Molecular Evolution: Producing the Biochemical Data Methods in Enzymology*, 224:456–487, 1993.

D. M. Hillis. *Molecular Systematics*, 2nd edn. Sinauer, Assoc. Inc., Sunderland, MA, 1996.

A. L. Himmelberger, T. F. Spear, J. A. Satkoski, D. A. George, W. T. Garnica, V. S. Malladi, D. G. Smith, J. L. Halverson, K. Webb, M. W. Allard and S. Kanthaswamy. Forensic utility of the mitochondrial hypervariable 1 region of domestic dogs, in conjunction with breed and geographic information. *Journal of Forensic Sciences*, 53:81–89, 2008.

M. Hoffmann, S. Zhao, J. Pettengill, Y. Luo, S. R. Monday, J. Abbott, S. L. Ayers, H. N. Cinar, T. Muruvanda, C. Li, M. W. Allard, J. Whichard, J. Meng, E. W. Brown and P. F. McDermott. Comparative genomic analysis and virulence differences in closely related *Salmonella enterica* serotype Heidelberg isolates from humans, retail meats, and animals. *Genome Biology and Evolution*, 6:1046–1068, 2014.

J. Kitching *et al.* Cladistics — The Theory and Practice of Parsimony, 2nd edn. The Systematics Association, Oxford University Press, New York, 1998.

A. J. Kluge. A concern for evidence and a phylogenetic hypothesis of relationships among Epicrates (Boidae, Serpentes). *Systematic Zoology*, 38:7–25, 1989.

S. Mirold, K. Ehrbar, A. Weissmüller, R. Prager, H. Tschäpe, H. Rüssmann and W.-D. Hardt. *Salmonella* host cell invasion emerged by acquisition of a mosaic of separate genetic elements, including *Salmonella* pathogenicity Island 1 (SPI1), SPI5 and *sopE2*. *Journal of Bacteriology*, 183(7):2348–2358, 2001.

K. C. Nixon and J. M. Carpenter. On simultaneous analysis. *Cladistics*, 12:221–241, 1996.

A. R. Ottesen, A. Gonzalez, R. Bell, C. Arce, S. Rideout, *et al.* Co-Enriching Microflora Associated with Culture Based Methods to Detect *Salmonella* from Tomato Phyllosphere. *PLoS ONE*, 8(9):e73079, 2013.

C.-Y. Ou, C. A. Ciesielski, G. Myers, C. I. Bandea, C.-C. Luo, B. T. M. Korber, J. I. Mullins, G. Schochetman, R. L. Berkelman, A. N. Economou, J. J. Witte, L. J. Furman, G. A. Satten, K. A. MacInnes, J. W. Curran and H. W. Jaffe. Molecular epidemiology of HIV transmission in a dental practice. *Science*, 256:1165, 1992.

R. D. M. Page and E. C. Holmes. *Molecular Evolution: A Phylogenetic Approach.* John Wiley & Sons, New Jersey, 2009.

J. B. Pettengill, Y. Luo, S. Davis, Y. Chen, N. Gonzalez-Escalona, A. Ottesen, H. Rand, M. W. Allard and E. Strain. An evaluation of alternative methods for constructing phylogenies from whole genome sequence data: A case study with Salmonella. *PeerJ*, 2:e620, 2014, http://dx.doi.org/10.7717/peerj.620.

A. B. Prasad and M. W. Allard. NISC comparative sequencing program and E. D. Green. Confirming the phylogeny of mammals by use of large comparative sequence data sets. *Molecular Biology and Evolution*, 25(9):1795–1808, 2008.

T. Read, S. Peterson, N. Tourasse, L. Baillie, I. Paulsen, K. Nelson, H. Tettelin, D. Fouts, J. Eisen, S. Gill, E. Holtzapple, O. Okstad, E. Helgason, J. Rilstone, M. Wu, J. Kolonay, M. Beanan, R. Dodson, L. Brinkac, M. Gwinn, R. DeBoy, R. Madupu, S. Daugherty, A. Durkin, D. Haft, W. Nelson, J. Peterson, M. Pop, H. Khouri, D. Radune, J. Benton, Y. Mahamoud, L. Jiang, I. Hance, J. Weidman, K. Berry, R. Plaut, A. Wolf, K. Watkins, W. Nierman, A. Hazen, R. Cline, C. Redmond, J. Thwaite, O. White, S. Salzberg, B. Thomason, A. Friedlander, T. Koehler, P. Hanna, A.-B. Kolsto and C. Fraser. The genome sequence of Bacillus anthracis Ames and comparison to closely related bacteria. *Nature*, 423(6935):81–86, 2003.

A. Riesgo, S. C. S. Andrade, P. P. Sharma, M. Novo, A. R. Pérez-Porro, V. Vahtera, V. L. González, G. Y Kawauchi and G. Giribet. Comparative description of ten transcriptomes of newly sequenced invertebrates and efficiency estimation of genomic sampling in non-model taxa. *Frontiers in Zoology*, 9:33, 2012.

G. J. Sharples and R. G. Lloyd. A novel repeated sequence located in the intergenic regions of bacterial chromosomes. *Nucleic Acids Research*, 18:6503–6508, 1990.

K. M. Webb and M. W. Allard. Identification of forensically informative SNPs in the domestic dog mitochondrial control region. *Journal of Forensic Sciences*, 54(2):289–304, 2009.

K. M. Webb and M. W. Allard. Mitochondrial genome DNA analysis of the domestic dog: identifying informative SNPs outside of the control region. *Journal of Forensic Sciences*, 54(2):275–288, 2009.

L. A. Wislon and P. M. Sharp. Enterobacterial repetitive intergenic consensus (ERIC) sequences in *Escherichia coli*: Evolution and implications for ERIC-PCR. *Molecular Biology and Evolution*, 23(6):1156–1168, 2006.

M. Wilson and M. W. Allard. Phylogenetic and mitochondrial DNA analysis in the forensic sciences. *Forensic Science Reviews*, 16:37–62, 2004.

M. Wilson, M. W. Allard, K. Monson, K. Miller and B. Budowle. Recommendations for consistent treatment of length variants in the human mitochondrial DNA control region. *Forensic Sciences International*, 129:35–42, 2002.

M. R. Wilson, M. W. Allard and E. W. Brown. The forensic analysis of food-borne bacterial pathogens in the age of whole-genome sequencing. *Cladistics*, 29:449–461, 2013.

M. Wise, G. R. Siragusa, J. Plumblee, M. Healy, P. J. Cray and B. S. Seal. Predicting Salmonella enterica serotypes by semi-automated, repetitive extragenic palindromic sequence-based PCR. *Journal of Microbiological Methods*, 76:18–24, 2008.

Supporting Webliography

(1) Redmine forum for members of the GenomeTrakr network. http://genomelc.jifsan.org/login?back_url=http%3A%2F%2Fgenomelc.jifsan.org%2Fprojects%2Fgenome-learning-community%2Fwiki, 2016.

(2) DNA based use for the identification of seafood. http://www.fda.gov/Food/FoodScienceResearch/DNASeafoodIdentification/, 2016.

(3) SRA format at the NCBI. http://www.ncbi.nlm.nih.gov/sra 2016.

(4) GenBank http://www.ncbi.nlm.nih.gov/genbank/, 2016.

(5) Pathogens available at the National Center for Biotechnology and Information. http://www.ncbi.nlm.nih.gov/genomes/lproks.cgi, 2016.

(6) FDA-CFSAN's homepage for The GenomeTrakr Program. http://www.fda.gov/Food/FoodScienceResearch/WholeGenomeSequencingProgramWGS/, 2016.

(7) GenomeTrakr Early Outreach Trailer. https://www.youtube.com/watch?v=4zMms2C6Yuk, 2016.

(8) The NIH-NCBI website for The GenomeTrakr Bioproject and database. http://www.ncbi.nlm.nih.gov/bioproject/183844, 2016.

(9) Published data analysis pipeline used in FDA outbreak investigations. https://peerj.com/articles/cs-20/, 2015.

(10) Greengenes taxonomic database. http://greengenes.lbl.gov/cgi-bin/nph-citation.cgi, 2016.

CHAPTER 23

Molecular Epidemiology and Evolution Concepts in Microbial Forensics

Fernando González-Candelas

Unidad Mixta Infección y Salud Pública FISABIO-Universidad de Valencia,
CIBER en Epidemiología y Salud Pública,
Instituto Cavanilles de Biodiversidad y Biología Evolutiva,
Edificio Institutos de Investigación. Parque Científico,
C/Catedrático José Beltrán,
2 46980-Paterna, Valencia, Spain

1 Evolutionary Principles in Microbial Forensics

Micro-organisms, especially viruses, and also some bacteria, can evolve very rapidly (Biek *et al.*, 2015; Drummond *et al.*, 2003). Humans have become fully aware of this possibility very shortly after the introduction and generalized use of new antibiotic and antiviral drugs. Only a few years, occasionally a few months, after the general-ized use of a new therapeutic drug physicians begin to notice the appearance of resistant strains or variants. Unless appropriately treated and/or managed, these resistant strains or variants may spread through the general population rendering the new drugs almost useless (Davies and Davies, 2010). Although very visible and

561

with undesirable consequences, this outcome is just a particular example of how fast new features or properties may arise and spread in a population of micro-organisms, occasionally jumping over well-delimited species. This fast pace of evolution in micro-organisms is a consequence of several factors. Some have very high mutations rates (Sanjuan *et al.*, 2010), usually because they lack proofreading mechanisms in the polymerases responsible for replicating the genetic material of the organism, but additional processes contribute to this general trend. Very short generation times, with replications occurring in a few hours or even minutes determine the production of very large numbers of progeny and the presence of additional mechanisms to increase hereditary variation, often involving the incorporation of foreign genetic material from the same or a different species, also help to increase the genetic variability of these organisms.

Microbial forensics — the analysis of micro-organisms and their products for attribution purposes can exploit the evolutionary processes that occur continuously in natural populations. In fact, the fast pace of evolution in microbial and viral populations can even be an advantage in a forensic analysis provided that the relevant evolutionary concepts, as well as the methodological and analytical tools needed for their adequate study and consideration, are incorporated into the analysis. In this chapter, it is shown how these general ideas were incorporated in a real forensic evidence and presented as expert testimony in court, in a case involving the continuous and massive infection of almost 300 patients with hepatitis C virus by an anesthesiologist for a decade (1988–1998) at two hospitals in the city of Valencia, Spain (González-Candelas *et al.*, 2013).

One of the goals of microbial forensics is to test whether a microorganism obtained from a person coincides with that derived from a presumed source of infection, which might be another person but also a surgical device, a vial containing a blood derivative, or any other substrate which can harbor at least temporarily a population of the infecting organisms and subsequently transfer it to the recipient. Relevant samples from the putative source and the recipient(s) are analyzed and compared. How to choose an appropriate marker or method of analysis and how to perform the relevant comparisons represents the first of a series of decisions which will lead to a scientifically robust conclusion or to a mere general comparison which can be almost useless for most serious and practical cases.

An immediate consequence of the intrinsic potential for rapid evolution of micro-organisms is that the chances of identifying two fully identical organisms, even when they are recently derived from the same biological source (technically when they share a relatively recent common ancestor), are very low. Naturally, this comparison depends critically on the level of resolution of the marker(s) used. Currently, complete genome sequences of bacteria, viruses and many lower eukaryotes can be obtained in a matter of hours or days (Casey *et al.*, 2013; Metzker, 2010). There is hardly a week in which new studies comparing hundreds or even thousands of genome sequences are not published. But this capacity has been the recent result of a long way paved with many different methodologies for typing and in which different micro-organisms were compared with very different markers. The genome revolution has led to standardization of the typing tools which, if not currently yet, will be the gold standard for all types of laboratories in a very near future. In the meantime, and for practical applications, we are still using a range of typing methodologies, most of which are molecular, but based on different features, structures or properties of the genomes of micro-organisms or the products encoded therein. Why and how can the choice of one or another marker be relevant for a forensic analysis?

The forensic analysis of human samples is the most frequent application of molecular typing results brought to courts all over the world. The problems being addressed in these cases are usually linked to blood or other bodily tissues and to establishing kinship in different types of trials and lawsuits. Given the essentially fixed genotype *conformation* of most eukaryotic organisms, including humans, it is not surprising that molecular forensics has been mainly focused at establishing the probability that two identical samples are actually derived from the same person (except for kinship but the principles are similar). The identity of the samples when analyzed with the corresponding markers (SNPs, microsatellites, etc.) is taken almost for granted. But this assumption is not the case for microbial samples, and, when a perfect match is obtained, it is more likely the result of using a marker with low resolution (PFGE, MLST, serotyping, among others) than a reflection of actual identity at the full genome level.

A recent review of mutation rates in pathogens shows that there is a relatively constant ratio between the mutation rate per nucleotide and the total genome size across a wide range of micro-organisms (Lynch, 2010). The product of these two parameters for RNA viruses is close to one (Drake and Holland, 1999), which implies that, on average, there is one error made by the replicative machinery every time a genome is copied to generate a new individual in the population. Even after assuming a Poisson distribution of these changes, which would conform a moderate sized class of offspring with no mutations, the great majority of offspring genomes will differ in at least one base from the corresponding progenitor. Naturally, most of these mutations will not remain in the population, because purifying selection will quickly remove those that have a deleterious effect, but they can remain around for a few generations before being completely eliminated. In addition, they will reappear once again in the following generation, and also in the next one and in every subsequent generation.

The analysis of genetic variation of most micro-organisms has not been driven by evolutionary or epidemiological interests. Instead, the primary goal in the development of new markers used in microbial typing has been the detection and identification of a pathogen. Only recently has there been a growing interest in characterizing the different variants and groups in which practically every living species can be subdivided. Occasionally there are good clinical reasons for this detailed analysis, as it is the case in which different groups of the same organism respond differently to a given drug or the prognoses of the corresponding infections are also different. This approach has resulted in the use of specific but also conserved markers, with many advantages for diagnostics but with severely limited potential for forensics (Maiden *et al.*, 1998).

They have proved so useful that many companies have developed semi- or even fully-automated procedures, along with the necessary hardware equipment and chemicals, which have been extensively adopted by many laboratories. This positive development and interesting application were some time ago considered as basic research but now are helping to diagnose faster and more reliably many infections. Furthermore, it has led to the widespread ability to establish reference collections of variants and to extend the screening of individual samples at a population level.

This shift from individual to population level is crucial in forensics applications. The reason is as follows. We already have commented on the difficulties of establishing a perfect identity between the complete genome sequences of two very closely related micro-organisms (even parent–offspring pairs). The use of low resolution markers creates a false sense of security in establishing those identities that can be translated in many cases to false positive identifications. Any organism in a population has only one (for most microbial forensics relevant cases) parent and with its offspring are necessarily the most closely related individuals to the target one in the population. This relationship means that they are also individuals with the highest probability of being fully identical to the target. However, the analysis of a large number of samples from that or even other populations with low resolution markers will reveal many identities to less or even completely unrelated individuals. On the basis of these analyses, it is not possible to derive any conclusion regarding the ancestry of any particular individual because that ancestry is reflected in the same level of identity with many other individuals.

What is the situation when the analysis is made with markers with a higher power of resolution? In this case, the problem is somewhat reduced, but not completely eliminated. Certainly, a marker with greater resolution will show fewer identities with unrelated individuals, thus reducing the number of false positives and increasing the chances that the true ancestor (or offspring) is included among those showing a perfect identity. This approach is a positive development but if we keep applying the same logic, we will end in the unpleasant position described above: when we actually compare using the marker with the highest possible resolution, i.e. the genome sequence, we will realize that many such parent–offspring pairs are not identical. They will be very similar, but not necessarily identical. The only way out of this "catch-22" situation is to abandon the search for identity as the most important criterion in establishing the link between parent and offspring (or between source and problem) and adopt a more flexible criterion that incorporates what we actually know about the expected similarities between such pairs of individuals.

Molecular phylogenetics and molecular population genetics developed as theoretical fields in the last decades of the 20th century, thanks to the insight of several pioneers (Felsenstein, 2004; Lewontin, 1985; Rosenberg and Nordborg, 2002). Both fields use extensively the concept of Most Recent Common Ancestor (MRCA) to denote the species (in phylogenetics) or the individual (in a genealogy) representing the last organism before the lineages leading to the members of a set of organisms being compared split into independent lines of descent. This approach can represent an unknown species, such as the MRCA of humans and our closest living relatives (chimpanzees and bonobos), or a known individual, as it is the case for most groups of siblings. What is evident is that any two individuals will show a level of identity which will be roughly proportional to their relatedness. Coalescence theory (Kingman, 1982) analyzes two independent processes, genealogical/phylogenetic descent and mutation, to infer the processes and their parameters occurring in a population or taxonomic group in the past. In consequence, it incorporates the consequences of selection, migration, or admixture as historical processes acting on natural populations (Neuhauser, 2001). They will have differential impacts on the levels and distribution of genetic variation which can be accommodated in what represents the most crucial task in the forensic setting, which is determining which organisms share a MRCA which is significantly different from that shared with other individuals from the general population.

In any transmission event or chain of events, a forensic expert must provide an assessment of how likely it is that the isolates obtained from the infected patients and those from the source(s) are so similar that they necessarily have to derive from one of those in the source (or a similar relationship). But it is not enough to show that they are related. All the organisms in a population are related to one another, but this does not imply a direct link among them. What is necessary is to show that their degree of relatedness is substantially and significantly higher than that with other organisms in the population. Naturally, this relationship cannot be achieved without evaluating the relatedness to a representative sample of the reference population. The range of situations and cases that have to be dealt with in the analysis of outbreaks and transmission chains and cases, provided that it can be defined, prevents a detailed treatment herein of how to obtain such a representative sample of the reference population.

In this regard, population structure can have a profound impact on the results obtained from a reference population (Morton, 1992; Nichols and Baldwin, 1991). Population structure denotes the presence of significantly different, at the genetic level, subgroups of organisms in a certain geographical area or temporal frame. Population subdivision is a natural consequence of many processes regularly occurring in natural populations. Colonization events, selection in an heterogeneous environment, genetic drift coupled with little migration, etc. can all lead to the differentiation of the global population which cannot be considered as a single unit but instead treated as composed of several of these smaller effective subunits in which changes at the appropriate genetic population scale occur. Furthermore, an infected organism may represent a sufficiently heterogeneous environment for many micro-organisms, especially those capable of establishing a chronic infection, leading to compartmentalization of the bacterial or viral population (Borderia *et al.*, 2007; Randow *et al.*, 2013; Roque-Afonso *et al.*, 2005; Sanjuan *et al.*, 2010; Schnell *et al.*, 2009). This possibility has to be considered when sampling and interpreting the results of a forensic analysis of a microbial or viral population. If compartmentalization exists, then it is possible that two recipients of an inoculum from a single source actually receive different initial populations which might even evolve quite differentially thereafter. In this case, searching for identity between the recipients to demonstrate a common source may be a futile effort.

2 A Real Case

All the preceding ideas and considerations were used in a large scale, massive outbreak of hepatitis C infection that occurred in the city of Valencia (Spain) during the last decade of the past century. The outbreak was originated by a single person, a practicing anesthesiologist, who infected almost 300 persons over a period of 10 years in medical services in two hospitals of the city. We were called to serve as expert scientists in the trial that led to a conviction of malpractice and a sentence of almost 2,000 years in prison.

Hepatitis C virus (HCV) is a RNA virus, which means that its genetic material is ribonucleic acid (RNA) rather than deoxyribonucleic acid (DNA). Other RNA viruses include influenza A, mumps, Ebola or human immunodeficiency (HIV) viruses. One feature common to all these viruses is that they evolve very rapidly, up to a million times faster than organisms with a DNA genome (Sanjuan *et al.*, 2010). This rapid mutation rate is one of the main reasons for the difficulties in finding an effective vaccine or, as for influenza, being necessary to revaccinate every year susceptible people. Furthermore, for those RNA viruses such as HCV and HIV that can establish a permanent infection, the viral population in a patient can rapidly develop new variants that are capable of escaping antiviral treatments. In fact, there is no cure yet for HIV and only recently new drugs have been developed that can eliminate HCV from infected persons, thus representing an effective, yet very expensive cure.

HCV infects about 170 million people world-wide. However, it has been estimated that about half of them are unaware of their condition (Lavanchy, 2011). This virus can establish a chronic, symptomless infection that, after a variable period between months and tens of years, develops into liver damage (hepatitis) and cirrhosis which may eventually progress to liver cancer (hepatocellular carcinoma), for which liver transplant is the only remedy. The virus is transmitted by blood, usually through sharing needles, transfusion or treatment with infected blood-derivatives and high-risk, unsafe sexual practices. There are some additional routes, such as mother-to-child or by professional exposure, but they are a small portion of the total number of cases. The prevalence of HCV infection varies widely from country to country, with the highest rates found in Egypt and Bolivia (above 10% of the population) and the lowest in central and northern European countries such as Denmark, Austria or the Czech Republic, with rates around 0.5%. The latest estimates indicate that prevalence of HCV infection in Spain is around 2.5% (Esteban *et al.*, 2008).

During the spring of 1998, several thousand people in the Valencia region were called to be tested for HCV infection. Many received positive results. The call was the result of an initial epidemiological investigation of what resulted to be one of the largest hepatitis C outbreaks in history, with at least 275 infected persons from a single source, an anesthesiologist named Juan Maeso (hereafter, IC, for index case). The outbreak was detected in early February of that year, when two physicians informed public health authorities of some possible linked cases of hepatitis C among some of their patients. The only common link among the patients was a relatively recent minor surgery in a private hospital in Valencia. The ensuing investigation found only one common link between the two physicians' patients, the IC. As the enquiries proceeded, it became clear that many more people had been exposed to this medical professional and, in consequence, to potential infection by HCV. Because the infection may not be noticed, it was decided that all the exposed people should be tested. However, since Dr. Maeso had a long professional career, the question became how long should his records be traced back in time to search for putatively infected patients? Another question pressed the investigators: what did it mean that someone tested positive for

HCV infection if the prevalence is about 2.5%? Could this investigation be taken as a certain case of this outbreak or should other sources of infection be discarded first? It became clear that additional analyses were necessary.

Regardless the consideration as living entities, a hotly debated issue in Biology, viruses certainly evolve and they do so under the same evolutionary principles followed by living organisms. Genetic variants arise in viral populations every generation which are then subjected to the same evolutionary processes of selection, migration and drift. The combination of these and similar processes results in evolutionary change, which can be easily observable, as in the case of influenza A strains spreading to pandemics every year or of HIV, with escape mutations that allow the virus to overcome the effects of antiviral drugs. These evolutionary changes occur at a very fast pace, as mentioned above, and, as consequence, it is possible to reconstruct the history of these events over very short periods of time, such as months or years. The general principles of phylogenetic reconstruction can be readily applied to viral features. However, viruses do not possess many structural, morphological or physiological features that can be compared and the only traits useful for these analyses are their genome sequences.

Public health authorities asked for our help to establish a genealogical link between those patients that were epidemiologically linked to the presumed source of the outbreak and the IC (González-Candelas *et al.*, 2013). This link would constitute a direct evidence of the common ancestry of the viruses found in each patient and the presumed source which, along with the epidemiological evidence, would provide very strong evidence for the direct infection from it. For this analysis, we had to use sequence information from two fragments of the HCV genome. One fragment corresponded to a 229 nucleotide (nt) long sequence from the viral RNA polymerase gene, called NS5B. The other fragment was a 406 nt portion of the genes coding for the envelop proteins 1 and 2, denoted E1 and E2, respectively. This part of the HCV genome includes three segments where the virus accumulates mutations very rapidly, even for RNA virus standards: they are known as hypervariable regions (HVRs). Genes and proteins do not evolve at the same rate, even those that are next to each other in the same genome. Rate variation among genes has to be considered when designing any molecular evolution analysis. Slowly evolving genes are useful for reconstructing evolutionary events in the distant past, whereas fast evolving ones can inform about recent events. Hence, it is very important to select an appropriate gene or protein for the problem trying to be solved. In this case, most of our inferences were based on the E1–E2 gene fragment, but we did use the NS5B gene sequences to perform a preliminary, quick analysis of who was likely infected by the IC which allowed for weekly updates of the size of the outbreak.

As outlined above, if the viruses obtained from one outbreak patient were derived from those in the presumed source, an appropriate phylogenetic analysis would reveal their shared ancestry. In order to differentiate between a common ancestor shared by only the outbreak-derived viruses and an ancestor common to the general population, it was essential to compare viruses derived from putative outbreak patients as well as those obtained from completely unrelated sources. These other sources will be used as population controls that will show a common ancestor much more distant in time than that of the viruses related to the same source in the outbreak.

Given the incidence of HCV in Spain, it was relatively easy to find unrelated samples from HCV-infected patients from the same location. However, in order to narrow down the analyses to relevant samples, one of the first tasks was to determine the viral subtype involved in the outbreak. There are seven major types of HCV, denoted as genotypes 1–7, and within these there are several subtypes, designated by letters. So, for genotype 1, there are subtypes 1a, 1b and so on. The classification of viral types and subtypes depends on the genetic relationships of the viruses (Smith *et al.*, 2014). So, HCV genotypes differ in about 40% of their genomes whereas differences between subtypes of the same genotype are around 25% of the genome sequence. Obviously, this variance is very important for outbreak investigations because all outbreak-related viruses (i.e. those derived from a common source) must share the same viral subtype. Furthermore, from a clinical perspective, these genetic differences are important, because they partially determine the viral response to antiviral treatment and, consequently, the prognosis of the infection for the patients. In this outbreak, we determined that the virus infecting the IC was subtype 1a, which allowed us to rapidly discard as not involved in the outbreak those patients who had different HCV subtypes. In the end, we were able to find 42 suitable population controls of this viral subtype for the following analyses.

The initial analyses were addressed at establishing the HCV subtype infecting each patient suspected to be involved in the outbreak. We sequenced 668 HCV samples of genotype 1 which included 374 of subtype 1a and 294 of subtype 1b. Since the IC subtype was 1a, the latter were discarded as not related to this outbreak. When we compared the nucleotide sequence of each HCV-1a sample with that of the source, we obtained an L-shaped distribution (Figure 1). Many of the sequences (about 170) were identical to that obtained from the IC, but there were also many sequences which differed in 1 or 2 positions. The number of suspected cases with 3 or more differences was also high when all the classes were grouped, and their distribution was similar to that obtained for the control sequences. None of these had fewer than 3 differences from the IC. This result indicated that many of the cases were likely linked to the source (and thus to the outbreak) but it was not possible to separate them into two clear-cut categories, i.e. in or out of the outbreak. But this resolution was already known from the classical epidemiology analysis.

The odds-ratio for the IC to be a factor responsible for the infection by HCV to the potential outbreak-affected patients was very high (28.50 with 95% IC = 9.83–82.59), being the only significant factor among the many candidates considered (González-Candelas *et al.*, 2013). With this information, it might have been tempting to define the outbreak from the number of differences observed between each sample and the IC, but a low number of such differences is not sufficient evidence for such a strong inference. We can be relatively sure that those patients with 0, 1 or even 2 differences were very likely infected by the IC (given the additional epidemiological evidence),

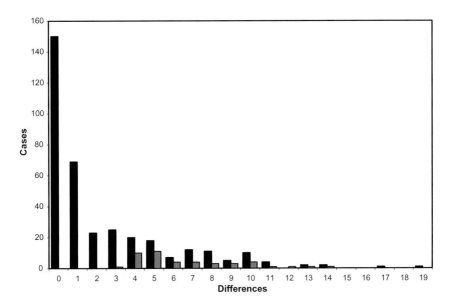

Figure 1: Distribution of the number of differences in the NS5B region to the index case.

Note: We sequenced 229 nucleotides from the NS5B region in each putative outbreak sample (blue) and control (brown) and compared them to the sequence obtained from the index case (IC). These results early revealed that the outbreak from a common source was real because many sequences had none ($N = 150$) or one difference ($N = 69$) to the IC, but it was not possible to know with precision how many people had been infected by him because there was no clear divide in two categories of the outbreak-suspected samples.

but this association was possible for samples with 3 differences in the region considered. Given that this number of differences was observed also for non-outbreak-related controls, could we support that none of the patients with 3 differences was infected by the IC? A more sensitive analysis was necessary.

The number of viruses infecting a human body can be staggering. For instance, about 100,000 million new HCV viruses are produced every day in an infected person. This large population, along with the high mutation rate of this virus, makes it likely that every single day in the life of an infected person, every possible mutation of the virus arises. Naturally, from the appearance of a mutation to its selection or elimination many things can happen, but chances are that any variant that can provide an advantage for the virus will spread in the infected organism. What is certain is that a viral population in an infected individual will consist of a huge swarm of similar but not necessary identical genomes. Given the appropriate methods, it is possible to analyze this diversity and use it to our benefit. For instance, it is now possible to use high-through-put sequencing technologies to reveal the presence of minority (in very low frequency) resistance variants in a virus sample before the start of therapy with the matching drug, thus preventing their selection and, consequently, treatment failure (Capobianchi *et al.*, 2013). In the case of this outbreak, the variability of the viral population was evidenced by sequencing several cloned PCR products of the E1–E2 region. This procedure is equivalent to isolating individual viruses and obtaining the sequence of a fragment of their genomes. The sequenced fragment, as mentioned above, is characterized by its high variability, which results from a high local mutation rate and diversifying selection. As a result, a few weeks after the initial infection it is possible to find variant viruses even when only a small sample of the total viral population is analyzed. As time proceeds, the likelihood of finding variants, and these being more and more divergent (accruing more differences among them) also increases. This capability is very useful for deriving a well-resolved phylogeny because as the number of changes increases, it is ever more difficult to find many instances of the same variations appearing independently (homoplasies, in technical jargon), which can mislead phylogenetic reconstructions.

We obtained an average of 10 clonal sequences from PCR products of a 406 nucleotide fragment in the E1–E2 region from each sample, both suspected outbreak and controls, and as many as possible (n = 134) from the IC. With the 4,184 sequences obtained, we derived a phylogenetic tree (Figure 2) which presented several interesting features. The most relevant in this case was a neat and statistically very significant separation between sequences obtained from the controls and many, but not all, the sequences derived from putative outbreak samples. Hence, it was possible to divide the phylogenetic tree into two monophyletic clades, one encompassing all

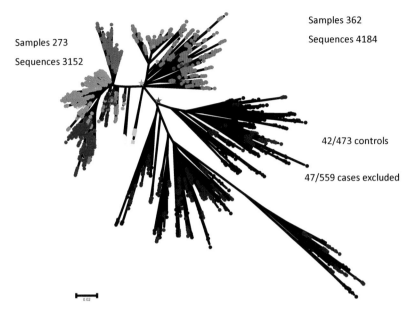

Samples 273
Sequences 3152

Samples 362
Sequences 4184

42/473 controls

47/559 cases excluded

Figure 2: A well-defined, statistically supported division between outbreak and not-outbreak samples was possible only after the analysis of sequence clones from the E1–E2 region, which revealed two mutually exclusive populations, one mono-phyletic (marked with a red asterisk) for all sequences derived from unrelated controls (dark blue), and which also included 560 sequences derived from 47 samples that were accordingly excluded from the outbreak (purple), and a monophyletic group which included sequences from 273 samples and from the index case (other colors). In fact, this cluster (marked with a green asterisk) was defined by the longest internal branch in the tree shown here, and by the co-occurrence in different clusters within these groups of sequences from the same sample, some of which were very close, even identical, to those obtained from the index case

the controls and some putative outbreak samples and the other which included the sequences derived from the IC and many out-break-related samples. This tree matched a likely scenario, one in which part of the patients epidemiologically linked to the IC had not been actually infected by him and with others having received the infecting virus from the putative source. Furthermore, for most of the possible outbreak samples more closely related to the con-trols, the genetic variability within patient was very similar to that of the controls whereas this relationship was not true for the other group of outbreak samples, whose genetic variation was substantially lower. This outcome was an indication of a more recent infection in the latter group, the outbreak, than in the controls and the patients that, from this moment, we considered to be excluded from the outbreak. In total, we identified 275 patients as included in the outbreak because the viruses obtained from them share a most recent common ancestor with those derived from the IC than with any control from the general population.

As noted above, a phylogenetic tree is a scientific hypothesis on the relationships among the sequences (or individuals or species) included in it. Any scientific hypothesis must be tested and science provides plenty of tools for such analyses. In the case of a phylogenetic reconstruction to be used for a forensic analysis, it is possible to obtain tests of many hypotheses by applying the following reasoning: if an individual has received the virus from the source, it is more likely that the sequences derived from him/her share a more recent common ancestor with the source sequences than with those derived from unrelated controls or other individuals not involved in the outbreak. This test can be performed under different statistical methodologies but the one we used is based on the evaluation of likelihood.

In the case of an outbreak, similarly to many court cases, there are essentially two hypotheses to be tested: a given person was infected by the source or not. If the source hypothesis is true, we expect that viruses infecting this person will share a more recent common ancestor with those obtained from the source and other outbreak patients than with the non-outbreak-related controls and outbreak-excluded patients. A nice property of molecular phylogenies is that these hypotheses can be easily translated into a special topology of the corresponding phylogenetic tree, by placing the target sequences in the appropriate group (Figure 3). In consequence, we tested these hypotheses for each individual included in the previously defined outbreak-group, thus providing the court with a statistical evaluation of the chances that the viruses obtained from that person were more closely related to the IC than to the

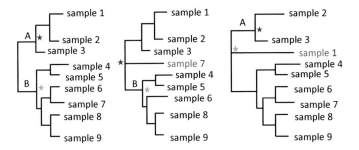

Figure 3: Tests of molecular epidemiological hypotheses.

Note: In the left tree, there are two groups of sequences which correspond to the general (Control) population (labeled A) and to the outbreak (labeled B), respectively. The tree in the middle represents the alternative hypothesis for sample 7, an outbreak sample which has been shifted to group with the control sequences (thus defining a new general population indicated by the red asterisk). The right tree represents the alternative hypothesis for a sample from the general population (or the group of outbreak-excluded sequences) which is now moved to group into the clade of outbreak sequences (defined now by the green asterisk). Each phylogenetic tree has a different likelihood for the observed alignment of sequences derived from each sample for the viral genome sequence considered.

general population (Figure 3). Furthermore, the testing can be done for the outbreak-excluded samples. In this case, the alternative hypothesis is that the individual was infected by the outbreak source and not by someone else, as the phylogenetic reconstruction suggests because the viral sequences derived from his/her group with the unrelated controls and not in the IC+outbreak group. By placing in this group the sequences derived from an outbreak-excluded patient, it is possible to obtain the likelihood of them being more closely related to the IC than to the general population (González-Candelas, 2010).

These tests were performed for all the outbreak-related samples, both those included and the excluded ones, testing the alternative hypothesis in each case. The results were fully confirmatory of the corresponding assignments (included or excluded from the outbreak) but now we had a quantitative evaluation of how strongly the data supported each individual assignment. This allowed us to report to the court that the molecular evidence for a particular case supported its inclusion in the outbreak up to 10^{60} times more (that is, a 1 followed by 60 0's) than the alternative possibility (exclusion from the outbreak). On an individual basis, values like this one represent such strong evidence that "absolute certainty" was the only term we could use to convey to the court an appreciation of how those values could be expressed in common language. The possibility of obtaining an individualized evaluation of the odds for each competing hypothesis is a very interesting property of molecular epidemiology. This approach has become quite usual in the reports of forensic experts dealing with the interpretation of DNA-based evidence (obtained from blood, saliva, semen or other body parts) as well as in kinship cases (Evett and Weir, 1998), but it had never been applied to virus transmission cases in courts. A similar idea was used to decide between two possible sources of infection (a surgeon and a blood donor) with HIV for a patient undergoing surgery (Holmes *et al.*, 1993). However, it must be stressed that this is only a part of the evidence to be considered in a trial and that other information must be considered and evaluated accordingly, without putting more confidence in a given analysis than is due.

Molecular phylogenetic analyses were introduced into courts at the beginning of the 1990s (Ou *et al.*, 1992). Most of them correspond to HIV-transmission cases (Banaschak *et al.*, 2000; Goujon *et al.*, 2000) that have been brought to criminal courts (Lemey *et al.*, 2005; Metzker, 2010; Scaduto *et al.*, 2010), but the same principles apply to many other viruses (Ikegaya *et al.*, 2008; Inoue *et al.*, 2014; Kato *et al.*, 2007; Velsko *et al.*, 2014). These and many other similar analyses have shown the power of molecular phylogenetics to disentangle the relationships among the infectious micro-organisms isolated from sources and recipients, thus providing the basis for forensic microbiology. However, the case described in detail also reveals that evolutionary concepts and principles can be applied to microbial forensics beyond the reconstruction of phylogenetic trees based on sequences. The increasing use of complete genome sequences to establish the relationships among transmitted isolates (Gardy *et al.*, 2007; Pérez-Lago *et al.*, 2014; Walker *et al.*, 2013) will make it even more necessary to incorporate evolutionary thinking in microbial forensics.

References

S. Banaschak, M. Werwein, B. Brinkmann and I. Hauber. Human Immunodeficiency Virus type 1 infection after sexual abuse: Value of nucleic acid sequence analysis in identifying the offender. *Clin Infect Dis*, 31:1098–1100, 2000.

R. Biek, O. G. Pybus, J. O. Lloyd-Smith and X. Didelot. Measurably evolving pathogens in the genomic era. *Trends Ecol Evol*, 30:306–313, 2015.

A. V. Borderia, F. M. Codoner and R. Sanjuan. Selection promotes compartmentalization in HIV-1; evidence from *gag* and *pol* genes. *Evolution*, 61:272–279, 2007.

M. R. Capobianchi, E. Giombini and G. Rozera. Next-generation sequencing technology in clinical virology. *Clin Microbiol Infection*, 19:15–22, 2013.

G. Casey, D. Conti, R. Haile and D. Duggan. Next generation sequencing and a new era of medicine. *Gut* 62:920–932, 2013.

J. Davies and D. Davies. Origins and evolution of antibiotic resistance. *Microbiol Mol Biol Rev*, 74:417–433, 2010.

J. Drake, W. and J. J. Holland. Mutation rates among RNA viruses. *Proc Nat Acade Sci USA*, 96:13910–13913, 1999.

A. J. Drummond, O. G. Pybus, A. Rambaut, R. Forsberg and A. G. Rodrigo. Measurably evolving populations. *Trends Ecol Evol*, 18:481–488, 2003.

J. I. Esteban, S. Sauleda and J. Quer. The changing epidemiology of hepatitis C virus infection in Europe. *J Hepatol*, 48:148–162, 2008.

I. W. Evett and B. S. Weir. *Interpreting DNA Evidence*. Sinauer, Sunderland, MA, 1998.

J. Felsenstein. *Inferring Phylogenies*. Sinauer, Sunderland, MA, 2004.

J. L. Gardy, J. C. Johnston, S. J. H. Sui, V. J. Cook, L. Shah, E. Brodkin, S. Rempel, R. Moore, Y. Zhao, R. Holt, R. Varhol, I. Birol, M. Lem, M. K. Sharma, K. Elwood, S. J. M. Jones, F. S. L. Brinkman, R. C. Brunham and P. Tang. Whole-genome squencing and social-network analysis of a tuberculosis outbreak. *New Engl J Med*, 364:730–739, 2011.

F. González-Candelas. Molecular phylogenetic analyses in court trials. In *Encyclopedia of Life Sciences*. John Wiley & Sons, Ltd, New York, 2010.

F. González-Candelas, M. A. Bracho, B. Wróbel and A. Moya. Molecular evolution in court: Analysis of a large hepatitis C virus outbreak from an evolving source. *BMC Biol* 11:76, 2013.

C. P. Goujon, V. M. Schneider, J. Grofti, J. Montigny, V. Jeantils, P. Astagneau, W. Rozenbaum, F. Lot, C. Frocrain-Herchkovitch, N. Delphin, F. Le

Gal, J. C. Nicolas, M. C. Milinkovitch and P. Dény. Phylogenetic analyses indicate an atypical nurse-to-patient transmission of Human Immunodeficiency Virus Type I. *J Virol*, 74:2525–2532, 2000.

E. C. Holmes, A. J. Brown and P. Simmonds. Sequence data as evidence. *Nature*, 364:766, 1993.

H. Ikegaya, H. Motani, K. Sakurada, K. Sato, T. Akutsu and M. Yoshino. Forensic application of Epstein-Barr virus genotype: Correlation between viral genotype and geographical area. *J Virolo Methods*, 147:78–85, 2008.

H. Inoue, H. Motani-Saitoh, K. Sakurada, H. Ikegaya, D. Yajima, S. Nagasawa and H. Iwase. Genotypic polymorphisms of hepatitis B virus provide useful information for estimating geographical origin or place of long-term residence of unidentified cadavers. *J Forensic Sci*, 59:236–241, 2014.

H. Kato, Y. Maeno, Y. Seko-Nakamura, J. Monma-Ohtaki, S. Sugiura, K. Takahashi, L. X. Zhe, T. Matsumoto, F. Kurvanov, M. Mizokami and M. Nagao. Identification and phylogenetic analysis of hepatitis C virus in forensic blood samples obtained from injecting drug users. *Forensic Sci Int*, 168:27–33, 2007.

J. F. C. Kingman. The coalescent. *Stoch Proc Appl*, 13:235–248, 1982.

D. Lavanchy. Evolving epidemiology of hepatitis-C virus. *Clin Microbiol Infec*, 17:107–115, 2011.

P. Lemey, S. Van Dooren, K. Van Laethem, Y. Schrooten, I. Derdelinckx, P. Goubau, F. Brun-Vezinet, D. Vaira and A. M. Vandamme. Molecular testing of multiple HIV-1 transmissions in a criminal case. *AIDS*, 19:1649–1658, 2005.

R. C. Lewontin. Population Genetics. *Annu Rev Genet*, 19:81–102, 1985.

M. Lynch. Evolution of the mutation rate. *Trends Genet*, 26:345–352, 2010.

M. C. Maiden, J. A. Bygraves, E. Feil, G. Morelli, J. E. Russell, R. Urwin, Q. Zhang, J. Zhou, K. Zurth, D. A. Caugant, I. M. Feavers, M. Achtman and B. G. Spratt. Multilocus sequence typing: A portable approach to the identification of clones within populations of pathogenic microorganisms. *Proc Nat Acad Sci USA*, 95:3140–3145, 1998.

M. L. Metzker. Sequencing technologies — the next generation. *Nat Rev Genet*, 11:31–46, 2010.

M. L. Metzker, D. P. Mindell, X. M. Liu, R. G. Ptak, R. A. Gibbs and D. M. Hillis. Molecular evidence of HIV-1 transmission in a criminal case. *Proc Nati Acad Sci USA*, 99:14292–14297, 2002.

N. E. Morton. Genetic structure of forensic populations. *Proc Nat Acad Sci USA*, 89:2556–2560, 1992.

C. Neuhauser and S. Tavar. The coalescent, In S. Brenner and J. Miller (eds.), *Encyclopedia of Genetics*, Vol. 1, pp. 392–397, Academic Press, New York, 2001.

R. A. Nichols and D. J. Baldwin. Effects of population structure on DNA fingerprinting analysis in forensic science. *Heredity*, 66:297–302, 1991.

C. Y. Ou, C. A. Ciesielski, G. Myers, C. I. BAndea, C. C. Luo, B. T. M. Korber, J. I. Mullins, G. Schochetman, R. L. Berkelman, A. N. Economou, J. J. Witte, L. J. Furman, G. A. Satten, K. A. MacInnes, J. W. Curran, H. W. Jaffe, Laboratory Investigation Group and Epidemiological Investigation Group. Molecular epidemiology of HIV transmission in a dental practice. *Science*, 256:1165–1171, 1992.

L. Pérez-Lago, I. Comas, Y. Navarro, F. González-Candelas, M. Herranz, E. Bouza and D. García de Viedma. Whole genome sequencing analysis of intrapatient microevolution. In *Mycobacterium Tuberculosis: Potential Impact on the Inference of Tuberculosis Transmission. J Infec Diseases*, 209:98–108, 2014.

F. Randow, J. D. MacMicking and L. C. James. Cellular self-defense: How cell-autonomous immunity protects against pathogens. *Science*, 340:701–706, 2013.

A. M. Roque-Afonso, D. Ducoulombier, G. Di Liberto, R. Kara, M. Gigou, E. Dussaix, D. Samuel and C. Feray. Compartmentalization of hepatitis C virus genotypes between plasma and peripheral blood mononuclear cells. *J Virol*, 79:6349–6357, 2005.

N. A. Rosenberg and M. Nordborg. Genealogical trees, coalescent theory and the analysis of genetic polymorphisms. *Nat Rev Genet*, 3:380–390, 2002.

R. Sanjuan, M. R. Nebot, N. Chirico, L. M. Mansky and R. Belshaw. Viral mutation rates. *J Virol*, 84:9733–9748, 2010.

D. I. Scaduto, J. M. Brown, W. C. Haaland, D. J. Zwickl, D. M. Hillis and M. L. Metzker. Source identification in two criminal cases using phylogenetic analysis of HIV-1 DNA sequences. *Proc Nat Acad Sci USA*, 107:21242–21247, 2010.

G. Schnell, S. Spudich, P. Harrington, R. W. Price and R. Swanstrom. Compartmentalized Human immunodeficiency virus type 1 originates from long-lived cells in some subjects with HIV-1–associated dementia. *PLoS Pathog*, 5:e1000395, 2009.

D. B. Smith, J. Bukh, C. Kuiken, A. S. Muerhoff, C. M. Rice, J. T. Stapleton and P. Simmonds. Expanded classification of hepatitis C Virus into 7 genotypes and 67 Subtypes: updated criteria and assignment web resource. *Hepatology*, 59:318–327, 2014.

S. P. Velsko, J. Osburn and J. Allen. Forensic interpretation of molecular variation on networks of disease transmission and genetic inheritance. *Electrophoresis*, 35:3117–3124, 2014.

T. M. Walker, C. L. Ip, R. H. Harrell, J. T. Evans, G. Kapatai, M. J. Dedicoat, D. W. Eyre, D. J. Wilson, P. M. Hawkey, D. W. Crook, J. Parkhill, D. Harris, A. S. Walker, R. Bowden, P. Monk, E. G. Smith and T. E. Peto. Whole-genome sequencing to delineate *Mycobacterium tuberculosis* outbreaks: a retrospective observational study. *The Lancet Infectious Diseases*, 13:137–146, 2013.

CHAPTER 24

Quality Assurance, Recommendations and Standards

Ingo Bastisch

BKA (Federal Criminal Police Office), Wiesbaden, Germany

Quality means doing it right when nobody is looking
(Henry Ford)

If you think Compliance is expensive, try Non-Compliance.
(Paul McNulty, U.S. Deputy Attorney General)

Forensic evidence plays a vital role in court or during the investigation of a crime regardless of the respective legal environment. Forensic scientists or practitioners are expected to examine and interpret evidence thoroughly, objectively, reliably and according to the state-of-the-art of their specific discipline. Although judges or juries make their final conclusions based on all the information and findings, a single forensic report might be the information that makes the difference between acquittal and conviction especially when the evidence — like in forensic genetics — directly links a person to a crime. As these forensic experts are the dedicated specialists in a certain area, it is very difficult for non-experts to evaluate, if the before mentioned characteristics apply to reported forensic findings.

The forensic community is very much aware of its role in the legal justice system and has continuously been implementing safeguards ensuring a certain level of reliability and robustness. But every method has its strengths and weaknesses, every machine its limits and uncertainties and every human being involved in this process can make mistakes. These issue are not only true for forensics but for every area of work or expertize. A well-trained expert is aware of limits and pitfalls and has implemented mechanisms and safeguards that will allow him or her to monitor the performance of his or her processes.

A very well established measure ensuring that minimum requirements of good forensic practice are met include principles, recommendations, guidelines etc. agreed by national, regional or international scientific or governmental bodies. Some examples of those will be discussed later. However, even the best guidelines only work if a laboratory in general and the individual comply. Otherwise issues may happen. Two examples are summarized in John Butler's book (Butler, 2009) (Chapter 13, Quality Assurance, D.N.A. Box 13.1). Issues of non-compliance with laboratory protocols were found in the FBI laboratory[1] and the Houston Police Crime Laboratory,[2] the latter with repeated incidents until 2014.[3] Both examples required serious and intensive independent investigations that resulted in a number of recommendations in order to re-create trust in the laboratory's professional ability to serve truth and justice.

The report of the National Research Council (NRC) (2009) identified several weaknesses within the forensic system including lack or vagueness of standards, their enforcement and oversight. That the recommended standards are sometimes vague has its reasons. They need to take into account the difference related to the legal environment, education programs, funding, etc. As a

---

[1] US DOJ, Office of the Inspector General. The FBI DNA Laboratory: A Review of Protocol and Practice Vulnerabilities, 2004. https://oig.justice.gov/special/0405/final.pdf.

[2] http://www.hpdlabinvestigation.org/.

[3] Houston Crinicle 2014. http://www.houstonchronicle.com/news/houston-texas/houston/article/Former-HPD-crime-lab-analyst-told-colleagues-of-5580097.php.

consequence, the least common denominator often is sought, meaning that guidelines on a national level are mostly more precise than those on an international level, and recommendations for a certain method can be more detailed than those covering principles that are applied at a broader spectrum of forensic disciplines. Furthermore, forensic processes undergo regular change due to advances in science. Standards or guidelines have to allow for flexibility to adopt the processes according to the current scientific knowledge.

1 Getting Started

Not every country in the world has the luxury of affording the full toolbox of forensic methods. But if one decides to implement forensic DNA analysis, there is a need for guidance on a very general and basic level. The INTERPOL DNA (2009) Monitoring Expert group published recommendations for the practical use of DNA and DNA data exchange. A hypothetical case illustrates the value of DNA and international data exchange for police investigations starting with the first responders at the scene of crime. A number of basic principles is summarized that help to use and preserve the evidential value of items and observations found including sampling material and procedures. A small part is dedicated also to the forensic laboratory and the findings. Altogether this book provides a good overview for decision makers who plan to implement or improve the use of DNA analysis in police investigations. It refers to training, databases, legislation and data protection, interaction with public and media, quality assurance and touches on other potential applications.

The International Forensic Strategic Alliance (IFSA), a cooperative partnership of the different regional forensic networks[4] taking

---

[4] American Society of Crime Laboratory Directors (ASCLD), European Network of Forensic Science Institutes (ENFSI), Senior Managers of Australian and New Zealand Forensic Laboratories (SMANZFL), Academia Iberoamericana de Criminalística y Estudios Forenses (AICEF), Asian Forensic Sciences Network (AFSN), Southern Africa Regional Forensic Science Network (SARFS).

care on global strategic matters in relation to forensic science, published the first of a number of basic documents for emerging laboratories. One of those minimum requirement documents deals with DNA collection, analysis and interpretation[5] and provides an overview of generally basic considerations like facilities, process design, training, education requirements, quality management etc. Although this document generally deals with principles that need to be implemented at a minimal level, some details are "nice to haves" like negative air pressure which is in fact not installed in many advanced laboratories.

The two mentioned documents provide a good resource for orientation of emerging laboratories. Nevertheless, it is highly recommended to seek guidance from an experienced institute that has similar legal and police structures and is ideally from the same area. Contacts may be established through the regional forensic laboratory networks (see footnote to IFSA). Especially in emerging countries, access to equipment, maintenance and consumables is sometimes limited and the processes are lengthy. Parallel to the set-up of a DNA laboratory, the processes of collection at the scene of crime and training of investigators and law persons need to be conducted. A laboratory can only do a good job if their partners in police and justice operate at a similar level.

2 Quality Systems and Accreditation

No matter which recommendation or guideline is considered, they all have in common that they refer to quality systems but what is generally meant is quality management systems. The most popular standard in this field is ISO 9001.[6] The key contents of this very generic standard are included in every quality management system.

---

[5] International Forensic Strategic Alliance (IFSA). *Minimum Requirements for DNA Collection, Analysis and Interpretation*, 2014. http://www.enfsi.eu/sites/default/files/documents/IFSA/ifsa_dna_mrd_2014.pdf.

[6] ISO 9001:2008. Quality management systems — Requirements. http://www.iso.org/iso/home/store/catalogue_tc/catalogue_detail.htm?csnumber=46486.

The main purpose is to ensure that a procedural system is implemented ensuring that the requirements of costumers related to products are met. The processes also need to ensure that there is a continuous improvement related to the customer's needs. Those key elements are included in ISO/IEC 17025[7] which defines the general requirements for the competence of testing and calibration laboratories and which is the standard mostly used in forensics. Other international standards used but not widely applied are ISO/IEC 17020[8] dealing with conformity assessments of bodies performing inspections and ISO/IEC 17024[9] dealing with the certification of individual experts.

Some countries may have their own guidelines that are used in addition or instead ISO/IEC 17025. In the United States, the Federal Bureau of Investigation (FBI) published two documents that define requirements for laboratories performing DNA testing/databasing.[10]

2.1 *ISO/IEC 17025*

As this is the standard most widely applied in forensics, some explanatory remarks are useful. While reading a standard, it is worthwhile to know the meaning of some key vocabularies used. A "shall" simply means you have to do it, a "should" means you better do it unless you have a good reason not to do it, a "may" means you may or may not do it and a "can" is an allowance. Although ISO/IEC 17025 is much more specific for use in forensics, it is still a generic standard.

---

[7] ISO/IEC 17025:2005. General requirements for the competence of testing and calibration laboratories. http://www.iso.org/iso/Catalogue_detail?csnumber=39883.

[8] ISO/IEC 17020:2012. Conformity assessment — Requirements for the operation of various types of bodies performing inspection. http://www.iso.org/iso/catalogue_detail?csnumber=52994.

[9] ISO/IEC 17024:2012. Conformity assessment — General requirements for bodies operating certification of persons. http://www.iso.org/iso/catalogue_detail?csnumber=52993.

[10] Federal Bureau of Investigation. Quality Assurance Standards for Forensic DNA Testing Laboratories and Quality Assurance Standards for Convicted Offender DNA Databasing Laboratories. Forensic Science Communications, 2(3), 2000. https://www.fbi.gov/about-us/lab/biometric-analysis/codis.

In order to provide more specific guidance, the International Laboratory Accreditation Cooperation (ILAC) published a document[11] that specifies some special forensic requirements in addition to those mentioned in ISO/IEC 17025 (and ISO/IEC 17020) and should be consulted accordingly.

The standard consists mainly of two parts, management requirements and technical requirements. The management requirements largely reflect the principles of ISO 9001, whereas the technical requirements define and deal with the necessities for laboratory testing. It would be useless to give a summary of the content but it might be useful to mention some additional resources that can give guidance on the implementation. Currently there are three websites[12] where regularly agreed guidelines or recommendations related to forensic genetics are published. It is useful to occasionally check for new documents.

2.1.1 Personnel

There are two helpful documents related to qualification and training of staff, the ENFSI DNA Working Group's Concept Training Document[13] and the SWGDAM's Training Guidelines.[14] Although the latter is not intended to be used for ISO/IEC 17025, it is a good resource for consideration. ISO/IEC 17025 does not prescribe a

---

[11] ILAC-G19:08/2014. Modules in a Forensic Science Process. http://ilac.org/publications-and-resources/ilac-documents/guidance-series/.

[12] DNA Working Group of the European Network of Forensic Science Institutes (ENFSI) http://www.enfsi.eu/about-enfsi/structure/working-groups/dna; the UK Forensic Science Regulator https://www.gov.uk/government/organisations/forensic-science-regulator; and the U.S. Scientific Working Group on DNA Analysis Methods (SWGDAM) http://www.swgdam.org/.

[13] ENFSI DNA Working Group. Concept Training Document, 2010. http://www.enfsi.eu/sites/default/files/documents/recommendations_for_the_training_of_dna_staff_-_v2010_0.pdf.

[14] SWGDAM. Training Guidelines, 2013 http://media.wix.com/ugd/4344b0_87b2b4a150aa433f9490b7113b1aa4a6.pdf.

certain way of qualifying and maintaining qualification; how this is achieved is to be decided by the laboratory if no additional rules exist. Generally requirements for different job roles (i.e. technical leader, reporting scientist, analyst) need to be defined, and for each role a specific training plan is to be documented. The details of the training plan are very much dependent on the previous education of trainees. Some countries have special education programs for forensics, such as a qualified education for lab technicians, etc.

2.1.2 Accommodation and environment

Some key principles are accepted across the community that are mainly based on safety, security, maintenance of the integrity of samples and contamination prevention: access control; separation of pre and post-PCR, separation of evidence and reference sample analysis; and separation of low template samples from samples containing large amounts of DNA. One has to keep in mind that the last recommendation is the most difficult to achieve as it is not always possible to estimate *a priori* if a sample has low or high DNA content. This issue will be more discussed later with regards to contamination.

2.1.3 Validation

Validation of instruments or methods shall demonstrate that a certain process or equipment is fit for a specific purpose in the given environment. This requirement can be differentiated into two different aspects of validation: developmental validation and user or internal validation. Developmental validation shall demonstrate that a new method or instrument is suitable for a certain purpose. The internal validation is required to check whether the method works as specified and will provide data to gain information on strengths and limitations of a method in the individual laboratory. Laboratories often are unsure about how much validation is needed in order to demonstrate fitness for purpose. A very useful and well understandable view was published by John Butler[15] who explains principles and misunderstandings around validation. Also SWGDAM and the ENFSI DNA Working Group published useful recommendations providing guidance for forensic DNA laboratories.[16]

Just recently SWGDAM issued new guidelines[17] for validation of probabilistic interpretation software which has not been considered in the other recommendations mentioned before.

2.1.4 Equipment, measurement traceability and assuring quality

Besides some formal requirements that must not be ignored, it is important to monitor the performance of instruments and reagents. There are certain ways of meeting this requirement: using proper controls, regular calibration of instruments, monitoring key data in order to recognize trends as early warning and taking part in proficiency tests and collaborative exercises. But it is also important to have well educated staff recognizing potential issues and taking responsibility for them. A good summary on quality control can be found in Ricky Ansell's article[18] on internal quality control in forensic DNA analysis.

2.1.5 Results, reports, interpretation and opinion

It is essential that reports on forensic DNA analysis make a clear distinction between results, interpretation and opinion. Interpretation

---

[15]J. M. Butler. Debunking Some Urban Legends Surrounding Validation Within the Forensic DNA Community in Profiles in DNA 9(2), 2006, pp. 3–6. http://www.promega.de/resources/profiles-in-dna/2006/debunking-some-urban-legends-surrounding-validation-within-the-forensic-dna-community/.

[16]SWGDAM. Validation Guidelines for DNA Analysis Methods, 2012. http://media.wix.com/ugd/4344b0_cbc27d16dcb64fd88cb36ab2a2a25e4c.pdf. ENFSI DNA Working Group. Recommended Minimum Criteria for the Validation of Various Aspects of the DNA Profiling Process, 2010. http://www.enfsi.eu/sites/default/files/documents/minimum_validation_guidelines_in_dna_profiling_-_v2010_0.pdf.

[17]SWGDAM. Guidelines for the Validation of Probabilistic Genotyping Systems, 2015. http://media.wix.com/ugd/4344b0_22776006b67c4a32a5ffc04fe3b56515.pdf.

[18]Ricky Ansell. Internal Quality Control in Forensic DNA Analysis, Accreditation and Quality Assurance 18, 2013, pp. 279–289. http://link.springer.com/article/10.1007%2Fs00769-013-0968-9.

shall be based on accepted scientific principles, and interpretation rules should be documented. Statistical interpretation is described in an earlier chapter in this book. But two recommendations should be mentioned that have broad acceptance: the ISFG mixture interpretation guidelines[19] and the recommendations for the interpretation of samples with probabilistic methods.[20] An example of a national interpretation guideline was made by SWGDAM.[21] Especially in statistical interpretation of DNA results, there has been a lot of progress within the recent years. Before adopting any of those guidelines and recommendations, it should be verified if they are still state-of-the-art.

Related to reporting, ENFSI recently published recommendations on evaluative reporting of forensic evidence.[22] Although the document focuses on a special type of report, it explains some reporting principles that always should be applied.

2.2 *Accreditation*

The United Kingdom Accreditation Service (UKAS) defines accreditation as follows[23]: "Accreditation is a formal, third party recognition of competence to perform specific tasks. It provides a means to identify

---

[19] P. Gill, C. Brenner, J. Buckleton, A. Carracedo, M. Krawczak, W. Mayr, N. Morling, M. Prinz, P. M. Schneider, B. Weir. DNA commission of the International Society of Forensic Genetics: Recommendations on the interpretation of mixtures. Forensic Science International, 160, pp. 90–101, 2006. http://www.isfg.org/Publication;Gill2006.

[20] P. Gill, L. Gusmão, H. Haned, W. Mayr, N. Morling, W. Parson, L. Prieto, M. Prinz, H. Schneider, P. M. Schneider, B. Weir. DNA commission of the International Society of Forensic Genetics: Recommendations on the evaluation of STR typing results that may include drop-out and/or drop-in using probabilistic methods. Forensic Science International: Genetics, 6(6), pp. 679–688, 2012. http://www.isfg.org/Publication;Gill2012.

[21] SWGDAM. Interpretation Guidelines for Autosomal STR Typing by Forensic DNA Testing Laboratories, 2010. http://media.wix.com/ugd/4344b0_da25419ba2dd4363bc4e5e8fe7025882.pdf.

[22] "ENFSI Guideline for Evaluative Reporting in Forensic Science", 2015. http://www.enfsi.eu/sites/default/files/afbeeldingen/enfsi_booklet_m1.pdf.

[23] http://www.ukas.com/about-accreditation/What_is_Accreditation/What_is_Accreditation.asp.

a proven, competent evaluator so that the selection of a laboratory, inspection or certification body is an informed choice. [...] accreditation means the evaluator can demonstrate to its customer that it has been successful at meeting the requirements of international accreditation standards..." That statement simply means that by assessment of a third party, it is verified that a laboratory meets the criteria of the standards, e.g. ISO/IEC 17025 in combination with ILAC G19. It must be clear that accreditation is a formal process. It does not mean that the accredited laboratory provides better results than a non-accredited laboratory, but it provides confidence to police, justice and society that a professional quality system is in place that meets at least some minimal criteria. Therefore, accreditation increases transparency and trust. Some countries have been requiring accreditation for forensic DNA laboratories for a long time. In 2009, a regulation[24] was decided making accreditation mandatory for DNA and fingerprint analyses in Europe.

3 Contamination, Prevention and Detection

Contamination happens! This is a fact. The forensic scientist and others related to forensics, such as police and justice, must not ignore this fact. If a laboratory claims it does not have contamination, this most likely means it does not recognize it. Especially since the introduction of the new generation STR typing kits, new and more sensitive instrumentation and the extended collection of contact traces contamination is more visible. The fact that contamination occurs does not mean it cannot be addressed. It is a combination of awareness, equipment, definition of processes, cleaning and training that can decrease the rate of contamination substantially. Those measures shall be in place even in the earliest part of the forensic process, i.e. the scene of crime, and must be continued to the end of the analytical work. Any direct or indirect contact may transfer

---

[24] Council framework Decision 2009/905/JHA of 30 November 2009 on Accreditation of forensic service providers carrying out laboratory activities. http://eur-lex.europa.eu/legal-content/EN/TXT/?uri=CELEX:32009F0905.

DNA from the people involved or between items. There are two helpful documents, currently still in a draft version, that deal with contamination prevention at the scene of crime and in the laboratory.[25] The ENFSI DNA Working Group also published some guidelines for contamination reduction.[26]

A further way by which contamination may be introduced is manufacturing-based contamination of consumables. Although this is by far less common than process-based contaminations, its effect is the same. The UK and Australian Standards organizations published requirements that include (UK)[27] or deal with (AU)[28] product requirements for forensic consumables. Recently, a special ISO standard[29] dealing with production requirements for forensic DNA consumables was published and customers may order their consumables in the future only if in accordance to this standard.

An additional process for improving the quality of results is detection of contamination. The most effective one is to compare results from evidence with DNA profiles of people (potentially) involved in the forensic process. These elimination profiles are mostly from staff or reference samples stored in local or in-house

---

[25] UK Forensic Science Regulator. The Control and Avoidance of Contamination in Crime Scene Examination involving DNA Evidence Recovery and The Control and Avoidance of Contamination in Laboratory Activities involving DNA Evidence Recovery and Analysis. https://www.gov.uk/government/publications?departments[]=forensic-science-regulator.

[26] ENFSI DNA Working Group. Contamination prevention guidelines, 2010. http://www.enfsi.eu/sites/default/files/documents/dna_contamination_prevention_guidelines_for_the_file_contamantion_prevention_final_-_v2010_0.pdf.

[27] British Standards Institution (BSI) PAS 377. Specification for consumables used in the collection, preservation and processing of material for forensic analysis. Requirements for product, manufacturing and forensic kit assembly, 2012. http://shop.bsigroup.com/ProductDetail/?pid=000000000030252063.

[28] Standards Australia AS 5481. Minimizing the risk of contamination in products used to collect and analyze biological material for forensic DNA purposes. http://infostore.saiglobal.com/EMEA/Details.aspx?ProductID=1530544.

[29] ISO 18385. Minimizing the risk of human DNA contamination in products used to collect, store and analyze biological material for forensic purposes. http://www.iso.org/iso/home/store.htm.

databases. The UK Forensic Science Regulator published a draft document on the use of elimination databases.[30] If no special legislation is in place, this database has to be in accordance with national law especially the data protection rules. It is further possible to compare questioned profiles against those of people working in the production of forensic consumables. Some manufacturers already have a collection of DNA profiles from their staff. The International Commission on Missing Persons (ICMP) recently launched a database[31] that allows for secure storage and query against DNA profiles of manufacturing personnel. This database also allows for storage of so-called unsourced profiles, i.e. profiles that appear in negative analytical controls and most likely result from manufacturing-based contamination. Additional laboratories should implement mechanisms to detect sample-to-sample contamination either within an analytical batch or between different batches.

The reporting scientist should always check for consistency of a DNA profile with the findings from evidence examination. For example, if a swabbing of a heavily burnt item shows a strong DNA profile in the analytical results, further analyses should support that this profile actually originates from the evidence.

Finally, investigators should be aware of the possibility of contamination. If two crime scene stains match that are from an intelligence perspective not linked, further investigation should be carried out before the police take further measures.

4 Databases and Data Exchange

The, by far, the most comprehensive document[32] on establishing and managing a database was published by the ENFSI DNA working

---

[30] UK Forensic Science Regulator. The Management and Use of Staff Elimination DNA Databases https://www.gov.uk/government/publications?departments[]=forensic-science-regulator.

[31] http://www.ic-mp.org/fdmsweb/index.php?w=intro EDB DNA Matching.

[32] ENFSI DNA Working Group. DNA database management — Review and Recommendations http://www.enfsi.eu/about-enfsi/structure/working-groups/dna.

group. This document has been updated regularly since its first release and contains the experience of many European and non-European institutions. A short and more generic brochure[33] to be used by police and stakeholders was published by INTERPOL. Only efficient database operation and management will make full use of the investigative power provided by DNA-testing.

5 Future Trends

Within the past decade, there has been a substantial increase of guidelines, recommendations and standards. This tendency is expected to continue. The Council of the European Union published a position paper on forensic science[34] aiming for a better level of forensics through accreditation, best-practice manuals, competency criteria, etc. that should be applied throughout Europe. The European Committee for Standardization (CEN) implemented a project committee on forensic science processes currently discussing the need of European Standards including collection, analysis and interpretation. Standards Australia already has some additional national standards on crime scene work, analysis, interpretation and reporting. The UK Forensic Science Regulator is working in parallel on a number of relevant documents, as well as is SWGDAM. ISO in 2015 implemented a special technical committee dealing with forensics. The trend for increased quality assurance, quality control, and standardization clearly continues and will result in more harmonization on a global level.

---

[33] INTERPOL DNA Monitoring Expert Group. Best Practice Principles: Recommendations for the Establishment of a National DNA Database. http://www.interpol.int/content/download/27993/375175/version/5/file/MEG_Recommendation_Establishing_DNA_Database.pdf.

[34] Council conclusions on the vision for European Forensic Science 2020 including the creation of a European Forensic Science Area and the development of forensic science infrastructure in Europe, 3135th JUSTICE and HOME AFFAIRS Council meeting Brussels, 13 and 14 December 2011.

References

J. M. Butler. *Fundamentals of Forensic DNA Typing.* Academic Press, 2009.

National Research Council. *Strengthening Forensic Science in the United States: A Path Forward.* The National Academies Press, 2009. http://www.nap.edu/catalog/12589.html.

INTERPOL DNA Monitoring Expert Group. *INTERPOL Handbook on DNA Data Exchange and Practice.* 2nd edn., Interpol 2009 (also available in Arabic, French and Spanish). http://www.interpol.int/content/download/8993/66934/version/6/file/HandbookPublic2009.pdf.

Index